# Hate Speech Law

Hate speech law can be found throughout the world. But it is also the subject of numerous principled arguments, both for and against. These principles invoke a host of morally relevant features (e.g., liberty, health, autonomy, security, non-subordination, the absence of oppression, human dignity, the discovery of truth, the acquisition of knowledge, self-realization, human excellence, civic dignity, cultural diversity and choice, recognition of cultural identity, intercultural dialogue, participation in democratic self-government, being subject only to legitimate rule) and practical considerations (e.g., efficacy, the least restrictive alternative, chilling effects). The book develops and then critically examines these various principled arguments. It also attempts to de-homogenize hate speech law into different clusters of laws/regulations/codes that constrain uses of hate speech, so as to facilitate a more nuanced examination of the principled arguments. Finally, it argues that it is morally fitting for judicial and legislative judgments about the overall warrant of hate speech law to reflect principled compromise. Principled compromise is characterized not merely by compromise over matters of principled concern but also by compromise which is itself governed by ideals of moral duty or civic virtue (e.g., reciprocity, equality, mutual respect).

**Alexander Brown** is Senior Lecturer in Contemporary Social and Political Theory at the University of East Anglia (UEA). He is the author of *Ronald Dworkin's Theory of Equality: Domestic and Global Perspectives* (2009) and *Personal Responsibility: Why It Matters* (2009).

# Routledge Studies in Contemporary Philosophy

*For a full list of titles in this series, please visit www.routledge.com*

30 **Feminism, Psychoanalysis, and Maternal Subjectivity**
*Alison Stone*

31 **Civility in Politics and Education**
*Edited by Deborah S. Mower, Wade L. Robison*

32 **Philosophical Inquiry into Pregnancy, Childbirth, and Mothering**
Maternal Subjects
*Edited by Sheila Lintott and Maureen Sander-Staudt*

33 **Authenticity as an Ethical Ideal**
*Somogy Varga*

34 **The Philosophy of Curiosity**
*Ilhan Inan*

35 **Self-Realization and Justice**
A Liberal-Perfectionist Defense of the Right to Freedom from Employment
*Julia Maskivker*

36 **Narrative Identity, Autonomy, and Mortality**
From Frankfurt and MacIntyre to Kierkegaard
*John J. Davenport*

37 **Contemporary Feminist Pragmatism**
*Edited by Maurice Hamington and Celia Bardwell-Jones*

38 **Morality, Self Knowledge, and Human Suffering**
An Essay on The Loss of Confidence in the World
*Josep Corbi*

39 **Contrastivism in Philosophy**
*Edited by Martijn Blaauw*

40 **Aesthetics After Metaphysics**
From Mimesis to Metaphor
*Miguel de Beistegui*

41 **Foundations of Freedom**
Welfare-Based Arguments against Paternalism
*Simon R. Clarke*

42 **Pittsburgh School of Philosophy**
Sellars, McDowell, Brandom
*Chauncey Maher*

43 **Reference and Structure in the Philosophy of Language**
A Defense of the Russellian Orthodoxy
*Arthur Sullivan*

44 **Civic Virtue and the Sovereignty of Evil**
*Derek Edyvane*

45 **Philosophy of Language and Webs of Information**
*Heimir Geirsson*

46 **Disagreement and Skepticism**
*Edited by Diego E. Machuca*

47 **Philosophy in Schools**
An Introduction for Philosophers and Teachers
*Edited by Sara Goering, Nicholas J. Shudak, and Thomas E. Wartenberg*

48 **A Philosophy of Material Culture**
Action, Function, and Mind
*Beth Preston*

49 **A Philosophy of the Screenplay**
*Ted Nannicelli*

50 **Race, Philosophy, and Film**
*Edited by Mary K. Bloodsworth-Lugo and Dan Flory*

51 **Knowledge, Virtue, and Action**
Essays on Putting Epistemic Virtues to Work
*Edited by Tim Henning and David P. Schweikard*

52 **The Ontology of Psychology**
Questioning Foundations in the Philosophy of Mind
*Linda A.W. Brakel*

53 **Pragmatism, Law, and Language**
*Edited by Graham Hubbs and Douglas Lind*

54 **Contemporary Dualism**
A Defense
*Edited by Andrea Lavazza and Howard M. Robinson*

55 **Reframing the Intercultural Dialogue on Human Rights**
A Philosophical Approach
*Jeffrey Flynn*

56 **How History Matters to Philosophy**
Reconsidering Philosophy's Past After Positivism
*Robert C. Scharff*

57 **The Affordable Care Act Decision**
Philosophical and Legal Implications
*Edited by Fritz Allhoff and Mark Hall*

58 **Realism, Science, and Pragmatism**
*Edited by Kenneth R. Westphal*

59 **Evidentialism and Epistemic Justification**
*Kevin McCain*

60 **Democracy in Contemporary Confucian Philosophy**
*David Elstein*

61 **Deleuze and Pragmatism**
*Edited by Sean Bowden, Simone Bignall, and Paul Patton*

62 **Mind, Language and Subjectivity**
Minimal Content and the Theory of Thought
*Nicholas Georgalis*

63 **Believing Against the Evidence**
Agency and the Ethics of Belief
*Miriam Schleifer McCormick*

64 **The Essence of the Self**
In Defense of the Simple View of Personal Identity
*Geoffrey Madell*

65 **Personal Autonomy and Social Oppression**
Philosophical Perspectives
*Edited by Marina A.L. Oshana*

66 **Domination and Global Political Justice**
Conceptual, Historical, and Institutional Perspectives
*Edited by Barbara Buckinx, Jonathan Trejo-Mathys, and Timothy Waligore*

67 **Hate Speech Law**
A Philosophical Examination
*Alexander Brown*

# Hate Speech Law
A Philosophical Examination

**Alexander Brown**

Routledge
Taylor & Francis Group
NEW YORK AND LONDON

First published 2015
by Routledge
711 Third Avenue, New York, NY 10017

and by Routledge
2 Park Square, Milton Park, Abingdon, Oxon OX14 4RN

*Routledge is an imprint of the Taylor & Francis Group,
an informa business*

© 2015 Taylor & Francis

The right of Alexander Brown to be identified as author of this work has been asserted by him/her in accordance with sections 77 and 78 of the Copyright, Designs and Patents Act 1988.

All rights reserved. No part of this book may be reprinted or reproduced or utilised in any form or by any electronic, mechanical, or other means, now known or hereafter invented, including photocopying and recording, or in any information storage or retrieval system, without permission in writing from the publishers.

**Trademark Notice:** Product or corporate names may be trademarks or registered trademarks, and are used only for identification and explanation without intent to infringe.

*Library of Congress Cataloging-in-Publication Data*
Brown, Alexander, 1974 December 27- author.
  Hate speech law : a philosophical examination / Alex Brown.
    pages cm. — (Routledge studies in contemporary philosophy ; 67)
  Includes bibliographical references and index.
  1. Hate speech—Law and legislation.  2. Hate speech—Philosophy.
I. Title.
  K5210.B76 2015
  345'.02501—dc23
  2014040617

ISBN: 978-0-415-88547-8 (hbk)
ISBN: 978-1-315-71489-9 (ebk)

Typeset in Sabon
by Apex CoVantage, LLC

**For Adriana**

# Contents

| | | |
|---|---|---|
| *Table of Cases* | | xi |
| *Acknowledgments* | | xv |
| **1** | **Introduction** | 1 |
| **2** | **Ten Clusters of Laws/Regulations/Codes That Constrain Uses of Hate Speech** | 19 |
| | 2.1 Group Defamation | 19 |
| | 2.2 Negative Stereotyping or Stigmatization | 21 |
| | 2.3 The Expression of Hatred | 23 |
| | 2.4 Incitement to Hatred | 26 |
| | 2.5 Threats to Public Order | 28 |
| | 2.6 Denying, etc. Acts of Mass Cruelty, Violence, or Genocide | 29 |
| | 2.7 Dignitary Crimes or Torts | 30 |
| | 2.8 Violations of Civil or Human Rights | 33 |
| | 2.9 Expression-Oriented Hate Crimes | 35 |
| | 2.10 Time, Place, and Manner Restrictions | 38 |
| **3** | **Principles of Basic Morality** | 49 |
| | 3.1 Health | 49 |
| | 3.2 Autonomy | 58 |
| | 3.3 Security | 66 |
| | 3.4 Non-Subordination | 75 |
| | 3.5 The Absence of Oppression | 86 |
| | 3.6 Human Dignity | 91 |
| **4** | **Principles of Personal Development** | 106 |
| | 4.1 The Discovery of Truth | 106 |
| | 4.2 The Acquisition of Knowledge | 116 |
| | 4.3 Self-Realization | 120 |
| | 4.4 Human Excellence | 127 |

| | | |
|---|---|---|
| **5** | **Principles of Civic Morality** | 142 |
| | 5.1 Civic Dignity | 142 |
| | 5.2 Assurance | 148 |
| | 5.3 Eligibility | 152 |
| **6** | **Principles of Cultural Diversity** | 160 |
| | 6.1 Culture | 161 |
| | 6.2 Misrecognition | 166 |
| | 6.3 Cultural Specificity | 174 |
| | 6.4 Intercultural Dialogue | 180 |
| **7** | **Principles of Political Morality** | 187 |
| | 7.1 Democratic Self-Government | 187 |
| | 7.2 Political Legitimacy | 201 |
| | 7.3 Citizens as Legal Subjects | 209 |
| **8** | **Principles of Balance** | 218 |
| | 8.1 Rights-Based Balancing | 218 |
| | 8.2 Interests-Based Balancing | 222 |
| **9** | ***Principia Juris*** | 239 |
| | 9.1 Pressing Social Need | 239 |
| | 9.2 Efficacy | 242 |
| | 9.3 The Least Restrictive Alternative | 251 |
| | 9.4 The Avoidance of Unintended Consequences for Free Speech | 263 |
| | 9.5 Neutrality | 269 |
| **10** | **Toward a Theory of Principled Compromise** | 276 |
| | 10.1 Why Overall Warrant Should Be Neither about Lexical Priorities among Principles nor Balancing between Principles | 277 |
| | 10.2 Overall Warrant as Compromise over Principles | 281 |
| | 10.3 Conjunction Compromise | 284 |
| | 10.4 Substitution Compromise | 285 |
| | 10.5 A Detailed Illustration: The Principle of Neutrality | 287 |
| | 10.6 The Ethics of Compromise | 297 |
| | 10.7 Two Possible Objections | 306 |
| **11** | **Conclusion** | 316 |
| | *References* | 321 |
| | *Index* | 347 |

# Table of Cases

### Australia

| | |
|---|---|
| Bryant v. Queensland Newspaper Pty Ltd. | 25 |
| Eatock v. Bolt | 25, 165, 184, 272 |
| Jones v. Toben | 48 |

### Brazil

| | |
|---|---|
| Case of Diane Soares da Costa | 32 |

### Canada

| | |
|---|---|
| Bou Malhab v. Diffusion Métromedia CMR Inc. | 237 |
| Canada (Human Rights Commission) v. Taylor | 11–12, 186, 271–2, 275 |
| Edmonton Journal v. Alberta (Attorney General) | 282 |
| Mugesera v. Canada (Minister of Citizenship and Immigration) | 28 |
| Ortenberg v. Plamondon | 31 |
| R. v. Keegstra | 11–12, 110, 138, 147, 164, 184, 186, 223–4, 244, 257, 266, 271–2, 274–5, 310 |
| R. v. Oakes | 18, 271–2 |
| R. v. Zündel | 97, 197, 216, 265 |
| Saskatchewan (Human Rights Commission) v. Whatcott | 93, 197, 216, 265, 272, 280 |
| Singer v. Iwasyk and Pennywise Food Ltd. | 34 |

### China

| | |
|---|---|
| Case of Chen and Wang | 31 |

### Committee on the Elimination of Racial Discrimination (CERD)

| | |
|---|---|
| TBB-Turkish Union in Berlin/Brandenburg v. Germany | 24 |

### European Court of Human Rights (ECtHR)

| | |
|---|---|
| Aksu v. Turkey | 11, 35, 47, 235 |
| Appleby and Others v. United Kingdom | 275 |

xii  Table of Cases

| | |
|---|---|
| *Balsytė-Lideikienė v. Lithuania* | 12, 45, 271, 275 |
| *Féret v. Belgium* | 12, 271–2, 275 |
| *Garaudy v. France* | 12, 46 |
| *Glimmerveen and Hagenbeek v. Netherlands* | 37 |
| *Handyside v. United Kingdom* | 243, 270, 275 |
| *Jersild v. Denmark* | 11 |
| *Mouvement Raelien Suisse v. Switzerland* | 275 |
| *Nilsen and Johnsen v. Norway* | 18 |
| *Peta Deutschland v. Germany* | 272 |
| *Refah Partisi (The Welfare Party) and Others v. Turkey* | 197 |
| *Ricci v. Italy* | 272 |
| *Soulas and others v. France* | 12, 270, 272, 275 |
| *Vejdeland and Others v. Sweden* | 11–12, 43, 66, 100, 145, 158, 271–2, 275 |
| *Willem v. France* | 12 |
| *X v. Federal Republic of Germany* | 171 |

### Germany

| | |
|---|---|
| *Case of the Fraudulent Asylum Seeker Poem* | 156 |
| *Case of Guenter Deckert* | 97, 219 |
| *Case of Kruzifix-Urteil* | 286 |
| *Case of National Democratic Party of Germany (or 'Auschwitz Lie')* | 146, 219, 286 |
| *Case of Germar Rudolf* | 96, 219 |
| *Case of Ernst Zündel* | 98, 219, 249 |

### Hungary

| | |
|---|---|
| *Case of György Nagy* | 135–6 |

### International Criminal Tribunal for Rwanda

| | |
|---|---|
| *Nahimana, Barayagwiza, Ngeze v. The Prosecutor* | 40 |

### Israel

| | |
|---|---|
| *Neiman and Avneri v. Chairman of the Central Committee for the Elections to the 11th Knesset* | 197 |

### South Africa

| | |
|---|---|
| *Islamic Unity Convention v. Independent Broadcasting Authority and Others* | 37 |
| *Mbatha v. Van Staden* | 32, 46 |
| *S. v. Mamabolo* | 215 |

### United Kingdom (UK)

| | |
|---|---|
| *Case of Keira McCormack* | 23 |
| *Hammond v. Director of Public Prosecutions* | 206 |

| | |
|---|---|
| Knupffer v. London Express Newspaper, Ltd. | 237 |
| Naik v. The Secretary of State for the Home Department | 29 |
| R. v. Ali, Javed, and Ahmed | 74, 140, 241 |
| R. v. Birdwood | 27 |
| R. v. El-Faisal | 65 |
| R. v. Heaton and Hannington | 71 |
| R. v. Osborne | 41, 159 |
| R. v. Sheppard and Whittle I | 68 |
| R. v. Sheppard and Whittle II | 272 |
| R. v. Stacey | 257 |

## The United States of America (US)

| | |
|---|---|
| Abrams v. United States | 137 |
| Agarwal v. Johnson | 32 |
| Anti-Defamation Association of Emigres from Post-1917 Russia v. FCC | 48 |
| Beauharnais v. Illinois | 147, 154, 158, 170, 184, 192, 216, 238 |
| Bendix Autolite Corp. v. Midwesco Enters., Inc. | 238 |
| Bradshaw v. Swagerty | 53 |
| Brandenburg v. Ohio | 100, 204 |
| Bullard v. Florida | 23 |
| Chaplinsky v. State of New Hampshire | 47, 290, 312 |
| Cohen v. California | 47 |
| Collin v. Smith I | 12, 203, 216 |
| Collin v. Smith II | 263–4, 272–3, 314 |
| Contreras v. Crown Zellerbach, Inc. | 52 |
| Corry v. Stanford | 47, 116 |
| Doe v. University of Michigan | 47, 62, 116, 231, 238, 265–6, 268, 273–4 |
| Downs v. Los Angeles Unified School District | 242 |
| EEOC v. AA Foundries Inc. | 34 |
| EEOC v. Caldwell Freight Lines | 87 |
| EEOC v. Tyson Foods, Inc. | 34, 76 |
| Gomez v. Hug | 53 |
| Irving v. J.L. Marsh Inc. | 237 |
| Korematsu v. United States | 198 |
| Kunz v. New York | 15 |
| Martin v. Parrish | 62 |
| Metro Broadcasting, Inc. v. FCC | 311 |
| Meritor Savings Bank v. Vinson | 274 |
| Minneapolis Star and Tribune Co. v. Minnesota Commissioner of Revenue | 272 |
| Murdock v. Pennsylvania | 238 |
| New York Times Co. v. Sullivan | 215, 224–5, 237 |
| Palmer v. City of Concord | 159 |
| Perry Education Association v. Perry Local Educators' Association | 18 |
| Phelps-Roper v. City of Manchester | 39, 273 |

Table of Cases

| | |
|---|---|
| Phelps-Roper v. Strickland | 39, 273 |
| Police Department of the City of Chicago v. Mosley | 275 |
| R.A.V. v. City of St. Paul | 36, 64, 100, 241, 256, 270–2, 275, 288–9, 293, 295–7, 300, 312–4 |
| Red Lion Broadcasting Co. v. FCC | 48 |
| Resident Advisory Board v. Rizzo | 61 |
| Rosenberger v. Rectors and Visitors of University of Virginia | 274 |
| Rosenblatt v. Baer | 142 |
| Roth v. United States | 238 |
| Rust v. Sullivan | 272 |
| Shanoff v. Illinois Department of Human Services | 46 |
| Shelton v. Tucker | 272 |
| Smith v. Collin | 12, 273 |
| Snyder v. Phelps | 33, 131, 141, 206, 217, 273 |
| State v. Klapprott | 68 |
| Terminiello v. City of Chicago | 197 |
| Taylor v. Metzger | 53 |
| Turley v. ISG Lackawanna Inc. | 33 |
| Ugalde v. W.A. McKenzie Asphalt Co. | 53 |
| United States v. Carolene Products | 197 |
| United States v. O'Brien | 272 |
| United States v. Progressive, Inc. | 230, 238 |
| Virginia v. Black | 72, 165, 184, 216, 264, 270–1, 273, 288, 295, 297, 312–3 |
| Wade v. Orange County Sheriff's Office | 52 |
| Walker v. Thompson | 53 |
| Ward v. Rock Against Racism | 272 |
| Watts v. United States | 72 |
| West Virginia State Board of Education v. Barnette | 215 |
| Whitney v. California | 139, 215 |
| Wiggs v. Courshon | 32 |
| Wilmington v. J.I. Case Co. | 52 |

# Acknowledgments

I would like to begin by expressing immense gratitude to Adriana, Eli, and Delphine for ensuring that any time I spent researching and writing this book amounted to mere interludes in the far more important vocation of husband and father and not vice versa. I am indebted to the University of East Anglia (UEA), and in particular the School of Political, Social and International Studies (as it then was), for two glorious semesters of more or less unmolested research leave, and to the UEA library's interlibrary loan system. No greater friend does a scholar possess than a good interlibrary loan system. Rudimentary versions of Chs. 5, 6, and 10 were presented at, respectively, the Third Annual Loyola Constitutional Law Colloquium 2012, the Annual Conference of the Centre for Research on Nationalism, Ethnicity and Multiculturalism 2012, and a workshop on themes from the work of Susan Brison at the University of Queensland in 2014. For their questions and insights on those occasions I thank Wayne Batchis, Susan Brison, Catherine Curtis, Rebecca Dew, Marguerite La Caze, Catriona Mackenzie, Tariq Modood, Bryan Mukandi, Robert Simpson, and Leonid Sirota. I would particularly like to thank Alexander Tsesis and Katharine Gelber not merely for their organizational dexterity but also for their largeness of spirit. I am also grateful to Judith Mehta for her convivial and intellectually stimulating politics, philosophy, and economics reading group. Its Norwich-based band of thinkers, including Alan Finlayson, Barbara Goodwin, Shaun Hargreaves Heap, Gareth Jones, Judith Mehta, Angus Ross, and Bob Sugden, indulged me on the subject of hate speech law on two separate outings, never once voicing contempt. During the process of writing up my ideas I also benefited from sporadic email exchanges with Raphael Cohen-Almagor, Eric Heinze, Mary Kate McGowan, and Jeremy Waldron. However, I owe my largest amount of thanks to Sylvie Bacquet, Eric Barendt, Katharine Gelber, Peter Jones, Alan Haworth, David Mead, Catherine Rowett, Adriana Sinclair, Simon Thompson, Alexander Tsesis, and Wayne Sumner, who each granted me the sizeable gifts of their time and intellectual prowess in critiquing draft chapters. Finally, for legal and/or linguistic expertise that enabled me to identify and/or translate relevant legislation and legal decisions into English, I am much obliged to Ilyas Cengiz, Elizabeth Cobbett, Hualing Fu, Christina Hall, Chris Hanretty, Tanya Katerí Hernández, Jennifer Karlsson, Zsolt Kortvelyesi, Fernanda Leite Lopez De Leon, Vitit Muntarbhorn, Macarena Saez, Pamela Schwikkard, Adriana Sinclair, Dorthe Sloth, and Jose Zalaquet.

# 1  Introduction

Hate speech law has been the subject of numerous principled objections. It has been denounced by some legal scholars and practitioners as, among other things, devastating to liberty, disrespectful to autonomy, stifling to the discovery of truth and the acquisition of knowledge, inhibiting to self-realization, antithetical to free participation in the formation of public opinion, a threat to the legitimacy of the state, ineffective, unnecessary, and responsible for chilling forms of valuable speech. But at the same time, it is difficult to name a single country that possesses no hate speech law whatsoever or, at least, a country that possesses no laws/regulations/codes that constrain uses of hate speech. If the detractors are to be believed, then almost the entire world is both deluded and gratuitously unfree.

For their part, proponents maintain that hate speech law can, among other things, help to avert damage to people's health (psychological and physiological), safeguard autonomy (substantive, if not formal), reduce insecurity (objective and subjective), emancipate people from subordination, stand as a bulwark against oppression, underpin human dignity, protect and give public assurances of civic dignity, ensure recognition of cultural identity, facilitate respectful intercultural dialogue, and furnish real access to participation in the formation of democratic public opinion for all. Not only that, many legislatures and courts across the world have determined that hate speech law can be effective, necessary, and limited in its chilling effects.

So the first main goal of this book is to articulate, clarify, and formalize these and other related principled arguments. I shall do so by grounding them in a collection of key normative principles. These are normative in the sense that they articulate propositions intended to serve as bases for chains of reasoning about whether or not legalistic constraints on uses of hate speech—which is to say, institutionally backed and more often than not coercive, legalistic, and quasi-legalistic restrictions—are *warranted*. Although I shall treat principles as the main units of evaluation, it bears emphasis that these principles are *only* important by virtue of safeguarding or serving normatively relevant features. I shall say more about the content of the latter in a moment. It also deserves mention that making a plurality of principles the main units of evaluation is not an uncommon strategy in normative philosophy. Principles have been used in similar ways in the theory of moral conduct (e.g., Audi 2004) and in the theory of social justice (e.g., Miller 1999), so why not in the theory of the moral limits of the criminal law (e.g., Feinberg 1984, 1988, 1989, 1990) and, more specifically, in the theory of freedom of expression and its limits? At any rate, I think it would be a serious error to presume that those people who reject hate speech law do so exclusively on the grounds of principle, whereas those people who defend hate speech law do so exclusively on the grounds of mere policy, with everything this implies about the relative normative importance of principle and policy (cf. Dworkin 1985; Heyman 2008). On the contrary, there are principled arguments on both sides of the debate.

I also believe that because there are principled arguments on both sides of the debate, in the end much comes down to which key normative principles are being used to attack or defend which hate speech laws, and in relation to which contextual circumstances. With this in mind, the second main goal of the book is to disaggregate hate speech law into different clusters of laws/regulations/codes that constrain uses of hate speech, so as to facilitate a more accurate and nuanced examination of the principled arguments. In other words, we must improve our understanding of the heterogeneity of hate speech law before we can hope to succeed in figuring out whether or not such law is warranted. In particular, I wish to combat two unwelcome tendencies in the literature. While much legal scholarship in this area concentrates on the intricacies of specific jurisdictions, laws, and legal rulings, and demurs from making broader generalizations about hate speech law, a good deal of the philosophical literature has been guilty of presenting overly generalized arguments about the merits and demerits of hate speech law, as though arguments that pertain to one sort of law/regulation/code must obviously pertain to all laws/regulations/codes. This matters because, as I shall try to show, principles that appear to warrant hate speech law typically lend greater justificatory credence to some clusters of laws/regulations/codes than others; conversely, principles that purport to rule out all hate speech law are, on closer inspection, devastating against some clusters of laws/regulations/codes but relatively helpless against, or inappropriately applied to, others. In addition to this, I shall seek to move beyond another oversimplification that says the only thing that matters is which principled argument is being used to attack or defend which type of hate speech law. As well as considering the nature, form, and content of hate speech, it is vital to consider the context in which hate speech occurs. In particular, I accept the line of thought that says whether or not hate speech law is warranted partly depends on whether or not, and how, law is applied to given contextual circumstances, not the least of which are the particular institutions and social practices in which hate speech occurs.[1]

Having said that, even if one adds specificity to the debate on hate speech law by distinguishing between different clusters of laws/regulations/codes and by pairing up clusters with the most germane normative principles, while also paying attention to the contextual circumstances in which hate speech occurs, this is unlikely to be sufficient to resolve principled dilemmas. More often than not, if institutional authorities decide to enact or enforce a certain hate speech law in a given context, they are bound to be honoring some normative principles but sacrificing others. But if they choose instead to refrain from enacting or enforcing a certain hate speech law in a given context, they are also bound to be honoring some normative principles while sacrificing others. Consequently, the third main goal of the book is to articulate and defend a particular way of resolving these sorts of principled dilemmas.

Before stating what my approach is, however, I first need to draw a distinction between two kinds of warrant. One kind of warrant is concerned with whether or not a law/regulation/code is *prima facie* justified, authorized, sanctioned, supported, or rendered permissible by the contribution it makes to a given normatively relevant feature, such as a right, interest, good, or value. When a principle specifies whether a law/regulation/code is *prima facie* warranted or unwarranted with reference to a given normatively relevant feature—meaning that the principle's verdict holds unless it is overridden or trumped by another principle which itself may highlight a different normatively relevant feature—I shall call this *narrow warrant* or *N-warrant*, for short. Of course, the larger the number of relevant principles, the lower the chances that any law/regulation/code will be N-warranted by each and every relevant principle. In the main, legislatures, courts, and regulators will be called upon to decide between a law/regulation/code that is N-warranted by one or more principles but also N-unwarranted by one or more principles. A second kind of warrant is tailored to addressing precisely these sorts of dilemmas. It requires overarching determinations of whether a law/regulation/code is warranted or unwarranted based on every relevant principle. I shall call this *all principles considered warrant* or *overall warrant*, that is, *O-warrant*, for short. Judgments of O-warrant can be *non-comparative*, such that it could be said of a law/regulation/code that it is overall warranted when viewed by itself, or *comparative*, such that it can be said of two laws/regulations/codes that one achieves greater overall warrant than the other. But either way, it seems to me that judgments of overall warrant lie at the heart of resolving dilemmas around hate speech law. One challenge for the legal philosopher, then, is to provide a compelling theory of the nature of these judgments.

By connecting overall warrant to a diverse range of principles, including not only principles concerned with basic human values but also legal principles that are concerned with issues of efficacy and justiciability, I am consciously situating the book in a tradition of scholarship on free speech and its limits that is alive to both moral and practical considerations (e.g., Packer 1968: 296; Cohen [Joshua] 1993: 262; Shiffrin [S.H.] 1999: 80–85; Sumner 2004: 185; Heyman 2008: 180). Nevertheless, the fact that judgments of overall warrant depend on assessments of different kinds of principles raises a question about whether or not such judgments can be meaningful and non-arbitrary. It may be tempting at this stage to say that the overall warrant of a given law/regulation/code is either a matter of satisfying an order of *lexical priority* among principles (such that the top principle must be satisfied come what may, and the next principle is only there to break ties) or about *balancing* principles (meaning that a little more success in satisfying one principle can be traded off against a little less success in satisfying another). I find neither alternative plausible. Instead, I shall argue that reaching judgments about the overall warrant of laws/regulations/codes that constrain uses of hate speech should be done on the basis of principled compromise. Principled compromise is characterized not merely by compromise over matters of principled concern but also by compromise that is itself governed by ideals of moral conduct. The ideals I have in mind are reciprocity, equality, and mutual respect (ideals that have been much discussed in various contemporary academic literatures, not the least of which is work on judicial ethics and virtue jurisprudence, deliberative democracy, discourse ethics, and communicative virtue). Articulating and defending a theory of overall warrant as principled compromise, then, is the third main goal of the book.

Before I can begin to pursue these three main goals in earnest, however, I first need to provide some important clarifications. For the purposes of this book I shall be guided by an essentially legalistic understanding of hate speech. Even putting to one side extralegal accounts of the nature of hate speech that have emerged from the disciplines of applied linguistics, discourse analysis, sociology, and social psychology, it is important to recognize that the jurisprudential literature alone contains numerous competing, sometimes contradictory characterizations of hate speech (e.g., Matsuda 1989b: 2357; Sherry 1991: 933; Coliver 1992: 363; Schauer 1992a: 1349; Smolla 1992: 152; Lawrence et al. 1993: 1; Glasser 1994: 1; Lederer and Delgado 1995: 4–5; Sullivan and Gunther 1995: 1131; Alexander 1996: 71; Brison 1998a: 313; 2013: 2332; Nockleby 2000: 1277; Vasquez and de las Fuentes 2000: 226; Corlett and Francescotti 2002: 1083; Miller 2003: 67, 218; Sumner 2003: 142; Parekh 2005–2006: 214; Cohen-Almagor 2006a: 153; Mahoney 2009: 325–326; Post 2009: 127; Lee 2010: 22; Waldron 2010: 1600; Fraleigh and Tuman 2011: 139; Yong 2011: 386; Gelber 2012a: 213; Langton 2012: 74–77). Nevertheless, I believe that in all of these cases the author is seeking, either explicitly or implicitly, to offer a characterization of the sort of speech or other expressive conduct that is, or has been at one time, the subject of laws or regulations. At any rate, the overall impression created by these characterizations is of speech or other expressive conduct that is in some sense intimately connected with hatred of members of groups or classes of persons identified by certain ascriptive characteristics (e.g., race, ethnicity, nationality, citizenship, origin of birth, war record, religion, sexual orientation, gender or transgender identity, disability, age, physical appearance), where this connection is exemplified by familiar tropes relating to hatred in the motive, content, or effect of the relevant speech or other expressive conduct.[2]

In the book I shall use the term 'speech or other expressive conduct' so as to cover not only words, written or oral, but also symbols, pictures, gestures, music, moving images, or any conduct that is intended to express or is reasonably regarded as expressive of meaning.[3] Of course, it is possible to give the word 'expression' a restrictive definition such that not all speech conduct counts as expression so defined. Under a restrictive definition, the putative conflict between the right to freedom of expression and laws/regulations/codes that constrain uses of hate speech that qualify as speech plus, illegal conduct, or speech conduct that has a purely emotional effect, for example, evaporates. This book does not seek to exploit such strategies, however.[4] Instead, I intend to treat all laws/regulations/codes that constrain uses of hate speech as potentially imposing a genuine cost in freedom of expression. Otherwise, any progress made in justifying legalistic constraints is liable to be rejected by civil libertarians as premised on a terminological sleight of hand.

Furthermore, I shall use the term 'hate speech law' in an inclusive way to mean laws/regulations/codes that tend, either directly or indirectly, to constrain at least some uses of hate speech. This concept or notional configuration is meant to capture not only laws/regulations/codes that are ostensibly aimed at constraining, suppressing or limiting hate speech but also laws/regulations/codes that impose incidental restrictions on some uses of hate speech, meaning laws/regulations/codes that, although aimed at the instruments or circumstances of speech or at certain forms of conduct, nevertheless thereby also restrict some uses of hate speech.[5] I shall also use the term 'laws/regulations/codes' in a deliberately broad way to capture various types of laws, regulations, rules, codes, and standards within both common law and civil law systems, and pertaining to public and private legal and quasi-legal institutions. The relevant means of coercion may include criminal punishments, civil liability, regulatory sanctions, regulatory rulings over the removal of content, orders to refrain from speech conduct of a certain sort, and even the prevention of speech through the denial or revocation of an individual's right to remain within the borders of a country.[6]

By referring to principles rather than to a single principle, I do not mean to overlook the fact that there are approaches to free speech and its limits that posit a single principle (or perhaps two principles) that serves or safeguards a single normatively relevant feature. Consider monist approaches that, respectively, concentrate on self-realization (e.g., Redish 1982), deliberative democracy (e.g., Sunstein 1993a), political legitimacy (e.g., Dworkin 2012), or autonomy (e.g., Baker 1989; 2009; 2011). Instead, I refer to principles to signal both the fact that I endorse principle pluralism and the fact that I am committed to value pluralism. Together, the key normative principles to be discussed in this book serve, protect, uphold, honor, enshrine, or enact a range of rights, interests, goods, and values. Some of the principles relate to a single normatively relevant feature, while others are concerned with multiple features. Some are fundamental principles, whereas others are derivative of, or instrumental for, fundamental principles (cf. Schauer 1982: 3–4; Dworkin 1977: 180; 1978: 116–117, 125–126). Although some are dependent upon a particular body of law or legal institution, others transcend any particular bodies of law or institutions (cf. Scanlon 1972: 205–206). Some, but not all, principles may strike people as self-evident, meaning that they do not require further evidence or support, but most are non-axiomatic. Some are rooted in mainstream traditions of legal and political thought, others less so. Some reflect legal thinking within certain countries, while some appear to be more universal. Some of the principles might be regarded as black letter laws within certain legal jurisdictions, but most remain open to dispute. Nevertheless, all of the normative principles that I shall discuss, in my view, have the potential to be epistemically justified in the sense that it may be appropriate to regard them not merely as the subjects of moral belief but as the objects of moral knowledge if the people who believe them have acted in epistemically responsible ways, meaning that they have done everything they should have done to hold true principles.[7]

The normatively relevant features to be discussed in this book will be the sorts of fundamental rights, vital interests, and basic human goods and values that are, or should be, matters of deep and enduring concern to all human beings: namely, liberty (negative and positive), health (psychological and physiological), autonomy (formal and substantive), security (objective and subjective), non-subordination, the absence of oppression, human dignity, the discovery of truth, the acquisition of knowledge, self-realization (in its various incarnations), human excellence, civic dignity, cultural diversity and choice, recognition of cultural identity, intercultural dialogue, participation in democratic self-government, and being subject only to legitimate rule. Of course, I do not mean to imply that this list is exhaustive or uncontroversial.[8] Instead, I simply wish to make clear what is to be considered in the course of this book, with its focus on hate speech law. Clearly this is also an eclectic list,[9] and I shall try to bring out some of the implications of this eclecticism in Chs. 8 [8.2] and 10 [10.1].

Now it might be worried that freedom of expression and equality are absent from the previous list of normatively relevant features. After all, hate speech law is often characterized as creating a conflict between freedom of expression and equality (e.g., Massaro 1991; Blim 1995; Hemmer 1995; Powell 1996–1997; Goodpaster 1997; Demaske 2004; Mahoney 2009). On closer inspection, however, both freedom of expression and equality are already implicit in the aforementioned list of features and may also be promoted by or play a role in the various principles that safeguard or serve those features. For one thing, it might be safe to assume that to promote and protect features such as liberty, autonomy, security, non-subordination, the absence of oppression, participation in democratic self-government, and being subject only to legitimate rule will be to promote and protect a good deal of freedom of expression. So even if there is no specific right to freedom of expression over and above a general right to liberty (cf. Schauer 1983), this does not mean that freedom of expression goes unprotected. For instance, one might think that a principle that limits coercive state intervention to the prevention of harm, or else a principle that demands respect for formal autonomy, ensures that people enjoy a protected sphere of freedom of expression. In a similar vein, features such as non-subordination, the absence of oppression, civic dignity, and the recognition of cultural identity can be interpreted as types of substantive equality. It might be thought that to treat someone as a subordinate or to subordinate someone is to treat that person as being unequal or to violate equality. Furthermore, many of the key normative principles to be outlined in the book embody types of formal equality. For example, some principles employ equality as a universal quantifier by insisting that particular normatively relevant features should be realized for *all* members of society and not just some. This type of formal equality is apparent in principles that require that no one exercise his or her fundamental rights or fulfill his or her vital interests or benefit from the realization of basic human goods and values in ways that can be expected to prevent other people from exercising their fundamental rights or block other people from fulfilling their vital interests or make it more difficult for other people to benefit from the realization of basic human goods and values. A closely related type of formal equality is embodied in the familiar legal principle that proclaims the right of all citizens to equal protection under the law. Yet another type of formal equality is embodied in the equally familiar legal principle that like cases should be treated alike.

Turning now to the structure of the book, Ch. 2 presents and distinguishes the following ten clusters of laws/regulations/codes that constrain uses of hate speech.

1. Laws/regulations/codes that proscribe public speech or other expressive conduct when it amounts to group defamation of members of groups or classes of persons identified by certain ascriptive characteristics.
2. Laws/regulations/codes that limit public speech or other expressive conduct that amounts to negative stereotyping or stigmatization of members of groups or classes of persons identified by certain ascriptive characteristics.
3. Laws/regulations/codes that disallow the public expression of hatred toward members of groups or classes of persons identified by certain ascriptive characteristics.
4. Laws/regulations/codes that ban the public use of speech or other expressive conduct with the intention (or likelihood) of stirring up, inciting, or promoting feelings of hatred or hostility toward or among members of groups or classes of persons identified by certain ascriptive characteristics.

5. Laws/regulations/codes that prohibit public speech or other expressive conduct that is directed at members of groups or classes of persons identified by certain ascriptive characteristics and that is a threat to public order.
6. Laws/regulations/codes that penalize public speech or other expressive conduct that constitutes denying, grossly trivializing, approving, justifying, condoning, or glorifying acts of mass cruelty, violence, or genocide perpetrated against members of groups or classes of persons identified by certain ascriptive characteristics.
7. Laws/regulations/codes that provide criminal sanctions or civil remedies that can be used to constrain speech or other expressive conduct directed at members of groups or classes of persons identified by certain ascriptive characteristics when that speech or other expressive conduct amounts to the enactment of a dignitary crime or tort.
8. Laws/regulations/codes that forbid speech or other expressive conduct when it amounts to conduct that violates or interferes with the exercise of the civil or human rights of members of groups or classes of persons identified by certain ascriptive characteristics.
9. Laws/regulations/codes that interdict speech or other expressive conduct that constitutes the enactment of an expression-oriented hate crime targeted at members of groups or classes of persons identified by certain ascriptive characteristics.
10. Laws/regulations/codes that can be used to indirectly constrain forms of public speech or other expressive conduct aimed at members of groups or classes of persons identified by certain ascriptive characteristics via time, place, and manner restrictions.

I shall argue that these ten clusters are interpretive, in the sense that they constitute idealizations of actual laws/regulations/codes that can be found in jurisdictions across the world. Their purpose in this book, however, is to provide a good starting position, as opposed to an endpoint, for normative evaluation of hate speech law. As stated previously, the hope is that attending to the heterogeneous nature of hate speech law will support a more fine-grained discussion of the principled arguments.

In Ch. 3 I examine arguments that appeal to principles of basic morality, which is to say, principles concerned with the fundamentals of how people ought to treat each other. These principles focus on the impact of hate speech on health, autonomy, security, non-subordination, the absence of oppression, and human dignity. Scholars from very different traditions of legal and political thought—critical race theory (e.g., Mari Matsuda, Charles Lawrence, Richard Delgado), subordination theory (e.g., Rae Langton, Ishani Maitra), and liberal theory (e.g., Susan Brison, Mary Kate McGowan), for example—agree that at least some conduct constituted by hate speech is regulatable given one or more of the aforementioned features. To say that conduct is regulatable is to say that it can meet a threshold that

Introduction  9

N-warrants the use of legalistic constraints whether or not it should actually be regulated all principles considered. I shall subject these lines of thought to critical scrutiny, highlighting gaps in empirical evidence and/or theoretical reasoning along the way. I will also try to draw inferences about which clusters of laws/regulations/codes are regulatable depending on which principle of basic morality is being underscored. For instance, I draw an inference from human dignity to the N-warrant of criminal sanctions or civil remedies against hate speech when it qualifies as a dignitary crime or tort.

In Ch. 4 I look at a range of principles of personal development that challenge the simplistic logic that says hate speech ought to be regulated because it is a force for moral bad. These principles purport to show that hate speech law is incompatible with the personal development of speakers, audiences, and even targets of hate speech. This is because (so the argument goes) even hate speech can be indispensable or else highly conducive to the discovery of truth, the acquisition of knowledge, self-realization (in its various forms), and human excellence. However, I argue that these principled considerations, once fully articulated, may indeed show that some hate speech law is N-unwarranted but fail to prove that all hate speech law is N-unwarranted, with reference to aspects of personal development. For example, I make the case that engaging in group defamation (*senso stricto*), discriminatory harassment, and Holocaust denial might open up pathways to greater knowledge and self-realization for speakers and audiences but may also close down pathways to truth discovery and self-realization for those people who are its targets. Drawing on insights from virtue jurisprudence, I also try to explain how even if hate speech law can in one sense remove opportunities for targets or victims to display stoical virtues, it remains the case that failing to restrict uses of hate speech can be a missed opportunity to deter the human vice of cruelty and promote the virtues of sympathy and empathy.

In Ch. 5 I investigate Jeremy Waldron's argument that hate speech law is N-warranted insofar as it protects civic dignity, which is a matter of whether or not citizens enjoy a high and equal social and legal status no matter their race, ethnicity, religion, gender, sexual orientation, physical disability, and other protected characteristics. In fact, Waldron argues that not merely can hate speech law protect civic dignity but it can also compel citizens to do their bit in providing the public good of assurance of civic dignity, meaning that we refrain from engaging in speech acts that lessen the extent to which members of vulnerable groups feel secure in their position as members of society in good standing. I shall make three critical arguments. First, I will argue that Waldron underestimates or undersells the applicability of his own approach by failing to recognize the full range of hate speech law that it has the potential to N-warrant. Second, I will suggest that hate speech law is neither a sufficient nor a necessary material condition for providing the good of public assurance. Third, I will argue that Waldron's approach has unwelcome consequences for which sorts of people are eligible for protection from laws/regulations/codes that constrain uses of hate speech. Specifically, I will argue that his approach falls short of N-warranting protection

10  *Introduction*

for resident non-citizens and people who are incapable of exercising the trappings of legal status—but it might be thought that both groups of people are in particular need of protection from hate speech.

In Ch. 6 I focus on principled arguments about hate speech law that relate to cultural diversity and choice, recognition of cultural identity, and intercultural dialogue. I argue that cultural diversity can be interpreted as a public good that we all have reason to care about, and that in order to provide this public good authorities may sometimes need to protect the hate speech of vulnerable groups but may sometimes need to impose constraints on the hate speech of groups who put at risk the provision of this public good. I also try to explain what it means to misrecognize cultural identity and how different clusters of laws/regulations/codes may be related to the avoidance of different forms of misrecognition. Finally, I interrogate Bhikhu Parekh's work on cultural specificity and intercultural dialogue. I argue that once disambiguated, his arguments tend to support laws/regulations/codes limiting hate speech when it amounts to negative stereotyping but that in places his own characterization of "the Muslim question" comes dangerously close to negatively stereotyping Muslims.

In Ch. 7 I turn to consider a set of principles that invoke distinctively political considerations relating to democratic self-government, participation in the formation of public opinion, political legitimacy, and political obligation.[10] James Weinstein and Robert Post, for example, underline the importance of freedom of expression, even hate speech, for public discourse, upon which more formal processes of democratic decision-making rest. But even they seek to draw distinctions between hate speech that is and hate speech that is not part of public discourse, properly understood. As I shall try to make clear, the attempt to draw these distinctions leaves their approaches vulnerable to attack from civil libertarians such as Eugene Volokh. For my part, I will argue that certain clusters of laws/regulations/codes may be N-warranted even if they suppress hate speech that *does* constitute public discourse by hate speakers. This is because some forms of hate speech, especially when carried out by a vociferous segment of the population, might leave members of targeted groups too vulnerable to themselves participate in the formation of public opinion—where this exclusion detracts from the richness of the cultural environment from which political decisions emanate. In this chapter I also discuss a recent debate between Waldron and Ronald Dworkin over the compatibility of hate speech law and political legitimacy. Whereas Dworkin highlights the need for unfettered speech in the collective authorization of anti-discrimination laws that benefit the very people who may also be tempted to claim protection from hate speech law, Waldron argues that the nature and effects of hate speech may be sufficiently serious to overshadow putative claims to political legitimacy. I argue that if one conceives of political legitimacy as a form of reasonable agreement, the case for some hate speech law is not difficult to understand. Finally, I examine C. Edwin Baker's argument that it would be incoherent for the state to expect citizens to obey the law if it did not at the same time respect their autonomous decisions regarding how to express themselves in public, including through hate speech. I propose that paying closer attention to traditional approaches to the question of political obligation can help to remove this apparent incoherence.

In Ch. 8 I explore another common idea in the literature: that balancing exercises can, and should, play a role in resolving dilemmas posed by hate speech (e.g., Special Committee on Hate Propaganda in Canada 1966: 60; Kretzmer 1987: 500; O'Neil 1989; Strossen 1990: 522; 2012: 384; Boyle 1992: 1–2; Anand 1997: 215; Chemerinsky 2003: 79; Sumner 2004: ch. 3; Braun 2004: 28; Barendt 2005: 30–36; Parekh 2005–2006: 220; 2006: 352; Cohen-Almagor 2006a: 6; 2009: 105; 2012: 44; McNamara 2007b: ch. 4; Tsesis 2009: 499; Grimm 2009: 13; Delgado and Stefancic 2009: 366; Bleich 2011: chs. 1–4; Berger Levinson 2013: 37–47).[11] Legal scholars are not alone in employing this metaphor. For example, Chief Justice Dickson of the Canadian Supreme Court has argued that balancing exercises are particularly well-suited to the application of s. 1 of the Canadian Charter of Rights and Freedoms[12] to hate speech law, provided that these exercises are accompanied by a careful scrutiny of the facts in particular cases. I have in mind his reasoning in *R. v. Keegstra* [1990][13] and *Canada (Human Rights Commission) v. Taylor* [1990].[14] For its part, the European Court of Human Rights (ECtHR) has sometimes made explicit reference to the careful balancing exercises undertaken by domestic courts in hate speech cases as grounds for upholding the decisions of these courts under its margin of appreciation doctrine. Consider *Jersild v. Denmark* (1994)[15] and *Aksu v. Turkey* (2012).[16] Indeed, in some cases the ECtHR has suggested ways in which those exercises might be expanded to encompass other rights, interests, goods, or values overlooked by domestic courts—for example *Vejdeland and Others v. Sweden* (2012).[17] However, the prevalence of the balancing metaphor is not always matched by the precision with which it is used. While scholars claim that the self-realization of hate speakers needs to be carefully balanced against the harms of hate speech, for instance, seldom do they provide a comprehensive theory of how this balancing ought to be performed (e.g., Gilmore 2011: 539), save for remarking that this is what judges are there for (e.g., Redish 1982: 623–625). The purpose of Ch. 8 is to shine a light on this lack of clarity where it exists and to add greater precision where possible. I try to do this by comparing and contrasting two main kinds of balancing: rights-based balancing, defended by Steven J. Heyman (2008); and interests-based balancing, exemplified in the work of Wayne Sumner (2004) and in a recent treatment of J.S. Mill's theory of free speech by Frederick Schauer (2012). I shall argue that interests-based balancing is the more justificatorily basic form of balancing among the two kinds, but that it faces the considerable problem of incommensurability.

In Ch. 9 I investigate some of the core legal principles employed by courts around the world in determining whether or not hate speech law is warranted.[18] The principles I will discuss focus on pressing social needs, efficacy, the least restrictive alternative, avoidance of unintended consequences for free speech, and neutrality. In many jurisdictions some or all of these principles are combined together to create complex, multipronged legal tests in free speech cases. For example, the Strict Scrutiny Test deployed by the US Supreme Court involves an assessment of whether or not law serves a compelling state interest (Is the law enacted for the sake of a pressing public end?), is necessary (Is the law the least restrictive means available of pursuing its end?), and is narrowly tailored (Is the law narrowly tailored to only that conduct which pertains to the relevant end?).[19] A good deal of hate speech law has run afoul of the Strict Scrutiny Test. Most famously, in the Skokie Affair of the late 1970s a set of municipal ordinances that restricted the activities of Nazi hate groups in Chicago (including content-based restrictions and time, place, and manner restrictions) were judged to be in violation of the First Amendment by a US District Court in *Collin v. Smith I* (1978).[20] This decision was confirmed by a US Court of Appeals in *Collin v. Smith II* (1978).[21] Shortly after a Writ of Certiorari was denied by the Supreme Court in Smith v. Collin (1978).[22] Both the content and application of multipronged tests differs in other jurisdictions, however. The Oakes Test employed by the Canadian Supreme Court requires an evaluation of whether or not law serves an important legislative objective (Is there a social need for the law of sufficient gravity to *prima facie* justify the restriction of rights it entails?), is rationally connected to the relevant social need (Have authorities demonstrated that the law will be an effective means of meeting the relevant social need?), is necessary (Is the law the least restrictive means available of pursuing its end?), and is proportional (Are the punishments specified by the law proportionate to the relevant social need?).[23] In both *R. v. Keegstra* and *Canada (Human Rights Commission) v. Taylor* the Canadian Supreme Court ruled that hate speech law did pass muster under the test. For its part, the ECtHR applies the Necessary in a Democratic Society Test—as articulated in Art. 10(2) of the European Convention on Human Rights (ECHR)—that calls for consideration of whether or not law serves a pressing social need (Does the law serve one or more of the interests articulated in Art. 10(2)?), is necessary (Has the state given sufficient reason for the use of the law in achieving its objectives such as by showing that it did not have other means at its disposal of accomplishing the same objective?), and is proportional (Are the punishments specified by the law proportionate to the relevant social need?).[24] In *Garaudy v. France* (2003),[25] *Soulas and others v. France* (2008),[26] *Balsytė-Lideikienė v. Lithuania* (2008),[27] *Féret v. Belgium* (2009),[28] *Willem v. France* (2009),[29] and, most recently, *Vejdeland and Others v. Sweden*, the ECtHR held that the relevant domestic courts had been justified in upholding and applying domestic hate speech law under the Necessary in a Democratic Society Test, and in accordance with its margin of appreciation doctrine. I shall argue that contrary to what several scholars have proclaimed or inferred, laws/regulations/codes that constrain uses of hate speech law can relate to pressing social needs, can be efficacious, can be the least restrictive alternative, can avoid unintended consequences for free speech, and can fall under well-established exceptions to the demands of content and viewpoint neutrality.

In Ch. 10 I shall defend a conception of overall warrant based on the ideals of principled compromise. This is a matter of parties to dilemmas over hate speech and freedom of expression arriving at compromise agreements in which matters of principled concern are addressed by both sides sacrificing at least one of their principles. In the case of *conjunction compromise* this is a matter of conjoining together a subset of principles taken from two or more original sets of principles. And in the case of *substitution compromise* it means substituting two or more opposing or contrasting principles with a third principle. What is more, using the core example of compromise among supreme court justices, I shall argue that a compromise (conjunction or substitution) is *principled* only if it is governed by the following ideals or standards: *reciprocity* (a matter of compromisers presenting reasons that are acceptable to both sides), *equality* (a matter of equal airing and consideration of alternatives), and *mutual respect* (a matter of compromisers displaying the virtues of honesty, integrity, good faith, open-mindedness, reasonableness, and magnanimity).

In short, my book will examine dilemmas of principle that surround hate speech law, and it will seek to do so in a way that is comparative (involving comparisons between laws/regulations/codes found in different jurisdictions), nuanced (seeking to separate hate speech law into differentiable clusters), interpretivist (directed toward not merely the description of law but the interpretation of law in its best light), normatively pluralist (aiming to subject hate speech law to normative evaluation by drawing on a range of moral, ethical, civic, cultural, political, and legal principles), critical (responsive to the goal of demasking relations of unequal power that underpin not only legal institutions and decision-making but also the social relationships and social practices on which the courts are asked to sit in judgment), linguistically pragmatic (concerned not simply with the meaning of words and symbols but also with what people do with words and symbols in interpersonal situations), and contextualist (sensitive to the point and purposes of the institutions and social practices that speech creates or in which speech is embedded, and motivated to assess the value of speech in the light of these contextual circumstances). In addition, the theory of overall warrant that I defend as a way of making decisions about hate speech law can be called a theory of principled compromise (by virtue of advocating not only compromise on matters of principle but also principled compromise) or even an aretaic theory of principled compromise (because it emphasizes the need for virtuous character among those people who are in a position to forge compromises).

## NOTES

1. Frederick Schauer (1998, 2005), for instance, insists that the degree of value or importance that courts do, and should, attach to particular constitutional principles or values relating to free expression is sensitive to the specific institutions in which speakers operate. For Schauer (2012) this means, for example, that the goods or values of truth discovery and knowledge acquisition associated with Holocaust denial may have a greater degree of value or importance

within the institution of the university than within other institutions. In a similar vein, Robert Post (1995: 1273) argues that 'speech makes possible a world of complex and diverse social practices precisely because it becomes integrated into and constitutive of these different practices; it therefore assumes the diverse constitutional values of these distinct practices.' Following on from this, Post suggests (1273–1280) that legalistic constraints on hate speech could be more readily justified in the context of the workplace than in other contexts because (in his view) the goods or values of self-expression and self-realization carry less weight or importance within the social practice of gainful employment than they do within the social practice of public discourse (i.e., the social practice of contributing to the formation of democratic public opinion). In short (2012: 12): 'Hate speech that is part of public discourse will receive the same protection that public discourse generally receives. Hate speech that is not part of public discourse will not receive this kind of protection. So, for example, hateful words addressed by one employee to another in the context of employment within the Social Security Administration will receive only the minimal forms of constitutional protection that we accord to speech expressed by employees in the context of government employment about matters of private concern.'
2. Importantly, I do not intend this as an analytical definition (i.e., a statement of necessary and sufficient conditions) of hate speech. It may be that hate speech is too close to being a 'family-resemblance' concept, in the Wittgensteinian sense, to admit of such a definition. Indeed, any attempt to pin-down this rather legalistic concept (i.e., one that emerges from the analysis of bodies of law) must depend on careful examination of hate speech law, going back and forth between alternative concepts of hate speech and alternative clusters of law until a coherent fit is found.
3. In this way burning crosses, making Nazi salutes, and even lynching may count as hate speech for the purposes of justification. Of course, law itself can express meaning, and many arguments against bodies of law that permit hate speech turn on what such laws say about our values and attitudes toward minorities. However, for the purposes of this book I shall not take a stand on whether or not it is right to treat law itself as hate speech. It is quite possible to assess the strength of the case for the symbolic meaning and value of hate speech law without having to settle that further issue.
4. One strategy could be to rely on the distinction between pure speech or mere speech, on the one hand, and speech conduct or speech plus, on the other (e.g., Emerson 1963: 917). More specifically, it would be to argue that when a particular hate speech law prohibits speech conduct or speech plus, there is no question of that law being incompatible with a constitutional guarantee of freedom of expression. I do not make anything of this distinction in this book, however, because I accept the counterargument that all forms of speech or expression are action or conduct, in the sense that all speech or expression necessarily has a performative dimension, whereas all action or conduct can be speech or expression, in the sense that it may have a declarative or communicative dimension. For further discussion of these issues, see Sunstein (1993b), Fish (1994: 124–126), Fiss (1996a: ch. 1), Butler (1997), Brison (1998b, 2004), Sadurski (1999: ch. 2), Lakoff (2000: 103–108), Collier (2001), Schaff (2002), and Neu (2008: ch. 6).

A second, related strategy is to accept that all speech or expression is action or conduct but to distinguish between expressive conduct that amounts to permissible or legal conduct and expressive conduct that constitutes impermissible or illegal conduct. The strategy is to stipulate that laws against expressive conduct that constitutes illegal conduct are always compatible with, that is to say, cannot violate, the right to freedom of expression. Incitement is often cited as an example in which, as Sunstein (1993a: 125) puts it, 'words actually amount to a way of performing independently illegal acts.' Similarly, it has been argued that hate speech that constitutes discriminatory harassment in the workplace or on a university campus does not merit *any* protection under, and is simply not relevant to, a constitutional guarantee of freedom of expression because it is not speech but rather illegal conduct (e.g., Marcus 2008). Once again, however, I shall not seek to exploit this strategy. Civil libertarians who care deeply about freedom of expression are unlikely to be reassured by the stipulation that illegal speech conduct is not really speech after all. Mere stipulation is no substitute for a justification as to why certain speech conduct should not be entitled to claim any protection as speech merely because it also happens to constitute illegal conduct. For further discussion of this strategy, see the work of Greenawalt (1989: chs. 12 and 15; 1995: 81–82), Strossen (1990), Volokh (1992), Sunstein (1993a: chs. 4 and 6), Murray (1997), Chemerinsky (2009), McGowan (2009, 2012), and Maitra and McGowan (2010).

A third strategy is to try to distinguish between expressive conduct that has (by intent) a cognitive, reason-based effect and expressive conduct that has a purely non-cognitive, emotional effect, where (so the strategy runs) the latter cannot claim protection under the First Amendment as 'speech.' This strategy is sometimes employed in thinking about the pornography question (cf. Schauer 1979; Sunstein 1986). It is also hinted at by Justice Jackson's dissent in *Kunz v. New York* (1951) 340 US 290. 'There, held to be "insulting or 'fighting' words" were calling one a "God damned racketeer" and a "damned Fascist." Equally inciting and more clearly "fighting words," when thrown at Catholics and Jews who are rightfully on the streets of New York, are statements that "The Pope is the anti-Christ" and the Jews are "Christ-killers." These terse epithets come down to our generation weighted with hatreds accumulated through centuries of bloodshed. [. . .] They are always, and in every context, insults which do not spring from reason and can be answered by none.' At 298–299. Once again, however, I do not think that this distinction does justice to the controversy around freedom of expression and hate speech law. As a practical matter, it seems highly unlikely that the average hate speaker intends or achieves *only* an emotional effect on the listener. Public expressions of hatred, such as through the use of insults, slurs, or derogatory epithets (e.g., "Black bastard!"), acts of incitement to hatred (e.g., "Please, I'm begging you, don't be scared to trust your feelings about just how much you hate Muslims"), and even acts of incitement to violence (e.g., "Death to Arabs!") can express messages of a cognitive as well as non-cognitive kind. This content may not be as obvious, explicit, sharply defined, or cerebral as in the case of group defamation or negative stereotyping (e.g., "Jews can't be trusted—they have all manner of schemes to capture the rest of us in their thrall"), but the ideational content is present nonetheless. So I think it would be wrong to lean too heavily on the notion that certain forms of hate speech do not deserve constitutional protection and are therefore regulatable because they have a purely non-cognitive, emotional effect on listeners. For conflicting views on this strategy, see Greenawalt (1989: chs. 8 and 17), Lawrence (1990), Strossen (1990: 547–549), and Cohen-Almagor (2012: 55–56). Indeed, one dimension of the current distinction often ignored in the literature is that it might tend to favor the speech of one socio-economic class over another. As Nicholas Wolfson (1997: 48) expresses it, 'if we limit censorship to the epithet, we create a two-tier approach: chilling of blue-collar muck and preservation of upper-crust mud.'

5. I am not alone in creating a new concept or notional configuration to discuss several different clusters of law under one umbrella. For example, in their edited volume, *Extreme Speech and Democracy* (2009) Ivan Hare and

James Weinstein employ the term 'extreme speech' to mean laws that suppress a range of forms of speech, including hate speech, blasphemy, religious speech that offends secular values, incitement to and glorification of terrorism, Holocaust denial, and obscenity. Weinstein and Hare (2009: 4) claim to be interested in 'current attempts to suppress various types of extreme speech that many believe pose an unacceptable threat to essential values in modern multicultural democracies, or in some cases, to democracy itself.' Based on this definition, something is extreme speech merely if enough people believe that it poses a threat to something they hold dear. As some of their contributors point out, however, from this definition it would be difficult to know where to draw the boundaries of what is or is not 'extreme speech' (e.g., Bodney 2009: 599; Rowbottom 2009: 608). My concept or notional configuration of hate speech law or, to be more exact, laws/regulations/codes that constrain uses of hate speech, pertains to speech or other expressive conduct that is intimately connected with hatred of groups or classes of persons identified by certain ascriptive characteristics. One distinctive feature of this concept is that it straddles the distinction that some academics draw between hate speech law and hate crime law (e.g., Jacobs and Potter 1998: 6). In particular, it includes laws/regulations/codes that constrain uses of hate speech when it amounts to a hate crime or a violation of civil rights, such as discriminatory harassment, intimidation, provocation, or incitement to crime. I regard the acts targeted by such laws/regulations/codes as expression-oriented, meaning they do not merely involve an expressive dimension but the expressive dimension is central to the way the act is performed. Like the concept of extreme speech, my configuration also includes Holocaust denial laws. However, my basis for inclusion is not that statements denying the Holocaust are believed to be a threat to democracy, but because they can be plausibly understood as forms of hate speech (e.g., Parekh 2006: 214–521; Cohen-Almagor 2006a: 12, 2009; Mahoney 2009: 325; Schauer 2012: 142–143).

However, I do not include as instances of hate speech law certain other sorts of law oriented toward the protection of religious beliefs, including laws against blasphemy, laws against apostasy, laws against insulting a religion or objects of religious worship of any class of persons, laws against denigrating the religious beliefs or values of sections of the population, and laws against offending religious believers or outraging religious feelings. Although some instances of blasphemy and outrage of religious feelings can be counted as hate speech, such as when blasphemous speech is used with intent to stir up hatred against religious believers, not all instances count as hate speech. It is quite possible for someone to deny, insult, offend, and outrage deities, sacred objects, and religious beliefs and believers without being motivated by hatred, without using hateful expressions, and without inciting or promoting hatred. Nor shall I include as instances of hate speech law, laws banning pornography or sexual harassment. I do not mean to deny that pornography and sexual harassment can be speech acts. Nor do I seek to deny that some pornography and sexual harassment is rooted in misogyny or hatred of women. But I believe that this may not be sufficient to lift them into the class of hate speech in an unproblematic way. As Catharine MacKinnon (1991: 808) writes: 'The fact that pornography so often presents itself as love, indeed resembles much of what passes for it under male dominance, makes its construction as hate literature a challenging exercise in demystification, to say the least.' Likewise, I draw a distinction between non-sexual discriminatory harassment based on gender and sexual harassment based on gender. No doubt both may involve elements of control, subordination, humiliation, and degradation. But sexual harassment is essentially or necessarily to do with sexual objectification and unwanted sexual attention, advances, or even blackmail.

Introduction 17

6. While it is not untypical to discuss the arguments for and against different forms of hate speech law, some thinkers use the term 'law' in a more restricted sense to mean only criminal law. For example, Bhikhu Parekh (1990b: 705–706) writes: 'Since the law can play only a limited part in creating a humane and gentle society, we need to explore other ways. A powerful press council along the lines recently proposed in Britain, non-punitive and declaratory laws laying down what may or may not be said publicly but attaching no penalties, and vigilant citizens' forums bringing to bear the organized pressure of enlightened public opinion on those responsible for corrupting and lowering the level of public discourse, indicate the direction in which we need to move.'
7. In its primary focus this is a book about the warrant of hate speech law as opposed to a book about moral epistemology. And so I shall not devote attention to comparing and contrasting leading approaches to the latter (e.g., foundationalist, coherentist, contextualist). That being said, it should be clear from the description of epistemic justifiability set out in the text that I favor a responsibilist-contextualist approach to moral epistemology. What matters in such an approach is whether or not agents act in epistemically responsible ways, meaning that they hold beliefs based on the standards or norms of logical reasoning, evidence gathering, the consideration of contrary evidence and counter arguments, and so on, found within the epistemic communities in which they are embedded. In the case of self-evident principles, these responsibilities may not be as extensive or onerous as other objects of moral knowledge. For more on these approaches, see, e.g., Lorraine Code (1987) and Mark Timmons (1999).
8. There are other lists in the literature that may not be identical with this list (e.g., Shiffrin [S.H.] 1983: 1197–1198; 2011a: 559; Nelson 2005: 143; Parekh 2005–2006: 216; Schauer 2012: 140).
9. The list is eclectic in at least three different ways. First, some of the features on the list represent an entire family or genus of normatively relevant features, while others constitute single species, and in some cases, species that fall under families or genera that themselves appear on the list. Second, some of the features are best realized at the level of the individual, some are best realized at the level of society, and some best realized in ways that are non-excludable and non-competitive. Finally, some of the features on the list are best conceived as rights, some as interests, some as goods (personal or public), and some as values (which may include virtues), while some of the features can be conceived as all of these things.
10. These considerations place distinctively political requirements on government action or may also be distinctively political ways of evaluating the very apparatus of the state. Nevertheless, in many instances they are also derivative of, or serve, more fundamental rights, interests, goods, or values, such as autonomy.
11. Jean Stefancic and Richard Delgado's (1993: 738) review of Sandra Coliver's edited volume *Striking a Balance* is instructive: 'All [the book's contributors] are struggling with the challenge encompassed in balancing liberty and community; freedom of expression and freedom from discrimination; and the marketplace of ideas and the right of minority groups to self-respect.'
12. 'The [Charter] guarantees the rights and freedoms set out in it subject only to such reasonable limits prescribed by law as can be demonstrably justified in a free and democratic society.'
13. 3 SCR 697 (relating to the prosecution of a teacher under s. 319(2) of the Canadian Criminal Code, which bans willful promotion of hatred against an identifiable group, for communicating anti-Semitic statements to his students, including described Jews as 'child killers', 'treacherous', and 'subversive', and using exams to test his students on their knowledge of these characterizations), at 733–734, 337.
14. 3 SCR 892 (involving an indictment under s. 13(1) of the Canadian Human Rights Act, which forbids acts of exposing persons to hatred on the grounds

18  *Introduction*

of race or religion, for distributing cards inviting telephone calls to a number answered by recorded messages containing statements denigrating the Jewish race and religion), at 921–922.
15. No. 15890/89 (ECtHR, 23 Sept.) (relating to the conviction of a Danish journalist for aiding and abetting hate speech offences committed on national TV), at para. 29.
16. Nos. 4149/04 and 41029/04 (ECtHR, 15 Mar.) (relating to decisions taken by domestic courts in Turkey not to uphold complaints made against the creators of dictionaries to be used for educational purposes that included a range of words the definitions of which expressed negative stereotypes of gypsies), at paras. 62, 74–77.
17. No. 1813/07 (ECtHR, 9 Feb.) (relating to the conviction of four members of an organization called National Youth under Ch. 16, s. 8 of the Swedish Criminal Code, for distributing leaflets containing homophobic statements within a secondary school), at paras. 34, 39, 51, 60, and, especially, Concurring opinion of Judge Yudkivska, at para. 9.
18. In the chapter I shall argue that although some of these principles do serve distinctively legal considerations, others function to realize other more fundamental rights, interests, goods, or values.
19. See, e.g., *Perry Education Association v. Perry Local Educators' Association* (1983) 460 US 37 (involving the constitutionality of a decision to grant exclusive access to one teaching union to an interschool mail system and teacher mailboxes), at 45.
20. 447 F. Supp. 676 (N.D. Ill.).
21. 578 F.2d 1197 (7th Cir.).
22. 439 US 916.
23. See *R. v. Oakes* [1986] 1 SCR 103 (relating to the constitutionality of an antinarcotics law that created a rebuttable presumption that the possession of a narcotic implies intention to traffic), at 138–139.
24. See *Nilsen and Johnsen v. Norway* (1999) No. 23118/93 (ECtHR, 25 Nov.) (relating to rulings by Norwegian courts in a defamation case pertaining to allegations of police brutality), at para. 43.
25. No. 65831/01, Adm. Dec. (ECtHR, 7 Jul.) (relating to rulings by French courts that the philosopher and writer Roger Gauardy was guilty of offenses of disputing the existence of the Holocaust, publicly defaming members of the Jewish community, and inciting hatred and discrimination against Jews, based on the contents of his book *The Founding Myths of Israeli Politics*).
26. No. 15948/03 (ECtHR 10 Jul.) (relating to the prosecution of two French authors under laws banning incitement to hatred and laws interdicting incitement to violence against persons based on certain ascriptive characteristics, for comments made about immigrant Muslim communities from northern and central Africa in their book *The Colonisation of Europe*).
27. No. 72596/01 (ECtHR, 4 Nov.) (relating to the prosecution of the creators of a nationalistic calendar containing anti-Semitic, anti-Polish, and anti-Russian statements, under Lithuanian incitement to hatred law).
28. No. 15615/07 (ECtHR, 16 Jul.) (relating to the prosecution of a leading politician and political magazine editor under Belgian laws banning incitement to hatred, violence, discrimination, or segregation against a person or group of persons because of race, color, origin or national or ethnic descent).
29. No. 10883/05 (ECtHR, 16 Jul.) (relating to the prosecution of the mayor of a French municipality under press laws interdicting incitement to discrimination against persons based on certain ascriptive characteristics, after he had publicly announced that he intended to call on municipal services to boycott Israeli products).

# 2 Ten Clusters of Laws/Regulations/Codes That Constrain Uses of Hate Speech

As stated in Ch. 1, this book is concerned with the following normative question. In which ways, if any, might it be possible to warrant hate speech law? This chapter clears the ground for that question by disaggregating hate speech law into different clusters. Moral debate on whether hate speech law can be justified, on what grounds, and covering which groups, has been simmering away, sometimes boiling over, for several decades. But in the meantime the variety of laws/regulations/codes implemented globally has grown to an extent, and in ways, that the debate has failed to capture. While many legal scholars have concentrated on one genus, one species, or even one instance of hate speech law, few have stepped back to look at the whole family. For their part, legal and political theorists have too often looked upon hate speech law as a homogeneous lump and have not paid attention to distinguishable clusters of laws/regulations/codes. Now in one sense Post is surely correct to say that 'hate speech regulations come in innumerable varieties' (2009: 127). Nevertheless, I believe that among the legalistic responses to the issue of hate speech that can be found across the world today, ten clusters of laws/regulations/codes are particularly prominent. But even though a list of ten clusters is longer than many lists found elsewhere in the literature, it is not intended to be exhaustive or static. While I think that large numbers of actual laws/regulations/codes can be fitted into one or more of these idealized clusters, I also acknowledge that there will be some specific laws/regulations/codes that cannot be fitted into any of them. And no doubt some clusters will become less, not more, prominent with the passage of time. Moreover, a significant proportion, albeit not all, of the illustrations that I offer in relation to these idealized clusters involve laws/regulations/codes as they are written as opposed to as they are interpreted and enforced. *Some* of the illustrations are, in that sense, only prospective, which is to say, concerned with how law could be applied.

## 2.1 GROUP DEFAMATION

The first cluster is exemplified by laws/regulations/codes that proscribe public speech or other expressive conduct when it amounts to group defamation of members of groups or classes of persons identified by certain ascriptive characteristics. In order to understand this cluster fully it is important to draw a distinction between two kinds of group defamation law: catchall and *sensu stricto*. David Riesman's pioneering article, 'Democracy and Defamation' (1942) exemplifies the former. In it he provided a genealogy of group defamation law in the US, the UK, and mainland Europe that included: law that proscribed the public expression of falsehoods that are damaging to the reputation of groups or classes of persons;[1] law that banned the use of inflammatory language in order to stir up hatred against groups or classes of persons or promote enmity between groups or classes of people, wherein truth is no defense;[2] and law that prohibited the public expression of any derogatory statements about groups or classes of persons that cause or are likely to cause a breach of the peace or riots, once again wherein truth is no defense.[3] This is 'group defamation law' in its catchall usage; that is, a broad category that encompasses a variety of different laws. Many First Amendment scholars have persisted in this usage (e.g., Tanenhaus 1950; Brown and Stern 1964; Kalven 1965; Downs 1985; Richards 1986, 1999; Matsuda 1989b; Hartman 1992; Walker 1994; Lasson 1995; Weinstein 2009; Shiell 2009). And this usage can also be found among scholars of hate speech law in France, Germany, and the UK (e.g., Belton 1960; Errera 1992; Modood 1993; Jones 1998; Eberle 2002; Parekh 2006; Mookherjee 2007; Morgan 2007; Mbongo 2009).

I believe that for many of these scholars, although not all, the rationale for this catchall usage has been to facilitate criticism. The greater the extent and variety of group defamation law, the easier it becomes to condemn it for being destructive of free speech values. Nevertheless, one of the drawbacks with this usage is that it stretches to breaking point the ordinary legal meaning of the term 'defamation', to wit, making false statements of fact that are damaging to reputation. Another is that it makes it much harder to explain what could be distinctive, normatively speaking, about a legal regime in which false damaging statements of fact may be prosecuted via group defamation law (e.g., "Every single one of the Jews living in this town is directly involved in the practice of kidnapping and murdering the children of Christians") but not crude abuse (e.g., "God damn those Kikes!"), nor the stirring up of hatred (e.g., "I hate Jews; you should too"), nor the expression of hyperbolic opinion (e.g., "The horrendous treatment of Palestinians by the State of Israel tells you everything you need to know about Jewish people; they are a vicious race hell-bent on stealing land and destroying other people's lives just to help themselves").

In contrast to its catchall usage, the term 'group defamation law' can also be used to mean group defamation law *sensu stricto*. Within this particular cluster of law, the offense of group defamation is limited to the following basic elements. First, the defendant has published or uttered in public a statement of fact (or claim, contention, assertion, or allegation that amounts to a statement of fact) pertaining to members of groups or classes of persons identified by certain ascriptive characteristics. Second, the statement admits of falsification (i.e., it can be proven true or false by recognized standards of evidence gathering and empirical inquiry) and is false. Often allied to this element, however, is a truth defense: that the speaker believed on reasonable grounds the statements to be true. Third, the statement is of the sort that tends to damage the good name or reputation of people, such as by lowering the esteem in which they are held by society; exposing them to contempt, ridicule, or obloquy; or causing them to be shunned or avoided. In civil proceedings, as opposed to criminal proceedings, two additional elements are necessary. Fourth, the statement not merely refers to or is of the group or class of persons to which the plaintiff belongs but also refers to or is of the plaintiff specifically. Fifth, the plaintiff can demonstrate or provide evidentiary proof of injury or damage to good name or reputation.

Criminal group defamation law (*sensu stricto*) is not uncommon among domestic criminal statutes and penal codes (e.g., the Netherlands,[4] Slovakia,[5] Spain,[6] several US states[7]). In addition to this, some countries possess criminal defamation laws that in principle could be used to constrain the use of group defamation (*sensu stricto*) even if prosecuting authorities utilize other laws instead (e.g., Germany,[8] Israel[9]). In addition, laws against group defamation (*sensu stricto*) can be found in press/media law (e.g., France,[10] Ivory Coast[11]). Finally, I shall outline civil laws relating to group defamation later in this chapter—the section dealing with dignitary crimes and torts [2.7].

The legal significance, or point of differentiation, of this cluster consists largely in its focus on false damaging statements of fact and, moreover, its use of a truth defense. One important implication of these features, as far as free speech values are concerned (see Chs. 4 and 7), is that persons cannot be punished under this cluster of laws for engaging in hate speech that amounts to mere hyperbole or opinionated bluster rather than statements of fact, or, conversely, if the speaker believed on reasonable grounds the statements of fact to be true. These features could make this cluster an attractive compromise alternative to clusters that are less narrowly framed by comparison (see [2.3, 2.4]). However, the full normative significance of this cluster will only be revealed in later chapters when I consider whether or not it could garner direct support from principles that invoke other normatively relevant features besides liberty, including but not limited to autonomy or the removal of undue influences (see Ch. 3 [3.2]) and civic dignity (see Ch. 5 [5.1]).

## 2.2 NEGATIVE STEREOTYPING OR STIGMATIZATION

The second cluster is focused around laws/regulations/codes that limit public speech or other expressive conduct that amounts to negative stereotyping or stigmatization of members of groups or classes of persons identified by certain ascriptive characteristics. Such law is regularly found in the sphere of media law and regulation. At the international level, both the United Nations (UN) Committee on the Elimination of Racial Discrimination (CERD), which is the body responsible for monitoring the implementation of the International Convention on the Elimination of All Forms of Racial Discrimination (ICERD), and the Council of Europe Advisory Committee on the Framework Convention for the Protection of National Minorities (FCPNM), have repeatedly criticized state authorities for not doing enough to impress upon their media the need to represent minority groups in balanced ways and to refrain from representing these groups wholly in terms of negative stereotypes. Particular emphasis has been placed on the reduction of stigmatizing portrayals of Roma people, for example.[12]

With or without the pressure of the international community, domestic media regulators (both statutory and non-statutory) often impose restrictions on the use of negative stereotyping or stigmatization of individuals on the basis of ascribed characteristics. By way of illustration, in the UK the communications regulator Ofcom includes within its Broadcasting Code for the content of TV and radio programs rules on 'harm and offence.' Rule 2.3 requires broadcasters to ensure that the broadcast of any material that includes discriminatory language relating to age, disability, gender, race, religion, beliefs, and sexual orientation must be 'justified by the context' including not merely the editorial content of the program but also the potential composition of the audience. Ofcom's guidance notes make it clear that the rule applies to 'the way that minority groups are presented.' To which it adds: 'If there is an under-representation [of a minority group], the use of stereotypes and caricatures or the discussion of difficult or controversial issues involving that community may be seen as offensive in that it is viewed as creating a false impression of that minority.' To cite one example, in March 2009 Ofcom ruled that Chris Moyles, a prominent BBC Radio 1 presenter at the time, was in breach of Rule 2.3 when during his breakfast show in January of that year he sang his own version of a song originally released by the recording artist Will Young with alternative lyrics poking fun at the singer's sexual orientation.[13] Ofcom reprimanded Moyles on the grounds that his actions 'could have reasonably been interpreted by listeners as promoting and condoning certain negative stereotypes based on sexual orientation.'[14]

The present cluster is also exemplified in codes of conduct adopted by broadcast companies themselves. So, for example, the Australian Broadcast Company (ABC) Code of Practice contains Rule 7.7: 'Avoid the unjustified use of stereotypes or discriminatory content that could reasonably be interpreted as condoning or encouraging prejudice.' To cite one case, in November 2011 a panel from the ABC Audience and Consumer Affairs division upheld a complaint made by a listener against one of its radio stations, 702 ABC Sydney, that during a discussion on the European sovereign debt crisis a presenter made a racist comment related to the behavior of Irish builders. It determined that although the presenter's comments were lighthearted and not intended to denigrate the Irish, they did replicate an unfortunate and inaccurate stereotype, and this being the case, were in breach of Rule 7.7.

Part of the raison d'être of this cluster of hate speech law is its potential for regulating statements that although do not amount to false statements of fact of the sort required under group defamation law (*sensu stricto*), do constitute unbalanced, oversimplified, or misleading impressions of reality. Generics are often used to negatively stereotype or stigmatize members of groups or classes of persons identified by certain ascriptive characteristics, where the exact meaning of the generic is sufficiently vague, ambiguous, or metaphysical to make the basic elements of defamation inapplicable. Media regulators often take the view that although not defamatory in the strict sense, generics can present a distorted depiction of reality that can also unfairly damage the reputation or social standing of the persons picked out. Interestingly, some principled arguments, such as those based on respect for cultural specificity and intercultural dialogue, purport to be defenses of group defamation law (*sensu stricto*) but on closer inspection are really about the necessity of regulating the use of negative stereotypes, especially in the media (see Ch. 6 [6.3, 6.4]).

## 2.3 THE EXPRESSION OF HATRED

The third cluster is characterized by laws/regulations/codes that disallow the public expression of hatred toward members of groups or classes of persons identified by certain ascriptive characteristics. This includes laws/regulations/codes that disallow, typically without a truth defense, one or more of the following types of conduct: directing insults, slurs, or derogatory epithets at such persons or otherwise ridiculing such persons; publicly disseminating ideas based on the inferiority of such persons; the public use of any words, signs, or symbols that are deeply insulting or offensive to such persons. Instances of this cluster can be found in domestic criminal statutes and penal codes (e.g., Belgium,[15] Bolivia,[16] Cuba,[17] Croatia,[18] Denmark,[19] Ecuador,[20] Greece,[21] Indonesia,[22] Italy,[23] Norway,[24] Rwanda,[25] Sweden,[26] Turkey,[27] some parts of the UK,[28] the US State of Connecticut[29]). In some countries the basic criminal offense of insult does not specify but can be applied to groups or classes of persons identified by certain ascriptive characteristics (e.g., Germany[30]). Examples of this cluster can also be found in the rules of contempt of court formulated and applied at the discretion of judges. In the US case *Bullard v. Florida* (1975),[31] for instance, a judge banned the use of the word 'chink', albeit this intervention was overturned on appeal (cf. Delgado and Stefancic 2004: 66–68). In addition, this cluster is instantiated in domestic civil and human rights law (e.g., Australia,[32] Mexico[33]). Examples can also be found in domestic press/media law (e.g., France,[34] Hungary,[35] India[36]) and the codes of practice written and enforced by media regulators (e.g., the UK[37]). In *Case of Keira McCormack* (2010),[38] for example, the UK's Press Complaints Commission (PCC) upheld a complaint against an article published in the Northern Ireland newspaper *Sunday Life*, which

## 24  Ten Clusters of Laws/Regulations/Codes

used the terms 'tranny', 'strapping', and 'burly' to describe the complainant in the context of reporting concerns about her employment as a rape counselor in Belfast. The Commission expressed its ruling thusly: 'While the newspaper was entitled to publish a story about people's concerns over the suitability of the complainant's employment, her gender identity should not have been open to ridicule.' '[T]he use of the word 'tranny'—which was a needless abbreviation, held by many to be offensive—was pejorative.'[39]

Furthermore, international law recognizes certain rights and responsibilities on the part of states to enact and apply the present cluster of law (e.g., the Conventions of the UN,[40] the protocols of the Council of Europe,[41] the decisions of the ECtHR[42]). (Of course, it remains the case that individual countries may upon signature and ratification of internal conventions or protocols enter reservations and interpretative statements that severely limit their extent in domestic law.[43] That being said, the community of states can censure states for entering such reservations or failing to enact laws.) Consider the case of Thilo Sarrazin who, as well as being a former Finance Senator of the Berlin Senate and former member of the Board of Directors of the German Central Bank, is an outspoken critic of Germany's immigration policy and its legacy. In 2009, a complaint was made against Sarrazin by members of the Turkish community in Berlin following an article he published in the journal *Lettre International* that carped at members of the Turkish community for failing to properly integrate into German society.[44] The Office of Public Prosecution in Berlin elected not to bring a case against Sarrazin under s. 130(1) of the German Criminal Code, which states that it is a punishable offense to incite hatred against or insult, maliciously malign, or defame segments of the population 'in a manner capable of disturbing the public peace.' Eventually the complainants took their case to the Committee on the Elimination of Racial Discrimination (CERD), the UN body charged with monitoring domestic compliance with the ICERD. In *TBB-Turkish Union in Berlin/Brandenburg v. Germany* (2013)[45] the Committee majority excoriated the state of Germany for its decision not to prosecute. It reminded the State Party of its obligations under Art. 4(a) of the ICERD, according to which '[states parties] [s]hall declare an offence punishable by law all dissemination of ideas based on racial superiority or hatred.' It also pointed out that 4(a) does not on its face contain the breach of the peace criterion.[46]

Of all the clusters of laws/regulations/codes to be discussed in this chapter the present cluster is liable to draw the strongest objection that it violates important free speech values (e.g., autonomy, self-realization, democracy). That being said, some of the laws in this cluster purport to protect such values by exempting statements published or broadcast for the purposes of public debate, artistic expression, journalistic reporting, or editorial commentary. In Australia, for example, s. 18C(1) of the Racial Discrimination Act 1975 (as amended by the Racial Hatred Act 1995) makes it unlawful conduct 'for a person to do an act, otherwise than in private, if: (a) the act is reasonably likely, in all the circumstances, to offend, insult, humiliate or intimidate another person or a group of people; and (b) the act is done because of the race, colour or national or ethnic origin of the other person or of some or all of the people in the group.' In addition, s. 18D sets out several exemptions including 'anything said or done reasonably and in good faith [. . .] such as for genuine academic, journalistic, artistic, scientific, or any other purposes in the public interest [. . .] or a fair and accurate report of any event or matter of public interest [. . .] [or] a fair comment on any event or matter of public interest if the comment is an expression of a genuine belief held by the person making the comment.' The Act also establishes a civil complaints mechanism, meaning that complaints are initially handled by the Australian Human Rights Commission (AHRC),[47] which can summarily dismiss cases or facilitate a private conciliation process between the parties. This process may result in agreed-upon remedies (e.g., apology, removal of material, payment of compensation, changes to policies and procedures, additional race-awareness training for staff). Once a case has been terminated (either way), if the complainant is unsatisfied he or she may seek a determination by the Federal Court of Australia or the Federal Circuit Court of Australia, either of which can also order remedies. In *Bryant v. Queensland Newspaper Pty Ltd.* [1997],[48] for example, the Commission dismissed a complaint relating to a newspaper's use of the pejorative terms 'Poms' and 'Pommies' on the grounds that journalists should enjoy a right of fair comment on public affairs, which includes some degree of mockery and inflammatory language.

Nevertheless, in a more recent case the Federal Court of Australia has determined that the aforementioned exemptions do not cover journalistic hate speech. In *Eatock v. Bolt* [2011][49] the Court considered a series of articles and blogs written by the journalist Andrew Bolt and published by the *Herald Sun* in its newspaper and on its website. Bolt claimed that light-skinned or mixed race Aboriginals were not genuinely Aboriginal and were only pretending to be Aboriginal so that they could access benefits intended for this group. Justice Bromberg held that the articles were written because of the race, color, or ethnic origin of a particular class of persons; that the statements made were likely to offend, insult, or humiliate such persons; that the statements did not fall under the relevant s. 18D exemptions because they contained distortions of the truth and errors of fact owing to a failure of due diligence to verify the facts;[50] and that the extent of mockery and inflammatory language used 'far exceeded that which was necessary to make Mr. Bolt's point.'[51] It is precisely these sorts of judicial determinations, however, that give rise to a fear among critics of hate speech law that they facilitate unwarranted press censorship. The fear is that overzealous judges will substitute their own personal views for those of professional journalists concerning what facts are required and what extent of mockery and

26   Ten Clusters of Laws/Regulations/Codes

inflammatory language is necessary in addressing issues of public interest. I shall return to these sorts of concerns in Ch. 9.

## 2.4  INCITEMENT TO HATRED

The fourth cluster comprises laws/regulations/codes that ban the public use of speech or other expressive conduct with the intention (or likelihood) of stirring up, inciting, or promoting feelings of hatred or hostility toward or among members of groups or classes of persons identified by certain ascriptive characteristics. A key feature of such law is that it permits prosecutions even in cases where no inchoate offense of inciting or encouraging a criminal act has been committed. Sophisticated hate speakers are often careful not to say things that could be construed as inciting acts of discrimination, assault, or murder, for example. What is more, unlike the offense of incitement to crime, the offense of incitement to hatred constitutes an independent offense, meaning that it is not dependent upon any principal offense. So incitement to hatred can be an offense even if hatred is not.

Instances of this cluster can found in domestic criminal statues and penal codes throughout the world (e.g., Armenia,[52] some Australian states,[53] Azerbaijan,[54] Bangladesh,[55] China,[56] East Timor,[57] Germany,[58] Hungary,[59] Ireland,[60] Kenya,[61] Kyrgyzstan,[62] Lithuania,[63] Macedonia,[64] Malaysia,[65] the Netherlands,[66] Pakistan,[67] Russia,[68] Singapore,[69] Switzerland,[70] the UK,[71] Uruguay,[72] the US State of West Virginia,[73] Uzbekistan,[74] Vietnam[75]). Instances can also be found in public gatherings law (e.g., South Africa[76]) and in immigration law (e.g., Canada[77]). In August 2008, for instance, Canadian authorities prevented members of the Westboro Baptist Church from entering Canada for the purpose of picketing a funeral on the basis that they had reasonable grounds to believe that the actions intended would constitute the offense of promoting hatred against homosexuals. Examples of this cluster can also be found in domestic civil and human rights law (e.g., Argentina,[78] China,[79] Mexico,[80] New Zealand,[81] South Africa[82]). In addition, instances of this cluster are present in domestic press/media law or broadcasting law (e.g., Chile,[83] France,[84] Germany,[85] Hungary,[86] Jordan,[87] Tunisia[88]), including codes of practice laid down by state media regulators (e.g., China,[89] Kenya[90]) and codes of practice adopted by media organizations under systems of self-regulation (e.g., the Democratic Republic of Congo[91]). In some countries the validity of laws banning incitement to hatred is explicitly recognized in written constitutions (e.g., Armenia,[92] Azerbaijan,[93] Turkmenistan[94]). Moreover, international law recognizes certain rights and responsibilities on the part of states to enact and apply such laws (e.g., the directives of the European Parliament and the Council of the European Union,[95] the framework decisions of the Council of the European Union,[96] the decisions of the ECtHR[97]).

The object of the present cluster can be distinguished from that of group defamation law (*sensu stricto*) in the following way. While hate speakers sometimes use false damaging statements of fact to stir up or promote hatred against members of groups or classes of persons, not all instances of such expression amount to stirring up hatred. Conversely, expressive acts of stirring up hatred can be performed, and often are performed, without the use of false statements of fact. Now in some countries the distinction between the two clusters is blurred by the presence of laws that penalize group defamation but only if it is used with the intention to excite hatred between citizens or residents (e.g., Senegal[98]) and laws that ban stirring up hatred but that at the same time specify a truth defense (e.g., Canada,[99] India,[100] Namibia[101]). But it is more common for legislatures and courts to detach the truth defense from incitement to hatred law. For example, the Hungarian Constitutional Court (citing the Supreme Court of Hungary) has clarified that for the purposes of applying Art. 332 (formerly Art. 269) of the Hungarian Criminal Code, 'it is totally irrelevant whether or not the facts stated are true; what matters is whether the specific composition of data, no matter whether true or false, is capable of arousing hatred'.[102] Similarly, in *R. v. Birdwood* (1995)[103] the Court of Appeal of England and Wales established the common law precedent that the truth of the content of speech is no defense against a prosecution for the offense of stirring up racial hatred under the Public Order Act 1986.

Many people who object to incitement to hatred legislation do so because they assume that it inevitably swallows up protected speech. They cite countries like Azerbaijan where authorities have exploited incitement to hatred law to punish journalists and writers for criticizing the role that Islam plays in the country's cultural, political, and economic affairs, or countries like China where laws banning the stirring up of ethnic hostility have been used to suppress political dissent in some regions. Yet this assumption belies the possibility of more nuanced wording in incitement to hatred legislation coupled with restraint by public prosecutors and courts in its application and interpretation. In the UK, for example, this nuance is reflected in the Racial and Religious Hatred Act 2006—which amends the Public Order Act 1986—by dint of the fact that the legislation limits the offense of incitement to religious hatred to the use of threatening words or behavior with the intent to stir up religious hatred and qualifies the offense with the following 'Protection of freedom of expression' proviso: 'Nothing in this Part shall be read or given effect in a way which prohibits or restricts discussion, criticism or expressions of antipathy, dislike, ridicule, insult or abuse of particular religions or the beliefs or practices of their adherents.'[104] Consequently, in the UK someone declaring in public "I hate what Muslims believe in" or publishing in a newspaper article the statement "I believe that Islam is a wicked faith and a danger to the finest institutions and traditions of this country" would be unlikely to face prosecution for, and extremely unlikely to be convicted of, the offense of incitement to religious hatred. Of course, even countries like the UK have been criticized by opponents of hate speech law for imposing any, albeit nuanced, restrictions on acts of expression.

28  *Ten Clusters of Laws/Regulations/Codes*

For example, it has been claimed that incitement to hatred laws are antithetical to free participation in the formation of democratic public opinion, political legitimacy, and the bases of political obligation. However, in Ch. 7 I shall put forward counterarguments to each of these claims.

## 2.5  THREATS TO PUBLIC ORDER

The fifth cluster is made up of laws/regulations/codes that prohibit public speech or other expressive conduct that is directed at members of groups or classes of persons identified by certain ascriptive characteristics and that is a threat to public order, in the sense that it causes or is likely to cause a public mischief, breach of the peace, or danger to public safety. This applies to the use of speech or other expressive conduct that causes or is likely to cause a police officer to start or continue an investigation unnecessarily; acts of violence or public disturbances perpetrated by those engaged in, incited by, or reacting to the words or conduct; or more generalized social unrest, damage to property, and breakdown in law and order. Some of the law in this cluster provides a narrow specification of the type of speech or other expressive conduct that is prohibited—for example, by requiring that a statements is both libelous and tends to raise disorder or unrest among the people (e.g., the Canadian Province of Manitoba[105]), while most of the law leaves the form of expression open. Either way, law in this cluster generally places a higher threshold for successful prosecution than does group defamation law (*sensu stricto*) or incitement to hatred law since it requires that speech or other expressive conduct must constitute a threat to public order. Unlike some of the other clusters to be discussed later, the ostensible purpose of such law is to protect not only the people targeted by hate speech but also the wider community.

Examples that epitomize the present cluster can be found in many domestic criminal codes (e.g., Canada,[106] Egypt,[107] Ethiopia,[108] Germany,[109] India,[110] Malaysia,[111] Singapore,[112] Turkey,[113] Venezuela[114]) and in some press/media law (e.g., France[115]). Examples are also present in some domestic immigration law. In the Canadian case *Mugesera v. Canada (Minister of Citizenship and Immigration)* [2005],[116] for instance, the Supreme Court held that the Minister of Citizenship and Immigration had acted lawfully when in 1995 he ordered the deportation of Léon Mugesera based on evidence of statements made by Mugesera to a gathering of approximately 1,000 party members at Kabaya, Rwanda, in November 1992.[117] The Court concluded that on the balance of probabilities the comments made not only constituted an offense under Rwandan law but if made in the same way in Canada would also constitute an offense under *inter alia* s. 319(1) of the Criminal Code. It states: 'Every one who, by communicating statements in any public place, incites hatred against any identifiable group where such incitement is likely to lead to a breach of the peace is guilty of [an offense].'

Similarly, in the UK, Art. 320(6) of the Immigration Rules sets out the following grounds on which entry clearance or leave to enter the country can be refused: 'where the Secretary of State has personally directed that the exclusion of a person from the UK is conducive to the public good.' In August 2005, in the wake of the 7/7 London bombings, the Home Secretary (Charles Clarke) set forth an indicative list of 'unacceptable behaviours' to be used as bases for such exclusions, including 'preaching' views that '[f]oster hatred which might lead to inter-community violence in the UK (cited in BBC News 2005).' This basis has been tested in administrative court. In *Naik v. The Secretary of State for the Home Department* [2010][118] the High Court of Justice ruled that an exclusion order against a Muslim writer and orator was a justified, proportional measure against a threat to public security and social harmony posed by his anti-Semitic speeches.[119]

While concerns about public order are front and center in this cluster, I think it would be wrong to suppose that such laws have a monopoly on serving the general interest in security. As I shall try to show in Ch. 3 [3.3], many principled arguments in favor of hate speech law that cite the insecurity or feelings of security caused by hate speech would naturally seem to support not merely laws in this cluster but also laws that ban incitement to hatred [2.4] and laws that forbid hate speech when it constitutes discriminatory intimidation, provocation, or incitement to violence [2.9]. (I shall go on to include cross burning statutes in the latter clusters.) Of course, it has often been said that all of these laws are essentially about balancing important rights or interests, most notably, liberty and security. In Ch. 8, however, I shall critically examine this common assumption by highlighting the problem of incommensurability.

## 2.6 DENYING, ETC. ACTS OF MASS CRUELTY, VIOLENCE, OR GENOCIDE

The sixth cluster is composed of laws/regulations/codes that penalize public speech or other expressive conduct that constitutes denying, grossly trivializing, approving, justifying, condoning, or glorifying acts of mass cruelty, violence, or genocide perpetrated against members of groups or classes of persons identified by certain ascriptive characteristics. Laws against the denial of the existence of such atrocities can be found in several domestic criminal statutes and penal codes (e.g., Canada,[120] Czech Republic,[121] Israel,[122] Romania,[123] Spain,[124] Switzerland[125]) and in press/media law (e.g., France[126]). Many of these laws make explicit reference to statements that deny the genocide committed by the National Socialist regime in Germany, namely, the Holocaust. Some laws in this cluster also name crimes against humanity committed by the Communist regime in Eastern Europe (e.g., Hungary[127]). Some cite no concrete examples of genocide, but it is not difficult to interpret which genocides are at stake (e.g., Rwanda[128]).

30   *Ten Clusters of Laws/Regulations/Codes*

In some instances, other laws have been used to penalize Holocaust denial, such as laws prohibiting speech capable of disturbing the public peace and laws providing sanctions against public speech that disparages the memory of the dead (e.g., Germany[129]). But an essential feature of the present cluster is that it provides protection against speech that denies, grossly trivializes, approves, justifies, condones, or glorifies acts of mass cruelty, violence, or genocide even when it does not rise to the level required for prosecutions under other hate speech laws. It is possible that Holocaust denial, for example, could in some circumstances constitute group defamation (*sensu stricto*) [2.1], the intent to stir up hatred [2.4], or even a threat to public order [2.5]. Yet none of these circumstances are necessary to support a prosecution under Holocaust denial law.

In addition to this, many of the laws found in the present cluster penalize not merely the denial of acts of mass murder or genocide but also the gross trivialization, approval, or justification of such acts (e.g., Austria,[130] Belgium,[131] Czech Republic,[132] Lithuania[133]), or even the glorification of such acts (e.g., Germany[134]). In addition to domestic law, elements of international law set out rights and responsibilities on the part of states to enact and enforce laws in this cluster (e.g., the protocols of the Council of Europe,[135] the framework decisions of the Council of the European Union,[136] the decisions of the ECtHR[137]).

One of the things that makes laws in this cluster stand out both legally and normatively is their focus on statements about historical events. At the same time, however, this also means that these laws are liable to face strong, principled objections, not the least of which is that they will sweep up or chill a significant amount of protected speech, including historical scholarship, artistic speech, and even political speech (see Ch. 4 [4.1, 4.2] and Ch. 9 [9.4]). On the other hand, because of the nature of Holocaust denial, for example, as an act of expression that "attacks" the fundamentals of Jewish dignity and identity, the present cluster is also backed by some powerful normative principles (see, e.g., Chs. 3 [3.6], 5 [5.1], and 6 [6.2]).

## 2.7   DIGNITARY CRIMES OR TORTS

Laws/regulations/codes in the seventh cluster center around criminal sanctions or civil remedies that can be used to constrain speech or other expressive conduct directed at members of groups or classes of persons identified by certain ascriptive characteristics when that speech or other expressive conduct amounts to the enactment of a dignitary crime or tort. This typically involves subjecting such persons to humiliation or degradation—in short, robbing them of their dignity. In some countries a subset of laws relating to dignitary crimes or torts are framed by specific reference to certain ascriptive characteristics. However, more often dignitary crimes or torts are widely conceived and so are merely capable of being used to constrain speech or other expression aimed at persons based on certain ascriptive characteristics but only incidentally. In other words, in many countries criminal and civil law has developed in such a way as to recognize cases in which hate speech rises to the level of a dignitary crime or tort, and it is these cases that I shall focus on here.

Defamation provides one possible avenue for lawsuits and class action lawsuits against hate speakers. In what is sometimes colloquially referred to as "America's first hate speech case", Aaron Sapiro filed a $1 million federal lawsuit against the *Dearborn Independent*, a popular newspaper under the control of Henry Ford, in relation to a series of anti-Semitic articles published in which it was claimed *inter alia* that Sapiro's plan to create farmers' cooperatives was the manifestation of a larger Jewish conspiracy to dominate and exploit the cooperative marketing system and American farmers in general. Ford's pragmatic response to the lawsuit was to close the newspaper and to issue a public apology for his anti-Semitic views. In the Canadian case *Ortenberg v. Plamondon* (1915)[138] the Quebec Court of Appeal gave judgment in favor of the plaintiff's claim for damages based on harm to his reputation as a Jewish businessman caused by a public lecture that, among other things, accused the Jewish race of routinely engaging in ritual murder and urged that 'the Jew, bear in mind, is the same in all places, and that which he has done elsewhere he will certainly do here' [trans.].[139] On the question of whether or not defamation of an entire race may count as defamation of one of its members, Judge Carroll stated: 'I am of opinion that [the Jewish community of Quebec] are sufficiently designated, that the plaintiff was included in this slander, that he has been injured in his sentiments and in his well-being, and that he ought to obtain judgment' [trans.].[140]

Moving beyond the narrow confines of defamation, some domestic human rights law (e.g., the Canadian Province of Saskatchewan[141]) and some domestic criminal law (e.g., Costa Rica,[142] Germany,[143] Switzerland[144]) disallows publicly making, publishing, or broadcasting statements pertaining to members of groups or classes of persons identified by certain ascriptive characteristics that under the circumstances amount to a violation of the dignity of members of the relevant groups. Along similar lines, Art. 250 of the Criminal Law of China makes it unlawful to publish an article 'designated to discriminate or humiliate an ethnic group, if the circumstances are flagrant and the consequences are serious' [trans.]. In the *Case of Chen and Wang* (1997)[145] the authors of a book about the sexual and matrimonial practices and customs among ethnic groups in China were convicted for humiliating some of the groups of people discussed in the book.

In other countries, the offense of *injuria*[146] relates to acts that affront the dignity of another person, including face-to-face interactions in which someone verbally abuses another person based on his or her membership of a group or class of persons identified by certain ascriptive properties (e.g., Brazil,[147] South Africa[148]). In South Africa the common law offenses of *injuria* (civil) and *crimen injuria* (criminal) have both been applied to the

32    *Ten Clusters of Laws/Regulations/Codes*

use of racially abusive language that under the circumstances constitutes humiliating or degrading treatment. For example, in *Mbatha v. Van Staden* (1982)[149]—a case heard even under the apartheid system—the plaintiff, a black South African male, sued the defendant, a white male, for *injuria* after the defendant had repeatedly called him a 'kaffer' and physically assaulted him following an argument about a parking place. Judge Didcott put the injury into context thusly:

> The tirade's worst feature was the use of the epithet 'kaffer'. Such alone can amount today to an actionable wrong, according to the decision of the Full Bench here in *Ciliza v. Minister of Police and Another* 1976 (4) SA 243 (N). Everything depends, of course, on the context in which the word is uttered. Settings which make it innocuous can no doubt be imagined. Ordinarily, however, that is not the case when, in South Africa nowadays, a Black man or woman is called a 'kaffer' by somebody of another race. Then, as a rule, the term is a derogatory and contemptuous one. With much the same ring as the word 'nigger' in the United States, it disparages the Black race and the person concerned as a member of that race. It is deeply offensive to blacks. Just about everyone knows that by now.[150]

In Brazil, Art. 140(3) of the Penal Code sets out a special type of *injuria*, which it refers to as *injuria racista*, in which someone offends or attacks another person's *dignidade* (dignity) or *decoro* (decorum), using statements pertaining to that person's race, color, ethnicity, religion, origin, or status as an older person or a disabled person. In cases of *injuria racista* the applicable penalty is increased from one to three years imprisonment. In *Case of Diane Soares da Costa* (2013),[151] for instance, the Court of Justice of the State of Sao Paulo dismissed an appeal against a conviction for *injuria* in relation to a defendant who had offended the dignity and decorum of a fellow employee by addressing her in the presence of other employees with statements including 'you are a monkey, you have no hair, your hair is hard; you are a bitch', 'you are a monkey and a black slut' [trans.].[152]

Finally, in the US, some victims of racist hate speech have successfully sued for damages using the tort of intentional infliction of emotional distress. *Wiggs v. Courshon* (1973)[153] and *Agarwal v. Johnson* (1979)[154] are early examples. There remain three major obstacles to recovery, however. First, the tort is reserved for 'extreme and outrageous conduct', the determination of which is at the discretion of the courts. Many courts have elected to regard the use of racial slurs or similar abuse as falling short of extreme and outrageous conduct (Delgado and Stefancic 2004: 12–16; Chamallas and Wriggins 2010: ch. 3). Second, due to the existence of federal laws against discrimination and harassment in the workplace, namely, Title VII of the Civil Rights Act of 1964, courts may be less likely to recognize or find in favor of plaintiffs for intentional infliction of emotional distress in the workplace. Courts could assume that there are alternative, more appropriate ways for individuals to pursue their grievances, despite federal laws containing clauses making it clear that they do not de-bar civil proceedings (Chamallas and Wriggins 2010: 81). Third, even lawsuits that are successful at the state level can be set aside by the US Supreme Court on First Amendment grounds (e.g., the special value of public protest). In *Snyder v. Phelps* (2011),[155] for example, the Court held that '[w]hat Westboro said, in the whole context of how and where it chose to say it, is entitled to "special protection" under the First Amendment and that protection cannot be overcome by a jury finding that the picketing was outrageous.'[156] Nevertheless, none of these obstacles are insurmountable. In *Turley v. ISG Lackawanna Inc.* (2013)[157] a US District Court upheld the damages awarded by a trial court to the plaintiff based on his having suffered years of extreme and outrageous racist abuse at work. This included being called 'boy', 'nigger', 'that fucking nigger', 'monkey'; having a 'dancing gorilla' sign and the letters 'KKK' placed at his workstation; having monkey noises made in his presence; having black grease applied to his work chair, door handles, and machine controls accompanied by the comment 'it must have been the boon that's doing it'; and having his work chair destroyed followed by the declaration 'That nigger ain't sitting in this chair'.[158]

The present cluster is often used to restrict hate-based insults, slurs, or derogatory epithets in face-to-face interactions, but an important point of differentiation between the present cluster and laws/regulations/codes that disallow the public expression of hatred [2.3] is that under the present cluster of laws the mere usage of such language is typically not enough by itself to attract criminal sanction or civil remedy. There must be proof of psychological or even physiological damage to an assignable victim, or it must be reasonable to assume that the speech humiliated or degraded the victim. Unsurprisingly, therefore, this cluster has been sustained *inter alia* by principles that appeal to emotional well-being (see Ch. 3 [3.1]) and human dignity ([3.6]).

## 2.8 VIOLATIONS OF CIVIL OR HUMAN RIGHTS

The eighth cluster is exemplified by laws/regulations/codes that forbid speech or other expressive conduct when it amounts to conduct that violates or interferes with the exercise of the civil or human rights of members of groups or classes of persons identified by certain ascriptive characteristics. The relevant rights include the right to non-discrimination, the right to fair accommodation, and the right not to be exposed to discriminatory harassment. As such, law in this cluster is often directed at particular settings (e.g., the workplace, public buildings and offices, schools, universities) and activities (e.g., employment, the provision and use of public services, education and learning). In the US, for example, the Equal Employment Opportunity Commission (EEOC) holds that Title VII of the Civil Rights Act of 1964 protects employees against employment discrimination *inter alia* when it involves '[h]arassment by managers, co-workers, or others in your workplace, because of your race, color, religion, sex (including pregnancy), national origin, age (40 or older), disability or genetic information.'[159] The EEOC enables employees to file charges, whereupon the Commission will investigate and may decide to offer mediation between the employee and employer, or to seek an out-of-court settlement with the employer. Failing that, the EEOC may decide to file a lawsuit in a court of law on behalf of the employee or send the employee notice of a right to sue. In *EEOC v. AA Foundries Inc.* (2012),[160] for instance, the US District Court for the Western District of Texas found in favor of the EEOC in relation to a lawsuit it had filed under Title VII on behalf of three African American employees who had been subjected to a racially hostile work environment. This included being called 'niggers' and 'mother-fucking boys', being accused of 'always stealing and wanting welfare', and having a noose displayed in the workplace.[161] In *EEOC v. Tyson Foods, Inc.* (2006),[162] a case redolent of the history of racial segregation in the US, the Court reached a Consent Decree and Final Judgment with respect to a lawsuit filed by the EEOC on behalf of several black employees who had been subjected to a racially hostile work environment in which a "Whites Only" sign had been placed on a bathroom in the maintenance department, the door padlocked, and keys given only to white employees. Occasionally courts have also protected the rights of employees when they have filed their own lawsuits under Title VII.[163]

More controversially, the present cluster also incorporates large numbers of campus speech codes across the US and associated complaints procedures and decisions forbidding hate speech that rises to the level of discriminatory harassment in classroom settings or even in other parts of the campus.[164] This is in spite of the fact that several campus speech codes have been struck down as unconstitutional by courts.[165] The various legal principles that have been used for assessing these codes will be discussed in Ch. 9, where I shall try to argue that despite what some courts have concluded, it is not necessarily the case that these codes are ineffective, not the least restrictive alternatives, and overbroad.

Examples of similar laws relating to discriminatory practices, including but not limited to discriminatory harassment and communication of hate messages, can be found in domestic civil and human rights law in several other countries (e.g., Canada,[166] New Zealand,[167] the UK[168]). In some instances human rights courts have moved beyond cases in which hate speech *enacts* discrimination (e.g., "Whites Only") or discriminatory harassment (e.g., having a noose displayed in the workplace) to cases in which hate speech *indicates* discrimination. In *Singer v. Iwasyk and Pennywise Food Ltd.* (1976),[169] for example, a Board of Inquiry of the Saskatchewan Human Rights Commission ruled that when a proprietor of a restaurant displayed an external sign depicting a small person with brown skin color wearing a chef's hat and a grass skirt and bearing the words 'Sambo's Pepperpot', this amounted to 'indicating discrimination.' Examples of the present cluster can also be found in the jurisprudence of supranational human rights courts. In *Aksu v. Turkey*, for instance, the ECtHR established the precedent that the right to respect for private and family life set forth in Art. 8 of the ECHR includes as a constitutive element 'an individual's ethnic identity' and that 'any negative stereotyping of a group, when it reaches a certain level, is capable of impacting on the group's sense of identity and the feelings of self-worth and self-confidence of members of the group' and as such 'can be seen as affecting the private life of members of the group'.[170]

It is an important feature of the current cluster of laws that they seek to constrain hate speech only when it constitutes an illegal act of discrimination or discriminatory harassment. As I shall try to show in Chs. 3 [3.5] and 7 [7.1], this feature has galvanized an important strand of thinking about hate speech law. People who instinctively reject hate speech law in the narrow sense captured by some of the previously mentioned clusters—because they regard hate speech law as anathema to free speech values—can nevertheless consistent with their beliefs defend laws that forbid hate speech when it is used to perform acts that are oppressive or exclusionary.

## 2.9 EXPRESSION-ORIENTED HATE CRIMES

The ninth cluster involves laws/regulations/codes that interdict speech or other expressive conduct that constitutes the enactment of an expression-oriented hate crime targeted at members of groups or classes of persons identified by certain ascriptive characteristics. This cluster may not constitute hate speech law under a narrow interpretation of that term, but nevertheless, it is comprised of laws/regulations/codes that indirectly constrain uses of hate speech and as such might be thought to implicate free speech values. It is certainly the case that civil libertarians in the US believe that cross burning statutes, for example, implicate the First Amendment even if cross burning can constitute an act of discriminatory intimidation, a type of expression-oriented hate crime. For my purposes, a hate crime is expression-oriented if it is essentially enacted through speech, symbols, gestures, or other expressive conduct, such as with the hate crimes of intimidation, provocation, or incitement to commit acts of discrimination, segregation, violence, mass murder or genocide.

Some of the laws in this cluster involve penalty enhancements, such as increased prison sentences or fines, for people found guilty of crimes or public order offenses when their offending was aggravated by hatred of people based on their ascriptive characteristics, such as race, ethnicity, religion, nationality, and so on (e.g., Croatia,[171] France,[172] Italy,[173] Russia,[174] the UK,[175] the US[176]). Other laws recriminalize existing crimes or offenses in order to create substantively new crimes or offenses relating to conduct

## 36  Ten Clusters of Laws/Regulations/Codes

that is aggravated by hatred of members of groups or classes of persons identified by certain ascriptive characteristics. These laws add the fact of being aggravated by hatred to the list of basic elements of the commission of the crime or offense. To give an example of expression-oriented crimes or offenses, it is not uncommon to find laws proscribing intimidation or harassment when targeted at members of groups or classes of persons in domestic penal codes and criminal statutes (e.g. the Australian State of Western Australia,[177] Slovakia,[178] some parts of the UK,[179] several US states[180]).

In some parts of the world, at certain times, authorities have attempted to recriminalize offenses relating to provocation in order to create separate offenses relating to provocation targeted at people identified by certain ascriptive characteristics. Consider the much-discussed City of St. Paul Bias-Motivated Crime Ordinance (1990): 'Whoever places on public or private property, a symbol, object, appellation, characterization or graffiti, including, but not limited to, a burning cross or Nazi swastika, which one knows or has reasonable grounds to know arouses anger, alarm or resentment in others on the basis of race, color, creed, religion or gender commits disorderly conduct and shall be guilty of a misdemeanor.'[181] At first glance, this ordinance sits foursquare within the cluster of laws/regulations/codes that disallow the public expression of hatred. Even so, the City of St. Paul insisted that this ordinance was intended to ban provocation under the rubric of the fighting words doctrine posited by the US Supreme Court in First Amendment cases.[182] The logic behind creating a subcategory of *racist* fighting words was essentially that in some contexts "You damn nigger" may operate like "I challenge you to a duel" may have once operated, in the sense that it fits within a social convention around the buildup to a fight (cf. Greenawalt 1989: 144; 1995: 50). In essence, the City of St. Paul argued that some expressions of hatred may constitute acts of discriminatory provocation, a type of expression-oriented hate crime. Of course, in *R.A.V. v. City of St. Paul* (1992)[183] the US Supreme Court struck down the ordinance. Yet the majority did so *not* because it was overbroad, in the sense of sweeping up the mere expression of hatred along with acts of discriminatory provocation. The majority did not see a reason to consider this point.[184] Instead, it argued that the ordinance involved content and viewpoint discrimination.

Moreover, the present cluster includes laws against the incitement of acts of discrimination, segregation, violence or genocide against members of groups or classes of persons identified by certain ascriptive characteristics. As one might expect, such laws can be found in international law and human rights instruments (e.g., the covenants of the United Nations General Assembly,[185] the American Convention on Human Rights (AmCHR),[186] the framework decisions of the Council of the European Union,[187] the Statute of the International Criminal Tribunal for Rwanda[188]). These laws are also developed through the jurisprudence of supranational human rights courts.

In *Glimmerveen and Hagenbeek v. Netherlands* (1979),[189] for instance, the ECtHR judged as inadmissible applications made by two Dutch nationals who had been found guilty by domestic courts of possessing with intent to distribute leaflets that incited racial discrimination. In addition, examples of the present cluster of laws can be found in domestic criminal statutes and penal codes (e.g., Argentina,[190] Belgium,[191] Brunei,[192] Cambodia,[193] Cuba,[194] East Timor,[195] Ecuador,[196] Finland,[197] Germany,[198] Greece,[199] Italy,[200] Kenya,[201] the Netherlands,[202] Spain[203]). They can also be found in media law (e.g., France[204]).

In some instances the relevant laws specify the form of words that constitute incitement to acts of discrimination or violence. For example, in *Islamic Unity Convention v. Independent Broadcasting Authority and Others* [2002][205] the Constitutional Court of South Africa opined that s. 2(a) of the Independent Broadcasting Authority's (IBA) Code of Conduct for Broadcasting Services (1993)[206]—which stated that '[b]roadcasting licensees shall [. . .] not broadcast any material which is [. . .] likely to prejudice the safety of the State or the public order or relations between sections of the population'—went beyond the exceptions to the right to freedom of expression outlined in s. 16(2) of the South African Bill of Rights, most notably s. 16(2)(c), which specifies that the right to freedom of expression does not extend to 'advocacy of hatred that is based on race, ethnicity, gender or religion, and that constitutes incitement to cause harm.'[207] Subsequently, the Independent Communications Authority of South Africa (ICASA), which was established in 2000, adopted a new Code of Conduct for Broadcasting Service Licensees (2009) containing s. 3(3)(c), according to which 'Broadcasting service licensees must not broadcast material which, judged within context, amounts to [. . .] the advocacy of hatred that is based on race, ethnicity, religion or gender and that constitutes incitement to cause harm.' This code of conduct interdicts only the use of advocacy of hatred that constitutes incitement to cause harm. Even in South Africa, however, the distinction between the offense of incitement to hatred and the offense of advocacy of hatred that constitutes incitement to cause harm remains intact. Consider s. 10(1) of the Promotion of Equality and Prevention of Unfair Discrimination Act 2000, which separates out the prohibition of hate speech into separate offenses. It prohibits the use of words targeted at people identified by certain ascriptive characteristics (or 'prohibited grounds') used with the intention to '(b) be harmful or to incite harm', and it prohibits words used with the intention to '(c) promote or propagate hatred.' So, whereas incitement to hatred only involves a speaker's intention to promote hatred of certain groups or classes of persons, the hate crime of incitement to cause harm is characterized by the speaker's intention to make someone else the instrument of his or her unlawful will in committing harmful acts.

It may be tempting to think that laws in the present cluster are among the most straightforward to defend because they piggyback on other laws that are already widely accepted. But the position is not so straightforward. Where laws specifically interdict hate-based forms of intimidation, provocation, or incitement to crime, for example, they do so in a way that discriminates between different content or viewpoints. As mentioned earlier, this means that they implicate free speech principles and values—most notably relating to neutrality—even if they are ostensibly directed at otherwise unprotected conduct. I shall return to discuss this complex issue in Chs. 9 [9.5] and 10 [10.5], where I shall argue that the ideal of neutrality is appropriately subject to exceptions that reflect other important principles and values.

## 2.10 TIME, PLACE, AND MANNER RESTRICTIONS

The tenth cluster is instantiated by a particular subset of laws/regulations/codes that impose time, place, and manner restrictions on speech. This cluster is qualitatively different from the others in the sense that normally such laws/regulations/codes are *not* intended to constrain speech or otherwise expressive conduct that is enacted through the use of hate speech. So this cluster is not hate speech law in the narrow sense. Nevertheless, I have included this cluster because in some circumstances authorities have attempted to utilize time, place, and manner restrictions in order to constrain the practices of hate speakers, including their uses of hate speech. Authorities have sought to constrain uses of hate speech, in other words, when they involve means or circumstances of communication that fall foul of relevant time, place, or manner restrictions. It might be true that even in these exceptional circumstances laws/regulations/codes only indirectly constrain uses of hate speech, but the fact that they do so is far from coincidental.

The US is a notable absentee from most of the previously discussed clusters, but arguably one example of a time, place, and manner restriction that had been used to constrain uses of hate speech was the Fairness Doctrine introduced in 1949 by the United States Federal Communications Commission (FCC). It made it mandatory for holders of TV and radio broadcast licenses to not merely broadcast controversial issues of public concern but also to do so in a manner that was honest, equitable, and balanced as determined by the FCC. In the late 1960s the US Supreme Court did not regard the Fairness Doctrine as a violation of the First Amendment, at least with respect to public service broadcasters.[208] More importantly, prior to the FCC's decision to repeal the Fairness Doctrine in 1987, associations representing groups or classes of persons had used the FCC complaints procedure to lodge complaints against broadcasters for violating the Doctrine through their use of hate speech, albeit with limited success.[209]

More recently, US courts have given a degree of leeway to authorities in tackling a new mode of hate speech via time, place, and manner restrictions. This form of hate speech is encapsulated in a practice adopted by Fred Phelps and other members of the Westboro Baptist Church of picketing the funerals of deceased US military personnel, the funerals of ordinary citizens who have died of AIDS, and the funerals of ordinary citizens killed in high-profile mass shootings, as a way of publicly conveying the Church's religious message that homosexuality is an abomination in the eyes of God. The practice has prompted lawmakers in various US states to enact time, place, and manner regulations concerning protests at funerals and burials, specifically, creating buffer zones or minimum distances for protests, written in such a way as not to run afoul of the First Amendment requirement of content and viewpoint neutrality (e.g., Arizona,[210] Kansas,[211], Missouri,[212] Ohio[213]). In several cases the Courts have looked upon these sorts of regulations not unfavorably from the perspective of free speech. In *Phelps-Roper v. Strickland* (2008)[214] and *Phelps-Roper v. City of Manchester* (2012),[215] for example, two US Courts of Appeal held that the laws or regulations adopted by the State of Ohio and the City of Manchester, Missouri, respectively to regulate protests and picketing at funerals and burials were legitimate time, place, and manner regulations consistent with the First Amendment. Of course, because time, place, and manner restrictions are broad in scope, they also constrain the activities of groups or classes of persons that have been the victims of hate speech and who are seeking to engage in direct forms of counterspeech. Thus, laws or regulations that create buffer zones around funerals apply equally to people who wish to mount counterprotests against picketers from the Westboro Baptist Church.

Because time, place, and manner restrictions do not pick out any particular content or viewpoint, there is a sense in which they pose less of a threat to free speech values than other clusters discussed previously. However, this does not mean to say that they are not subject to objections. There are civil libertarians who argue that sometimes these laws are exploited for purposes that do violate free speech values, and that the aim of confronting hate speakers would be better pursued by allowing counterspeech to find its own path, without legalistic constraints. I shall discuss at length the counterspeech argument against hate speech law in Ch. 9 [9.3].

\* \* \*

I wish to draw this chapter to a close by making some general observations about these ten clusters. My first observation is that together they span three jurisdictional levels: laws/regulations/codes at the level of a sovereign state, including laws issued by national, state, county, city, and even village governmental authorities (e.g., constitutional law, criminal law, civil law, administrative law, immigration law, public gatherings law, law on contempt of court, various kinds of local or municipal laws, codes, regulations, or ordinances); laws/regulations/codes at the international level (e.g., conventions, declarations, protocols, the jurisprudence of supranational human rights courts); laws/regulations/codes at the level of subnational institutions, organizations, and commercial companies (e.g., speech codes enforced by employers, schools, universities; rules on permissible content imposed by independent media and internet regulators;

standards or codes on acceptable content adopted and enforced by newspapers, TV and radio broadcasters, internet service providers, social networking websites, internet messaging services). So in that sense one can plausibly say that as a corpus of law hate speech law is not merely variegated in form but also broad in scope.

My second observation is that many of these clusters are recognized, implicitly or explicitly, by courts themselves. At times courts have taken a dim view of attempts to transplant arguments appropriate to some clusters of law into the pastures of other clusters. So, for example, in *R. v. Birdwood*, the Court of Appeal of England and Wales rejected a truth defense relating to the offense of incitement to racial hatred partly on the grounds that the point and purpose of such law differs from that of group defamation law (*sensu stricto*). More generally, courts of review have often been asked to consider whether or not lower courts have paid due attention to relevant distinctions between clusters of laws, including relevant differences between the types of conduct proscribed by those laws. Thus, in *Nahimana, Barayagwiza, Ngeze v. The Prosecutor* (2007)[216] the Appeal Chamber of the International Criminal Tribunal for Rwanda judged that the Trial Chamber had not blurred the distinction between statutes banning incitement to hatred, statues interdicting incitement to discrimination and violence, and statutes prohibiting direct incitement to commit genocide.[217]

My third observation acts as a counterweight to the second. It is that, like all ideal types, the precision these clusters promise is not always matched by actual law. For one thing, it is evident that some laws/regulations/codes are articulated in such a way as to render punishable a disjunctive form of conduct (conduct that is comprised of either conduct A *or* conduct B) and others a conjunctive form of conduct (conduct that is comprised of conduct A *and* conduct B), and as a result these laws/regulations/codes can be fitted into more than one of the ten clusters outlined in this chapter. Consider Ch. 11, s. 8 of the Finnish Penal Code, which prohibits 'ethnic agitation.' 'A person who spreads statements or other information among the public where a certain race, a national, ethnic or religious group or a comparable group is threatened, defamed or insulted shall be sentenced for ethnic agitation to a fine or to imprisonment for at most two years [trans.].' The reference to threat, defamation, and insult could conceivably mean that the law could be placed in the cluster of laws banning hate speech when it amounts to discriminatory intimidation, laws prohibiting group libel (*sensu stricto*), and laws restricting the expression of hatred. Furthermore, there are many occasions when cases have been pursued by appealing to one cluster of law when arguably the facts of the case might have best suited a different cluster that was also available to public prosecutors in the relevant jurisdiction. Holocaust denial literature has often been tackled using laws other than dedicated Holocaust denial laws.[218]

Finally, it is one thing to say that particular laws are open to interpretation and can be fitted into different clusters; it is quite another to say that

## Ten Clusters of Laws/Regulations/Codes  41

when it comes to legal interpretation, there are no holds barred. Sometimes key elements of laws/regulations/codes delimit which clusters they can be reasonably interpreted as belonging to, and so it would be naive to think that any particular law/regulation/code that constrains uses of hate speech can be identified with any one of the aforementioned clusters. Laws banning incitement to hatred have often been subject to gross misinterpretations, for example. A *Newsweek* article from 1988, which is cited by the *Oxford English Dictionary* as containing the earliest published use of the term 'hate speech', repeatedly conflates laws banning incitement to hatred with laws proscribing incitement to violence (Jacoby 1988: 48). The author of a best-selling undergraduate textbook on political ideologies at best misleadingly and at worst erroneously explains that '[s]tates such as the UK have [. . .] introduced laws banning expressions of religious hatred' (Heywood 2012: 322). Similarly, Waldron writes that '[i]n Britain, there are laws forbidding the expression of racial hatred' (Waldron 2010: 1642). These statements belie the true nature of incitement to hatred law in the UK, both as it is written and as it is interpreted and applied by the courts. It would be far more accurate to say that public order law in the UK forbids the intentional stirring up of hatred on the grounds of race, religion, or sexual orientation, and that depending on their interpretation of the facts in particular cases the courts might or might not regard a defendant's public expression of hatred as amounting to the intention to stir up hatred. This level of specificity helps to honor distinctions between different clusters of laws/regulations/codes that constrain uses of hate speech, such as between laws/regulations/codes disallowing the public expression of hatred [2.3] and laws/regulations/codes banning the use of speech or other expressive conduct with the intention of stirring up hatred [2.4].

But why does this specificity matter normatively? Because normative principles that appear to N-warrant hate speech law typically lend greater N-warrant to some clusters of laws/regulations/codes than others; conversely, principles that purport to rule out all hate speech law are, on closer inspection, devastating against some clusters of laws/regulations/codes but relatively helpless against, or inappropriately applied to, others—this, at least, is what I aim to demonstrate in Chs. 2–9.

## NOTES

1. David Riesman cites the example of Decree-Law of 17 Jul. 1931 (as amended by Decree-Law of 10 Aug. 1931), which the German state used to stem the flow of published attacks on 'democrats', 'Reds', 'socialists', 'Jews', 'liberals', and 'Catholics.' The need for this legislation reflected the fact that such attacks (Riesman 1942: 729) 'ran little risk of a prosecution for libel, since vague groups of this sort, it was held, could not be defamed.'
2. Riesman (1942: 742) cites the case of *R. v. Osborne* (1732) 25 Eng. Rep. 584 (involving a printed libel that members of the Portuguese Jewish community

living in London had murdered a Jewish woman and her illegitimate child by a Christian lover) as evidence of the fact that the English common law offense of seditious libel 'was occasionally invoked to curb attempts "to promote feelings of ill-will and hostility between different classes" of His Majesty's subjects.' Note that the English common law offense of seditious libel was abolished by s. 73 of the Coroners and Justice Act 2009.
3. Riesman (1942: 743) cites a nineteenth-century French law, Art. 10 of the Law of 25 Mar. 1822, 'which punished those who publicly sought to disturb the peace by inciting citizens to contempt or hatred against one or more classes of persons.' As Riesman himself concedes (ibid.), '[t]his, of course, was not a libel law in the American sense, for it covered mere derogatory expressions like "down with the priests", or the "aristocrats", or the "bakers."'
4. Art. 137c of the Penal Code (as amended in 1992).
5. s. 423 of the Penal Code.
6. Art. 510(2) of the Penal Code.
7. See, e.g., Ch. 38, para. 27 of the Illinois Revised Statutes; Ch. 272, s. 98C of the Massachusetts General Laws; s. 609.765 of the Minnesota Statutes; s. 45-8-212 of the Montana Code; Ch. 200, s. 510 of the Nevada Revised Statutes.
8. ss. 186 and 187 of the Criminal Code.
9. Art. 1(4) and 4 of the Prohibition of Defamation Law of 1965.
10. Art. 32 of Law on the Freedom of the Press of 29 Jul. 1881 (as amended by the Law of 1 Jul. 1972, the Law of 30 Dec. 2004, and the Law of 6 Aug. 2012).
11. Art. 81 of Law No. 2004-643 of 14 Dec. 2004.
12. See, e.g., the Advisory Committee on the Council of Europe Framework Convention for the Protection of National Minorities, Opinion on Austria, 16 May 2002, para. 85; Opinion on the Former Yugoslav Republic of Macedonia, 27 May 2004, para. 55; Second Opinion on Estonia, 24 Feb. 2005, para. 73. See also the Committee on the Elimination of Racial Discrimination, General Recommendation No. 27: Discrimination against Roma, 16 Aug. 2000, para. 9.
13. It including the following lyrics: 'Oooh Will Young here, mmmmh. I'm here, it's Will's birthday and as the years go by I get more very gay. When you saw me years ago you didn't know, but now I'm the gayest fella you probably know. Mmmm I like to wear a silly hat, I get camper by the hour, oh would you look at the muck in here. I'm Will Young and I'm gay.'
14. Ofcom Broadcast Bulletin, Issue 130 (23 Mar. 2009).
15. Art. 21 of the Law of 30 Jul. 1981.
16. Art. 16 of Law No. 045 of 8 Oct. 2010.
17. Art. 295(2) of the Penal Code (as enacted by Law No. 62 of 29 Dec. 1987).
18. Art. 174(3) of the Criminal Code.
19. s. 266(b)(1) of the Penal Code.
20. Art. 212(a)(1) of the Penal Code (added by Supreme Decree 2636 of 1978).
21. s. 2 of Act 927/25.6.1979.
22. Art. 156 of the Penal Code.
23. Art. 3(a) of Law No. 654 of 1975 (as amended by Art. 1 of Decree-Law No. 122 of 1993, converted with amendments into Law No. 205 of 1993).
24. s. 135(a) of the Penal Code.
25. Art. 393(a) of the Penal Code.
26. Ch. 16, s. 8 of the Criminal Code.
27. Art. 216(2) of the Criminal Code.
28. In England and Wales, s. 3 of the Football (Offences) Act 1991 (as amended by s. 9 of the Football (Offences and Disorder) Act 1999).
29. See, e.g., s. 53-37 of the Connecticut General Statutes.
30. s. 185 of the Criminal Code.

## Ten Clusters of Laws/Regulations/Codes 43

31. 324 So.2d 652.
32. s. 18C of the Racial Discrimination Act 1975 (as amended by the Racial Hatred Act 1995).
33. Art. 9(15) in conjunction with Art. 4 of the Federal Law for the Prevention and Elimination of Discrimination.
34. Art. 33 of the Press Law of 1881 (as amended the Law of 1 Jul. 1972, the Law of 30 Dec. 2004, and the Law of 6 Aug. 2012).
35. Art. 17(2) of Act CIV of 2010 on the Freedom of the Press and the Fundamental Rules on Media Content.
36. s. 3(2)(b) of the Information Technology (Intermediaries Guidelines) Rules, 2011, which supplements the Information Technology Act 2000 (as amended by the Information Technology (Amendment) Act 2008).
37. Rule 12(i) of the Editors' Code of Practice issued by the Press Complaints Commission (PCC).
38. 80 Adjudication issued 04/01/10.
39. Full text available at: http://www.pcc.org.uk/cases/adjudicated.html?article=NjEyNw== (last accessed 28/11/14).
40. Art. 4(a) of the International Convention on the Elimination of All Forms of Racial Discrimination (ICERD).
41. Art. 5 of the Additional Protocol to the Convention on Cybercrime, Concerning the Criminalization of Acts of a Racist and Xenophobic Nature Committed through Computer Systems.
42. See, e.g., *Vejdeland and Others v. Sweden*.
43. Consider the reservations entered by Japan and the US in relation to Art. 4(a) of the ICERD.
44. For example (Sarrazin 2009): 'Integration is an accomplishment of those who integrate. I don't have to accept anyone who doesn't do anything. I don't have to accept anyone who lives off the state and rejects this very state, who doesn't make an effort to reasonably educate their children and constantly produces new little headscarf girls. That is true for 70% of the Turkish and for 90% of the Arab population in Berlin. Many of them don't want any integration, they want to live according to their own rules. Furthermore, they encourage a collective mentality that is aggressive and ancestral [. . .].'
45. No. 48/2010 (CERD, 26 Feb.).
46. At para. 12.8.
47. Formerly the Human Rights and Equal Opportunities Commission (HREOC).
48. HREOCA 23 (involving a complaint made against a newspaper for the use of epithets referring to English people under s. 18C(1) of the Racial Discrimination Act 1975).
49. FCA 1103 (involving a complaint made against a journalist and newspaper for remarks made about mixed-race Australians, under s. 18C(1) of the Racial Discrimination Act 1975).
50. At paras. 370–393.
51. At para. 414.
52. s. 226 of the Criminal Code.
53. See, e.g., ss. 76–80 of the Criminal Code of the State of Western Australia (as amended by s. 6 of Law No. 80 of 2004); s. 4 of the Racial Vilification Act 1996 of the State of South Australia; s. 8 of the Racial and Religious Tolerance Act 2001 of the State of Victoria.
54. Art. 283(1) of the Penal Code.
55. s. 153A of the Penal Code.
56. Art. 249 of the Criminal Law and Art. 47 of the Public Security Administration Punishments Law.
57. s. 135(2) of the Penal Code.

58. s. 130(2) of the Criminal Code.
59. Art. 332 of the Criminal Code (as amended by Act C of 2012, formerly Art. 269 of the Criminal Code).
60. s. 2(1) of the Prohibition of Incitement to Hatred Act, 1989.
61. s. 13(1) of the National Cohesion and Integration Act 2008.
62. s. 299 of the Penal Code.
63. Art. 170 of the Criminal Code.
64. Art. 319 of the Criminal Code.
65. s. 298A(a) of the Criminal Code.
66. Art. 137(d) of the Penal Code.
67. s. 153A of the Penal Code.
68. Art. 282(1) of the Criminal Code.
69. s. 298A(a) of the Criminal Code.
70. Art. 261 of the Criminal Code.
71. Pt. 3, ss. 17–29, and Pt. 3A, ss. 29A-29N of the Public Order Act 1986 (as amended by the Racial and Religious Hatred Act 2006 and s. 74 and Sch. 16, para. 14 of the Criminal Justice and Immigration Act 2008).
72. Art. 149a of the Penal Code (enacted by Law No. 9.155 of 4 Dec. 1933).
73. s. 61-10-16 of the West Virginia Code.
74. s. 156 of the Criminal Code.
75. s. 87(1)(b) of the Criminal Code.
76. s. 8(5) of the Regulations of Gatherings Act 205 of 1993.
77. s. 19 of the Immigration Act.
78. Art. 3 of Law No. 23.593 of 9 Sept. 1988.
79. s. 46 of the Disability Discrimination Ordinance, Hong Kong Special Administrative Region of China.
80. Art. 9(27) in conjunction with Art. 4 of the Federal Law for the Prevention and Elimination of Discrimination.
81. Art. 61 of the Human Rights Act 1993.
82. s. 10(1)(c) of the Promotion of Equality and Prevention of Unfair Discrimination Act 2000.
83. Art. 31 of the Statute on Freedom of Opinion and Information and the Performance of Journalism.
84. Art. 24 of the Press Law of 29 Jul. 1881 (as amended the Law of 1 Jul. 1972, the Law of 30 Dec. 2004, and the Law of 6 Aug. 2012).
85. Art. 3(1) of the Interstate Broadcasting Agreement.
86. Art. 17(1) of Act CIV of 2010 on the Freedom of the Press and the Fundamental Rules on Media Content.
87. Art. 7 of the Printing and Publications Act, No. 8.
88. Art. 69(1) of the Press Code and Ordinance 2011 (replacing Arts. 53–54 of the Press Code of 1975).
89. See, e.g., Art. 26(4) of the Regulations on the Administration of Publication; Art. 25(4) of the Regulations on the Administration of Movies; Ch. 3, para. 2(b) of the Generic Code of Practice on Television Programme Standards; para. 7(b) of the Radio Code of Practice on Programme Standards, Hong Kong Special Administrative Region of China.
90. s. 19(d) of the Kenya Information and Communications (Broadcasting) Regulations, 2009.
91. Art. 5 of the Code of Ethics of the Congolese National Press Union.
92. Art. 47 of the Constitution.
93. Art. 47 of the Constitution.
94. Art. 30 of the Constitution.
95. Art. 6 of the Audiovisual Media Services Directive of 2010 (replacing Art. 3b of the Television without Frontiers Directive).

96. Art. 1(a) of the Framework Decision on Combating Racism and Xenophobia by Means of Criminal Law.
97. Consider the decision in *Balsytė-Lideikienė v. Lithuania*.
98. Arts. 261 and 262 of the Penal Code.
99. ss. 319(2) and 319(3)(a)(c) of the Criminal Code (as amended by An Act to Amend the Criminal Code (Hate Propaganda) of 2004).
100. ss. 505(2) and 505 Exception of the Penal Code.
101. ss. 11(1)(b) and 14(2)(a)(c) of the Racial Discrimination Prohibition Act 26 of 1991, as amended by the Racial Discrimination Amendment Act 26 of 1998.
102. Decision 30/1992 (V. 26.) AB (Hung. Const. Ct.), at IV, 5.
103. No. 94/2421/X2 (EWCA, 11 Apr.), 6 Archbold News 2 (involving the dissemination of anti-Semitic written materials).
104. s. 29J of the Racial and Religious Hatred Act 2006.
105. s. 19(1) of the Defamation Act 2002.
106. ss. 181 and 319(1) of the Criminal Code.
107. s. 176 of the Penal Code.
108. Art. 486(b) of the Criminal Code (as amended by Proclamation No. 414/2004).
109. s. 130(1) of the Criminal Code.
110. s. 153A(b) of the Penal Code.
111. s. 298A(b) of the Criminal Code.
112. s. 298A(b) of the Criminal Code.
113. Art. 216(1) of the Criminal Code.
114. Art. 286 of the Penal Code (enacted by Law No. 5494 of 20 Oct. 2000).
115. Art. 27 of the Press Law of 1881.
116. 2 SCR 100 (involving the deportation of a member of a hard-line Hutu political party with respect to charges brought by Rwandan authorities for incitement to murder, genocide, and hatred).
117. These included the following: 'Something else which may be called "not allowing ourselves to be invaded" in the country, you know people they call "Inyenzis" (cockroaches), no longer call them "Inkotanyi" (tough fighters), as they are actually "Inyenzis"' [trans.]. 'These people called Inyenzis are now on their way to attack us' [trans.].
118. EWHC 2825 (Admin.).
119. At para. 83.
120. s. 318(1) of the Criminal Code.
121. s. 261a of the Law against Support and Dissemination of Movements Oppressing Human Rights and Freedoms.
122. Denial of Holocaust (Prohibition) Law 5746-1986.
123. Emergency Ordinance No. 31 of 13 Mar. 2002.
124. Art. 607(2) of the Criminal Code.
125. Art. 261 of the Criminal Code.
126. Art. 24(2) of the Press Law of 1881 (as amended by the Law of 13 Jul. 1990 and the Law of 16 Dec. 1992).
127. Art. 333 of the Criminal Code (as amended by Act C of 2012, formerly Art. 269C of the Criminal Code).
128. Art. 3(2) of Law No. 18/2008 of 23/07/2008 Relating to the Punishment of the Crime of Genocide Ideology.
129. ss. 130(3) and 189 of the Criminal Code.
130. s. 3h of the National Socialism Prohibition Law of 1947 (as amended in 1992).
131. Art. 1 of Negationism Law of 23 Mar. 1995 (as amended in 1999).
132. s. 261a of the Law against Support and Dissemination of Movements Oppressing Human Rights and Freedoms.
133. Art. 170(2) of the Criminal Code.
134. s. 131 of the Criminal Code.

## 46 Ten Clusters of Laws/Regulations/Codes

135. Art. 6(1) of the Additional Protocol to the Convention on Cybercrime, Concerning the Criminalization of Acts of a Racist and Xenophobic Nature Committed through Computer Systems.
136. Art. 1(c)(d) of the Framework Decision on Combating Racism and Xenophobia by Means of Criminal Law.
137. See, e.g., *Garaudy v. France.*
138. 24 B.R. 69, 385 (Quebec) and reported in the *Canadian Law Times* 35 (1915): 262–273.
139. At 264.
140. At 268.
141. s. 14(1)(b) of the Saskatchewan Human Rights Code.
142. Art. 3 of Law No. 7711 of 22 Oct. 1997.
143. s. 130(2) of the Criminal Code.
144. Art. 261 of the Criminal Code.
145. Cited in Fu (2012: 7).
146. The term 'injuria' or 'iniuria' can be defined as an act of indignity or an act that is prejudicial to another person's dignitary rights (cf. de Villiers 1899: 21–22).
147. Art. 140(3) of the Penal Code (introduced by Law No. 9.459, 1997, as amended by Law No. 10.741, 2003).
148. Common law offense or delict of *injuria* (civil) or *crimen injuria* (criminal).
149. (2) SA 260 (N) (involving a lawsuit for *injuria* after the defendant repeatedly called the plaintiff a 'kaffir' and assaulted him)
150. *Mbatha v. Van Staden*, at 262–263.
151. No. 0098040-18.2010.8.26.0050 (Sao Paulo Ct. of Just., 23 May) (involving an appeal against a conviction for racial *injuria* under Art. 140(3) of the Penal Code).
152. Original text available at: http://tj-sp.jusbrasil.com.br/jurisprudencia/116077758/apelacao-apl-980401820108260050-sp-0098040-1820108260050/inteiro-teor-116077768 (last accessed 27/11/14).
153. 355 F. Supp. 206 (S.D. Fla.) (involving a black lawyer and his family who were racially abused with the word 'nigger' by a restaurant waitress).
154. 25 Cal.3d 932 (involving a plaintiff's claim of damages *inter alia* for intentional infliction of emotional distress as a result of being subjected to racist abuse).
155. 562 US __ (Docket No. 09-751).
156. At __.
157. No. 1:2006-cv-00794, Doc. 251 (W.D.N.Y.) (involving an African American steel worker who had suffered years of expressive abuse at the hands of fellow employees and supervisors).
158. At 2-5.
159. See the website of the EEOC. Available at: www.eeoc.gov/employees/index.cfm (last accessed 10/08/14).
160. No. 11-792 (W.D. Tex.) (involving a lawsuit brought by the EEOC in relation to discriminatory harassment in the workplace).
161. At 1-2.
162. No. cv-05-BE-1704-E (N.D. Ala.) (involving a lawsuit brought by the EEOC in relation to discriminatory harassment in the workplace).
163. See, e.g., *Shanoff v. Illinois Department of Human Services* (2001) 258 F.3d 696 (7th Cir.) (involving a lawsuit brought by a white Jewish employee alleging that his supervisor, a black female, had subjected him to a hostile work environment because of his race and religion, including referring to him as a 'haughty Jew', in violation of Title VII).
164. See, e.g., Pennsylvania State University's *Policy on Discrimination, Harassment, Sexual Harassment and Related Inappropriate Conduct* (2014); Middle

## Ten Clusters of Laws/Regulations/Codes  47

Tennessee State University's *Discrimination and Harassment –Complaint and Investigation Procedure* (2008).
165. See, e.g., Stanford University's Fundamental Standard and Fundamental Standard Interpretation: Free Expression and Discriminatory Harassment (1990), which was struck down in *Corry v. Stanford* (1995) No. 740309 (Cal. Super. Ct., 27 Feb.); the University of Michigan at Ann Arbor's *Policy on Discrimination and Discriminatory Harassment by Students in the University Environment* (1988), which was struck down in *Doe v. University of Michigan* (1989) 721 F. Supp. 852 (E.D. Mich.).
166. s. 13(1) of the Canadian Human Rights Act 1985 (formerly the Canadian Human Rights Act 1976–1977).
167. Art. 63 of the Human Rights Act 1993.
168. s. 26 of the Equality Act 2010.
169. Unreported (Bd. of Inq. of the Sask. Hum. Rights Comm., 5 Nov.) (involving a contravention of Art. 4(1) of the Canadian Province of Saskatchewan's Fair Accommodation Practices Act 1965).
170. *Aksu v. Turkey*, at para 58.
171. Art. 174(1) of the Penal Code.
172. Arts. 132–176 of the Penal Code (as amended by Law of 3 Feb. 2003, Law 239 of 18 Mar. 2003, and Law 204 of 9 Mar. 2004).
173. Art. 2 of Decree-Law No. 122 of 1993 (converted with amendments into Law by Law No. 205 of 1993).
174. Art. 63(f) of the Criminal Code.
175. ss. 145 and 146 of the Criminal Justice Act 2003.
176. See, e.g., the Violent Crime Control and Law Enforcement Act 1994; the Matthew Shepard and James Byrd, Jr. Hate Crimes Prevention Act 2009.
177. Pt. 2, ss. 80A–80J of the Criminal Code of the State of Western Australia (as amended by s. 6 of Law No. 80 of 2004).
178. ss. 424 and 424a of the Penal Code.
179. In England and Wales, ss. 31–32 of the Crime and Disorder Act 1998. In Scotland, s. 50A of the Criminal Law (Consolidation) (Scotland) Act 1995 (as amended by s. 33 of the Crime and Disorder Act 1998).
180. See, e.g., s. 18-9-121 of the Colorado Revised Statutes; s. 45-5-221(1)(b) of the Montana Code; s. 2927.12 of the Ohio Revised Code; s. 1456 of the Vermont Statutes and Codes; s. 18.2-423 of the Virginia Code.
181. City of St. Paul, Minn., Code of Ordinances, s. 292.02.
182. See, e.g., *Chaplinsky v. State of New Hampshire* (1942) 315 US 568, at 572; *Cohen v. California* (1971) 403 US 15, at 20.
183. 505 US 377 (involving the application of the City of St. Paul's Bias-Motivated Crime Ordinance to a case of cross burning on the property of an African American family).
184. At 381.
185. See, e.g., Art. 20(2) of the International Covenant on Civil and Political Rights (ICCPR).
186. Art. 13(5).
187. See, e.g., Art. 1(a) of the Framework Decision on Combating Racism and Xenophobia by Means of Criminal Law.
188. Art. 2(3)(c).
189. Nos. 8348/78 and 8406/78 (ECtHR, 11 Oct.).
190. Art. 3 of Law No. 23.593 of 9 Sept. 1988.
191. Art. 20 of the Law of 30 Jul. 1981.
192. s. 505 of the Penal Code.
193. s. 61 of the Criminal Code.
194. Art. 295(1) of the Penal Code (as enacted by Law No. 62 of 29 Dec. 1987).

48  Ten Clusters of Laws/Regulations/Codes

195. s. 135(2) of the Penal Code.
196. Art. 212A(2)(3) of the Penal Code (added by Supreme Decree 2636, 1978).
197. Ch. 11, s. 10(a) of the Criminal Code.
198. s. 130(2) of the Criminal Code.
199. s. 1(1) of Act 927/25.6.1979 (supplemented by s. 24 of Act 1419/8.3.1984 and amended by s. 72 of Act 2910/2001).
200. Art. 3(a)(b) of Law No. 654 of 1975 (as amended by Art. 1 of Decree-Law No. 122 of 1993, converted with amendments into law by Law No. 205 of 1993).
201. s. 62 of the National Cohesion and Integration Act 2008.
202. Art. 137(e) of the Criminal Code.
203. Art. 510(1) of the Penal Code.
204. Arts. 23 and 24 of the Press Law of 1881.
205. ZACC 3 (involving an application made by an Islamic community radio station against the way that the Broadcasting Monitoring and Complaints Committee had handled a complaint made by the South African Jewish Board of Deputies about a program in which an author asserted that Jewish people were not gassed in concentration camps during World War II but died of infectious diseases, particularly typhus, and that only a million Jews had died).
206. Set out in Schedule 1 to the Independent Broadcasting Authority Act 153 of 1993.
207. At paras. 33–36.
208. See, e.g., *Red Lion Broadcasting Co. v. FCC* (1969) 395 US 367 (involving an on-air personal attack on the reputation of a journalist). In this case the US Supreme Court made a unanimous decision to uphold the constitutionality of the Fairness Doctrine, taking into account the First Amendment. It pointed to 'the right of the public to receive suitable access to social, political, esthetic, moral, and other ideas and experiences.' At 390.
209. Consider the decision of the FCC in January 1986 to reject a complaint made by the Anti-Defamation Association of Emigres from Post-1917 Russia that an episode of the public affairs television program *Frontline* titled 'The Russians Are Here', aired by several broadcasters, portrayed émigrés from Russia in a demeaning way and unfairly denied them a chance of a rebuttal in the program. This decision was upheld by the courts. See *Anti-Defamation Association of Emigres from Post-1917 Russia v. FCC* (1987) 831 F.2d 831 (D.C. Cir.).
210. s. 13-2930 of the Arizona Revised Statutes.
211. s. 21-4015a of the Kansas Statutes.
212. See, e.g., s. 210.264 of the City of Manchester Municipal Code; s. 578.501(2) of the Missouri Revised Statutes.
213. s. 3767.30 of the Ohio Revised Code (on which many other statues are based).
214. 539 F.3d 356 (6th Cir.).
215. 697 F.3d 678 (8th Cir.).
216. No. ICTR-99-52-A (Int. Crim. Trib. for Rwan., 28 Nov.) (involving an appeal against prosecutions for direct and public incitement to commit genocide and persecution and extermination as crimes against humanity).
217. At paras. 692–696.
218. Consider the Australian Holocaust denial case *Jones v. Toben* [2002] FCA 1150 (involving the application of s. 18C(1) of the Racial Discrimination Act 1975 to Holocaust denial).

# 3 Principles of Basic Morality

In this chapter, I examine principles of basic morality. I use the word 'basic' not because I think these principles are simple or uncontroversial, but because of the fundamental nature of the normatively relevant features they purport to safeguard or serve: namely, liberty, health, autonomy, security, non-subordination, the absence of oppression, and human dignity. These principles are 'moral' in the sense that they go to the heart of how at a rudimentary level human beings ought to be treated and to how such expectations bear upon the N-warrant of legalistic constraints on hate speech. Intriguingly, many of these principles have been invoked by both defenders and critics of hate speech law. So this makes the task of clarifying their character and scope all the more crucial. This task is complicated, however, by the fact that often the content and application of these principles rests upon empirical or quasi-empirical premises about how certain uses of hate speech impact other people's well-being and decision-making. Hitherto, some of the basic moral arguments in favor of hate speech law have been weakened by a failure to acknowledge the presence of incomplete or inconclusive empirical evidence. In this chapter I attempt in some small way to rectify that potential shortcoming. Finally, the chapter is intended to feed into the first and second main goals of the book. These are to clarify the principled arguments for and against hate speech law and to show that virtually all principled arguments are improved by attending more closely to the heterogeneity of such law.

## 3.1 HEALTH

Well-being, in the sense of what makes a human life go well, can be defined in many different ways and may contain numerous elements (cf. Griffin 1986). Nevertheless, one typical element of well-being that seems to have obvious relevance to assessments of the basic moral status of hate speech, and to the N-warrant of hate speech law, is people's psychological and physiological health (e.g., Delgado 1982: 166–167). Clearly, any attempt to further specify the nature of health is fraught with familiar problems and challenges. Suppose health includes emotional tranquility. If so, would framing free speech policy in terms of protecting emotional tranquility entail banning the use of certain words simply because some listeners dislike, disapprove of, or feel offended by them? Alternatively, suppose psychological and physiological health is defined as the absence of medically defined disorders and pathologies. If so, is health the complete absence of all disorders and pathologies or simply the absence of the worst of these? How is "worst" determined? Indeed, what happens if, bowing to social or political pressure, the medical profession radically alters its understanding of what constitutes "pathology" and "disorder" in order to help or hinder certain claims for legal redress? Or suppose the concept of health is understood to be a matter of normal human functioning. In which case, how is "normal" defined? These are all important questions, to which I have no straightforward answers. Instead, I want to focus on a more immediate concern. If people's health is to figure in the decisions we make about the N-warrant of hate speech law, what principle best captures this feature?

A fairly obvious choice might seem to be the Harm Principle. 'That the only purpose for which power can be rightfully exercised over any member of a civilized community, against his will, is to prevent harm to others' (Mill [1859] 1972: 78). Ostensibly, the Harm Principle is a principle that safeguards liberty: it functions to furnish people with a protected sphere of negative liberty in which their thoughts, speech, and self-regarding actions are not impeded by external constraints. Then again, the Harm Principle also recognizes circumstances in which it is permissible to restrict liberty, to wit, harm prevention. And, what is more, several academics (myself included) have had recourse to the Harm Principle in thinking about whether or not at least some of the conduct that is constituted by hate speech can cause harm in the relevant sense (e.g., Cohen-Almagor 1993; Kateb 1996; Kernohan 1998; Brink 2001; Sumner 2004; Simpson [E.] 2006; Morgan 2007; Brown 2008). However, there are two drawbacks with putting all the eggs in this one basket. To begin with, it is not clear whether the Harm Principle, at least on Mill's reading, is consistent with the recognition of emotional distress as harmful in the relevant sense. On the one hand, to omit severe emotional distress from the list of relevant harms may seem overly restrictive. Then again, if it is acceptable to legislate against any threats to emotional tranquility, then the Harm Principle might turn out to be a surprisingly low hurdle—one that a vast amount of speech-restricting law could potentially clear. In addition to this, the Harm Principle states that harm prevention is the only aim that can justify coercive interference. But even people who maintain that the psychological, psychosomatic, and physiological harms resulting from uses of hate speech provide a powerful reason to legislate against it, might also accept that harm does not exhaust the legitimate grounds for legislation. Of course, given the potentially capacious meaning of the word 'harm', it might be meaningful to speak of the harm of subordination or even the harm of violating human dignity. But this could seem to rely on conceptual gymnastics and still might not adequately capture the fact of value pluralism: that several very different kinds of moral arguments can be made for and against hate speech law.

In the remainder of this section, therefore, I shall examine the argument from health through the lenses of a bespoke principle, which I label the Principle of Health, that legalistic constraints on uses of hate speech are (N-)warranted if they function to protect people from severe damage to their psychological or physiological health. Not just any sort of harm is relevant to the Principle of Health, as I shall define it. Building on suggestions made by Sumner (2004: 159–160) and Erik Bleich (2011: 146), I assume that in order to pass muster under the Principle of Health the relevant damage to health must be reckonable (amenable to measurement using established techniques and methods in the social sciences), assignable (attributable to particular individuals and not merely to an entire group of people en mass), and severe (beyond the level of mild irritation or feelings of offense). In addition to this, I want to stress at this stage that the Principle of Health is concerned with N-warrant. Would a given piece of hate speech law be *prima facie* warranted or unwarranted by *this* particular normatively relevant feature? As described in Ch. 1, the question of overall warrant is a different matter. In order to evaluate overall warrant, legislators and judges would also need to consider a range of other principles that invoke practical as well as moral considerations, such as whether a particular law would be effective in preventing the relevant harms, would be the least restrictive method of achieving that result, and would not have serious unintended consequences for free speech. I shall return to discuss these practical considerations in Ch. 9. Based on these and other principles, they will need to frame judgments of overall warrant. I will consider such judgments in Ch. 10.

## Short-Term Severe Emotional Distress

What potential harms to people's health resulting from uses of hate speech could be regarded as reckonable, assignable, and severe? For critical race theorists such as Delgado, Matsuda, and Lawrence the first item on the list is the immediate or short-term severe emotional distress suffered by some people as a result of experiencing interpersonal racist abuse (e.g., Delgado 1982: 137; Matsuda 1989b: 336). In the case of "You black bastard" uttered to someone on the street, for example, an individual is left in no doubt that he or she is being picked out by this generic term of abuse. And it is not difficult to comprehend how such abuse could evince severe emotional distress of one sort or another, such as anxiety, panic, shame, or fear. But it is also important to recognize that mental states associated with emotional distress can be complex. The immediate mental sensation of being verbally abused need not be restricted to an impression of how others feel about oneself; being subjected to hate speech also implicates how one feels about oneself. As Delgado explains, '[t]he psychological responses to [racial] stigmatization consist of feelings of humiliation, isolation, and self-hatred' (Delgado 1982: 137; cf. Goffman 1963).

Delgado writes that '[i]mmediate mental or emotional distress is the most obvious direct harm caused by a racial insult' (Delgado 1982: 143). Based on this, he advocates judicial recognition of a new tort for racial insult partly on the basis of the need to protect 'emotional well-being' (166). Eric Barendt goes so far as to say that '[t]he best argument for restricting racist hate speech is undoubtedly that a state has a compelling interest to protect members of target groups against the psychological injuries inflicted by the most pernicious forms of extremist hate speech' (Barendt 2005: 174–175). But what makes emotional distress the 'most obvious' harm? And, what makes this harm the 'best argument' for restricting hate speech? For one thing, the relevant sorts of psychological injuries are most commonly associated with abuse of an interpersonal and personal nature. The conduct is interpersonal in the sense of being performed in direct or face-to-face encounters and personal in the sense of being perpetrated against particular victims. Both aspects could tend to make these harms reckonable, assignable, and severe. Moreover, if the case for hate speech law can be made by drawing on a relatively uncontroversial construal of harm, namely, psychological injuries, then it means that defenders of such law need not rely on more controversial assumptions about diffuse or generalized harmful effects.

What does the foregoing imply about which clusters of laws/regulations/codes that constrain uses of hate speech have the necessary qualities to pass muster under the Principle of Health? Laws/regulations/codes that provide sanctions or remedies against uses of hate speech that qualify as dignitary crimes or torts; that forbid the use of hate speech when it amounts to a violation of civil or human rights (e.g., discriminatory harassment); that interdict the use of hate speech when it constitutes the enactment of expression-oriented hate crimes (e.g., provocation through the use of racist fighting words)—these are certainly among the candidate clusters for passing muster. To give one concrete example, consider the way civil courts in the US confront the psychological effects of racist hate speech. Mindful of the First Amendment, courts do not find for plaintiffs lightly in cases involving expressive conduct. Yet some courts have been persuaded that racist abuse can cause mental injury of a sort that is reckonable, assignable, and severe. Matsuda (1989b: 2336n.83) cites *Wade v. Orange County Sheriff's Office* (1988)[1] and *Wilmington v. J.I. Case Co.* (1986)[2] as two such cases.[3] Delgado (1982: 133) also cites *Contreras v. Crown Zellerbach, Inc.* (1977)[4] as a case in which the plaintiff was able to demonstrate to the satisfaction of the Supreme Court of Washington injuries under the tort of intentional infliction of emotional distress, or the tort of outrage as it is sometimes called. The Court relied on s. 46(1) of *The Restatement of Torts (Second)*, which defines the tort thusly: 'One who by extreme and outrageous conduct intentionally or recklessly causes severe emotional distress to another is subject to liability for such emotional distress.' In fact, Delgado and Matsuda were not the first to express optimism about the use of tort law to tackle racist verbal abuse in the US. In the mid-1960s James Jay Brown and Carl L. Stern (1964) proposed the tort of intentional infliction of emotional distress as a remedy for the psychological harms of racist hate speech. Later, Dean M. Richardson (1982) declared that the tort of outrage has 'great potential' as a means of recovery for people injured by racist verbal abuse.

It is not all plain sailing, however. It is possible to cite numerous failed lawsuits across the US involving racist verbal abuse and the tort of outrage. Consider *Bradshaw v. Swagerty* (1977),[5] *Gomez v. Hug* (1982),[6] *Ugalde v. W.A. McKenzie Asphalt Co.* (1993),[7] and *Walker v. Thompson* (2000).[8] The key sticking point has been a particular interpretation of the tort of outrage that is described in s. 46(1), comment d of *The Restatement of Torts (Second)*: the tort 'does not extend to mere insults, indignities, threats, annoyances, petty oppressions, or other trivialities' but only to 'extreme and outrageous conduct.' Courts have tended to interpret racist verbal abuse as the former rather than the latter (Delgado and Stefancic 2004: 12–16; Chamallas and Wriggins 2010: ch. 3). Then again, the optimism of critical race theorists has not proven entirely misplaced. Not all courts have summarily excluded racist verbal abuse or similar hate speech from the class of extreme and outrageous conduct. Consider the opinion of Judge Handler in *Taylor v. Metzger* (1998).[9]

> We recognize that many jurisdictions have held that a supervisor's utterance of racial slurs toward his subordinates is not, as a matter of law, extreme and outrageous conduct that would give rise to an intentional infliction of emotional distress cause of action. [. . .] We disagree. In this day and age, in this society and culture, and in this State, an ugly, vicious racial slur uttered by a high-ranking public official, who should know better and is required to do better, cannot, in light of this State's strong and steadfast public policy against invidious discrimination, be viewed as a picayune insult. That view would be blind and impervious to the lessons of history.[10]

As a basis for his interpretation of the tort of outrage Judge Handler was able to draw on another part of s. 46(1), namely, comment d: conduct must be 'so outrageous in character, and so extreme in degree, as to go beyond all possible bounds of decency, and to be regarded as atrocious, and utterly intolerable in a civilized community.' In Judge Handler's eyes, there is nothing in this specification *per se* that blocks recovery for injuries caused by racist verbal abuse given contemporary understandings of what is intolerable in a civilized community.

At this stage, however, it might be objected that if courts utilize the test of what is intolerable in a civilized community, then the tort of intentional infliction of emotional distress is less a tool for the prevention of harm than an instrument for the imposition of civility norms about the appropriate tone of public speech (e.g., Post 1991: 286; 2009: 135). However, I find this objection unpersuasive. Arguably, the role of the test is to provide courts with a rule of thumb that helps them to identify modes of expression that are *most likely* to produce emotional distress or modes of expression that tend to produce the *most intense* forms of emotional distress. No doubt it could be argued that the test will sometimes fail to track the likelihood or intensity of emotional distress. But that is to make a point about the empirical assumptions underpinning the use of the test; it is not to demonstrate that harm prevention has been downgraded from a fundamental purpose to a subordinate purpose or to show that the real goal of the test is the imposition of civility norms. So long as courts are making a good faith effort to employ a test (even if it is a very crude test) that helps them to better home in on reckonable, assignable, and severe psychological damage, surely there is much less cause for the present line of criticism.

By comparison, I think it is far more difficult to justify criminal statutes that disallow any and all public expressions of hatred through the use of insults, slurs, or derogatory epithets by appealing to psychological symptoms. Some of the difficulties are evidential, which is to say, finding valid evidence. For example, in their study into the prevalence and effects of 'ethnoviolence' Howard J. Ehrlich et al. (1995) made use of phone interviews of a stratified sample of 2,078 people. They asked respondents questions that would disambiguate their experiences of ethnoviolence over the previous twelve months. One form was 'group defamation', which Ehrlich et al. defined as insulting verbal, written, or symbolic statements (e.g., a spray painted "KKK" sign on a public wall) that are not directed at respondents individually but at the groups to which they or people close to them belong based upon ascriptive characteristics. As the authors explained, '[w]e asked our respondents whether, because of their own background or that of someone close to them, they had been insulted by either leaflets or posters, spray painted signs or slogans, radio or television programming, newspaper or magazine materials, teasing jokes or other comments' (Ehrlich et al. 1995: 65). Ehrlich et al. then compared these results against the respondents' responses to questions about whether they had suffered any negative psychological symptoms during the same period, from a list of nineteen symptoms. They found that among white, black, and Hispanic respondents that had reported experiencing group defamation, the average reported symptoms was 4.02 compared to 2.85 for non-victims (67). However, the way in which Ehrlich et al. defined the experience of group defamation meant that the relevant victim-group included *only* people who self-selected as having been insulted by statements. But arguably this might have skewed the results. After all, this sub-group could have an increased tendency toward negative psychological symptoms (on the grounds that persons who feel insulted might also be more likely to feel other negative emotions). People who experienced what is objectively describable as group defamation but who did *not* experience it as insulting, in contrast, might have a decreased tendency toward negative psychological symptoms. In addition, the fact that this type of study is heavily reliant on respondents' perceptions and memories of past experiences and their reflexive understandings of their psychological symptoms raises issues of epistemic validity. Perception and memory of potentially traumatic experiences might not be as reliable as other sorts of perception and memory. Plus, respondents' reflexive understandings of their psychological symptoms could be susceptible to underreporting, exaggeration, or misidentification.[11] Of course, some of these weaknesses in the evidence could be overcome by conducting laboratory experiments. But, as Timothy Jay points out, '[o]n ethical grounds, psychological research does not permit us to construct empirical research to test the harm thesis for hate by exposing one group to hate speech and comparing its reaction to a control group that is not maligned' (Jay 2009: 84).

More generally, from the fact that given forms of hate speech produce emotional distress in *some* individuals, it does not follow that all instances of that type should be criminalized; after all, some individuals have developed admirable coping mechanisms for hate speech (e.g., Strossen 2012: 378). Evan Simpson goes so far as to say that there is a division of responsibility for dealing with hate speech and that potential addressees have a responsibility to cultivate the rational capacities needed to 'reject unreasonable views and feigned threats' (Simpson [E.] 2006: 169). Whether or not Simpson overstates the argument, there certainly is evidence to suggest that in the US severe emotional distress is *not* the most common reaction to being subjected to hate speech in face-to-face encounters. Using field observations and in-depth interviews of 100 participants recruited from northern California, Laura Beth Nielsen (2002) found that 17% of people of color who had been targets of racist speech reported being afraid or fearful, the same proportion reported feeling anger, and a very small percentage reported feelings of sadness. Yet the most common reaction, 49%, was to ignore the remark and simply leave the situation. If being subject to racist verbal abuse is a daily occurrence for members of racial/ethnic minorities, it is feasible that some individuals may become desensitized to it and no longer feel the intense emotional distress that they may have once felt. Ironically, the indomitable human capacity to endure and adapt to adversity might pull the rug from underneath an attempt to justify the criminalization of the use of racist or other hate-based epithets by appealing to the problem of severe emotional distress.

But that need not be the end of the matter. For, it might be countered that the most common response to being racially abused, ignoring it and walking away, is itself symptomatic of unwelcome psychological coping mechanisms – for example, emotional suppression, emotional transference, cognitive dissonance reduction by means of self-deception and self-delusion. And, if the only reason why exposure to hate speech does not cause someone emotional distress is due to one or more pathological coping mechanisms that he or she has developed as a response to earlier episodes of hate speech, then this surely constitutes yet another psychological injury that ought to be taken seriously. Emotional suppression, for example, has been shown to have an adverse influence on affect, relationships, and well-being (e.g. Gross and John 2003). Of course, not all individuals employ the same emotional regulation strategies. Someone might be able to ignore racist abuse not by suppressing his or her negative emotions, which is *ex hypothesi* unhealthy, but through other strategies and coping mechanisms, such as using positive affirmations or engaging in cognitive reappraisal of the situation. This person might tell himself or herself every morning, "I am a beautiful and talented black person." Or the person might reappraise the situation as a case of the speaker's ignorance: "Poor stupid fool, he doesn't know any better." Or the person might reason, "If I get upset, then I am giving the hate speaker exactly what he wants, and I just don't want to give him that satisfaction." Then again, hate speakers cannot guarantee that their addressees will regulate their emotions in healthy rather than pathological ways. Hate speakers must take their addressees as they find them, in that sense, and are rightly held responsible for the consequences of their conduct. In tort law this is commonly known as 'the eggshell skull rule.'

It might also be countered that even if exposure to racist abuse triggers emotional distress or unwelcome psychological coping mechanisms only among a relatively limited proportion of individuals, this alone could be enough to N-warrant legal intervention under the Principle of Health. Assuming that each person's well-being matters on its own terms—this is the distinctness of persons doctrine in moral and political philosophy—it means that the existence of a relatively small proportion of actual sufferers is not a decisive barrier to the relevant mode of justification. For that matter, it could be argued that everyone who is targeted by the use of racist epithets faces an increased risk of suffering severe emotional distress as compared to a baseline of not being targeted. This increased risk might be enough to N-warrant the criminalization of the usage of racist epithets under the Principle of Health, despite the fact that relatively few people actually go on to suffer severe emotional distress.

## Medium- to Long-Term Psychological and Physiological Health Complications

For some victims, the harmful impact of hate speech lasts much longer than short-term severe emotional distress. There are also medium- to long-term psychological and physiological health complications to be factored into the evaluation. These potential consequences of hate speech have been underscored for some time. In the early 1960s, for example, Brown and Stern blamed 'our discriminatory-defamatory society' for traumatic experiences which can produce 'migrainous headaches and hypertension' and 'psychoneurotic or psychopathic behavior and psychosomatic disease' (Brown and Stern 1964: 27–28; cf. Kardiner and Ovesey 1951; Adams 1958). Along similar lines, in the 1980s Delgado claimed that 'the stresses of racial abuse may have physical consequences', including 'mental illness and psychosomatic disease' and 'high blood pressure' (Delgado 1982: 137–139; cf. Harburg et al. 1973; Kiev 1973). For her part, Matsuda pointed to evidence of a link between the experience of racial prejudice and alcoholism (Matsuda 1989b: 2336n.84; cf. Kitano 1974). She also cited a study that identified 'psychological symptoms including headaches, dizziness, social withdrawal, chronic depression, and anxiety neurosis in survivors of extreme persecution' (Matsuda 1989b: 2336n.84; cf. Hafner 1968). As recently as 2004 Delgado and Stefancic asserted a connection between the experience of racial discrimination and 'increased levels of stress, suffering, depression, and life dissatisfaction' (Delgado and Stefancic 2004: 14; cf. Feagin et al. 2001).

However, on closer examination the cited evidence often falls short of demonstrating a causal connection between exposure to hate speech specifically and medium- to long-term psychological and physiological health complications. Consider the various studies cited by Delgado. It is certainly true that Ernest Harburg et al. (1973) notes higher levels of suppressed hostility and high blood pressure among blacks living in high-stress areas (racial discrimination is used as one marker of an area being high stress); that Ari Kiev (1973) pinpoints high rates of psychiatric disorder among minority groups and posits a correlation with discrimination (among many other correlates); and that Joe Feagin et al. (2001) cites three studies of Mexican immigrants that found stress, depression, and life dissatisfaction to be correlated with discrimination (among other correlates). Yet *none* of these studies explicitly refer to racist verbal insults as illustrative examples of discrimination, and most of the examples of discrimination they do mention concern *overt* discriminatory practices in the workplace, housing allocation, and treatment by police. Delgado seems to assume that surveys of people's experiences of racist discrimination will automatically catch exposure to racist hate speech in their nets, and that such exposure must be playing a part in this larger causal story. But these assumptions are not made by the authors of the studies that Delgado cites, and he himself offers no grounds for them. Similarly, on the issue of alcoholism, Matsuda cites Harry Kitano (1974), but this study contains only an unsupported generalization about Native American drinking habits accompanied by a conjecture that cultural exclusion is easier to live with when inebriated. Likewise, Matsuda's reference to Heinz Hafner (1968) obscures the fact that this was a study of 1,000 people liberated from Nazi concentration camps, whose experiences of anti-Semitic hate speech were inextricably linked with imprisonment, violence, torture, starvation, physical pain and suffering, such that forming reliable conclusions about the impact of hate speech in isolation would seem virtually impossible. The problem of incomplete evidence persists. A recent review of studies on the

## 58  Principles of Basic Morality

health impacts of racism on adults found a positive correlation between the experience of racism and increased levels of blood pressure reactivity to stress (when combined with a lack of intragroup support) (Brondolo et al. 2011). But the studies considered in this review typically fail to disaggregate racist episodes and so ignore possible differences between the effects of expression-oriented hate crimes (e.g., discriminatory harassment, discriminatory intimidation) and other sorts of hate crimes (e.g., aggravated assault).

That being said, some studies *do* focus on hate speech specifically. Brendesha Tynes et al. (2008) looked at the psychological impact upon adolescents of exposure to online racist discrimination defined mainly in terms of exposure to racist hate speech of a personal nature (e.g., 'People have said mean or rude things about me because of my race or ethnic group online', 'People have threatened me online with violence because of my race or ethnic group') and of a vicarious nature (e.g., 'People have cracked jokes about people of my race or ethnic group online', 'People have said things that were untrue about people in my race or ethnic group') (566). The authors found that increased exposure to online racist hate speech of a personal nature was positively correlated with increased depression. Of course, one study does not constitute sufficient evidence. These results would need to be replicated, both among adolescents and adults, many times before the burden of proof is met. But if it could be met, defenders of the harm thesis would expect legislators and courts to forget the saying "Sticks and stones may break my bones but words will never hurt me", and think more in terms of "The straw that broke the camel's back." Some critical race theorists, for example, have been cautiously optimistic that plaintiffs might in the future have greater success in civil proceedings when it comes to proving that their psychological, psychosomatic, and physiological health complications resulted from their subjection to discriminatory harassment in the workplace (e.g., Matsuda 1989b: 2336n.84). Perhaps this relies on civil courts accepting parallels between the cumulative effects of hate speech and the cumulative effects of asbestosis or industrial deafness or other dose-based diseases, all of which are not uncommon in the modern workplace.

## 3.2  AUTONOMY

Like health, human autonomy cannot be left out of any serious debate about the basic moral status of hate speech and the N-warrant of hate speech law. Unsurprisingly, this non-instrumental human good or value holds a magnetic attraction for people seeking to justify the inclusion of the right to free speech within a legitimate constitution. It has been argued that free speech is indispensible to the development and exercise of individual autonomy and that autonomy is among the permanent interests of man as a progressive being in the Millian sense (e.g., Gray 1983). Other scholars maintain that autonomy is the only source of rights and duties within a Kantian system of basic morality, not the least of which is the right to free speech (e.g., Fried 1992; Rostbøll 2011). More concretely, under Baker's well-known formulation of the Principle of Autonomy, '[t]he key ethical postulate is that respect for individual integrity and autonomy requires the recognition that a person has the right to use speech to develop herself or to influence or interact with others in a manner that corresponds to her values' (Baker 1989: 59). In a subsequent chapter I shall say more about how Baker relates this idea of autonomy to the value of self-realization (see Ch. 4 [4.3]) and to the concept of citizens as legal subjects (see Ch. 7 [7.3]). For now it is enough to focus on his core contention that 'the ethically autonomous individual' has a right to use speech 'to influence or interact with others in a manner that corresponds to her values' (ibid.).[12]

What is the relationship between autonomy and hate speech? Consider the following argument, developed with the autonomy of the hate speaker in mind. (1) Autonomy is a basic human good or value. (2) Autonomy requires that hate speakers should be free to choose how and when they will try to influence the beliefs and attitudes that their audiences hold about certain groups of people. (3) The mere fact that some hate speakers attempt to influence audiences in ways that some authorities and some audiences disfavor is not sufficient to justify the suppression of such speech. Therefore, (4) the value of autonomy yields a defense of freedom of expression that includes the right to engage in hate speech (cf. Baker 1989: 59, 73; 2009: 64). Another argument focuses on the autonomy of the hate speaker's intended audience. (1) Autonomy is a basic human good or value. (2a) Autonomy requires that audiences should be free to decide for themselves which depictions of certain groups of people are true and which are false and whether or not they are willing to let themselves be influenced by hate speakers in coming to harbor certain beliefs, attitudes, or feelings toward members of those groups. (3a) By banning hate speech authorities fail to treat citizens as beings who are capable of autonomous and responsible decisions about whether or not to partake of certain beliefs, attitudes, or feelings. Therefore, (4a) the value of autonomy yields a defense of freedom of expression that includes the right to receive hate speech (e.g., Hare 2006: 532; cf. Nagel 1995: 96). Nadine Strossen, former president of the American Civil Liberties Union (ACLU), puts the argument in simpler, more forceful terms. '[I]t is kind of insulting to suggest that we lack critical capacity to evaluate and reject ideas' (Strossen 2012: 379).

However, I believe that it would be a mistake to assume that the value of autonomy supports a blanket protection of freedom of expression. A good illustration of why this would be a mistake can be found in the evolution of T.M. Scanlon's thinking on the subject. Initially Scanlon defended what he called 'the Millian Principle', which states that the following harms cannot be taken as part of a justification for legalistic constraints on acts of expression: '(a) harms to certain individuals which consist in their coming to have false beliefs as a result of those acts of expression; (b) harmful consequences of acts performed as a result of those acts of expression, where the connection between the acts of expression and the subsequent harmful acts consists merely in the fact that the act of expression led the agents to believe (or increased their tendency to believe) these acts to be worth performing' (Scanlon 1972: 213). According to Scanlon, these are harms that a truly autonomous person could not permit the state to protect him or her from by means of restricting acts of expression. This is because '[t]he contribution to the genesis of his [or her] action made by the act of expression is, so to speak, superseded by the agent's own judgment' (212). In a later article, however, Scanlon recanted the idea that the audience interest in autonomy acts as a side constraint upon legalistic constraints on acts of expression. For, as Scanlon pointed out, this idea 'prevents us from even asking whether these interests might in some cases be better advanced if we could shield ourselves from some influences' (1979: 534). Other academics have followed Scanlon's lead. David Partlett, for instance, accepts both that '[t]he interest served by free speech is the individual's interest of autonomy' and that 'speech may be constrained when it invades the basic value it was designed to protect' (1989: 453).

Following on from this, surely some laws/regulations/codes that constrain uses of hate speech can garner direct support from the goal of shielding autonomous human beings from undue influences. Thus, consider a third argument that concentrates on the autonomy of the listener, a broad class that is intended to include both the audience of hate speech and individuals on the receiving end of hate speech. (1) Autonomy is a basic human good or value. (2b) In some instances hate speech amounts to an exercise of undue influence on the listener: namely, it can inhibit an audience from deciding for itself what to think about certain groups of people, and it can compel its targets to react in ways that reflect the will of the speaker rather than their own will. (3b) The notion of undue influence can be used to draw a line between autonomy-violating restrictions on acts of expression (i.e., restrictions that prevent speakers from choosing how to influence others or that reflect the paternalistic idea that the state does not trust listeners to think for themselves) and autonomy-protecting restrictions on acts of expression (i.e., restrictions that address only forms of speech or other expressive conduct that significantly thwart attempts on the part of listeners to think for themselves). Therefore, (4b) the value of autonomy yields a limited defense of freedom of expression consistent with laws/regulations/codes that constrain uses of hate speech that constitute undue influences on listeners. This third argument underpins what I shall call the Nuanced Principle of Autonomy, that legalistic constraints on uses of hate speech are (N-)warranted if they function to protect listeners against undue influences on their impulses, decision-making, or conduct.

Of course, in order to get the Nuanced Principle of Autonomy off the ground the defender of hate speech law needs a convincing and workable account of undue influence. The remainder of this section is devoted to exploring three alternative accounts of undue influence and how each might be applied to particular clusters of laws/regulations/codes that constrain uses of hate speech. According to the first account, speech or other expressive conduct rises to the level of undue influence when it constitutes *coercion*. On Baker's definition, '[s]peech used to influence another person may be coercive if the speaker manifestly disrespects and attempts to undermine the other person's will and the integrity of the other person's mental processes' (Baker 1989: 59). However, Baker resists the idea that hate speech is coercive. '[T]he use of speech (normally) ought not to be viewed as coercive—even if the person's expression, for example, her racist or sexist speech, reflects and perpetuates an unjust order and affirms or promotes a much more stunted view of the person' (ibid.). Perhaps hate speech that amounts to no more than the expression of hatred or a denial of the humanity of the targeted groups is not coercive. But it seems implausible to say the same about hate speech that constitutes discriminatory harassment, for example. Surely this type of hate speech is coercive precisely in the Bakerean sense that it seeks to manipulate the mind or decision-making processes of its targets. Discriminatory harassment in the workplace can alter the circumstances that feed into or inform listeners' thoughts about their positions as members of the workforce and any decisions about future life plans that hinge on their work status.

Interestingly, Baker does concede that prohibitions on racist speech are permissible 'in special, usually institutionally bounded, limited contexts where the speaker has no claimed right to act autonomously, such as when, as an employee, she has given up her autonomy in order to meet role demands that are inconsistent with expressions of racism' (Baker 2009: 143). Even so, his reason for allowing the exception to the general injunction against restrictions on hate speech has to do with the fact that the speaker effectively alienates his or her right to expressive autonomy within certain institutional domains. I do not seek to deny that particular point. (But, note, some people might think that the right to expressive autonomy is inalienable.) Instead, I want to make the different point that prohibitions on hate speech can be N-warranted quite apart from the speaker's implicit consent to alienate his or her right to expressive autonomy. The relevant N-warrant has to do with the coercive or autonomy-undermining character of discriminatory harassment itself.

It might be pointed out that under normal circumstances employees also voluntarily accept offers of employment. Even so, surely employees cannot be regarded as thereby also giving their implicit consent to whatever hate abuse comes their way during the course of a day's work. They do not alienate their right not to be subjected to discriminatory harassment. Moreover, as employees they are expected or required to be at work, within the confines of certain spaces, at certain times, and so forth. So they are in that sense a *captive audience*, which is normally viewed as inimical to being an autonomous speech-recipient. Indeed, in *Resident Advisory Board v. Rizzo*

## 62  Principles of Basic Morality

(1980)[13] employees were recognized by the court as a captive audience. Interestingly, much the same has been said about students attending classes on university campuses (e.g., Matsuda 1989b: 2372; Lawrence 1990: 456–457; Sadurski 1999: 186; Shiell 2009: 110, 155). The idea that student-on-student hate speech is unprotected speech under the First Amendment because students are a captive audience was also put forward by the University of Michigan's defense team in *Doe v. University of Michigan* (cited in Shapiro 1990: 216–217n.73). Although not accepted by that court, in *Martin v. Parrish* (1986)[14] another court ruled that the captive audience doctrine did apply to the abusive, in-class speech of a college lecturer.

In addition to this, Baker cites several examples of what he *does* consider to be coercive speech, or 'speech designed to disrespect and distort the integrity of another's mental processes or autonomy' (Baker 1989: 59–60). Speech used in the enactment of fraud, perjury, blackmail, espionage, and treason is coercive speech (60). For Baker, when speech becomes no more than someone's intended method of performing an act of espionage, it loses its First Amendment protection (66). It is worth pausing to reflect a little more upon why speech used in the performance of espionage counts as coercive under Baker's definition. I believe that doing so further weakens his contention that hate speech is non-coercive. Suppose a spy or espionage agent has been tasked with conducting clandestine operations with two main goals: first, to obtain secret or confidential information without the permission of the holder of the information and without being detected; second, to communicate that information to a foreign government that intends to use that information to coerce the country from which the information was taken. Speech can be as vital in the first stage as the second. Suppose the spy gains access to a government information store by telling a security guard, "My name is General Jones and I am here to deposit a file on military clothing procurement." In fact, his name is Smith and he has come to copy information on US missile bases that he lacks permission to copy. If this is accurate, then deception and failure to obtain consent are key mechanisms through which espionage speech attempts to undermine the integrity of the other person's mental processes. But if deception and failure to obtain consent are key mechanisms through which speech becomes coercive, it is inexplicable why Baker does not recognize that at least some forms of hate speech could be included under his own definition of coercion because arguably some uses of hate speech exhibit the same mechanisms. Suppose a speaker spreads false rumors about a practice of murdering Christian children among a Jewish community in an attempt to promote feelings of mistrust and hostility between Jews and gentiles and to bring an end to the official policy of tolerance toward Jews. The speaker uses falsehoods to manipulate the audience's mental processes and circulates a stolen coroners' report about the death of a child without obtaining the consent of the parents concerned. Surely this is no more than the speaker's intended method of involvement in an act of seditious libel and is coercive.[15]

## Principles of Basic Morality 63

A second account defines undue influence as getting other people to think or feel things *without going through cognitive channels of persuasion*. David A. Strauss, for example, defends the Principle of Persuasion, according to which 'the government may not suppress speech on the ground that the speech is likely to persuade people to do something that the government considers harmful' (Strauss 1991: 335). But at the same time he clarifies that this principle excludes from its range of protection 'two categories of speech that move people to action by means other than the rational process of persuasion: namely, false statements and speech that seeks to elicit action before the hearer has thought about the speech and possible answering arguments' (335–336). At first glance, it would seem that several forms of hate speech can be fitted squarely within these two categories. First, it would seem that group defamation (*sensu stricto*), which involves the dissemination of false damaging statements of fact about protected groups, circumvents the rational process of persuasion by moving people to action through non-autonomous agency based upon false beliefs. The spreading of false rumors about outgroups over the Internet is one example. I have in mind what Cass Sunstein calls 'cybercascades', where individuals are influenced to believe certain false rumors as a result of coming into contact with large numbers of believers online. Cascades can exist when individuals possess one or more of the following tendencies: to rely on information provided by other people because they lack access to the information themselves; to substitute the judgment of speakers they esteem for their own personal judgment; and/or to want or even emotionally need the good opinion of other people (adopting and spreading other people's beliefs is one way to endear oneself to members of an ingroup community) (Sunstein 2007: 83–90). Indeed, according to Sunstein, '[t]he internet is an obvious breeding ground for cascades, and as a result, thousands or even millions of people who consult sources of a particular kind will move in one or another direction or even believe something that is quite false' (90–91). To give a second example, consider the use of hate-based insults, slurs, or derogatory epithets directed at individuals in face-to-face encounters, and that under the circumstances create feelings of humiliation and an urgent desire to extricate oneself from the situation. Third, consider hate-based fighting words, which are used in order to elicit an angry or violent response. Surely, in both these examples hate speech is capable of moving the intended targets to action or reaction at an emotional level (i.e., the flight or fight response) before the intended targets have had a chance to think about any ideas being expressed, to articulate more thoughtful responses, or to supersede the words of the hate speaker with their own rational judgments (e.g., Brison 1998a: 328: Brink 2001: 138–140; Shiffrin [S.V.] 2011: 437).

However, Strauss is reluctant to place hate speech into either of these exempted categories. For example, he insists that when the State of Illinois added s. 224a to its Criminal Code—a group defamation law (catchall)—it did so either partly or wholly on the grounds that hate speech can persuade people to adopt attitudes that *it* considered to be unwelcome or harmful (Strauss 1991: 340n.14). So it is not enough to say that the State of Illinois did or could have also banned hate speech partly on the grounds that it involves the spreading of false statements of fact or moves people to action by means other than the rational processes of persuasion. 'If the government offers more than one justification, or if there is a risk that the government may be relying on an impermissible justification, doctrinal rules must take into account the danger that government action purporting to have a proper justification in fact violates the persuasion principle' (ibid.). Likewise, if Strauss were to apply his approach to *R.A.V. v. City of St. Paul*, he would probably insist that even if the City of St. Paul justified its Bias-Motivated Crime Ordinance partly on the grounds that racist fighting words seek to elicit action before the hearer has thought about the speech, there is also the danger that it banned this subcategory of proscribable speech because of the undesirable ideas it expresses (cf. Wells 1997: 193–194). This take on doctrinal rule foreshadows Justice Scalia's position in *R.A.V. v. City of St. Paul*: namely, that content discrimination among proscribable speech is permissible only if 'there is no realistic possibility that official suppression of ideas is afoot.'[16]

I intend to return to these issues in the chapter on compromise [10.5], but let me briefly anticipate one of my arguments. It is far from obvious that *any* risk of official suppression of ideas should suffice to strike down statutes or ordinances involving content discrimination among proscribable speech. Surely what matters is whether or not a given level of risk of official suppression of ideas is acceptable given the nature of the valid bases for content discrimination. Therefore, if the City of St. Paul can be interpreted as banning certain forms of hate speech that fall under general categories that Strauss himself claims are excluded from the reach of the Principle of Persuasion, and, more generally, if banning certain forms of hate speech can be justified by appealing to the present conception of undue influence under the Nuanced Principle of Autonomy, then this might be enough to N-warrant the St. Paul ordinance in spite of there being a small risk that official suppression of ideas is afoot.

A third possible account, that I should now like to propose, defines undue influence in terms of a failure to discharge *positional responsibilities*. The sorts of responsibilities I have in mind are associated with speakers who occupy positions of authority, power, privilege, or trust. When speakers occupy such positions, we often say that they have a responsibility not to abuse their positions for personal gain or interest, including the furtherance of personal viewpoints or ideological agendas. We might use the term 'undue influence' to describe cases in which speakers fail to live up to this responsibility. Some responsibilities stem from the fact that the audience is epistemically dependent upon the speaker, some from the fact that the audience is particularly impressionable, some from the fact that the speaker has signed a code of professional ethics, and so forth. Consider

*Principles of Basic Morality* 65

two examples. The first involves teachers who are in a position of trust and epistemic authority in relation to young, impressionable minds. Arguably, teachers have a responsibility to present issues in an open, unbiased way, ensuring that students are exposed to a variety of information and perspectives. This might imply that teachers fail in their positional responsibilities if they decide to teach only a one-sided version of the Holocaust, based solely upon the creed of denial, revisionism, and conspiracy theory (e.g., Cohen-Almagor 2008: 225, 235–236). The second hypothetical example concerns an expert on national security and terrorism who elects to appear in the mainstream media warning that there is an imminent threat of terrorist attack from young male Muslims radicalized as a result of watching hours of Jihadist videos downloaded from the Internet. The expert might have a responsibility to make a good faith effort to present the facts in an objective manner. This responsibility could rest on the assumption that it is unreasonable to expect lay people to come to form their own judgment on the threat level or to cultivate the capacities necessary to be in a position to check or verify the evidence utilized by the expert (cf. Shiffrin [S.V.] 2011: 437n36). Indeed, it could also flow from the fact that he has signed a code of practice written by his employer (e.g., a government agency, a university, or a think tank) or any professional body to which he belongs. If the expert is found to have deliberately exaggerated the relevant threat level so as to give effect to his own personal prejudices, biases, or hatred toward Muslims, then his speech could be lifted out of the protected category of expert testimony and into the proscribable category of incitement to hatred.

The present account has been implicitly accepted by some courts. In their application of incitement to hatred legislation, for example, some English courts have held that religious leaders have special responsibilities toward those under their spiritual guidance or pastoral care. Consider *R. v. El-Faisal* (2003).[17] In this case police investigating possible al-Qaeda links in the UK found tape recordings of speeches given by the Jamaican-born Muslim cleric Abdullah el-Faisal labeled 'No peace with the Jews' and 'Jewish Traits.' He was convicted *inter alia* of two counts of distributing threatening recordings with intent to stir up racial hatred—the first Muslim cleric to be convicted of such offenses in the UK. For each of the two counts el-Faisal received a sentence of twelve months imprisonment. In his sentencing remarks Judge Beaumont touched upon el-Faisal's special responsibilities. 'In my judgment, your offending was aggravated by the fact that as a cleric you were sent to this country to preach and minister to the Muslim community in London, and so had a responsibility to the young and impressionable within that community at times of conflict abroad and understandable tensions in the communities here over the period which is spanned by the indictment.'[18] It is unclear whether Judge Beaumont meant to lump the young and impressionable into a single class. Perhaps it is possible that anyone receiving extensive guidance and pastoral care from someone in a position of religious authority is to some degree impressionable. Either way, English courts are not alone in looking at the nature of the speaker-audience relationship in evaluating cases of incitement to hatred. *Vejdeland and Others v. Sweden* was an ECtHR case involving the decision of Swedish courts to uphold convictions for agitation against a national or ethnic group against three members of a Swedish organization called National Youth after they had distributed leaflets containing homophobic messages in a secondary school. The ECtHR considered whether the domestic application of the relevant section of the Swedish Criminal Code was consistent with the 'necessary in a democratic society' test articulated in Art. 10(2) of the ECHR. In doing so, the Court made clear that it took into consideration the fact that 'the leaflets were left in the lockers of young people who were at an impressionable and sensitive age and who had no possibility to decline to accept them.'[19]

Now, I do not presume to know which of the foregoing accounts of undue influence is superior. No doubt each has its advantages and disadvantages.[20] Nor do I think that I have provided an exhaustive list of possible examples of undue influence. Instead, my aim has merely been to show that whichever account one picks, it is likely that at least some forms of hate speech might qualify as undue influence.

## 3.3 SECURITY

After having considered health and autonomy, it is now time to examine a third basic human good, security. I take it as read that positing a connection between hate speech and insecurity is not merely stating a hypothesis about an objective or external state of affairs of heightened insecurity that might be induced, directly or indirectly, by some uses of hate speech; it is also about paying attention to increases in subjective or internal feelings of insecurity that might be evinced by hate speech. No doubt internal feelings of insecurity sometimes track external states of insecurity, but not always.[21] Therefore, in this section I intend to explore how security-centered arguments might factor into the debate on hate speech law. In particular, I want to investigate how what I shall call the Principle of Security—that legalistic constraints on uses of hate speech are (N-)warranted if they significantly reduce insecurity (subjective as well as objective)—might be fleshed out and applied to particular clusters of law.

### The Threat from a Climate of Hatred

One notable security-centered justification for hate speech law points to the acts of discrimination, violence, damage to property, and so forth, which are more likely to occur within a climate of hatred and to the contribution that some uses of hate speech make to the creation and maintenance of such a climate. In other words, if people are permitted to stir up hatred against members of vulnerable groups with impunity, this could contribute

*Principles of Basic Morality* 67

to the creation of a climate of hatred that threatens the security of members of these outgroups. In Brown (2008: 13) I defined a climate of hatred as a widespread attitude of hatred that is partly the product of an accumulation of hate speech and that is associated with an increased chance of acts of discrimination, violence, damage to property, and so forth. One feature of a climate of hatred that I did not properly explore, however, is *intragroup* contact. I now realize that it would be naive to think of a climate of hatred simply as the product of a large number of isolated individuals who just so happen to possess similar beliefs, attitudes, or emotions. In fact, a climate of hatred is more plausibly conceived as being rooted in a community of hatred. A community of hatred will feed on intragroup contact as well as on shared hatred of, and lack of contact with, outgroups. Like other communities, it is also likely to possess ringleaders and organizers who sit at the epicenter of its activities and play key roles in facilitating intragroup contact.[22] What is more, emerging academic research into how new technologies are shaping contemporary social formations has the potential to reveal much about the means of this intragroup contact. In the case of far right movements in Europe and the US, researchers have pointed to the fact that groups have been assisted in building large networks based on shared racist ideologies by using the Internet and related forms of electronic communication (e.g., Solomos and Schuster 2002: 45–46). Similarly, Sunstein maintains that what is particularly striking about the activities of online hate groups is that they 'provide links to one another, and expressly attempt to encourage both recruitment and discussion among like-minded people' (Sunstein 2007: 57–58). 'It is,' as Sunstein puts it, 'clear that the internet is playing a crucial role in permitting people who would otherwise feel isolated, or move on to something else, to band together and spread rumors, many of them paranoid and hateful' (58).

Another characteristic feature of the sort of climate of hatred to which hate speech can be a significant contributor is that feelings of hatred toward members of outgroups are apt to spill over into acts of discrimination, destruction of property, violence, and so forth, in entirely predictable ways (e.g., Hauptman 1995: 11; Tsesis 2002: 138; Sumner 2004: 162–163; Parekh 2005–2006: 217–218; Morgan 2007: 136–137; Brown 2008: 13). This second feature of the argument from a climate of hatred furnishes one possible response to a criticism that is often leveled against law banning incitement to hatred. The criticism is that it is peculiar to have an offense of incitement to hatred when there is no principal offense, hatred, on which it can rest (e.g., Nash and Bakalis 2007: 367). The possible response is that incitement to hatred should be criminalized because of the substantive evils of the climate of hatred to which it contributes—substantive evils that legislatures have an obligation to try to prevent.

It might be countered that in the US any law restricting freedom of expression on the grounds of protecting public security must satisfy well-known juridical tests requiring that the relevant harms must be *direct* in the

68  *Principles of Basic Morality*

sense of involving relatively short chains of connection between conduct and harm. This requirement finds powerful expression in Justice Holmes' 'clear and present danger' test and its more recent incarnation, the 'imminent lawless action' test. Under the latter test, 'the constitutional guarantees of free speech and free press do not permit a State to forbid or proscribe advocacy of the use of force or of law violation except where such advocacy is directed to inciting or producing imminent lawless action and is likely to incite or produce such action.'[23] Thus David Richards takes it as read that law banning incitement to hatred of the sort found outside of the US would be extremely unlikely to satisfy relevant First Amendment tests due to the causal distance between acts of stirring up hatred and the eventual harms visited upon members of hated groups (e.g., Richards 1986: 178–187; 1999: 144). This assumption is backed up by case law. In *State v. Klapprott* (1941),[24] for example, the Supreme Court of New Jersey ruled as unconstitutional a state incitement to hatred statute partly on the grounds that it criminalized speech in violation of the clear and present danger test.[25]

Even so, I believe that the argument from a climate of hatred is important precisely because it forces one to rethink the role and importance of the imminent lawless action test. I do not deny that concern for *imminence* has exerted a powerful influence over American scholars, even those who actually defend hate speech law. Kammy Au, for example, urges 'that authorities ban all slogans or remarks which carry even the slightest incitement to racial hatred, because they are no longer just views, but, threaten, clearly and imminently, to ripen into conduct which our spirit will not allow' (Au 1984: 52). Nonetheless, the argument from a climate of hatred works in an importantly distinct way from Au's argument precisely because it *limits* the role and importance of imminence. Although the argument from a climate of hatred *does* claim that the harmful effects of a climate of hatred are imminent and likely, it does *not* attempt to claim that hate speech itself has the imminent effect of producing a climate of hatred. On the contrary, the argument proceeds on the assumption that a climate of hatred builds up slowly over time (e.g., Parekh 2005–2006: 217). But on the present line of argument, the lack of imminence of the effects of hate speech, to wit, the climate of hatred, is not a decisive factor.[26]

One upshot of all this is that making good on the argument from a climate of hatred requires two distinct steps.[27] The first involves establishing a connection between the existence of hate speech and the existence of a climate of hatred. The second has to do with establishing a connection between a climate of hatred and the increased incidence of hate-based discrimination, destruction of property, violence, and so forth.[28] A key feature of this argument is that there is no requirement to demonstrate that a particular piece of hate speech caused a particular act of discrimination, destruction of property, violence, and so forth. Interestingly, some judges in England seem to have embraced this two-stage justification for law banning incitement to hatred. Consider *R. v. Sheppard and Whittle I* (2009).[29] In this case the defendants were found guilty of offenses relating to posting content on the website *The Heretical Press* that is threatening, abusive, or insulting, and likely to stir up racial hatred. After the guilty verdicts were returned, the defendants jumped bail and fled to California—where the remote server hosting the website was physically located—and claimed political asylum. Their claims were denied and they were deported back to the UK for sentencing. In his sentencing remarks Judge Grant expressed the rationale for the legislation thusly:

> I have no doubt whatsoever that in the present climate which pervades the country that [the website content's] effect has the potential of doing great harm to our society. [. . .] I am also asked [by your Counsel] to take into account that there is no evidence of harm actually having been caused to individuals or people [. . .]. But as I said earlier, the mischief of such offences is the potential which it has to cause social harm of the kind that I have mentioned.[30]

Nevertheless, if the current argument is to succeed, there must exist sufficiently strong evidence to support each of the aforementioned two steps. And, as with the sorts of damages discussed earlier in the chapter [3.1], the challenge of producing sufficiently strong evidence is great. To begin with the connection between hate speech and a climate of hatred, the greatest concentration of social scientific research falls within the field of communication studies and media effects research. For example, numerous experiment-based studies have found that exposure to negative stereotypes of racial/ethnic outgroups is positively correlated with increased levels of adverse judgments, attitudes, and emotions toward members of these groups (e.g., van Dijk 1987; Peffley et al. 1996; Ford 1997; Johnson [J.] et al. 1997; Mastro 2003; Dixon and Maddox 2005; Mastro et al. 2009; Das et al. 2009). Similar effects have been associated with negative stereotypes found in video games (e.g., Burgess et al. 2011). Any strong conclusions about media effects must be treated with a degree of caution, however. Many other studies in this area have harnessed theories of intergroup contact (e.g., Allport 1954; Pettigrew 1997) in order to qualify the role of media effects. These studies show that the extent to which exposure to negative stereotypes of outgroups produces adverse judgments is highly sensitive to the degree of real-world interaction with members of these groups (e.g., Kawakami et al. 2000; Dovidio et al. 2003; Mastro et al. 2007; Ortiz and Harwood 2007; Ramasubramanian 2013). Some people might choose to read this alternative research as demonstrating that the *proximate* cause of racial/ethnic prejudice is lack of contact with members of other racial/ethnic groups rather than negative stereotypes in the media. They might further conclude that the correct solution to the relevant problem is not tighter regulation of the media but more effective enforcement of laws proscribing racial/ethnic discrimination in the workplace, more imaginative strategies for promoting racial/ethnic integration in educational settings, better management of housing policy and town planning to reduce the problem of racial/ethnic ghettoization, and so on. Then again, other people might insist that what this shows is that society is likely to need all of these other policies *alongside* regulation of negative stereotypes in the media.

Turning next to the connection between a climate of hatred and hate-based behavior, the challenge is to show that a climate of hatred constitutes a genuine threat, such as an increased probability of hate-based discrimination, destruction of property, violence, and so forth. One part of this challenge is to counter the commonsense observation that since not everyone who possesses adverse beliefs, attitudes, or feelings about racial/ethnic outgroups acts upon them, there is no cause to regulate the public dissemination or broadcast of negative stereotypes of these outgroups (e.g., Richards 1986: 190–193; 1999: 144). Indeed, in his seminal review of social scientific research on the nature of prejudice, Ehrlich (1973) found that the connection between prejudiced attitudes and prejudiced behaviors is frequently weak. Another part of the challenge has to do with the demands of research ethics. The challenge is to conduct experiments that adequately test the connection between mental states of hatred and hate conduct while at the same time refraining from creating in the laboratory actual, other-affecting behavior. Recent studies have sought to meet this challenge in imaginative ways. For example, Unkelbach et al. (2008) used an experiment based on a computer game in which participants made rapid decisions to shoot at armed characters. The researchers discovered a significant bias for shooting at Muslim targets, who in the game were represented as non-white people wearing turbans. This reveals a correlation between implicit negative stereotypes/prejudices about Muslims and increased aggressive tendencies toward Muslims in simulated settings. Then again, it is one thing to show that under laboratory conditions implicit racial/ethnic prejudice is a strong predictor of increased willingness to shoot simulated Muslims; it is another thing to prove that this accurately predicts a willingness to shoot actual Muslims or even a bias toward shooting actual Muslims over actual non-Muslims.

What of the hypothesis that a climate of hatred supervenes upon intragroup contact? In an attempt to get at this issue, one might look at Peterson et al. (2004) in which participants were asked to make reward-allocation decisions affecting members of their own ingroup and members of outgroups. It was found that members of strongly cohesive ingroups (measured in terms of participants' judgments, the group atmosphere, the degree of group cooperation, the absence of conflict, and interest in future cooperation) displayed a stronger bias against members of outgroups than did individuals acting in isolation. One possible implication of this research vis-à-vis the Principle of Security is that the case for hate speech law is particularly strong when applied to regulations designed to tackle whichever forms of hate speech are most commonly used by hate groups to build cohesion. With that in mind, consider, for example, Art. 5(1) of the Council of Europe Additional Protocol to the Convention on Cybercrime, Concerning the

Criminalization of Acts of a Racist and Xenophobic Nature Committed through Computer Systems.

> Each Party shall adopt such legislative and other measures as may be necessary to establish as criminal offences under its domestic law, when committed intentionally and without right, the following conduct: insulting publicly, through a computer system, (i) persons for the reason that they belong to a group distinguished by race, colour, descent or national or ethnic origin, as well as religion, if used as a pretext for any of these factors; or (ii) a group of persons which is distinguished by any of these characteristics.

Of course, any sound application of the Principle of Security to internet regulation is reliant upon further research identifying hate groups and analyzing their most commonly utilized forms of hate speech. But this is by no means an insurmountable obstacle. Hate groups that are predominantly active online have already been the subject of several social scientific studies (e.g., Schafer 2002; Gerstenfeld et al. 2003; Weatherby and Scoggins 2005; Daniels 2008). What is more, courts in England are already showing an awareness of the ways hate speakers use words to stir up hatred among a hard core of followers or like-minded individuals. Consider *R. v. Heaton and Hannington* (2010).[31] In this case the defendants were members of an organization called the Aryan Strike Force (ASF), and had played an active role in its website and associated forums. Both were found guilty of offenses relating to using words or behavior with intent to stir up racial hatred. In his sentencing remarks Justice Irwin offered the following observations about the close interaction between their hate speaking and their group membership:

> [Mr. Heaton] I have no doubt that for a period, and quite an extended period, you saw yourself as a leader of a potentially significant active national socialist [indecipherable], and this sustained racist ranting was intended to build up that group. You were stirring up racial hatred with a direct purpose in mind. As you said in the course of the evidence, you wanted to start a race war.

> [Mr. Hannington] You were a lonely man with little in your life. You lived in a shambles. You habitually told lies about your non-existent Army career, your non-existent serious criminal past, your knowledge of survival techniques, and so forth. All of that in a vain attempt to gain status. You, too, made many hundreds of racist statements often foul in language and sentiment [. . .][32]

## Protecting a Sense of Personal Security

The idea that human beings have a right to a sense of personal security, the right not to be afraid, is another potentially powerful N-warranting instrument for law interdicting hate speech. This at least has been the view of the

General Assembly of the United Nations since the mid-1960s. The preamble to the Universal Declaration of Human Rights states only that 'the advent of a world in which human beings shall enjoy freedom of speech and belief and freedom from fear and want has been proclaimed as the highest aspiration of the common people.'[33] That an absolute right to freedom of speech is most likely incompatible with the human right to freedom from fear is not mentioned. But this omission was rectified in 1966 by the International Covenant on Civil and Political Rights (ICCPR). Its preamble recognizes that 'the ideal of free human beings enjoying civil and political freedom and freedom from fear and want can only be achieved if conditions are created whereby everyone may enjoy his civil and political rights.'[34] Consequently, Art. 20(2) declares: 'Any advocacy of national, racial or religious hatred that constitutes incitement to discrimination, hostility or violence shall be prohibited by law.' Within this human rights covenant, then, the right to a sense of personal security is invoked as a basis for calling upon all states to enact law interdicting uses of hate speech when it amounts to the performance of the expression-oriented hate crime of incitement to discrimination or violence. Put simply, how could racial/ethnic minorities fail to be afraid when hate speakers incite acts of discrimination or violence against them?

I believe that similar arguments can be made for law interdicting hate speech when it constitutes intimidation or true threat. Intimidation is a menace to security in the sense that its intended purpose is to undermine feelings of safety. The fact that intimidation produces fear of bodily harm or even death is owed to a belief that the threat is credible. This means that the persons being intimidated must possess a reasonable belief that the speaker doing the intimidating is willing and able to carry it out his or her threat or implied threat. Consequently, in *Watts v. United States* (1969)[35] the US Supreme Court held that speech does *not* fall into the category of intimidation, a category of proscribable speech under the First Amendment, if given the context it amounts to mere 'political hyperbole' and not a 'true "threat."'[36]

Perhaps the opponents of hate speech law would seek to characterize a good deal of hate speech, if not all hate speech, as falling short of true threat. Even hate speech that takes the form of threatening words or behavior (so they might argue) is no more than exaggeration; an extravagant proclamation, rhetorical device, or figure of speech that is intended to be taken seriously but not intended to be taken literally. Nevertheless, in *Watts v. United States* the Court made it clear that whether speech counts as hyperbole or true threat is not to be settled in the abstract, based on the transcendental meaning of the words used, but instead must be grounded in contextual interpretation. For example: 'Taken in context, and regarding the expressly conditional nature of the statement and the reaction of the listeners, we do not see how it could be interpreted otherwise.'[37] Given this, it is highly implausible to suppose that hate speech could never rise to the level of true threat, given the context. For example, in *Virginia v. Black* (2003)[38] Justice

O'Connor reasoned that although cross burning should *not* be regarded as *prima facie* evidence of an intent to intimidate a person or group of people, there are certainly *some* instances in which it can amount to intimidation or a threat that rings true in the context of a history of violence against African Americans and the repeated conjunction of violence and cross burning by the Ku Klux Klan.[39] Once again, she insisted that an attempt to intimidate must be read off 'the contextual factors' of the situation and cannot be defined *ex ante*.[40] Nevertheless, the key point here is that there is no knockdown reason to think that the First Amendment bars laws that interdict the use of cross burning as a deliberate menacing threat, one that makes people justifiably scared for their safety given the cultural and historical meanings of cross burning (e.g., Tsesis 2009, 2010, 2013).

It is another question how much further this line of argument could be stretched without its becoming unsustainably thin. For example, Matsuda makes a case for laws restricting the dissemination of racist propaganda on the basis of the vital interest in having a sense of personal security. 'As much as one may try to resist a piece of hate propaganda, the effect on one's self-esteem and sense of personal security is devastating' (Matsuda 1989b: 2337–2338). Similarly, Au defends criminal group defamation law (catchall) partly on the grounds that at a fundamental level the 'Bill of Rights is aimed at assuring us freedom from fear' and that 'freedom of speech should yield to freedom from fear' (Au 1984: 49–50). According to Au, the fact that hate speech can create a sense of insecurity of among American Asians is based upon their perception of what forms of discrimination and violence are waiting at the end of a causal chain that begins with racist propaganda claiming that an increased presence of Asians is responsible for depressed wages, lack of jobs, unemployment, and even a generalized moral corruption (50).

But there is a problem with this line of argument. The putative N-warrant for criminal group defamation law (catchall) says nothing about why particular forms of hate speech should be legally recognized sources of fear. From the mere fact that an expressive act induces fear, it does not follow that legal sanctions are N-warranted. If American Asians feared the sound of Sanctus bells because of an association between the sound of such bells and historical attacks by Irish Americans, should the use of Sanctus bells be prohibited? Arguably there must be a non-accidental connection between the expressive act and the fear it induces. If the sound of Sanctus bells is merely coincidental to attacks by Irish Americans on American Asians, then the fact that it induces fear should not be sufficient to N-warrant its regulation. If, on the other hand, the Sanctus bells had been used as a signal of impending attacks, this might be another matter. Consider once again the case of cross burning. The original significance of a burning cross has been traced back by Klan members themselves to the practice of cross burning in Scotland—the *Crann Tara* (or fiery cross)—as a declaration of war to strike fear in the hearts of one's enemies. In this way the connection between the burning cross and the fear it induces is non-accidental. Fear is intended; it as an essential part of the meaning and purpose of cross burning.

This point about non-accidental connections might also help to explain why incitement to hatred law in the UK has the particular wording it has. Together, the Racial and Religious Hatred Act 2006 and the Criminal Justice and Immigration Act 2008 make it an offense to use 'threatening words or behaviour' to stir up hatred against people on the grounds of their religion or sexual orientation. At first glance, this restrictive wording is hard to understand. If the concern is ultimately with the likelihood of hatred being stirred up, why restrict the offenses to only threatening words or behavior? Why not also include insulting, derogatory, stigmatizing, or defamatory words? One possible answer is that these offenses are designed to pinpoint the subjective element of insecurity, that is to say, to deter attacks on people's sense of personal security. What is more, the legislative focus on threatening words or behavior reflects the logical connection between such words or behavior and the fear they induce. It is part of the point and purpose of threatening words or behavior that they instill fear in others. This interpretation seems to be shared by judges in English trial courts. Consider *R. v. Ali, Javed, and Ahmed* (2012).[41] In July 2010 three devout but also socially conservative members of the Muslim faith distributed leaflets on the streets of Derby titled 'Turn or Burn', 'GAY—God Abhors You', 'Death Penalty?' as a protest to the Gay Pride Festival taking place that day. The defendants became the first people to be successfully prosecuted for offenses relating to stirring up hatred on the grounds of sexual orientation in England and Wales. In his sentencing remarks Judge Burgess articulated the law's rationale as follows:

> For the vast majority of the time the vast majority of us get along together very well, and the greatest freedom that we all enjoy is to live in peace and without fear. The law has evolved and adapted to protect that freedom. In particular, laws have been passed to prevent written material being distributed which is intended to stir up hatred. This has proved necessary because a small minority of our broad community sometimes seeks to stir up hatred against their fellow citizens merely because those fellow citizens are perceived to be different in some way.[42]

Speaking to the local press after the sentences had been handed down, Chief Inspector Sunita Gamblin of the Derbyshire Constabulary echoed Judge Burgess' rationale:

> When opinion and beliefs spill over into hatred as seen in this case it makes people feel threatened. No-one should be made to feel fearful simply because of their sexual orientation or any other characteristic. (quoted in This Is Derbyshire 2012)

I have argued that, adequate empirical evidence permitting, some clusters of laws/regulations/codes that constrain uses of hate speech may be N-warranted under the Principle of Security either according to a logic that says the relevant hate speech contributes to the creation of a climate of hatred, which itself threatens people's civil rights, private property, physical safety, and so forth, or according an argument that says the relevant hate speech violates people's right to a sense of personal security. However, I want to finish this section by acknowledging that security is a protean concept, one that can be easily subdivided into different kinds. So, for example, it might be possible to defend campus speech codes that forbid acts of discriminatory harassment by appealing to the context of the relevant institutions or social practices, and to the claim that students have a right to *educational security*, which is to say, a right to freedom from fear in pursuing their personal goal of getting a college education (e.g., Lawrence 1990: 464–465; Hartman 1992: 875–876; Tsesis 2010: 620–621). Furthermore, in Ch. 5 [5.2] I shall explore Waldron's argument that criminal group defamation law (catchall) is N-warranted by virtue of providing an assurance of civic dignity, which is to say, conveying to citizens a sense of security that they are seen as members of society in good standing.

## 3.4 NON-SUBORDINATION

Yet another way of thinking about the basic moral standing of hate speech and how this bears upon the N-warrant of hate speech law takes its lead from subordination theory: an attempt to uncover the ways in which certain social practices tend to support or even constitute the subordination of certain groups of people. Subordination theory has a great many things to teach us about hate speech, some of which I shall try to bring out in this section. My aim is to explore possible instantiations of what I shall call the Principle of Non-Subordination, that legalistic constraints on uses of hate speech are (N-)warranted if they serve to protect individuals from acts of expression that also constitute acts of subordination.

It is useful to begin by recalling some claims made by critical race theorists in the late 1980s and early 1990s about hate speech and subordination. According to Matsuda, '[r]acist speech is particularly harmful because it is a mechanism of subordination, reinforcing a historical vertical relationship' (1989b: 2358). For his part, Lawrence characterized the practice of racially segregated schools as *speech*—speech that conveys a particular message of subordination, 'that black children are an untouchable caste, unfit to be educated with white children' (1990: 439). At first glance, Matsuda and Lawrence seem to be suggesting that racist utterances either have subordination as among their *negative consequences* (i.e., speech acts that have perlocutionary effects) or have subordination as *the idea they express* (i.e., speech acts that have locutionary force), and only these things. According to Andrew Altman, however, Matsuda and Lawrence are also suggesting 'that hate speech can inflict a wrong by virtue of its illocutionary acts, the very speech acts performed in the utterances of such speech' (Altman 1993: 309).[43]

I shall say more about the relationship between different forms of hate speech and illocutionary acts of subordination in a moment, but first I want to try to excavate the intellectual roots of Altman's intervention. Matsuda herself acknowledged some of these roots as follows: 'In an analogous context, the work of Catharine MacKinnon recognizes subordination of women and calls for laws addressing that subordination' (Matsuda 1989b: 2362n.214). Matsuda had in mind not only MacKinnon's work on pornography (Mackinnon 1987, 1991; see also MacKinnon and Dworkin 1988) but also her work on discriminatory harassment in the workplace and other forms of hate speech (1979, 1993). In the latter work MacKinnon moved beyond the First Amendment to suggest that the Fourteenth Amendment's equal protection clause N-warrants the protections set out in Title VII of the Civil Rights Act of 1964 vis-à-vis discriminatory harassment in the workplace, even if these protections have the effect of constraining some speech (e.g., MacKinnon 1979: 6). But she also insisted that contemporary thinking about both the First and Fourteenth Amendments shows a 'substantial lack of recognition that some people get a lot more speech than others' and of the fact that 'the more the speech of the dominant is protected, the more dominant they become and the less the subordinated are heard from' (1993: 72). In addition to this, Altman's point about hate speech and illocutionary acts is intellectually rooted in Rae Langton's (1990a, 1990b, 1993; see also Langton and West 1999) seminal argument that pornography does not simply *cause* the subordination of women as a perlocutionary consequence but also *constitutes* the subordination of women as an illocutionary act. On Langton's analysis, this act has the following dimensions: *ranking* women relative to men, *legitimating discrimination* against women, and *depriving* women of rights and powers.

In fact, several philosophers besides Altman have sought to extend Langton's argument about pornography to the case of hate speech, including Langton herself (e.g., Maitra and McGowan 2010; Maitra 2012; Langton 2012; Langton et al. 2012). The existence of this extension project makes sense given the fact that Langton employed an example of racial discrimination in order to explain her central thesis that some speech acts can be subordinating in the illocutionary sense. Specifically, Langton pointed to discriminatory speech acts during the apartheid era in South Africa—for example, a legislator declares, "Blacks are not permitted to vote"; an official signpost reads, "Whites only" (Langton 1993: 302). As she put it, these discriminatory speech acts '*rank* blacks as having inferior worth'; '*legitimate* discriminatory behavior on the part of whites'; and '*deprive* blacks of some important powers: for example, the power to go to certain areas and the power to vote' (303). Indeed, as *EEOC v. Tyson Foods, Inc.* demonstrates (see Ch. 2 [2.8]), this sort of racist speech retains its power to discriminate even in contemporary US society. In her more recent work on the topic, Langton has argued that hate speech is also used to perform other potentially subordinating acts, most notably, *inciting* and *assaulting (insulting)* (e.g., Langton 2012: 74–77; Langton et al. 2012: 758–759).

For reasons of space, the remainder of this section focuses on two of the aforementioned classes of speech act that are said to be constitutive of subordination: *ranking people* and *depriving people of rights and powers*. But before I begin the examination, however, three general issues require immediate attention. First, I want to raise and then immediately discount one line of objection to arguments for hate speech law that appeal to subordination theory. It is the objection that to say that *prima facie* certain forms of hate speech may be regulated if they constitute acts of subordination is to say no more than that according to certain norms or social conventions relating to treating people in a civilized manner hate speech is beyond the pale and should not be tolerated. This basis for restricting speech (so the objection runs) is inimical to any true regime of freedom of expression (e.g., Alexander 1996: 89–90). I discount this objection on the grounds *tu quoque*. *If*, and it is by no means clear-cut that they are, subordination theorists are defending hate speech law simply by appealing to norms or social conventions relating to what is uncivilized conduct, then arguably *so are* critics of hate speech law. *Their* norms or social conventions just happen to be concerned with a very broad range of speech that in their view ought to be protected in a civilized society.

Second, in my discussions of health [3.1] and security [3.3] I tried to interrogate some of the evidential bases for key empirical assumptions underpinning claims about the effects of hate speech. In some instances I found the evidence incomplete. So it might be asked, does subordination theory rely on empirical assumptions, and, if not, is that a strength or weakness of the approach? Abigail Levin has suggested that 'the illocutionary hypothesis, while still a causal hypothesis, is nonetheless causal in a way that veers significantly away from the traditional model of causality and would tend to preclude in principle its confirmation or falsification by traditional social science methodology, due to the near simultaneity of cause and effect that it posits' (Levin 2010: 113). I disagree. It is certainly the case that 'subordinating' is an abstract verb and one that is defined (by Langton and other theorists) in terms of yet other abstract verbs: 'ranking', 'legitimating', 'depriving', 'inciting', 'promoting', 'assaulting', and 'insulting'. But one should not forget that 'harm' and 'security' are themselves abstract nouns. Of course, when the concept of harm is defined in terms that can be specified descriptively, such as high blood pressure, clearly it becomes reckonable by public health scientists. They can ask, does exposure to hate speech increase the incidence of high blood pressure for a large proportion of people? And, does it raise the probability of high blood pressure for an individual when all other factors besides the presence or absence of exposure to hate speech are held constant? By the same token, however, when ranking people or depriving people of rights and powers is defined in terms of sets of formal linguistic qualities occurring under sets of sociolinguistic conditions, they too are amenable to social scientific assessment by linguists and sociologists. They can ask, do uses of hate speech possess certain formal and pragmatic linguistic properties consistent with ranking people or depriving people of rights and powers? And, do uses of hate speech render it more likely that an individual is being ranked or being deprived of rights and powers when all other factors besides the presence or absence of certain formal and pragmatic linguistic properties are held constant?

Third, and this follows on from the last point about speech pragmatics, subordination theorists face the particular challenge of explaining how it could be that mundane instances of hate speech performed by average citizens could, in the particular contexts of performance, constitute acts of subordination (as defined by Langton and others) even though average citizens lack the particular types of authority exemplified in the apartheid case. The assumption here is that authority is a necessary condition of illocutionary acts of ranking, depriving, and so on. In Langton's apartheid example the constitution of South Africa conferred authority upon the legislator's utterance in the context of domestic lawmaking, and the official signposts carried the authority of the governmental regime that created them. How could ordinary hate speakers plausibly be said to have authority for their public speech? (e.g., Sadurski 1999: 122–124). Much of the work currently being done by subordination theorists is devoted to addressing this Authority Problem in one way or another.

## Subordination as Ranking People

In her discussion of hate speech as ranking Maitra (2012) offers an ingenious solution to the Authority Problem. In doing so she relies on insights from speech pragmatics and, in particular, Robert Stalnaker's account of how assertions work (cf. Stalnaker 1878, 2002). Suppose an Arab woman is sitting in a crowded subway carriage minding her own business. Unprompted, an older white male approaches her and utters, "Fucking terrorist, go home—we don't need your kind here." The other passengers in the carriage hear the older man's rant but say nothing. Neither does the Arab woman (Maitra 2012: 100–101). Maitra's intuition is that this hate speaker succeeds in ranking as inferior the Arab woman in the context of that conversation and subordinates her in that sense. He does so by changing the background of shared information or 'common ground' that provides the basis for the remainder of the conversation: the other passengers do not have to *believe* that Arabs are inferior; all they must do is *accept* it for the purposes of the conversation (112, 116). The challenge posed by the Authority Problem is to explain how the hate speaker is able to *authoritatively* perform this illocutionary act of ranking given that he occupies no official position of authority, or at least no position of authority that equates to the position of the legislator or signpost creator in the apartheid

Principles of Basic Morality 79

case. In Maitra's example the older white male is just an ordinary (bigoted) citizen. Maitra claims that the key to meeting this challenge rests in the acquiescence of the other people in the subway carriage, who, like it or not, are participants in a conversation (115). She argues that in the context of this conversation the other people are free to reject the older man's claims about the woman. That they fail to do so by remaining silent amounts to 'licensing', in the sense of granting authority. It is due to this licensing that 'the speaker in this case succeeds in ranking his target' (ibid.).

Although there is much that I find plausible in this account of licensing-based authority, there are significant weaknesses in what Maitra says (or does not say) about the conditions that must be satisfied in order for licensing to take place. Maitra gives scant guidance on these conditions and, moreover, some of the conditions that seem obvious appear to disqualify Maitra's conclusion. Wojciech Sadurski offers two conditions. First, parties to a conversation must 'see a speaker as having a right to issue a particular type of illocution' (1999: 131). Second, the speaker must perform the putatively subordinating illocutionary act 'with a special kind of intention peculiar to this kind of act, and with the purpose that this intention be recognized as such by a hearer' (ibid.). Even if one accepts that the old man in Maitra's subway carriage example speaks with the intention of ranking Arabs, it is debatable whether he is seen by people on the carriage as having a *right* to rank, and thereby subordinate, Arabs in this way. What is more, I think that a third, extralinguistic condition must be satisfied. An act or omission on the part of participants in a conversation may legitimately count as licensing or granting authority to a speaker to perform some other illocutionary speech act (e.g., ranking) only if the participants enjoy a reasonable opportunity to refrain from performing the act or omission that purports to license or grant authority. If the participants would face an unreasonably high burden as a result of performing whichever act or omission counts as withholding license or refusing to grant authority, then they do *not* enjoy a reasonable opportunity.[44] Let us suppose for the sake of argument that in the subway carriage example the only thing that counts as withholding license or refusing to grant authority to the hate speaker is standing up and objecting to his speech. Let us also suppose that the burden of this act is an increased probability of the hate speaker coming over and hurling abuse at the objector (e.g., "You know what, you're even worse than this Arab bitch because you're selling out your own people—that's right, you're a lousy traitor") multiplied by the resulting harm if he does so (e.g., the psychological harm of being called a traitor) plus the increased probability of the speaker coming over and physically assaulting the objector (e.g., repeatedly punching the objector around the head and face), multiplied by the concomitant harm of being assaulted in this way (e.g., the physical damage and psychological harm of being punched). Finally, let us suppose for argument's sake that this burden is unreasonably high. In which case, remaining silent *cannot* be legitimately taken to constitute the licensing or granting of authority to the hate speaker to engage in ranking. If it is generally the case that the expected burdens of sticking up for the victims of hate speech are unreasonably high, then remaining silent will generally fail to qualify as licensing or granting authority.[45]

Nevertheless, the deeper question that drives my interest in subordination theory is how well the Principle of Non-Subordination fits with the different clusters of laws/regulations/codes that I outlined in Ch. 2, as distinct from hate speech law understood as a non-disaggregated lump. Sticking with the first dimension of subordination, *ranking,* and assuming for argument's sake that the Authority Problem can be resolved satisfactorily, it would seem reasonable to suppose that the Principle of Non-Subordination could buttress the normative case for laws/regulations/codes that proscribe group defamation (*sensu stricto*); that limit the use of hate speech when it amounts to negative stereotyping or stigmatization; and that disallow the public expression of hatred, including through the use of insults, slurs, or derogatory epithets directed at members of groups or classes of persons identified by certain ascriptive characteristics, and through the public dissemination of ideas based on the inferiority of such persons. How it is that the various forms of hate speech constrained by these different clusters of law can constitute acts of ranking could be explained both directly and indirectly: directly, by virtue of the fact that degradation is built into the very meaning of certain words or ideas; indirectly, because of what the decision to employ such words against some groups of people but not others says about the relative status of those groups (e.g., Delgado 1982: 144n.65; Lawrence 1987: 350–351; 1990: 461, 461n.112; Neu 2008: vii; Saunders 2011: 132; Langton et al. 2012: 758).[46]

## Subordination as Depriving People of Important Rights and Powers

As well as associating hate speech with *ranking,* subordination theorists believe that some uses of hate speech *deprive* members of targeted groups of important rights and powers (Langton et al. 2012: 758). How does this work? Part of the answer can be borrowed from the work of critical race theorists, specifically the observation that racist hate speech can *change the psychological traits and behavioral dispositions* of members of targeted groups in such a way as to make them effectively surrender their own rights and powers by withdrawing from mainstream society. Another part of the answer is to be found in subordination theory itself, relating specifically to the phenomenon of *silencing.* More on this later. However, it is not sufficient to provide an account of how this depriving works. Subordination theorists must also furnish a *theory* of the fundamental nature and importance of the rights and powers at stake. Otherwise they will have failed to motivate the belief that depriving people of rights and powers is serious enough to N-warrant restrictions on the relevant forms of hate speech.

Consequently, in order to assist subordination theorists in answering this more fundamental question about rights and powers I propose to introduce an *intermezzo theory*, the purpose of which is to forge a link between an abstract normative principle and the case for particular clusters of laws/regulations/codes. Specifically, I intend to repurpose Martha Nussbaum's (1988, 1993, 2000, 2003, 2006, 2011) work on the ten 'central capabilities' as a model for thinking about the nature and importance of those rights and powers that can be deprived by some uses of hate speech. In short, I think that capability theory can help to bridge the gap between the detailed insights of critical race theorists and subordination theorists about the evils of hate speech and the more abstract claim made by subordination theorists that some uses of hate speech deprive intended targets of important rights and powers.[47]

Before turning to the detailed insights of critical race theorists and subordination theorists, I need to say more about the intermezzo theory. For the purposes of this theory, to be deprived of important rights and powers is to be deprived of central capabilities, where this means to be deprived of having real access to basic human functionings. It is to be deprived of having regular, reliable, and uncoerced access to the valuable doings and beings that are part and parcel of any worthwhile human existence, including but not limited to healthy emotions (e.g., having a sense of self-worth); senses, imagination, and thought (e.g., developing and exercising intellectual abilities); play (e.g., partaking of public spaces and events); control over one's environment (e.g., operating in the workplace, participating in the formation of public opinion and influencing political decisions); and affiliation (e.g., enjoying friendships and loving relationships with other human beings).[48] With the help of this theory I translate the abstract claim that some uses of hate speech deprive intended targets of important rights and powers into the claim that some uses of hate speech deprive intended targets of real access to basic human functionings by imposing upon them various unwanted impediments to and undue influences on the achievement of basic human functionings. As will become clear, these unwanted impediments and undue influences can be psychological as well as social and linguistic in nature. What is more, this intermezzo theory provides a way of translating the point, insisted on by some subordination theorists, that hate speech can have illocutionary as well as perlocutionary force vis-à-vis depriving intended targets of important rights and powers. Under the proposed translation, some uses of hate speech can have illocutionary force in depriving intended targets of real access to basic human functionings in the moment of hate speech as well as perlocutionary force in producing changes in intended targets' psychological traits and behavioral dispositions which in turn deprive them of real access to basic human functionings.

Now to the detailed insights, of which three stand out. First, Lawrence claims that racist hate speech 'inflict[s] psychological injury by assaulting a person's self-respect' (Lawrence 1987: 351). Similarly, Delgado maintains that 'it is neither unusual nor abnormal for stigmatized individuals to feel ambivalent about their self-worth and identity' (Delgado 1982: 137). 'This ambivalence,' he continues, 'arises from the stigmatized individual's awareness that others perceive him or her as falling short of societal standards, standards which the individual has adopted' (ibid.). To place these harms in the conceptual framework of capability theory, it might be said that some uses of hate speech cause changes in psychological traits that deprive victims of real access to *healthy emotions* (cf. Nussbaum 2011: 33–34). Extrapolating from Nussbaum's own description of this capability, one might say that some uses of hate speech adversely affect the ability to love and respect oneself. Being deprived of real access to healthy emotions might also adversely impact the proper exercise of another central capability, *senses, imagination, and thought* (33). When exposure to hate speech changes a person's emotional default setting to one of self-hatred, ambivalence, and diffidence, one knock-on effect could be that he or she is less likely to think, reason, and develop positive ideas, still less to take pleasure in the public articulation of ideas. "What good are my ideas either to myself or to other people if I am less than human?" a victim of hate speech might conclude. By way of evidence for these theoretical claims, research in the field of media effects has uncovered the phenomenon of 'stereotype threat', in which exposure to media content containing negative stereotypes about the intellectual abilities of African Americans or Latinos in certain settings (e.g., educational settings) leads to impaired performance in tests of these abilities in the relevant settings by members of these groups (e.g., Steele and Aronson 1995; Gonzales et al. 2002). Subsequent research in this field has found that among the coping mechanisms adopted by some individuals in response to stereotype threat has been to disengage with the relevant settings and/or to dis-identify with the stereotyped group (e.g., Major et al. 1998; Cohen [G.] et al. 2008).[49]

If capability theory does provide a cogent framework for understanding this first detailed insight, and for grounding the abstract claim that some uses of hate speech deprive intended targets of important rights and powers (i.e., central capabilities), then this opens up a pathway to applications of the Principle of Non-Subordination, which is to say, the N-warrant of clusters of laws/regulations/codes that constrain uses of hate speech. One place to start is with laws/regulations/codes that limit uses of hate speech that constitute negative stereotyping and stigmatization. Another place to look is laws that provide sanctions or remedies against uses of hate speech that amount to dignitary crimes or torts. Couched in the capability framework, the thesis is that when hate speech is used to humiliate and degrade its victims, this can bring about changes in their psychological traits which in turn makes their access to creative thinking and their taking pleasure in creative thinking less reliable.

At this stage, it might be objected that Nussbaum herself describes the central capability of senses, imagination, and thought in terms of '[b]eing able to use one's mind in ways protected by guarantees of freedom of expression with respect to both political and artistic speech' (Nussbaum 2011: 33). In which case, surely there is something incoherent about appealing to this central capability in the articulation of a principle designed to N-warrant restrictions on freedom of expression. But it is telling that Nussbaum herself only mentions two, high-value categories of speech in First Amendment jurisprudence, to wit, political and artistic speech. Hate speech is not mentioned, and perhaps for good cause.

Second, critical race theorists believe that (cumulative) exposure to hate speech has the power to change victims' behavior for the worse. This insight begins with the observation that racial minorities can be subject to hate speech at any time, while carrying out any activity. As Matsuda explains, 'African Americans have been subjected to racist attacks while engaging in commonplace activities such as changing a tire or attending a church picnic' (Matsuda 1989b: 2336n.84). Consequently, '[i]n order to avoid receiving hate messages, victims have had to quit jobs, forgo education, leave their homes, avoid certain public places, curtail their own exercise of speech rights, and otherwise modify their behavior and demeanor' (2337). Matsuda (2337n.86) cites Lieberson (1985) as a source of evidence for this phenomenon, which looks at the impact of exposure to negative stereotypes and stigmatization on the behavior of members of beleaguered groups.[50] At stake here, I propose, is deprivation of real access to *play* and *control over one's environment* (cf. Nussbaum 2011: 34). Delgado also highlights the way in which racial stigmatization worsens victims' relationships with others. Being subjected to racist hate speech over an extended period of time, perhaps starting from childhood, can make some individuals more chary, defensive, or aggressive in their interactions with members of other races, and even cause them to be emotionally needy in their relations with members of the their own group (Delgado 1982: 137; cf. Allport 1954; Hayakawa 1966). This implicates deprivation of real access to *affiliation* (cf. Nussbaum 2011: 34). Another concern raised in the literature is about self-fulfilling prophecies. When confronted with negative stereotypes about the group to which one belongs, one response is to simply act out the behaviors unfairly attributed to the group: to become delinquent, unemployed, alcohol or drug dependent, involved in crime, incarcerated, an absent father or mother, and/ or uninterested in civil society or political affairs (e.g., Delgado 1982: 146; cf. Deutsch et al. 1968; see also Matsuda 1989b: 2336n.84; Clark 1995: 6–7). Once again, one potential implication of these unwelcome changes to character traits and behavioral dispositions is that the individuals concerned lack real access to *control over one's environment*—such as if exposure to hate speech causes a withdrawal from public life. A related implication is that some victims of hate speech may be unable or unwilling to participate in the formation of the very sort of public opinion that could lead to the introduction of hate speech law, which *ex hypothesi* would help to protect their central capabilities.

As for the appropriate legal response to this sort of deprivation, it seems natural to point once again to laws/regulations/codes that limit uses of hate speech that constitute negative stereotyping and stigmatization. Focusing on the insight about self-fulfilling prophecies, the argument for media regulation of this form of hate speech might be that the use of generics like "Latinos are lazy" or "Muslims are violent"—'characteristic generics' that entail or strongly imply that all members of a group possess an essential nature or innate set of characteristics (cf. Langton et al. 2012: 760–765)—are implicated in depriving Latinos and Muslims of real access to basic human functionings. The thesis is that if the objects of negative stereotyping and stigmatization internalize the meaning of these generics, they may come to think that their behavior is inevitable because of their possession of an essential nature or may even come to actively embrace their essential nature as badges of identity.

Third, critical race theorists and subordination theorists alike have had much to say about the putative *silencing effect* of hate speech. Lawrence puts the point thusly: '[w]hen racial insults are hurled at minorities, the response may be silence or flight rather than a fight' (Lawrence 1990: 452). Essentially, Lawrence's claim is that some uses of racist hate speech have the perlocutionary effect of silencing intended targets via feelings of fear and intimidation, or a simple desire for self-preservation in a racist society. This idea remains at the forefront of current thinking about hate speech and is by no means restricted to critical race theorists and subordination theorists. According to Katharine Gelber, for example, the psychological effects of hate speech 'would *ordinarily* act to deter or perhaps even prevent a targeted person or community or their supporters from responding to the hate speech with (unsupported) counterspeech' (Gelber 2012a: 213, emphasis added).

However, this version of the silencing argument faces the objection that other factors besides racist hate speech may in fact be causing the relevant perlocutionary effects, not the least of which is the broader and more complex practice of racism in all its manifestations. Therefore, the empirical basis (so the objection runs) for concluding that racist hate speech is a material cause of silencing remains unproven (e.g., Post 1991: 310). Echoing Jay's point presented earlier in this chapter [3.1], it may be simply unfeasible to perform controlled experiments in which one group is exposed to racist hate speech but not the more generalized experience of racism, while another group is exposed to both racist hate speech and the more generalized experience of racism.

Nevertheless, in response to this methodological objection, some subordination theorists would insist that speech can deprive intended targets of important rights and powers by virtue of its illocutionary force, independently of producing perlocutionary effects via changes to psychological traits and behavioral dispositions. By analogy, Langton (1993; see also Langton and Hornsby 1998) argues that pornography reinforces a norm of verbal communication according to which when a woman says "no" in the context of sexual interaction she really means "yes." So when a male user of pornography is attempting to force himself on a woman sexually, she can utter the word "no", but this might not perform the illocutionary act of *refusal* by virtue of a lack of uptake by her assailant.⁵¹ This particular argument has attracted a good deal of critical attention (e.g., Jacobson 1995, 2001). Nevertheless, I believe that a similar argument can be made about hate speech. Suppose the white foreman of a cardboard box factory announces to his staff in a fit of pique, "For the rest of the week no goddam nigger will use the public address system." His positional authority is devolved to him by the company's owners. Or suppose instead that one of the employees makes the following utterance in the canteen to his workmates, "Hey, the next time that nigger gets on the public address system let's ignore him." His fellow workmates do not object even though (let us stipulate for the purpose of the example) they have a reasonable opportunity to do so. In that sense they license or grant him authority to speak for them. Either way, now suppose that later in the day an African American employee sits at the public address system microphone, flicks the switch, and says, "All packers are to be advised that there is no more cardboard glue in the dispenser." By this utterance he intends to *advise* his colleagues of this state of affairs, to *warn* them not to expect to find glue, and perhaps to *prompt* someone to order more glue. But acting in solidarity with the comments made earlier in the day, other employees in the factory simply go on as though he had not uttered a word. Since there is no uptake of his attempt, his utterance does not count as the illocutionary act of advising, warning, prompting, and so on. No doubt similar examples could be constructed in which students on university campuses are deprived of the illocutionary power of speech by forms of discriminatory harassment. The speech act approach to theorizing such examples sheds new light on the claim made by critical race theorists that 'minorities often report that they find themselves speechless in the face of discriminatory verbal attacks' (Lawrence 1990: 452). What is more, I believe that capability theory adds a philosophical foundation to the claim that important rights and powers are at stake. It can do so by translating these examples as uses of hate speech depriving intended targets of real access to *control over one's environment* and *senses, imagination, and thought*.

Drawing upon these varied observations about the silencing effect of hate speech (perlocutionary and illocutionary) would seem to facilitate an argument in favor of at least laws/regulations/codes that forbid hate speech when it amounts to discriminatory harassment in the workplace or in educational institutions. So, for example, Lawrence (1990: 472) lists silencing as among the various destructive consequences of racist hate speech within universities, which N-warrants the enactment and effective enforcement of campus speech codes. Much the same line of thinking would seem to fit with an argument in favor of laws/regulations/codes that interdict uses of hate speech that constitute the performance of the expression-oriented hate crime of discriminatory intimidation, not the least of which are cross burning statutes. Thus, Lawrence (1990, 1992) defends cross burning statutes, including the City of St. Paul Bias-Motivated Crime Ordinance, *inter alia* on the grounds that the expressive conduct it prohibits constitutes 'a threat that silences a potential speaker' (1990: 472) and is 'an act intended to silence through terror and intimidation' (1992: 790).

## 3.5 THE ABSENCE OF OPPRESSION

Few people would deny, I think, that not being oppressed is ultimately good for a human being. To be oppressed is, among other things, to be systematically discriminated against or denied the fundamentals of justice. It is not difficult to see connections between the good of non-oppression and free speech. For one thing, it might be argued that one of the central purposes of a constitutional guarantee of freedom of expression and the free press is to protect the speech of journalists, and citizens when they have a voice, should they attempt to speak truth to oppressive public officials about the forms of discrimination and injustice for which the latter are responsible (e.g., Shiffrin [S.H.] 1999: 42, 91; 2011a: 562).[52] There is, however, a danger in going to the other extreme: namely, that free speech can itself be used as a tool of oppression by powerful members of society over less powerful members. If society embraces a constitution that requires that government shall make no law abridging free speech and freedom of the press, and if society chooses to interpret this constitutional right in an absolutist way, society may well be complicit in the oppression which is allowed to flourish as a result. In other words, society may be accepting a regime of unfettered speech that operates not to emancipate the weak but to empower the strong (Shiffrin [S.H.] 1999: 77, 85–86). This line of thought points toward what I shall call the Principle of Non-Oppression, that legalistic constraints on uses of hate speech are (N-)warranted if they serve to inhibit the oppression of some members of society by other, more powerful members.

In the mid-1990s Clay Calvert gave expression to the oppressive nature of hate speech when he analyzed hate speech as a particular form of *ritual*: an attempt to maintain and reinforce the values and traditions of racism and discrimination (Calvert 1997: 7). As he put it, 'ritualistic use of racist epithets facilitates and promotes disparate, unequal treatment of particular groups' (11). This echoes MacKinnon's observation that racial-based group defamation is 'a practice of discrimination in verbal form' (1993: 99).[53] Thus, in this section I want to critically examine the idea that some uses of hate speech are oppressive not because they legitimate or incite discrimination but because they *enact* discrimination. Few academics have done more to elucidate this idea than McGowan (2009, 2012; see also Maitra and McGowan 2010). On her account, some forms of hate speech constitute illegal acts of discrimination by virtue of *enacting norms of activity*. One need *not* think of racist hate speech as simply changing the terms of a racist *conversation*. It can also be conceived as changing the terms of a collective human activity of *racism*. In other words, McGowan believes that racism is a 'norm-governed' activity and that some contributions to this activity, like moves in a game, can 'enact' facts about what is subsequently permissible or impermissible within the activity. This means that participants in a social practice of racism can, by their utterances, enact facts about the permissibility or impressibility of certain sorts of behavior within that activity ('permissibility facts') (McGowan 2009: 395–397; 2012: 132–136).

How so? McGowan invites us to consider two cases that build on MacKinnon's original example of a "Whites Only" sign in a restaurant— a sign that enacts racial discrimination in that restaurant (MacKinnon 1987: 194). In the first case, the boss of a company declares to his human resources department, "From now on we don't hire blacks." Because the boss has the authority to make moves in the practice of racism in his company, he creates a new permissibility fact, which is racially discriminatory and illegal (McGowan 2012: 123, 136). In fact, one need not think of this as a purely hypothetical example. Consider *EEOC v. Caldwell Freight Lines* (2012).[54] In the second case, an elderly white man is traveling on a public bus somewhere in the US, when he turns to an African American man who just boarded the bus and says, "Just so you know, because I realize that your kind aren't very bright, we don't like niggers around here." All the other *passengers* on the bus are white, and they each nod with approval after the utterance (McGowan 2012: 121, 139). According to McGowan, by his utterance the elderly white man enacts a permissibility fact for the activity of racism on that public bus: that African Americans are not permitted on the bus (136–137), or that any African Americans who do board the bus are not welcome (137n.28). What is more, '[e]ven if the enacted permissibility facts are highly localized (pertaining only to that particular bus), and, even if they are merely temporary (lasting only for a short while), the enacting of such permissibility facts nevertheless constitutes an illegal act of racial discrimination' (142).[55] There is an obvious justificatory link between McGowan's line of argument and laws/regulations/codes that forbid hate speech when it amounts to a violation of civil rights, including rights to non-discrimination. Not only that, the argument purports to show how this cluster of hate speech law could be, and should be, utilized to restrict not merely the discriminatory speech of institutions and office holders but also the hate speech of ordinary members of the public when it rises to the level of enacting discrimination within the context of particular activities. The potential of this approach to shed new light on some familiar cases of hate speech should not be underestimated. Although McGowan does not do so, it is worth pausing to reflect on what her account of oppression and the enactment of discrimination would say about the infamous Skokie Affair of the late 1970s. In particular, consider the placards that Frank Collin and his associated intended to march with (in full Nazi costume) through the streets of Skokie, partly as a protest over the municipal ordinances enacted by local authorities to curb such marches, namely, "Free Speech for White America." If they had been permitted to march, carrying this placard might have constituted an incitement to discrimination, assuming that the implied message of the placard in the context of the march was not merely that white Americans ought to be granted free speech rights but that *only* white Americans ought to be granted free speech rights (e.g., Bollinger 1986: 27). More significantly, applying McGowan's approach, carrying this placard might have *enacted* discrimination within the activity of racism in Skokie at that time.

However, I also believe that McGowan's account leaves some important questions unanswered, and this is what I wish to explore in the remainder of the section. McGowan assumes that the elderly white man has the authority he requires to enact relevant permissibility facts only if two conditions are met: 'First, he must be a player in the game (that is, a participant in a system of racism) and, second, he must be capable of making that move at that time' (McGowan 2012: 138). For McGowan, it is clear that each of these conditions is met in the case of the elderly white man on the public bus (ibid.). However, in attempting to explain why it is that he is 'a player in the game' (in satisfaction of the first condition) McGowan merely offers some general observations about how society is racist and how we each make some level of contribution to the collective human activity of racism (ibid.). Strictly speaking, these general observations are beside the point. The question here is what makes it the case that the elderly white man is a participant in *the activity of racism on that public bus*. It might seem reasonable to expect, I think, that this is a matter of the elderly white man establishing his credentials as a racist on that public bus prior to his making this particular utterance. He might possess credibility as a participant in the activity of racism on that public bus by dint of previous qualifying participations—for example, making other racist remarks, standing at the door of the bus attempting to block the entry of non-whites, attempting to assault non-white passengers. What I am suggesting, then, is that possessing sufficient authority to change the norms of any norm-governed social activity is about building up credibility within the activity over time, as though serving an apprenticeship. Hence, a hate speaker could lack the requisite authority to make utterances that enact new permissibility facts for a particular activity of racism if he or she lacks prior credentials as a participant in that activity.

Or maybe McGowan is intending to claim instead that the elderly white man qualifies as a participant in the activity of racism on that public bus purely by virtue of making the racist remarks he did. Indeed, she writes: 'Since uttering racist hate speech is one way to mistreat a person by virtue of her race, the uttering of racist hate speech is clearly and uncontroversially a move in the system [of racism]' (McGowan 2012: 136). But then again, it seems hard to believe that simply making a racist utterance is a sufficient condition. To see this, suppose a young white woman also sitting on the bus has spent the previous half hour helping African Americans onto the bus and welcoming them on board. Inexplicably, she suddenly turns to one such person and utters the very same words uttered by the elderly white man, "Just so you know, because I realize that your kind aren't very bright, we don't like niggers around here." Surely it would be a stretch to say that she

*Principles of Basic Morality* 89

is a *participant* in the activity of racism on that public bus simply by virtue of making the utterance. Apart from anything else, her previous behavior means that she lacks the credentials to be taken seriously as a participant. The point is that patterns of behavior as opposed to single utterances will be decisive in deciding if someone is a true participant in racist activity. McGowan does say that when it comes to the potential application of her account of racist utterances to the law, courts will have to take a 'contextual' approach to interpreting whether a given utterance does in fact constitute an act of racial discrimination (143). This may well be true, but it is also likely that courts will have to construct rules of thumb about how to determine what it means to be a genuine participant in an activity of racism. And McGowan gives insufficient guidance on this score, I believe.

Another question left unanswered is the scope of the permissibility facts supposedly enacted by the elderly white man. McGowan asserts that 'the elderly white man's utterance covertly enacts *the same* (racially discriminatory) permissibility facts that a proprietor's posting of a "Whites Only" sign would' (McGowan 2012: 137–138, emphasis added). But this is far from obvious. In the case of a restaurant proprietor posting a "Whites Only" sign, the permissibility fact that he enacts has *wide scope*: that is to say, its scope is the totality of activities comprising the full functioning of a restaurant, namely, allowing entry, sitting patrons at tables, selling food and beverages, providing restroom facilities, and so on. Since the proprietor has authority over the restaurant, the scope of the permissibility fact that he enacts covers the totality of activities that comprise its full functioning. Hence, the relevant permissibility fact is that non-whites are not permitted to gain access to the restaurant, sit at tables, purchase food and beverages, use the restroom, and so on. In the case of the elderly white man on the public bus, in contrast, the permissibility fact that he enacts has *narrow scope*: its scope is *not* the totality of activities comprising the full functioning of that public bus, namely, the bus operator posting schedules, the driver stopping to pick up passengers from bus stops, the driver accepting payments for journeys, waiting for passengers to take their seats, endeavoring to carry passengers safely to their chosen points of departure, and so on. Since the elderly white man lacks authority over the bus, the scope of the permissibility fact that he enacts does not cover the totality of activities that comprise its full functioning. Instead, the immediate scope of the permissibility fact that he enacts is limited to just those participants in and those activities comprising the activity of racism on that public bus, such as the holding of racist beliefs, uttering racist remarks to non-white passengers, making non-white passengers who do board the bus feel unwelcome or refraining from making them feel welcome, not lifting a finger to protest against the aforementioned, and so on. This means that the list of activities comprising the activity of racism on that public bus is non-identical with the activities comprising the full functioning of that public bus. And this in turn means that from the mere fact that the elderly white man enacts racially discriminatory permissibility facts for the activity of racism on that public bus, it does not automatically follow that he thereby also enacts racially discriminatory permissibility facts for the activities comprising the full functioning of that public bus. Putting it another way, the non-identity between the activity of racism on that public bus and the activities comprising the full functioning of that public bus creates a gap that the enactment of the norm must somehow span if it is to constitute an act of racial discrimination for the full functioning of that public bus.

Perhaps McGowan might respond by accepting that this gap exists but denying that it matters. She might reason that the norm is enacted by the utterance, that the scope of the norm covers activities comprising the complex activity of racism on that public bus, that these activities have the character of racial discrimination, and, therefore, that it does not matter whether or not there is identity between the activities comprising the complex activity of racism on that public bus and the activities comprising the full functioning of that public bus. However, suppose that even though the activities comprising the complex activity of racism on that public bus are racially discriminatory *in and of themselves*, the activities comprising the full functioning of that public bus are *not* racially discriminatory—for example, the bus company posts schedules to be read by white and non-white passengers, the driver always stops to pick up white and non-white passengers who wait together at non-segregated stops, the driver accepts payment for journeys from white and non-white passengers, the driver waits for white and non-white passengers to take their seats before driving off, the driver endeavors to carry white and non-white passengers safely to their chosen points of departure, the driver intervenes to admonish and stop anyone who interferes with or threatens to interfere with other passengers getting on or off the bus, and so on. Under these conditions, the elderly white man might succeed in enacting racially discriminatory permissibility facts for the complex activity of racism on that public bus, but surely fails to enact racially discriminatory permissibility facts for activities that comprise the full functioning of that public bus. Of course, it could transpire that the elderly white man's utterance, perhaps when combined with lots of other racist activities, intimidates the driver and the bus operators sufficiently to make *them* adopt racially discriminatory policies and practices. But in that eventuality one could only affirm that the elderly white man's utterance *indirectly brings about* the enactment of racially discriminatory permissibility facts for that public bus. One could not say, as McGowan perhaps wants to say, that the elderly white man's utterance *in itself enacts* racially discriminatory permissibility facts for the full functioning of that public bus.

The upshot of all this is that even though McGowan's approach to theorizing oppression may lend support to law forbidding hate speech when it amounts to the violation of civil rights, including rights to non-discrimination, there is still more work to be done in showing how this argument can be extended from the speech or expressive conduct of people in authority, such

*Principles of Basic Morality* 91

as holders of public office or restaurant owners, to the hate speech of ordinary citizens. Here, at least, it may be that other fundamental human values possess less technically problematic N-warranting power. It is to another of these values that I turn in the final section.

## 3.6 HUMAN DIGNITY

It is widely supposed by legal scholars that human dignity is the inherent worth or value borne by all human beings (e.g., Schachter 1983: 849; Beschle 2004: 966; Knechtle 2006: 551; Heyman 2008: 39; McCrudden 2008: 679; Glensy 2011: 76). These scholars take themselves to be paying their intellectual dues to Kant.[56] It is also commonly assumed that showing respect for human dignity means respecting fundamental rights, not the least of which is the right to freedom of expression (e.g., Eberle 2002). And not without valid reason. If, for example, one believes that human dignity is grounded in the capacity of human beings to determine for themselves what it is about human beings that gives them inherent value, then one is likely to conclude that only with the strongest guarantee of free speech will human beings be able to develop and exercise this capacity (e.g., Dworkin, 2011). However, stacked up against these ideas is the equally compelling thought that far from being the enemy of human dignity some hate speech law can be its guardian angel. This is because some uses of hate speech 'violate', 'assault', 'damage', 'compromise', 'undermine', 'threaten', 'affront', 'deny', 'infringe', or 'fly in the face of' human dignity (e.g., Schachter 1983: 850–852; Lasson 1995: 277; Corlett and Francescotti 2002: 1097; Parekh 2005–2006: 217; Wright 2006: 544–549; Cortese 2006: 16; Heyman 2008: ch. 10; Weinrib 2009: 187).[57] Another of Matsuda's many pleas springs to mind. 'However we choose to respond to racist speech, let us present a competing ideology, one that has existed in tension with racism since the birth of our nation: there is inherent worth in each human being, and each is entitled to a life of dignity' (Matsuda 1989b: 2381).

In what follows I attempt to articulate this line of thought more fully and to put flesh on the bones of what I shall call the Principle of Human Dignity, that legalistic constraints on uses of hate speech are (N-)warranted if they serve to thwart people from violating the human dignity of others. I mean to ask two questions. What does it mean to say that hate speech 'violates' human dignity? And, what would it mean to say that hate speech law can 'protect' human dignity? Having answered these abstract questions I turn to consider more particular arguments connecting the protection of specific aspects of human dignity with specific clusters of laws/regulations/codes.

So, to begin with the first question, on one level it might be tempting to think that some uses of hate speech violate human dignity simply as a matter of stipulation. For example, in defending a new tort for racial insult Delgado writes the following.

> Moreover, a tort for racial insults contains an indisputable element of harm, the affront to dignity. Professor Michelman and others have argued that the intangible quality of novel interests should not, by itself, preclude valuing them for purposes of compensation. Juries always can assign a value to such interests and their infringement. (1982: 166)
>
> If racial invective is aimed at a victim, an infringement of the plaintiff's dignity, at the least, has occurred. (171)

Delgado provides no conceptual analysis of dignity and no explanation of how or why it is the case that racial insults constitute an infringement of dignity. His use of the term 'indisputable' would seem to suggest that he is simply relying on stipulation. The problem with stipulation, however, is that it can often lack persuasive force. To insist that racial insult is an affront to dignity may have little or no impact on civil libertarians who reject the idea of a new cause of action for racial insult as unconstitutional because it involves content discrimination. Essentially one could choose to define human dignity in all manner of ways, but the real question is what makes one stipulation superior to its alternatives (cf. Waldron 2011).

Perhaps better progress could be made by exploiting another intermezzo theory. In the present case, the purpose of the intermezzo theory would be to explain the sense in which some uses of hate speech infringe human dignity and, in turn, the sense in which certain clusters of laws/regulations/codes protect human dignity. I shall now provide two instances of such a theory.

## The Categorical Imperative and Hate Speech Law

The first theory is based on Kant's Categorical Imperative. Kant classifies backbiting ([1797] 1996: 212), mockery (212–213), and hatred (161–162) as *immoral* acts because they are an affront to human dignity. Although Kant does not pause to explain *how* these acts contravene the Categorical Imperative, it is not difficult to construct an explanation. The Formula of the Law of Nature calls on agents to consider whether or not particular maxims could be consistently willed as universal laws of nature, bearing in mind the facts of rational nature ([1785] 1948: 84). For Kant, rational nature consists in three 'predispositions': 'a predisposition to *animality*' in the natural world (innate instincts directed toward self-preservation, procreation, and society with other human beings); 'a predisposition to *humanity*' in the world of human society (the drive to be esteemed and honored in the eyes of other people); and 'a predisposition to *personality*' (a receptivity to moral action) ([1793] 2009: 27–30). Drawing on these predispositions, Kant's reasoning might be explained as follows. A being with rational nature could not consistently will that the maxim "Let individuals backbite,

*Principles of Basic Morality* 93

mock, and express hatred toward other people whenever they feel inclined to do so" holds everywhere as a law of nature given people's natural predisposition to animality (the instinct for society) and to humanity (the drive for esteem and honor in the eyes of others) (cf. Hill 1980: 97; Korsgaard 1996: 211). It is it not difficult to apply this sort of reasoning to some uses of hate speech. For instance, a being with rational nature could not consistently will that the maxim "Let individuals publicly express hatred toward members of outgroups with the use of insults, slurs, or derogatory epithets or through the dissemination of ideas based on the inferiority of such people whenever they feel inclined to do so" holds everywhere as a law of nature given people's natural predisposition to animality (the instinct for society) and to humanity (the drive for esteem and honor in the eyes of others).

With this intermezzo framework in place we can reflect on how the duty to respect human dignity could lend credence to particular forms of hate speech law. Consider laws/regulations/codes that constrain uses of hate speech when they amount to a dignitary crime or tort. In the area of domestic human rights codes, for example, one might think that this framework justifies s. 14(1)(b) of the Saskatchewan Human Rights Code, which prohibits any speech or other expressive conduct 'that exposes or tends to expose to hatred, ridicules, belittles or otherwise affronts the dignity of any person or class of persons on the basis of a prohibited ground.' I believe that placing the focus on the duty to respect human dignity gives pause for thought on a recent decision on s. 14(1)(b) by the Canadian Supreme Court. In *Saskatchewan (Human Rights Commission) v. Whatcott* (2013)[58] a unanimous Court teased apart two different strands of s. 14(1)(b). It determined that prohibiting any representation 'that exposes or tends to expose to hatred' any person or class of persons on the basis of a prohibited ground, which is the first strand of s. 14(1)(b), *is* a reasonable limit on freedom of speech and is demonstrably justified in a free and democratic society, but that prohibiting any representation that 'belittles or otherwise affronts the dignity' of any person or class of persons on the basis of a prohibited ground, which is the second strand of s. 14(1)(b), is *not* a reasonable limit on freedom of speech and is *not* demonstrably justified in a free and democratic society. Writing the opinion of the Court, Justice Rothstein argued that the first strand is, and the second strand is not, rationally connected with the core objectives of the Saskatchewan Human Rights Code, specifically 3(b) 'to further public policy in Saskatchewan that every person is free and equal in dignity and rights and to discourage and eliminate discrimination'.[59] He argued that '[i]f a group of people are considered inferior, subhuman, or lawless, it is easier to justify denying the group and its members equal rights or status.'[60] In that sense '[h]ate speech lays the groundwork for later, broad attacks on vulnerable groups [. . .] [including] discrimination, to ostracism, segregation, deportation, violence and, in the most extreme cases, to genocide.'[61] This is a textbook example of the argument from a climate of hatred that I outlined earlier in the chapter [3.3]. Nevertheless, it is far from obvious

94 *Principles of Basic Morality*

that it was the only possible line of reasoning open to the Court. Arguably, the Court could have paid closer attention to the other core objective of the Saskatchewan Human Rights Code, namely, 3(a) 'to promote recognition of the inherent dignity and the equal inalienable rights of all members of the human family.' It could have interpreted this core objective as reflecting an imperative not to affront human dignity. It could have chosen to regard this core objective as essential to a free and democratic society. It could have viewed the second strand of s. 14(1)(b)—prohibiting any representation that belittles or otherwise affronts the dignity of any person or class of persons on the basis of a prohibited ground—as being rationally connected with this core objective. And, it could have judged Whatcott's flyers—which, among other things, described homosexuals as 'sex addicts' with 'sick desires', who 'want to share their filth and propaganda with Saskatchewan's children', and who are '430 times more likely to acquire AIDS and 3 times more likely to sexually abuse children'—as an affront to the dignity of gays and lesbians. I shall say more about this case in Ch. 10 [10.1].

It may be possible to develop similar arguments about laws/regulations/codes that penalize forms of speech that grossly trivialize, condone, or glorify acts of mass murder and other atrocities committed against groups or classes of persons identified by certain ascriptive characteristics. Kant explains that the predisposition to personality includes 'the (natural) human being's feeling himself compelled to revere the (moral) human being within his own person' (Kant [1797] 1996: 187). Looking at this natural compulsion from the perspective of the Formula of the Law of Nature, it is hard to see how a human being could consistently will that the maxim "Let individuals grossly trivialize, condone, or glorify the wonton destruction of human beings whenever they feel so inclined" holds everywhere as a law of nature given that human beings possess a natural compulsion to revere the human capacity for moral action. Universalizing this maxim would cut against the grain of the human personality, as Kant would say. This line of argument lends moral support to s. 131 of the German Criminal Code, for example, which makes it an offense to disseminate or present material that 'describe[s] cruel or otherwise inhuman acts of violence against human beings in a manner which expresses a glorification or rendering harmless of such acts of violence or which represents the cruel or inhuman aspects of the event in a manner which injures human dignity' [trans.].

R. George Wright identifies a potential banana skin for this interpretation of the Categorical Imperative in the shape of the hate speaker who believes that 'the target group lacks the requisites for Kantian dignity, and therefore does not qualify for respect on Kant's own terms' (Wright 2006: 546). Although Wright does not make this connection, there is a basis in current theories of social psychology for this phenomenon. Consider what Susan Opotow calls 'moral exclusion', a process in which 'individuals or groups are perceived as outside the boundary in which moral values, rules, and considerations of fairness apply' (Opotow 1990: 1). According to Melba

Vasquez and Cynthia de las Fuentes, it is likely that hate speech is 'one of the behavioural consequences of that process' (Vasquez and de las Fuentes 2000: 231). However, even if it is a recognizable phenomenon in which hate speakers deny that Africans and Jews, say, are human beings in the relevant Kantian sense, the Categorical Imperative is not predicated upon being applicable in a world created in the minds of hate speakers. Indeed, in such cases the hate speaker might be violating the Categorical Imperative through the vice of 'contempt' (i.e., judging other human beings to be without dignitary worth) (e.g., Kant [1797] 1996: 209).

The challenges do not end there, however. For one thing, some scholars would insist that human dignity requires the guarantee of free speech, even speech that affronts human dignity. Dworkin puts the argument thusly: 'Living in a just society—a society whose government respects human dignity— means that I must accept the right of others to hold me in contempt' (Dworkin 2012: 342). On closer inspection, however, Dworkin's grounds for affirming what he calls the right of others to hold me in contempt turns on his account of political legitimacy. For Dworkin, political legitimacy depends on governmental respect for the fact that individuals are ethically independent: namely, individuals are capable of developing their own *ideas* about human dignity and morality. The aim of the right to free expression is to offer speakers a degree of protection from governmental officials who might be inclined to suppress whichever ideas *they* believe to be misguided. Hate speech typically expresses ideas about morality and human dignity, and governmental authorities may not suppress these ideas on pain of being illegitimate. Nevertheless, the present line of argument assumes that what it means to respect human dignity is knowable through reason, and that when legislators and judges act on that reason to ban hate speech, they *prima facie* act legitimately. The fact that hate speech also expresses ideas about human dignity and morality is beside the point. Of course, Dworkin insists otherwise. He argues that unless there is free expression of *all* ideas, no lawmaking can be legitimate. For this reason, I shall postpone a full treatment of his approach until Ch. 7 [7.2].

That being said, there exists a further, exegetical objection to the current intermezzo theory that cannot be postponed. The objection is that it is an affront to Kant's own philosophy to transplant the Categorical Imperative and what it says about the immorality of certain forms of speech into juridical affairs. To do so runs counter to Kant's distinction between the doctrine of (private) morality and the doctrine of (public) right. Thus, Kant is very careful to distinguish between backbiting, which is an immoral act, and slander, which is an offense within the arena of public right: 'a false defamation to be taken before a court' (Kant [1797] 1996: 212). Nevertheless, it strikes me that this objection misunderstands the point of the current intermezzo theory. Its point is not to faithfully bring together different parts of Kant's moral, political, and legal philosophy. If it were, it would probably fail. Instead, its purpose is to provide a theoretical framework that can connect the abstract idea that hate speech violates human dignity with concrete arguments in favor of particular clusters of laws/regulations/codes that constrain uses of hate speech. Arguably it performs that purpose quite well.

At any rate, it may yet be possible to interpret some legalistic constraints on hate speech through the lenses of Kant's doctrine of (public) right, most notably Holocaust denial law. And this is what I wish to discuss now.

## The Dignity of the Dead and Holocaust Denial Law

For Kant, 'a good reputation is an innate external belonging'—one that in his view even applies to the dead (Kant [1797] 1996: 76). False statement of fact about the dead can be rightly taken before the courts (212), even if doing so thereby constrains freedom of expression. Like a case involving theft of property, this is a matter of the law deciding upon conflicting claims upon valuable goods. Indeed, Kant sometimes refers to slander of the dead using the metaphor of robbery (76n). What is more, the claim to a good reputation after death not merely takes effect under a regime of constitutional law but is 'conceivable a priori in a state of nature' and, therefore, something to which statutes should be adapted (73). Following on from this, Helga Varden argues that there is a way of viewing Holocaust denial law (i.e., a matter of public right) as a special case of the more general category of defamation of the dead. As she puts it, '[b]y defaming the dead, a person aims to falsify the public opinion, upon which everyone is dependent for rightful honor' (Varden 2010: 45).

This is precisely what *some* German prosecutors have argued when bringing Holocaust denial cases before the courts. In *Case of Germar Rudolf* (2007),[62] for example, the Regional Court Mannheim accepted the public prosecutor's argument that Holocaust denial amounted to a violation of the constitutionally protected right to human dignity—Art. 1 of the Basic Law of Germany states that '[h]uman dignity shall be inviolable' and that '[t]o respect and protect it shall be duty of all state authority.' More than that, the Court accepted the prosecutor's argument that Holocaust denial constitutes a clear violation of s. 189 of the Criminal Code, which makes it a punishable offense to disparage the memory of a deceased person.[63] This ruling is very far from being uncontroversial, of course. From Holocaust deniers will come the riposte that s. 189 is invalid because it prohibits Holocaust denial by invoking the dignitary rights of the very deceased persons whose existence Holocaust deniers are attempting to disprove or cast doubt upon. But German courts have tended to counter by insisting upon the self-evidentness of the facts surrounding the mass murder of Jews in gas chambers. I shall examine in the next chapter [4.1] whether or not this amounts to the more nuanced claim that the chances of Holocaust denial propositions being true are so tiny that it is reasonable to regard them as having little or no value vis-à-vis the discovery of truth.

At any rate, if this line of argument concerning the right to dignity even among the deceased is plausible, then one notable implication is that the case for banning Holocaust denial literature does *not* rest on the precarious assertion that all Holocaust denial is by definition an instance of incitement to hatred. At present a bill to introduce Holocaust denial legislation is making its way through both houses of Russia's parliament. The bill's main sponsor, Irina Yarovaya, offers the following warning about this form of speech by way of a justification for the new legislation. 'It is also a shot fired at the future, an instigation for new crimes against peace and security' (quoted in RT News 2014). Yet on closer reflection it is hard to escape the truth that not all Holocaust denial is an instance of incitement to hatred. This, at least, was a truth insisted upon by the German Federal Court of Justice in March 1994, when in *Case of Guenter Deckert* (1994)[64] it ordered a re-trial of a case involving a conviction for Holocaust denial under s. 130(1) of the German Criminal Code. The Court's reasoning was essentially that since it is conceivable that a historian could deny the Holocaust without intending to incite hatred of Jews, and since neo-Nazis exploit various other means of inciting hatred against Jews besides Holocaust denial, it is unsafe to stipulate that Holocaust denial equals incitement to hatred (cf. Dworkin 1996: 224). What I wish to suggest, however, is that it is also unnecessary as far as the project of morally justifying this sort of legislation is concerned to suppose that Holocaust denial equals incitement to hatred. Instead, prosecutors may draw on bespoke laws against Holocaust denial or laws against violating the memory of the dead—laws that can be tolerably well anchored to principles and values of human dignity.

A further, related implication is that the case for criminalizing Holocaust denial need not be reliant upon the potentially problematic assumption that Holocaust denial must be capable of disturbing the public peace. In *R. v. Zündel* [1992][65] the Canadian Supreme Court overturned Ernst Zündel's conviction for spreading false news under s. 181 (formerly s. 177) of the Criminal Code.[66] The Court received a written submission from the Attorney General for Canada explaining that the purpose of the section was 'to ensure that meaningful public discussion is not tainted by the deleterious effects of the wilful publication of falsehoods which cause, or are likely to cause, damage to public interests, to the detriment of public order.'[67] In response the Court pointed out that s. 181 was not to be found in the part of the Code dealing with sedition but rather in part dealing with nuisance. In the eyes of the Court, this implied that s. 181 was not really about public order after all. What is more, the Court remarked upon the fact that the enactment of s. 181 was *not* preceded by parliamentary committee debate on the matter of its purpose, including debate (and presumably the gathering of evidence) on the extent to which Holocaust denial literature is actually detrimental to public order.[68] As per the dissent by Justices Cory and Iacobucci, I would say simply that injury to human dignity might be sufficient to N-warrant Holocaust denial legislation quite apart from the existence or non-existence of evidence proving that Holocaust denial poses a threat to public order.[69]

## 98  Principles of Basic Morality

To finish the story of Zündel, in 2003 the Canadian Citizenship and Immigration Minister ordered the deportation of Zündel under the Canadian Immigration and Refugee Protection Act, which gives the Minister the right to deny access to any Canadian territory to persons, including refugee claimants, who are 'security risks.' Interestingly, the Minister did not postulate any automatic connection between Holocaust denial and the security risk but instead relied upon Zündel's association with members of extremist neo-Nazi groups. Upon deportation to Germany Zündel was immediately arrested and charged with offenses under ss. 130(1), 130(3), and 189 of the German Criminal Code for posting Holocaust denial material on his website *The Zündelsite*. In the *Case of Ernst Zündel* (2007),[70] the Regional Court of Mannheim convicted Zündel and handed down a prison sentence of five years, which was the maximum permitted under ss. 130(1) and 130(3). Both sections require that the dissemination of material is done 'in a manner capable of disturbing the public peace.' In his verdict Judge Meinerzhagen maintained that Zündel's conduct was capable of disturbing the public peace not merely because of its ulterior motive ('Zündel aims to return to the fascist state' [trans.]) but because of his chosen means, namely, the unlimited numbers of individuals who could access *The Zündelsite* ('Therein especially lies the danger of that medium' [trans.]).[71] By tethering its decision to the social impact of posting Holocaust denial material on the Internet the Court invited incredulity from those Germans who remained unpersuaded that this sort of mediated speech conduct amounts to a clear and present danger of a return to a fascist state, much less a threat of imminent lawless action. Perhaps the very same people would have been incredulous in a different way in the face of the argument that Holocaust denial law is justified by virtue of upholding the dignitary rights of the dead. But at least public prosecutors would not have carried an evidential albatross around their necks, that of proving that Holocaust denial posted on the Internet causes or is likely to cause a disturbance of the public peace.

\* \* \*

In this chapter, I have attempted to articulate what many scholars take to be the most important moral arguments in favor of hate speech law. I have also tried to weave together particular strands of thinking, both my own and that of others, about important features of basic morality—namely, liberty, health, autonomy, security, non-subordination, the absence of oppression, and human dignity—and observations about which clusters of laws/regulations/codes that constrain uses of hate speech these features most naturally point toward. I have not attempted to enumerate all possible concatenations of strands and clusters. Instead, I have concentrated on those that strike me as among the most plausible or at least most worthy of further study. But I also hope it is clear from what I have said that I do not think these particular arguments are unproblematic. Moreover, the mere fact that some of the previously discussed principles can N-warrant given clusters of laws/regulations/codes does not make those principles decisive in judgments of overall warrant. For, these principles must be stacked up against contrary, free speech protecting principles. I shall try to set out some of these principles in Chs. 4, 8, and 9. Finally, in Ch. 10 I will outline and defend a compromise-based approach for resolving these principled dilemmas.

## NOTES

1. 844 F.2d 951 (2d Cir.) (involving a lawsuit brought by an African American sheriff's deputy for emotional distress and humiliation caused by racial harassment at work).
2. 793 F.2d 909 (8th Cir.) (involving an African American welder who suffered several years of racial harassment in the workplace).
3. Of course, one potentially relevant factor in these decisions was the fact that the racist abuse had occurred in the context of the workplace where standard assumptions about the epistemic, developmental, and political values of expression might have less traction.
4. 88 Wn.2d 735 (involving a lawsuit brought by a Mexican American against his employer for damages relating to humiliation and embarrassment caused by the racial jokes, slurs, and comments of his fellow employees).
5. 1 Kan. App. 2d 213 (involving an African American lawyer racially abused with the slur 'nigger').
6. 7 Kan. App. 2d 603 (involving a lawsuit brought against a member of the Board of County Commissioners of Shawnee County for referring to the Plaintiff, an employee of Shawnee County, as a 'fucking spic').
7. 990 F.2d 239 (5th Cir.) (involving a supervisor who repeatedly uttered epithets toward a Mexican American employee).
8. 214 F.3d 615 (5th Cir.) (involving an employee who was subjected to a daily barrage of demeaning, racist remarks and comments in the workplace).
9. 152 N.J. 490 (involving an African American sheriff's officer who was addressed with the words 'There's the jungle bunny' during an official firearm training event).
10. At 510.
11. I am not suggesting that Howard J. Ehrlich et al. themselves are attempting to use their study in order to justify criminal group defamation statutes (catchall). Instead, my points are addressed to those who might try to use this study to that end.
12. Notwithstanding C. Edwin Baker's reference to the ethically autonomous individual, it would be a mistake to think of his defense of free speech as applying only to the domain of moral expression (cf. Brison 1998a: 323).
13. 503 F. Supp. 383 (E.D. Pa.) (involving the use of loud speakers by local residents to harass workers on a construction site in an urban area), at 402.
14. 805 F.2d 583 (5th Cir.) (involving the termination of the employment contract of a college instructor following formal complaints by two students about his inveterate use of profane language during class).
15. That being said, Baker (1989: 66–67) also argues that if a citizen steals secret military information and passes it on to an unauthorized agent—be it a foreign government or the press—with the aim of improving public debate or political decision-making processes within his own country, then this should not be counted as coercive speech and ought to be protected under the First Amendment. (The case of Chelsea Manning, formerly Bradley Manning, is one

100  *Principles of Basic Morality*

recent high-profile US military whistleblower example.) The rationale seems to be that even autonomy-denying speech is permissible provided that it is being used ultimately to improve general conditions of autonomy. So perhaps Baker would want to say the same about any hate speech which, albeit involving deception and failure to obtain consent, is nevertheless used with the aim of improving public debate or political decision-making processes. This would be to place hate speech in the protected category of political speech. I shall return to the connection between political speech and autonomy in Ch. 7 [7.3].

16. *R.A.V. v. City of St. Paul*, at 390.
17. No. T20027343 (Central Crim. Ct., 7 Mar.) (involving the prosecution of a Muslim cleric for several public order offenses including using threatening, abusive or insulting words or behavior with intent to stir up racial hatred).
18. Transcript obtained from Smith Bernal Reporting Ltd.
19. *Vejdeland and Others v. Sweden*, at para. 56.
20. One way of evaluating competing accounts of undue influence would be to reflect on which are justiciable: namely, which accounts of undue influence can be adequately utilized by courts. Another consideration is which are vulnerable to 'the tyranny of the majority.' If one is the sort of liberal who believes that freedom of expression is a vital check against the tendency of popular opinion to suppress undesirable speech, then one is also likely to be mindful of the possibility that popular opinion could find a way to suppress undesirable speech through the back door by exploiting juridical uses of the concept of undue influence (e.g., Brown 2008: 12).
21. Here I take inspiration from security studies and, in particular, Arnold Wolfers (1952: 485) canonical distinction between 'objective' and 'subjective' elements of security: 'security, in objective sense, measures the absence of threats to acquired values, in a subjective sense, the absence of fear that such values will be attacked.'
22. So it should perhaps come as no surprise that when the Race Relations Bill—which became the Race Relations Act 1965, notable for creating for the first time in the UK a criminal offense of stirring up racial hatred—was debated in the House of Lords, Lord Stonham, the Joint Parliamentary Under-Secretary of State for the Home Office, clarified that the legislation was 'designed to operate selectively against the leaders and organisers' of racial hatred. House of Lords, 26 Jul. 1965, Hansard, vol. 268, col. 1011. He went on to say: 'As an additional safeguard, therefore, Clause 6 requires that the Attorney General's consent must be obtained before proceedings may be instituted. This is an important safeguard against proceedings being taken in circumstances which would penalise or inhibit legitimate controversy, and will ensure that their use is confined to the ringleaders and organisers of incitement to racial hatred. This clause will serve to check effectively the emergent Fascist leader.' col. 1012.
23. *Brandenburg v. Ohio* (1969) 395 US 444 (involving the conviction of a Ku Klux Klan leader under Ohio's criminal syndicalism statute for his participation in a televised rally in which Klan members wore robes and hoods, carried firearms, burnt crosses, and made threatening racist speeches), at 447.
24. 127 N.J.L. 395 (involving an indictment of members of the German American Bund under s. 157B of the New Jersey Annotated Statutes 1935 for making disparaging remarks about Jewish people).
25. At 403.
26. As Richard Posner puts it (2006: 122), '[a] huge harm unlikely to materialize for several more years is not a lesser threat to the nation than a much smaller harm likely to materialize tomorrow.' Indeed, Posner suggests (124) that incitement to racial and religious hatred might constitute a long-term threat to national security of sufficient magnitude to N-warrant legal sanction, particularly if a raised incidence of incitement to hatred against American Muslims

*Principles of Basic Morality* 101

increases the chances over the long term of terrorist attacks by American Muslims on home soil. This argument puts a different complexion on an argument that was made by some UK politicians (e.g., Charles Clarke) in favor of legislation banning incitement to religious hatred: namely, that doing so is required to keep the country safe from terror attacks that from flow hatred against the Christian world stirred up by radical Muslim clerics.

27. I owe this particular way of understanding what is distinctive about the argument to Simon Thompson.
28. These two steps are often conflated in the literature on hate speech, and in a way that the argument from a climate of hatred discourages. According to Brown and Stern (1964: 8): 'It is ironic, indeed, that in the United States, guardian and protector of individual rights and champion of justice, eighteen years after fighting a global war which was largely the result of group hatred and defamations, there is no law to combat these same evils.' In a similar vein, Matsuda (1989b: 2335) asserts that '[t]he racially motivated beating [to] death of Vincent Chin by unemployed white auto workers in Detroit, during a time of widespread anti-Asian propaganda in the auto industry, was no accident.' Picking up on the problem of homophobic hate speech, Morgan (2007: 136) writes: 'One of the reasons why Dutch civil rights groups wanted the state to crack down on homophobic Islamic preachers was due to the sharp rise in physical assaults on gays in Dutch cities by Dutch-Moroccan youths.' Indeed, similar claims are increasingly being made about Islamophobic hate speech. In her book *The 9/11 Backlash*, Nicoletta Karam draws a direct link between an increase in negative stereotyping and stigmatization of American Muslims and American Asians post-9/11 and rising levels of hate crimes committed against individuals perceived to be members of these groups. For example, Karam (2012: 61) suggests a causal connection between a hate-based attack on a Sikh man in New Jersey in January 2008 and the airing of an Islamophobic episode ('Rachel Ben Natan') of the popular series *Nip/Tuck* in the same month. Similarly, in December 2012 Mark Potok, a regular contributor to the website of *HateWatch* (an American non-governmental organization [NGO] that monitors online bigotry and hatred of various forms) posted a piece claiming that the 50% increase in hate crimes against perceived Muslims recorded by the FBI from 2009 to 2010 was 'largely as a result of anti-Muslim propagandizing.' As for the 31% drop in anti-Latino hate crimes from 2010 to 2011, he concludes (2012): 'It's not clear what might be behind that drop, other than an apparent diminution in anti-Latino and anti-immigrant propaganda as negative attention focused on Muslims.' However, since this evidence does not relate to controlled experiments, it is not possible to discount other factors.
29. No. T20080094 (Leeds Cr. Ct., 10 Jul.) (involving offences of stirring up racial hatred).
30. Transcript obtained from J.L. Harpham Ltd.
31. No. T20107203 (Liver. Cr. Ct., 25 Jun.) (involving offences of stirring up racial hatred).
32. Transcript obtained from Cater Walsh Transcription Ltd.
33. Available at: www.un.org/en/documents/udhr/ (last accessed 27/11/14).
34. Available at: http://www.ohchr.org/en/professionalinterest/pages/ccpr.aspx (last accessed 27/11/14).
35. 394 US 705 (involving a conviction of knowingly and willingly threatening the President).
36. At 708.
37. Ibid.
38. 538 US 343 (involving the application of a State of Virginia statute against cross burning to the case of Barry Black, who in August 1998 had orchestrated

102  *Principles of Basic Morality*

       a Ku Klux Klan rally among like-minded people on private property complete with a cross burning ritual).
39. At 352–357, 363.
40. At 366–367.
41. No. T20110109 (Derby Cr. Ct., 10 Feb.) (involving offences of stirring up hatred on the grounds of sexual orientation).
42. Transcript obtained directly from Judge Burgess.
43. The architecture of Altman's analysis is based on J. L. Austin's distinction between the act of *saying* something, a *locutionary act* (I *said* to him, "You can't do that!"); what one is *doing* when one says something, an *illocutionary act* (I *commanded* that he must not do that); and the effect on the listener of what one is doing when one says something, a *perlocutionary act* (My words *brought him to his senses* and *stopped him* from doing that) (e.g., Austin 1962: 102). According to Altman (1993: 309–310), 'hate speech involves the performance of a certain kind of illocutionary act, namely, the act of treating someone as a moral subordinate.' This involves treating targeted members of an academic community (310), say, as though their interests and lives are inherently less important than those of other members. Based on this, Altman concludes (317) that universities can and should try to regulate such instances with campus speech codes, even at a cost to freedom of expression. However, Altman (310n.22) also argues that 'the speech act of treating someone as a moral subordinate is not characteristic of all forms of racist speech.'. He draws a distinction (311) between, on the one hand, the use of insulting or degrading epithets like 'kike', 'faggot', 'spic', and 'nigger', which are 'verbal instruments of subordination', and, on the other hand, 'scientific or philosophical' modes of hate speech such as 'describing, asserting, stating, arguing, and so forth' (e.g., '[t]o assert that blacks are genetically inferior to whites'), which are not subordinating in the relevant sense. That being said, he also adds (ibid.) that he 'would not rule out a priori that in certain contexts even scientific or philosophical hate speech is used in part to subordinate.'

    I should like to make two points about Altman's contribution. First, it may be that his particular way of expressing the relevant illocutionary act is less than optimal. To say that some instances of hate speech perform the act of *treating someone as a moral subordinate* could be to deemphasize at least one way in which hate speech is itself *subordinating*. Often, uses of hate speech do not merely treat members of certain groups as having a lower rank but actually make it the case that members of certain groups have a lower rank; to put it bluntly, some hate speech does not merely assume but performs an act of ranking. Second, I believe that it is central to subordination theory that the distinction between speech acts that subordinate and speech acts that do not subordinate cuts across other formal distinctions that are characteristic of some scholarship on freedom of expression. This means that the initial presumption should not be that describing, asserting, stating, arguing, and so forth do not constitute acts of subordination. Rather, the initial presumption should be that *any* type of speech act could amount to an act of subordination.
44. Note, I am influenced here by accounts of tacit consent in the theory of political authority (e.g., Simmons 1979: 81; Greenawalt 1987: ch. 5).
45. Interestingly, Maitra (2012: 116) herself acknowledges that whether or not people who remain silent in the presence of hate speakers can be accused of being '*complicit* in what the hate speaker does' depends on the weight we attach to 'concern for personal safety.' Yet she does not think to use this insight as a condition for licensing as I have sought to do.
46. Indeed, according to Mark Richard (2008: 1), '[w]hat makes a word a slur is that it is used to do certain things, that it has (in Austinian jargon) a certain illocutionary potential.'

*Principles of Basic Morality* 103

47. Of course, I am not the first to look to the work of Nussbaum and capability theory for sources of insights about free speech issues. Most notably, Gelber (2010, 2011, 2012a, 2012b) utilizes capability theory to build up a picture of the harms of hate speech vis-à-vis opportunities of speaking back. According to Gelber (21012a: 213), hate speech 'enacts harms that imperil the realization of central human functioning capabilities by, among other things, disempowering, marginalizing, and silencing.' Gelber puts an emphasis on those central capabilities that are involved with or implicated in the phenomenon of persons speaking back to hate speech. Because some hate speech 'can do bad things' in terms of blocking persons from speaking back (ibid.), 'there is a justification for some kind of policy response to it.' However, Gelber is skeptical as to the efficacy of a response characterized by legalistic restriction, limitation, and punishment, or, at least, she finds the evidence for this efficacy lacking. Instead she defends a 'speaking back policy', in which governmental agencies and officials assume responsibility for speaking back on behalf of the victim's of hate speech. I shall return to the reasons for Gelber's skepticism about the efficacy of traditional legalistic responses and for her alternative approach in Ch. 9 [9.3]. At this stage, I simply want to note the originality of Gelber's approach but also to flag the nature of my departure from it. While we are both agreed that some hate speech can undermine the exercise of central capabilities, I part company from Gelber about what the best policy response should be. I believe that the Principle of Non-Subordination captures an important truth about the N-warrant of hate speech law. And I utilize capability theory as a model for thinking about the rights and powers that are deprived by some uses of hate speech.
48. This list borrows from Nussbaum's list of ten central capabilities: life; bodily health; bodily integrity; senses, imagination, and thought; emotions; practical reason; affiliation; other species; play; and control over one's environment (e.g., Nussbaum 2000 78–80; 2011: 33–34). Moreover, I take a degree of inspiration from Wolff and de-Shalit's (2007: 37) concept of 'genuine opportunities for secure functionings' as well as from Nussbaum's (2011: 42–44, 145–146) tentative approval of that concept. However, whereas Wolff and de-Shalit focus on opportunities that do not require for their exercise the sacrifice of other functionings (genuine), and functionings that are not subject to threats or risks beyond the control of the agent (secure), I am particularly interested in the ways in which some uses of hate speech can render access irregular, unreliable, or coerced, not only by changing the target's psychological traits and behavioral dispositions but also by directly silencing the target by manipulating the sociolinguistic or pragmatic context of speech. Of course, when fear and insecurity play a role in depriving people of rights and powers in this sense, then there is significant overlap between the argument from subordination and the previously discussed argument from security [3.3].
49. Having said that, some of this research has also been challenged for overstating its case, such as by intimating that stereotype threat is singularly responsible for poor achievement (e.g., Sackett et al. 2004). Moreover, some recent studies have failed to replicate findings of stereotype threat in earlier studies (e.g., Ganley et al. 2013).
50. This phenomenon is echoed by research on the effects of hate crimes, where victims can report moving to an alternative neighborhood or simply trying to be less visible (e.g., Weiss et al. 1991–1992).
51. Langton (1993: 315) refers to this as 'illocutionary disablement.' She also expresses the idea by saying that the illocutionary act is metaphorically 'unspeakable', as in, even if the words can be spoken, the illocutionary act of withholding consent or refusing cannot be successfully performed.
52. This is captured in the following statement about the rationale for the right to freedom of expression made by delegates to the Continental Congress of

26 Oct. 1774: 'The importance of [the freedom of the press] consists [in] its ready communication of thoughts between subjects, and its consequential promotion of union among them, whereby oppressive officials are shamed or intimidated into more honorable and just modes of conducting affairs.' Available at: www.heritage.org/constitution/#!/amendments/1/essays/140/freedom-of-speech-and-of-the-press (last accessed 27/11/14).
53. For MacKinnon's more recent thinking about racist speech, see her (2012).
54. No. 5:11CV00134 (W.D.N.C.) (involving a lawsuit filed by EEOC on behalf of a large group of African American job applicants who had suffered discriminatory hiring practices and an implicit discriminatory hiring policy as evidenced by a high-level manager allegedly stating that he 'didn't want any [B]lacks on the dock'), at 1-2.
55. In an interesting departure from Langton's subordination theory and its focus on illocutionary acts, McGowan (2012: 132) claims that in order for the elderly white man's speech to possess 'exercitive force' it is *unnecessary* that it satisfies the necessary conditions of 'standard exercitive force': that the speaker intends to introduce permissibility-norms and that the other putative participants in the activity of racism are aware of this intention. She dubs (132–133, 137) this alternative, 'covert exercitive force'. Indeed, she claims (132n.20) that because covert exercitives operate independently of speaker intention and listener awareness of intention, they are neither perlocutionary nor illocutionary phenomena.
56. It is a question for the art of translation whether or not the English term 'human dignity' is the best rendering of the German expressions actually used by Kant: namely, 'Menschenwürde,' 'Würde der Menschheit,' 'innern Werth,' and 'absoluten Werth des Menschen.' Either way, analyzing the term 'human dignity' in terms of the concept of inherent value itself has the potential to obscure at least three distinct ideas found in Kant's work. The first is that human beings are valuable for their own sake or as ends in themselves. This means that they possess *final end value* as opposed to instrumental value (e.g., Kant [1785] 1948: 90–91). The second is that by virtue of being the bearers of rational nature (or some such ground of human dignity) human beings possess an *unconditional worth*. This worth does not depend on any prior qualifying status except for the rational nature (or some such ground) that is said to be characteristic of the human species: it does not depend on social position or inherited rank or nobility (i.e., social *dignities*); persons do not acquire it through their actions, achievements, qualities, or relations; a person can never lose his or her human worth so long as he or she remains a human being (e.g., Kant [1797] 1996: 210). The third idea is that as the bearers of the capacity for morality human beings possess not merely a worth or value but a value *beyond comparison*, which is a particular type of worth to be distinguished from mere price (e.g., Kant [1785] 1948: 96–97; [1797] 1996: 186).

Much attention has already been paid to the interplay between these ideas by Kantian scholars (e.g., Korsgaard 1996: 256–262; Wood 1999: 132–139), and it is not my intention to rehearse their insights. Instead, I shall simply assume for the sake of argument that it is theoretically possible to hold both that human beings possess final end value and that they possess unconditional value without at the same time subscribing to the further view that human beings carry a sort of value beyond comparison. I believe that this possibility may have implications for how we think about the respect that is owed to human dignity in matters of free speech. For, if it is the case that human beings do not carry a sort of value beyond comparison, this might suggest that it is possible to formulate balancing-act principles that strike a balance between human dignity and various other sorts of human goods. I shall explore this

## Principles of Basic Morality 105

possibility in Ch. 7. Indeed, it also opens up the possibility of compromise between principles of human dignity and other sorts of principles. I will examine this in Ch. 10.
57. Indeed, some scholars suggest that human dignity is liable to become more virulent as a source of limitations on the right to freedom of expression than as a justification for that right (e.g., Schauer 1992b: 178–184; Carmi 2007: 982).
58. 1 SCR 467 (involving the circulation of flyers containing a mixture of anti-homosexuality and homophobic messages).
59. At 505.
60. At 506.
61. At 506–507.
62. 2 KLs 503 17319/01 (Reg. Ct. Mann., 15 Mar.) (involving Holocaust denial).
63. For an account of other cases in Germany involving protection of the dignity of the dead, see Eberle (2002: 117–118n.102).
64. 1 StR 179/93 (Fed. Ct. Jus., 15 Mar.) (involving Holocaust denial).
65. 2 SCR 731 (involving Holocaust denial).
66. The Court also pointed to its overbreadth. I shall return to that finding in Ch. 9 [9.4].
67. At 763.
68. Ibid.
69. At 806–807.
70. 6 KLs 503 4/96 (Reg. Ct. Mann., 15 Feb.) (involving Holocaust denial).
71. Original text available at: http://dejure.org (last accessed 26/11/14).

# 4 Principles of Personal Development

The purpose of this chapter is to examine what can be said for and against hate speech law from the perspective of the human goods or values of personal development. My working hypothesis is that there is a positive relationship between personal development and the right to freedom of expression but that even freedom of expression may be regulated in order to uphold or safeguard real access to personal development for all. In the first two sections I look at intellectual and epistemic development, specifically the discovery of truth and the acquisition of knowledge. Here I question the assumption that personal development is only feasible within a constitutional regime that rules out *any* legalistic constraints on uses of hate speech. I do so pointing to the toxic effect of some uses of hate speech vis-à-vis the discovery of truth and the acquisition of knowledge. In the remaining sections I consider two broader aspects of personal development: namely, self-realization (which I take to be a matter of self-fulfillment, self-definition, and self-respect) and human excellence (which, I shall assume, has to do with developing and practicing virtues and avoiding vices). I shall try to show that while some laws/regulations/codes that constrain uses of hate speech may be at odds with self-realization and human excellence, others may be compatible with or even necessary for their protection and promotion.

## 4.1 THE DISCOVERY OF TRUTH

It might be thought that truth is indispensible to many things, but among them is surely personal development. Without access to true information, how can individuals develop themselves? Personal development is a highly complex and abstract notion, of course, and as such it can be taken to involve many different things. Rather than providing an overall definition of that concept, therefore, I shall simply focus on a number of things that I assume are constituent components of personal development. The first is the discovery of truth. Thus, I shall take it as read that to demonstrate the significance of freedom of expression to the discovery of truth is to demonstrate the significance of freedom of expression to personal development.

## Principles of Personal Development   107

As I understand it, the discovery of truth defense of freedom of expression is *partly* an argument for guaranteeing the unfettered exchange of information between trailblazers, visionaries, heretics, dissenters, and radicals. For those seeking to challenge the veracity of conventional beliefs collaboratively, free speech is essential. No doubt this is how *some* hate groups are apt to see themselves.[1] *In addition*, the truth defense of freedom of expression says that suppression of radical speech makes it harder for ordinary people to discover the truth. As Mill famously put it, '[i]f the opinion is right, they are deprived of the opportunity of exchanging error for truth' (Mill [1859] 1972: 85). On one version of the argument, 'the discovery and spread of truth on subjects of general concern [. . .] is possible only through absolutely unlimited discussion' (Chafee 1941: 31). But this does not appear to be Mill's version. Mill seems to be claiming not that it is literally impossible for ordinary people to exchange false opinions for true opinions without the opportunity for listening to radicals but rather that freedom of expression provides people with invaluable opportunities for exchanging error for truth. One might say, therefore, that the discovery of truth is more likely to thrive within a rich or diverse ecosystem of ideas. Or, to use Justice Holmes' mercantile metaphor, 'the ultimate good desired is better reached by free trade in ideas—that the best test of truth is the power of the thought to get itself accepted in the competition of the market'.[2] Putting aside what the metaphor of the marketplace might wrongly imply about the nature of truth,[3] and inherent problems with the metaphor itself,[4] the underlying principle seems to match what Mill was also getting at. Call it the Principle of Truth, that legalistic constraints on speech or other expressive acts, including constraints on uses of hate speech, are (N-)unwarranted if they deprive people of valuable opportunities for exchanging error for truth.[5]

Why is the discovery of truth so important? Some people might say that if one has to ask the question, something has already gone wrong. For, the discovery of truth is self-evidently valuable. Others seek to motivate the importance of the discovery of truth by emphasizing its process aspects: by uncovering the valuable human intellectual capacities that go into the discovery of truth (e.g., Marshall [W.] 1995). Even if one accepts that the discovery of truth possesses *final end value*, however, the question remains: why is the discovery of truth *so much more* important than other final end values? When pondering this question one cannot help but call to mind Willmoore Kendall's famous observation that Mill's great mistake was to assume that society is a 'debating-club, devoted above all to the pursuit of truth' (Kendall 1963: 112). At any rate, it is not difficult to think of counter-examples to the generalization that suppressing any speech, and thereby removing opportunities for exchanging truth for error, is *never* a price worth paying. Consider Scanlon's classic case of the misanthropic inventor who wishes to broadcast his household recipe for nerve gas on television (Scanlon 1972: 211).[6] Is the discovery of truth *really* more important than averting a nerve gas catastrophe? Or consider a different sort of example due to

Larry Alexander. 'Knowing what Tony Blair wears to bed is undoubtedly not worth the embarrassment the revelation might cause, even if unbridled expressions about it might converge on the truth of the matter in a short time' (Alexander 2005: 130). Is the discovery of truth *really* more important than personal dignity? Finally, an example of hate speech. Suppose a self-confessed Islamophobe intends to appear on a popular French television program in order to communicate various generics or negative stereotypes about Muslims, such as that "Muslims are criminals." He plans to achieve this with the help of the factually correct statistic that 65% of the French prison population is Muslim, while Muslims account for only 12% of the general population. While the Islamophobe's script includes some generics or negative stereotypes about Muslims that do not amount to statements of fact, it also contains an accurate statistic about the prison population. Since this statistic might be informative to some audience members, it is at least arguable that his script does fall under the umbrella of the Principle of Truth.[7] But is protecting the discovery of truth *really* more important than seeking to prevent the sort of discrimination, damage to property, violence, and so on, which is rendered more likely within a climate of hatred to which Islamophobic speech contributes?

Clearly, in order to answer these questions definitively we require some sort of measuring device to evaluate the weight of the different interests, rights, or values at stake (e.g., Schauer 1982: 17). Thus, in his recent work Schauer (2012) envisages what he calls 'a post-Millian calculus' that would enable us to balance the discovery of truth against various non-epistemic goods relating to dignity, security, and so on. I shall discuss this calculus in Ch. 8 [8.2]. In this section, however, I want to explore more fully a different response that could be made to the idea that legalistic constraints on uses of hate speech are N-unwarranted because they deprive people of the opportunity of exchanging error for truth. It is to disaggregate hate speech and to distinguish between those uses of hate speech that do and those uses of hate speech that do not constitute genuine opportunities for exchanging error for truth.

The Principle of Truth does not guarantee any uses of hate speech that do not amount to or do not contain statements of fact that possess truth conditions or that could be adjudged to be true or false by a competent thinker using established methods of evidence gathering and evaluation. If a law restricting such uses of hate speech existed, it would not run afoul of the Principle of Truth. Among the various clusters of laws/regulations/codes identified in Ch. 2, perhaps the most obvious cluster of law that would *not* run afoul of the Principle of Truth is law proscribing hate speech that constitutes group defamation (*sensu stricto*). Such law proscribes the public expression of false damaging statements of fact about members of protected groups or classes of persons. When the basis for the prohibition consists partly in the fact that the prohibited statements are false, no significant danger of depriving people of the opportunity of exchanging error for truth

## Principles of Personal Development    109

exists.[8] Of course, at this juncture it can be observed that falsehoods may yet have value when considered from the perspective of the acquisition of knowledge. In other words, when it comes to having justified true beliefs, it could be that exposure to false statements is a good thing. It is, as Mill famously put it, a matter of 'the clearer perception and livelier impression of truth, produced by its collision with error' (Mill [1859] 1972: 85). I shall return to that particular argument in the next section [4.2].

There is, however, a further complication. It is possible to interpret the Principle of Truth in more or less demanding ways based on the chance that the opinion being suppressed is true. In its most demanding form, the Principle says that the suppression of an opinion is N-unwarranted so long as there is *any* chance *whatsoever* of its being true. In its moderate form, it says that the suppression of an opinion is N-unwarranted only when the chance of its being true reaches a minimum threshold. The case for the moderate reading can be put thusly. If the rationale is to ensure that people have a reasonable opportunity of exchanging error for truth, it seems unnecessary to protect a statement that has only a tiny chance of being true. Schauer illustrates the point thusly: 'If I am prosecuted for selling as "Pure Orange Juice" a liquid containing only water, sugar, and artificial flavouring and colouring, it is not and should not be a defence that some extreme sceptics would be reluctant to exclude completely the possibility that we could be mistaken about when a liquid is orange juice and when it is something else' (Schauer 1982: 32–33). Surely we would want a prosecution for false advertising or mis-selling of pure orange juice to proceed even if there is a 1% chance that the expert witnesses are in fact mistaken about the produce not being pure orange juice. How might this logic apply to hate speech law? Take the case of criminal group defamation law (*sensu stricto*). Like criminal defamation law in general, the courts place the burden on the prosecution to prove beyond a reasonable doubt that an offense of defamation was committed.[9] The threshold of reasonable doubt concerns all elements of the offense of group defamation, including the element that says the statement made was false. And in practice it means that the prosecution need not prove that there is a 0% chance that the statement is false.

A similar sort of logic might also be applied to Holocaust denial law. The courts, I believe, could reasonably take the view that the probability of statements denying the Holocaust being true is so tiny that there is no genuine risk that by suppressing them the state is taking away genuine opportunities for exchanging error for truth. They could take this view not merely in relation to abstract statements claiming simply that the Holocaust never took place but also when it comes to more specific, nuanced, and convoluted propositions that challenge the conventional wisdom of mainstream historians (cf. Brown 2010: 866). These propositions might include: that the number of Jews killed by the Nazis is large but still a fraction of the 6 million that has been claimed; that the large amount of Jewish civilian displacement and death during the relevant period was the effect of excessive militarism and the disruption caused by the Allied advancement as opposed to anti-Semitism, much less a coordinated plan to exterminate the Jews; that there were no gas chambers in German concentration camps during the period; that there was nothing unique or historically exceptional about the killing of Jews in Nazi Germany; and that the suppression of these facts and the spreading of the Holocaust myth is largely the result of a Jewish conspiracy.[10] Perhaps these propositions are so unlikely to be true that they cannot claim protection under the Principle of Truth, given a moderate reading of the Principle.

So far, so plausible.[11] But now for a fly in the ointment. The moderate version of the Principle of Truth must be augmented with a judgment about where to set the threshold below which the probably of truth is too low for the speech to claim protection under the Principle. After all, there could be statements made by Holocaust deniers that carry a greater than infinitesimal probability of being true, if still only a very small probability. (Consider the proposition that until late in 1943 Hitler had been unaware of the true extent of the mistreatment and murder of the Jews, and at that stage he made reasonable efforts to minimize the excesses of his subordinates.) However, these sorts of judgments about thresholds are vulnerable to an instance of a familiar philosophical challenge known as the sorites paradox. If statements that only have a 1% chance of being true need not be protected against suppression because their being suppressed is perfectly compatible with giving people a reasonable chance of exchanging error for truth, and if adding 1% to the chance of a statement being true is not sufficient to show that it ought to be protected against suppression, then by an iteration of these premises one could end up being committed to the paradoxical conclusion that a statement with a 100% chance of being true also need not be protected against suppression. In order to avoid falling into this paradox (so the argument runs), we must protect virtually all statements against suppression since virtually all statements have some chance of being true, no matter how tiny. Putting all this a simpler way, since we have no reliable or uncontroversial means of knowing what percentage chance is the cutoff for acceptable suppression, it is better not to permit any suppression.

I should like to offer two replies to this argument. The first reply points out that there are dangers on both sides of the equation. Suppose courts permit virtually all statements simply because there is virtually always a tiny chance that they could turn out to be true. This precautionary approach results in the granting of permission to a good deal of spreading of false statements, and the circulation of falsehoods may turn out to be a hindrance to the discovery of truth. So if what matters ultimately is enabling people to exchange error for truth, perhaps what is required is the opposite precautionary approach: namely, working on the basis that a given statement is probably false and that permitting its expression could be harmful to the discovery of truth. This seems to have been the position advocated by Justice Dickson in *R. v. Keegstra*. In this case a public school teacher had been convicted of the criminal offense of willfully promoting hatred against an identifiable group having made a series of anti-Semitic statements to his students, including statements describing Jews as 'treacherous', 'subversive', 'sadistic', 'money-loving', 'power hungry', and 'child killers', and alleging that Jews had 'created the Holocaust to gain sympathy.' Justice Dickson offered this insight:

> Taken to its extreme, [the Principle of Truth] would require us to permit the communication of all expression, it being impossible to know with absolute certainty which factual statements are true, or which ideas obtain the greatest good. The problem with this extreme position, however, is that the greater the degree of certainty that a statement is erroneous or mendacious, the less its value in the quest for truth. Indeed, expression can be used to the detriment of our search for truth; the state should not be the sole arbiter of truth, but neither should we overplay the view that rationality will overcome all falsehoods in the unregulated marketplace of ideas. There is very little chance that statements intended to promote hatred against an identifiable group are true, or that their vision of society will lead to a better world. To portray such statements as crucial to truth and the betterment of the political and social milieu is therefore misguided.[12]

The second reply is that when it comes to the moderate version of the Principle of Truth, what matters is not merely the magnitude of probability of a statement being true but also the reason or epistemological basis for thinking that it has a chance of being true. Take the case of statements denying the Holocaust. One might think it wrong or inappropriate to protect Holocaust denial under the banner of the Principle of Truth if the *only* viable reason or epistemological basis for doubting personal testimonies relating to the Holocaust is philosophical doubt as to the veracity of all human sense perception. This, at least, is the view of Alan Haworth:

> I think readers will agree with me it is not a reason which will hold much appeal for historians, for Holocaust survivors, or for the relatives of victims. Nor should it. (Haworth 1998: 49)

Haworth does not pause to say why Cartesian doubt lacks appeal for such persons. But I suspect the problem stems from the fact that Descartes' method of doubt furnishes a generic reason to be skeptical that anything whatsoever has actually taken place out there in the world, whereas perhaps a more fitting reason for doubting a proposition rests on the nature of that proposition itself and the sorts of reasons we have for affirming it (cf. Brown 2010: 866). So, for example, it might be thought that Cartesian skepticism is unsuitable as grounds for doubting the Holocaust because it ignores the special nature of the evidence upon which knowledge of the Holocaust is based, including the personal testimony of survivors. Ironically, then, it may be more 'respectful' of the evidence surrounding the

## 112  Principles of Personal Development

Holocaust to rest the determination of whether or not the Principle of Truth extends its protection to statements denying the Holocaust upon the particular reasons we might have for supposing that such statements are in fact true. These reasons might include pointing to the potentially unreliable testimony of "partisan" witnesses or witnesses who have suffered severe trauma, or to the inherently unreliable nature of hearsay testimony, such as testimony by means of documentary films whose creators are no longer around (cf. Douglas 1995: 109). Of course, if these reasons for thinking that statements denying the Holocaust could be true turn out to be feeble in the face of the overwhelming corroborating evidence for the existence of the Holocaust,[13] then the probability of statements denying the Holocaust being true will be very small and could not claim protection under the Principle of Truth. Of course, these arguments may also be vulnerable to the sorites paradox. However, the current reply is essentially that wielding the sorites paradox is sophistic and debilitating to respectful epistemic judgment of probabilities. Try telling the survivors, loved ones, or descendants of the Holocaust, or any Jewish person for that matter, that the reason why the state is inclined to permit Holocaust denial is because as yet the state does not have a philosophically valid response to the sorites paradox. Not only that, of course, but one might also think that Holocaust denial legislation can be N-warranted on the basis of other principles, including the Principle of Human Dignity discussed in Ch. 3 [3.6].

Thus far the debate has focused on hate speech as a potential vehicle for truth discovery in general. It is worth reflecting for a moment, however, on a different argument that focuses on the discovery of truths about freedom of expression itself and other fundamentals of justice. One version of the argument says that banning hate speech could suppress valuable public debate about the meaning of free expression, including how to tackle the issue of hate speech, and about other forms of injustice suffered by the targets of hate speech (e.g., Downs 1985: 117–120; Strossen 2012: 382–383). Suppressing hate speech might be bad for citizens who would be denied opportunities for exchanging error for truth. Consider a situation in which hate speakers are permitted to talk in their own terms, which then promotes further questioning and discussion that reveals them for what they really are, and in turn reaffirms to people why freedom of expression is so valuable. Suppression could also be bad for authorities who may have less chance of arriving at correct laws or policies for dealing effectively with acts of discrimination and violence perpetrated against vulnerable groups. By permitting hate speech they come to learn more about the complex nature of the bigoted beliefs, attitudes, and feelings that are the root causes of some acts of discrimination and violence.

While I accept this argument may strike a chord with critics of hate speech law, I also think it is easily overcome. I do not, however, intend to dispute the empirical assumption that underpins the argument: namely, that permitting hate speech can spark a better public debate about the nature, value, and limits of free speech and about other forms of social injustice. Instead, I want to make these two critical points. The first is that it may be possible to make the same type of argument on behalf of other forms of speech that we do not think ought to be unregulated. Suppose for the sake of argument that permitting people to falsely shout "fire" in a crowded theater with intent to create unnecessary panic would improve the quality of public debate about free speech and specifically whether or not there should be laws banning people from falsely shouting "fire" in a crowded theater with intent to create unnecessary panic. No doubt it would give the victims a first-hand appreciation of the issues. Nevertheless, it would be strange to think that this argument could justify deregulating harmful speech. Second, it might just as easily be argued that banning hate speech can spark public debate about free speech and about hate speech law specifically. The public debate instigated by the ban could increase the chances of truth discovery, even with participants in that debate being debarred from utilizing hate speech.

Another version of the argument says that permitting racist hate speech has positive benefits for the discovery of facts about the prevalence of racism. For example, Strossen argues that racist hate speech on university campuses across the US 'undoubtedly [has] had the beneficial result of raising public consciousness about the underlying societal problem of racism' (Strossen 1990: 560). What is more, '[i]f these expressions had been chilled by virtue of university sanctions, then it is doubtful that there would be such widespread discussion on campuses, let alone more generally, about the real problem of racism' (ibid.). But once again it is not difficult to identify a hole in this argument. Surely few people would find persuasive an argument that said it is permissible not to prosecute cases of domestic violence for the sake of heightening the public's awareness of the true nature and extent of marital problems in society. Instead, they would argue that prosecutions should continue while relevant public authorities and other organizations find alternative, less harmful ways to enliven public debate about marital problems. The health of victims should not be sacrificed no matter if decriminalizing harmful acts somehow benefited public discourse on the subject (cf. Brink 2001: 142).

The Principle of Truth tells us when hate speech law is N-*unwarranted* because of the value of truth discovery. I now want to turn to another truth-based principle, one that tells us when hate speech law is N-*warranted* because of the value of truth discovery. According to the Nuanced Principle of Truth, as I shall dub it, legalistic constraints on uses of hate speech are (N-)warranted if they restrict speech or other expressive conduct that substantially hinders the discovery of truth. I offer two possible examples. The first is hate speech that rises to the level of group defamation (*sensu stricto*). The claim is not merely that engaging in such expression fails to provide conducive opportunities for exchanging error for truth but that engaging in it can create a genuine hindrance to the discovery of truth (cf. Sadurski 1999: 12; Brink 2001: 130). As Rhonda G. Hartman puts it, '[b]y making

## 114  *Principles of Personal Development*

little pretense toward persuasion but much toward prejudice, group defamatory hate speech [. . .] perpetrates falsehoods that serve only to impede the advancement for truth' (Hartman 1992: 858–859). Hartman does not elaborate upon the mechanics of this hindrance, but perhaps her idea is that finding out the truth about certain groups or classes of persons is harder when one first has to wade through a quagmire of lies and false rumors than if one begins with a blank page, so to speak.

The second example has to do with hate speech that amounts to discriminatory harassment. It is not uncommon for critics of campus speech codes to say that attempts to restrict discriminatory harassment invariably deny people opportunities for exchanging error for truth, especially in the classroom. It is quite possible (so they will argue) for a college professor or student to express complex ideas about the inferiority of certain racial/ethnic groups or complex ideas about the sinful nature of homosexual activity. And for the expression of these complex ideas to contain *both* true statements of fact that might be conducive to the discovery of truth of some audience members (e.g., statistics on average IQ results for different racial/ethnic groups or statistics on the rates of HIV AIDS among different groups in society) and words that university authorities might regard as disciplinable. However, there is a tendency for such critics to concentrate on the general audience and to fail to fully consider the discovery of truth of those members of the audience who are being cast as inferior or sinful. Campus speech codes are N-warranted (according to this counter argument) precisely because discriminatory harassment hinders the discovery of truth on the part of students who are its intended targets (e.g., Lawrence 1990: 436; Hartman 1992: 858).

Since the term 'campus speech code' covers a range of potentially very different regulations, it is worth reflecting on some concrete examples. Consider first the University of Michigan's *Policy on Discrimination and Discriminatory Harassment of Students* (1988).

> Any behavior, verbal or physical, that stigmatizes or victimizes an individual on the basis of race, ethnicity, religion, sex, sexual orientation, creed, national origin, ancestry, age, marital status, handicap or Vietnam-era veteran status, and that
>
> a. Involves an express or implied threat to an individual's academic efforts, employment, participation in University sponsored extra-curricular activities or personal safety; or
> b. Has the purpose or reasonably foreseeable effect of interfering with an individual's academic efforts, employment, participation in University sponsored extra-curricular activities or personal safety; or
> c. Creates an intimidating, hostile, or demeaning environment for educational pursuits, employment or participation in University sponsored extra-curricular activities.[14]

Part b. captures stigmatizing speech that has the 'purpose or reasonably foreseeable effect of interfering with an individual's academic efforts.' Arguably, a large proportion of this academic effort is oriented toward the discovery of truth. Consequently, it is possible that stigmatizing speech, which is guaranteed by the Principle of Truth insofar as it possesses truth conditions, would be rendered impermissible given the University of Michigan's definition of discriminatory harassment. The further suggestion is that the University of Michigan's speech code would be N-warranted under the Nuanced Principle of Truth.

Now consider Stanford University's *Fundamental Standard* or, more specifically, *Fundamental Standard Interpretation: Free Expression and Discriminatory Harassment* (1990).

> Speech or other expression constitutes harassment by personal vilification if it:
>
> a) is intended to insult or stigmatize an individual or a small number of individuals on the basis of their sex, race, color, handicap, religion, sexual orientation, or national and ethnic origin; and
> b) is addressed directly to the individual or individuals whom it insults or stigmatizes; and
> c) makes use of insulting or "fighting" words or non-verbal symbols.
>
> In the context of discriminatory harassment, insulting or "fighting" words or non-verbal symbols are those "which by their very utterance inflict injury or tend to incite to an immediate breach of the peace," and which are commonly understood to convey direct and visceral hatred or contempt for human beings on the basis of their sex, race, color, handicap, religion, sexual orientation, or national and ethnic origin.[15]

Part c) associates harassment by personal vilification with the use of insulting or fighting words. Some people argue that such words do not merely lack truth conditions but are an active impediment to the discovery of truth on the part of the people to whom they are directed (e.g. Lawrence 1990: 452; Brink 2001: 140). This might occur if, say, the words trigger a psychological self-preservation mechanism, the fight or flight response. In such an eventuality, the emotional impact of hate-based insulting or fighting words, namely, distress, humiliation, fear, or rage, consume the addressee's attention, making the discovery of truth the furthest thing from his or her mind. Consequently, the use of insulting or fighting words would not be guaranteed by the Principle of Truth and would be subject to disciplinary action under Stanford University's definition of discriminatory harassment. Moreover, Stanford University's speech code would be N-warranted under the Nuanced Principle of Truth.

116  *Principles of Personal Development*

Having said all that, determining the overall warrant of campus speech codes requires an all principles considered assessment of the aforementioned truth-based principles along with various other legal principles that animate judicial interpretations of the constitutional right to freedom of expression. Interestingly, Sunstein maintains that the University of Michigan's speech code is a 'broad ban' that 'forbids a wide range of statements that are part of the exchange of ideas' (Sunstein 1993b: 815; see also his 1993a: 198), but he asserts that Stanford University's speech code 'is quite narrowly defined' and focused upon speech that does *not* contribute to the exchange of ideas (1993b: 816). It strikes me, however, that both speech codes prohibit speech acts of a complex nature (either conjunctively or disjunctively complex), and that both speech codes could potentially prohibit speech that conveys the speaker's ideas as well as his or her contempt. Consider this hypothetical rant directed at a female student by a male student: "God damn you bitch, just shut up a listen to me, because you know there's a reason why God made you weaker and dumber, that's so everyone knows what role they are supposed to play, so run along back home to your father's house and do your duty like a grateful daughter, because Lord knows I don't know why you're even here, you're turning everything upside down." It strikes me that this example of speech could have run afoul of both the University of Michigan's and Stanford University's speech codes, and that it not only exhibits many of the familiar tropes of discriminatory harassment (stigmatizing, derogatory, demeaning, or humiliating face-to-face speech motivated by prejudice, bigotry, or hatred of its target) but also contains ideas (e.g., patriarchalism, filial duty, theology of gender). In any event, both speech codes were ultimately struck down as unconstitutional with respect to the First Amendment. In *Doe v. University of Michigan* and *Corry v. Stanford* the courts held that these campus speech codes swept up protected as well as unprotected speech and that they lapsed into vagueness in some of their parts, providing students with insufficient guidance as to what is and what is not disciplinable. I shall return to these issues in Ch. 9 [9.4].

## 4.2   THE ACQUISITION OF KNOWLEDGE

Naturally there is more to personal development than truth discovery; even sticking within the realm of epistemic human goods, there are many valuable activities and practices that go into the acquisition of knowledge. This line of thought intertwines with the second key strand of Mill's famous defense of free speech: namely, that even if the opinions being suppressed are wrong, members of the potential audience still 'lose, what is almost as great a benefit, the clearer perception and livelier impression of truth, produced by its collision with error' (Mill [1859] 1972: 85). What Mill was getting at is the idea that there is something of inherent worth in the 'manner' in which our beliefs are held and not simply in the holding of true beliefs. This manner involves acquiring knowledge or justified true belief (as it has come to be defined within epistemology). What is more, for Mill, epistemic justification is dependent upon on having been confronted with, and providing answers to, opposing opinions. In short, the legalistic suppression of false opinions reduces opportunities for *a form of* Socratic dialectic: coming to *know* that which is true by 'exposing the contradictions and muddles of an opponent's position' (Blackburn 1996: 104). Or, as Mill puts it, in the absence of collision with error we cannot expect individuals to develop the enthusiasm necessary to ascend 'to something of the dignity of thinking beings' (Mill [1859] 1972: 102).

I am particularly interested in a general principle that is implied by the second key strand of Mill's famous defense of free speech. According to what I shall call the Principle of Knowledge, legalistic constraints on speech or other expressive acts, including constraints on uses of hate speech, are (N-)unwarranted if they obstruct the acquisition of knowledge. Among other things, this means that even specious racist statements should not be suppressed if doing so would obstruct the acquisition of knowledge. Consider: "Every single one of the Jews living in this town is either directly involved or complicit in the widespread practice of kidnapping and murdering the children of Christians for the purposes of using their blood for Jewish rituals and holidays." It is not inconceivable that exposure to this defamatory rumor could encourage critical reflection on whether or not there are *any* hidden cases of child abuse in the town (whatever the background of the perpetrators) and on the values that Jews and Christians have in common when it comes to the importance of child protection. This might happen if the statement sparks an exchange of information and ideas between Jews and Christians that leads both communities to redouble their commitment to uncovering hidden cases of child abuse in the town and to clearly articulate their shared theological, cultural, and moral commitments to child protection. As Steven Shiffrin puts it, even racist speech 'may contribute to "the clearer perception and livelier impression of truth, produced by its collision with error"' (Shiffrin [S.H.] 1999: 78). This means, for example, that criminal laws proscribing group defamation (*sensu stricto*) might be N-unwarranted under the Principle of Knowledge even though they are not ruled out by the Principle of Truth.

However, there is a well-known problem with Mill's understanding of knowledge, which should not be ignored, since it has implications for what the Principle of Knowledge might say about hate speech law. As stated earlier, Mill appears to assume that a sort of dialectic is a necessary condition of knowledge. But that assumption is controversial. It is arguable that even if opposing opinions are suppressed, individuals can still manage to acquire justified true beliefs based upon either direct familiarity with the evidence or reasonable reliance on professionals who themselves have direct familiarity with the evidence, where the gathering and evaluation of evidence utilizes widely accepted norms or standards. As Geoffrey Marshall puts it, '[w]e have at the moment rational assurance that the earth is roundish in shape from photographs produced by astronauts, and we should still have it if the Flat Earth Society were an illegal organization' (Marshall [G.] 1971: 158).[16] Following this broader, evidence-based understanding of knowledge, it seems feasible that ordinary people could possess true beliefs about certain events, events that are the subject of denial by hate speakers (e.g., the Holocaust), but do *not* need to be exposed to the contradictions and muddles of the hate speaker's opposing position in order for these beliefs to reach a level of epistemic justification sufficient for knowledge. This is because ordinary people may have first-hand experience of the events in question or direct access to witness accounts of people with first-hand experience or access to evidence uncovered by well-respected historians. Knowledge that the Holocaust occurred might well be of this order. If this rival account of knowledge is accurate, it means that Holocaust denial laws are not necessarily N-unwarranted by the Principle of Knowledge. Of course, the same goes for law proscribing group defamation (*sensu stricto*).

Having said that, it might be argued on Mill's behalf that what really counts in favor of the right to freedom of expression is that people develop their epistemic virtues to the best of their ability, that they endeavor to rise to the dignity of thinking beings. Although there is a sense in which someone could acquire knowledge of the Holocaust without ever consulting radical, opposing opinions on the subject, if they did so, they would not be realizing the full extent of their powers of critical reflection. They would not have acted in an epistemically virtuous way, as a matter of personal epistemic justification. And so, for Mill, suppressing opinions might not hinder all aspects of epistemic personal development, but it will certainly hinder some aspects, and aspects that matter. As J.K. Miles puts it, '[c]ensorship prevents individuals from justifying their opinions precisely because it prevents them from applying the practices of justification to the strongest arguments against their position' (Miles 2012: 223). This line of reasoning may be applied not just to hate speakers but also to those wishing to respond to hate speech either on their own behalf or on behalf of others. Consider the words of Jeanne Craddock.

> Through the active, engaging, and often relentless debate on issues of social and political concern, holders of minority opinions learn the strengths of their own arguments and the weaknesses of their opponents'. With this knowledge, these groups are better able to strike at the heart of a bigoted argument with all of the fervor and force necessary to combat hateful ideas. (Craddock 1995: 1089)

However, can this argument be made to work for all hate speech, even hate speech composed of false statements of fact damaging to reputation? It is worth delving a little deeper into the connection between the spreading of false rumors and the acquisition of knowledge. In the previous section I took into consideration the idea that group defamation (*sensu stricto*) could be a hindrance to the discovery of truth. Might the same be said for certain forms of hate speech and their relationship to the acquisition of knowledge, even on the broader, confronting-counter-evidence-based understanding of

## Principles of Personal Development 119

knowledge? According to Schauer, a major part of Mill's grounds for playing down the potential harmfulness of the free dissemination of false beliefs is his unbridled optimism or confidence that the collision of true belief with specious beliefs will invariably result in the triumph of truth over falsehood (Schauer 2012: 139).[17] Schauer regards this confidence with some incredulity—describing it as 'quaint' (140). '[T]he persistence of so many so-called urban legends is a valuable caution against assuming too quickly that truth is a highly effective remedy against false belief' (ibid.). For example, people who defend Holocaust denial law on the grounds of the harmful consequences of permitting the dissemination of Holocaust denial material (e.g., the argument from a climate of hatred, the argument from human dignity) do so precisely because they recognize the fact that 'belief that the Holocaust never occurred persists in the face of overwhelming and widely accessible evidence to the contrary' (142). Schauer seems to be assuming that the resistance of false beliefs to falsification involves a process by which people are confronted with widely accessible evidence to the contrary and continue to believe as they do. But this might not be an entirely accurate picture of the circumstances surrounding belief in the non-existence of the Holocaust. It seems to me that the work of Sunstein (2007) offers a more plausible hypothesis: that people who believe that the Holocaust never occurred are often people who regularly and exclusively look at Holocaust denial and other hate group websites. They exist within these deliberative conclaves such that they simply choose not to look at sites that present a more comprehensive range of evidence or present the evidence in a different light, and are not encouraged to do so by the sites they do look at. What access they do have to evidence that could potentially contradict their beliefs is mediated by the sites they are familiar with—sites that partially select, edit, or omit evidence for the existence of the Holocaust in order to present the opposing position in its weakest possible light. The corollary of these observations is that some uses of hate speech involve the editing and repackaging of evidence such that the audience is unable to form justified true beliefs based on complete information.

Recall that the Principle of Knowledge states that legalistic constraints on free speech are (N-)unwarranted if they obstruct the acquisition of knowledge. It is not difficult to imagine a different knowledge-based principle that takes the current problem more seriously. According to what I shall call the Nuanced Principle of Knowledge, legalistic constraints on uses of hate speech are (N-)warranted if they target speech or other expressive conduct that substantially obstructs the acquisition of knowledge, such as through the circulation of partial or misinformation. I believe that this alternative principle might justify, in educational settings for example, rules governing the content of school curricula, the selection of teaching materials, and the presentation of facts and issues to students—rules designed to ensure that lessons always provide students with a variety of viewpoints. Enforcement of these rules would prevent rogue teachers from exposing pupils to one-sided, biased agendas or ideologies in the teaching of the subject of the Holocaust, for example (e.g.,

120  *Principles of Personal Development*

Cohen-Almagor 2008). This principle may even justify internet regulators (independent internet regulators or regulators working at the behest of internet service providers) imposing special time, place, and manner restrictions on agents responsible for creating and maintaining Holocaust denial websites. For example, regulators might force agents to place in prominent positions links to other websites detailing all of the available evidence supporting the existence of the Holocaust, or forcing them to declare whenever they have partially selected, edited, or omitted evidence.[18] This echoes calls made by some politicians, pressure groups, and scholars in the US for the reinstantiation of federal restrictions on the manner in which talk radio stations may address controversial social issues, making it mandatory for any broadcasters who exploit hate speech to attack minority groups to also present opposing views (e.g., Delgado and Stefancic 2004: 159–170; Cortese 2006: 96–97).

Now it might be objected that defending the regulation of Holocaust denial websites based on the fact that some individuals may be deterred from gathering complete information as a result of being bound up in particular informational enclaves, is appealing to the lowest common denominator. Putting it another way, to allow the existence of a relatively small number of narrow-minded individuals to become a supporting premise in an argument that justifies censorship of false statements of fact or misleading presentations of evidence, despite the fact that these statements and presentations could help to bring about a clearer and livelier perception of the truth among a more enlightened, intellectually curious majority, is to embrace a *numbskull's veto*. The Nuanced Principle of Knowledge need not concern itself with the knowledge acquisition of individuals who choose to look at Holocaust denial websites (so the objection runs) precisely because such individuals access these websites of their own volition, often because they are already minded to think that the Holocaust was probably a hoax, and are perfectly free to look at other, mainstream websites, on which can be found a comprehensive inventory of evidence clearly demonstrating that the Holocaust did in fact take place. However, it should not be overlooked that people responsible for Holocaust denial websites might exert an undue influence over users, even users who choose to enter these sites. For, those responsible for these sites could be undermining the integrity of users' mental processes by exploiting false statements of fact or misleading presentations of evidence, or could be circumventing cognitive channels of persuasion by taking advantage of users' emotional need to feel part of a group. These observations about autonomy—see also Ch. 3 [3.2]—may render the point about volition moot.

## 4.3 SELF-REALIZATION

The *locus classicus* of the self-realization defense of free speech is a passage from the work of Thomas Emerson which begins '[the right to freedom of expression] derives from the widely accepted premise of Western thought that the proper end of man is the realization of his character and potentialities as a human being' (Emerson 1963: 879). The take-home message is not simply that free speech is an indispensable means to self-realization but that self-realization is exactly the sort of value upon which a constitutional guarantee of free speech can, and should, be based.[19] What is more, Samuel P. Nelson is not atypical in thinking that the self-realization defense of free speech is particularly relevant to domains in which the realization of self is most conspicuous, such as in the domains of artistic or dramatic speech (e.g., Nelson 2005: 62). This is contrasted with commercial speech, for instance, where there is 'no self to realize or to develop' (84). The case of political speech is more complex. 'Everyday political speech motivated by self-interest [. . .] may not contribute to self-realization' (ibid.). In contrast, 'political expression is important to the self-realization of those for whom politics takes the form of active engagement in public life' (85).[20]

Now it might be thought that focusing on artistic or dramatic speech has the effect of turning hate speech into an outlier category as far as the self-realization defense of free speech is concerned. But this is not necessarily true. For, as Marjorie Heins has argued, '[h]ate-filled or degrading epithets can be a powerful part of artistic or dramatic expression' (Heins 1983: 590). If satirical speech ought to be protected for the sake of self-realization, for example, surely the same applies to satirical hate speech or hate-satire. The point being that anti-Semitic or Islamophobic satire (e.g., Louis-Ferdinand Céline's book *Trifles for a Massacre*, Kurt Westergaard's cartoons of the prophet Muhammad, Geert Wilders' short film *Fitna*, Sacha Baron Cohen's feature film *The Dictator*, Dieudonné's comic performances) contains no less realization of creative capacities than any form of satire. Even putatively scientific forms of hate speech (e.g., Fred A. Leuchter's *The Leuchter Report*) involve the realization of at least some distinctively human capacities, if only the capacity for pseudoscience. Indeed, Post argues that '[a]ny communication can potentially express the racist self', and thus a law that sought to 'suppress racist manifestations of racist personality' would leave no category of speech untouched (Post 1991: 270). So, according to what I shall call the Principle of Self-Realization, legalistic constrains on speech or other expressive acts, including constraints on uses of hate speech, are (N-)unwarranted if they significantly impede self-realization.

The purpose of this section is not to undermine this principle directly. Rather, I wish to defend its supplementation with a second principle. The rationale for the second principle can be captured with a simple question. Assuming that self-realization is a fundamental human value, why should constitutional essentials guarantee even speech that has no value vis-à-vis self-realization or that embodies the self-realization of some people at the expense of the self-realization of others? According to the Nuanced Principle of Self-Realization, as I shall label it, legalistic constraints on uses of hate speech are (N-)warranted if the hate speech in question fails to embody values of self-realization or if the imposition of constraints is necessary for the sake of protecting or promoting real access to self-realization for all. In order to fully explain the Nuanced Principle of Self-Realization, however, I need to distinguish between three distinct dimensions or aspects of self-realization, albeit interconnected in practice.[21] I contend that each dimension puts pressure on the simplistic notion that permitting hate speech is good for self-realization.

## Self-Fulfillment

The first aspect of self-realization is self-fulfillment, which is nothing less than the fulsome development of our potential capacities as human beings. To say that freedom of expression is indispensible to self-realization in this sense is to say that the development and exercise of a range of distinctively human capacities, such as thinking, feeling, communicating, imagining, culture building, and so on, would be practically impossible, if not inconceivable, without freedom of expression given the expressive nature of the human capacities in question. Even ostensibly internal capacities, such as thinking, feeling, and imagining, require freedom of expression. For starters, we often think, feel, and imagine via the external articulation of thoughts, feelings, and ideas (e.g., Gilmore 2011: 531–533). What is more, few complex thoughts, feelings, and ideas originate entirely in our own minds. Typically, we learn about their constituent parts through dialogue with others (e.g., Nelson 2005: 65).[22]

At first glance, the claim that free speech is necessary for the development of distinctively human capacities would appear to have a wide scope, as wide as the range of capacities that can be distinctively human. Yet on closer inspection it is not clear that respecting the value of self-fulfillment requires granting a privileged status to *all* capacities. Consider Emerson's assertion that the proper end of man is the realization of his character and potentialities as a human being. The term 'character' can be understood in different ways. Alan Gewirth, for example, has recently portrayed self-fulfillment as a matter of 'carrying to fruition one's deepest desires or one's worthiest capacities' (Gewirth 2009: 3). The inclusion of one's deepest desires within the account of self-fulfillment would certainly shed light on Heins' intriguing statement that 'even within Emerson's framework, gutter language, including racially-charged gutter language, is not wholly unrelated to "individual self-fulfillment"' (Heins 1983: 590). But the mere fact that it is possible to make sense of Heins' statement does not make it any less controversial. For, as Delgado argues, even if it is possible that 'she means that some persons derive pleasure from browbeating blacks and other minorities', 'it seems unlikely that this is self-fulfillment envisioned by Emerson and other first amendment theoreticians' (Delgado 1983: 594). After all, the strong desire of hate speakers to browbeat their targets soon butts up against the equally strong desire of their targets not to be browbeaten. Moreover, it is not clear that achieving self-fulfillment, or semipermanent potentialities of the self, is intended to be a matter of satisfying transient, perhaps pathological pleasures.

Indeed, it might be argued that true self-realization rests upon the development of not just any distinctively human capacities but instead the development of *virtuous* qualities. I shall say much more about personal development through the cultivation of virtues in the final section of this chapter [4.4]. But to briefly anticipate the nature of that argument, I would rephrase Delgado's argument using the following question. What aspects of good character or which ethical virtues could be promoted by allowing people to publicly express their hatred of other races through the use of racist insults, slurs, or derogatory epithets or through the dissemination of ideas based on the inferiority of other races? If the answer to that question is "none" or "far fewer then would be promoted by not allowing it", then this may lend support to laws/regulations/codes that disallow this sort of public expression of hatred.

## Self-Definition

A second aspect of self-realization—call it self-definition—has to do with 'the affirmation of self', as Emerson puts it, a matter of someone finding 'his meaning and his place in the world' (Emerson 1963: 879). The capacity for self-definition is itself a distinctive human capacity, of course, but it is also a capacity with special functions. Among other things, self-definition helps us to make sense of why we develop, possess, and exercise the distinctive human capacities we do. For, it is partly as a result of thinking, feeling, communicating, imagining, culture building, and so on, that we come to make it clear to ourselves and to others who we really are. No doubt the relationship also works in the other direction, so that an individual's emerging self-definition can shape his or her decisions to concentrate on some capacities rather than others. Self-definition depends on free speech both directly and indirectly. Without free speech the development and exercise of the human capacities upon which self-definition is predicated would be practically impossible. Freedom of expression is also important for explicit acts of self-definition, such as when we tell other people who we are by telling them about what we can do.[23]

But consider forms of self-definition that attack the self-definition of others. Take the hate speaker who denies the personhood of others with such statements as, "Think about 9/11, think about what they did, and you will see that Muslims are not like us, they are animals, not human." Does this denial constitute a violation of the right to self-definition of Muslims? Heyman argues that it does (drawing on the work of Hegel). When confronted by other human beings (so Heyman's reading of Hegel goes), we suffer a crisis of personhood and we look for ways of asserting ourselves *to others*. We find property wanting in this regard and so we turn to language (Heyman 2008: 54, 172). We might, for example, declare to others, "I am a person." On Heyman's analysis, when people assert themselves by denying the personhood of others, this amounts to the non-recognition of personhood (54). He cites the case of hate speakers who deny the humanity or affirm the subhuman status of certain groups of persons (274n.33). For Heyman, the mere fact that such speakers might be simultaneously affirming their own personhood or self-definition as white supremacists or anti-Semites, for example, would not be sufficient to excuse the fact that they are violating the rights of others to their personhood or self-definition (172).

In response to Heyman, it might be argued that the right to self-definition extends only as far as the right to express one's identity; it does not extend so far as to disallow other people the right to make public statements the propositional content of which denies core aspects of one's identity (e.g., that one is human). That is taking the right too far. I find this response to Heyman marginally persuasive. Nonetheless, I also think that there are other sorts of cases in which hate speakers *do* impede other people from exercising their own right to expressive self-definition. Suppose some university students are members of an on-campus, conservative religious group and claim an entitlement to condemn, criticize, and admonish whichever students they perceive to be gay or lesbian, whenever they see fit, and whether or not the university authorities classify this as discriminatory harassment. They argue that they are simply using speech to work through a self-conception based on their religious beliefs, where being a true believer (as they conceive it) means partaking in vehement face-to-face condemnation of suspected gays and lesbians and attempting to teach such people the error of their ways through the recitation of scripture. It seems to me that if their speech disables, discourages, or hinders members of targeted groups from asserting their own self-definition, perhaps by silencing such locutions as "I am gay and proud of it", this would constitute a failure to achieve real access to self-realization for all. As such, university authorities would be N-warranted in intervening (cf. Heyman 2008: 182).

To say that the Nuanced Principle of Self-Realization N-warrants restrictions on hate speech for the sake of the victims of hate speech is not to say that it unfairly discriminates against hate speakers. On the contrary, the Principle is concerned with achieving real access to self-realization for all. The working assumption is that hate speakers do not strictly need to engage in hate speech in order to achieve access to self-definition, since they are free to use a range of other words to similar effect. But when hate speech rises to the level of silencing its victims—and I do not mean to suggest that everything that could be called "hate speech" will be capable of doing this— then characteristically this has an all-embracing effect, blocking several means and avenues of expressive self-definition. In this event, intervention is N-warranted to restore real access to self-definition for all (i.e., for hate speakers and their victims alike). Therefore, rather than pitting the value of self-realization against other constitutional values, the present argument is internal to the value of self-realization unless, of course, real access for all is deemed to constitute an independent value. It is a matter of guaranteeing each student's access to self-realization compatible with similar access for all (e.g., Lange 1990: 128; Gale 1991: 164).

## Self-Respect

If self-definition has to do with a generalized practice of finding one's meaning and one's place in the world, a third aspect of self-realization—call it self-respect—involves attempts to affirm the self as something good or worthy of approval. The relationship between self-respect and free speech is once again multidimensional. Attitudes that individuals form about their own capacities and persona will depend partly on what approval they receive from other people. If those other people are not permitted to speak, this removes one potential source of self-respect. What is more, the very fact that other people are prepared to listen to what individuals have to say, including what they have to say using their capacities, and about their capacities, can bolster their sense of themselves as being valuable. Suppression of speech would also undercut these processes. Indeed, Meir Dan-Cohen argues that our self-respect may depend on our thinking of ourselves, and having others think of ourselves, as the types of beings who are strong enough and self-aware enough to be able to listen to "home truths" about who we are, even if critical and uncomfortable to listen to. That hate speech can be hurtful is part of the reason why it should *not* be banned, for the simple fact that the willingness to listen to hate speech that contains useful, albeit critical, information about ourselves bespeaks or indicates a certain sort of self-respect (Dan-Cohen 2002: 189). Nevertheless, it seems reasonable to suppose that not all hate speech can deliver useful information or "home truths." Consider hate speech that comprises false statements of fact or blunt expressions of revilement or enmity and, therefore, no useful information to speak of. What is more, as discussed in Ch. 3, even hate speech that does contain "home truths" may, in the case of prolonged or cumulative exposure, tend to undermine the self-respect of its intended targets. In these cases exposure to hate speech does not evince a feeling of self-respect that one is the sort of person who can hear bad things about oneself without falling apart, but instead produces emotions of self-hatred, especially when the victim internalizes the negative perception of who he or she is. For some theorists, these effects are a powerful reason to defend hate speech law (e.g., Delgado 1982: 137; Lawrence 1987: 351; Anderson 1995: 201). What we have, then, is a scorecard on which hate speech scores plusses and minuses for self-respect.

Interestingly, Thompson (2012) argues that banning incitement to hatred can be a justified way of safeguarding a positive attitude toward self on the part of those people against whom hatred is being stirred up. Drawing on Axel Honneth's theory of recognition,[24] Thompson affirms that one of the prerequisites for developing a positive attitude toward self is the recognition by others that the capacities one has developed or is in the process of realizing are valued by the rest of society. According to Honneth, social esteem has to do with 'the degree of recognition the individual earns for his or her form of self-realization by thus contributing, to a certain extent, to the practical realization of society's abstract goals' (Honneth 1995: 126). 'Once confronted with an evaluation that downgrades certain patterns of self-realization, those who have opted for these patterns cannot relate to their mode of fulfillment as something invested with positive significance within their community' (1992: 191). Thompson concludes from this that 'for Honneth, being esteemed should be understood negatively: it is the opportunity to be valued which exists when one's identity is not ridiculed or one's achievements scorned' (Thompson 2012: 225–226). Based on the premises that everyone's self-realization matters equally, that being esteemed is a precondition of adequate self-realization, and that the protection of self-realization may therefore N-warrant limitations on free speech, Thompson concludes that the UK government was justified in extending law banning incitement to racial hatred to include incitement to religious hatred. As he puts it, one 'reason for criminalizing incitement to religious hatred would be to combat the collective denigration of particular religious groups, since such denigration undermines the opportunities for their members to be esteemed for their contributions to society's collective goals, and this in turn undermines their opportunities for self-realization' (228).

There is much to commend in Thompson's argument, but I would also argue that it contains two important omissions. First, Thompson is vague about the exact nature of the barriers to individual self-realization created by hate speech. It seems to me that the barriers could be *internal* and *external*. If, as a result of being exposed to hate speech, someone has a low opinion of the capacities that partly define his personality, it may be natural for him to be less inclined to devote the requisite time and effort to developing those capacities to their fullest extent. Doing so may seem pointless, and its seeming so constitutes an internal or psychological barrier to self-realization. On the other hand, when a society has a low opinion of the capacities that partly define the personality of an entire group or class of persons, then society may inevitably deny the space, time, and money that such people need in order to develop their capacities to the fullest extent. This might include denying them platforms to communicate their beliefs, opinions, and ideas through the media; removing sources of funding to build their culture; and/or limiting the moments in which they can express their affective states in important contexts such as schools, workplaces, and parliaments. This is an external or social barrier to self-realization. Suppose it were possible to break down the internal or psychological barriers with the help of special cognitive therapy or counseling. Would this innovation render law banning incitement to hatred redundant on Thompson's view?

Second, Thompson's exclusive focus on law banning incitement to hatred, and the UK Racial and Religious Hatred Act 2006 in particular, appears unmotivated. According to s. 29B(1) of the Act, '[a] person who uses threatening words or behaviour, or displays any written material which is threatening, is guilty of an offence if he intends thereby to stir up religious hatred.' The fact that the offense is restricted to 'threatening' modes of expression as opposed to insult, derision, and denigration creates a disconnect between the actual law Thompson defends and his claim that one 'reason for criminalizing incitement to religious hatred would be to combat the collective denigration of particular religious groups.' Thompson is aware of this disconnect and his response is to say that he does not support the Act as it stands. Instead, he defends a modification; that 'the offence should refer to words and behaviour which are intended to incite hatred, in whatever tone or manner they are delivered' (Thompson 2012: 220). But then why stop there? If the core of the argument from positive relation to self is plausible, then surely it would also lend strong support to several other clusters of laws/regulations/codes that constrain uses of hate speech. Consider laws/regulations/codes that proscribe group defamation (*sensu stricto*), laws/regulations/codes that limit speech or other expressive conduct when it amounts to negative stereotyping or stigmatization of groups or classes of persons identified by certain ascriptive characteristics, and even laws/regulations/codes that disallow the public expression of hatred toward members of protected groups, including through the use of insults, slurs, or derogatory epithets or through the dissemination of ideas based on the inferiority of protected groups. So, the second omission is an account of the scope of the argument, not the least of which is an indication of where to draw the line between those clusters of laws/regulations/codes that the approach does N-warrant and those it does not—assuming, that is, the approach draws a line.

## 4.4 HUMAN EXCELLENCE

In this final section of the chapter I focus on the idea of personal development through the cultivation of human excellence, and on the idea that the proper role of lawmakers and legal professions is not simply to exemplify aspects of human excellence in their decision-making but also to create laws that promote aspects of human excellence among the population. There are, of course, many different ways of understanding the nature of human excellence, but one natural place to begin is with Aristotle's conception of *eudaimonia*, which is a matter of living a life of reason-governed virtue within a political community. What is more, in both Aristotle's *Ethics* and *Politics*, we find that legitimate constitutions, just laws, and right-acting magistrates are directed toward the promotion of human excellence. Some law *facilitates* doing and living well—for example, law relating to currency, exchange, contract, and gift giving enable the realization of virtues in the sphere of getting and spending, not the least of which are the virtues of liberality (*eleutheriotes*) and magnificence (*megaloprepeia*) (Aristotle [c. 350 BC] 1976: 104, 142–145,

149–152). Other law *discourages* doing and living badly—for example, Aristotle claims that 'there is nothing which the legislator should be more careful to drive away than indecency of speech' (Aristotle [c. 340 BC] 1996: 193). Since I have adopted principles as the primary units of analysis throughout this book, some might question the possibility of taking an aretaic turn. If virtue ethics and virtue jurisprudence in particular are focused on the good agent rather than the good action, how can principles tell us what constitution drafters, supreme court justices, trial court judges, legislators, policymakers, and regulators should or should not do in given situations? However, I follow the lead of Rosalind Hursthouse (1999) in supposing that principles (or what she terms 'v-rules') can be part of the normal vocabulary of virtue ethics. Of course, there are philosophers who will insist that the adoption of Hursthousean principles has no place within virtue ethics properly understood.[25] But my central focus is not excavating virtue ethics but in working through what a human excellence-centered approach to hate speech law might look like. Consequently, in what follows I shall concentrate on what I call the Principle of Human Excellence, that legalistic constraints on uses of hate speech are (N-)warranted if the lawmakers and legal professionals who are responsible for creating them not only display human excellence in their decision-making but also promote human excellence through the creation of these constraints.

As with other principles, I believe that the application of the Principle of Human Excellence to dilemmas posed by hate speech law is improved by de-homogenizing the latter. Robert P. George's book *Making Men Moral* (1993) is a good illustration of the failure to do so. In it he defends a virtue-centered approach to jurisprudence according to which 'sound politics and good law *are* concerned with helping people to lead morally upright and valuable lives, and, indeed, that a good political society may justly bring to bear the coercive power of public authority to provide people with some protection from the corrupting influence of vice' (George 1993: 20). Based on this, George argues that '[s]omeone who appreciates the human values served by free speech should be unwilling to authorize content-based restrictions on speech unless [. . .] the speech to be restricted is not the sort of speech that makes for true communication and co-operation, but, rather, is something else, such as gratuitous abuse (as when the neo-Nazis march through a neighborhood populated by Holocaust survivors shouting "send the Jews to the ovens")' (198–199). Although his treatment of the neo-Nazi march example suggests that a perfectionist defense of free speech has the wherewithal to justify hate speech law, George is not explicit about the particular sort of law he has in mind. His reference to shouting "send the Jews to the ovens" could imply various different clusters of laws/regulations/codes that constrain uses of hate speech, including: laws/regulations/codes that criminalize the glorification of mass murder; laws/regulations/codes interdicting hate speech that amounts to the hate crime of incitement to mass murder; laws/regulations/codes that disallow the public expression of hatred through the use of deeply insulting or offensive words or symbols;

and laws/regulations/codes that provide sanctions or remedies against hate speech that comprises a dignitary crime or tort (e.g., the tort of intentional infliction of emotional distress). Consequently, in the remainder of this section I try to flesh out the connection between the Principle of Human Excellence and particular clusters of laws/regulations/codes, wherever I believe the justificatory link is especially strong.

Before doing so, however, I need first to address an immediate objection. It is that there may be many different forms of human excellence implicated in cases of hate speech, and not all these forms would seem to support hate speech law. On the contrary, it might be argued that the victims of hate speech themselves demonstrate considerable human excellence through virtues such as self-control, forbearance, endurance of suffering, not playing the victim, independence, and rugged individualism. This being the case, could not institutional authorities who are motivated by the Principle of Human Excellence decide not to resort to hate speech law for the sake of promoting these stoical virtues? For example, Henry Gates Jr. argues that when institutional authorities give people legalistic avenues for responding to hate speech—for example, campus speech codes that enable victims to make complaints against discriminatory harassment and courts that grant plaintiffs the right to sue for intentional infliction of emotional distress in cases of discriminatory harassment in the workplace—they infantilize the victims of hate speech and undermine 'the older and much-beleaguered American tradition of individualism' (Gates 1993: 46). Likewise, Donald E. Lively denounces hate speech law 'as paternalistic methods that reinforce the imagery and reality of black dependence upon white kindness' (Lively 1994: 68–69). Similarly, writing of the Skokie Affair, Edward L. Rubin declares that '[t]here is a certain dignity and virtue in refusing to respond to provocation of this kind' (Rubin 1986: 250). Indeed, John Durham Peters (2005) argues that turning to the law represents a squandered opportunity to look into the abyss of evil and neither jump into it (by allowing it to conquer one's soul) nor shy away from it (by banning it). To stand up against it without relying on the law is to make a virtue out of a bad situation, as a kind of 'abyss-redemption.'

What these thinkers would prefer, it seems, is for targets of hate speech to be left to get on with the job of dealing with abuse on their own. However, Delgado and David H. Yun resist this sort of 'toughlove' argument on two grounds: first, there is an element of virtuous personal responsibility in choosing whether or not to bring a complaint or file a lawsuit and, second, the people who press this argument would not seriously propose that individuals deal with theft of their property on their own, even though the levels of harm are equally serious (Delgado and Yun 1994: 1819). From the perspective of virtue jurisprudence, I would add that if a university authority or a municipal government *does* decide to enact and enforce campus speech codes that constrain uses of hate speech, for example, then this would not necessarily be problematic if it could be shown to be a good-faith attempt to act in accordance with the Principle of Human Excellence. Thus,

130  *Principles of Personal Development*

an impartial, wise, and judicious university dean might conclude that since uses of hate speech that constitute acts of discriminatory harassment always realize unwanted human vices but elicit the virtues of stoicism and rugged individualism only to some extent and only some of the time, then it may indeed be appropriate to introduce and enforce campus speech codes.

## Intentional Infliction of Emotional Distress as Cruelty

In Ch. 3 [3.1], I examined the optimism of critical race theorists that the tort of intentional infliction of emotional distress could be used as a means of recovery for persons injured by racist verbal abuse. I also noted the fact that US courts have reserved this tort for 'extreme and outrageous conduct,' and in many instances have chosen to see racist verbal abuse as falling short of that abstract test. It strikes me that taking an aretaic turn in the operationalization of the extreme and outrageous conduct test could bear fruit. In particular, I would argue that judges (and juries) guided by the Principle of Human Excellence might conclude that the human vice of *cruelty* should be at least one of the things that qualifies conduct as extreme and outrageous,[26] and interpreting the tort of intentional infliction of emotional distress in terms of cruelty can be useful in N-warranting the application of that tort to cases of hate speech.

If the current proposal is going to work, however, the task must be to capture what cruelty means in the sorts of spheres in which the tort of intentional infliction of emotional distress currently operates, and to relate the vice of cruelty to certain uses of hate speech. Judith Shklar has defined cruelty as 'the deliberate infliction of physical, and secondarily emotional, pain upon a weaker person or group by stronger ones in order to achieve some end, tangible or intangible, of the latter' (Shklar 1989: 29). I believe that this definition comes close to the sort of conception of cruelty that could be put to use in defining the tort of intentional infliction of emotional distress, particularly in cases of hate speech. For one thing, it acknowledges emotional pain and not merely physical pain. For another, it captures a typical element of cruelty, an unequal relationship. In cases of cruelty the perpetrator tends to be in a position of strength or dominance, and has it within his or her choice to behave compassionately, while the victim is in a position of weakness or vulnerability, subject to the arbitrary choice of the other person. Nevertheless, I think it would be a mistake to interpret this to mean that only members of powerful ethnic/racial groups can be cruel, and that, for example, if a black person verbally abuses a white person with the terms 'honky', 'whitey', 'redneck' or 'cracker', this cannot be cruel. On the contrary, there are surely contexts of speech in which a member of a powerful ethnic/racial group becomes vulnerable, in which the tables are turned, even if momentarily.

In fact, I propose that the courts should see cruelty as involving a range of *characteristic elements*. In cases involving the use of insults, slurs, or

## Principles of Personal Development 131

derogatory epithets based on someone's race, ethnicity, nationality, citizenship, origin of birth, war record, religion, sexual orientation, gender or transgender identity, disability, age, physical appearance, and so on, these elements might be the following. One is that the injured party did not give consent to the speech acts that are alleged to have been cruel. This might occur if the plaintiff was a 'captive audience', for example, in the workplace, a classroom, a dormitory, or a public transit vehicle. A second is that the injured party was in a position of vulnerability, which may have subjective and objective dimensions. A plaintiff may have been vulnerable if, for example, he was the only non-white person in the workplace and felt socially anxious about being "the odd one out." Alternatively, an injured party may have been vulnerable if her coworkers had an ingroup bias or they looked upon her as somehow weaker or inferior. A third is that the defendant showed indifference toward, or lack of empathy for, the victim's vulnerable position and for any emotional distress that might be caused by the conduct, choosing to exploit that vulnerability for self-gratification or to cement his or her own status or position. In an extreme case this might involve taunting or ridiculing a person because of his disability. A fourth is that the injured party suffered severe emotional distress as a result of the conduct in question.

I hope that the applicability of the aforementioned elements of the cruelty test to typical cases involving intentional infliction of emotional distress, such as discriminatory harassment in the workplace and on campus, is obvious. After all, anecdotally, it is not uncommon for unions, citizens' advice agencies, lawyers, and university authorities to invoke the idea of cruelty in an effort to explain the nature of discriminatory harassment to potential injured parties or complainants using layperson's terms. Potentially this idea can give ordinary people a better handle on what discriminatory harassment involves than the more arcane, technical legal concept of extreme and outrageous conduct.

I also believe that my proposed cruelty test could be usefully applied to a different sort of case involving hate speech and the intentional infliction of emotional distress. In *Snyder v. Phelps* the plaintiff claimed that the homophobic hate speech (e.g., banners reading 'God Hates Fags') employed by Fred Phelps and other members of the Westboro Baptist Church while picketing the funeral of his deceased son (a US Marine) contributed to the intentional infliction of emotional distress. According to the operationalization that I am suggesting, the court could have ruled that the conduct was cruel, showing no mercy toward a vulnerable, grieving father.[27] Of course, in the end the Supreme Court ruled that the First Amendment guarantees even speech that intentionally inflicts emotional distress if it pertains to a matter of public interest. On the other hand, Justice Alito insisted that since Snyder was not a public figure, the Court should not have privileged First Amendment values over the right to mourn in peace.[28] On my proposed analysis, the distinction between public figures and private persons is less important than whether or not persons are vulnerable. Private persons can be vulnerable for all manner of reasons, including their emotional state.[29] In the case of public figures, the issue is perhaps more complex. One argument is that they are not vulnerable because they can use their name to attract an audience should they choose to defend themselves with counterspeech. Another is that their vulnerability consists in the fact that their tormentors know far more about the details of their lives than vice versa.

## Empathy and Sympathy as a Framework for Innovations in Hate Speech Law

For David Hume, human excellence takes the form of agreeable character traits or virtues, whereas lack of excellence has to do with vices that we find displeasing. But that is only part of the story. Finding character traits agreeable or displeasing will often rest on deeper sentiments, such as love and hatred. Hume maintains that we tend to find virtues agreeable among the people we love and vices displeasing among the people we hate by virtue of our possession of certain psychological mechanisms, notably empathy and sympathy toward others (Hume [1739–1740] 1984: 625–642). My own interest in the work of Hume is not his meta-ethics *per se*. Instead, I want to explore whether the psychological mechanisms he identifies might be usefully put to work in the N-warranting of hate speech law. In particular, I wish to propose that empathy and sympathy are not merely *causes* of people's judgments of human excellence but are themselves *constituent features* of human excellence (*qua* virtues). What is more, I propose that these features should be not simply exercised but also promoted by lawmakers and legal professionals in their handling of hate speech cases. This, once again, speaks to the rationale behind the Principle of Human Excellence.

I take some inspiration for the approach I have in mind from Jacqueline Taylor's illuminating essay 'Humean Humanity Versus Hate' (2006). In it Taylor attempts to show how appealing to Hume's moral philosophy can provide the resources for explaining how group hatred emerges and what authorities should do to counter it. Taylor suggests that the Humean concept of sympathy 'works by enlivening a belief about another's emotion so that we feel the same emotion ourselves, or have some other emotional response to them, for example, admiration in response to someone's pride in accomplishing a difficult feat' (Taylor [J.] 2006: 193). However, the nature and direction of a person's sympathies can be often mediated by bias or prejudice. 'According to Hume, we naturally love and hate others for features such as their character, their physical appearance and abilities, and their wealth and power—or lack of these' (187). Moreover, it is a distinctive tendency of human beings to construct and follow 'general rules' about what to think and feel about others; that is to say, we put people in boxes. Yet in many instances we classify or judge other people due to factors that do not actually bear upon their character or virtue. Here 'Hume's description lines up with contemporary psychological theory, which refers to the tendency to evaluate one's own group more favorably in comparison with another, as "in-group bias"' (190; cf. Crocker and Luhtanen 1990). When our natural emotions are combined with these sorts of prejudices or biases, what results are 'perverted' forms of sympathy and even contempt (Taylor [J.] 2006: 187–189). 'Those who hate others on the basis of perceived membership in a group exhibit a failure to take up or appreciate the perspective of members of the targeted group' (184). Indeed, '[t]he prejudice reflected in hate activity is a particularly virulent form of stereotyping, involving the misattribution of negative traits (e.g., associating skin color with intellectual inferiority) or stigmatizing a feature (such as sexual orientation) shared by members of a group' (189; cf. Goffman 1963). In addition to this, 'attitudes of respect and contempt are intensified and sustained by the creation of social distance' (Taylor [J.] 2006: 190). The systematic use of negative stereotypes and stigmatizing epithets plays a major part in creating and maintaining this artificial gap in understanding and regard (188, 191). According to Taylor, 'Hume's moral philosophy is notable for advocating extending our natural sympathy in order to adopt a view we can hold in common with others' (184–185). Put simply, breaking down hatred is a matter of helping people to cut through or discard their biases or prejudices by means of adopting the point of view of others. 'Social psychologists refer to this adoption of the point of view of others as "perspective taking," and it is often associated with empathy' (ibid.; cf. Underwood and Moore 1982). In practical terms, the taking up of this common perspective often depends upon conversation (Taylor [J.] 2006: 196). In Hume's words, '[t]he more we converse with mankind, and the greater social intercourse we maintain, the more we shall be familiarized to these general preferences and distinctions, without which our conversation and discourse could scarcely be rendered intelligible to each other' (Hume [1751] 2006: 63).

Following on from this, Taylor argues that 'Hume's virtue ethics helps us to appreciate the value of [an] educational remedy to hate' (Taylor [J.] 2006: 183). She has in mind 'community education about perceived social differences' (ibid.). Taylor has much less to say about legalistic instruments for addressing the problem of biased sympathy, such as the restriction of some uses of hate speech. This is partly explained by her focus on the US and her assumption that hate speech is protected by the First Amendment (183). It might also reflect a particular reading of Hume's political writings on free speech (cf. Hume [1741–1777] 1994; [1768] 1932). It seems to me that Taylor is correct to focus on the inculcation of empathy and sympathy but wrong to ignore regulation. One way to bring both elements together is for institutional authorities to make it a statutory or regulatory requirement that anyone, including lawmakers, judges, and regulators, tasked with the responsibility of deciding or reviewing hate speech cases, undertake race awareness training or, more generally, equality and diversity training, part of the purpose of which is to challenge negative stereotypes of minority groups (cf. Vasquez and de las Fuentes 2000).[30]

With this in mind, imagine a world in which when it comes to the training as well as the selecting of the judiciary, what matters most is not that they share our political beliefs but that they have acquired the psychological mechanisms appropriate for standing in judgment of citizens, not the least of which are empathy and sympathy (cf. Henderson 1993; Colby 2012). According to critical race theorists, empathy for the victims of hate speech is crucial in deciding cases involving hate speech law. Matsuda, for example, urges the legal profession to make 'a deliberate choice to see the world from the standpoint of the oppressed' (Matsuda 1989a: 9). 'We can choose to know the lives of others by reading, studying, listening, and venturing into different places' (ibid.; see also Lawrence 1990: 436). Let us imagine, then, that judges are both equipped and motivated to honor the Principle of Human Excellence. How could empathy for the victims of hate speech appropriately be reflected in judicial decision-making? It might be easier to recognize empathetic decision-making in its absence. Consider the Justice Scalia majority opinion in *R.A.V. v. the City St. Paul*. The case involved the act of burning a cross on the property of an African American family. The Court considered the fact that the City of St. Paul Bias-Motivated Crime Ordinance targeted only fighting words based on race, creed, color, or gender, and had to evaluate whether or not this ordinance fell into recognized exceptions to the First Amendment doctrine of content neutrality. Justice Scalia summarily rejected the argument that the effects of racist fighting words are relevantly dissimilar from other subcategories of fighting words as mere 'wordplay.'[31] 'What makes the anger, fear, sense of dishonor, etc., produced by violation of this ordinance distinct from the anger, fear, sense of dishonor, etc., produced by other fighting words is nothing other than the fact that it is caused by a distinctive idea, conveyed by a distinctive message.'[32] Arguably this reflects a failure to see the world from the eyes of those subjected to cross burning: a failure to understand the meaning of cross burning as a symbol both of historic oppression and of persisting racist discrimination; a failure to understand the increased latent anxiety of members of groups that have suffered and continue to suffer oppression, discrimination, and hatred; and a failure to understand the particular type and severity of emotional trauma caused by the use of such symbols given this social and psychological environment (cf. Lawrence 1992).

Building on this, imagine that the Humean judge, legislator, and policymaker have each embraced the Principle of Human Excellence. What innovations in the regulation of hate speech could he or she adopt? I offer three illustrations, the first of which I am unaware of having been proposed elsewhere. It has to do with internet regulation. The Humean regulator might reason that hate speech on the Internet puts virtual and physical distance between the speaker and the subject, making the development of any feelings of sympathy through contact even less likely. It is not merely that the hate speaker cannot see or experience the effect of his or her words on the target online, it is also that by deciding whom to accept or not accept as friends on social networking websites, or who to reveal or not to reveal the initiator's true identity to, perpetuates distance. So based on the goal of cultivating unbiased sympathy and the adoption of a common point of view, there might be a powerful case for the regulation of hate speech on the Internet. This regulation might, for example, focus on the use of negative stereotypes or stigmatization of people based on their race, ethnicity, nationality, citizenship, origin of birth, war record, religion, sexual orientation, gender or transgender identity, disability, age, or physical appearance. Why? Because this sort of hate speech reinforces people's prejudices and makes bias-changing conversation less likely. George argues that virtue jurisprudence is about establishing a healthy 'moral ecology' (1993: 45). The present innovation would seek to improve the moral ecology of the Internet.

The second innovation concerns the use of imaginative sentencing in the criminal law. In *Case of György Nagy* (2012)[33] the Pest Central District Court convicted the defendant under a section of Hungary's criminal code that prohibits denying or belittling crimes against humanity, for holding up a sign with the message 'The Shoah did not happen' penned in Hebrew during a public demonstration on October 23, 2011, in Budapest. The Court's decision was later upheld by the Budapest-Capital Regional Court (2012).[34] Apart from being Hungary's first conviction for Holocaust denial, what was particularly striking about the case was the nature of the sentencing. Judge Dénes handed down an eighteen-month suspended prison sentence with the requirement that the defendant must visit one of three named Holocaust memorial centers and write an essay on his reflections on the visit(s). It is hard to imagine a more appropriate way to promote greater empathy among perpetrators of Holocaust denial.

The third innovation revolves around the use of restorative justice in the arena of campus speech codes. Suppose the Humean university dean wants to promote empathy on campus. Based upon his or her understanding of the essential character of a university, the dean casts empathy as the human capacity to interact with others in a constructive dialogue to discover the contents of one another's distinctive feelings, needs, and rights; this has consequences not merely for how one understands the force of hate speech but also for how one conceives the just response to it. Following on from this, the dean reimagines the institution of campus speech codes not as a narrowly defined set of verbal or pictorial behaviors that are to be prohibited but instead as something that could provide a space in which hate speakers and victims of hate speech could be brought together to work through their differing views on the right to freedom of expression and the right not to be subjected to discriminatory harassment. Exactly in this spirit, Diana Tietjens Meyers (1995) has proposed that the problem of campus hate speech should be dealt with by university authorities not by imposing a punitive scheme of retributive justice on perpetrators but by creating a system of victim-focused

136  *Principles of Personal Development*

reparative justice. Within the system she envisages, the victims of discriminatory harassment would be given the right to confront their tormentors in a university-managed process of arbitration and reconciliation, as well as the right to claim personal compensation from the university, such as in the form of a refund of tuition fees for the relevant year or credit toward any remaining tuition fees. Through the process of arbitration and reconciliation, perpetrators of hate speech might come to realize that discriminatory harassment can silence the very people with whom a dialogue is vital in challenging latent biases and prejudices. But even if not, at least within the process of restorative justice communication between persons would be regulated by specialists in mediation, and the victims of discriminatory harassment would be given a safe environment in which to speak out.[35]

In response to these innovations, however, it might be argued that if agents take on the Principle of Human Excellence as a guiding light of regulatory design, this will constitute an attempt to legislate morality: it is to expect them to become agents of change in moral sentiments through the inculcation of empathy and sympathy. If this is an accurate interpretation of these sorts of innovations—and it is certainly one that some theorists have embraced (e.g., Delgado 1982: 148–149; Meyers 1995: 233)—then it invites this familiar objection. "You cannot legislate morality." I take this to mean not that it is literally impossible to effect change of moral sentiments through legislation but that it is N-unwarranted to attempt to effect change in moral sentiments because trying is bound to involve an excessive or disproportionate amount of interference in freedom.[36] For example, Suzanne Sherry argues that if the purpose of campus speech codes in American universities is to inculcate civic virtues, they are 'bound to fail' (Sherry 1991: 944). First, 'students have already acquired a nearly unalterable belief system' even before they reach university (ibid.).[37] Second, 'virtue requires taking responsibility for one's actions, and taking responsibility requires choice' (ibid.). However, what is noticeable about the three innovations outlined previously is that they are each designed to leave space for an exercise of choice and responsibility on the part of people in whom a change in moral sentiments is desired. First, the plan to improve the moral ecology of the Internet gives users of hate sites the choice to click onto other sites that provide a different perspective, absent the negative stereotypes that tend to create sympathy bias. Second, the judge in *Case of György Nagy* did not order the defendant to publicly recant his beliefs about the Holocaust, and presumably because doing so would have been futile and contrary to the fundamental principles of a liberal society. Instead he ordered the defendant to visit one of three named Holocaust memorial centers and write an essay on his reflections on the visits, thus leaving space for the defendant to make a leap of imagination into the experience of people who do not deny the Holocaust. Third, the proposal for a process of arbitration is intended to deal with the issue of hate speech by personalizing it, by promoting mutual understanding and recognition, and by giving hate speakers an opportunity

*Principles of Personal Development* 137

to take responsibility for their actions and emotions without fear of being penalized for doing so.

\* \* \*

In conclusion, there are people for whom one of the primary purposes of free speech rests in its being practically indispensible, or at least highly conducive, to personal development. Such people tend to think that this applies as much to a freedom to engage in hate speech as to a freedom to engage in any speech that authorities may be minded to ban because they deem it to be undesirable or insidious in its effects. But this blanket assumption often belies a lack of specificity as to how a given bit of regulatory suppression would undermine a given constituent feature of personal development. I hope to have shown that once specificity is provided, both about what constitutes personal development and about which clusters of laws/regulations/codes are at stake, this blanket assumption starts to appear dogmatic. For, in some instances hate speech law can be the friend, as opposed to the enemy, of the values of personal development.

## NOTES

1. Consider the website *The Heretical Press* (www.heretical.com) (last accessed 20/09/14).
2. *Abrams v. United States* (1919) 250 US 616 (involving leaflets thrown onto the street from a building in New York City which denounced the Allied intervention into the Russian Civil War), at 630.
3. According to Schauer (1982: 20), the marketplace of ideas metaphor is 'most apt' when combined with a survival theory of truth (that truth is by definition whatever emerges by consensus, having survived a process of open discussion among a group of people).
4. For one thing, it is difficult to understand how the marketplace of ideas could have been a suitable metaphor for the First Amendment at the time of its enactment. The marketplace analogy implies not merely a location where large numbers of ordinary consumers can access ideas freely and easily but also a place where large numbers of ordinary producers can sell their ideas (e.g., Lee 2010: 16–17). Yet at the time of the drafting of the Bill of Rights very few ordinary Americans had the opportunity to express their ideas in print. Newspapers were often the mouthpieces of intellectual elites, not the least of which were Thomas Jefferson and James Madison (e.g., Chafee 1947: 17). Even Holmes' use of the metaphor seemed to be more focused on the power of patterns of consumption to change what ideas survive in the marketplace of ideas than on popular access to inexpensive public dissemination of new ideas. It may be, therefore, that the metaphor has become more, not less plausible in the age of the Internet. In addition to this, the marketplace of ideas metaphor presupposes a framework of competition and the pursuit of self-interest, yet it may be more appropriate to think of the discovery of truth as functioning best through dialogical cooperation (e.g., Gordon 1997: 246). Nevertheless, for a defense of both the marketplace of ideas metaphor and the search for truth as a basis for the constitutional right to free expression, see Eugene Volokh (2011a).
5. The general claim that free speech provides valuable opportunities of exchanging error for truth strikes me as consistent with a range of theories of truth,

138  *Principles of Personal Development*

including not only the survival theory of truth (that truth is by definition whatever emerges by consensus, having survived a process of open discussion among a group of people) but also the correspondence theory of truth (freedom to listen to new opinions might provide valuable opportunities of making statements that correspond to actual state of affairs), the coherence theory of truth (freedom to listen to new opinions might provide valuable opportunities of expressing propositions that form part of a coherent system of beliefs), or even deflationary theories of truth (freedom to listen to new opinions might provide valuable opportunities of falling into line with a pattern in the usage of the predicate 'is true' that can be observed among a population of users, such to assert "snow is white" if and only if snow is white).

6. Interestingly, not long after the publication of T.M. Scanlon's article a US District Court was faced with a real dilemma along these lines. See *United States v. Progressive, Inc.* (1979) 467 F. Supp. 990 (W.D. Wis.) (involving the publication of information relating to the creation of the atomic bomb).
7. Of course, not all hate speech amounting to negative stereotypes and stigmatization will be guaranteed by the Principle of Truth. Suppose the Islamophobe still intends to negatively stereotype Muslims, portraying them as depraved, oppressive toward women, and prone to terrorism, but on this occasion is minded to offer no supporting statements of fact. What he will say remains entirely within the terrain of opinion, judgment, and hyperbole. The Principle of Truth says that laws restricting hate speech are N-unwarranted if they deprive persons of opportunities for exchanging error for truth. Yet in the realm of opinion, judgment, and hyperbole there is no possibility of exchanging error for truth because there is no truth or falsity to be had. Indeed, even when stigmatizing generics purport to be grounded in statements of fact, on closer inspection these statements can be statements of interpretation, on a par with opinion or judgment. Consider the utterance, "Because of what the Qur'an says, Muslim people have to fight Christians and Jews, they have to attack and humiliate them until they accept true religion—that's why Muslims can't be trusted." This is opinion in the sense that it offers a reading of the Qur'an that cannot be falsified. This, like all representations of a theology, can scarcely claim refuge under the Principle of Truth (cf. McNamara 2007a: 163–164). Contrast this with, "A recent survey of Muslims shows that n percent believe that it is their religious duty to fight Christians and Jews under certain circumstances—that is a statistic we should all take note of and think about."
8. Interestingly, in his 'Law of Libel and Liberty of the Press' Mill opposed the use of libel law to suppress statements of opinion but not the use of libel law to suppress false statements of fact (e.g., Mill [1825] 1984: 14).
9. In the case of civil proceedings, the burden falls upon the plaintiff.
10. I thank Alan Haworth for his expertise regarding these propositions.
11. Of course, it is a matter of perspective whether the fact that the Principle of Truth would not extend its guarantee of free expression to some uses of hate speech is a minus or plus point for that Principle. Nor do I mean to suggest that issues of truth are the most important considerations in all hate speech cases. As Lee Bollinger points out (1986: 54): 'In a case such as *Skokie*, the chance that the Nazi messages may turn out to be "true" is hardly a persuasive basis on which to defend such speech, and few if any free speech advocates turned to this kind of argument in that context.'
12. *R. v. Keegstra*, at 762–763.
13. Evidence such as large quantities of human remains (including decomposed bodies, skeletons, and ashes) found at Nazi concentration camps (as reported in the personal testimonies of, and motion pictures captured by, Allied troops); the confessions of perpetrators of orchestrated acts of mass murder; letters between Nazi

*Principles of Personal Development* 139

officials either directly or indirectly discussing operational plans for genocide; the special layout of concentration camps; aerial photos and partial remains of gas chambers; and demographic statistics, including records kept by Nazis of diminishing Jewish population sizes.
14. Document obtained by the author directly from the University of Michigan.
15. Document obtained by the author directly from Stanford University.
16. Of course, it might be pointed out that it is possible to fake photographs of the Earth. Nevertheless, the key point here is that there is a way of having knowledge that is not based on first-hand experience but on reasonable reliance on professionals. In the case of the roundish shape of the Earth, *pace* Geoffrey Marshall, these are likely to be professionals in the centuries old scientific discipline of observational astronomy.
17. Although Schauer provides no textual evidence in support of this interpretation, such evidence is not hard to come by. Consider this passage from Mill's 'Law of Libel and Liberty of the Press' ([1835] 1984: 7–8): 'Under a free system, if error would be promulgated, so would truth: and truth never fails, in the long run, to prevail over error.' Of course, that truth will prevail over error under a repressive system is another matter entirely. Consider this famous passage from *On Liberty* (Mill [1859] 1972: 96). 'But, indeed, the dictum that truth always triumphs over persecution, is one of those pleasant falsehoods which men repeat after one another till they pass into commonplaces, but which all experience refutes.'
18. Of course, in an ideal world the education system would produce adults who were intellectually curious and epistemically virtuous enough to not rely on limited sources of information. So in that sense the proposal is partly a response to failures in the education system.
19. In fact, it is argued by some scholars that self-realization is a justificatorily foundational value in relation to which other First Amendment values are derivative (e.g., Redish 1982: 594; Baker 1989: 47–51; Blim 1995: 481–484). I shall not discuss here the further, disputed issue of the relationship between the values of self-realization and autonomy (cf. Baker 1978: 990–921; Raz 1986: 375–377). There is also a lively debate within the literature about whether or not self-realization is capable of explaining why speech acts should deserve dedicated constitutional protection when other types of intentional acts that are also causally related to, or constitutive of, self-realization, do not receive such special protection (e.g., Bork 1971; Schauer 1983; cf. Redish 1982: 600–601; Greenawalt 1989: 12; Murchison 1998: 447–449; Nelson 2005: 68–86). The main purpose of this chapter is to consider what might be said for and against hate speech law from the perspective of the goods or values of personal development. So the fact that certain of these values might be more or less credible as justifications for the special constitutional protection afforded to speech conduct (as compared to other sorts of conduct) need not be resolved here.
20. At least in that regard Anita Whitney would seem to be an exemplar. Consider the words of Justice Brandeis in *Whitney v. California* (1927) 274 US 357: 'Those who won our independence believed that the final end of the state was to make men free to develop their faculties.' At 375.
21. I do not have in mind Redish's (1982: 593) distinction between self-realization as the development of one's capacities and self-realization as participation in the making of life-affecting decisions. Nor do I have in mind Samuel P. Nelson's (2005: 64) distinction between the individual's journey toward the realization of his or her own capacities based on his or her experience of performing expressive acts and the role played by the individual in contributing to a rich environment of expressive acts upon which other people may draw in taking their journeys toward self-realization.

140  *Principles of Personal Development*

22. There are echoes here of Charles Taylor's account of the relationship between human agency and language. For example, Taylor (1985: 270) argues that 'adequate' articulation of our affective states and feelings can lead these states to become 'clearer, less fluctuating, have steadier boundaries.'
23. Taylor also believes that dialogue with others is essential to the shaping of self-identity. In his words (Taylor [C.] 1991: 33): 'We define [our identity] always in dialogue with, sometimes in struggle against, the identities our significant others want to recognize in us.' Indeed, for Taylor (1985: 233), the articulation of our mental states can become 'self-shaping recognitions' in the sense that '[l]anguage realizes man's humanity' and '[m]an completes himself in expression.' For more on the implications of Taylor's work for how we think about the right to freedom of expression, see Murchison (1998: 462–476) and Nelson (2005: 75–76).

    Note, in the main paragraph I focus on the connection between self-definition and self-fulfillment (i.e., the definition of self through the development of capacities), for the purpose of enabling a briefer, simplified analysis of self-realization. I do not mean to say that this is all there is to self-definition or the self-definition defense of free speech. For more expansive accounts, see Murchison (1998) and Nelson (2005: ch. 3).
24. I focus here on only one of the three lines of argument that Simon Thompson develops off the back of Axel Honneth's theory of recognition.
25. It might be thought, for example, that if virtue ethics has to do with wise judgment and other forms of virtuous attitude, character, or disposition, then this precludes principles because any rule or principle can in principle be broken if that is what wise judgment or virtuous character dictates in the circumstances.
26. The fact that international law recognizes the human right not to be subjected to cruel treatment or punishment and in many countries divorce courts recognize mental cruelty as a grounds for divorce is both an indication of how seriously we take the vice of human cruelty and of the work that this concept can do in sophisticated legal regimes. That being said, I do not mean to suggest that cruelty can provide an exhaustive definition of extreme and outrageous conduct. Other scholars have proposed affront to dignity as another subcategory of extreme and outrageous conduct (e.g., Love 1990: 158; Chamallas and Wriggins 2010: 84). Moreover, I do not mean to suggest that perfectionism lays sole claim to concern with cruelty. Judith Shklar (1984: 44), for example, defines what it means to be a liberal partly in terms of the belief that cruelty is 'the worst thing we do.'
27. Several thinkers have examined whether or not the Phelps' conduct did in fact fall within recognized categories of proscribable speech under the First Amendment (e.g., Volokh 2010; Fishman 2011; Zipursky 2011; Berger Levinson 2013). Others have considered whether or not the conduct would have constituted an offense if, contrary to fact, it had been performed in other countries (e.g., McAllister 2010; Heyman 2012). In the UK, for example, the conduct might have constituted an offense of incitement to hatred on the grounds of sexual orientation. There are certainly similarities with the case *R. v. Ali, Javed, and Ahmed*, in which the defendants were found guilty of the offense of incitement to hatred on the grounds of sexual orientation for distributed material in a city center containing, among other things, the words 'G.A.Y. God Abhors You.' Indeed, in February 2009 the Secretary of State issued an exclusion order against Fred Phelps and Shirley Phelps-Roper on the basis that if permitted entry into the UK, they would have publicly expressed views about homosexuality that were likely to have fostered hatred and might have led to intercommunity violence. This came in response to a post on the 'picket

*Principles of Personal Development* 141

schedule' of their website *GodHatesFags* (www.godhatesfags.com) declaring an intention to picket a performance of the gay rights awareness play *The Laramie Project* at Queen Mary's College, a sixth-form college in Hampshire. The words of the posting were as follows: 'Central Studio Queen Mary's College—God H8s Ur Queen! Cliddesden Road In Merry Old England they plan to further enrage the Living God by putting on the farce known commonly as "The Laramie Project". Now that is so interesting. We will picket them, and see if they actually believe those lies they tell about how tolerant and accepting Brits are. RIIIGHT! Just because you rage against God and make laws that say you cannot use "hate speech" (a/k/a—you may not speak of the Bible standards) in the UK does NOT mean you will not get the message that God Almighty intends for you to get. God Hates England; Your Queen Is A Whore; You Hate God; God Hates You; You're Going to Hell; Matt Is In Hell; Hell Is Real Ask Matt; God Hates Fags (Buggers); Obey God, etc. Some of the best Bible preaching in the history of the world came out of that dark dismal land, but now it is full of all abominations! God will shortly destroy the UK and the world, but not until they have gotten the plain, clear message so that they will be WITHOUT EXCUSE!' In Germany, the funeral picketing might have been prosecuted under s. 189 (the offense of violating the memory of the dead) of the Criminal Code.

28. *Snyder v. Phelps*, at _.
29. Along these lines, Justice Alito writes: 'They first issued a press release and thus turned Matthew's funeral into a tumultuous media event. They then appeared at the church, approached as closely as they could without trespassing, and launched a malevolent verbal attack on Matthew and his family at a time of acute emotional vulnerability. As a result, Albert Snyder suffered severe and lasting emotional injury. The Court now holds that the First Amendment protected respondents' right to brutalize Mr. Snyder. I cannot agree.' *Snyder v. Phelps*, at _.
30. After all, it is not uncommon for judges trying particular types of cases to be required to undergo special training. Consider the system of 'rape ticketing' for judges in cases dealing with allegations of rape.
31. *R.A.V. v. the City St. Paul*, at 392.
32. At 392–393.
33. No. 13.B.V.24.755/2012/8 (Pest Cen. Dist. Ct, 12 Jun.).
34. No. 23.Bf.10.283/2012/4 (Budapest-Capital Reg. Ct., 7 Dec.).
35. For a critical response to the proposal, however, see Thomas Peard (1999).
36. Ronald Dworkin maintains that a legitimate state is one that respects ethical independence, and this 'means that no individual citizen may be forced to accept any official ethical conviction or be prevented from expressing one's own ethical convictions' (Dworkin 2012: 342). I shall return to this argument in Ch. 7 [7.2].
37. It is not clear whether Sherry would extend the same point to school pupils. For the view that teachers ought to inculcate virtues of tolerance, understanding, and respect to school pupils (on the basis that ought implies can), see Cohen-Almagor (2008).

# 5 Principles of Civic Morality

The idea that a just society is one in which even speech may be regulated in order to protect the rights of other citizens can be motivated via the example of the right to reputation. We want to say that speakers have a right to comment on the character and conduct of other people, and in ways that may adversely affect the reputation of those people in the eyes of society. Yet we also want to say that persons should enjoy a right to reputation, which means, among other things, the right not to be defamed. Why is this right important? One answer is that it is intimately connected with personal dignity, which is a matter of how high or low people are esteemed based upon their personal qualities, achievements, and so on. Moreover, as touched upon in Ch. 3 [3.6], some courts have justified the right to reputation ultimately in terms of the value of human dignity. On this account, protecting people against unjustifiable attacks on their reputation constitutes an affirmation of their worth as human beings. However, these are not the only ways of thinking about the nature and importance of reputation. Another approach that has emerged in the hate speech literature (I have in mind the work of Jeremy Waldron) focuses on how some forms of hate speech can undermine *civic dignity*, which is a matter of whether or not citizens enjoy a high and equal social and legal status no matter their race, ethnicity, religion, gender, sexual orientation, or other protected characteristics. On this account, hate speech law serves to protect the fundamentals of people's reputations as members of the political community in good standing and also provides the public good of *assurance*. This chapter is devoted to critically examining this alternative approach to the theory of reputation, dignity, and hate speech law.

## 5.1 CIVIC DIGNITY

In *Rosenblatt v. Baer* (1966)[1] Justice Stewart offered the following account of the special importance of reputation. 'The right of a man to the protection of his own reputation from unjustified invasion and wrongful hurt reflects no more than our basic concept of the essential dignity and worth of every human being—a concept at the root of any decent system of ordered

Principles of Civic Morality    143

liberty.'[2] In his 2009 Tanner Lectures, 'Dignity, Rank, and Rights', however, Waldron claims that this Kantian definition of dignity (as the fundamental worth of every human being) 'has had a deplorable influence on philosophical discussions of dignity and it has led many lawyers, many of whom are slovenly anyway in these matters, lazily to assume that "dignity" in the law must convey this specific Kantian resonance' (Waldron 2011: 221). Instead, Waldron insists that the sort of dignity that matters in the law, especially in the law dealing with reputation-damaging speech, is intimately connected with social rank or status, something which is an essential feature of the ancient concept of dignity or *dignitas* (225). As described by Marcus Cicero in the context of the Roman Republic, for example, '*dignitas est alicuius honesta et cultu et honore et verecundia digna auctoritas*' ('rank is the possession of a distinguished office which merits respect, honour, and reverence') (Cicero [c. 84 BC] 1949: 333).

However, Waldron also argues that there is a key difference between the ancient use of the concept of dignity—with its emphasis on a person's role (*personae*) in the republic and on a hierarchy of social ranks or statuses—and the modern use of this concept. '[T]he modern notion of *human* dignity involves an upwards equalization of rank, so that we now try to accord to every human being something of the dignity, rank, and expectation of respect that was formerly accorded to nobility' (Waldron 2011: 229). As evidence of this upward equalization of rank, he cites the fact the modern concepts of human dignity and human rights entail the sort of protection of the right to bodily integrity, the right to privacy, and the prohibition of humiliating or degrading treatment of prisoners that was once granted only to the nobility (230–231).

If the modern notion of dignity formally means a high and equal rank or status, what is the currency of this status or what forms does it take? At this stage, Waldron appeals to the idea of 'social and legal status' (Waldron 2010: 1612). When he speaks of 'social status', he has in mind such things as the esteem in which one is held by one's fellow citizens and the various signs of respect received from them. In the case of 'legal status', he is referring to what it means to be a full rights-bearing member of society and to partake of the fundamental benefits and privileges of a system of law. As he puts it, '[i]f our modern conception of human dignity retains any scintilla of its ancient and historical connection with rank—and I think it does: I think it expresses the idea of the high and equal rank of every human person—then we should look first at the bodies of law that relate status to rank (and to right and privilege) and see what if anything is retained of these ancient and historical conceptions when dignity is put to work in a new and egalitarian environment' (2011: 210).[3] Putting these two aspects together, Waldron is centrally concerned with the ways in which enjoying a high and equal socio-legal status furnishes citizens with a package of fundamental rights.

For Waldron, included among this package of fundamental rights is the right to protection against group libel (catchall). Consider the following passages.

144  *Principles of Civic Morality*

> [I]t helps to view hate speech laws as protecting vulnerable minorities against the evil of *group defamation*. These days we tend to think of defamation as a tort. But [. . .] historically the law of criminal libel has been used to support and express a collective commitment on the part of society to uphold the fundamentals of people's reputations as members of society in good standing—vindicating, as I shall say, the rudiments of their civic *dignity* as a necessary ingredient of public order. (2010: 1600)
>
> The United States abolished titles of nobility in 1787, but it did not necessarily abolish that sort of concern for status. A democratic republic might equally be concerned with upholding and vindicating important aspects of legal and social status—only now it would be the elementary dignity of even its non-officials as citizens—and with protecting that status (as a matter of public order) from being undermined by various forms of obloquy. And that is what I think is the concern of laws regarding group defamation. (2010: 105)
>
> In countries where hate speech and group libel are prohibited, people are required to refrain from the most egregious public attacks on one another's basic social standing. A great many countries use their laws to protect ethnic and racial groups from threatening, abusive, or insulting publications calculated to bring them into public contempt. (2011: 234)

These passages indicate Waldron's implicit commitment to what I shall call the Principle of Civic Dignity, that legalistic constraints on uses of hate speech are (N-)warranted if they protect the rudiments of people's civic dignity.

At the heart of Waldron's argument is the claim that certain uses of hate speech are a threat to the esteem in which targeted groups are held by fellow citizens and the system of law. In itself, this is not a new claim, of course. In the 1980s and 1990s critical race theorists such as Matsuda pointed to evidence showing that racist negative stereotyping and stigmatization (or 'racist hate propaganda') affects how a society views members of racial/ethnic minorities, for the worse (e.g., Matsuda 1989b: 2339–2340; cf. Gardner and Taylor 1968; Greenberg and Pyszczynski 1985). Research into this phenomenon has continued apace in the intervening years, and now also includes research on the impact of negative stereotyping and stigmatization on the grounds of gender, religion, and sexual orientation, to name only a few characteristics (e.g., MacRae et al. 1996; Schneider 2004).

So what is original in Waldron's work? The answer, I think, rests in his accounts of *protection* and *assurance* of civic dignity. I shall return to assurance in the next section, but for now I shall focus on protection. When Waldron claims that it is helpful to think of hate speech law as protecting the high and equal sociolegal status of members of vulnerable groups, he means something that runs deeper than the brute fact that in a society where such law is effectively enforced, victims can expect the criminal justice system to punish people who engage in group libel (catchall) against them. He also means, I think, that laws/regulations/codes that constrain uses of hate speech are at their best when they focus on forms of expression that deny possession by members of targeted groups of qualities or attributes that are prerequisites for their enjoying a high and equal social status or which deny their possession of legal rights that are the trappings of a high and equal legal status. This interpretation is supported by Waldron's three concrete illustrations of 'the ways in which a group might be libeled' (Waldron 2010: 1609). First, 'the *Beauharnais* pamphlet, with its imputation that "rapes, robberies, knives, guns and marijuana" were somehow typical of "the negro"' (ibid.). Second, 'the characterization of minority members as animals' (ibid.). Third, 'a group and its members can be libeled by signage associating group membership with prohibition or exclusion: "No blacks allowed"' (1610).[4] The first two examples do not involve false statements of fact and so do not amount to group libel (*sensu stricto*). Instead, they seem to be a matter of negative stereotyping or stigmatization, and so constitute group libel in the catchall sense of covering a range of types of hate speech. At first glance, the third example looks like the enactment of discrimination (e.g., Asquith 2009; McGowan 2009, 2012). But perhaps Waldron regards this speech as group libel (catchall) because the signage asserts or implies that "blacks" lack some of the basic constitutional rights granted to other persons (i.e., the right not to be discriminated against). This is negative stereotyping and may even be group libel (*sensu stricto*). At any rate, what really matters is what all of these examples share in common, and that is a denial of the fact that members of certain groups possess qualities or attributes necessary for a high and equal social status or a denial of the fact that these people possess rights that suggest a high and equal legal status. And so part of the function of what Waldron calls 'hate speech regulation' is to protect vulnerable minorities against such group libel (catchall) (Waldron 2010: 1600, 1612, 1628). In his words, '[t]he issue is publication and the harm done to individuals and groups through the disfiguring of our social environment by visible, public, and semi-permanent announcements to the effect that in the opinion of one group in the community, members of another group are not worthy of equal citizenship' (1601).[5]

Certainly Waldron's way of thinking is plausibly applied to *some* European hate speech law. Consider laws/regulations/codes that disallow the public expression of hatred against protected groups, such as Ch. 16, s. 8 of the Swedish Criminal Code ('A person who, in a disseminated statement or communication, threatens or expresses contempt for a national, ethnic or other such group of persons with allusion to race, colour, national or ethnic origin or religious belief shall, be sentenced for *agitation against a national or ethnic group* to imprisonment for at most two years or, if the crime is petty, to a fine' [trans.]). It is not difficult to see how this law could do much to protect the rudiments of the civic dignity of members of protected groups. Indeed, in *Vejdeland and Others v. Sweden* the ECtHR upheld the decision of the Swedish Supreme Court to sustain convictions for agitation against a national or ethnic group in the case of a group of defendants who had circulated leaflets containing powerful expressions of homophobic beliefs, in a secondary school. The leaflets included the statements that homosexuality was a 'deviant sexual proclivity,' had 'a morally destructive effect on the substance of society,' was responsible for the 'modern plague' of HIV and AIDS, and was associated with those lobbying for the legalization of pedophilia. The Court declared that in its view 'the interference served a legitimate aim, namely "the protection of the reputation and rights of others", within the meaning of Article 10 § 2 of the Convention.'[6] This would seem to be an example of restricting statements that deny that members of protected groups possess qualities or attributes necessary for a high and equal sociolegal status.

However, I believe that Waldron can be fairly criticized for overlooking other kinds of law that might also be said to protect the high and equal sociolegal status of members of vulnerable groups. I offer two illustrations. The first is Holocaust denial law. It is not difficult to see how such law could protect the civic dignity of Jews—over and above protecting the dignitary rights of the dead (see Ch. 3 [3.6]). Consider the most famous Holocaust denial case of all, *Case of National Democratic Party of Germany* (or '*Auschwitz Lie*') (1994).[7] Here the Constitutional Court of Germany upheld a prior restraint on the National Democratic Party of Germany in relation to a public event it was planning to hold that included a lecture by David Irving. The Party was required to ensure that nothing would be said about the persecution of the Jews during the Third Reich that would deny or call into question that persecution and in contravention of ss. 130, 185, 189 and 194 of the German Criminal Code. In doing so the Court quoted with approval an earlier opinion of the Federal Court of Justice of Germany (1979)[8] in which the latter had stated the following.

> Whoever seeks to deny these events denies vis-à-vis each individual the personal worth of [Jewish persons]. For the person concerned, this is continuing discrimination against the group to which he belongs and, as part of the group, against him. [trans.] (cited in Kommers 1997: 386)

Surely part of what the Court is getting at here is precisely what Waldron seems to be concerned with in the case of the "No blacks allowed" signage: namely, a denial of the fact that certain groups or classes of persons possess legal rights that are the trappings of a high and equal legal status. Put in Waldronian terms, Holocaust denial is a threat to the rudiments of each Jewish person's civic dignity. Interestingly, Waldron explicitly mentions the fact that statements claiming that the Holocaust is a hoax invented by Jewish people for nefarious purposes can be damaging to the 'social and cultural reputation' of Jews (Waldron 2012: 57–58). Yet he chooses to make this point not as a part of an additional justification for Holocaust denial law but as part of his discussion of *R. v. Keegstra*, a case involving

s. 319(2) of the Canadian Criminal Code, which makes it a punishable offense to willfully promote hatred against an identifiable group of persons. Interestingly, Waldron introduces his approach with the following declaration. 'Mostly, what I want to do is offer a characterization of the laws we find in Europe and in the other advanced democracies of the world, and also as we have found them in America from time to time' (2010: 1598). So it is unclear why he has not sought to defend Holocaust denial law *as well*.

Perhaps Waldron would say that when he uses the term 'hate speech regulations', he also has in mind Holocaust denial law (cf. Waldron 2008). But there is a second dimension to the present criticism that cannot be so easily accommodated. In contrast to critical race theorists, Waldron focuses on criminal law and consciously places civil libel law outside of the frame of the argument. He claims that whereas civil defamation law is concerned with 'the intricate detail of each person's reputation and its movement up or down the scale of social estimation' (Waldron 2010: 1607), criminal defamation law is 'oriented to protecting the basic social standing [ . . . ] of members of vulnerable groups' (1646). He also uses *Beauharnais v. Illinois* (1952)[9] to illustrate the distinction. In his dissenting opinion in that case Justice Black rejected the majority's analogizing s. 224a of the Illinois Criminal Code with criminal libel law on the grounds that the latter 'has provided for punishment of false, malicious, scurrilous charges against individuals, not against huge groups.'[10] According to Waldron, Justice Black 'neglects an important difference between the concern for personalized reputation in civil cases and a broader social concern for the *fundamentals* of anyone's reputation or civic dignity as a member of society in good standing' (Waldron 2010: 1607).[11] However, the sorts of civil proceedings that might be used to protect vulnerable groups against attacks on their civic dignity are not limited to the tort of libel. There is also the tort of intentional infliction of emotional distress, and Delgado's proposed tort for racial insult. Waldron acknowledges that a strong argument can be made for other regulatory approaches to hate speech, but he assumes that the relevant justificatory project is different from his civic dignity rationale (1614). But this assumption is premature, and for the simple reason that when critical race theorists have sought to justify such law, they too have sometimes made an explicit appeal to the way in which racist insults threaten people's sociolegal status. In the words of Delgado, '[t]he wrong of this dignitary affront consists of the expression of a judgment that the victim of the racial slur is entitled to less than that to which all other citizens are entitled' (Delgado 1982: 144). Indeed, in his review of Waldron's *The Harm in Hate Speech* (2012) Delgado argues that although 'nothing is wrong with focusing, as Waldron does, on monuments, writings, and other tangible symbols of hatred and contempt', 'face-to-face vituperation can pollute the environment in ways almost as damaging as billboards and monuments' (Delgado 2013: 233). All of this suggests that Waldron is too hasty in de-emphasizing the role of civil proceedings in protecting the civic dignity of

148  *Principles of Civic Morality*

vulnerable groups, especially given the fact that these proceedings have also been found in America from time to time, as several critical race theorists have pointed out (see Ch. 3 [3.1]).

## 5.2 ASSURANCE

A second claim to originality in Waldron's approach rests in his account of assurance. Waldron insists that hate speech law functions not merely to protect vulnerable minorities against group libel (catchall) and the concomitant public denials of their civic dignity, but also to provide an important *public good*: namely, the 'assurance' of civic dignity. As Waldron puts it, assurance is 'a pervasive, diffuse, ubiquitous, general, sustained, and reliable underpinning of people's basic dignity and social standing, provided by all for all' (Waldron 2010: 1630). The use of the word 'underpinning' is significant for two reasons. First, the word 'underpinning' indicates that the public good of assurance is a process or something we *do*. And so I read Waldron as using the word 'assurance' to mean *the act of assuring*. Second, Waldron argues that law has an important part to play in this process of underpinning (1623). What he means is that, although assurance is the responsibility of all citizens and this means that all citizens have a responsibility to refrain from doing anything to undermine the action of assuring, including the responsibility to refrain from engaging in group libel (catchall), law plays in important role in the collective action problem of ensuring that everyone does their fair share in contributing to the provision of this public good. In other words, hate speech law serves to enforce the responsibility to refrain from engaging in group libel (catchall) (1630). This line of argument might seem to support what I shall call the Principle of Assurance, that legalistic constraints on uses of hate speech are (N-)warranted if they provide the public good of assurance.

I take it that when Waldron describes assurance as a public good he does *not* mean to suggest that it is something that cannot be excluded from certain vulnerable groups once it has been afforded to other groups. After all, there are plenty of hate speech regulations, such as those found in Russia, that provide protection to some groups (e.g., race, ethnicity, religion, nationality) but not to others (e.g., sexual orientation, gender, physical disability). Instead, he means to say that once it has been provided to some individual members of a protected group, it cannot be excluded from other members. Even so, what is the object of this action of assuring? What is it that beneficiaries of hate speech law are being assured of? Waldron says various things about this, ranging from the more abstract to the more concrete. First, beneficiaries of hate speech law are being assured that they are worthy of a high and equal sociolegal status; that they are members of society in good standing (Waldron 2010: 1601, 1605, 1626–1627). Second, they are being assured that because they are members of society in good standing, they enjoy fundamental rights;

*Principles of Civic Morality* 149

that their high and equal sociolegal status will translate into entitlements to just treatment (1613, 1626–1627). Third, they are being assured that their fundamental rights include the right not to be subjected to group libel (catchall) (1599, 1627–1628). Waldron gives no guidance on the sequencing of these assurances. Is hate speech law supposed to give all three forms of assurance simultaneously? Or is it supposed to give assurances of the most abstract form, which itself underpins the second and third forms of assurance, working from the abstract to the concrete? Or is it supposed to give assurances of the third, most concrete form, which itself underpins the second and first forms of assurance, working from the concrete to the abstract? What is relatively clear, I think, is that what people are being assured of is not merely ideas but also states of affair—for example, not merely the idea that their fundamental rights include the right not to be subjected to group libel (catchall) but the state of affairs that hate speakers will be denied the luxury of thinking that what they are doing is perfectly legal.

In addition to this, Waldron maintains that the action of assuring should be undertaken in such a way as to create a sense of being assured or a feeling of security, so that citizens can be confident that they will not be subjected to group libel (catchall) when they step out of their homes (Waldron 2010: 1626–1627, 1629–1630). Importantly, however, Waldron does not say whether he regards hate speech law as a necessary and sufficient condition of the action of assurance and the related sense of being assured. It only takes a moment of careful reflection to see that the enactment of hate speech legislation alone could never be sufficient. For, the mere enactment of hate speech legislation alone is unlikely to constitute an action of assurance or to create an effortless sense of being assured if there are low levels of police enforcement and public prosecution (cf. Young 1990: 62). Something that the UK experience of incitement to hatred legislation demonstrates is that cases are relatively infrequently referred to public prosecutors by the police, rarely proceed to prosecution, and very rarely result in successful prosecutions; at least, that is, in the first few decades of enactment (e.g., McNamara 2007b: 177–178; Nash and Bakalis 2007: 357). This means that, as McNamara explains, '[t]here is often an "expectation gap" between the circumstances in which individuals and groups call for the invocation of hate speech laws and the circumstances in which the CPS determines that it can initiate a prosecution' (McNamara 2007b: 178). More importantly, the existence of this expectation gap might tend to support the case *against* these sorts of laws/regulations/codes insofar as the disillusionment it creates could undermine the power of hate speech legislation to create a sense of being assured. If legislatures enact hate speech statutes that are difficult to enforce and to win convictions for, for example, this could be worse, from the point of view of assuring people that they are members of society in good standing, than not having these statutes on the books. Every high-profile decision not to prosecute and every high-profile acquittal might be greeted with anger and dismay by the minority group, who would be forgiven for seeing these results not as a valiant but ultimately failed attempt on the part of the state to defend their rights but as yet further evidence that their rights do not matter or even that in some sense the state implicitly sanctions, endorses, or approves of hate speech. In this scenario of civic disillusionment, the assuring action of legislation is outweighed by the disquieting omission of enforcement and prosecution.[12]

Of course, nowhere does Waldron claim—and nor does he think—that actions of assurance begin and end with legislation. He cites the example of a sign 'on the New York subway, in English and Spanish, telling people that they do not have to put up with unwanted sexual touching in a crowded subway car' (Waldron 2010: 1629). Then again, perhaps this sign constitutes a compelling act of assurance only because there are laws underpinning it, making it the case that unwanted sexual touching in a crowded subway car is illegal. But suppose a government enacts a law/regulation/code that constrains uses of hate speech and at the same time a government official publicly declares, "Be warned, in this country we shall take a zero tolerance attitude toward hate speech—all hate speakers can expect to be prosecuted to the fullest extent of the law." Would this constitute the sort of assurance that could lead persons to have a sense of being assured or a feeling of security when they leave their homes? Potentially not. When it comes to having a sense of being assured, members of vulnerable groups may know from experience that ministerial declarations do not always produce changes on the ground. Actions speak louder than words. And so neither the enactment of legislation nor the declaration as to enforcement will be sufficient. What matters practically is whether or not the minister is successfully able to orchestrate, with the help of the police, public prosecutors, and magistrates/judges, high levels of police enforcement of hate speech law and a high percentage of successful prosecutions for hate speech offenses.

Furthermore, it would be naive to think that instituting and rigorously enforcing hate speech law alone can be sufficient to provide the sort of public assurance that Waldron is concerned with. After all, there exists all manner of subtle, implicit, veiled, and unspoken ways in which members of society can cause other members of society to feel that they are not held in good standing (cf. Rice 1994: 91; Strossen 2012: 387; Simpson [R.] 2013: 724). For example, someone who graciously holds a door open for the next person when entering or leaving a building but not if the next person happens to be wearing a headscarf may send a clear signal to that person that she is not an equal. But such discourtesies are beyond the reach of any sensible hate speech law.

No doubt Waldron would willingly concede that hate speech law is not a sufficient condition for the public assurance of civic dignity. But, more worryingly for his argument, it can also be difficult to understand why laws/regulations/codes that constrain the use of group libel (catchall) are a necessary condition for public assurance of civic dignity. Suppose for the sake of argument that supreme courts are the final arbiters of what it means to have high and equal sociolegal status and of what fundamental rights should belong to citizens who enjoy this status. This would seem to entail that if a supreme court routinely upholds hate speech regulations, and in that sense assures the members of affected groups of their right not to be subjected to group libel (catchall), then at the same time this constitutes an act of assuring that being a member of society in good standing does entail the right to protection from group libel (catchall). However, it would also seem to entail that if a supreme court, such as the US Supreme Court, routinely strikes down hate speech regulations, it is saying that what it means to have high and equal sociolegal status and what fundamental rights follow from enjoying this status does *not* entail the right to protection from group libel (catchall). This, I think, opens up the possibility that even if hate speech law is necessary for providing an assurance that citizens enjoy a right to protection from group libel (catchall), it is not the case that hate speech law is necessary for providing an assurance that citizens are members of society in good standing, at least in the eyes of the supreme court.

Of course, Waldron could counter that there is an essential subjective dimension to the public good of assurance, which has to do with whether or not individuals *perceive* that they are members of society in good standing. Imagine that the US were a country in which racial/ethnic and religious minorities, not to mention gays and lesbians, could all count on authorities to unfailingly protect their civil rights in the political arena, the workplace, and in educational settings. Imagine as well that civil rights extended to rigorously enforced laws forbidding discriminatory harassment. But now also imagine that these groups do *not* enjoy legal rights against group libel (catchall). This means that someone could wear a T-shirt in a public park depicting an African American as an ape or post a piece on the Internet declaring "All Muslims are terrorists" or picket a funeral with a placard reading "God hates fags" or paint a Swastika on a public wall without fear of prosecution (other than for the generic offense of vandalism). Waldron is inviting the reader to entertain the possibility that the targets of these expressive acts could lack a sense or a feeling of being assured that they are members of society in good standing even if they enjoy the aforementioned civil rights.

> When a society is defaced with anti-Semitic signage, burning crosses, or defamatory racial leaflets, that sort of assurance evaporates. A vigilant police force and Justice Department may still keep people from being attacked or excluded, but people no longer have the benefit of a general public assurance to this effect, provided and enjoyed as a public good, furnished to all by all. (Waldron 2010: 1627)

If that is the case, however, then it appears that the damage to assurance done by group libel (catchall) is mediated through the thoughts, attitudes, and feelings of its targets. At this point, critics of hate speech law will probably argue that there is nothing predetermined or necessary about these sorts of thoughts, attitudes, and feelings. It is equally possible (so they might say) for members of vulnerable groups to continue to feel assured that they are members of society in good standing in spite of the fact that they do not enjoy the right to be protected against group libel (catchall)—perhaps they can feel this because whenever they see or hear public displays of hatred, they have trained their minds to concentrate upon all of the civil rights that they do enjoy. Indeed, critics of hate speech law might insist that targets of group libel (catchall) ought to bear some responsibility for their own mental attitude. For, there is a sense in which their failure to develop the right sort of mental attitude makes them susceptible to lacking a sense or feeling of being assured of their civic dignity. Of course, at this stage Waldron might retort that individuals should not have to bear the responsibility of developing the right sort of positive mental attitude: because the time and mental effort involved is an unreasonable burden. Then again, there seem to be burdens on both sides, for if persons do not seek to develop the right sort of mental attitude and go on to lack a sense of assurance, then the state may be forced to step in, and this comes at a cost to the interests of hate speakers. One possible solution to this dilemma might be to ask a question about what individuals could reasonable reject in terms of being asked to bear the practical burdens of cultivating the necessary cognitive capacities (assuming they can) to avoid lacking a sense or feeling of assurance of civic dignity (cf. Scanlon 1998). I shall return to this contractualist idea of reasonable rejection in Ch. 7 [7.2].

## 5.3 ELIGIBILITY

Assuming that the point of hate speech law is to protect and assure a high and equal sociolegal status, there is a prior question that cannot be put off any longer. Who is eligible for civic dignity and the package of fundamental rights that customarily follow in its wake? At certain points Waldron implies that eligibility for an equal and high sociolegal status depends on those familiar aspects of humanity that tend to crop up in the literature on human rights and human dignity, such as the capacity for rational behavior, for autonomy, for morality, or simply the ability to give meaning to life. Thus, he cites with approval Locke's idea that 'the rank of equality applies to all humans in virtue of their rationality' (Waldron 2011: 223). And he writes that '[w]e accord people dignity on account of the sorts of beings human individuals are, and we are gravely concerned when it is said publicly that some people, by virtue of their membership in a racial, ethnic, or religious group, are not really beings of that kind and so are not entitled to that dignity in one way or another' (2010: 1628). However, on closer inspection we find that Waldron's idea of a high and equal sociolegal status, or civic dignity, is very different from the Kantian notion of the inherent worth or value borne by all human beings, and this has important consequences for the issue of eligibility—or, so I shall now try to demonstrate.

*Principles of Civic Morality* 153

For one thing, Waldron explains that his concept of dignity 'involves the active exercise of a legally-defined status' (Waldron 2011: 223). This means that dignity is a status not to be passively possessed but to be dynamically carried forth. It involves wielding, as opposed to merely bearing, a package of rights, privileges, powers, authorities, roles, responsibilities, duties, and expectations. On the assumption that eligibility for civic dignity supervenes on the ability to actively exercise the incidents of a legally defined status, it would seem to follow that only a being capable of functioning as a citizen in that special sense could qualify for such a status. Take the case of rights. According to Waldron, '[r]ight bearers stand up for themselves; they make unapologetic claims on their own behalf; they control the pursuit and prosecution of their own grievances' (236). Accordingly, the only persons who can meaningfully possess rights are those capable of standing up for themselves, making claims and taking control of their grievances. Consider the citizen who actively exercises his or her right to protection from group libel (catchall) by reporting to the police a case of group libel and by appearing in court to give evidence in a subsequent criminal trial. Waldron also argues that 'the very nature of law' presupposes a certain kind of dignity-bearing being. Drawing on a range of jurisprudence he contends that law characteristically involves *self-application* (237–238), which presupposes beings who are capable of self-control or living in accordance with rules; *standards* such as the reasonable person test (238), which assumes the existence of beings capable of reflecting on the meaning of indeterminate rules in given contexts; *hearings* (239), which involves beings capable of explaining and justifying their behavior to others; and *argumentation* (239–240), which entails being able to think and contend.

So where does all this leave persons who are unable to exercise rights or meaningfully partake of the aforementioned aspects of a legal system? Tackling this question head-on Waldron writes the following.

> Certainly we do have to give an account of how human dignity applies to infants and to the profoundly disabled. My own view is that this worry should not necessarily shift us away from a conception that involves the active exercise of a legally-defined status. But it does require attention. I believe it can be addressed by the sort of structure that John Locke introduced into his theory, when he said of the rank of equality that applies to all humans in virtue of their rationality: "Children, I confess, are not born *in* this full state of equality, though they are born *to* it." Like heirs to an aristocratic title, their status looks to a rank that they *will* occupy (or are destined to occupy), but it does not require us to invent a different sort of dignity altogether for them in the meantime. (Waldron 2011: 223–224)

The implication is that eligibility for civic dignity depends not on the *actual* possession of the capacity for a high and equal sociolegal status but instead on the *potential* to develop that capacity in the future.

However, this is at best only a partial answer. While it may be straightforward to see how children pass this eligibility test, it is much less obvious in the case of adults who have been diagnosed with severe and permanent learning difficulties, emotional impairment, mental illness, or damage to core brain functioning. If this group or class of persons does not satisfy the eligibility test for civic dignity, the logic of Waldron's position would seem to suggest that they are *not* entitled to the rights associated with a high and equal sociolegal status, including the right to protection against group libel (catchall). Why does this matter? For the simple reason that members of this group or class of persons are often subjected to hate speech of various kinds, and in many countries have been subjected to some of the most extreme and sustained campaigns of hate speech suffered by any minority group (e.g., Mencap 1999; Equality and Human Rights Commission 2009; Saxton 2009). Consequently, we are left with a theory that says it helps to view laws/regulations/codes as protecting vulnerable minorities against the evil of group defamation (catchall), but that, at the same time, cannot account for how a particular section of our society who may be particularly vulnerable to this sort of speech could be eligible for the very civic dignity that is foundational for the right to protection under the terms of that theory. If, as seems plausible, it is arguable that the disabled should have just as much right to protection from hate speech as other groups or classes of persons who receive this protection, such as people identified by the characteristics of race/ethnicity (cf. Cram 2005), then surely the lack of eligibility must be counted as a weakness of Waldron's theory.

A second feature of civic dignity, namely, citizenship, might attract a related criticism. Waldron cites s. 224a of the Illinois Criminal Code, the statute implicated in *Beauharnais v. Illinois*, as exactly the sort of hate speech law that protects the rudiments of civic dignity. As noted earlier, Waldron rejects Justice Black's dissent 'with its perverse implication that the very large number of people defamed in the White Circle League's leaflet meant that the leaflet could not be subject to any sort of regulation at all' (Waldron 2010: 1609). However, it is important to recognize that the relevant statute refers not to 'people' but to 'a class of citizens.' And so, in Illinois at least, the right to protection from group libel (catchall) was bestowed only upon citizens. Indeed, it may be fitting to understand libel law as a way of society passing judgment on who is eligible to be thought of as members of the society in good standing (cf. Post 1986: 711). Citizenship is one criterion for this eligibility. This criterion seems to be implicitly accepted by Waldron when he refers to 'speech that in its content and tone runs counter to the assurances that citizens are supposed to have of one another's commitment to equality' (Waldron 2010: 1620n.108) and when he claims that the point of hate speech law is 'the conveying of an assurance to all citizens that they can count on being treated justly' (1628).

Once again, why does this matter? Because throughout the world it is common for undocumented immigrants (a class of resident *non*-citizens) to be the targets of group libel (catchall). Couched in the official-sounding language of "illegal aliens," members of this group are routinely associated with immorality and criminal behavior (in addition to their immigration status); cast as inhuman or animals, guilty of introducing inhuman or animalistic practices into a country; accused of arriving in such large numbers as to constitute an "invading horde" or of using illegal immigration as a staging post for "taking over" new lands (Anti-Defamation League 2006). It is extremely difficult to motivate a concern for this sort of group libel (catchall) within the framework of a theory that is focused on providing protection and assurance to *citizens* only. That we ought to look upon this as a weakness of the theory can be further motivated by reflecting on the Catch-22 in which undocumented immigrants could find themselves. Without eligibility for citizenship and civic dignity, undocumented immigrants would not benefit from the protection from group libel (catchall) that Waldron defends on behalf of citizens. Yet being victimized by this sort speech with impunity would only weaken their social standing and decrease the chances of their coming to be viewed by the general population, politicians, and key policymakers as deserving of citizenship. Matsuda once said that '[w]hen hundreds of police officers are called out to protect racist marchers, when the courts refuse redress for racial insult, and when racist attacks are officially dismissed as pranks, the victim becomes a stateless person' (Matsuda 1989b: 2338). This was probably meant in a metaphorical sense, but in the case of hate speech directed at undocumented immigrants it might be literally true.

Once again, Waldron is not oblivious to this potentially exclusionary feature of civic dignity. On the one hand, he writes this:

> If I were to give a name the status I have in mind, the high rank or dignity attributed to every member of the community and associated with fundamental rights, I might choose the term "legal citizenship." What I have in mind is something like the sense of citizenship invoked by T. H. Marshall in his famous book *Citizenship and Social Class* [. . .]. (Waldron 2011: 244)

But, on the other hand, he qualifies this by saying that he is conscious of Gerald Neuman's (1992) plea that political theorists should refrain from defining and using the term 'citizenship' in such a way as to entail or imply the acceptability of intolerant behavior toward resident non-citizens and undocumented immigrants (Waldron 2011: 244n.114). Yet Waldron does not pause to elaborate further on this. Perhaps in addition to his argument about the various rights associated with legal citizenship Waldron believes that there is a set of even more basic or fundamental rights, such as human rights, that a government owes even to undocumented immigrants. The question of what rights are owed to such persons must be answered, in other words, outside of the scope of the theory of civic dignity and hate speech regulations. However, I believe that it is an error to think that this question can be postponed or set aside precisely because hate speech directed at undocumented immigrants is a core example of the issue that any adequate theory must confront. After all, as noted in Ch. 2, several international conventions and protocols classify hate speech as an issue of human rights and call on states to adopt such legislative and other measures as may be necessary to prohibit hate speech directed at all persons under their care.

Notwithstanding this last point, Waldron begins by saying that he wants to offer a justificatory characterization of the hate speech law 'we find in Europe and in the other advanced democracies of the world', and it is certainly true that in some European countries hate speech law does serve to protect citizens only. Consider the case of Italy. Art. 3 of its constitution states, 'All citizens have equal social dignity and are equal before the law, without distinction of sex, race, language, religion, political opinion, personal and social conditions.' In accordance with this aspiration toward the *dignità sociale* of all *citizens*, previous Italian governments have enacted laws that grant special protection to those minority groups who have earned their right to a high and equal sociolegal status by becoming "good" citizens of Italy. Thus, Law No. 482 of 1999 relating to the protection of the linguistic minorities (as amended in 2001[13]) ensures that Art. 3(a) of Law No. 654 of 1975 (as amended in 1993[14]), which is a law prohibiting the dissemination of ideas based on racial or ethnic superiority or hatred, also applies to citizens belonging to linguistic minorities. What the law is saying here is that the Italian state recognizes and protects the rights of the Slovene minority living within its borders as it does the Italian citizenry in general. In contrast, the European Commission against Racism and Intolerance has strongly criticized the Italian state for its failure to adopt and enforce measures to protect migrants without a legal status, such as Roma and illegal immigrants from Africa, from hate speech in the media and on the Internet (European Commission against Racism and Intolerance 2012: paras. 54–61). Nevertheless, in other parts of Europe hate speech law explicitly protects persons against incitement to hatred on the grounds of citizenship (or lack thereof). In the UK, for example, Pt. 3 of the Public Order Act 1986 makes it an offense to use threatening words or behavior with the intention of stirring up racial hatred, where 'racial hatred' is defined as 'hatred against a group of persons in Great Britain defined by reference to colour, race, nationality (including citizenship) or ethnic or national origins.' Along similar lines, in *Case of the Fraudulent Asylum Seeker Poem* (1994)[15] the Bavarian Supreme Court ruled that the creation and distribution of a poem that contained defamatory statements about and negative stereotypes of asylum seekers in Germany amounted to incitement to hatred for the purposes of s. 130(2) of the German Criminal Code, even though asylum seekers do not enjoy the sociolegal status of citizens. Waldron may be unable to account for why non-citizens ought to be eligible for this sort of protection.

\* \* \*

In conclusion, I believe that Waldron has provided an original and important justification for hate speech law, one that might compliment or work alongside justifications based around values such as human dignity. However, I also believe that the force of the putative argument from protection and assurance of civic dignity extends into other areas of hate speech law that are either ignored or dismissed by Waldron, including Holocaust denial law and tort law. Moreover, I believe that Waldron ought to be more circumspect in claiming that it helps to view hate speech law as protecting vulnerable minorities against the evil of group defamation. Perhaps what he ought to say about his theory is that it helps to view hate speech law as protecting *some but not all* vulnerable minorities against the evil of group defamation. This in turn represents an important difference between the sorts of arguments for legalistic constraints on uses of hate speech that appeal to the concept of human dignity and those that turn on the concept of civic dignity. The latter apes both the egalitarianism and the universal applicability of the former but in the end cannot deliver on these promises, for it is rooted in eligibility criteria, such as the active exercise of legal status and citizenship, that discriminate between human beings.

## NOTES

1. 383 US 75 (involving a newspaper column criticizing fiscal mismanagement of a county recreation area).
2. At 92.
3. Interestingly, Waldron devotes far more textual space to charting the contours of the legal status than to providing a detailed sociological account of the nature of the social status being protected.
4. Waldron discusses a similar, although slightly expanded, set of examples elsewhere in the same article (Waldron 2010: 1618) and at greater length in his *The Harm in Hate Speech* (2012: 56–61).
5. There is a further complication, however. At times Waldron (2010: 1605, 1612, 1613, 1646) uses the terms 'protect', 'protecting', and 'protection', but at other times (1600, 1605, 1620) he uses 'vindicate', 'vindicating', and 'vindication.' Indeed, at one stage he claims (2011: 233) that historically certain laws would 'protect and vindicate dignity in the sense of rank or high status', whereas modern laws, including hate speech law, provide 'protection and vindication of the high rank or dignity of the ordinary person.' It is not clear, however, if he intends 'vindicate', 'vindicating', and 'vindication' to mean something *in addition to and different from* 'protect', 'protecting', and 'protection.' He does not pause to explain or define what he means by 'vindicate', 'vindicating', and 'vindication.' In ordinary English usage, 'to vindicate' can mean to clear one's good name or to seek exoneration from charges of guilt. Along these lines, one could say that civil libel law is a mechanism by which individual persons (or groups of persons in a class action lawsuit) may vindicate their reputations. However, Waldron is explicit that this sort of civil vindication is *not* the purpose of criminal group defamation law (catchall) (e.g., Waldron 2010: 1607). In another sense of the word, 'to vindicate' can be to justify or support the truth of a proposition by evidence or argument or through the giving of reasons or the pointing out of relevant facts, typically in the face of suspicion or doubt. In the case of hate speech law, the thing putatively being removed from suspicion or doubt is the social standing of the groups protected by such laws.

*Principles of Civic Morality*

How could this be the case? Starting with dignity as a legal status, it is not difficult to see how the very existence of hate speech law vindicates the dignity of those protected by such laws. For, if enjoying a certain legal status entails having rights to protection from group libel (catchall), then the mere fact that these laws protect members of certain groups from such speech provides the wider community with a reason to believe that the members of these groups are rights-bearing members of society in the relevant sense. That they are the beneficiaries of the enactment, maintenance, and effective application of these laws proves that they enjoy a high and equal legal status by virtue of the meaning of that status. Yet this proves only that hate speech law vindicates civic dignity in a trivial, tautological sense. In the case of dignity as a social status, it is more difficult to see how the mere existence of hate speech law could furnish reasons to believe in the high and equal social status of members of targeted groups. The mere fact that persons will be punished if they deny or call into question the humanity or civility of members of a minority group does not in itself provide evidence for the proposition that members of the group enjoy good standing in the society, particularly in the face of suspicion or doubt as to that standing. Both the hate speaker and the general audience could consistently retain their suspicion and doubt despite legal sanctions. Arguably very few laws have *this* sort of power to vindicate. Laws against theft will not provide reasons to believe that certain property is privately owned to persons who deny that it is, for example. Consequently, attempts to disambiguate the words 'vindicate', 'vindicating', and 'vindication' might detract from rather than reinforce Waldron's main contention. It may be that I have simply misinterpreted Waldron, however. Perhaps what he has in mind by 'vindicate', 'vindicating', and 'vindication' is nothing more than or different from 'protect', 'protecting', and 'protection.' He uses both to mean that hate speech law serves to uphold, defend, or guard the fundamentals of people's reputations as members of society in good standing. If I am right, then the language of vindication performs only a rhetorical function, and so it would be wrong to read Waldron as claiming more for hate speech law in terms of vindication than it can deliver.

6. *Vejdeland and Others v. Sweden*, Majority opinion at para. 49.
7. 1 BvR 23/94 (Const. Ct. of Germany, 13 Apr.) (involving the constitutionality of a local authority's imposition of a prior restraint on the National Democratic Party of Germany).
8. VI ZR 140/78 (Fed. Ct. of Just., 18 Sept.) (involving the constitutionality of a Holocaust denial law).
9. 343 US 250 (involving a prosecution of the founder of the White Circle League of America under s. 224a of the Illinois Criminal Code for distributing on street corners lithograph leaflets that exposed black Americans to contempt, derision, or obloquy).
10. *Beauharnais v. Illinois*, at 271–272.
11. Two further wrinkles are worth mentioning. First, in some countries both criminal and civil proceedings can be launched against the same transgression. For example, in France a public prosecutor may initiate criminal proceedings against persons suspected of defaming or insulting people on the grounds of their race, ethnicity, nationality, religion, gender, sexual orientation, and physical disability under ss. 32 and 33 the Press Law of 1881. What is more, Art. 2 of the Code of Criminal Procedure (in conjunction with s. 48 of the Press Law of 1881) grants both individual victims and interest groups representing groups of individuals the power to bring civil proceedings under ss. 32 and 33. Courts will hear both cases simultaneously and can hand down criminal penalties and award civil damages at the same time (see Janssen 2009). This would seem to suggest that at least forms of defamatory or insulting speech

## Principles of Civic Morality 159

could undermine both an individual's personal reputation (and its movement up or down the scale of social estimation) and the fundamentals of people's reputations as members of society in good standing.

Second, Waldron (2010: 1608) also recognizes the fact that in many jurisdictions the erstwhile mode of distinguishing between civil and criminal defamation law has been to say that the main purpose of the latter is to prevent breach of the peace or danger to public safety. See also Thomas Jones (1998: 88) and Patrick Milmo and W.V.H. Rogers (2008: 767). Thus, in *R. v. Osborne* an English court convicted the defendant of seditious libel for making accusations of child murder against Portuguese Jews living in London in the context that similar accusations had already produced an outbreak of anti-Jewish rioting. *Pace* Justice Black, there is nothing conceptually strange about the idea of a criminal law that prohibits defamation of a relatively large group of people (e.g., Portuguese Jews living in London) for the purposes of preventing breach of the peace or danger to public safety. Far from it. It would seem likely that the larger the group defamed the greater the risk of large-scale or widespread violence or unrest. Likewise, in the US case *Palmer v. City of Concord* (1868) 48 N.H. 211 (involved accusations of cowardice made against a body of soldiers relating to their conduct in the Civil War) the Court explained the purpose of criminal libel law as follows. 'Indictments for libel are sustained principally because the publication of a libel tends to a breach of the peace, and thus to the disturbance of society at large.' At 215.

12. The argument that legislation banning incitement to hatred should not be introduced for fear of raising false hopes is not hypothetical. In 1994 two members of the House of Lords in the UK suggested amendments to the Criminal Justice and Public Order Bill to include an offence of inciting religious hatred. Among the many arguments made against the amendments was the raising false hopes argument. On June 16 during the Committee Stage of the House of Lords debate on the Criminal Justice and Public Order Bill the most reverend Primate the Archbishop of York argued as follows: 'The point is that legislation arouses expectations. If a new criminal offence is put on the statute book without a reasonable expectation that it will prove effective, it may do more harm than good. That is particularly important in this case, where we are very properly seeking to protect and reassure groups which feel themselves to be vulnerable. If the legislation proves to be ineffective or is found to be directed toward the wrong target, such groups, which may be placing great hopes in Parliament to do something for them, will feel particularly let down.' House of Lords, 16 Jun. 1994, Hansard, vol. 555, col. 1894. The same argument was articulated on July 12 by Earl Ferrers during the Report stage of the Bill: 'The amendment could raise expectations that religious belief is now going to be protected against criticism or insult. That would not be its effect and the Government do not believe that it should be. But without very careful consultation over the purposes and the effect of any change in this area, many people and, I fear, many Moslems in particular, might be deeply critical of any law when they realised that the expectation that religion was to be protected from vilification was not going to be met. They might well feel let down and mislead.' House of Lords, 12 Jul., 1994, Hansard, vol. 556, col. 1749.
13. As amended by Art. 23 of Law No. 38 of 2001.
14. As amended by Art. 1 of Decree-Law No. 122 of 1993 and converted with amendments into law by Law No. 205 of 1993.
15. Cited in Brugger (2003: 29–30).

# 6 Principles of Cultural Diversity

If one believes that culture is part of the lifeblood of individual and communal life, one is bound to take a keen interest in free speech and its limits. First, one might think that to be human is to be able to choose between, or perhaps to make choices that are rendered meaningful by, culture (i.e., configurations of beliefs, values, customs, social arrangements, venerated objects, memories, narratives, and so on) and that free speech is indispensible to such choices. One might also think that certain cultural choices can be informed by hate speech, in constructive as well as destructive ways. Second, one could believe that real value resides in the actual cultural configurations that result from human activity and the capacity for choice such as it is. And so, because particular cultural identities have special value, they must not be misrecognized, including misrecognition through hate speech. Third, one could argue that to be truly human is to engage in culturally specific interpretations of minimum universal values and to enter into intercultural dialogue with other people concerning their competing interpretations, including competing interpretations of how these minimum universal values bear upon the complex issue of hate speech law. What is more, one could insist that in order to be fully responsive to ideals of mutual respect between cultures this sort of intercultural dialogue should not merely be about hate speech law but also, where necessary, governed by it. Some of the aforementioned arguments have already been expressed by champions of the politics of identity, the politics of recognition, multiculturalism, and interculturalism. Others have not, and I shall do my best to develop them here. It is also the case that the variety of legalistic constraints on hate speech that are currently implemented through media and internet laws and regulations, local statutes, national criminal codes, and human rights instruments is much greater than many cultural theorists have hitherto imagined. Hence, another goal of this chapter is to show how certain principled arguments are more naturally suited to some clusters of laws/regulations/codes than others.

## 6.1 CULTURE

Liberal approaches to culture differ as to whether culture is principally viewed as an object of choice or as a context of meaningful choice. But either way, informed choice seems to depend on access to information about one's own or different cultural configurations and this access may be predicated upon the right to free expression and an associated right to receive information. If other people are not permitted to communicate to us what is distinctive and valuable about our own or alternative cultures, how can we make either informed choices about which cultures to adopt or culturally embedded choices about how to live? But free speech is not merely important for learning about the essentials of any given culture; it is also indispensible for those seeking to build or maintain languages that are constitutive of their chosen cultures. So, for example, Will Kymlicka (1995) argues that a 'societal culture' is one that provides its members with meaningful ways of life across a full gamut of human activities and that societal cultures are typically based on a shared language. Building on this idea, it might be argued that if the state suppresses a particular language, then it is suppressing a societal culture, and for Kymlicka at least this means reducing the opportunities for members of those societal cultures to make meaningful choices. The fact that culture is intersubjective and temporal provides another possible justification for guaranteeing free expression. Insofar as culture relies upon and is partly embodied in an intersubjective practice of communicating and re-communicating a body of shared beliefs, ideas, stories, perspectives, feelings, and so on, over time and from one generation to the next, the suppression of these practices can make culture whither on the vine. Whether culture is something persons choose to adopt or something persons find themselves enveloped in or a subtle mixture of both, to suppress the communicative practices through which culture is created, transmitted, and embodied is bad for cultural diversity and bad for persons who find it difficult and costly to give up a culture and take on a new one. The effect of banning storytelling in cultural communities constituted by and through their oral traditions is an extreme but indicative example of this danger. For his part, Joseph Raz argues that the freedom to portray in public a given cultural way of life serves three main purposes: to 'familiarize' the wider society of things it may have in common with a given cultural way of life; to 'reassure' the adherents of a given cultural way of life that they are not alone or invisible; and to provide 'validation' that a given cultural way of life is among the acceptable options in that society (Raz 1991: 311). Conversely, 'censoring expression normally expresses authoritative condemnation not merely of the views or opinions censored but of the whole style of life of which they are a part' (310).

This family of arguments for freedom of expression supports the Principle of Culture, that legalistic constraints on speech or other expressive acts, including constraints on uses of hate speech, are (N-)unwarranted if they undermine the existence of a plurality of cultures or deny people opportunities for choosing between cultures or else choosing ways of life amidst culture. But just how far does this argument extend? Raz extends his argument for freedom of expression even to 'critical or hostile portrayals of Muslims or gays' (Raz 1991: 320) or what he calls 'hostile speech' (321n.36), which he characterizes as speech that expresses hostility, condemnation, or criticism for other ways of life (320). This is partly because 'criticism of rival ways of life is a part of any way of life in the sense that it is implied by it, and is felt by its adherents' (320–321). For Raz, if familiarization, reassurance, and validation are important reasons to defend the public portrayal of different cultures, the same reasons apply to hostile speech that is partly constitutive of some cultures. Consider the religious conservative for whom engaging in hostile speech, not merely on the subject of homosexuality but directed toward homosexuals, is an important dimension of *his* way of life. Alon Harel comes to a similar conclusion. He argues that 'hate speech should not only be considered as part of free-speech jurisprudence, but also as part of the literature concerning multiculturalism and the toleration of communal practices' (Harel 2012: 326). For Harel, there are special reasons to protect hate speech that have to do with the particular value of culturally rooted lifestyles or what he calls 'comprehensive forms of life' (323). These reasons find (partial) expression in law. For example, in both Australia (the State of Victoria, State of Western Australia) and Canada, legislation banning incitement to hatred sets out exemptions for speech that has a religious purpose or is motivated by sincerely held religious beliefs.[1] I say 'partial' expression because these laws do not offer wholesale exemptions for speech with a cultural purpose, and clearly culturally embedded or comprehensive ways of life do not begin and end with religion. If one fully accepted the aforementioned family of arguments, it would be hard not to grant exemptions for acts of incitement to hatred performed by speakers for the avowed purpose of expressing their 'white culture' or, to take a more extreme example, a neo-Nazi comprehensive way of life (cf. McNamara 2007a: 164). Indeed, it might be difficult to think of any examples of incitement to hatred that are not rooted in at least *one* comprehensive form of life.

Notwithstanding this last point, does ensuring a plurality of different cultures *really* necessitate a constitutional guarantee of freedom to engage in hate speech? Interestingly, Anna Elisabetta Galeotti puts forward an argument in favor of hate speech law that mirrors the arguments that Raz presents on behalf of free speech.

> Literally, it is demanded that citizens in a still weak social position be spared the position of racist abuse. But, more importantly, the claim concerns the stabilization of the public presence of identities that have previously been excluded and discriminated against, a process which is undermined by the persistence of unchecked racist speech. The

destabilizing effect of widespread racist speech is symbolically reinforced by its public tolerance. The argument for restrictions is thus aimed also at institutionalizing some form of public stand against racism which symbolically delegitimizes it. (Galeotti 2002: 156)

Consequently, if one focuses on the validation function of speech, what we are being presented with, in effect, is a conflict between competing claims to the validation of culture. For example, just as suppressing anti-homosexual or homophobic speech (e.g., "I hate gays, and if you have any morals you should too") might be said to constitute an authoritative validation of homosexual culture and the condemnation of homophobic culture, so a failure to suppress homophobic speech might be said to constitute an authoritative validation of homophobic culture and a condemnation of homosexual culture. So what is to be done?

It might be possible to settle these conflicts between competing claims to validation on behalf of different cultural communities by appealing to some sort of common interest or public good. On this approach, a legalistic scheme of speech freedoms and restrictions is N-warranted just in case it serves a common interest or public good that benefits everyone, either directly or indirectly. Consider rules of conduct associated with the practice of public debating. These rules are N-warranted (so the argument runs) if they succeed in ensuring that everyone can partake of the public good of constructive debate (Hart 1973: 544–545). Based on this analogy, one might start to think of the existence of a plurality of cultures or comprehensive ways of life as being itself a public good. Since most people nowadays are immersed in many different cultures at the same time, the maintenance of a plurality of cultures is something that the representative individual is likely to want. Indeed, even someone who is entirely embedded in only a single culture and has no immediate interest in the maintenance of a plurality of cultures, might be thought to have a rational interest in being able to choose to change culture at a later date if he or she so desires. Because human beings can be fundamentally mistaken about which comprehensive way of life is most valuable, it is rational to prefer having the option to change, even if for the foreseeable future one has no intention of doing so. Even so, my point about a plurality of cultures potentially being a public good under a liberal approach to these issues is not intended as a defense of preserving the current set of cultures exactly as they are, simply because they happen to exist, but ensuring that *some* set of diverse cultural communities exist so as to provide a range of options for culture construction and for culturally embedded choices.

Following on from this, if the existence of a plurality of cultures or comprehensive ways of life is a public good, the operative question becomes which scheme of speech freedoms and restrictions best promotes or protects that public good. I do not pretend that the answer to this question is straightforward. Maintaining cultural diversity may depend upon achieving something like an equilibrium in the interaction among different, overlapping cultures, so that no one culture or limited set of cultures dominates and monopolizes the others, but what this equilibrium looks like in practice and which cultures or comprehensive ways of life should be safeguarded will be difficult to pin down and open to controversy. Nevertheless, my own hunch is that the common good of a plurality of cultures or comprehensive ways of life need not be ill-served by a legalistic scheme of speech freedoms and restrictions that includes *some* restrictions on hate speech. For example, there seems to be a partial analogy between an argument that says Amish and Mennonite communities in the US should have the right to exclude pornography from their settlements in order to protect the purity of their way of life within the wider society and an argument that says Muslims living in the US should have the right to impose on the wider population laws banning incitement to hatred on the grounds of religious identity so as to safeguard the long-time survival of Muslim culture in the wider, non-Muslim society (cf. Levy 2000: 140). To give another example, it could be the case that the extent to which the survival of gay culture is put at risk from instances of incitement to hatred on the grounds of sexual orientation is greater than the extent to which the survival of homophobic culture (a broad church including some conservative Muslims) is put at risk by the prohibition of such speech.

These observations might support the Nuanced Principle of Culture, that legalistic constraints on hate speech are (N-)warranted if they serve to protect a plurality of cultures and opportunities for making choices between cultures or choices embedded in culture. The idea that hate speech law is N-warranted in the name of safeguarding cultural diversity was certainly part of the Canadian Supreme Court's thinking in *R. v. Keegstra*. Invoking s. 27 of the Canadian Charter of Rights and Freedoms ('This Charter shall be interpreted in a manner consistent with the preservation and enhancement of the multicultural heritage of Canadians'), Chief Justice Dickson put the following argument for a law banning incitement to hatred.

> This Court has where possible taken account of s. 27 and its recognition that Canada possesses a multicultural society in which the diversity and richness of various cultural groups is a value to be protected and enhanced. [. . .] The value expressed in s. 27 cannot be casually dismissed in assessing the validity of s. 319(2) under s. 1, and I am of the belief that s. 27 and the commitment to a multicultural vision of our nation bear notice in emphasizing the acute importance of the objective of eradicating hate propaganda from society.[2]

But what does it mean to say that a cultural group can be put at risk by hate speech? One possibility is that hate speech compels persons to reject the identity that causes them to become the objects of ritual humiliation (cf. Matsuda 1989b: 2337). If sufficient numbers of people alienate themselves from their communal cultural identity, this could in the long term weaken

*Principles of Cultural Diversity* 165

the ability of that culture to withstand external pressures to radically change or even cease being. Indeed, this possibility was one of the avowed rationales behind the Federal Court of Australia's decision in *Eatock v. Bolt*, in which the Court found against a journalist who made allegations in print that mixed race Aboriginals were unscrupulously pretending to be genuinely Aboriginal merely to claim benefits reserved for Aboriginal peoples. Justice Bromberg articulated the rationale thusly.

> In seeking to promote tolerance and protect against intolerance in a multicultural society, the RDA [Racial Discrimination Act] must be taken to include in its objective tolerance for and acceptance of racial and ethnic diversity. At the core of multiculturalism is the idea that people may identify with and express their racial or ethnic heritage free of pressure not to do so. Racial identification may be public or private. Pressure which serves to negate it will include conduct that causes discomfort, hurt, fear or apprehension in the assertion by a person of his or her racial identity. Such pressure may ultimately cause a person to renounce their racial identity. Conduct with negating consequences such as those that I have described, is conduct inimical to the values which the RDA seeks to honour.[3]

Ostensibly Justice Bromberg is making the point that individuals should not be persecuted for their cultural membership and bullied into giving it up, but this might also be interpreted as a wider point about what is required to safeguard the persistence of cultural diversity or a multicultural society over time: namely, that alternative cultural communities can continue to exist only if members and potential members of those communities are not subjected to persecution in the form of hate speech.

Having said all of that, it might also be the case that some hate speakers are members of cultural communities that are themselves vulnerable to external pressures such that banning *their* use of hate speech could threaten to wipe out that particular culture or comprehensive way of life. Consider law interdicting uses of hate speech when it amounts to discriminatory intimidation, such as cross burning statutes. In *Virginia v. Black* the US Supreme Court considered the constitutionality of the State of Virginia's cross burning statute, according to which burning a cross on or near the property of another person, or across from a highway or other public place 'shall be *prima facie* evidence of an intent to intimidate a person or group.' Writing for the majority, Justice O'Connor struck down this *prima facie* evidence provision, remarking that '[a]s the history of cross burning indicates, a burning cross is not always intended to intimidate.'[4] Justice O'Connor goes on to explain how the burning cross has been, and continues to be, for certain groups of people 'a statement of ideology', 'a symbol of group solidarity', 'a ritual', and something that is 'directed at a group of likeminded believers'.[5] What she describes bears all the hallmarks of a cultural community or comprehensive way of life. Perhaps part of what is at stake here is a conflict between competing claims to the validation of culture on behalf of white and black Americans. What is more, there may be a sense in which what Justice O'Connor is describing is a particular white culture that is under siege, whose continued existing might be threatened by statutes banning its core rituals (in the context of wider social, economic, and cultural progressiveness). No doubt critics of Holocaust denial legislation might wish to say the same about people for whom denying the Holocaust has become a way of life, replete with its own beliefs, values, customs, rituals, language, domains, and so on.

Does this mean, therefore, that even someone embedded in an African American or Jewish culture has an indirect interest in a legal regime that validates the culture and the cultural hate speech of white supremacist or neo-Nazi groups by virtue of the fact that he or she might at some point in the future wish to join this group? No doubt it would be extremely difficult to find anyone who would report having this interest, but it does not follow that this interest is not rational. On the other hand, it may be rational to not favor the protection of the culture of a group whose raison d'être is the destruction of all cultures save one. For, it is likely that persons currently belong to cultural communities or could potentially belong to cultural communities that are under attack from this group. What we have, then, is a complex interplay between the demands of the Principle of Culture and the implications of the Nuanced Principle of Culture. Together they call for a nuanced assessment of whether or not a particular hate speech law or a specific application of hate speech law to a cultural community is N-warranted given its likely overall impact on cultural diversity and choice.

## 6.2 MISRECOGNITION

Culture figures in the above arguments for and against hate speech law as a part of a public good. But this is not the only way that culture can figure in such arguments. Another means of approaching the topic is to adopt a deontological perspective and to ask what it means to respect the culture or cultural identity of human beings. The literature on the politics of identity and the politics of recognition contains various terms for the absence of respect, including 'cultural imperialism' (Young 1990), 'nonrecognition' or 'misrecognition' (Taylor [C.] 1994), 'cultural hegemony' (Modood 1993), 'cultural injustice' (Fraser 1995), and 'disrespect' (Honneth 1992, 1995; Parekh 2006; Appiah 2005). According to Charles Taylor, for example, 'identity is partly shaped by recognition or its absence, often by the *mis*recognition of others' (Taylor [C.] 1994: 25). By defining misrecognition in terms of an attack on identity Taylor can plausibly claim that 'recognition is not just a courtesy we owe people [ . . . ] [but] a vital human need' (ibid.).

What is more, unlike some of the liberal approaches to cultural diversity discussed in the previous section, Taylor argues that what really matters and what should be the object of recognition is not the putative capacity of human beings to autonomously choose or acquire cultural identity but 'what they have made of this potential in fact', as in, the actual cultural identities of different groups of people (42–43).

For some theorists working in the politics of identity or the politics of recognition traditions, a key part of what is troubling about the use of hate speech in the performance of misrecognition (e.g., the use of negative stereotypes in the media, the use of speech that constitutes incitement to hatred) is the fact that the ascription of identities to persons or groups of persons on the basis of (arbitrary) characteristics is performed by more powerful groups (working through oppressive institutions and structures), and invariably this means that less powerful groups are given lower status identities (e.g., Young 1990: 60, 135–136; Thompson 2012: 228).

These sorts of approaches point in the direction of what I shall call the Principle of Recognition, that legalistic constraints on uses of hate speech are (N-)warranted if they limit misrecognition and promote recognition. In the remainder of this section I shall try to flesh out this principle through an exposition of four main forms of misrecognition (inspired by but not limited to the work of Taylor) and their connection with particular clusters of laws/regulations/codes that constrain uses of hate speech.

## Misrecognition as the Oppressive Ascription of Identity

One form of misrecognition has to do with oppressively ascribing an identity to, or arbitrarily imposing an identity upon, individuals. First, this is a matter of that identity being ascribed externally (by other agents, institutions, structures) against the will of the person, meaning that it is an identity that people have not chosen and would not chose to adopt if they had been given the choice. Second, the content of an identity can be oppressive if it forecloses the possibility of other joint identities that someone might want to adopt; that is to say, if it closes down rather than opens up the possibility of other, elective identities. Hate speech can be, and often is, used to enact this form of misrecognition. In extreme cases, legal-political institutions can externally designate the identity of people using ethnophaulisms or other forms of hate speech, and in ways that have serious implications for not merely their identity but also the various legal-political rights, statuses, and capacities that hinge on identity. Consider the use of the word "nigger" to impose an identity on African slaves and former slaves both before and after abolition in the US, the use of the term "kaffir" to ascribe an identity to black South Africans both under the system of apartheid and in the post-apartheid settlement, or the use of the term "illegal alien" to fix the identity of certain groups of resident non-citizens in many Western democracies. In these contexts when someone's identity is ascribed to her on the basis of perceived racial, ethnic, nationality, or citizenship characteristics, both the ascription of identity is involuntary and the content of that identity limits her options of giving herself other meaningful identities. Thus, in a deeply racialized and racist society, once someone's identity is settled with the term "nigger", she may find it extremely difficult to attribute other identities to herself. She may call herself "lawyer", "school governor", "mother", "citizen", or even "mixed race", but in the eyes of society she is just a "nigger."[6]

But then again what of persons who embrace ethnophaulisms in the construction of their own identity? Consider the rapper who proclaims "I'm a bad nigga" in a conscious (commercial) attempt to tap into negative stereotypes about African Americans and to project a public image that is thought to be appropriate or authentic for artists in that genre of music. If such a person uses the term "nigger" or even "nigga" to fix his own identity, or at least his artistic persona, then how could it possibly amount to misrecognition for other people to subsequently address him using those terms? Perhaps in this exceptional case—assuming that it is not an involuntary or pathological internalization of an inferior identity—the use of the term "nigger" is not oppressive. But then again, the problem is that when African Americans with a high public profile use the term "nigger" or even or "nigga", this can send a message to other Americans that it is permissible to use these terms in reference to, or as a mode of address for, African Americans *in general*. And it is certainly not the case that other African Americans have somehow asked to be labeled in these ways. On the contrary, there are large numbers of African Americans who, given a free choice in the matter, would prefer not to be called "nigger" or even "nigga"—and would even prefer it if other African Americans did not refer to themselves using such terms. Their preference is revealed in various ways, not the least in their decision on a point of principle not to use, and not to purchase music or consume other forms of media that use the words "nigger" or "nigga."

In short, so long as people remain the objects rather than the coauthors of social practices whereby identities (that they would not choose for themselves) are ascribed to them using hate speech, there is an argument to say that they are the victims of misrecognition. What is more, insofar as the politics of recognition or the politics of identity enjoins interference in individual liberty where it is necessary to curb the grosser forms of misrecognition, focusing on the present form of misrecognition might support laws/regulations/codes that disallow the public expression of hatred toward protected groups, including through the use of insults, slurs, or derogatory epithets and the dissemination of ideas based on the inferiority of protected groups. Then again, what reason is there to think that misrecognition *qua* the oppressive ascription of identity constitutes one of the grosser forms of misrecognition? Perhaps because it makes sense to demand, as a matter of right, that the practice of other people ascribing identity to oneself, insofar as there is a place for that practice, is limited to terms that one cannot reasonably object to because they

Principles of Cultural Diversity 169

do not ascribe an identity that imposes severe social, political, legal, and economic disadvantageous on the bearer and because they do not preclude the possibility of other identities that one might elect to adopt if one had the choice. It is this right to consensual identity-ascription (along with many other rights) that was so grotesquely violated under the system of slavery and to a lesser extent during the Reconstruction era in the US, and under the apartheid regime and to a lesser extent in the post-apartheid settlement in South Africa.

## Misrecognition as Tarnishing an Identity

A second form of misrecognition often goes hand in hand with the first form but *in itself* involves tarnishing an identity, such as by subjecting an identity to a systematic campaign of denigration, negative stereotyping, stigmatization, and defamation. If successful, this campaign can transform the *content* of an identity, making it synonymous with what is bad, unjust, unsuitable, inhuman, evil, out of place, and other. To borrow the words of Taylor: 'a person or group of people can suffer real damage, real distortion, if the people or society around them mirror back to them a confining or demeaning or contemptible picture of themselves' (Taylor [C.] 1994: 25). In other words, the present form of misrecognition of cultural identity can 'inflict a grievous wound, saddling its victims with a crippling self-hatred' (26). For this reason, argues Honneth, it is appropriate for a minority communal culture to demand protection 'from forms of public degradation, disrespect, and humiliation' (Honneth 2003: 166).

Applying this form of misrecognition to the case of hate speech puts a new spin on the familiar argument (made by critical race theorists) that stigmatizing people on the grounds of their racial or ethnic identity is morally unacceptable in part because over time members of the targeted group may come to internalize this stigmatization and develop low self-esteem or self-hatred. Parekh, for example, associates damage to social identity with damage to self-esteem (Parekh 2005–2006: 218). Although he is not explicit in this regard, he appears to believe that the mechanics of damage to social identity and adverse esteem effects are rooted in the connection between social identity and personal identity. According to Parekh, personal identity has to do with how we as individuals define ourselves or identify the kinds of person we are (2008: 10). It is also 'the source of such powerful and action-guiding emotions as pride, shame, embarrassment and guilt, and is closely bound up with one's sense of self-worth' (13). Insofar as an individual's sense of who he or she is, or personal identity, is based on a particular social identity, hate speech that damages the standing or reputation of that identity can in turn diminish a person's sense of self-worth.

If this form of misrecognition is understood to be sufficiently serious and there are no less restrictive ways of curbing it—an issue to which I shall return in Ch. 9 [9.3]—there may be a case for legalistic constraints on the uses of hate speech that constitute this form of misrecognition. Consider the regulation of the use of negative stereotyping and stigmatization in the media and on the Internet, or even criminal law proscribing forms of group defamation (catchall). How could it be right to stop governmental authorities from giving people legal protections against attempts by hate speakers to tarnish their group identities? This line of argument is implicit in parts of Justice Frankfurter's justification for his finding in *Beauharnais v. Illinois*. 'It would [. . .] be arrant dogmatism, quite outside the scope of our authority in passing on the powers of a State, for us to deny that the Illinois legislature may warrantably believe that a man's job and his educational opportunities and the dignity accorded him may depend as much on the reputation of the racial and religious group to which he willy-nilly belongs, as on his own merits.'[7]

At this stage, however, it must also be observed that using hate speech to tarnish an identity is only possible so long as the relevant words possess negative meaning or connotation, and that it is quite possible for groups of persons to turn words with negative meanings into positive affirmations (or symbols of defiance) through processes of 'transformation', 'resignification', or 'reclaiming' (e.g., Fraser 1995: 82–83; Butler 1993: 226–233; Abel 1998: 243; Kennedy 1999–2000: 90–91; Modood 2007: 40). In other words, if, as Taylor argues, '[m]y own identity crucially depends on my dialogical relations with others' (Taylor [C.] 1994: 34), then it is quite possible that these dialogical relations can support the creation of a positive self-identity even if terms such as "queer" or "nigger" are involved in that creation. The existence of this possibility has been seized upon by some thinkers as reason to believe that all hate speech law should be rejected since there is always a chance that it can be used against persons faithfully involved in projects in which they seek to resignify their own identity. Instead, what is needed (so the argument goes) is a guaranteed space for freedom of expression—a space for hate speakers and reclaimers alike (e.g., Karst 1990: 108–109; Richards 1999: 134–137; Stopford 2009: 71). However, this particular conclusion seems to overlook the fact that reclaimers are often in a subordinate or less powerful position in society, and so it may not be a "fair fight." Indeed, some words may be beyond salvation and cannot be resignified despite the best efforts of reclaimers. Worryingly, in some instances words are resignified by a minority group, only for that group to embrace meanings that themselves constitute the subordination of a "minority" within that minority, such as in the case of the misogynist language used in gangsta rap (e.g., Williams Crenshaw 1993; Buckner Inniss 2007). Finally, the conclusion also ignores the plight of persons who must suffer misrecognition while the battle for resignification rages on. They would be collateral damage in an experiment conducted by the government to see if reclaimers can win a battle without support.

## Misrecognition as Existential Threats to Identity

A third form of misrecognition is best described as existential threat to identity. Some uses of hate speech undermine or threaten the very existence of the cultural identities they target in ways other than by coercing adherents to abandon their own culture. This is perhaps most obvious in the case of Holocaust denial, which I believe poses three existential threats to the cultural identity of Jews. First, Holocaust denial may constitute an existential threat to the cultural identity of deceased Jews. Existential misrecognition of their cultural identity takes the form of the denial that they ever existed, such as through the denial of the testimony of eyewitnesses and other evidence supporting the fact of their existence. Here it is the expressive act of refusal to say the names of the victims of the Holocaust that amounts to hate speech. As William James Booth puts it, 'until their names are restored to them, until those names live again in the light of memory, these people remain among the lost, in nothingness' (Booth 2006: 77).[8]

Second, Holocaust denial may constitute an existential threat to the cultural identity of living Jews, by denying the memories that are partly constitutive of their identity as members of Jewish cultural communities. A large part of what binds together a cultural community and the members of that community, both in the present moment and over time, is cultural memory. Following the work of Jan Assmann on cultural memory and cultural identity, I shall assume that cultural memory 'preserves the store of knowledge from which a group derives an awareness of its unity and peculiarity' (Assmann 1995: 130) and that cultural memory 'is maintained through cultural formation (texts, rites, monuments) and institutional communication (recitation, practice, observance)' (129). Interestingly, cultural formation and institutional communication are often placed in the hands of specialists who are recognized as bearing a special epistemic authority over the meaning, interpretation, and reconstruction of texts, rites, monuments, recitations, practices, observances, and so on (131). How does all this relate back to Holocaust denial? When Holocaust deniers or revisionists misrecognize or fail to recognize certain texts, archives, and written and recorded testimonies, and also misrecognize or fail to recognize the epistemic authority of specialists in the management of the cultural memory associated with the Holocaust, this constitutes an existential threat to the cultural identity of Jews insofar as that identity is bound up with this cultural memory. An extreme example would be claiming that certain "experts" on the Holocaust far from preserving for posterity certain buildings and sites involved in the Holocaust actually manufactured or created those things. In this way Holocaust denial law might be a justified response to the fact that Holocaust denial constitutes misrecognition of memory, which is a significant part of the identity of members of the Jewish culture. Indeed, in *X v. Federal Republic of Germany* (1982)[9] the European Commission for Human Rights supported a conviction under Germany's defamation laws against an individual who had displayed pamphlets denying the Holocaust. The Court found that this expressive conduct attacked the reputation of Jews as persons whose personal testimony and collective memory of historical events can be trusted.

Third, Holocaust denial may constitute an existential threat to the persistence of Jewish cultural identity over time. Suppose one takes the view that 'the memory criterion' is a necessary condition not just of personal identity but of the persistence of cultural communities over time. On this criterion, a cultural community that exists now is identical with another cultural community that existed at a previous time just in case the cultural community that exists now can remember experiences that the other cultural community actually had at that previous time. It might be argued that Holocaust denial threatens the chain of cultural memory linking bearers of the Jewish cultural identity now to bearers of the Jewish cultural identity at a previous time because it denies that the memories of Jews living now are memories of the actual experiences of Jews at the time. This is by virtue of the fact that (according to Holocaust deniers) the Jews at the time did not experience the Holocaust (because the Holocaust did not take place). In this third way Holocaust denial law might be a justified response to the fact that Holocaust denial constitutes misrecognition or a failure to recognize the persistence of Jewish cultural identity over time.

However, what about cases in which interpersonal communication does throw up inaccuracies and incompleteness in personal testimony? Should we say that this form of communication constitutes hate speech? Consider Dori Laub's (1992) seminal account of his interview of a woman who was an eyewitness to events at Auschwitz during the Holocaust. He notes how historians involved in the project identified both factual inaccuracies in her account of the Auschwitz uprising (she had been in error about the number of chimneys burnt down) and incompleteness in her account of her act of resistance in appropriating clothes and shoes for fellow inmates (she said nothing about where the clothes and shoes had come from). What is more, they were inclined to dismiss her testimony as unsound for fear that it could become grist for the mill of Holocaust deniers and revisionists. However, Laub argues that there is a sense in which what survivors of the Holocaust are *really* testifying to is not empirical or historical facts but the narratives they create in relation to these traumatic events (Laub 1992: 60–62). Why do these narratives matter? One reason, mentioned by Laub, is that they give people the will to survive, to make it through the immediate traumatic period and to go on with their lives after it has ended (62). A second, equally important reason, it seems to me, has to do with identity. The narrative of the woman Laub describes is central to the identity that she has constructed for herself as someone who was an eyewitness to Jewish resistance and as a person who tried to do good in an environment of evil. As Laub puts it, '[t]his was her way of being' (62). How then should we judge those historians who were likely to label her testimony "unsound"? Would the use of this label have been proscribable hate speech? I would suggest that insofar as the intended aim would not have been to destroy an individual identity but instead to protect the identity of the Jews in general, calling her testimony "unsound" would not have amounted to misrecognition and would not have constituted proscribable hate speech (under the present account). This is contrasted with the speech of Holocaust deniers who claim that personal narratives are "lies" or "deliberate inventions told for the purposes of attracting sympathy." Here the aim is to destroy both the identity of the Holocaust survivor and the identity of Jews in general, and as such this counts as proscribable hate speech (under the present account).

## Misrecognition as Oversimplifying the Cultural Identity of the Individual

A fourth form of misrecognition has to do with attributing only one or two basic identities to an individual when in fact he or she may partake of a multitude of cultural identities, to differing degrees and in idiosyncratic concatenations. The point here is that an individual may have reason to care about a plethora of cultural identities, including even identities associated with cultural groups with which he or she is no longer substantially connected (e.g., individuals brought up in religious communities but who no longer practice any religion).[10] It is often argued that hate speakers are guilty of precisely this sort of oversimplification of people's identity (e.g., Delgado 1982: 144). Parekh, for example, notes that hate speech not only stigmatizes its target group 'by ascribing to it a set of constitutive qualities that are widely viewed as highly undesirable' (Parekh 2005–2006: 214) but also involves a secondary attack on the individuals concerned by falsely intimating that they have only one social identity, thereby 'reducing them to uniform specimens of the relevant racial, ethnic or religious group' (217). Monica Mookherjee makes a similar point in relation to negative stereotyping on the basis of race, ethnicity, religion, and so on. 'Such a reductive assessment of complex human beings [. . .] falsely unifies their identities' (Mookherjee 2007: 117).

Nevertheless, it must also be asked whether our responses to hate speech perpetuate this form of misrecognition. The politics of recognition developed by Taylor connects together the concepts of recognition, cultural identity, and positive attitudes to self. This means that claims about recognition and misrecognition are themselves mediated through certain assumptions about the cultural identities of the groups to which individuals putatively belong. Critics of Taylor, however, have argued that these assumptions may themselves constitute forms of misrecognition (e.g., Caws 1994; Blum 1998; Honneth 2003; Phillips 2009: ch. 2). The struggle for recognition may be important, but, as Nancy Fraser puts it, 'the routes such struggles take often serve not to promote respectful interaction within increasingly multicultural contexts, but to drastically simplify and reify group identities' (Fraser 2000: 108). What should be recognized, then, is not so much the cultural identity of the group(s) to which an individual belongs as the personalized way in which the individual construes his or her own identity partly in relation to group identities. This means that an individual may choose to embrace the cultural identity of various groups on his or her own terms, as part of a wider project of defining his or her own identity sometimes in concert

174  *Principles of Cultural Diversity*

with but also sometimes in opposition to group identity (e.g., Appiah 1994: 149–156; Blum 2002: 193n.6; Honneth 2003: 174; Parekh 2008: 28–30).

Following on from these observations, critics of hate speech law might argue that it is hard to see how such law could deliver on the expectation that individuals are entitled to define their own identities given the fact that, in order to claim protection, someone's identity must first be fixed using one of the protected characteristics enshrined in the relevant body of law, such as race, ethnicity, nationality, citizenship, origin of birth, war record, religion, sexual orientation, gender or transgender identity, disability, age, or physical appearance. As Parekh himself says, 'we need to be extremely careful how we categorize people officially, and should leave room for those who wish to identify themselves in terms of more than one category or none at all' (Parekh 2008: 17). Given the nature of law and the need for justiciability, predictability, and enforceability, authorities tend to create offenses defined by social categories capable of being applied to large numbers of individuals. Even when statutes refer to speech that is likely to promote hatred among groups or classes of persons, it is left to case law to figure out which particular groups or classes of persons are covered, at which point these designations become precedential. It would be impossible to draw up laws that explicitly recognized the microidentity of every individual since the number is potentially infinite and the tremendous variety of identities is unforeseeable. And so those individuals who do wish to have their right not to be subjected to hate speech recognized and enforced will be compelled to refer back to the main cultural identities enshrined in law. So while it may be the case that individuals are pigeonholed, and in that sense misrecognized, by certain uses of hate speech, it may also be the case that the beneficiaries of hate speech law are similarly pigeonholed and misrecognized. This may be a particular problem for identities that are poorly understood, such as transgender identities.

## 6.3  CULTURAL SPECIFICITY

Yet another way in which cultural diversity can figure in arguments about free speech and its limits is through variations in the ways different cultural communities understand and valorize normatively relevant features such as liberty, health, autonomy, security, and dignity. Some multiculturalists maintain that in the context of culturally diverse societies, what majority cultural communities owe to minority cultures is an acknowledgment that the way the latter interpret the meaning and importance of minimum universal values can be as *valid*, and certainly deserve to receive as much *careful consideration*, as the interpretations favored by the majority cultural community. For example, Parekh argues that much of the disagreement between sponsors and critics of hate speech law emanates not from disagreement about which human values are at stake but from divergent beliefs about the content and relative importance of these values, where people's beliefs, and their sense of epistemic surety in holding their beliefs, is rooted in the particulars of their own cultural communities (i.e., histories, experiences, sensitivities, institutions, practices, authorities). As Parekh puts it, in recent controversies over putative Islamophobic and anti-Islamic speech, a belief that free speech values have absolute priority in comparison to other values 'came naturally to philosophers, creative writers and others with an understandable occupational bias in favour of free speech' (Parekh 2006: 353). In contrast, a belief in the preeminence of the values of dignity and reputation came naturally to the traditional, religious cultural communities who believed themselves to be under attack (2009: 63–66).[11]

I wish to explore this line of thought more fully using the example of dignity. Parekh highlights two kinds of dignity that could be (re-)interpreted by particular cultural communities to support their case for legal protection from hate speech. The first is *human dignity*. Parekh suggests that having a sense of human identity and with it a sense of human dignity is partly a realization 'of the fact that human beings differ from the rest of the natural world in their physical and mental constitution, can do things and form relationships that are beyond the reach of even the most developed animals' (Parekh 2008: 26). In other words, human dignity is a 'hierarchical concept and describes a privileged status' (2006: 130). 'This is why every discussion of human dignity directly or indirectly contrasts humans with animals, emphasizes their superiority, and insists that they may not be treated as if they were animals' (ibid.). What is more, Parekh points to human dignity as one of several 'important values' that might justify limits on free speech (2005–2006: 216). The logic of this argument is that hate speech can be an affront to human identity/dignity when it denies or challenges the humanity of the intended group of persons. Among the few concrete examples of hate speech cited by Parekh (215) the one that comes closest to an affront to human identity/dignity in the aforementioned sense is the example of football fans making monkey noises and chanting racist slogans at black football players (ibid.).

At this stage, it might be wondered what an acknowledgment of cultural specificity brings to the table since the aforementioned argument from human dignity would appear to be transcultural. However, Parekh is at pains to point out the close relationship between human dignity and culture. For starters, it is relatively clear from Parekh's description of the capacities that underpin human identity/dignity—'the ability to think, reason, use language, form visions of the good life, enter into moral relations with one another, be self-critical and achieve increasingly higher levels of excellence' (Parekh 2006: 129)—that many of these capacities are oriented toward the acquisition of culture. More importantly, Parekh maintains that human identity/dignity 'is not inherent in human beings, but is a status they confer on themselves' through the various beliefs and values of the cultural communities to which they belong (130; see also 2008: 27). Parekh cites the example of religious beliefs. 'Since the concept of human dignity is based on a sharp distinction between humans and non-humans, it is central to those traditions of thought such as the Greek, the Christian and the Islamic which set much store by that distinction' (2006: 131). In that sense, it is through the lenses of our different cultural communities that we come to give detailed substance to our latent sense of human identity/dignity and to our expectations of dignified treatment from others, including the expectation not to be targeted by hate speech that reduces us to animals.

Parekh believes that a second kind of dignity is also 'central to the good life and deserve[s] to be safeguarded' (Parekh 2005–2006: 216). This is *social dignity* or the 'protection of one's good name and honour' (ibid.). At the heart of this kind of dignity stands 'social identity.' All individuals identify themselves, and are in turn identified by others, with a variety of relationships and with various occupations, roles, and memberships in a multitude of organizations, groups, and communities (2008: 15). Parekh claims that social identity weighs heavily on some individuals, as a cross they bear or something they would rather forget, whereas other individuals actively seek it out and embrace it (17–21). For example, some British Muslims (according to Parekh) have turned toward faithful Islamic practice in order to give themselves 'a sense of dignity and identity, a particularly noticeable trend among college and university students' (2009: 77). Parekh suggests that one of the key ways in which social identity/dignity can be safeguarded is through libel law. Libel is an offense, according to Parekh, 'not because it causes pain to or offends the feelings of the individual concerned [. . .] but because they [sic] lower him in the eyes of *others*, lower his *social* standing, and harm his *reputation*' (2006: 313). For Parekh, this explains why '[m]any Muslim, Jewish and other minority spokesmen in Britain, the USA and elsewhere have argued that [the offense of libel which is generally restricted to individuals] should cover racial, religious, ethnic and other communities as well' (ibid.).[12] 'Like individuals, communities too can be objects of libel, for one can make public, untruthful and damaging remarks about them which lower them in their own and others' eyes, harm their reputation and social standing, and go beyond fair comment' (ibid.). Parekh cites the example a poster of a woman wearing a Burka with the accompanying text: 'Who knows what they have under their sinister and ugly looking clothes: stolen goods, guns, bombs even?' (2005–2006: 215). He claims that such hate speech 'damages their sense of dignity' (223).

In what sense is this an argument about cultural specificity? For one thing, every cultural community will have its own ideas about which social identities merit protection from damaging hate speech. It is no accident, for example, that in the UK just a few years after religious groups (including Muslims) were granted legal protection against incitement to hatred on the grounds of religious affiliation, gays and lesbians were given the same protection against incitement to hatred on the grounds of sexual orientation. This is because in the UK gay and lesbian identity/dignity was recognized as something valuable and equally deserving of legal protection, alongside racial and religious identity/dignity. This may not be true of other cultural communities. In Russia, for instance, Art. 282 of the Criminal Code prohibits incitement to hatred on the grounds of religion, national, or racial affiliation only. Neither gender nor sexual orientation are recognized.[13] In addition to this, Parekh's observations about group libel diverge from those of Waldron, and they do so partly because of the space that Parekh leaves for culture. As discussed in Ch. 5, Waldron views social dignity, at least the sort that justifies criminal laws proscribing group defamation, as essentially a matter of civic dignity. Civic dignity has to do with one's place in the political community, meaning that citizens who enjoy civic dignity have a right to the protection of their reputation as members of the community in good standing. However, as discussed in Ch. 5 [5.3], eligibility for a high and equal sociolegal status might be thought to depend on whether or not persons have contributed or will contribute to the civic life of the community, and, if so, this narrows the range of characteristics that qualify persons as being entitled to legal protections. For Parekh, in contrast, social identity, of the sort that merits protection, can be based around membership of cultural communities (Parekh 2008: 24–25).

Nevertheless, Parekh also fails to disambiguate the different clusters of laws/regulations/codes that might be used to deal with attacks on human and social dignity, and this has unforeseen consequences for the plausibility of the aforementioned culturally sensitive arguments in favor of hate speech law. As already mentioned, Parekh cites the example of football fans making monkey noises and chanting racist slogans at black football players. In the context of the UK, this example would come under s. 3(1) of the Football (Offences) Act 1991 ('It is an offence to engage or take part in chanting of an indecent or racialist nature at a designated football match'). Then again, laws/regulations/codes that disallow the public expression of hatred, including through the use of insults, slurs, or derogatory epithets, are among the hardest to justify within the cannon of hate speech law. They are set on a collision course with some important free speech principles, including the Principle of Self-Realization (see Ch. 4 [4.3]) and the Principle of Democracy (see Ch. 7 [7.1]). This is because even racist chanting at football matches cannot be automatically dismissed as being wholly inarticulate or having no ideational content, even if it can be dismissed on the grounds of weighing its costs and benefits (cf. Posner 2002: 145–146). Indeed, if, as seems likely, football fans form their own cultural communities with their own stadium patois, then even the Principle of Culture might rule out legal restrictions that threaten the survival of this culture.

Furthermore, Parekh presents as an argument for law proscribing 'communal libel or group defamation' (Parekh 2006: 313) the fact that such speech can damage social identity/dignity. But he conflates the two different uses of the term 'group libel law' that I distinguished in Ch. 2 [2.1]. He defines 'libel' as making 'public, untruthful and damaging remarks about an individual that go beyond fair comment' (ibid.) and draws a direct parallel

178  *Principles of Cultural Diversity*

between libel law and group libel law. This implies that he has in mind law proscribing group libel (*sensu stricto*). But then this makes it hard to accept his claim that '[t]o say that "all Jews are secretive, greedy, vindictive and conspiratorial", that "all blacks are stupid, unruly, licentious and unreliable", or that "all Indians are devious, cheats, manipulative and undependable" is clearly to libel these communities in the sense defined earlier' (ibid.). In order to count as group libel (*sensu stricto*) statements must amount to false statements that can be falsified on issues of fact. The expression of opinion, judgment, or hyperbole does not count, and the examples Parekh offers would all seem to be instances of opinion in that sense. Indeed, they point not in the direction of criminal group defamation law (*sensu stricto*) but toward laws/regulations/codes that constrain uses of hate speech when it amounts to negative stereotyping or stigmatization. This is further supported by Parekh's claim that '[g]iven the deep streak of anti-Semitism and anti-black racism in western societies, (as indeed in many others), and given the need to counter the malicious stereotypes to which they have both been subjected over centuries with disastrous results, Jews and blacks would seem to qualify for anti-libel laws in most western countries' (2006: 316).[14]

Further grounds for thinking that the aforementioned culturally sensitive arguments are really arguments for laws/regulations/codes that constrain negative stereotyping or stigmatization comes from Parekh's 2009 article on Muslims in Europe. Here he asserts that '[t]he twelve Danish cartoons that lampooned the Prophet Muhammad [. . .] and the commentaries that accompanied them led Muslims to conclude that their community and religion were regarded as backward and unfit to be part of civilized Europe' (2009: 55). Specifically, he describes the article, 'Something Rotten in Denmark?', published in the Danish magazine *National Post* as an attempt 'to demonize Muslims and generate powerful feelings against them' (58). Among other things, the article included the statement, 'Muslims are only 4 percent of the Denmark's 5.4 million but make up a majority of the country's convicted rapists.' If, as Parekh seems to think, Muslims had a valid reason to request legal action against the publication of this article, what cluster of hate speech law would have been useful? Although s. 266b(1) of the Danish Penal Code prohibits forms of expression 'by which a group of people are threatened, insulted or degraded on account of their race, colour, national or ethnic origin, religion, or sexual inclination', public prosecutors in Denmark elected not to bring charges against the authors of the article under this law. They viewed it as being unlikely that a court would deem its content to have reached the requisite level of threat, insult, or degradation. Moving from actual Danish law to possible law, perhaps the statement could have constituted incitement to religious hatred.[15] Then again, it might be hard to prove intent to incite hatred. Finally, it seems unlikely that a conviction for an offense of group defamation (*sensu stricto*) would have been possible. Its authors might have been able to use a truth defense (either that the statistic was true or that they had cited the statistic in good faith and in reasonable belief that it was true). It seems far more plausible to say that this sort of statement could fall under the remit of media regulators whose rules and guidelines require newspapers, magazine, TV production companies, and so on, to place reasonable limits on uses of hate speech when it amounts to negative stereotyping or stigmatization. The statement counts as negative stereotyping and stigmatization because it depicts Muslims in a wholly adverse light and presents only a narrow or one-sided picture of reality, such as by failing to point out the fact that only a tiny minority of Muslims are convicted rapists and omitting to mention other possible explanations besides religious affiliation as to why conviction rates for rape might be higher for Muslims than for non-Muslims in Denmark.

Indeed, Parekh himself insists that from the mere fact that some uses of hate speech are morally unacceptable under culturally sensitive interpretations of minimum universal values such as dignity, it does not follow that criminalizing hate speech is warranted all principles considered. He argues that the overall warrant of using the criminal law to deal with the problem depends on the wider options open to targeted groups and on the general level of development of the society. Wherever possible a cultural community targeted by hate speech should 'rely on other forms of pressure, such as a powerful press council, organized disapproval by enlightened public opinion, social or economic sanctions against individuals and organizations shown to be guilty of communal libel, and a declarative and non-punitive law' (Parekh 2006: 316–317). This reference to 'a powerful press council' speaks to the sorts of media regulations limiting the use of negative stereotyping and stigmatization that can be found in media law and regulation in many parts of the world.

Interestingly, Parekh also draws a distinction between, on the one hand, developed Western societies that enjoy 'several mechanisms to cope with hate speech and its consequences, such as an open and competitive economy, a vibrant civil society, a reasonably cohesive and integrated society, a varied media representing a wide spectrum of views, and a plural and self-limiting public culture', and, on the other hand, developing countries that 'are composed of ethnic, religious and racial groups with little experience of working together and a long legacy of mistrust, ignorance, misunderstanding and hostility' and where '[e]xtralegal mechanisms on which the developed societies rely are not yet strong enough to cope with the consequences of hate speech' (Parekh 2005–2006: 223). In the latter case, 'law [is] the only reliable means of introducing a measure of civility and buying time until the society acquires reasonable cohesion and stability' (ibid.).[16] Unfortunately, Parekh does not specify here what he means by 'law', but it seems as though he is equating law with criminal law, including group defamation law (*sensu stricto*) and law banning incitement to hatred, viewed only as a last resort.

For all of these reasons, it seems appropriate to read Parekh as accepting, other things remaining equal, the need not for criminal law but for other

180  *Principles of Cultural Diversity*

measures, such as media laws and regulations, to limit the use of negative stereotyping or stigmatization of cultural communities. However, this reading creates its own potential banana skin for Parekh. For, it is hard to square his assertion that negative stereotyping and stigmatization is objectionable because it has exacerbated the anger felt by '[a] small but deeply alienated group of young Muslims' (Parekh 2009: 77) with his own portrayals of *this particular* subgroup of Muslims. He describes them as 'boys and young men', 'rioters', as showing 'active disloyalty to their country of settlement', 'among the poorest', who 'underachieve educationally', have 'limited emotional intimacy' with their parents, 'loud, rigid, and uncompromising in their religiosity', for whom 'Islam is the sole basis of their personal and public identity', 'a sulking Muslim underclass', 'available for mobilization by militant groups', and 'a legitimate source of concern' (60, 77–79). If negatively stereotyping and stigmatizing entire groups of individuals based on their religious beliefs, gender, age, and various other ascribed characteristics counts as hate speech, then Parekh's own words are hate speech or dangerously close to it.

## 6.4  INTERCULTURAL DIALOGUE

Parekh argues that the sorts of minimum universal values that do most of the heavy lifting in debates around free speech and its limits have no foundations in the sense of indisputable and objective bases but do have grounds in the form of intersubjectively discussable reasons, and are, therefore, not arbitrary (e.g., Parekh 2006: 128). 'Although we might try to arrive at universal values by analyzing human nature, universal moral consensus and so on, as philosophers have done over the centuries, the more satisfactory way to arrive at them is through a universal or cross-cultural dialogue' (ibid.; cf. Gutmann and Thompson 1996: 55–56). Moreover, this intercultural dialogue is to be understood as an ideal that embodies virtues of 'sensitivity and empathy' (Parekh 2006: 77) as well as 'respect for other cultures' (128). Each side is to recognize that the other is drawing on its own culture as reasons for holding human values and that the other has a right to give its reasons as well as a responsibility to listen to opposing reasons (128–129). 'If they offer no reasons or ones that are flimsy, self-serving, based on crude prejudices or ignorance of relevant facts, they are being unreasonable and have in effect opted out of the dialogue' (129). In other words, intercultural dialogue requires 'such essential political virtues as mutual respect and concern, tolerance, self-restraint, willingness to enter into unfamiliar worlds of thought, love of diversity, a mind open to new ideas and a heart open to others' needs, and the ability to persuade and live with unresolved differences' (340).

According to Parekh, the exercise of these virtues is not a sufficient condition for full intercultural dialogue. New forums may be required: dedicated spaces for intercultural dialogue open to all but especially to minorities who 'lack enough political and economic power to be a significant political presence' (Parekh 2006: 306–307).[17] These dedicated spaces for intercultural dialogue must be provided in addition to familiar legal institutions, not least the institution of free speech (340). But does this mean, then, that there is to be a moratorium on any new hate speech legislation pending the outcome of intercultural dialogue on such legislation? If so, surely that would put at a disadvantage those cultural communities who are already subject to hate speech: they may find it more difficult to get their point across or to be heard if the larger ecosystem of intercultural dialogue is already polluted with hate speech. I would say that Parekh should support no such moratorium. For one thing, his vision of intercultural dialogue is not exhausted by the willingness to listen; it is also exemplified in ways in which people address each other, including in their speech. Intercultural dialogue is very far from being a dialogical anarchy, in other words.

Consider the Rushdie Affair as an illustration of when, in Parekh's eyes, Western democracies failed to live up to the ideals of intercultural dialogue in both the content and manner of their discourse. Parekh's concerns refer not to the content of *The Satanic Verses* but rather to the content and manner of the public discussion that ensued. At the time Parekh was critical of the British press for vilifying those Muslims who objected to the publication of Rushdie's book. 'Muslims were called "barbarians", "uncivilised", "fanatics", and compared to the Nazis' (Parekh 1990a: 62), which are forms of negative stereotyping and stigmatization.[18] What is more, Parekh lamented the fact that the cultural communities that clashed on the issues remained at arm's length from one another. 'Rarely did the two meet together to debate *as fellow-citizens* the kind of Britain they wished to create and the terms of their membership of it' (73). What this suggests is that the deeper threat to society posed by the Rushdie Affair was not so much an attack on a tradition of free speech or on the human rights of an author or even public peace but a departure from a process of intercultural dialogue in which different identities come together to contest and work through the right response to controversial written material in a spirit of mutual respect (cf. Modood 1990: 160). Following on from this, Parekh proclaims that under certain circumstances 'the law might need to intervene' if doing so 'helps create a climate of civility and mutual respect' (Parekh 2006: 317). Unfortunately, once again Parekh does not pause to explain what he means by 'the law', but sticking with the example of the British press, one relevant distinction is between media regulation, wherein persons can make complaints to the press regulator about British newspapers negatively stereotyping Muslims, and the Public Order Act 1986 as amended by the Racial and Religious Hatred Act 2006, wherein persons can make complaints to the police and ultimately public prosecutors could decide to prosecute newspapers for committing offenses relating to stirring up religious hatred.

At any rate, I read Parekh as arguing that regulatory and in some instances criminal law approaches to hate speech are not merely an appropriate *subject matter* of intercultural dialogue (i.e., the debate between cultural communities who defend free speech and those who back the protection of groups through hate speech law); they are also potentially a *precondition* of mutually respectful intercultural dialogue (i.e., shared rules that forbid certain forms of hate speech as modes of expression that are unacceptable in the context of intercultural dialogue).[19] In these ways Parekh's argument is an instance of what I shall call the Principle of Intercultural Dialogue, that legalistic constraints on uses of hate speech are (N-)warranted if they serve to protect and promote the public good of intercultural dialogue.

But why is intercultural dialogue a public good? In his recent work Parekh has suggested that intercultural dialogue—in particular when both sides in public disputes, including public disputes over free expression and its limits, choose to honor the values or ideals of mutual cultural respect—has two main advantages for Western societies that contain significant Muslim populations. First, '[i]t reassures Muslims that their culture is valued by the wider society and that they need not panic, turn inward, or become intransigent' (Parekh 2009: 73). 'It also reassures the wider society that it remains in charge of its civic and cultural institutions, that Muslims will not seek to undermine it by irresponsible demands, and that the differences between the two can be resolved through a rational dialogue' (ibid.). The relevant advantages, then, belong to everyone. Nevertheless, if what I have said previously is correct, then the values of mutual cultural respect must also extend to how Muslims are represented by Parekh as he attempts to articulate the particular challenges and opportunities for intercultural dialogue in societies that contain significant Muslim populations.

There is, then, a way of seeing the types of laws/regulations/codes dealing with hate speech that can be found in Europe, Canada, Australia, and other parts of the world as supporting not merely the values and concerns of the politics of recognition and multiculturalism but also interculturalism. At this stage, however, these laws face a further objection. According to Post, 'hate speech regulation must necessarily enforce social norms that represent the well-socialized intuitions of the hegemonic class that controls the content of the law' (Post 2009: 132).[20] According to Post, this is true 'even in a society that purported to adopt a "multicultural" perspective enforcing norms of respect among disparate groups' (ibid.). If correct, it means that when in the late 1990s the Canadian Supreme Court affirmed that hate speech law is N-warranted partly by virtue of safeguarding cultural diversity and harmonious relations within a multicultural society,[21] what it was actually doing was enforcing 'hegemonic community norms' (ibid.). The decisions of the US Supreme Court are another matter, or so Post would have us believe. The Court 'pressures the state to be neutral with respect to the many competing communities that seek to control the law by enforcing their own particular ways of distinguishing decency from indecency, critique from hatred' (133). Since civility norms 'always reflect the view of some particular community', to regulate speech on the basis of one particular set of norms would be to favor one community over another (ibid.).

What is particularly striking about Post's argument, however, is that having made the suggestion that legalistic constraints on uses of hate speech must necessarily enforce social norms, Post does not reflexively consider the possibility that even the absence of legalistic constraints on uses of hate speech must also enforce social norms. He depicts the First Amendment as standing above the fray, like a referee, steadfastly refusing to choose between competing cultural communities and their social norms. He seems to believe in the unencumbered First Amendment. But if his own observations are correct, there is no such thing. Post also criticizes defenders of hate speech law for being blind to the power dynamic underpinning the enactment of hate speech law. 'Hate speech regulation imagines itself as simply enforcing the given and natural norms of a decent society [. . .] but from a sociological or anthropological point of view we know that law is always actually enforcing the mores of the dominant group that controls the content of law' (Post 2009: 130). Yet arguably the First Amendment, or the Supreme Court's interpretation of the First Amendment in striking down hate speech law, is as much a product of hegemonic community norms as any hate speech law. This logic applies to Post's own belief that speech acts that constitutes public discourse or contributions to the formation of public opinion ought to receive full First Amendment protection by way of protecting core democratic values (2012: 12). But what else is this belief if not the statement of a kind of social norm? It is no less a social norm simply because Post happens to endorse it as showing the First Amendment in its best light. So if the present objection is well founded, it would seem to afflict all justificatory approaches to free speech and its limits, not just multiculturalism and interculturalism. That is because all of these views reflect ideological commitments or value choices of one sort or another (cf. Gerber 2004: 37–38).[22]

\* \* \*

By way of summary, in this chapter I began by investigating what liberals who take culture seriously might say on behalf of the right to free expression and how this relates to arguments about hate speech law. Here, the arguments turned on the importance of cultural diversity as a public good that is important for choice between cultures or choice embedded within culture. I also suggested that cross burning statutes and Holocaust denial legislation may in fact undermine the diversity and richness of cultural communities. I then sought to consider what the advocates of the politics of recognition have said, and could say, on behalf of hate speech law. Given that misrecognition is a multifaceted phenomenon, it turned out that these sorts of arguments support an array of hate speech law: from laws/regulations/codes that disallow the public expression of hatred through to Holocaust denial legislation. Finally, I considered the perspectives of multiculturalism and interculturalism on the issue of hate speech. Some of the principled arguments turned out to favor the use of media regulators to limit negative stereotyping of protected groups. In one sense, this result is as one might expect given the existence of words and images spread through the media that subvert the self-perceptions, perspectives, and narratives that are prominent in the lives of members of cultural communities, making intercultural dialogue so fraught.

## NOTES

1. In the case of the State of Victoria, see ss. 11(b)(i) and 11(2) of the Racial and Religious Tolerance Act 2001. In the case of the State of Western Australia, see s. 80G(1)(b)(i) and 80G(1)(b)(i) (as amended by s. 6 of Law No. 80 of 2004). With respect to Canada, see s. 319(3)(b)of the Criminal Code (as amended by An Act to Amend the Criminal Code (Hate Propaganda) of 2004).
2. *R. v. Keegstra*, at 757.
3. *Eatock v. Bolt*, at para. 334.
4. *Virginia v. Black*, at 365.
5. At 365–366.
6. Consider the historical 'one-drop' rule in the US.
7. *Beauharnais v. Illinois*, at 262–263.
8. Having said that, Kenneth Lasson (1997: 66) argues that deceased victims of the Holocaust may equally become lost in history as a result of banning Holocaust denial. He writes: 'If reason is to prevail, the existence of racism in all forms must be documented. This is true of both fact and fiction. If we are to learn from history, what is the difference between the Nazis' foul deeds and their descendants' denial of them? It is as important for later generations to witness the propaganda of genocide as to see its effects, to hear the exhortations of racism as well as its results. Both the propaganda and the facts depict the personification of evil. To expurgate either would blur the facts of history and blot out the memory of all those martyred because of their ethnicity, murdered because of their race.'
9. No. 9235/81 (Eur. Comm. of Hum. Rights decision, 16 Jul.) 29 DR 194 (involving a Holocaust denial case).
10. Surveys of ethnic minorities in the UK (Modood et al. 1998), for example, reveal that a high proportion of individuals will accept ethnoidentity identifiers such as 'Caribbean' and 'Pakistani' despite lack of adherence to traditional practices associated with those identifiers
11. Ironically, Parekh's own generalizations could be regarded as misrecognition by oversimplifying the identity of members of religious cultural communities, some of whom might in fact share the views of civil libertarians on matters of free speech. Perhaps for this reason, Parekh (2009: 65) is careful in his discussion of Muslim views on free speech to point out that 'there is no unanimity among Muslims.' Parekh also declares (63) that, putting to one side a small group of disaffected young Muslims, the West has much less to fear from Islam than it thinks because Muslims 'do not have much difficulty with many' of the minimum universal values that are found in the West and throughout the world. 'Human dignity, and equal human worth, equality of the races, civility, peaceful resolution of differences, and reciprocity are all either enjoined by Islam or can be read into it' (ibid.). This is, perhaps, Parekh's own attempt to provide a balanced depiction of the attitudes and behavior of European Muslims, and to offset simplistic stereotypes of Muslims as violent opponents of Western values, including free speech. These simplistic stereotypes are not rendered true of all Muslims even in the wake of the terror attacks on the offices of *Charlie Hebdo* in January 2015.

12. For critics of multiculturalism, this type of gendered language ('spokesmen') only serves to illustrate the problem this ideology has in recognizing the unequal position of women within some cultural minorities.
13. Indeed, a recent amendment (Federal Law No. 135-FZ of 29 Jun. 2013) to the Federal Law On Protection of Children from Information Harmful to Their Health and Development (Federal Law No. 436-FZ of 23 Dec. 2010) means that 'propaganda' of 'non-traditional sexual relationships' is now included within the class of harmful information under the law.
14. It is interesting that Parekh chooses to use the word 'malicious', which may be an unconscious attempt to harness the connotation of the 'actual malice' test in libel law.
15. Indeed, Parekh (2006: 314) also states that 'several legal systems disallow [group libel] in one form or another', and he (314–315) cites laws banning incitement to racial and religious hatred as well as laws forbidding incitement to harmful actions against particular groups. This also suggests that he is using the term 'group libel law' in the catchall sense.
16. There are echoes here of Mill's declaration in *On Liberty* ([1859] 1972: 79) that his doctrinal defense of free speech is not meant to apply to 'those backward states of society in which the race itself may be considered as in its nonage.' 'Liberty, as a principle, has no application to any state of things anterior to the time when mankind have become capable of being improved by free and equal discussion.'
17. Parekh (2006: 306–307) clarifies that public forums must be found in which 'representatives of different communities can meet regularly to explore contentious issues, acquire a better understanding of each other's ways of thinking and living, and hopefully arrive at a consensus on what issues are at stake and what arguments and considerations are relevant to their resolution which can then be fed into the wider public debate.' While Parekh does not explicitly mention any specific examples of new public forums, it is likely that among the possibilities he has in mind are quasi-autonomous national organizations, such as the Commission for Racial Equality and its successor the Equality and Human Rights Commission (on which he served as a Vice-Chairman), to which governments devolve limited powers but which are essentially non-departmental or independent public bodies with a remit of investigating, discussing, and making recommendations on controversial issues of public interest and policy. He might also have in mind forums for the examination and discussion of issues set up by non-profit policy institutes, such as the Commission on the Future of Multi-Ethnic Britain (for whom he also served as a Chairman). In fact, Parekh is not alone in preaching the virtues of intercultural dialogue or the need for special, extrapolitical public forums in which it can take place. See, e.g., Tariq Modood (1993, 2005) and Nasar Meer and Modood (2012).
18. Parekh was not the only one to criticize the media in this way. The then Chair of the Commission for Racial Equality, Michael Day (1990: 107) declared that '[t]he worst kind of racial stereotyping has been in evidence with Muslims portrayed as religious fanatics intent on denying freedom of speech.' The Labour Party politician, Gerald Kaufman (1989: 20) made a similar point writing in *The Independent*.
19. This dual purpose has been echoed by the Council of Europe (Council of Europe Ministers of Foreign Affairs 2008: 20). Its 2008 *White Paper on Intercultural Dialogue* states that '[i]ntercultural dialogue entails a reflexive disposition, in which one can see oneself from the perspective of others'. But it also stakes out its position that hate speech is a barrier to intercultural dialogue (21). 'Racism, xenophobia, intolerance and all other forms of discrimination refuse the very idea of dialogue and represent a standing affront to it.' Therefore (39), '[s]tates should have robust legislation to outlaw "hate speech" and

racist, xenophobic, homophobic, anti-Semitic, Islamophobic and anti-gypsy or other expressions, where this incites hatred or violence.'
20. Others make a similar point regarding campus speech codes (Sherry 1991: 942), that they are part of an 'enforcement of "politically correct" orthodoxy.'
21. See, e.g., *R. v. Keegstra*, at 757; *Canada (Human Rights Commission) v. Taylor*, at 919.
22. This reply to Post echoes my reply to Alexander in Ch. 3 [3.4].

# 7 Principles of Political Morality

In this chapter I focus on arguments for and against hate speech law that are rooted in distinctively political principles, which is to say, principles that speak directly and explicitly to the values and structures of democratic self-government, political legitimacy, and political obligation. I seek to challenge a conventional wisdom that says because the right to freedom of expression is indispensable to democratic self-government, political legitimacy, and political obligation, absolutely no hate speech law can be tolerated within spheres of public discourse. Instead, I argue that some clusters of laws/regulations/codes that constrain uses of hate speech are N-warranted, not in spite of distinctively political principles and values, but because of what these things demand of constitutional essentials and the fundamentals of justice. Specifically, I shall argue that bodies of law involving freedom of expression but also *some* hate speech law are at their most democratic, legitimate, and supportive of political obligation when they manage to do each of the following: guarantee that all citizens enjoy genuine opportunities to participate in public discourse; realize a form of political legitimacy that is based on the goal of reasonable agreement; and ground political obligation in a fair distribution of benefits and burdens.

## 7.1 DEMOCRATIC SELF-GOVERNMENT

It is sometimes said that the main reason why we ought to value free speech is because it is indispensible to citizens playing their part within an organized system of democratic self-government. This argument has two elements. First, democracy has to do with the ability of the 'self' that is portrayed in the concepts of collective self-determination and democratic self-government 'to make its will effective' (Meiklejohn 1960: 14). Second, in order to partake of the various mechanisms of collective decision-making that constitute democratic self-government citizens must be well-informed on issues of public concern. 'That is why no idea, no opinion, no doubt, no belief, no counterbelief, no relevant information, may be kept from them' (75). This second line of thought supports what I shall call the Principle of Democratic Self-Government, that legalistic constraints on speech or other expressive acts, including constraints on uses of hate speech, are (N-)unwarranted if they deny people the information they need in order to contribute to processes of collective decision-making on issues of public concern. On this approach, free speech has special importance precisely because it is a collective as opposed to an individualistic value. If what really matters is collective decision-making on issues of public concern, then free expression has a 'constitutional status which no pursuit of an individual purpose can ever claim' (55).

The constitutional status of free speech might be further enhanced if one considers that partaking of mechanisms of collective decision-making is not merely a right but a civic duty. It would be wrong to insist that all citizens have a duty to be well-informed on issues of public concern, say, but at the same time restrict the practice of free expression that is a precondition of their fulfilling that duty. What is more, the present arguments are not limited to the idea of well-informed citizens dutifully voting in periodic elections. After all, processes of collective decision-making carry on in between elections. As such, freedom of speech may be seen as crucial to enabling both governments to continuously hear and respond to the will of the people, and citizens 'to meet the responsibilities of making judgments, which that freedom to govern lays upon them' (e.g., Meiklejohn 1961: 255). Finally, Alexander Meiklejohn interprets the scope of the Principle of Democratic Self-Government as extending beyond the narrow confines of political speech to all categories of speech protected under the First Amendment, which is to say, the full range of human communications from which the voter derives 'the capacity for sane and objective judgment' (ibid.). As Emerson puts it, the principle that free speech is essential for participation in collective decision-making 'embraces the right to participate in the building of the whole culture, and includes freedom of expression in religion, literature, art, science, and all areas of human learning and knowledge' (Emerson 1970: 7).[1]

The aforementioned justifications for the First Amendment are ones that the US Supreme Court has at times explicitly embraced.[2] But there is no reason to think that the relevance and force of these arguments is limited to the US. For example, the Constitutional Court of South Africa has argued that the right to freedom of expression is especially important given its country's history of apartheid, in which the majority of the population was subject to both censorship and disenfranchisement. 'It could actually be contended with much force that the public interest in the open market-place of ideas is all the more important to us in [South Africa] because our democracy is not yet firmly established and must feel its way.'[3]

Although tantalizing, this family of arguments suffers from two stumbling blocks in the case of hate speech. First, even in a representative democracy in which each citizen enjoys an equal right to vote, it would be delusional to imagine that everybody enjoys the same level of access to, and influence on, the formal decision-making processes of chambers of elected representatives.

Some groups or classes of persons are much better represented in these chambers than others. Some have more sway over the editorial decisions of, and the content carried by, the press, TV broadcasters, radio stations, and online media platforms than others. Some have greater lobbying capacity than others. Some have better social networks that can be harnessed to impact, or directly engage in, political campaigning during and in between elections than others. Consider once again the words of Catherine MacKinnon, 'some people get a lot more speech than others' (MacKinnon 1993: 72). Given such conditions, an argument that claims that hate speakers should be granted the right to say whatever they please for the sake of the collective value of democratic self-government might seem bitterly ironic to the point of ludicrousness (e.g., Shiffrin [S.H.] 1999: 164–165n.174). In response to this putative stumbling block it might be insisted that even if an ideal of democratic self-government is yet to be realized, it remains an appropriate ideal for which society should strive (cf. Post 1991: 326–327). As such, a democratic argument for freedom of expression can still be made. Yet this response may ignore the distinctness of persons (or groups of persons). For, the response assumes that it is acceptable to sacrifice the good of one group of persons in society for the sake of striving for a yet to be fully realized collective value. But why should people like us allow ourselves to be subjected to hate speech (some might ask) simply in the hope that at an unspecified time in the future the value of democratic self-government will become fully realized for everyone? Indeed, what guarantees do we have that permitting hate speech now will make that future more, not less, likely?

Second, if democracy is about living by rules that we give ourselves, then surely this ought to apply as much to rules or policies on free expression as to any other area of law or public policy. Accordingly, what is to stop citizens from voluntarily choosing through a democratic process to limit their own free expression by giving themselves hate speech law? If, for instance, the idea of democratic self-government actually means that where there are differences of opinion the majority view should hold sway, then '[a]ny distinct restraint on majority power, such as a principle of freedom of speech, is by its nature anti-democratic, anti-majoritarian' (Schauer 1982: 40). In a constitutional democracy such as the US a majority can be thwarted in its attempts to legally constrain hate speech by a sacred constitutional right to freedom of expression. But if the constitutional protection of free speech makes certain forms of expression untouchable irrespective of any democratic judgment concerning where the basic threshold for democracy falls in the case of free speech, this may seem to undermine rather than bolster the claim that the system of government is democratic (cf. Dahl 2001). It may even embody a form of 'mistrust' on the part of the authors of the constitutional protection of free speech concerning the good intentions and rationality of those involved in democratic legislative processes: namely, a view that any alternative vision of the extent of fundamental rights 'that might be concocted by elected legislators next year or in ten years' time is so likely to be wrong-headed or ill-motivated that *his own* formulation is to be elevated immediately beyond the reach of ordinary legislative revision' (Waldron 1999: 222). Consequently, it might seem more, not less, democratic if supreme courts permit societies acting through their legislative agents to choose to adopt hate speech law through appropriate democratic mechanisms (e.g., Bleich 2011: 12–13). Michael Sandel makes the same argument with his customary illustrative finesse.

> [P]rotecting speech by insisting that local communities bracket moral judgments carries costs for self-government. [. . .] Although the Holocaust survivors had most at stake in preventing the Nazis from marching, it was the citizens of Skokie who agreed to the ordinance the court overturned [. . .]. Not only the good of communal respect but also the good of self-governing communities acting to secure this end is frustrated by the strictures of the procedural republic. (Sandel 1996: 89)

## The Right of Individuals to Participate in the Formation of Public Opinion

Cognizant of these stumbling blocks both Post (1990, 1991, 1993a, 1993b, 2009, 2011, 2012) and James Weinstein (2001, 2009, 2011a, 2011b) have sought to recast the relationship between the right to freedom of expression and the ideal of democratic self-government by highlighting an earlier stage in the democratic process. On their approach, what really matters is the rights of individuals to participate in the formation of public opinion upon which the familiar mechanisms of democratic decision-making are based.[4] This vision of democratic self-government borrows from both deliberative and participatory theories of democracy. From the former it borrows the ideas that democracy is essentially a matter of genuine deliberation of issues (i.e., not merely saying yea or nay on a given issue), that deliberation is not the preserve of parliaments but occurs throughout the public sphere, and that political speech should not be understood in narrow terms but rather as encompassing speech on innumerable areas of public concern, everything from prominent legal cases and rights to broader issues around public goods and even the sort of ethos or culture a society should have. From the latter it takes the notion that democracy by the people means some sort of popular participation in politics. But it also emphasizes the role that individuals play in contributing their authentic beliefs, ideas, opinions, and so on, to the processes in and through which public opinion is formed (i.e., public discourse), where public opinion is the bedrock of the familiar mechanisms of democratic decision-making. What matters, then, is that the state responds to public opinion and that citizens feel that they are in some sense the authors or coauthors of public opinion by contributing to public discourse. Thus, the state must be 'constitutionally prohibited from preventing its citizens from participating in the communicative processes relevant to the formation of democratic public opinion' (Post 2002: 166). This approach does not turn its back on the value of collective self-government. Instead, it redirects the intuitive force of this value through a different channel, namely, the right of each person to participate in public discourse (Weinstein 2009: 29–30). In a nutshell, '[p]reventing a current majority from suppressing the discourse that allows for the creation of new majorities thus promotes rather than inhibits democracy' (Weinstein 2001: 147).

The approach advocated by Post and Weinstein seems to support what I shall call the Principle of Democracy, that legalistic constraints on speech or other expressive acts, including constraints on uses of hate speech, are (N-)unwarranted if they deny individual citizens the right to engage in speech acts or other expressive conduct that amount to public discourse or contributions to the formation of democratic public opinion. What if a majority decides that it wants to exercise its basic democratic right by banning group defamation or incitement to hatred in the public sphere? Post and Weinstein respond as follows. Such a decision is effectively a decision to confine or hinder all further discussion on the issue since participants in the evolving formation of public opinion may well be apt to use hate speech in articulating their thoughts and ideas. This means that it may not be safe to assume that a particular hate speech law once enacted through a majoritarian decision could be repealed just as swiftly through a similar democratic process if public opinion changed. The law could make the minority less inclined to participate under threat of punishment. The basic point is that public discourse on legislation is never settled once and for all even when the legislation has been enacted. It is telling that both Post (1991: 281) and Weinstein (2009: 27) quote the same passage from the work of Hans Kelsen in which he likens a democracy to 'a running discussion between majority and minority.'

Skeptics might wonder, however, whether hate speech plays such a significant role within a functioning democracy as to mean that banning hate speech effectively changes the nature of public discourse: namely, that it could skew the debate on whether or not hate speech law is N-warranted, making the repeal of such law unlikely. This seems to assume that detractors of hate speech law have no alternative means of getting their message across than engaging in hate speech. This may seem far-fetched. So I wish to put this issue to one side for a moment and focus on another key feature of the current approach.

Post calls on judges to evaluate particular laws/regulations/codes dealing with hate speech as acceptable or unacceptable using the yardstick of whether or not they suppress speech acts that comprise public discourse (i.e., contributions to the formation of democratic public opinion) (Post 2012: 12).[5] According to Post, in practical terms this is about courts determining whether or not the context in which speech occurs can be conceived as being part of the social practice of public discourse in the public sphere (2011: 482).[6] Consider group libel (catchall) enacted through the distribution of leaflets on street corners. Post argues that this context or domain does take a form within the institution of democracy or the social practice of public discourse and therefore banning it may be incompatible with the Principle of Democracy. Thus, according to Post, 'the leaflet at issue in *Beauharnais v. Illinois*, which was an effort "to petition the mayor and council of Chicago to pass laws for segregation," was plainly an effort to engage in public discourse, despite its overt and virulent racism' (1991: 289–290). In contrast, consider racial insults directed toward individuals in the workplace. 'There is a significant difference,' argues Post, 'between proscribing racial insults directed toward individuals in the workplace and proscribing them in a political discussion or debate' (302). The key difference comes to the fact that the point and purpose of the institution of the workplace or the social practice of going about one's duties as an employee differs from that of the institution of democracy or the social practice of public discourse: the point and purpose of the former is about providing business owners with opportunities to employ labor and workers with opportunities to earn money to live, whereas the point and purpose of the latter is nothing less than democratic self-government. 'Thus even if the first amendment were to immunize from legal regulation the circulation of certain racist ideas in newspapers, it would not follow that the expression of those same ideas could not be restrained by the government within the workplace, where an image of dialogue among autonomous self-governing citizens would be patently out of place' (289). Of course, once restrictions on discriminatory harassment in the workplace are N-warranted, the next logical step is to draw analogy with campus speech codes that forbid discriminatory harassment in the context of the university (e.g., Lange 1990; Cox 1995). Post is not unsympathetic to this strategy yet insists that one must dissect campus speech codes using the distinction between what is and what is not part of the sphere of public discourse. This means that such codes ought to be sensitive to the different meanings or functions of classrooms, dormitories, and open spaces on university campuses vis-à-vis public discourse (Post 1991: 324–325; see also Smolla 1990: 217–224; 2011: 125–128).

There are civil libertarians, however, who question whether Post and Weinstein can afford to be agnostic about what happens in the workplace and classrooms given their own overarching concern for public discourse and democratic self-government. For example, like Post, Weinstein has suggested that for the most part workplace speech will not contribute to the formation of democratic public opinion (Weinstein 1992: 203). Eugene Volokh disagrees. Since the workplace is where we spend a significant proportion of our waking hours, and where we do in fact participate in the formation of public opinion (if only the public opinion of our coworkers), it is unfitting to think of this domain as being somehow outside of the sphere of public discourse (Volokh 2011b: 578). Volokh is certainly not alone in making this point (e.g., Browne 1991: 515; Greenawalt 1995: 83; Estlund [C.] 1997: 718–741). Of course, an employer might have commercial reasons for frowning on employees talking politics when they are supposed to be performing their work duties. But that still leaves all the times when people are at work and permissibly not working, such as during coffee and lunch breaks, or even when traveling in lifts together. Thus, according to Volokh, there is a danger that workplace speech restrictions, not the least of which are laws forbidding discriminatory harassment, could conceivably undermine people's ability to participate in the formation of public opinion and *ex hypothesi* democratic self-governance (Volokh 2011b: 577–579). Presumably the danger is that an employer could exploit laws against discriminatory harassment in the workplace in order to launch a moral crusade against racist ideologies that he or she finds abhorrent, such as by banning his or her employees from mentioning meetings of organizations such as the Ku Klux Klan in the workplace (1992: 1848). Accordingly, Volokh believes that workplace harassment *qua* hate speech neither falls under existing categorical exceptions to First Amendment protection nor constitutes a *sui generis* categorical exception.

Volokh is equally critical of Post's attempt to distinguish between domains of the university campus that are and are not parts of the sphere of public discourse. Post characterizes the relation between teacher and student as being 'outside public discourse' (Post 2011: 483). But Volokh insists that it is ludicrous to suppose that speech between teacher and student is not part of the formation of public opinion, whether that be a teacher in a publicly funded school or university or a teacher in a privately funded school or university (Volokh 2011b: 571–573). This may be true of all university disciplines but especially so in the social sciences and humanities where topics directly and consciously bear upon public affairs. Indeed, one might ask: if teachers are *not* saying anything that students may at the time or later draw on in forming and expressing their opinions on public affairs, then what exactly is it that teachers are doing and what would be their point?

Of course, even if the workplace is accepted as being within the domain of public discourse, it does not automatically follow that workplace speech cannot be regulated. Some legal scholars have faith—perhaps more faith than the courts themselves have—that courts can draw distinctions between what is political comment and what is hate speech. This might be based on a contextual reading of the speaker's intentions and how the speech was taken by the audience: namely, whether the intention was simply an effort to harass, humiliate, or bring persons into contempt or instead as an attempt to contribute to social deliberation (e.g., Sunstein 1993a: 198; Lasson 1995: 281–282). However, Volokh insists that 'trying to distinguish "nonpolitical" bigoted jokes from political speech would be virtually impossible' (Volokh 1992: 1847). The question comes down to how much can be read off the context. Suppose a worker turns to another and says, "The problem with you bloody Irish is that you're always drunk on the job." If they are good friends, inside and outside of work, who share daily banter with each other, back and forth, then it seems highly unlikely that any court would find against the speaker or the employer in a lawsuit for discriminatory harassment (and highly unlikely that any such case would be brought). On the other hand, if the speaker and the addressee are not friends, and if the addressee has experienced a pattern of derogatory comments about his or her Irish heritage, from various workers, then this may be a different story. But here is the rub. Would an employer instruct his or her workers, who are neither friends nor locked into a pattern of harassment, to desist from making any comments about the social problem of high-functioning alcoholism for fear of being sued? It is the risk of a chilling effect on speech if such delicate decisions are placed into the hands of courts that Volokh warns against (1797, 1811). Because these distinctions are so difficult to make, workers and their employers may not be able to predict accurately enough what decision a court would make in order for them to feel reasonably secure to permit commentary on controversial matters.

## Real Opportunities to Participate in the Formation of Public Opinion

Notwithstanding these arguments against hate speech law, I believe that it may yet be possible to mount a democratic defense of such rules by reflecting further on the ideal of participation that Post and Weinstein purport to uphold. Even if one accepts that the state has a duty to protect the rights of citizens to participate in the formation of public opinion, it does not follow from this that adopting a laissez-faire approach to public discourse is ultimately justified. In order to motivate the place of hate speech law within a democratic theory of free expression we might appeal to another consideration that arguably any democratic vision must take seriously: namely, the need to ensure that all citizens enjoy real opportunities to contribute to the formation of democratic public opinion.

Now Post and Weinstein certainly accept that the demands of democratic equality go beyond the idea that every member of the political community is to be treated as having the capacity to be involved in familiar mechanisms of democratic decision-making (e.g., voting). It also includes the formal doctrine of non-exclusion, meaning that every citizen has the right to participate in the formation of public opinion, meaning that nobody's voice is intrinsically less important than anybody else's and therefore no individual may be formally excluded from participating in the formation of public opinion. But needless to say these doctrines may end up cutting both ways. In one direction it suggests that persons may not be formally excluded from participating in the formation of public opinion simply because the state or indeed other citizens deem their ideas to be repugnant, outmoded, and uncivilized. This implies that even hate speech should be tolerated. In the other direction it suggests that certain groups of people should not be formally excluded from participation in the formation of public opinion simply because the state or indeed other citizens hold the bigoted idea that anything they could conceivably say is less valuable because of their race, ethnicity, religion, sexual orientation, disability, gender, and so on. So far, so uncontroversial. The real sticking point comes when we turn our attention away from formal scenarios of exclusion in which it is the state that excludes certain persons from participation in the formation of public opinion and toward informal or substantive scenarios of exclusion in which it is the speech of other citizens that excludes certain persons from participating in the formation of public opinion. It seems to me that good faith democratic concern about these scenarios might lead one to endorse what I shall call the Nuanced Principle of Democracy, that legalistic constraints on uses of hate speech are (N-)warranted if they operate for the sake of ensuring that all citizens enjoy real opportunities to participate in public discourse.

What does this principle mean? And what does it tell us about particular clusters of laws/regulations/codes that constrain uses of hate speech? Starting with the first question, Meiklejohn holds up as a democratic ideal 'the traditional American town meeting' (Meiklejohn 1960: 24). This, according to Meiklejohn, is not a setting in which there are no holds barred, verbally; it is not a 'dialectical free-for-all' where 'abusive' speech or expression 'that threatens to defeat the purpose of the meeting' is freely granted its place along with respectful and purposive speech (25). On the contrary, the meeting involves a group of free and equal citizens 'cooperating in a common enterprise, and using for that enterprise responsible and regulated discussion' (ibid.). Because '[t]he final aim of the meeting is the voting of wise decisions', its participants 'must be made as wise as possible' (26)—and the regulation of speech is orientated to that end with the sharpest focus of intent. *If* this is how wider processes of democratic public opinion formation ought to be viewed, then equal opportunities should mean 'responsible and regulated discussion.' Pursuing this line of thought to its logical end, one might suppose that the Nuanced Principle of Democracy is designed to enforce norms of responsible and regulated discussion—the sort of discussion, therefore, to which all citizens have genuine access.

Post anticipates this line of argument and rejects it on the following grounds. It is wrongheaded to think (argues Post) that the formation of public opinion in a modern democracy is akin to a town meeting where it is cooperation in a common enterprise that makes responsible and regulated discussion an appropriate governing rule. When members of large and diverse democratic societies contribute to public opinion formation, their disagreements are not confined to the various matters of public concern in relation to which those opinions are formed. On the contrary, their disagreements also extend to any reflexive procedures, including rules and regulations on speech, that might be thought to govern how people should contribute to public opinion formation. Therefore, to choose one set of rules is to favor one community over another and therefore violates the governmental duty to remain neutral or nonpartisan (e.g., Post 1993b: 1113–1114; 2002: 166–168). However, the present argument does not seek to deny that there will be controversies over the rules governing the formation of public opinion, both at the level of abstract statements of these rules and at the level of contextual application. But this alone is no reason to reject such rules out of hand. If it were, then surely it would be impossible to justify any rules relating to the institutions and social practices of democracy. On the contrary, it is enough that those who participate in the formation of public opinion understand and agree that the formation of public opinion is a common enterprise at least in the minimal sense that it serves a democratic purpose. The fact that vast numbers of individuals belonging to very different communities bother to speak in public on matters of public concern is evidence that they are agreed on this point.[7] And, if processes of public opinion formation do have this minimum function, then this opens the door to appropriate reflection upon what forms of regulation might be necessary in order guarantee that these processes possess and continue to possess this function in a similar way for all citizens. Arguably this is where hate speech law comes in. It mitigates against, to steal a phrase from Meiklejohn, the 'mutilation of the thinking process of the community' (1960: 27).

Critics, however, would argue that what Meiklejohn is getting at is nothing more than the imposition of norms of civility or the mores of polite society, meaning that the moderator is within its rights, as the guardian of public decorum or civility, to forbid speech merely because it is deemed disrespectful to, or beneath the dignity of, civilized democracy. The problem is that for every lawmaker, judge, journalist, or citizen who affirms that '[h]ate speech of any sort has no place anywhere in a civilized society' (Bolotin 2011), there is another who draws the line between what is civilized and uncivilized speech conduct differently. This is, in other words, 'endlessly controversial' (Post 2002: 167). However, another way to come at the question of regulated public discourse is to recognize that what makes public opinion or the formation of public opinion 'democratic' is not merely the democratic function it serves but also how it is produced, which is to say, whether or not it is the product of, or associated with, with fair access to the formation of public opinion. This insight is enshrined in the Nuanced Principle of Democracy.

Support for the Nuanced Principle of Democracy might also flow from what in 1937 Karl Loewenstein dubbed the theory of 'militant democracy.' Loewenstein was exiled from Nazi Germany and was cognizant of the dangers that Nazi hate speech had posed to democracy in Germany. This experience contributed to his belief that sometimes free speech needs to be curtailed precisely to protect democracy. On Loewenstein's analysis, a democracy turns militant when for pragmatic reasons it turns its back on the sort of 'democratic fundamentalism' that upholds liberal rights such as free speech no matter the cost to democracy itself and embraces the need to restrict even free speech for the sake of safeguarding democracy (Loewenstein 1937a: 430–431). Among the many illustrations of militant democracies cited by Loewenstein are authorities in Czechoslovakia, the Netherlands, and the Canadian province of Manitoba, who during the 1930s enacted laws banning incitement to hatred, laws proscribing group libel (*sensu stricto*), and laws prohibiting hate speech that causes or is likely to cause a breach of the peace, as measures against behavior that is corrosive of democracy because it is connected with the 'excesses of political strife' (1937b: 651). Scholars still describe the approach of German courts to free speech issues, including the constitutional status of Holocaust denial law, as an exercise in militant democracy (e.g., Kahn 2004: 148–151). This idea also resonates with the reasoning of the Israeli Supreme Court. In *Neiman and Avneri v. Chairman of the Central Committee for the Elections to the 11th Knesset* (1985),[8] for example, Justice Barak defends the authority of the electoral committee to remove from electoral lists parties whose racist ideology is contrary to democracy itself. As if to demonstrate Loewenstein's assertion that militant democracy takes hold when 'legalistic self-complacency and suicidal lethargy' give way to 'a better grasp of realities' (1937a: 430–431), Justice Barak concludes that '[d]emocracy must not commit suicide in order to prove its existence [trans.].'[9] The idea that democracy is too important for its defense to be left to such a blunt and lumbering instrument as an absolute right to free expression also persists in the hate speech jurisprudence of the Canadian Supreme Court. In *Saskatchewan (Human Rights Commission) v. Whatcott*, for example, the Court upheld aspects of the ruling of the Human Rights Commission partly on the grounds that hate speech 'impacts on that group's ability to respond to the substantive ideas under debate, thereby placing a serious barrier to their full participation in our democracy.'[10] Likewise, in their dissenting opinions in *R. v. Zündel* Justices Cory and Iacobucci stressed that democracy is founded upon ideals of equal participation and consensus building, which they found to be incompatible with spreading false news about the Holocaust.[11] These ideas are also present in some of the relevant decisions of the ECtHR. In *Refah Partisi (The Welfare Party) and Others v. Turkey* (2003),[12] for example, the Court upheld a ruling that the Turkish government was within its rights to order the dissolution of an Islamist political party because some of its senior office holders had advocated holy war against, and the imposition of Islamic law on, non-Muslims in Turkey. The Turkish government argued that the party posed an imminent and serious threat to democracy and democratic institutions.

At first glance, these ideas of militant democracy may seem far removed from First Amendment jurisprudence. But on closer reflection perhaps they are not so very foreign. Consider Justice Jackson's famous dissent in *Terminiello v. City of Chicago* (1949),[13] in which he issued the following warning. 'There is danger that, if the Court does not temper its doctrinaire logic with a little practical wisdom, it will convert the constitutional Bill of Rights into a suicide pact.'[14] Or consider one of the main bases given by the Court for the Strict Scrutiny Test, which is a feature of its approach to First Amendment cases. The Test itself originated in Footnote 4 of *United States v. Carolene Products* (1938),[15] in which Justice Stone asserted that a high level of scrutiny may be appropriate in cases involving 'the review of statutes directed at particular religious [. . .] or national [. . .] or racial minorities.'[16] The rationale given was that 'prejudice against *discrete and insular minorities* may be a special condition, which tends seriously to curtail the operation of those political processes ordinarily to be relied upon to protect minorities, and which may call for a correspondingly more searching judicial inquiry.'[17] The Court famously applied the test in *Korematsu v. United States* (1944).[18] The prejudice involved the disenfranchisement of Japanese American citizens who were denied the opportunity to vote during their internment. By analogy, it might be argued that certain forms of hate speech seriously curtail the operation of political processes by preventing minorities from participating normally or as other citizens do in the formation of democratic public opinion and any such mutilation of public debate is pathological for democracy. The irony here is that the Strict Scrutiny Test is assumed by civil libertarians to fatally undermine the constitutionality of hate speech law.

But what are the mechanisms by which hate speech can undermine genuine access to the formation of public opinion? In what does the mutilation of the thinking process of the community consist? One answer to these questions extends the silencing effect argument discussed in Ch. 3 [3.4]. Here the claim is that, if left unchecked, certain forms of hate speech can deter or inhibit members of targeted groups from functioning as ordinary deliberative democrats. What is at stake is a sort of deliberative exclusion in which out of fear for their personal safety or livelihood or as a result of an impaired sense of their status some, perhaps many, victims of hate speech tend to refrain from participating in the formation of public opinion; adapt their expressed preferences in order to fit their reduced circumstances; and/or find that even when they do decide to speak up what they say falls on deaf ears because of the low opinion that others have of them, partly as a consequence of the negative stereotypes carried and reinforced by hate speech (e.g., Lawrence 1992; Delgado and Stefancic 1992; Michelman 1992; Delgado and Yun 1995; Musselman 1995; Fiss 1996a: ch.1; 1996b: ch. 6; Ogletree 1996; Brison 1998a; Brink 2001; Demaske 2004; Parekh 2005–2006; Tsesis 2009; Gelber 2011: ch. 1). Delgado expresses the point most eloquently.

> I mean the daily, low-grade largely invisible stuff, the hassling, cruel remarks, and other things that would be covered by rules. This kind of behavior keeps nonwhite people on edge, a little off balance. We get these occasional reminders that we are different, and not really wanted. It prevents us from digging in too strongly, starting to think we could really belong here. It makes us a little introspective, a little unsure of ourselves; at the right low-grade level it prevents us from organizing on behalf of more important things. (Delgado 1991: 380n.319)

Of course, the silencing effect argument also faces objections. One is that it is supported by a paucity of evidence. For example, Weinstein explicitly acknowledges the possibility that a society could be so fundamentally racist and racial minorities so oppressed or dominated that hate speech does have a silencing effect and is used to the detriment of the rights of such persons to participate in the formation of public opinion. Under those circumstances he concedes that democratic values could N-warrant hate speech law (e.g., Weinstein 2001: 158). Nevertheless, Weinstein points to a lack of undeniable and overwhelming evidence of these effects in the US, and concludes that in the absence of such evidence one is left with the strong suspicion that attempts to ban racist speech are motivated by an official abhorrence of racist ideology (158–159). However, it might be argued in response to this objection that we should think of the Nuanced Principle of Democracy in terms of the adoption of a type of precautionary approach to silencing. So, for example, an authority may adopt laws forbidding hate speech when it amounts to discriminatory harassment in the workplace or on campus, or laws interdicting hate speech when it constitutes discriminatory intimidation, because having identified the possibility of the catastrophic anti-democratic outcome that a proportion of the individuals targeted by hate speech will not participate in the formation of public opinion, and bearing in mind the conditions of uncertainty that surround these outcomes, it errs on the side of precaution.[19]

A second objection begins with the observation that the silencing effect is produced not simply by hate speech alone but by hate speech that is mediated through certain attitudes and beliefs among targeted groups or classes of persons. The likely sequence of effects runs like this: social attitudes and beliefs on the part of hate speakers, the occurrence of hate speech, social attitudes and beliefs on the part of the victims of hate speech, the silencing of the speech of the victims of hate speech. This means that silencing would not occur but for the social attitudes and beliefs of hate speakers and would also not occur but for the social attitudes and beliefs of the victims of hate speech.[20] These include believing that their opinions do not matter, feeling too scared to air their views in public, and losing interest in public discourse on public affairs. But restricting speech because of its mediated effects is a dangerous precedent (so the objection runs). There are any number of social attitudes and beliefs that can be responsible for making persons inclined to act or omit to act in certain ways, but this does not mean that it is right to curtail the forms of speech that trigger the social attitudes and beliefs that bring about these consequences (Alexander 1996: 74–75; cf. Scanlon 1972: 213; Strauss 1991: 335). Suppose the publication of humdrum information about political affairs produces or exacerbates an attitude of apathy in a significant minority of citizens such that they are led not to vote. Surely these mediated effects are not grounds to suppress the publication of this information. However, it is clearly not the case that we never think it right to make decisions about whether to protect or constrain speech on the basis of social attitudes that play a crucial part in the causal story (e.g., Scanlon 1979: 534). Most people concede that it should be illegal to shout 'fire' in a crowded theater, but here the effects are mediated through a sort of social attitude, namely, *hear the word 'fire' and start panicking*. And, even those who object to hate speech law on the grounds of its having a chilling effect assume a chain of causes including an attitude, *feeling scared to speak out for fear of prosecution* (e.g., Laird 1994: 392; Michelman 1995: 274). So sometimes social attitudes are parts of chains of events that do not justify legalistic constraints on speech, but sometimes they are parts of chains of events that do justify legalistic constraints on speech. Therefore, what matters is the moral standing of the chain of events, for example, not the social attitude itself.

Assuming that the aforementioned objections can be defeated roughly in the ways I have suggested, I now wish to focus on the clusters of laws/regulations/codes that might be N-warranted under the Nuanced Principle of Democracy. To take one example, Owen Fiss agrees with some of the democratic theorists discussed earlier in this chapter that collective self-governance should be seen as the principal rationale for First Amendment protection of free expression, but he insists that sometimes, such as in some cases of hate speech, the state will need to constrain the speech of some in order to protect the quality of public debate and the rights of all citizens to participate in the formation of public opinion. In his view, this may require granting media regulators the right to regulate hate speech (Fiss 1986: 1415, 1421) and governmental authorities the right to legislate against hate-based fighting words (1996a: ch. 1). Just as the regulation of public highways through speed limits serves 'a worthy public end' of setting out the background rules required for everyone to travel safely, so the regulation of public discourse through hate speech law serves the end of establishing 'essential preconditions for collective self-governance by making certain all sides are presented to the public' (17–18). 'The state is simply acting as a fair-minded parliamentarian, devoted to having all views presented' (21). Such a parliamentarian would be sensitive to the need for time, place, and manner restrictions on public discourse and, in particular, 'sensitive to the excesses of advocacy and the impact of such excesses on the fullness of debate' (1996b: 118). 'Ugly, hateful speech may force some participants to withdraw and may be as destructive to the full airing of an issue as speaking out of turn' (118–119). According to Fiss, emphasizing the silencing effect of hate speech can 'transform what at first seemed to be a conflict between liberty and equality into a conflict between liberty and liberty' (Fiss 1996a: 15) under 'a democratic conception of freedom' (17).[21]

No doubt some people are skeptical that it is possible to regulate speech so as 'having all views presented' (e.g., Jacobson 2007: 75–76). But this skepticism misses the point I think. The current suggestion is for the state to *strive* for the goal of enabling all sides to participate in the debate. The fact that a magical outcome in which all sides speak exactly when, where, and how they prefer is unfeasible does not render the goal undesirable as a basis for regulation. What matters is whether it is possible for all sides to be presented to the public in some shape or form, that is, in a sufficiently fair way, under the framework of time, place, and manner restrictions.

Principles of Political Morality 201

To offer another example, I believe that embracing the Nuanced Principle of Democracy could lend support to laws interdicting provocation or intimidation of members of groups or classes of persons identified by certain ascriptive characteristics. Heyman cites the example of a neo-Nazi march through a Jewish neighborhood, arguing that 'it fails to meet the minimum standards of respect that citizens are entitled to demand of one another in public discourse' (Heyman 2008: 181). Another relevant example might be cross burning statutes. It seems to me that embracing the Nuanced Principle of Democracy and perhaps even the ideal of militant democracy should lead the US Supreme Court to reconsider its stance on these statutes. In *Virginia v. Black*, for example, the Court presented the following distinction.

> The act of burning a cross may mean that a person is engaging in constitutionally proscribable intimidation. But that same act may mean only that the person is engaged in core political speech.[22]

Some scholars have interpreted the Court to mean that when cross burning can be interpreted as core political speech, democratic values dictate that it must be protected under the First Amendment (e.g., Brettschneider 2013: 609–610). But arguably even when acts of cross burning are pregnant with political messages and are performed for political purposes, it does not follow from this that democratic values dictate their protection. For, even this sort of cross burning may have the intended consequence of deterring other people from engaging in politics or the formation of public opinion. Justice O'Connor's own brief history of the Ku Klux Klan and its use of cross burning makes that point very eloquently. 'The Klan fought Reconstruction and the corresponding drive to allow freed blacks to participate in the political process.'[23] 'Soon the Klan imposed "a veritable reign of terror" throughout the South.'[24] Indeed, studies of the cultural and historical significance of black churches among African Americans also reveal the particular significance of acts of church burning by Klan members. To burn down spaces where African Americans tend to 'organize politically' as well as 'persist spiritually' (SimmsParris 1998: 133) is to perform an act of intimidation that directly undermines values of equal political participation.

## 7.2 POLITICAL LEGITIMACY

I now wish to turn directly to the question of political legitimacy. One crude concern one might have about hate speech law has to do with the issue of who in practice decides that hate speech is sufficiently bad to (N-)warrant the use of legalistic constraints. If this is ultimately to be decided by national governments, what if an illegitimate government chooses to forbid hate speech because it deems it to be 'dangerous', 'harmful', or simply 'irresponsible'? Surely then hate speech law must also be illegitimate (Malik

[K.] 2005). This may be true, but it is not a counterargument that is in any sense distinctive to hate speech law. We do not suppose that all defamation law is N-unwarranted simply because it just so happens that in the hands of illegitimate regimes the application of such law can be illegitimate. However, it might be insisted that even those of us fortunate enough to live in true democracies cannot afford to be complacent about who decides how hate speech law is administered. For, what if we collectively deliver extremists into elite positions of lawmakers, judges, attorney generals, university deans, chief executives of media regulators, and so on? Surely it would be better to have no hate speech law so that extremists could not abuse the law (Holmes 2012: 350). Yet this is an unsatisfactory argument, for the simple fact that it proves too much. If the argument is right, then it would seem to imply that we should permit no law that we would have cause to regret if it fell into the hands of extremists. It is hard to think of any law that would not qualify. Consider the words of Justice Frankfurter.

> We are warned that the choice open to the Illinois legislature here may be abused, that the law may be discriminatorily enforced; prohibiting libel of a creed or of a racial group, we are told, is but a step from prohibiting libel of a political party. Every power may be abused, but the possibility of abuse is a poor reason for denying Illinois the power to adopt measures against criminal libels sanctioned by centuries of Anglo-American law.[25]

So the real question is whether there is something about hate speech law in particular that impairs political legitimacy even in otherwise legitimate political regimes. We might capture this with the Principle of Political Legitimacy, as I shall call it, that legalistic constraints on speech or other expressive acts, including constraints on uses of hate speech, are (N-)unwarranted if they decisively impair political legitimacy. Critics of hate speech law have argued that such law runs afoul of the Principle of Political Legitimacy in a variety of ways. The present section is dedicated to critically assessing leading arguments about these ways.

## Ensuring That Citizens Do Not Feel Alienated from Political Decisions

One argument linking free speech to political legitimacy highlights the need for collective authorization of the political order. Post, for example, maintains that political legitimacy depends on whether or not citizens can regard themselves as the coauthors of the public opinion that informs political decisions. If the state decided to ban certain persons from participating in the formation of public opinion, then those persons would be 'alienated' from political decisions (Post 2005: 144). They would not be able to identify with political decisions but would 'instead feel controlled and manipulated by the external force of the collectivity' (145). 'The state thereby loses its claim to democratic legitimacy with respect to those citizens' (147). In fact, Post argues that legitimacy depends not only on formal equality but also on substantive equality, that is, laws and public policies that treat citizens as equals by seeking to eliminate or reduce gross material inequality (152).

What is perplexing about this argument, however, is Post's failure to see that legitimacy might be about more than the way in which the state treats its citizens vis-à-vis formal and substantive equality. Surely it is also about the sorts of intercitizen relationships that a state permits. If infringements of formal and substantive equality can alienate citizens and impair the forms of identification that are necessary for democratic legitimacy, then surely the same can be said of unequal communicative relationships in which some citizens are denied real opportunities to partake of public discourse by and through the speech of other citizens. The more that minority citizens are silenced or marginalized by the hate speech of others, the less likely it is that they will identify with the state in the manner required by democratic legitimacy (cf. Gelber 2011: 19).[26]

Post, of course, might insist that for the state to apply the same standard of non-exclusion both to its treatment of citizens and to the regulation of citizens' communicative treatment of each other would amount to taking control of 'the intimate and independent processes by which citizens evaluate the ideas of others' and 'would verge on the tyrannical' (Post 2005: 148). This is why, other things remaining equal, the First Amendment protects citizens' right to choose the ways, manner, and circumstances of their participation in the formation of public opinion (e.g., Post 2002: 167; 2005: 148). This connection between any constraints on free speech and political tyranny has been echoed by some judges in the US. Consider *Collin v. Smith I* in which Judge Decker opined that '[t]he ability of American society to tolerate the advocacy even of the hateful doctrines espoused by the plaintiffs without abandoning its commitment to freedom of speech and assembly is perhaps the best protection we have against the establishment of any Nazi-type regime in this country.'[27]

However, talk of tyranny seems peculiar or perhaps exaggerated in the context of the innumerable democratic societies throughout the world that have collectively chosen to embrace laws/regulations/codes that constrain uses of hate speech. Suppose the relevant supreme courts started to systematically overturn this democratic legislation. Surely in that scenario citizens would feel alienated from authoritative decisions, feeling as though they are controlled and manipulated by the external force of the judiciary. This boils down to a disagreement between politicians (and citizens who elect them) who are directly or indirectly responsible for enacting hate speech law and supreme court justices who are appointed to be the custodians of constitutional rights. But suppose the enactment of laws banning incitement to hatred, say, reflect the careful and lengthy decision-making of one democratic chamber, containing elected representatives doing their best to act upon public opinion, and taking into account the perspectives and concerns of a second chamber. Together the two chambers have taken the view that such law is necessary for protecting democratic values and the legitimacy of the political regime. Perhaps these facts could stave off a feeling of alienation that hate speakers might have. As Waldron phrases it, 'if an institution which *is* elected and accountable makes the wrong decision about what democracy requires, it is not silly for citizens to comfort themselves with the thought that at least they made their *own* mistake about democracy rather than having someone else's mistake foisted upon them' (Waldron 1999: 293–294).

## Freedom to Voice Concerns and the Political Legitimacy of Downstream Laws and Policies

Another variant of the argument from collective authorization of the political order starts from the slightly different premise that the legitimacy of a constitutional democracy depends upon the ideal of citizens who, even if they are not free to exit the political community without incurring unreasonably high costs, can at least freely voice in public their concerns about everything from constitutional essentials and key democratic institutions and practices to the decisions and legislation of the government of the day. On this argument, it is through the exercise of their opportunities to voice objections that individuals may ultimately come together to collectively authorize or unauthorize the basic ingredients of their political order. It is further argued that the more legislation, including hate speech law, constrains this sort of voicing of concerns, the greater the deficit in legitimacy. In the words of Dworkin, '[t]he majority has no right to impose its will on someone who is forbidden to raise a voice in protest or argument or objection before the decision is made' (Dworkin 2009: vii; see also his 1996: 200–201; 2011: 372). In applying this reasoning to the case of hate speech law, the claim is that countries that have adopted such law are sliding into totalitarianism. Dworkin cites with approval what he takes to be America's exceptionalism in this regard. For example, he claims that the Ohio law overturned by the Supreme Court in *Brandenburg v. Ohio* violated the rights of the local Ku Klux Klan leader 'because it prohibited him from attempting to rally other citizens to his political opinions' (2011: 373).

Consider also the role of free speech in facilitating demands for greater civil rights. According to Parekh, '[i]t is a little odd for law to prohibit religious, racial or ethnic discrimination but grant more or less absolute immunity to utterances that feed the attitudes and nurture the practices leading to such discrimination' (Parekh 2006: 317). For critics of hate speech law, however, there is nothing odd about this whatsoever. On the contrary, several scholars point to the fact that historically US citizens have utilized their rights, protected under the First Amendment, to campaign for the civil rights legislation that prohibits religious, racial, ethnic, and other forms of

## Principles of Political Morality    205

discrimination (e.g., Walker 1990, 1994; Rubenstein 1994; Richards 1999). On one interpretation of these events, for these groups to now claim an entitlement to hate speech law would not merely demonstrate breathtaking short-term memory; it would be tantamount to a gross betrayal of the very institution that enabled them to achieve the advances they have made (e.g., Strossen 2001: 262–266). However, surely the question is not whether or not the groups who now claim entitlement to hate speech law could have fought for and won their other civil rights without the institution of freedom of expression. Rather, it is whether they could have done so with anything less than a civil libertarian conception of the right to freedom of expression. Indeed, it might be argued that the aforementioned advances in civil rights were made *even though* many US states and cities possessed group defamation laws (catchall).

Nevertheless, Dworkin's response to all this is to insist that it remains necessary in the here and now to protect hate speech precisely because the most comprehensive spectrum of expression is a precondition for the continued collective authorization of laws prohibiting discrimination. He puts this point in the following way.

> We may and must protect women and homosexuals and members of minority groups from specific and damaging consequences of sexism, intolerance, and racism. We must protect them against unfairness and inequality in employment or education or housing or the criminal process, for example, and we may adopt laws to achieve that protection. But we must not try to intervene further upstream, by forbidding any expression of the attitudes or prejudices that we think nourish such unfairness or inequality, because if we intervene too soon in the process through which collective opinion is formed, we spoil the only democratic justification we have for insisting that everyone obey these laws, even those who hate and resent them. (Dworkin 2009: viii)

However, two responses are available to Dworkin's argument about the connection between upstream free speech and the political legitimacy of downstream laws and policies. The first is that the democratic justification of downstream laws and policies is simply not the sort of thing that can validate upstream decisions not to enact or to strike down hate speech law. Laws and policies that provide protection to members of identifiable groups against discrimination, disenfranchisement, and hate crime embody fundamental rights. In other words, the provision of these laws and policies is a matter of fundamental rights rather than discretionary privileges. And precisely because of this fact, there is no sense in which the beneficiaries of these rights must feel grateful or indebted to governmental authorities. It is not the case, therefore, that they can be expected to suffer other forms of unjust treatment in return for being lucky enough to have been granted protection through civil rights legislation. Thus, it might be argued that it is entirely inappropriate to expect racial minorities, for example, to endure racist hate speech as the price they must pay for laws and policies banning racist discrimination, especially when those laws and policies are not yet perfectly enforced (cf. MacKinnon 2012: x).

The second response is that even if the democratic justification of downstream laws and policies could justify a decision not to enact upstream hate speech law, it is doubtful that this argument applies to all hate speech law equally. On the contrary, it may be possible to draw a distinction between hate speech law that does and hate speech law that does not thwart a substantial amount of public discourse. Weinstein, for example, maintains that if a citizen is excluded from political debate because government deems his or her speech disturbing or offensive, then 'any decision taken as a result of that discussion would, as to such an excluded citizen, lack legitimacy' (Weinstein 2009: 28). Consequently, he condemns the decision of the High Court of England and Wales (Admin.) in *Hammond v. Director of Public Prosecutions* [2004][28] to uphold a conviction under s. 5 of the Public Order Act 1986[29] of a defendant who had stood in a public square wearing a double-sided sign bearing the words 'Stop Immorality', 'Stop Homosexuality', and 'Stop Lesbianism.' Weinstein regards this as the sort of public demonstration against government policy on homosexuality that ought to be protected as public discourse. Yet he also insists that '[i]n any system of freedom of expression there must be a line separating the highly protected realm of public discourse from the rest of the speech in human society, particularly those words that often accompany or even instigate disputes having little or nothing to do with public affairs' (36). Thus, he maintains that '[i]f Hammond had directed anti-gay epithets at a particular individual or even towards a group of individuals immediately in front of him, he could have been punished for his speech consistent with the core democratic precept underlying freedom of expression' (ibid.). Of course, when it comes to evaluating the plausibility and usefulness of Weinstein's distinction, the devil is in the detail. Consider the US Supreme Court's decision in *Snyder v. Phelps* to strike down as unconstitutional the application of the tort of intentional infliction of emotional distress to a case in which the defendants were engaged in a public demonstration against government policy on homosexuality.[30] Even if one accepts that Weinstein's distinction ought to have been operative in this case, it is not immediately obvious whether the Court should have interpreted the actions of the Westboro Baptist Church as comprising a contribution to public discourse (protesting governmental policies on homosexuality and the rights of homosexuals) or as actions that constituted the discriminatory harassment of the family, friends, and colleagues of a deceased US Marine in the context of his funeral.

At this stage, however, it might be objected that the legitimacy of a constitutional democracy depends upon more than just the protection of free expression when it comprises the direct and explicit voicing of ideas relating

*Principles of Political Morality* 207

to public affairs, including dissent against or challenges to established governmental policies. It also depends upon the right to freely contribute to the 'moral and cultural environment' that spawns direct and explicit voicing of challenges. Dworkin explains it as follows.

> A community's legislation and policy are determined more by its moral and cultural environment, the mix of its people's opinions, prejudices, tastes, and attitudes than by editorial columns or party political broadcasts or stump political speeches. It is as unfair to impose a collective decision on someone who has not been allowed to contribute to that moral environment, by expressing his political or social convictions or tastes or prejudices informally, as on someone whose pamphlets against the decision were destroyed by the police. This is true no matter how offensive the majority takes these convictions or tastes or prejudices to be, nor how reasonable its objection is. (Dworkin 2009: viii)

Nevertheless, in response to Dworkin the defender of hate speech law can raise the issue of the effect that hate speech has on this wider cultural environment. Put simply, what if the speech in question is not merely offensive but is toxic to the sort of moral and cultural environment that is required in order to support the collective authorization of policy and legislation? Waldron puts it thusly.

> A motivation oriented purely to protect people's feelings against offense is one thing. But a restriction on hate speech oriented to protecting the basic social standing—the elementary dignity, as I have put it—of members of vulnerable groups, and to maintaining the assurance they need in order to go about their lives in a secure and dignified manner, may seem like a much more compelling objective. And the complaint that attempting to secure this dignity damages the legitimacy of other laws may be much less credible as a result. (Waldron 2010: 1646)

Presumably what makes this complaint much less credible is the belief that a relatively minor reduction in the collective authorization of downstream laws and policies can be justified on the basis of serious considerations that justify the relevant upstream laws. In other words, political legitimacy has greater but not absolute weight in comparison to other goods or values, meaning that a sufficiently large extent of the realization of other goods or values, most notably the assurance of civic dignity, can be of equal or greater value than the realization of political legitimacy.

One fairly obvious reply to this line of thinking, however, is that the goods or values of political legitimacy and the assurance of civic dignity cannot be traded off against each other in this sort of way. Political legitimacy is not the sort of thing that can be placed on balancing scales with things other than itself. But now consider the following, final response. It is possible that the aforementioned assessment of hate speech law is being made from the sole perspective of political legitimacy. This is not about trading off political legitimacy with the assurance of civic dignity but about the way in which the assurance of civic dignity is constitutive of the realization of political legitimacy. Suppose—and here I might be *reading into* Waldron more than *reading from* Waldron—that political legitimacy, including the legitimacy of the legal system, itself depends upon its being possible, at least in principle, to justify that system to each citizen bound by it on the basis of fundamentals of justice that they cannot reasonably reject (cf. Waldron 1999: ch. 10). Applying this general view of political legitimacy to the issue of hate speech, it might be argued that members of minority or vulnerable groups could reasonably reject the following justification of an absolutist free speech doctrine. "For fear that hate speech law may put at risk the collective authorization and political legitimacy of downstream laws from which you benefit, we shall neglect to utilize the measures at our disposal to curb forms of hate speech that can be corrosive of a shared, public sense of the basic elements of your reputation, status and dignity as members of society in good standing." In other words, insofar as political legitimacy is a matter of interpersonal justification and consensus among equal citizens, sometimes this requires authorities to limit free expression for reasons of assuring civic dignity even though in many other cases it requires authorities to protect free expression for the sake of the collective authorization of downstream laws. If this is a plausible interpretation of what a Waldronian view might be, then it means that political legitimacy is among the values underwriting the arguments discussed in Ch. 5 that connect the public good of assurance of civic dignity with several clusters of laws/regulations/codes, including laws proscribing group defamation (*sensu stricto*), laws banning incitement to hatred, regulations limiting the use of negative stereotyping or stigmatization, and perhaps even Holocaust denial legislation. It also means that the disagreement between Dworkin and Waldron is not simply a disagreement about what political legitimacy implies for the status of hate speech law but also about the nature of political legitimacy itself.

## Political Legitimacy and Ethical Independence

A third argument for illegitimacy of hate speech law directly challenges the idea that government has the right to engage in the business of banning speech if it expresses unethical opinions about particular groups being subhuman or unworthy of equal citizenship. Dworkin, for instance, urges that political legitimacy depends upon governmental respect for the fact that individuals are ethically independent or have a responsibility to develop their own understanding of ethical values, including values of what counts as a human being and how human beings should be treated.[31] Consequently, governmental authorities must respect even the free speech of persons who use that right to express unethical views (Dworkin 1996: 200–201; 2011:

372–373; 2012: 342). Among other clusters of laws/regulations/codes, this argument challenges the political legitimacy of hate speech law that disallows the dissemination of ideas based on the inferiority of members of groups or classes of persons identified by certain ascriptive characteristics, or hate speech law that limits the use of negative stereotyping or stigmatization, such as the characterization of such persons as criminals or animals. Thus, Dworkin asserts that Waldron's defense of hate speech law conflates the question of what a legitimate government owes to its citizens in matters of policy and legislation with the different question of what individuals owe to each other as they conduct their affairs within the structure of legitimate law. In Dworkin's words, Waldron gives to government the power 'to enforce a particular collective opinion about what forms of respect individual human beings owe one another just as human beings' (Dworkin 2012: 343). 'But a government is not fully legitimate that claims it' (ibid.).

However, Dworkin's criticism of Waldron mischaracterizes the nature of the latter's argument, at least as it might be interpreted. Waldron could respond that a truly legitimate government has responsibilities with respect to creating or maintaining a public environment conducive to assurance of the equal standing of all citizens. This includes a legislative responsibility to establish laws that compel citizens to do their part in providing the assurance of civic dignity. This is not a matter of illegitimately imposing an ethical doctrine on citizens anymore than implementing a system of taxes in order to combat gross material inequality is illegitimately imposing an ethical doctrine on citizens. Instead, it is about delivering on the fundamentals of justice. If this does constitute the imposition of an ethical doctrine (albeit a political ethical doctrine), then this is a charge that can be leveled against virtually all political theories, including the liberal egalitarianism defended by Dworkin himself. For, it too seeks to impose its vision of the fundamentals of justice on citizens.

## 7.3 CITIZENS AS LEGAL SUBJECTS

Yet another potential argument against hate speech law starts by asking what it means for the state to recognize citizens as legal subjects, that is, as autonomous agents capable of holding rights and duties, and then infers from this implications about the particular sorts of rights and duties citizens ought to be furnished with, including rights and duties relating to freedom of expression. This argument reintroduces into the discussion the Principle of Autonomy, that legalistic constraints on speech or other expressive acts, including constraints on uses of hate speech, are (N-)unwarranted if they fail to respect the formal autonomy of those subject to them. One version of this argument can be inferred from the work of Axel Honneth.[32] According to Honneth, to say that a system of law makes citizens legal subjects is to say that it makes what happens to citizens and what is expected of them, to a greater or lesser, sensitive to their autonomous choices. As beneficiaries of legal rights citizens are placed in possession of a degree of control over other people's duties and can make choices about what to do with their rights. And as subjects of legal duties citizens are held responsible both for limiting their behavior in the light of legal constraints and for the choices they make in that regard. For Honneth, this means that 'adult subjects acquire, via the experience of legal recognition, the possibility of seeing their actions as the universally respected expression of their own autonomy' (Honneth 1995: 118). 'In obeying the law,' in other words, 'legal subjects recognize each other as persons capable of autonomously making reasonable decisions about moral norms' (110). When persons are excluded from legal rights and duties, in contrast, they are denied this possibility. 'For the individual, having socially valid legal rights withheld from him or her signifies a violation of the person's intersubjective expectation that he or she will be recognized as a subject capable of reaching moral judgments' (1992: 191). This constitutes a type of misrecognition—misrecognition that can damage 'moral self-respect' (1995: 133) and in extremity bring about a sort of 'social death' (135).

Now it may be tempting to infer from Honneth's theory that withholding legal rights to protection against hate speech, such as by failing to enact laws banning incitement to hatred, constitutes misrecognition of autonomy (cf. Thompson 2012: 225–228). For, it denies citizens control over other people's duties to refrain from hate speech. But this inference may be too hasty, and for two good reasons. The first is that some of the rights protected by criminal laws banning hate speech, such as the right not to have hatred stirred up against oneself, can be exercised independently of the will of the objects of hate speech. A case can be brought to the attention of the police and taken to court without the objects of the stirring up of hatred ever choosing to be involved in the collection of evidence or to provide testimony or victim impact statements. In which case, this argument may be ill-suited to criminal laws banning uses of hate speech. The second, more general reason is that arguably denying hate speakers the right to free expression would seem to constitute, under Honneth's conceptual framework, a violation of the hate speaker's intersubjective expectation that he or she will be recognized as a subject capable of reaching moral judgments. This is because the right to free expression gives an individual the space to develop his or her own moral judgment about what to say, to whom, and when to say it.

There are parallels here with Baker's (2012) argument against hate speech law. His argument starts with the premise that the legitimacy of the political order depends upon the ideal of citizens who are capable of understanding and fulfilling their political obligation including an obligation to obey the law (Baker 2012: 63). 'The state cannot coherently ask a person to obey its laws unless it treats the person as capable of making choices for herself, for example, the choice to obey the law' (ibid.). Therefore, any law that *formally* treats citizens as anything less than capable of making choices for himself or herself cannot be legitimate. A second premise is that among the other sorts of choices that define this general autonomy, which must be formally respected, are choices pertaining to personal values and, what is more, choices over whether or not and how to embody one's values through speech or expression (ibid.).[33] 'A person is not treated as formally autonomous if the law denies her the right to use her own expression to embody her views' (ibid.). A third premise is that hate speech law formally treats citizens as less than autonomous with regard to such choices. It does this by substituting a governmental choice for a personal choice about how and when to embody one's values in speech, including a personal choice as to what is appropriate and what is inappropriate public speech (64). Baker concludes from this that hate speech law is politically illegitimate.

But now consider three possible lines of response to this argument. The first stresses the fact that hate speech can itself, if left unchecked, impede the *substantive autonomy* of its targets, such as by reducing their actual capacity and real opportunities to make choices about how to embody their values in speech. Baker freely admits this possibility, but he insists that the question of political legitimacy—as distinct from the question of the justification of governmental policy—*is* focused on the government's treatment of citizens vis-à-vis their formal autonomy (Baker 2012: 64).

A second line of response, due to Shiffrin, denies that political legitimacy must be tied to formal rather than substantive autonomy. Shiffrin asks the reader to assume for the sake of argument that racist speech creates unjust conditions for people of color, including conditions that reduce substantive autonomy (Shiffrin [S.H.] 2011b: 339). Following on from this, he argues that 'it is a little odd to be told that injustice must be maintained in order to protect the legitimacy of the government' (ibid.). Conversely, it may be perfectly consistent with the idea of political legitimacy for a degree of realization of the value of formal autonomy to be forsaken in order to achieve minimum realization of other goods or values that are constitutive of political legitimacy, not the least of which is substantive autonomy. In other words, using the law to intervene against hate speech that creates unjust conditions, including conditions that tend to make it more difficult for people of color to exercise their substantive autonomy, 'can make the government more legitimate' (ibid.). 'If the facts warranted intervention in the context of racist speech, I would rather explain to the racist why his moral theory is defective and why the state need not respect it than try to explain to people of color that they must live in unjust conditions' (340). But once again Baker has an answer to this response. It is that the value of formal autonomy and the ideal of political legitimacy that it embodies are simply not the sorts of values and ideals that can be outweighed by other goods or values, such as those that are purported to be realized by hate speech law,[34] as Shiffrin advocates (Baker 2011: 252–253). To think that it could be outweighed is to fail to understand the deontological nature of these values and ideals. In Baker's own words, formal autonomy is 'a side constraint on law necessary for legal legitimacy and appropriate for constitutional theory'

(253). Interestingly, in an earlier formulation Baker frames the argument as a Kantian interpretation of the respect owed to citizens. 'For the community legitimately to expect individuals to respect collective decisions, i.e., legal rules, the community must respect the dignity and equal worth of its members' (Baker 1978: 991–992). '[T]he state's policy must respect people's integrity as rational, equal, autonomous moral beings, it must respect people as ends and not just as means' (ibid.).

Nevertheless, I would like to propose a third possible line of response to Baker's argument that I believe may be harder to answer. It focuses on political obligation. As normally conceived, the question of political legitimacy has to do with whether or not governing authorities stand in a special kind of relationship with their citizens such that authorities may rightfully claim a right to rule and a right to expect that citizens have an obligation to obey the law. For Baker, the hallmark of this relationship is one in which governments treat their citizens as autonomous agents formally speaking, meaning that they respect citizens' rights to use their own expression to embody their views. But this does not exhaust the essential ingredients of this relationship, especially in the case of political obligation. Traditionally political obligation has been justified by philosophers on the basis of tacit consent, a debt of gratitude for the voluntary receipt of benefits, and/or a duty of fair play relating to the generation of benefits that citizens voluntarily receive. But it is arguable that under each of these accounts certain conditions of justice must be satisfied in order for individuals' conduct to be transformed into obligation-grounding conduct. And it seems to me that hate speech law may be partly constitutive of those conditions.

Suppose tacit consent is the principal basis of political obligation and that such consent is usually signaled by or grounded in the conduct of not exiting the political community despite having reasonable opportunities to do so or in voting in elections for particular candidates rather than ticking the box marked 'none of the above' or spoiling the ballot paper. Nevertheless, conduct that might otherwise qualify as tacit consent may fail to do so for certain groups or classes of persons if they are systematically treated as second-class citizens vis-à-vis the fundamentals of justice. This might happen if they are denied legalistic protection from group defamation (*sensu stricto*) or incitement to hatred. Because they are subject to hate speech and other forms of unjust treatment, they could lack the material wherewithal required to exit the community. They might also be deficient in the access to education, specialist knowledge about law, or even group consciousness they need in order to fully appreciate that being denied the aforementioned protection is an injustice. And so they do not think to register a protest vote. If the conduct that might otherwise qualify as tacit consent does not do so in their special case, they cannot be said to have an obligation to obey the law. Or suppose instead that other things remaining equal, political obligation is grounded either in a straightforward debt of gratitude for receiving benefits from government or in a slightly more complex duty of fair play based on receiving benefits from the political community in the circumstances that other individuals have submitted themselves to the law in order to generate those benefits. Once again, this may not be enough to ground political obligation for all groups or classes of persons in the event that some groups or classes of persons unfairly receive fewer benefits than others (e.g., Greenawalt 1987: ch. 7). Even if the obligation to obey the law falls as a burden on everyone more or less equally, the benefits of membership of the political community can be fewer for the targets of hate speech than for others. In other words, for groups or classes of persons who are disproportionately subject to hate speech, the benefits of membership are not 'presumptively beneficial'[35] in the sense that we cannot safely and reasonably presume that the burden of submitting to the law, such as having to endure hate speech protected under a constitutional regime of free expression, is worth its while given the level of benefits they receive in return, such as being able to engage in hate speech if they so desire. For the most frequent victims of hate speech this benefit is tempered by the fact that in a political community in which discrimination and hatred cast a pall over the communicative environment, they may be more likely to fall prey to defamatory, demeaning, degrading, or stigmatizing hate speech than other groups.

Assuming these lines of analysis are plausible, what they suggest is that even if it is accurate to say that the expectation of political obligation is bound up with treating citizens as formally autonomous, it is also the case that under traditional theories of political obligation no citizen can be plausibly said to possess an obligation to obey the law if he or she is not treated as an equal member of the community vis-à-vis the fundamentals of justice. Indeed, it is normally supposed that to treat citizens as capable of obeying the law must mean to treat them as capable of obeying *just* law (e.g., Simmons 2001: ch. 1). So the proper recognition of autonomy comes in the shape of treating citizens as capable of exercising the qualified nature of their political obligation with respect to just laws. If laws proscribing group defamation (*sensu stricto*) or incitement to hatred, for example, are essential parts of a just political settlement, then this too is something the autonomous citizen is assumed to understand.

\* \* \*

In this chapter I have examined several arguments of political morality relating to freedom of expression and hate speech law. In the past it might have been supposed that principles of political morality support free speech only in a narrow way, applying exclusively to the limited category of political speech. The task of courts would then be to determine the nature and boundaries of political speech, that is, to specify what are and are not political figures, platforms, contexts, and subject matters. However, many of the arguments explored in this chapter have a deliberately broad scope, applying to numerous categories of speech insofar as they help to inculcate the capacities necessary for citizens to perform their civic responsibilities and

214 *Principles of Political Morality*

contribute to the formation of public opinion or the building of the cultural environment. Nevertheless, if forms of hate speech are located within the panoply of human communications that are essential to democratic self-government, political legitimacy, and even political obligation, then this poses a significant challenge for defenders of hate speech law.

Be that as it may, I have tried to show that this challenge can be met by at least some laws/regulations/codes. In the case of the formation of public opinion, even thinkers who are generally skeptical of the merits of hate speech law acknowledge that democratic values are not incompatible with hate speech law when it is sensitive to the difference between acts of hate speech that comprise public discourse and acts of hate speech that do not, with the touchstone being the wider social practices or institutions in which speech acts are embedded. Yet this argument tends to be limited to certain clusters of hate speech law and the contexts they cover, such as laws/regulations/codes forbidding discriminatory harassment in the workplace. So to this argument I added the proposition that some clusters of hate speech law, including laws/regulations/codes interdicting speech when it constitutes discriminatory intimidation (e.g., cross burning statutes), laws/regulations/codes banning incitement to hatred, laws/regulations/codes proscribing group libel (*sensu stricto*), and laws/regulations/codes prohibiting hate speech that causes or is likely to cause a breach of the peace, can be justified on the democratic basis of ensuring that all citizens enjoy real opportunities for contributing to the formation of public opinion. I also explored various arguments connecting freedom of expression with political legitimacy. Once again, it emerged that hate speech law is not necessarily incompatible with political legitimacy, particularly laws/regulations/codes forbidding discriminatory harassment, laws/regulations/codes proscribing group defamation (*sensu stricto*), laws/regulations/codes banning incitement to hatred, and regulations limiting the use of negative stereotyping or stigmatization. Finally, I looked at free speech arguments based on the idea of citizens as legal subjects who are capable of autonomous decisions about their own speech. Here I argued that even if we assume that where there is a reasonable expectation of legal rights and duties, not the least of which is the obligation to obey the law, there ought to be an assumption that citizens are capable of making autonomous decisions about their own speech, there is also a sense in which there can be no political obligation unless certain other just grounding conditions are in place. I suggested that these just grounding conditions may include the enjoyment of laws proscribing group defamation (*sensu stricto*) and laws banning incitement to hatred.

**NOTES**

1. The idea that arguments about democratic self-government justify the protection of categories of speech other than political speech is not universally shared, however. cf. Bork (1971: 26–31) and Schauer 1982 (ch. 3).

*Principles of Political Morality* 215

2. See, e.g., *Whitney v. California*, at 375; *West Virginia State Board of Education v. Barnette* (1943) 319 US 624, at 641; *New York Times Co. v. Sullivan* (1964) 376 US 254, at 301.
3. *S. v. Mamabolo* [2001] ZACC 17, para. 37.
4. Post and Weinstein believe that adopting this sort of approach has three important implications for how we think about freedom of expression. One is that we should think of freedom of expression not as a fundamental right but as something that derives from the right to participate in the formation of public opinion. A second implication is that we end up with an argument not for a general right to free speech but instead an argument for particular rights to speech acts: according to Post (2011: 483), 'those speech acts and media of communication that are socially regarded as necessary and proper means of participating in the formation of public opinion'. A third implication (Weinstein 2011a: 513) is that because it is rights-based, this approach places a renewed emphasis on what we may not reasonably ask any individual of a democratic society to give up even if it is as a result of a democratic process in which he or she finds himself in the minority; and this includes the right to contribute to public discourse. Of course, there may be other reasons to value participation in democratic self-government besides rights-based reasons. One is that it is morally desirable to promote the sort of personal development that flows from acting as a citizen in a democratic order (cf. Dahl 1989: 104–105).
5. In fact, the Principle of Democracy might also provide a basis for legal doctrines and principles that themselves make it more difficult to legitimize hate speech law. One way of using the Principle of Democracy to motivate the doctrine of overbreadth, for example, is to consider what could happen to the formation of public opinion in its absence. Suppose that whenever protected speech acts are combined with sanctionable acts, the result is that the protected speech act becomes sanctionable. It would then be possible to ban almost any protected speech act, no matter its value, simply by banning speech acts that were a combination of the protected and the sanctionable. Consider the act of expressing in public the belief that one cannot trust a black person to be an elected representative of the student body because he or she will inevitably favor black students to the detriment of white students. This is protected speech. But in the absence of the Principle of Overbreadth a campus code banning discriminatory harassment could be used to sanction the act of racially harassing someone by expressing the aforementioned belief every time one sets eyes on that person. This would seriously hamper the ability of a member of the student body to participate in the formation of public opinion during hustings and public debates for the election of student representatives.

Similarly, it might be argued that the Principle of Democracy supports the doctrine of neutrality. As Weinstein (2001: 155) puts it, 'there is something troubling with government imposing a restrictive view of public discourse on those expressing views with which it disagrees, while allowing those with who it agrees to engage in more freewheeling and abusive discourse'. For Weinstein, other things remaining equal, this concern also applies to laws that discriminate between different forms of unprotected speech on the basis of racist content or viewpoints (157).
6. According to Weinstein (2011a: 493n.9), this marks one of the differences between his view and that of Post. In the determination of whether or not something counts as public discourse Post places an emphasis on the context, on whether or not the speech is *in* the public sphere, whereas Weinstein errs more on the side of the content, on whether or not the speech is *of* public concern.
7. Indeed, in order for Post's own argument for free speech to make any sense it *must* be the case that there is sufficient agreement as to the existence of public

discourse and the public spheres in which it occurs and sufficient agreement as to the status of public discourse as something that is bound up with the formation of democratic public opinion in order to justify the existence and particular interpretation of the constitutional right to free speech. If there were not this minimum agreement over the fact that public opinion functions in at least this way even if it functions in other ways as well, then Post's theory of free speech would be dead in the water.

8. 39 P.D. II 225.
9. At 315.
10. *Saskatchewan (Human Rights Commission) v. Whatcott*, at 507.
11. *R. v. Zündel*, at 806, 814–815.
12. Nos. 41340/98, 41342/98, 41343/98 and 41344/98 (ECtHR, 13 Feb.).
13. 337 US 1 (in which the US Supreme Court ruled as unconstitutional a City of Chicago breach of peace ordinance).
14. At 37.
15. 304 US 144.
16. At 155.
17. Ibid.
18. 323 US 214 (involving the constitutionality of an executive order relating to the internment of Japanese Americans during World War II).
19. Based on this line of analysis, it may appear at first sight that by striking down hate speech law the US Supreme Court has tended to reject the use of precautionary principles when it comes to speech behavior no matter the catastrophes imagined. Recent First Amendment doctrine, as Schauer puts it (2009: 305), 'requires us to accept the uncertain risk of a catastrophe rather than restrict the speech that might cause it'. However, Schauer also argues that the answer to the question of whether US free speech doctrine rejects or accepts precautionary principles depends on how one frames the catastrophe. Thus (ibid.), 'if we were to define the catastrophe as the large-scale restriction of speech, then we could understand existing free speech doctrine, not as a rejection of the precautionary principle, but instead as an embodiment of the precautionary principle—albeit with a different conception of the catastrophe.'
20. Of course, it would also not occur but for a range of other causes, including government policy, a culture of intimidation, social and civic exclusion, and so on. But here for the purposes of argument I am interested in teasing out the role of the beliefs and attitudes of targets themselves. I thank Alexander Tsesis for suggesting I make this clarification.
21. This echoes Langton's (1990a: 332n.61) suggestion that if the argument against pornography were based on the principal claim that pornography silences women, then it 'might lead to an argument of a rather different kind, which saw the issue as presenting a conflict, not between liberty and equality, but between the liberty of men and the liberty of women.'
22. *Virginia v. Black*, at 365.
23. At 352.
24. At 353.
25. *Beauharnais v. Illinois*, at 263.
26. It is also worth pointing out that legitimacy is likely to be a function not merely of the inclusion of all citizens in public discourse but also of the overall quality of that discourse. And there is every reason to suppose that ensuring high levels of inclusion will only improve the overall quality of public discourse (e.g., Seglow 2003: 90–91).
27. *Collin v. Smith I*, at 702.
28. EWHC 69 (Admin).

29. This section makes it an offense to display any writing or sign that is threatening, abusive, or insulting within the hearing or sight of a person likely to be caused harassment, alarm or distress.
30. Much of the action in *Snyder v. Phelps* was around the question of whether or not Phelps' speech pertained to a matter of public interest *and* even whether or not Snyder was a public figure. For critical discussion of this case, see Volokh (2010), Deana Pollard Sacks (2010), and Heyman (2012).
31. According to Dworkin, the fact that individuals are ethically independent in this sense is one of the fundamental principles of human dignity from which legal and political rights flow (Dworkin 2006: 10; 2011: 14).
32. I thank Simon Thompson for pointing this out to me.
33. Elsewhere Baker (2009: 42) formulates this in terms of bodily ownership: that in order for autonomy to be respected a person 'must have a general right over the value-expressive uses of herself—her own body.'
34. Baker (2012) also expresses skepticism as to the truth of the empirical assumptions necessary to support the belief that hate speech law can actually realize significant goods or values. I shall discuss his main lines of skepticism in Ch. 9.
35. This is George Klosko's terminology. See Klosko (1992: ch. 2).

# 8 Principles of Balance

Thus far I have examined principles focused on a single type of interest, right, good, or value. However, several critics and defenders of hate speech law alike have suggested that the fitting resolution to these dilemmas rests upon striking a balance between different types of interests, rights, goods, or values. While the metaphor of balance is not always used in these debates with precision as to what is being balanced, the mechanics of balancing, what constitutes an optimum balance, and whether balancing exercises will yield similar results for all hate speech law, some scholars at least have attempted to turn balancing into a principle-governed exercise. This chapter takes a close look at two kinds of balancing principles that have been proposed in the literature: rights-based balancing and interests-based balancing. The differences are not limited to that which is being balanced (balanceanda) because the balanceanda often have an impact on the nature of balancing itself. I shall argue that interests-based balancing is the more justificatorily basic of the two kinds of balancing. However, I shall also try to show that interests-based balancing is dogged by the problem of incommensurability: namely, that for many of the vital interests at play in dilemmas over hate speech law there is not a true trade-off ratio between interests. Taking this problem seriously casts new light on the claims that certain scholars have made on behalf of some of the values discussed in previous chapters, including autonomy, human dignity, or even the democratic values of public discourse: namely, that these values cannot be traded off against other values.

## 8.1 RIGHTS-BASED BALANCING

Heyman argues that when it comes to conflicts between freedom of expression and other considerations that seem to support hate speech law, the conflict is best understood through the lenses of what he calls liberal humanism, according to which legalistic constraints on speech are N-warranted only if they protect 'fundamental rights' (Heyman 2008: 2), which must themselves be founded on respect for 'the inherent freedom and dignity of human beings' (38). His account of what it means to respect human freedom and dignity combines the Kantian notion of the inherent and absolute worth of human beings (39), which is rooted in the capacity for autonomy (ibid.), with a particular reading of the state of nature theories of Hobbes, Locke, and Hegel (7–8, 171–172). On Heyman's reading of this tradition, when persons come face-to-face with each other in the state of nature, they are motivated by a concern for their sense of worth, a need for security, and an awareness of their natural freedoms to agree upon a set of fundamental rights that ought to be respected as constitutional rights or 'the bond that constitutions the political community' (171). Included among the fundamental rights that flow out of the inherent freedom and dignity of human beings as well as state of nature theories are the right to freedom of speech, rights of personal security, rights of personality, and the right to recognition (44–45, 170–171).

Heyman makes it clear that although these fundamental rights may be valuable as aspects or instantiations of human freedom and dignity, not all fundamental rights are absolutely valuable or even equally valuable and not all laws realize fundamental rights to the same degree. In other words, no fundamental right and no fundamental right-instantiating law has value beyond comparison. This in turn ensures that even if it might appear to be the case that drawing on fundamental rights rather than individual interests stymies any meaningful talk of balancing (Heyman 2008: 33), balancing remains possible (70–71). The view that it is possible to balance even fundamental rights is not without legal precedent. For example, when German courts have dealt with Holocaust denial cases (e.g., *Case of Guenter Deckert*, *Case of National Democratic Party of Germany* (or '*Auschwitz Lie*'), *Case of Germar Rudolf*, *Case of Ernst Zündel*) under sections of the Criminal Code, perhaps it could be said that they have tried to balance the right to freedom of expression, which is protected under Art. 5(1) of German Basic Law, against the right to personal honor, which is protected under Art. 5(2), all under the rubric of Art. 1(1), which states that '[h]uman dignity shall be inviolable.' Similarly, in *Aksu v. Turkey* the ECtHR affirmed that in dealing with cases of negative stereotyping of groups or classes of persons identified by certain ascriptive characteristics, 'the Court will need to balance the applicant's right to "respect for his private life" against the public interest in protecting freedom of expression, bearing in mind that no hierarchical relationship exists between the rights guaranteed by [Arts. 8 and 10 of the ECHR].'[1]

As one component of his approach to conflicts between fundamental rights,[2] Heyman defends a rights-based balancing approach. '[W]hen an act of expression comes into conflict with another right, the balancing approach seeks to determine whether regulation is warranted by weighing (1) the value of the speech and (2) the extent of the restriction against (3) the value of the other right and (4) the impact of unregulated speech on that right' (Heyman 2008: 71). In order 'to assess the value of competing rights, one needs a common standard by which to measure them' (70). Heyman lights upon the moral good or value of 'human freedom and dignity' (ibid.).

Specifically: 'Rights have value as aspects of (1) external freedom, (2) freedom to develop and express one's personality, (3) freedom to participate in the social, political, and cultural life of the community, and (4) intellectual and spiritual freedom' (ibid.). Following on from this, Heyman supports what I shall call the Principle of Rights-Based Balancing, that legalistic constraints on uses of hate speech are (N-)warranted only if they 'harmonize the competing rights by protecting both as far as possible and, to the extent they conflict, by protecting the right that at the margin constitutes the most important form of [human freedom and dignity]' (71).

Heyman subsequently applies this principle to the following hate speech problem. He asks the reader to imagine a group of neo-Nazis or a group of Klansmen who wish to march through a Jewish American neighborhood or an African American neighborhood wearing special costumes, uttering hate-based verbal insults, and making wounding gestures—all in an effort to express their view that Jewish Americans or African Americans are subhuman and are not entitled to the same civic rights as others (Heyman 2008: 169). According to Heyman, this case involves a conflict between the right to freedom of speech and three other highly valuable rights. First, there is the right to personal security (170, 179). People living in the area will have group memory of atrocities committed by the Nazis in Europe and by Klansmen across the US but especially in the southern states. This collective memory will generate reasonable fear or feelings of insecurity insofar as the expressive behavior of the marchers 'amounts to a threat of or incitement to violence' (170). Similarly, Heyman argues that racist fighting words, including cross burning when it amounts to racist fighting words, may severely impact a highly valuable right shared by not merely the direct targets of such speech but also by the community as a whole: namely, the right to security (168, 180). Second, there are rights of personality (or dignitary rights) (170), including the right to mental tranquility and the right to reputation (170, 179). In terms of the right to mental tranquility, Heyman draws an analogy between the neo-Nazis' or Klansmen's march and forms of discriminatory harassment in the workplace that attract civil action under the tort of intentional infliction of emotional distress (144–146, 165, 170).[3] In terms of the right to reputation, Heyman maintains that insults or verbal injuries may be the subject of lawsuits 'because of the "outrage" they inflict on the victim's sense of honor, which derives from his inherent dignity as a human being' (145).[4] In short, whether or not the march inflicts severe emotional distress or even lasting psychological trauma, 'it constitutes a fundamental attack on their right to personal dignity' (170). Third, and '[a]bove all', there is the right to recognition (170–171, 179), which 'is the most fundamental right that individuals have' (171). '[I]ndividuals have a duty to recognize one another as human beings and citizens' (ibid.). By denying the very humanity of their targets, some group-based insults violate this duty (ibid.).[5] Heyman maintains that, even taking into consideration the idea that the march might also constitute political speech or more simply a contribution to public discourse, it is nevertheless a type of hate speech that given the particular context 'is not deserving of constitutional protection' (179). Interpreted through the lenses of the Principle of Rights-Based Balancing, this judgment reflects the high value of the other rights violated by this type of hate speech and the extent of the impact on those rights should it go unregulated (179–181).

Heyman has provided a sophisticated theoretical framework that honors the complexity of the issue of hate speech, but it also leaves some questions unanswered. First, Heyman is not explicit about which forms of hate speech law the foregoing argument is supposed to support. Reflecting on the details of the march example and the fundamental rights implicated, it seems that the argument is intended to support a range of laws/regulations/codes, including those that interdict discriminatory provocation; that disallow the public expression of hatred, including through the use of insults, slurs, or derogatory epithets and through the dissemination of ideas based on the inferiority of protected groups; that provide sanctions or remedies against hate speech when it qualifies as a dignitary crime or tort; and/or that limit negative stereotyping or stigmatization. It strikes me, however, that the logic behind Heyman's argument would also lend support to other clusters of laws/regulations/codes that constrain uses of hate speech, including those that ban incitement to hatred; that interdict hate speech when it constitutes discriminatory intimidation or incitement to discrimination or violence; and that proscribe group defamation (*sensu stricto*). For, it may be that stirring up hatred or using hate speech to intimidate or using hate speech to incite acts of discrimination or violence infringes on the right to personal security as much as racist fighting words, and that group defamation may do as much to violate the right to reputation as verbal insults or insulting gestures.

Second, Heyman may not be justified in focusing exclusively on the four freedoms he does. For one thing, why only external freedom (negative liberty) and not also freedom from subordination? Surely non-subordination ought to be considered just as central to human freedom and dignity as any other sort of freedom. Indeed, it seems that any plausible balancing act is likely to take on board a multiplicity of basic human goods or values, some of which may not be equivalent with, or easily be reduced to, Heyman's four freedoms (e.g., Shiffrin [S.H.] 1983: 1197–1198; 2011a: 559; Nelson 2005: 143; Parekh 2005–2006: 216; Schauer 2012: 140).

Third, Heyman remains conspicuously silent on how the four types of freedom that together make up the value of human freedom and dignity are to be traded off against each other in cases of conflict. Suppose for the sake of argument that the fundamental right to free expression, specifically the right to racially insult other people, has significant value as an aspect of (1) external freedom and (2) freedom to develop and express one's personality, but much less value as an aspect of (3) freedom to participate in the social, political, and cultural life of the community and (4) intellectual and spiritual freedom, whereas the fundamental right to mental tranquility, specifically the right not to be subjected to racist insults, has significant value as an aspect of (3) and (4) but much less value as an aspect of (1) and (2). How is the balance to be struck? It seems that in this difficult case the balancing exercise will ultimately depend on judgments of the relative value or importance of these freedoms. Yet Heyman provides scarcely any guidance on how to make such judgments. He writes, '[i]n such cases, while the rights-based approach does not yield clear, uncontroversial results, it does serve to focus our attention on the crucial issue—the relative value and importance of different forms of liberty' (Heyman 2008: 73). What this seems to indicate, therefore, is that (Heyman's version of) rights-based balancing is not justificatorily basic. On the contrary, performing rights-based balancing exercises would appear to depend upon more fundamental balancing exercises involving aspects of human freedom and dignity.

## 8.2 INTERESTS-BASED BALANCING

One way of thinking about these aspects of human freedom and dignity, and perhaps many other goods or values, is to think of them as *interests*. For the purposes of this discussion, interests are not necessarily things that someone has preferences for, likes, cares about, or desires. Rather, they are things that are good or valuable for someone, in the sense that they make his or her life go better, whether or not he or she prefers them. As Joel Feinberg puts it, '[t]hese interests, or perhaps more accurately, the things these interests are *in*, are distinguishable components of a person's well-being: he flourishes or languishes as they flourish or languish' (Feinberg 1984: 34). Feinberg also suggests that a person's interests are likely to be 'a miscellaneous collection' (ibid.). One need only reflect on the various normatively relevant features discussed in this book to see how this could be the case: namely, liberty, psychological and physiological health, autonomy, security, non-subordination, the absence of oppression, human dignity, the discovery of truth, the acquisition of knowledge, self-realization, human excellence, civic dignity, cultural diversity and choice, recognition of cultural identity, intercultural dialogue, participation in democratic self-government, and being subject only to legitimate rule.

The need for balancing stems from the fact that any system of constraints on, and permissions for, hate speech is likely to enable the realization of some interests and disenable the realization of others. A decision to strike down a hate speech law can be a decision to protect speech that enables the realization of some interests but at the same time to protect speech that disenables the realization of others. Conversely, a decision to uphold a hate speech law can be a decision to suppress speech that disenables the realization of some interests but at the same time to suppress speech that enables the realization of others.[6] How is the point of optimum balance determined then? One answer might be that legislators and judges should attempt to

Principles of Balance 223

reach a point where no more could be done to enable the realization of interests than is being done. This is encapsulated in what I shall call the Principle of Interests-Based Balancing, that legalistic constraints on uses of hate speech are (N-)warranted only if they achieve an optimum balance between the interests in play, where an optimum balance represents the point at which increasing the degree of constraint on hate speech is likely to enable the realization of interests of a combined extent of realization and value or importance that is no greater than that of the interests the realization of which is likely to be disenabled by this increase, while decreasing the degree of constraint on hate speech is likely to enable the realization of interests of a combined extent of realization and value or importance that is no greater than that of the interests the realization of which is likely to be disenabled by this decrease. In short, this approach calls for the maximum realization of interests.

The previous statement of the Principle of Interests-Based Balancing takes its inspiration from the work of Sumner. As part of his detailed analysis of the Canadian Supreme Court's approach to hate speech cases, Sumner argues that the Court balances rights on the basis of 'the interests they are meant to enhance or protect' (Sumner 2004: 60). According to Sumner, the interests-based approach is best exemplified by the balancing of the following 'constellations' of interests. On the side of free speech there are speaker interests in self-expression, communication, and self-fulfillment (e.g., being a competent speaker); audience interests in partaking of communication, being better informed, being exposed to new ideas, and achieving self-realization (e.g., coming to posses deeper convictions); third-party interests in living in a society that enjoys the benefits of communication, free inquiry, and well-informed debate. On the side of hate speech law there are addressee interests in avoiding emotional distress (e.g., feelings of humiliation, exclusion, and self-hatred) and victim interests in not being subject to insecurity (e.g., increased risk of violence, discrimination, and injustice) (60–61). Sumner interprets the Court as seeking not merely to balance interests but also to 'locate the optimal balance between conflicting interests when the costs of a departure in either direction exceeds its benefits [. . .] that is, the point at which the balance of benefits over costs is maximized' (63). 'Whether the existing hate propaganda statute properly locates that balance point is, of course, the issue on which the majority and the minority on the *R. v. Keegstra* court took opposing sides' (ibid.).

The form of maximizationalist consequentialism that Sumner has in mind is, I believe, an instance of the Principle of Interests-Based Balancing. As I interpret his view, a legalistic constraint on hate speech is N-warranted only if it achieves an optimum balance between interests, where the optimum balance is achieved at a point such that introducing any additional constraints on hate speech for the sake of fulfilling relevant addressee or victim interests would reduce net interest-realization because of the expected reduction in the realization of speaker, audience, and third-party interests, while removing constraints on hate speech for the sake of speaker, audience, and third-party interests would reduce net interest-realization because of the expected reduction in the realization of addressee and victim interests (cf. Sumner 2004: 33, 63). As Sumner indicates, the majority in *R. v. Keegstra* opined that the existing hate propaganda statute did achieve an optimum balance, meaning that any change to the law up or down the scale of constraint would result in a reduction in net interest-realization. To explain this sort of reasoning, the statute makes it a criminal offense to willfully promote hatred against any identifiable group of persons by communicating statements in public. To say that the statute achieved an optimum point may be to say two things. First, if the statute were changed so as to constrain hate speech even further, such as by dropping the *mens rea* element captured by the term 'willfully', then this might increase the realization of victims' interests by curbing even more speech that could contribute to a climate of hatred, but it might also have the effect of reducing net interest-realization due to a cost in speakers' interests in having the freedom to make comments that could contribute to a climate of hatred but without intent to promote hatred or knowledge of the substantial certainty of such a consequence. Second, if the statute were revised or repealed with the consequence of constraining hate speech even less, then this might increase the realization of speaker interests, but it might also have the effect of reducing net interest-realization by virtue of a cost in victims' interests in not living in a climate of hatred, a cost in audience interests in not being exposed to undue influences (assuming that children are among the audience members), and a cost in third-party interests in not living within a society marked by hatred and the results of hatred, including exclusion, radicalization, and balkanization.

In this section, I wish to focus less on Sumner's specific take on the Court's reasoning in *R. v. Keegstra*[7] and more on the general approach he outlines and how it differs from the approach adopted by the US Supreme Court. According to Sumner, the latter approach is an instance of what he calls 'indirect consequentialism.' Here consequentialist balancing of interests is utilized in order to frame certain rules, principles, tests, doctrines, or definitions for dealing with issues of free speech, after which cases are adjudicated by reference to those precepts rather than direct balancing of consequences (Sumner 2004: 75–77).[8] US defamation law may provide an illustration of this indirect approach. In *New York Times Co. v. Sullivan* the US Supreme Court defended the need for constitutional protection for press reports about public officials even if they contain inaccuracies or untruths. This reflects the democratic interests served by political speech, which often touches upon the character and conduct of public officials. At the same time, the Court also allowed for less protection in the case of statements that show 'actual malice': namely, if 'the statement was made with knowledge of its falsity or with reckless disregard of whether it was true or false'.[9] The adoption of this test might be said to strike an optimal balance between *inter alia*: speaker interests in participating in the formation of public opinion; public officials' interests in social reputation; third-party interests in public officials being able to carry out their duties unmolested; and third-party interests in public officials being held to account so that government is legitimate. Building on *New York Times Co. v. Sullivan*, some academics have suggested as a response to the problem of defamatory hate speech a sort of aggravated malice test to cover defamatory statements made about members of groups or classes of persons identified by certain ascriptive characteristics (e.g., Partlett 1989: 488; Lawrence 1990: 463n.119). Under this test, other things remaining equal, the public expression of a false damaging statement about such persons should benefit from First Amendment protection. This reflects the democratic interests served by social commentary, which may often touch upon the character and conduct of groups or classes of persons identified by certain ascriptive characteristics. At the same time, if the social commentator made the statement with knowledge of its falsity or with reckless disregard for whether it was true or false, then the plaintiff (or plaintiffs in a class action lawsuit) would have a reasonable expectation of success. Again, the adoption of this test might be thought to strike an optimal balance between *inter alia*: speaker interests in participating in the formation of public opinion; objects' of hate speech interests in civic dignity; and third-party interests in the effects of all citizens enjoying civic dignity. Of course, it goes without saying that even if courts adopted this new aggravated malice test, there would remain substantial technical difficulties around proving a case for damage to reputation relating to defamatory statements made about a group or class of persons to which the plaintiff belongs.[10]

Interestingly, Schauer has also recently developed a version of the interests-based balancing approach with respect to balancing epistemic goods or values like discovery of truth and acquisition of knowledge against other non-epistemic goods or values such as security and freedom from oppression (Schauer 2012: 132). Schauer levels a criticism against Mill that is familiar within Millian scholarship, namely, that Mill erred in neglecting to take seriously the possibility that sometimes authorities may choose to suppress an opinion without doing so because they believe that opinion to be false but instead because they believe that it is true, and permitting its circulation would disenable the realization of non-epistemic goods or values (ibid.). On Schauer's version of this criticism, Mill's omission amounted to his assuming a trade-off ratio wherein epistemic goods or values possess absolute weight over non-epistemic goods or values; that is to say, Mill's mistake was 'presupposing that the intrinsic good of knowledge is of greater value than any other human good, and is so much greater that no amount of non-epistemic benefit is worth the cost of even the smallest sacrifice of increased knowledge' (133). According to Schauer, this fault can be corrected by adopting what he calls 'the post-Millian calculus.' According to this calculus, which I take to be an instance of the Principle of Interests-Based Balancing, the official suppression of speech 'can be justified only when (but not always when) it is predicted that the consequential losses from the spread of false opinions that might be accepted and acted upon despite their falsity will be greater than the consequential gains that will come from the discovery of previously unknown truths and the increase in knowledge that is the corollary of that discovery' (138).

How might this calculus be applied to the case of Holocaust denial material, for example? It is not difficult to see how permitting such material might enable the realization of epistemic goods or values: if not discovery of truth (assuming that Holocaust denial material has limited value as a step to truth because the probability of Holocaust denial material being true is vanishingly slim), then perhaps acquisition of knowledge (assuming that Holocaust denial material has considerable value to the acquisition of knowledge because it promotes greater epistemic surety in holding true beliefs about the Holocaust through exposure to, and debunking of, fatuous challenges to those beliefs). That being said, Schauer is at pains to point out that permitting Holocaust denial material may also come at a cost in epistemic goods or values in the event that exposure to false beliefs about the Holocaust only perpetuates ignorance among sections of the population who are unreceptive to rational argument and factual demonstration (Schauer 2012: 136). It may also be the case that permitting Holocaust denial disenables the realization of non-epistemic goods or values (or enables the realization of non-epistemic bads or disvalues). Schauer avers the possibility that 'accepting the fact and the size of the Holocaust is important in lessening the manifestations of anti-Semitism' (132). There is also the good or value of human dignity to be borne in mind (see Ch. 3 [3.6]), and perhaps even civic dignity (see Ch. 5 [5.1]). Based on this, when it comes to permitting the unregulated public airing of Holocaust denial material, it might prove to be the case in many situations that the expected losses in terms of disenabling the realization of epistemic and non-epistemic goods or values (or enabling the realization of epistemic and non-epistemic bads or disvalues) are greater than the expected gains in terms of enabling the realization of epistemic and non-epistemic goods or values.

Consider another example. In Ch. 7 [7.2] I examined Dworkin's argument that the political legitimacy of downstream laws and policies that protect identifiable groups from discrimination and other injustices necessitates decisions not to enact upstream hate speech law. Waldron has argued that it might be reasonable to build into this argument sensitivity to the distinction between hate speech law that chills ongoing public debates and hate speech law that chills public debates that are to all intents and purposes over or concluded. Suppose for the sake of argument that debate on whether or not all racial/ethnic groups should be afforded equal status in the political community is the only debate to which group defamation (catchall) or incitement to hatred contributes. According to Waldron, banning this sort of hate speech would not pose a problem for political legitimacy because '[t]here is a sense in which the debate about race is over, won, finished' (Waldron 2010: 1647). As Waldron also acknowledges, however, this suggestion has the potential to put the Principle of Political Legitimacy on a collision course with the Principle of Knowledge. In Waldron's own words, 'I am mindful of John Stuart Mill's point about the importance of sustaining a "living apprehension" of the truths on which our social system is organized' (1648).[11] Nevertheless, Waldron, like Schauer, insists that we should part company with Mill when it comes to his implicit assumption that epistemic goods or values such as knowledge acquisition have absolute weight in comparison with other goods or values. Waldron does not deny that knowledge acquisition is important or valuable, but he insists that providing assurance of civic dignity for vulnerable members of society is more so (1649).

However, all of these forms of interests-based balancing face similar challenges, of which I mention three. The first comes from defenders of the First Amendment, who believe that such balancing exercises will not grant sufficient protection to free speech, including even hate speech. Forms of interests-based balancing (according to one version of the first challenge) carry with them an implicit assumption that free speech interests are no different than other interests, in the sense that they are so many more interests to be placed onto the balancing scales or into the net interest-realization calculation machine. This stands in direct opposition to the view that free expression is 'in a preferred position.'[12] Of course, under the indirect approach the US Supreme Court could perform a balancing exercise that results in the adoption of a rule, principle, or test that is designed to give effect to the First Amendment and that protects certain categories of speech and not others. But absolutists insist that the First Amendment *is* the operative rule to be applied, and its absolute nature ('Congress shall make no law . . . ') clearly indicates that it precludes balancing free speech interests against other sorts of interests. In the words of Meiklejohn, '[t]he essential meaning of the First Amendment is that, already, in the making and maintaining of the Constitution, the procedure of "balancing" has been undertaken and completed' (Meiklejohn 1951: 485). That being said, it is still incumbent upon absolutists to justify why, aside from the language of the First Amendment, free speech interests should be granted absolute weight. After all, it seems equally plausible to believe that First Amendment interests could be weighed in the balance with other interests provided that they 'weigh very heavily in the scale' (Chafee 1941: 31). The First Amendment might be interpreted as giving binding force to that more nuanced belief.[13] In any event, it seems likely that in order to justify why free speech interests ought to be granted either absolute or very heavy weight, one needs to call upon more fundamental interests. So, for example, a critic of hate speech law might seek to argue that free speech interests ought to weigh heavily on the scales because they are rooted in or embody a fundamental interest in self-realization or a fundamental interest in participation in the formation of public opinion or a fundamental interest in autonomy. Then again, those on the other side of the debate may also hope to call on these or other fundamental interests to support the claims of those subjected to hate speech. But who is to say which sets of fundamental interests are more weighty? In addition to this, it might be argued that any balancing exercise that requires lawmakers and judges to place on the scales epistemic interests, such as truth discovery and knowledge acquisition, related to hate speech is bound to require those lawmakers and judges, at some point, to engage in personal assessments of whether in their view the ideas expressed by hate speech are true or valuable. But such assessments (according to this second version of the first challenge) 'will be partisan and controversial through and through' and so inimical to the purpose of the First Amendment (e.g., Alexander 2005: 57–59).

The second challenge comes from defenders of hate speech law who believe that forms of interests-based balancing do not grant sufficient protection to the victims of hate speech. Sumner's account of interests-based balancing focuses on the individual interests of three constituencies of the population, namely, speakers, audiences, and third parties, and enjoins the maximization of net interests-realization. No doubt Sumner views this as a matter of quality and not just quantity, in the sense that only two interests of equal weight or importance will level the balancing scales, but some interests are of greater weight or importance than others, other things remaining equal. Yet the very notion of achieving an optimum point of balance that delivers greater benefits (interest-realization) than costs (interest-non-realization) when everything is added up may be problematic for what it says about what may happen to individual persons who find that the optimum balance of benefits and costs entails that *their* interests are not to be fulfilled. This, it might be argued, violates the distinctness of persons in the sense that it treats persons or their interests as things that may be sacrificed for the sake of the larger goal of achieving an optimum balance of interests.

Arguably, concern for the distinctness of persons lies behind Schauer's own counterargument to the view that under the First Amendment, the harms resulting from speech are the price "we" must pay for the benefits of enjoying freedom of expression: namely, that it is 'troubling whenever the cost of a general societal benefit must be borne exclusively or disproportionately by a small subset of the beneficiaries' (Schauer 1992a: 1322). Schauer cites the harms caused by hate speech (e.g., an increase in the chances of being subjected to discrimination or violence) as one instance. As he puts it, '[t]he increases in the amount of violence and discrimination are the marginal costs of increased First Amendment protection, marginal costs not borne proportionately by all those who benefit from that increased protection' (1351). Indeed, it might be argued that part of the point of a bill of rights must be to protect the interests of minorities on whom the costs of the institutional regime of freedoms and restrictions are disproportionally visited.[14]

The other side of the coin, however, is that it also seems quite possible that a large enough amount (quantity and quality) of interest-realization associated with laws banning hate speech could outweigh a smaller amount of interest-non-realization associated with such laws. Reflecting on this possibility, critics of hate speech law might insist that it would be contrary to the basic purpose of the First Amendment to sacrifice speaker interests for the sake of audience or third-party interests. Perhaps, then, the present challenge to interests-based balancing is not that this sort of balancing is more likely to disadvantage the victims of hate speech but instead that there is something fundamentally immoral in grounding decisions about whether or not to ban hate speech in the maximization of interest-realization. In which case, both of the foregoing challenges may come to the same thing: namely, that there is something special about values such as autonomy and human dignity, which means that it is not appropriate to regard them solely as "interests" in the sense of constituents of people's well-being or things that people have a stake in. Rather, they are values that should be respected in themselves, over and above the sense in which they make people's lives go better. In other words, they place demands on how people should be treated; they are side constraints, in that sense. Thus, as observed in Chs. 3 [3.2] and 7 [7.3], Baker argues that the requirement to respect formal autonomy operates as a principled side constraint on government action, not because it is an interest but because it is a deontological requirement. Then again, as suggested in Ch. 3 [3.6], some people think that the value of human dignity places side constraints on how people may talk to one another, such as by not denying the Holocaust.

Interests-based balancing approaches also face a third major challenge. This is to explain how it is possible to measure the combined extent of realization and value or importance of interests the realization of which is enabled or disenabled by a system of constraints or permissions. Starting with the extent of realization, one might understand this to be a matter of *how much* realization of relevant interests is enabled or disenabled by constraining or permitting hate speech. For some interests, such as the discovery of truth, it may be natural to view realization as a matter of degree because the relevant interest comes in degrees. So, for example, it might be thought that permitting some types of hate speech enables the realization of more discovery of truth than permitting other types of hate speech because more or fewer truths can be discovered. For other interests, in contrast, realization may be all or nothing. Thus, it might be thought that permitting a certain type of hate speech either does or does not disenable the realization of recognition of cultural identity because given forms of hate speech either do or do not involve such recognition.

Turning to the comparative value of different interests, an obvious challenge is to explain how a list of miscellaneous interests can possess commensurable value. One simple definition of commensurability says that two interests possess commensurable value if and only if there is a true trade-off ratio between them in the whole range of situations in which they are compared (cf. Wiggins 1997: 59). This true trade-off ratio might be linear, such as when two interests have equal value or weight, meaning that if the realization of the two interests is equal, then the two realizations are equally valuable, but if the extent of the realization of one interest is greater than the extent of realization of a second interest, then the realization of the first interest is greater in value than the realization of the second interest. Or it might be non-linear, such as when an interest has absolute weight in comparison to a second interest, meaning that no amount of the realization of the second interest can be equal to or greater in value than any amount of realization of the first interest, or when an interest has greater but not absolute weight in comparison to a second interest, meaning that if the extent of the realization of two interests is equal, the value of the realization of the first interest is always greater than the realization of the second interest, but a sufficiently large extent of the realization of the second interest can be of equal or greater value than the realization of the first interest. What matters is that there is *some* true trade-off ratio between the interests. In the absence of such a ratio the interests are incommensurable. Although it may still be possible to compare the differing extents to which alternative legal responses to the issue of hate speech realize interests, if it proves to be the case that there is no true trade-off ratio between these interests, the comparison remains only superficial and talk of balancing is highly misleading or nonsensical (e.g., George 1993: 199).

To clarify, the problem is not that it is impossible to come up with some or other ratio that will functionally determine the relative weight of very different interests. Rather, it is that there is no single *true* ratio. So the problem of incommensurability is a claim about the arbitrariness, rather than any strict impossibility, of measurement. Indeed, there is often a suspicion that courts pluck ratios out of the sky from any number of ratios they could have lighted upon, without a rational or non-arbitrary basis for doing so. Of course, it might be argued that there are at least some commensurable interests at stake in free speech debates. Consider the words of District Judge Warren in *United States v. Progressive, Inc.* 'Faced with a stark choice between upholding the right to continued life and the right to freedom of the press, most jurists would have no difficulty in opting for the chance to continue to breathe and function as they work to achieve perfect freedom of expression.'[15] However, the commensurability of these particular rights or interests seems to be the exception rather than the rule, especially in hate speech cases.

Of course, some schemes for judging the relative weight or importance of miscellaneous human interests deliberately incorporate two or more ratios. But the challenge for proponents of these complex schemes will be to provide some sort of overarching index or ratio of ratios that could explain how attributing more or less weight or importance to given interests according to one ratio is traded off against attributing more or less weight or importance to the same interests according to another ratio. For example, Feinberg (1984: 204–206) argues that in order to measure the overall weight or importance of interests other than interests in liberty, legislators must

*Principles of Balance* 231

consider at least three ways in which interests can differ in their weight or importance: first, there is their importance to the interest holder, which is to say, their 'vitality' within his or her total system of personal interests; second, there is the degree to which interests are reinforced or backed up by other interests, both personal and community interests; third, there is the inherent moral quality of interests. Then, there are additional ratios for interests in liberty, depending on whether these are specific interests in liberty or the general interest in liberty (i.e., an interest in having as many open options as possible) (207), not least the ratio of 'fecundity', which is a matter of assessing how many further options are opened up by a given open option (208). If all of these interests and all of these ratios matter, then the interests-balancer is faced with the difficult task of creating an overall index (or ratio of ratios). At this point Feinberg states simply that the task of interests-based balancing is 'difficult' and 'delicate' (205). Not only that, but '[i]t is impossible to prepare a detailed manual with the exact "weights" of all human interests' (203). 'In the end, it is the legislator himself, using his own fallible judgment rather than spurious formulas and "measurements," who must compare conflicting interests and judge which are the most important' (ibid.). Some people might respond that this is an implicit admission that in most cases there is no one true measurement of importance and *ex hypothesi* interests are incommensurability. A related response is that for a legislator or judge to say that he or she has engaged in a balancing exercise and achieved the optimal balance is really just a rhetorical device designed to lend credence to what is in fact a personal judgment call. Putting it another way, the statement "I choose option A because it is strikes a more optimal balance of interests than option B" is extensionally equivalent to "I have thought about it and I reckon that option A is better than option B but there is no reason to think that my reckoning is any more or less sound than a very different reckoning that I, or other people for that matter, could have arrived at taking exactly the same things into consideration."

Interestingly, some US Supreme Court justices have wholeheartedly embraced the skeptical position that when it comes to comparing constitutional values there is no single true trade-off ratio. In the famous words of Justice Scalia, '[i]t is more like judging whether a particular line is longer than a particular rock is heavy.'[16] Of course, this position is not shared by all judges. In *Doe v. University of Michigan*, for example, District Judge Cohn described the dilemma of whether or not to use legalistic constraints in responding to the problem of campus hate speech as one of balancing.

> It is an unfortunate fact of our constitutional system that the ideals of freedom and equality are often in conflict. The difficult and sometimes painful task of our political and legal institutions is to mediate the appropriate balance between these two competing values. Recently, the University of Michigan at Ann Arbor (the University) [. . .] adopted a Policy on Discrimination and Discriminatory Harassment of Students

## 232  Principles of Balance

> in the University Environment (the Policy) in an attempt to curb what the University's governing Board of Regents (Regents) viewed as a rising tide of racial intolerance and harassment on campus. [...] However laudable or appropriate an effort this may have been, the Court found that the Policy swept within its scope a significant amount of "verbal conduct" or "verbal behavior" which is unquestionably protected speech under the First Amendment.[17]

Then again, District Judge Cohn said nothing in his judgment about how ideals of freedom and equality are rendered commensurable, philosophically speaking.

Contemporary philosophers of value have presented some ingenious solutions to the problem of incommensurability. I shall consider one such solution in Ch. 10 [10.1]. Nevertheless, one pragmatic as opposed to philosophical solution is to take the problem of measuring very different normative features out of the hands of judges and put it into the hands of democratic institutions. Bleich explains the nature and putative merits of this proposal as follows.

> At the societal level, I stress that the most legitimate outcomes are most often reached when democratically elected legislatures take responsibility for passing laws that represent citizens' perspectives, rather than having outcomes determined by courts. Because these decisions force us to confront trade-offs between core liberal democratic values, no country has an approach that has been stable over time or that is grounded in a coherent overarching philosophy. This is the natural result of diversity of citizen opinion and of diverse national circumstances. That is not only an acceptable outcome, it is also a desirable one for those who believe in the core principles of democracy. (Bleich 2011: 12–13)

However, there is a sense in which this response to the problem of balancing is more radical than Bleich seems willing to admit. For, once one accepts the fact that there is no coherent overarching philosophy bearing upon the comparative value of the interests at stake in hate speech cases and, therefore, no true trade-off ratios between those interests, then whatever emerges from a public debate channeled through democratic institutions might reasonably be called 'democratic' or even 'legitimate' (Bleich 2011: 8), but surely it cannot be termed "rationally optimal." So, for example, when Bleich asserts that the UK's introduction of incitement to religious hatred legislation in 2006 'capped half a decade of debate about the appropriate balance between punishing religious incitement—as an extension of Britain's 1965 racial incitement laws—and protecting freedom of expression' (23) and that '[t]aking into account the context and likely effects in early twenty-first century Britain, a law curbing religious incitement—which would target aggressive statements against groups and not religious jokes or criticisms of doctrine—appeared justified' (29), this must be read as commentary on the fairness of the democratic processes that produced this decision rather than on the substantive fairness of the balance that was struck.

What is more, even if it could be somehow rationally demonstrated that the numerous interests implicated in the issue of hate speech are commensurable with each other, a further complicating factor is that the relevant trade-off ratios are unlikely to be transcontextual. This is to say that comparisons of value may be sensitive to the contexts in which interests are realized, such as institutions and social practices, meaning that each context will exhibit its own set of ratios.[18] So, for example, Schauer suggests that epistemic interests such as discovery of truth and acquisition of knowledge may possess higher value when realized as parts of the social practice of public discourse (Schauer 2012: 132–133) or within the institution of academic inquiry and research (140–141), as compared to when they are embedded in other social practices or institutions. Similarly, Nelson argues that because the values of self-realization or expressivism may be the most appropriate justifications for free speech in the context of art, these values will weigh particularly heavily on the balancing scales within that particular context (Nelson 2005: 86). On this general approach to the theory of comparative value, the weight or value attached to the realization of a given interest is likely to depend on the extent to which it serves the point and purpose of the particular institution or social practice that it constitutes or helps to create or is embedded in, and within which it is realized.[19]

Of course, appealing to the point and purpose of particular institutions or social practices does not make the task of comparing value any more straightforward. There are a range of conflicting views on the primary mission of a university, for example (cf. Smolla 1990: 216–217; Post 1991: 318–325; Sunstein 1993a: 201–202). Even if one accepts the basic proposition that discovery of truth and acquisition of knowledge have special value on university campuses, there is still the matter of how to choose between different understandings of that special value, including how that value compares to the value of other goods and values—understandings that will be rooted in competing interpretations of the primary mission of a university.[20] Donald Downs, for example, claims that at one time the assumption among major research universities in the US was that 'the university's primary mission is to ensure the academic freedom of properly trained professors and their students' (Downs 2005: 4). Based on this, it would seem natural to believe that a university may legitimately seek to protect as far as possible activities of truth discovery and knowledge acquisition if these activities flow from the exercise of academic freedom (e.g., Smolla 1990: 216–217; Gunther 1990: 7; Rosenberg 1991: 586–587). What is more, if properly trained professors and their students are themselves unconcerned with observing other, non-epistemic standards of conduct in their scholastic endeavors, then (it might be reasoned that) any campus speech codes that are oriented toward imposing such standards upon professors and students would be illegitimately repressive. In contrast, it might be thought instead that a university is a community of scholarship where the term 'community' implies that '[t]he university is an island of equality, civility, tolerance, and respect for human dignity; a place where the contemplative and rational faculties of man should triumph over blind passion and prejudice' (Smolla 1990: 217). Hartman, for instance, affirms that the university's primary mission is to ensure that scholastic endeavors adhere to 'a recognition of inherent civility and dignity toward each individual', as dictated by 'the inherent dignity of the academic community' (Hartman 1992: 858). Reflecting this understanding, it might be thought that a university should grant its professors and students only as much freedom to engage in truth discovery as is consistent with this inherent dignity. And so campus speech codes may limit freedom for the sake of dignity (e.g., Klaff 2010).

Faced with this dilemma, one suggestion has been to zone university campuses into different kinds of areas, serving different primary functions, reflecting different balancing ratios between the relevant interests at stake, and regulated by different speech management regimes (e.g., Smolla 1990: 217–224; 2011: 125–128). Alternatively, both Sunstein and Sadurski have proposed the solution of granting universities the discretion to conduct balancing exercises relating to campus speech codes as they see fit, making as much or as little of the aforementioned zone-based differentiations as they prefer—provided, that is, that prospective students have a real choice to make between universities that have balanced the considerations in meaningfully different ways (Sunstein 1993b: 832; Sadurski 1999: 185–186). The result is that 'the students themselves may decide whether they will be more comfortable in a permissive-libertarian, or a protected, learning environment' (Sadurski 1999: 185–186).[21] At first glance, this may sound like an eminently pragmatic, even reasonable solution. But it also carries certain dangers, I believe. Sunstein opines that '[c]olleges that restrict a large amount of speech may find themselves with few students' (Sunstein 1993b: 832). My own suspicion is that the "let students vote with their feet" approach could result in the balkanization of the university sector. One possible eventuality is that a majority of actual and potential hate speakers prefer to attend a permissive-libertarian learning environment while a majority of actual or potential targets of hate speech favor a protected learning environment. If the split between hate speakers and the targets of hate speech mirrors the split between different racial/ethnic groups, this could lead to *de facto* intercollegial racial/ethnic segregation.

* * *

In this chapter I have examined two different kinds of balancing exercise based on rights and interests respectively. I have suggested that interests-based balancing, when it involves miscellaneous fundamental human goods and values the realization of what makes people's lives go better, is not based on any more fundamental balanceanda. But I have also shown that interests-based balancing faces a serious philosophical challenge in the shape of the problem of incommensurability. This problem tells us something about the difficulty of sustaining the claim that a given governmental or institutional authority has struck the right balance between interests in dealing with the issue of hate speech. It also casts in a new light Baker's argument (see Chs. 3 [3.2] and 7 [7.3]) that a legitimate government always treats its citizens as formally autonomous and this value cannot be outweighed by any goods or values that might be realized by hate speech law. At first glance, this argument might seem to be saying that there *is* a true trade-off ratio between democratic values and other goods or values consisting in the fact that no amount of the realization of other goods or values can be equal to or greater in value than any amount of the realization of democratic values. But on closer inspection, the argument might be expressing the more profound idea that any talk of democratic values being outweighed by other goods or values is strictly speaking meaningless because the goods or values in question are incommensurable with democratic values. In Ch. 10, therefore, I defend a different kind of approach to dilemmas over whether or not hate speech law can be warranted all principles considered, one that is based on principled compromise.

More generally, in Chs. 3–8 I have set forth a range of principles of basic morality, personal development, civic morality, cultural morality, and political morality. It is important to bear in mind, however, that the debate about whether or not laws/regulations/codes that constrain uses of hate speech law are warranted does not begin and end with these sorts of principles. There still remains a set of vexed legal issues to be borne in mind, including identifying pressing needs for hate speech law, determining how effective hate speech law is in reducing hate speech/the evils of hate speech, showing that hate speech law is the least restrictive alternative available, bearing in mind any potential unintended consequences of hate speech law for freedom of expression, and dealing with the requirement that any law that restricts freedom of expression is content and viewpoint neutral. The fact that all of the principles discussed so far are framed in terms of whether or not legalistic constraints on hate speech are N-warranted is partly owing to the need to consider these legalistic issues in arriving at judgments of overall warrant. And it is to these issues that I now turn.

## NOTES

1. *Aksu v. Turkey*, at para. 62.
2. Heyman (2008: 71–72) argues that rights-conflicts can be resolved not merely through balancing exercises but also through an appeal to 'internal relationships between rights' and to the preservation of 'the system of constitutional liberty' itself. In this section, however, I focus on balancing.
3. Heyman (2008: 145) recognizes that the tort of intentional infliction of emotional distress cannot be used, under its customary conditions for successful action in the US, in cases where speech does not cause the plaintiff 'to suffer *severe* distress, either because he had great strength of character or because he

had become inured to repeated abuse.' 'Yet it seems clear he would have suffered a serious injury to personality,' argues Heyman. 'Regardless of whether it causes severe distress, [insulting speech] infringes the right to "an inviolate personality" in the same way that offensive battery infringes the right to bodily integrity.' Therefore, Heyman (146) argues that 'insults should be unlawful [ . . . ] when they inflict emotional or dignitary injury.' However, he does not provide much guidance on how the notion of dignitary injury is to be justicized. He points to the 'extreme and outrageous' test used by American courts in interpreting the tort of intentional infliction of emotional distress (266n.81). Yet the courts have tended to regard insulting speech as falling short of extreme and outrageous conduct. See Ch. 2 [2.7] and Ch. 3 [3.1]. It is also puzzling why Heyman makes no reference to Delgado's proposed tort for racial insult given Delgado's insistence that this proposed tort could be used to address racial insults that cause dignitary injury, whether or not they damage emotional well-being (e.g., Delgado 1982: 171).
4. Note, however, that at times Heyman (2008: 145) appeals to the notion of social personality, which is akin to reputation. 'When the speech degrades an individual in front of others, it also constitutes an attack on social personality that is analogous to defamation.' This enables Heyman to retain the publicity requirement (that hate speech must occur in public to qualify as such) alongside the appeal to interests in personality. At any rate, the public nature of Heyman's march example would seem to suggest that he has social personality in mind.
5. The right to recognition, as conceived by Heyman, partly foreshadows Waldron's idea of protecting civic dignity. See Ch. 5 [5.1].
6. The notion of enabling or disenabling the realization of interests (i.e., things such as goods or values in which people have a stake) is deliberately abstract. I use it as a placeholder for one or more of the following three types. First, speech can enable the realization of interests in the sense of being constitutive of the realization of those interests. This is to say that speech can be an embodiment of interests even if that relationship is not describable in causal terms. Conversely, speech can also disenable the realization of interests in the sense of being constitutive of the absence of interests (or constitutive of harms to interests). Second, speech can enable the realization of interests in the sense of being indispensable to or a necessary causal prerequisite for the realization of interests. Here it might be fitting to think in terms of thresholds of speech, meaning that without a minimum amount of speech the interests simply could not exist. In contrast, speech can disenable the realization of interests in the sense of being a sufficient causal condition for the non-existence of those interests (or the existence of harms to interests). Third, speech can enable the realization of interests in the sense of being a means to or instrumentally useful for the realization of interests. This instrumentality may consist in the fact that speech facilitates or provides opportunities for interests. It is not the case that the interests are impossible without speech but it is the case that speech provides resources for or removes obstacles to the attainment of interests. On the other hand, speech can disenable the realization of interests by impeding the attainment of interests.
7. For an argument that in fact the Court adopted a form of qualified deontology rather than consequentialism, see Richard Mullender (2007: 246–247).
8. This distinction is on a par with standard distinctions between 'balancing' and 'categorical' approaches and between 'ad hoc' and 'definitional' balancing approaches to constitutional analysis. For more on these approaches and the differences between them, see, e.g., Frantz (1962), Fried (1963), Nimmer (1968), Aleinikoff (1987), Greenawalt (1989), Shiffrin [S.H.] (1990: ch. 1), Post (1995), Shaman (2001), and Deutsch (2006).

9. *New York Times Co. v. Sullivan*, at 279–280.
10. For one thing, it must be shown that specific individuals are covered by defamatory statements made about an entire group or class of persons. For example, courts will not necessarily interpret the statement "All Arabs are thieves" as applying literally to each and every Arab in spite of the presence of the universal quantifier "all." This is because in some situations the statement could signify the generic (i.e., generalization) "Many Arabs are thieves." In order for a cause of action to be successful it must be demonstrated that the statement is "of the plaintiff", so to speak, such as if an ordinary person would reasonably understand the statement to be picking out individual members of the relevant group and specifically the plaintiff. The statement "Mahmoud is a thieving Arab" printed in a newspaper or the words "Thieving Arab" daubed on Mahmoud's door leave less scope for doubt in this regard than "All Arabs are thieves." This issue was summed up by Lord Atkin in *Knupffer v. London Express Newspaper, Ltd.* [1944] AC 116 (involving a lawsuit brought against a newspaper by a Russian resident of London in response to libelous statements printed about an émigré group called *Mlado Russ* who were accused of being agents of Hitler). 'The reason why a libel published of a large or indeterminate number of persons described by some general name generally fails to be actionable is the difficulty of establishing that the plaintiff was, in fact, included in the defamatory statement, for the habit of making unfounded generalizations is ingrained in ill-educated or vulgar minds, or the words are occasionally intended to be a facetious exaggeration.' At 122.

    In addition to this, courts will require not merely that the defamatory statements were made of the plaintiff but also that the plaintiff did in fact sustain a dignitary injury (i.e., damage to reputation) as a result of being a member of the defamed group. So, for example, in the Canadian case *Bou Malhab v. Diffusion Métromedia CMR Inc.* [2011] 1 SCR 214 (involving a class action lawsuit for damages resulting from racist comments made by Andre Arthur during a radio broadcast concerning Montréal taxi drivers whose mother tongue is Arabic or Creole) the Supreme Court of Canada ruled that the plaintiffs had failed to demonstrate that they had suffered personal injury. As Justice Deschamps explained: 'The size of the group is the factor to which the courts have attached the greatest importance in Quebec and elsewhere. Generally speaking, it is recognized that the larger the group, the more difficult it is to prove that personal injury has been sustained by the member or members bringing the action.' At 245.

    Finally, a cause of action brought for malicious defamation is unlikely to succeed simply in virtue of the fact that the defendant used certain epithets. This is because epithets such as "black bastard", "stupid mulatto", and "dirty faggot" could be interpreted by an ordinary person merely as vulgar expressions of hatred rather than as false damaging statements of fact. For instance, in *Irving v. J.L. Marsh Inc.* (1977) 46 Ill. App.3d 162 (involving an African American architecture student who was passed a document to sign by a shop assistant with the annotated remark "Arrogant nigger refuses exchange") an Appellate Court of Illinois dismissed a cause of action for defamation on the grounds that the word "nigger" is not defamatory in its ordinary meaning. 'In arguing that the racial slur "nigger" implies that an individual is generally lacking in the virtues of honesty, intelligence or creativity, we believe plaintiff attributes a definition to the words that is far in excess of its meaning. The words used by defendant's salesman do not impute an inability to perform or want of integrity in the discharge of the duties of office or employment.' At 166.
11. I also happen to think that Waldron's suggestion is at odds with a vision of political legitimacy that says that democratic decision-making is legitimate not

because of a structure of free speech that facilitates the reaching of final agreements and, therefore, a terminus in debate, but because of a structure of free speech that enables debate without any end—as Post (1991: 283) notes, 'upon which the legitimacy of all political arrangements depends.'

12. See, e.g., *Murdock v. Pennsylvania* (1943) 319 US 105, at 115; *Roth v. United States* (1957) 354 US 476, at 514.
13. See, e.g., Justice Jackson's dissent in *Beauharnais v. Illinois*, at 295.
14. Of course, it might also be asked whether other versions of interests-based balancing could do any better at avoiding the objection from the distinctness of persons. Roscoe Pound (1915: 344), for example, distinguished between three different types of interests, namely, individual, public, and social, and insisted that the true purpose of law is to serve social interests identified as 'interests of the community at large'. Then again, he also made it clear (1943: 39) that based on his scheme, the law may serve social interests 'through delimitations or compromises of individual interests, so as to give effect to the greatest total of interests.' More recently, Peard (2004: 147) envisages a form of nuanced interests-based balancing in which the interests of the targets of hate speech are granted additional weight when placed on the balancing scales insofar as such persons represent an 'innocent party' and hate speakers harm their interests 'intentionally'. However, saying that victims' interests should be given more weight might still be compatible with saying that a sufficient amount of interest-realization on the part of hate speakers could outweigh victims' interests.
15. *United States v. Progressive, Inc.*, at 995.
16. *Bendix Autolite Corp. v. Midwesco Enters., Inc.* (1988) 486 US 888, at 897.
17. *Doe v. University of Michigan*, at 853.
18. It is a further question, one that I shall not seek to address in this book, how the distinction between acontextual and contextual value maps onto the more familiar distinctions within the theory of value between 'endgood' and 'instrumental' value and between 'intrinsic' and 'extrinsic' value. For more on the latter two distinctions, see Korsgaard (1983).
19. Interestingly, Post goes even further than this. He argues that because the value or importance of an interest depends to a large extent on the point and purpose or 'internal logic' of the social practice constituted by it or into which it is integrated or which it helps to create, it can be misleading to use the metaphor of balancing interests. In fact, as Post (1995: 1280) notes, 'the question for decision is what social practice ought to be legally recognized in a particular context.'
20. Of course, this does not only apply to the institution of the university. One might also take the view that getting clear about the primary function of the institution of an independent media will determine how much importance or value should be attached to the different interests that are realized by the speech of that institution, and that there are competing interpretations of that primary function (e.g., Rowbottom 2009).
21. For a critical discussion of the related idea that campus speech codes could be N-warranted if universities seek and obtain voluntary consent from students upon joining the university, see Phil Cox (1995: 120–123).

# 9 *Principia Juris*

In this chapter I wish to focus on legal principles. Many of the legal principles to be discussed embody, crystallize, or give effect to some of the principles discussed in previous chapters, thus providing courts with guidance on how more fundamental principles should be applied to free speech issues. Others are independent principles in the sense that they speak to the particular function of domestic supreme courts and international human rights courts in reviewing, and where necessary, overturning domestic law. Some legal principles are a mixture of both these things. That being said, I do not regard courts as somehow separate from the firmament of moral reflection from whence all normative principles spring, but rather as a source of one corpus of principles. Importantly, all of the legal principles to be discussed in this chapter are general in the sense that they apply to various areas of free speech jurisprudence. But at the same time the courts have also applied these principles to cases dealing with hate speech law in a particular fashion, giving them a specific sort of meaning in the terrain of such cases. Finally, what follows is not intended as an inventory of all legal principles that have been, or might be, called upon in reviewing hate speech law. But they do reflect a rich jurisprudence on this body of law, not only in the US but also in domestic and international courts in other parts of the world.

## 9.1 PRESSING SOCIAL NEED

A cornerstone of legal thinking about free speech is the Principle of Pressing Social Need, as I shall term it, that legalistic constraints on speech or other expressive acts, including constraints on uses of hate speech, are (N-)warranted only if the objective is sufficiently important to support the constraints such as when they serve a pressing social need. This principle is partly reflected in the first part of the US Supreme Court's Strict Scrutiny Test known as the 'compelling state interest' test. It is also instantiated in the first part of the Canadian Supreme Court's Oakes Test: 'At a minimum, an objective must relate to societal concerns which are pressing and substantial in a free and democratic society before it can be characterized as sufficiently important.'[1] And it is present in s. 10(2) of the ECHR, which requires the ECtHR to consider whether or not restrictions on free speech have the objective of serving one or more core interests of a democratic society.

Of course, there are those who would wish to say that there can be no pressing need for hate speech law due to the relatively limited number of individuals affected by hate speech so extreme that their complaints stand a chance of not only reaching courts or disciplinary panels but resulting in convictions or disciplinary findings. As Lively puts it, 'in a functionally segregated society, points of interracial contact are relatively scarce, and beneficiaries of regulation constitute a relatively discreet subgroup' (Lively 1994: 63). Yet Lively misses the point on two levels. For one thing, the section of society that stands to benefit from hate speech law is not limited to those who bring complaints nor even to those who have the option of bringing complaints but potentially the whole society, for the public goods of cultural diversity, assurance, and harmony benefit everyone. Moreover, the presence of hate speech might be one of the things that explains why the society remains functionally segregated, by virtue of the fact that persons "keep to their own kind" for fear of being racially or ethnically abused. Thus, the fact that society is functionally segregated could make the need for robust institutional responses to hate speech more, not less, pressing.

Interestingly, courts in Canada, Australia, and Europe have recognized various types of pressing social need as appropriate grounds for upholding hate speech law, including many of the grounds discussed in previous chapters of this book. These pressing social needs include shielding persons from, or giving them a formal means of redress for, the psychological damage wrought by hate speech as well as the increased chances of acts of discrimination or violence within a climate of hatred,[2] supporting the equal participation in public debate of all members of society,[3] safeguarding cultural diversity and harmonious relations between groups,[4] respecting the equal dignity of all human beings,[5] and protecting civic dignity or the rudiments of people's reputation as members of society in good standing.[6]

Now it may be tempting to assume that institutional authorities always and only intend for laws/regulations/codes to serve pressing social needs through their *coercive function*, to assume that institutions of law enforcement will impose such punishments as to deter people from engaging in illegal conduct. But this assumption is narrow sighted. Authorities may also attempt to pursue a pressing social need by relying on the *expressive* and *educative functions* of law. 'A legal response to racist speech is,' as Matsuda puts it, 'a statement that victims of racism are valued members of our polity' (Matsuda 1989b: 2322). Others have pointed to the way in which hate speech law can carry messages of disapproval (Partlett 1989: 469), solidarity (Kretzmer 1987: 456), delegitimization (Galeotti 2002: 156), assurance (Waldron 2010: 1622–1623), and even remembrance (Suk 2012: 154). This claim about the expressive function of law is not peculiar to legal scholars;

it is also embraced by some law enforcement professionals. Consider the UK case, *R. v. Ali, Javed, and Ahmed*. Welcoming the Derby Crown Court's decision to hand down prison sentences to the defendants (ranging from fifteen months to two years), who had been found guilty of offenses relating to the stirring up hatred on the grounds of sexual orientation, Chief Inspector Sunita Gamblin of the Derbyshire Constabulary declared that '[t]hese sentences send a very strong and clear message that this type of activity is a criminal offence and it is not acceptable or tolerated' (cited in This Is Derbyshire 2012). In addition to the expressive function of law, Delgado has argued that the introduction of a tort for racial insult 'would discourage such harmful activity through the teaching function of the law' (Delgado 1982: 148–149). 'Laws,' as Allport proclaims in his seminal book on prejudice, 'restrain the middle range of mortals who need them as a mentor in molding their habits' (Allport 1954: 439). The upshot of all this is that decisions taken by supreme courts to strike down laws/regulations/codes that constrain uses of hate speech can mean denying authorities the chance to utilize the expressive and educative functions of lawmaking. In the words of an anonymous contributor to the Harvard Law Review, 'forbidding localities to interfere with the public advocacy of group hatred affirms individual liberty, but denies the political community the opportunity to express through law the central commitments and ideals that unite its members' (Harvard Law Review 1988: 683).

Then again, some scholars insist that banning hate speech *merely* for the symbolic message that doing so carries is impermissible, especially under the First Amendment (e.g., Weinstein 1992: 223, 245). Likewise, in *R.A.V. v. City of St. Paul*, Justice Scalia reasoned that 'the only interest distinctively served by the content limitation is that of displaying the city council's special hostility towards the particular biases thus singled out.' To which he added: 'That is precisely what the First Amendment forbids.'[7] Justice Scalia is denying that the message that was to be transmitted by the ordinance N-warranted the use of a criminal sanction to transmit it given that the ordinance frustrated the free speech rights of ordinary citizens. Presumably the reason for this injunction against using the criminal law purely for symbolic purposes has to do with the seriousness of the sanctions involved in such law. In other words, if the state is going to threaten to incarcerate lawbreakers or harm their vital interests in other ways, it better have a very powerful reason, including but not limited to preventing or deterring people from harming the vital interests of other people.

But putting aside uses of the criminal law in which symbolism is the sole rationale, is there any reason why it is wrong *per se* for an elected government to use the criminal law for the supplementary purpose of publicly expressing or declaring its particular conception of fundamental values given that it will undoubtedly draw on such a conception in determining the shape of its non-declarative laws? Is there any reason why elected governments must be self-effacing in the sense that they may select laws based on their best understanding of the core values of their country but may not select laws partly based on their desire to express or declare to the public their best understanding of the core values of their country? The short answer is that I can see no such reason. Indeed, with respect to government speech, US courts have developed the government speech doctrine, according to which governmental authorities have the right to transmit official messages or ideas to the public without adhering to principles of content or viewpoint neutrality, precisely because there can be a compelling state interest in getting particular messages across.[8] So, for example, in *Downs v. Los Angeles Unified School District* (2000)[9] a US Court of Appeals upheld the decision of a high school board to deny a member of the staff the privilege of posting anti-homosexual material on bulletin boards set up by other members of the staff for the purposes of recognizing Gay and Lesbian Awareness Month. The Court affirmed that the school had every right to use the bulletin boards, and the rules surrounding what material or content may or may not be placed on those boards and by whom, in order to communicate its own favored message. And that the appellant did not have a First Amendment right to dictate what that message should be.

Nevertheless, it might be countered that the US Bill of Rights was intended by its framers as a limitation on the power that governmental authorities exercise over citizens, including exercise of power that constitutes government speech. This means that the First Amendment protects citizens against governmental censorship or suppression of speech even when acts of censorship or suppression constitute government speech. Could governmental authorities in the US realistically claim First Amendment protection for this particular sort of censorship *qua* government speech? No. To think that governmental authorities may censor or suppress speech insofar as doing so constitutes an act of government speech that is protected under the First Amendment would be to turn the First Amendment on its head. But having said all that, not every constitution around the world that encompasses a right to freedom of expression does so using the absolutist language of the First Amendment. On the contrary, in many countries the codified constitution explicitly recognizes exceptions to the right to freedom of expression in the case of hate speech (e.g., Armenia,[10] Azerbaijan,[11] Kenya,[12] South Africa,[13] Turkmenistan[14]). Clearly in these countries it would not turn the constitution on its head for governmental authorities to use hate speech law in order to transmit an official message about the evils of hate speech.

## 9.2 EFFICACY

The no less important desideratum of effectiveness may be crystallized in the Principle of Efficacy articulated by Sumner as follows: '[E]mploy only measures of harm reduction that promise to be effective' (Sumner 2004: 185). Sumner offers this partly as an interpretation of a key component of the

Oakes Test, which states that legal measures 'must be rationally connected to the objective.'[15] On this interpretation, effectiveness in reducing hate speech and the harms associated with hate speech is one such rational connection. Sumner's use of the word 'promise' indicates that legislation must have a reasonable chance of limiting the behavior in question and in that sense have the desired harm-reducing impact. But it is a further question how this reasonable chance is to be measured. Turning away from the Canadian Supreme Court and toward the decisions of the ECtHR, in *Handyside v. United Kingdom* (1976)[16] Judge Mosler opined that '[a] measure likely to be effectual under normal conditions cannot be deprived of its legal basis after the event by failure to attain the success which it might have had in more favourable circumstances.'[17] This suggests that the Principle of Efficacy should be read as meaning effective under normal circumstances. What is more, it would seem unhelpful to interpret the Principle as indicating that a law banning conduct of a given type is only effective if it eradicates all instances of that type. Few, if any laws, could meet such a stringent standard. Instead, the Principle may be read as requiring that there is a reasonable chance of the law having a minimally acceptable degree of success in achieving its objectives, where that minimum reflects the nature of the restrictions and the nature of the objectives.

Be that as it may, it is quite common for critics of hate speech law to claim that such law is 'ineffective' (e.g., Strossen 1990; Lively 1994; Baker 2009, 2012; Hare 2006, 2009, 2012). Far less frequently are they precise about the measure of ineffectiveness they are using. Sometimes ineffectiveness is associated with whether or not legislation will support an unspecified target number of successful prosecutions. Critics argue that if, as should be the case, legislation is written in such a way as to safeguard free speech values (i.e., with various limitations, caveats, and excusing conditions), then its frame of reference becomes a very limited set of examples of hate speech rather than the broad class of hate speech that motivated the creation of the legislation in the first place. This seems to be true of legislation banning incitement to hatred in the UK, for example (e.g., Leopold 1977; Bindman 1992; Nash and Bakalis 2007; Hare 2006). If cases are infrequently referred to public prosecutors by the police, rarely taken to trial by prosecutors, and produce only a small number of convictions over a significant period of time, the efficacy of the legislation is called into question (e.g., Hare 2006: 522). However, it deserves mention that low prosecution rates need not be decisive evidence of ineffective law. After all, legislation banning incitement to racial hatred, say, might cause hate groups to tone down their rhetoric for fear of being prosecuted even if, objectively, the likelihood of being successfully prosecuted is low. Ironically, the people who criticize legislation banning incitement to hatred for being ineffective in curbing hate speech are often the same people who object to such legislation on the grounds that it creates a chilling effect (e.g., Hare 2006, 2012).[18] This point about deterrence is certainly not restricted to the UK. Delgado, for example, implies that the rise of 'shock jocks' and 'hate radio' in the US since the late 1980s can be partly explained by the FCC's decision to repeal its Fairness Doctrine in 1987 (Delgado and Stefancic 2004: 160). This is despite the fact that the FCC complaints procedure resulted in very few complaints being upheld against broadcasters in relation to programs that defamed or demeaned entire groups or classes of person.

Of course, at this point critics of hate speech law are liable to insist that such law has a very limited deterrence effect. They may point out that the relevant legislation tends to impose maximum prison sentences of two to three years but in many instances courts issue suspended sentences or prison sentences of a few months, and that this does not deter hard core offenders. They might also point to the existence of certain high-profile cases in which hate speakers did not desist in their hate speech despite several prosecutions to their names. Consider Lady Jane Birdwood, Harry Taylor, and Simon Sheppard in the UK or Brigitte Bardot in France. However, one should not forget that what makes these cases high-profile is partly the fact that the individuals have received a degree of public notoriety for their offending, which in some instances may contribute to their persistent offending. This only serves to underscore the relevance, I think, of Judge Mosler's point that effectiveness should be judged under normal circumstances. Legislators can hardly be expected to desist from legislating against hate because of a hard-to-predict cocktail of prejudice, attention seeking, and media interest, which creates a repeat offender such as Brigitte Bardot. What might be relevant is if critics of hate speech law could produce evidence demonstrating that the rate of repeat offending among people found guilty of hate speech offenses is much higher than for other offenses, so high in fact as to lift hate speech law into a category of hopelessly ineffective legislation.

At any rate, it seems to me that a far more commonsensical approach to evaluating the effectiveness of hate speech laws is to examine whether or not they actually reduce the amount of hate speech of whatever sort they are intended to restrict. In *R. v. Keegstra* Justice McLachlin dissented on several grounds including efficacy. 'Historical evidence,' she claimed, 'gives reason to be suspicious of the claim that hate propaganda laws contribute to the cause of multiculturalism and equality.'[19] The evidence she cites is a passage from the work of Alan Borovoy, the general counsel of the Canadian Civil Liberties Association (CCLA).

> Remarkably, pre-Hitler Germany had laws very much like the Canadian anti-hate law. Moreover, those laws were enforced with some vigour. During the fifteen years before Hitler came to power, there were more than two hundred prosecutions based on anti-Semitic speech. And, in the opinion of the leading Jewish organization of that era, no more than 10 per cent of the cases were mishandled by the authorities. As subsequent history so painfully testifies, this type of legislation proved ineffectual on the one occasion when there was a real argument for it. (Borovoy 1988: 50)

This is a bold piece of inductive reasoning—one that Borovoy himself subsequently attested to be not engaged in (Borovoy et al. 1988–1989: 343–344)—drawing as it does a conclusion about the likely ineffectiveness of Canadian laws based on evidence gathered concerning *one* particular instance of the same genus of law. But the fact that hate speech law did not contribute to the maintenance of ideals of multiculturalism and equality in pre-Hitler Germany could predict that such law will not contribute in that way in contemporary Canada only if the circumstances are the same. And there may be reasons to think that the circumstances are not the same. In pre-Hitler Germany anti-Semitism was a significant feature of public life and was actively supported not merely by various strands of *völkisch* populist, nationalist movements but also by the actions of state institutions, including the 1916 census of Jews that fed the 'stab-in-the-back legend' in the aftermath of World War I. This culture supported a rich tapestry of group defamations against Jews (e.g., Blain 1995). Hence, the fact that there were so many prosecutions for published attacks or libels against Jews may tell us something important about the ferocity of the anti-Semitic climate at that time. The Weimar Republic's decree-laws against group libel may have been on a par with the legendary story of King Canute. The circumstances in contemporary Canada may seem far more favorable in contrast. Canada possess a very high per capita immigration rate, is a haven for very large numbers of refugees from around the world, and benefits from a range of official policies designed to promote its ideals of multiculturalism and equality under the Canadian Charter of Rights and Freedoms, including anti-racism educational policies and practices.

To give another illustration, Rwanda ratified the ICERD in 1975 and wasted no time in amending its criminal code accordingly. Art. 75 was replaced with Art. 393(a) of the Penal Code, which states 'Any person who, by defamation or public insult, manifests aversion or hatred toward a group of persons or a given race or religion, or commits an act likely to provoke such aversion or hatred, shall be liable to imprisonment for a term of one month to one year and to a fine not exceeding 5,000 francs, or to one of these penalties.' Throughout the 1970s and 1980s the Committee on the Elimination of Racial Discrimination (CERD) reported that in terms of meeting its responsibilities under ICERD Rwanda's progress was 'exemplary' because racial discrimination was 'totally prohibited' (cited in Viljoen 2012: 91). What followed was the genocide in 1994. According to Baker, this is more evidence of ineffectiveness. '[L]egal prohibitions on racist speech—to the extent that they would (often did) exist where "needed" but given how much and against whom these laws most likely would be (or were) enforced—would not have, or perhaps rather might not have, prevented the occurrence of the genocide in Rwanda or elsewhere' (Baker 2012: 78). What is most telling in Baker's diagnosis is the implicit admission that the real problem was one of inadequate and misdirected *enforcement*. Once again, this calls to mind Judge Mosler's point that a measure cannot reasonably be called ineffective simply because of its failure to attain the success that it might have had in more favorable circumstances—adequate and properly directed enforcement, for example.

Putting to one side putative evidence showing the inefficacy of hate speech law, what about evidence supporting its efficacy? Some scholars claim to have searched in vain to find evidence demonstrating that there is a reasonable chance of the types of laws/regulations/codes dealing with hate speech that can be found in Canada, Australia, and Europe actually reducing hate speech/the evils of hate speech to a minimally adequate degree (e.g., Sumner 2004). Others condemn defenders of hate speech law for failing to cite hard evidence (e.g., Heinze 2006, 2013). Now it is certainly the case that there is a dearth of useful evidence comparing the extent of hate speech in countries that do possess hate speech law with the extent of hate speech in countries that do not. One barrier to this sort of research is the lack of shared metrics and methods for collecting data on the extent of hate speech among the agencies, organizations, and institutions based in different countries that do collect data on hate speech (e.g., B'nai Brith in Canada, the Umati Project in Kenya, Bytes for All in Pakistan, the Simon Wiesenthal Center in the US). Future research may depend on the success of international projects seeking to bring together and harmonize statistics from different countries (e.g., International Network Against Cyber-Hate, the Sentinel Project's 'Hatebase' initiative). A second is the difficulty of unearthing a suitable control group (country) where the independent variable being tested (the presence of hate speech law) cannot influence the extent of hate speech. The fact is that scarcely any countries possess no laws/regulations/codes that constrain uses of hate speech.

However, following in the tradition of Delgado (1991: 374n.270), I find it hard to accept that there is zero evidence to support the view that hate speech law can effect changes in hate speech behavior. Some evidence can be found in studies of the discourse of young people in which speech is compared across more or less regulated settings. For example, in Tynes et al. (2004) the researchers looked at the discourse around race and ethnicity used by adolescents in internet chat rooms on popular teen websites. It compared the discourse used in monitored chat rooms, defined by the presence of an adult monitor and declared rules on speech, including rules against uses of hate speech, with the discourse used in unmonitored chat rooms, defined by the absence of an adult monitor and rules on hate speech. The researchers found that racial or ethnic slurs were significantly more frequent in the unmonitored than in the monitored chat rooms. Similarly, in its 2011 survey of the climate in US schools, the Gay, Lesbian and Straight Education Network (GLSEN) (2012) reported a decline between 2001 and 2011 in the percentage of LGBT school students reporting hearing homophobic remarks, being verbally harassed, or being physically assaulted because of their sexual orientation. GLSEN puts this decline down to an increased availability of LGBT school-based support networks, more inclusive curricula, more supportive school staff, and an increase in comprehensive anti-bullying/anti-harassment policies, including speech codes. According to GLSEN, students attending schools with comprehensive anti-bullying/anti-harassment policies report hearing homophobic remarks less frequently and report experiencing significantly lower severities of victimization related to their sexual orientation than schools without (Gay, Lesbian and Straight Education Network 2012: 68–70).

Clearly the evidence I have cited is limited in its size and scope, but at the same time clearly it cannot be said that there is *no* evidence that laws/regulations/codes are effective in curbing hate speech. Indeed, it may even be that the appropriate standard of evidence is lower than some critics of hate speech law would have us believe. For, it might be appropriate to adopt a precautionary approach in the face of uncertainty about how to reduce hate speech/the evils of hate speech. The approach I have in mind focuses not on evidential uncertainty about the evils of hate speech (cf. Schauer 2009; 2012: 139) but rather on evidential uncertainty about the effectiveness of laws/regulations/codes in reducing hate speech/the evils of hate speech. According to what I shall call the Precautionary Principle, where the effects of doing nothing to reduce hate speech/the evils of hate speech are sufficiently grave or serious, evidential uncertainty about what measures are minimally effective in reducing hate speech/the evils of hate speech ought not to be used as a basis for not pursuing measures that could be effective. This means, for example, that if the threat to people's health and security of doing nothing to reduce discriminatory intimidation or harassment or the threat to cultural diversity of doing nothing to reduce incitement to hatred are grave or serious, then a lack of evidential certainty as to the most effective means of combating these forms of hate speech should not be a barrier to the application of relevant hate speech law. This principle stands in opposition to the view that says in the absence of firm evidence about the efficacy of hate speech law, the right thing to do is to favor freedom of expression since its effects *are* known (e.g., Baker 2009: 157).

The debate about evidence does not end there, however. The preliminary findings of an important study by Katharine Gelber and Luke McNamara (2012, 2014) on the effects of hate speech law on public discourse in Australia has revealed uneven or asymmetrical impacts across types of speaker. The study examined the content of newspapers over a twenty-year period and found that anti-vilification law has tended to alter the content found in broadsheet newspapers to a greater degree than in tabloid newspapers, which often find ways to avoid violating the letter of the law while ignoring its spirit. Perhaps tabloid newspapers have been more resistant to change because they regard it as essential to their point of differentiation from competitor broadsheet newspapers that the discourse found within their pages is more sensationalist, extreme, unmeasured, or occasionally beyond the pale of civility. However, from the fact hate speech law has had a differential impact on different types of speaker, it does not necessarily follow that such law runs afoul of the Principle of Efficacy. That tabloid newspapers are avoiding flagrant violations of the law may be enough to demonstrate a minimally adequate degree of effectiveness.

A related concern is that hate speech law might have an unwelcome asymmetrical impact on old and new media. The worry is that more established press organizations will come under greater pressure to conform, because they are easier, more stable targets, leaving other hate speakers to use social networking websites, internet messaging services, and web-based forums with impunity. The state would end up clamping down heavily on the established press, while finding itself impotent in the face of hate speech on the Internet. As Sumner puts it, '[t]o the extent that restrictions can be readily circumvented, by an underground market or by technological innovations such as the internet, the case for them is weakened' (Sumner 2004: 34). It is not easy to determine whether these concerns are powerfully prophetic or misguidedly alarmist. In the UK at least, incitement to hatred law has been successfully used against hate speech circulated on the Internet, and courts have rejected grounds for appeal seeking to exploit the special nature of the Internet, including that publication on the Internet takes place wherever the Web server on which it is hosted is located rather than wherever the persons uploading the material are located, that Web activities are not 'publication', and that electronically manufactured words posted on the Internet are not 'written material.'[20]

What of the expressive and educational functions of law? It is not hard to think of ways in which some clusters of laws/regulations/codes may be less effective than others in the state getting its message across about hate speech. Consider time, place, and manner restrictions, such as statutes banning public protests or demonstrations within a certain specified distance of funeral services or municipal ordinances requiring organizations that intend to hold public marches or demonstrations in populated areas to purchase liability insurance. These sorts of restrictions may be a clumsy way of sending out the message that the state finds hate speech intolerable, for example. Some people might misinterpret the state's intentions and take these restrictions as a sign that the state does not find hate speech intolerable after all. In comparison, hate speech law that is ostensibly or directly targeted at hate speech could send out a more clear-cut message. Speaking of group defamation law (catchall), for example, Parekh remarks that '[b]y affirming the community's collective disapproval of certain forms of utterances, it both reassures the minorities and lays down norms of public debate made effective by selective enforcements' (Parekh 1990b: 705).

However, this sort of claim is susceptible to its own version of the objection from inefficacy. Suppose a governmental or institutional authority wishes to use law to make a statement that it regards certain hate speech conduct as unacceptable. How effective hate speech law will be in making such a declaration depends on both the law and the context. If, for example, a law banning incitement to hatred is drafted in such a way that there will be low levels of police enforcement and few successful public prosecutions, it may be asked whether having the law on the books is worse from the point of view of getting the intended message across than having no law at all. Given the negative symbolism of low enforcement and prosecution, the unintended message might be that the government does not regard the problem as a serious one or even worse that it implicitly believes hate speech is acceptable (e.g., Strossen 2012: 392). A related concern is that hate speakers will get their message out regardless of enforcement. If hate speech law is enacted but not properly enforced, it could provide an unwelcome encouragement to hate speakers, sending them a signal that they are free to proceed. If it is properly enforced, however, then hate speakers might in response choose to tone down their message, and this ironically could enable them to reach a broader, more mainstream audience (Coliver 1992: 373–374; Strossen 2001: 259). However, I suspect that for the true believer in hate speech law, this second scenario would still be seen as a victory. It could be that former hate speakers turn to find more subtle, implicit, veiled, and unspoken ways to influence public opinion, but for the defenders of hate speech law this is preferable to their using hate speech. This is because there is (in their book) something especially wrong, harmful, pernicious, or detrimental about hate speech as compared to other ways of influencing public opinion.

Nonetheless, many critics worry that courtrooms give hate speakers a public platform in which they can turn themselves into martyrs or send out their message to a larger audience at the expense of the message that the state wants to send (e.g., Riesman 1942: 755–756; Borovoy 1988: 50; Strossen 1990: 559; 2001: 257; 2012: 382; Bindman 1992: 17–18; Feldman 1993: 812; Greenawalt 1995: 63; Shiffrin [S.H.] 1999: 83; Braun 2004: 148–149; Crossman 2005: 9; Krotoszynski 2006: 131; Nash and Bakalis 2007: 359; Knechtle 2008: 64; Heinze 2009a: 199). Lawrence Douglas cites the case of Ernst Zündel, who 'turned his trial into a small media circus, arriving at court each day in a flak jacket and hard-hat emblazoned with the words "Freedom of Speech"' (Douglas 1995: 100). Or consider the recent case of Ezra Levant, a Canada-based conservative political activist who in 2006 was investigated by the Alberta Human Rights Commission regarding his alleged violation of s. 13(1) of the Canadian Human Rights Act, which forbids the communication of hate messages, pursuant to complaints made against him and his newspaper *The Western Standard* following its republication of the Danish cartoons of the prophet Muhammad. Levant exploited the Commission's investigation along with his own access to and prowess with printed and internet news platforms, Facebook, Youtube, and Twitter to draw wider public attention toward himself and his derogatory messages about Muslims (Edger 2010). Nevertheless, I think that there is a sense in which this particular line of objection underdetermines its own conclusion. For, there are plenty of other kinds of law that racists, anti-Semites, Islamophobes, homophobes, misogynists, and so forth could choose to break that would also give them these sorts of declarative opportunities, vandalism being one example, but nobody seriously suggests that these laws should be repealed for fear of facilitating courtroom grandstanding (cf. Posner 2006: 124). What is more, as much as legal cases may provide a platform for perpetrators of hate speech, they also provide a platform for victims of hate speech, and this too is a valuable opportunity for them to get out their message (e.g., Partlett 1989: 469).

In other instances authorities may seek to engage in lawmaking with an educative purpose. In other words, they may wish to ban hate speech in an attempt to reeducate the population about what is morally or socially unacceptable speech conduct. Of course, some people believe that any such attempt to use hate speech law to change hearts and minds is doomed to failure. Since it is not possible to legislate changes in moral conscience (so the objection goes), it is wrong to try because in the trying there is bound to be excessive interference in freedom of expression.[21] Interestingly, Harel argues that laws banning incitement to hatred are even more likely to be ineffective in the case of people whose hate speech is motivated by, or rooted in, their comprehensive ways of life. Think of religious conservatives who stir up or promote hatred against people on the grounds of their sexuality. 'When hate speech is deeply rooted in individuals' long-term customs, ways of life, and ideological commitments, when it is bound up with their identity, external direct intervention—in particular, criminal law, tort law, and other forms of coercive intervention—are unlikely to succeed in eradicating the sentiments of hatred' (Harel 2012: 306–307).

I wish to make two responses to Harel's argument. The first relates to the evidence (or lack of it) that Harel offers in support of his core assertion that '[i]t seems evident that an external effort to eradicate hatred is less likely to be effective when the hatred is deeply rooted' (Harel 2012: 322). Harel cites evidence from the disciplines of theology and the sociology of religion relating to the ways in which customary sentiments, beliefs, and practices are closely intertwined among members of certain religions or religious communities (318–322). But he does not cite any evidence from the disciplines of developmental psychology, social psychology, the psychology of change management, educational psychology, or even the sociology and social psychology of offender rehabilitation—surely all disciplines or fields of social scientific study that are indispensable to the task of demonstrating that criminal sanctions are likely to be ineffective in changing the sentiments of individuals whose sentiments happen to be rooted in comprehensive ways of life. While there is limited evidence to draw on in the case of hate speech offenders specifically, there is at least one major international study of programs for the rehabilitation of hate crime offenders. Iganski et al. (2011) reports on a range of programs across the world, including a specialist program in Germany that targets individuals whose hate conduct is deeply rooted in a comprehensive communal way of life, namely, skinhead far right white nationalism. The German program uses group-based cognitive behavioral therapy and for a decade has been highly effective in reducing rates of re-offending and re-imprisonment. 'The recidivism rate is under 30% (in terms of known re-offending) and under 10% (for re-imprisonment) compared with a 78% recidivism rate for comparable offenders' (Iganski et al. 2011: 28).

My second point is that even if Harel were justified in assuming that hate speech law is likely to fail in significantly reducing sentiments of hatred when they are rooted in comprehensive ways of life, I think it is naive to presuppose that the educative function of such law is simply to get rid of feelings of hatred. On the contrary, it may be that the true function of such law is to significantly reduce the take-up of certain norms about the appropriateness of hate speech conduct. Although hate speech conduct is sometimes motivated by sentiments of hatred, it is not identical with those sentiments. Hate speech conduct may result from idleness or a desire to belong as much as from deep-rooted feelings of enmity or hostility. Since a failure to significantly reduce sentiments of hatred does not necessarily mean a failure to significantly reduce the take-up of certain norms about the appropriateness of hate speech conduct, it would be wrongheaded to conclude that hate speech law is ineffective simply because it is unlikely to significantly reduce sentiments of hatred.

## 9.3 THE LEAST RESTRICTIVE ALTERNATIVE

Another key legal principle is the Principle of the Least Restrictive Alternative, as it is commonly referred to, that legalistic constraints on speech or other expressive acts, including constraints on uses of hate speech, are (N-) warranted only if they are the least restrictive alternative among two or more methods of achieving the same objective. This principle is part of the Strict Scrutiny Test applied in First Amendment cases in the US,[22] present in the Oakes Test employed by the Canadian Supreme Court,[23] and implicit in some ECtHR interpretations of the Necessary in a Democratic Society Test.[24] Civil libertarians doubt that hate speech law can be the least restrictive alternative, but it is important to be clear from the start that their reason for thinking this depends on both what they regard as the highly restrictive nature of hate speech law and what they view as the comparatively less restrictive nature of other methods. In the former respect, civil libertarians are at pains to point out that hate speech law restricts speech behavior even in cases when it does not attract prosecution. Consider the words of Borovoy.

> On the streets of Toronto in the mid-1970s you had some young people handing out leaflets at a visiting Shriners Parade. The leaflets bore the words "Yankee Go Home." I hope that isn't too unpopular a message here. And for that, they were arrested by the police on a charge of distributing hate propaganda. Now the prosecuting attorney had the good sense subsequently to withdraw the charge. But I always hasten to tell

people, particularly lawyers who measure things too often in terms of judicial decisions and not enough in terms of the actual experience of real people, don't derive too much consolation from the fact that the charge didn't proceed. Those activists wound up suffering the suppression of their legitimate protest, and they spent a couple of days in jail. (Borovoy et al. 1988–1989: 340)

According to the Principle of the Least Restrictive Alternative, however, a law will not be the least restrictive alternative if there is another law that is less restrictive. Unsurprisingly, the idea of 'less restrictive' is comparative. Take three examples. First, it might be argued that creating a university-managed process of arbitration and reconciliation for dealing with complaints about hate speech on campus is a less restrictive alternative to the top-down imposition of campus speech codes and punitive sanctions for code violators. But some people may think that relying on the power of social disapprobation toward hate speakers on campus is an even less restrictive but no less effective alternative to a university-managed process of arbitration and reconciliation. Second, authorities could opt to impose time, place, or manner restrictions on the activities of hate groups in an effort to limit their hate speech. Then again, some people may argue that although this is a less restrictive alternative than banning speech altogether, counterspeech remains a less restrictive but no less effective alternative. Third, if the objective is not to limit hate speech *per se* but instead to send out a message that the state is committed to values of tolerance and equality, then some people might be inclined to think that the state could adopt an alternative approach of simply permitting hate speech to occur unfettered and then rigorously enforcing laws prohibiting the acts of discrimination, destruction of property, and violence that are associated with a climate of hatred. This approach purports to be as effective in sending out the desired message but at the same time leaves speech untouched (e.g., Heins 1983: 587n.11; Greenawalt 1995: 63; Strossen 2012: 380–382).

It is important to note, however, that the Principle of the Least Restrictive Alternative only calls on authorities to consider efficacious alternatives. This means that, under the Principle, the existence of a less restrictive but non-efficacious method of achieving the objective would not invalidate a given law. But insofar as both restrictiveness and efficacy are a matter of degree, this is liable to generate some challenging conundrums for those applying the principle. If an alternative to the preferred law is slightly less restrictive and significantly less effective, then it may not be a good enough alternative to invalidate a given law. If the alternative is significantly less restrictive and only slightly less effective, then this could be good enough to invalidate a given law. But it may be a much closer call if the alternative is both slightly less restrictive and slightly less effective. This means that applying the principle may require lawmakers and judges to make sophisticated and nuanced compromises between restrictiveness and efficacy.

Moreover, it will require a significant amount of acumen and perspicacity in recognizing that what purport to be reasonable alternatives may turn out not to be so if they are not as unrestrictive or not as efficacious as they first appeared to be. Thus, in the remainder of the section I wish to discuss in greater detail three putatively reasonable alternatives to hate speech law: namely, government intervention to discourage hate speech short of banning it; social disapprobation, censure, and boycott of hate speech and hate speakers; and counterspeech to hate speech.

## Interventions Short of Banning

It is often said that there are many things that institutional authorities (e.g., national or local governments, university authorities) can do to reduce hate speech/the evils of hate speech short of banning it. These include: requiring teachers and lecturers to cover certain historical events that may be the target of hate speech or to cover social issues relating to prejudice and hate speech; requiring students to take classes educating them about the nature of prejudice and hate speech; regulating the education sector to ensure that schools and universities impress upon teachers the value of promoting communicative virtues in classrooms, such as tolerance and respect for others, that could act as counterweights to the tendency toward hate speech and the pernicious attitudes underpinning it; funding NGOs that specialize in raising consciousness about or combating hate speech; impressing upon museums and other public institutions that they have an important role to play in educating their patrons about the potentially hateful roots of their artworks; hiring trained officers to work as mediators between conflicting social groups within institutions or communities; providing a framework for behind-the-scenes processes of dispute resolution; and/or compelling persons convicted of hate crimes, say, to undergo compulsory overcoming-hatred classes (e.g., Rice 1994: 93–95; Schachter 1983: 853–854; O'Neil 1989; McGowan and Tangri 1991: 917–918; Strossen 2001: 272–273; Sumner 2004: 34; 2009: 207; Weinman 2006; Molnar 2010: 263; 2012: 185–192).

However, that these are all less restrictive but no less effective measures in comparison to banning hate speech is much harder to demonstrate than it might be assumed. Starting with efficacy, take the provision of a statutory framework for private processes of dispute resolution, such as can be found in Australia. Adopting these methods as opposed to more straightforward laws banning hate speech may limit the state's role as a mouthpiece for declaring unequivocally that hate speech is unacceptable. What these statutes are effectively saying is not that the state regards hate speech to be intolerable but that the state thinks it is a good thing if individuals can, in private and with the help of mediators, thrash out a resolution to their differing views on what hate speech is and whether or not it is acceptable conduct. According to Gelber, this approach also creates a disconnect between the aim of addressing what are public acts of hate speech and the use of a mechanism that is largely private (Gelber 2002: 19–25). Moreover, in terms of the educative function of the law, there may be a sense in which 'to educate publicly would require publicity' (Partlett 1989: 482).

With regard to restrictiveness, for governmental authorities to instruct schools and colleges to teach certain historical facts or to inculcate particular social values, for instance, only seems slightly less restrictive than some hate speech law itself. An educational institution's freedom to decide what it will teach would be limited, and so would its expressive rights: it may no longer use the curriculum to send out its desired message to parents and the wider community about what really matters in the education of children because the state has usurped its right to decide the curriculum. Moreover, university authorities could require students to attend special classes on the nature of prejudice and hate speech or else face disciplinary proceedings. Hate speakers, then, would not face a disciplinary panel for refusing to desist from engaging in hate speech but they could be brought before such a panel if they refused to attend the classes. Either way, they are being coerced by university authorities to change their conduct.

## Social Disapprobation, Censure, and Boycott

The approach of social disapprobation, censure, and boycott may involve various methods, including: TV companies refusing to give airtime to hate speakers or sacking presenters who engage in hate speech; newspapers refraining from the publication of material that constitutes hate speech; consumers deciding to stop buying newspapers that publish editorials containing hate speech; NGOs campaigning for boycotts of broadcast media and internet companies that permit hate speech on their platforms; voters electing to throw out politicians who engage in hate speech in any areas of their public discourse; university administrators refusing to engage in any sort of public debate with hate speakers; and/or more enlightened members of society choosing to verbally attack hate speakers, giving them a taste of their own medicine by exposing them to ridicule, humiliation, denunciation, castigation, marginalization, and plain contempt (e.g., Borovoy et al. 1988–1989: 344; Strossen 2012: 388). At times the mainstream media in the UK, for example, have employed some of these techniques for dealing with the question of hate speech. According to Tariq Modood, 'it is how the British media responded to the Danish cartoons affair, recognizing that they had the right to republish the cartoons but that it would be offensive to do so' (Modood 2007: 57). Indeed, Peter Horrocks, the BBC's editor of TV News, explained that the BBC had made a decision not to republish the cartoons 'in order not to gratuitously offend the significant number of Muslims in Britain but also—because we make decisions for our pieces to be broadcast internationally—the very significant numbers of Muslim viewers of BBC World television' (cited in Plunkett 2006). Of course, the true test of whether or not the cartoons constituted *hate speech* is not their offensiveness but if they exhibited or conformed to familiar tropes of hate speech. Thus, scholars of hate speech have predictably focused their attention on whether or not typecasting or denigrating the image and character of the prophet Muhammad can amount to an act of group defaming or negatively stereotyping all Muslims (e.g., Bleich 2006: 21; Modood 2006: 4; Brahm Levey and Modood 2009: 236–241).

Once again, however, whether or not social disapprobation, censure, and boycott are reasonable alternatives to hate speech law depends on whether they are less restrictive but at the same time no less effective. To begin with the question of restrictiveness, several scholars in the liberal cannon, not the least of whom is Mill, have pointed out that people can be, and often are, as much compelled by fear of social disapprobation or censure into not acting or speaking as they would like as they are compelled by fear of criminal sanction or state censorship into not acting or speaking as they would like (e.g., Mill [1859] 1972: 73). What is more, some of these scholars insist that it would be a mistake to think that social disapprobation, censure, and boycott involve less restriction merely because they engage restriction of a different kind than state censorship. As Lee Bollinger puts it, '[w]hen we compare our reluctance to impose legal restraints against speech with our readiness to employ a host of informal, or nonlegal, forms of coercion against speech behavior, the paradox is striking' (Bollinger 1986: 12). Therefore, the choice in how agents attempt to bring about a reduction in hate speech is *not* between legalistic restraints and non-legalistic non-restraints. Rather, it is arguably, as Hadley Arkes puts it, 'a choice between two forms of restraint: one carried out by private groups operating outside of the law, and another, of a more limited nature, carried out by legal authorities under the constraints of a formal structure' (Arkes 1974: 284).

Nevertheless, it might be insisted that there are morally relevant differences between the two forms of restraint (e.g., Packer 1968: 320; Schauer 1982: 121–122). Schauer, for example, argues that if private individuals and companies bow to social disapprobation, censure, or boycotts and refrain from saying certain things in public 'it is because [they] *choose* to respect the views of the majority, or because they choose to place their faith in particular arbiters of communicative value' (Schauer 1982: 121). They could choose instead to respect the view of the minority, or to place their faith in different arbiters of communicative value. The implication of Schauer's argument seems to be that if private individuals and companies adhere to laws backed up by the threat of punishment, it is not because they choose to respect the laws of the land. It is not as though there is a different set of laws they could choose to adhere to within *their* geographical territory. However, I would argue that there is a sense in which both forms of restraint limit the choices of private individuals and companies by virtue of limiting their options. Both forms of restraint effectively remove the conjunctive option of not complying with what the restraining force is telling them to do (or not do) and avoiding the serious consequences of non-compliance. In the case of law, the serious consequences may be fines or prison sentences; in the case of social disapprobation, censure, and boycott, the serious consequences may be subjection to contempt or derision, social ostracism, or financial ruin.

In terms of effectiveness, it strikes me that these approaches can be piecemeal, contingent, and unreliable. Perhaps they can work in societies where powerful elites or influential shapers of public opinion do *not* share values or interests with hate speakers, but what of those societies in which the majority of media companies, newspapers, and consumers do happen to share *some* basic values or interests with hate speakers? Think of all the newspaper editors who feel no particular need to refrain from printing articles that group-libel Muslims because it just so happens that relatively few of their patrons are Muslim and their readership likes to read this sort of material. This approach also involves a free rider problem, in that citizens may have an interest in living in a society in which there is social disapprobation or censure of hate speakers, as a public good, but also an interest in not contributing to the creation of that public good since putting their own heads over the parapet to confront hate speakers may harm their personal interests. In that sense at least, uses of hate speech law may be a more effective solution to this collective action problem.

What is more, there is an issue here about how effective these approaches can be in realizing the wider objective of reducing the net amount of hate speech. Social disapprobation or censure directed toward hate speakers often exhibits a race to the bottom, with hate speakers being attacked with yet more hate speech. As Delgado and Stefancic point out, it seems unlikely that countering with logic will have the same force or power as the hate speech itself.

> How could one respond to: "N, go back to Africa. You don't belong at the university"? Would one say: "Sir, you do not understand. According to prevailing ethics and constitutional interpretation I, an African American, am of equal dignity and entitled to attend this university in the same manner as others. Now that I have explained this, will you please modify your remarks in the future?" (Delgado and Stefancic 1996: 481)

To expect the victims of hate speech not to use hate speech in response to hate speech could be—to recycle a metaphor used by Justice Scalia in striking down a content-based cross burning ordinance in *R.A.V. v. City of St. Paul*[25]—to expect them (the victims of hate speech) to follow Marquis of Queensberry rules while their opponents (hate speakers) fight freestyle. However, the net result of this unregulated verbal frenzy is likely to be that the amount and level of hate speech is ratcheted up, with each side having to make ever-more extreme statements in order to gain the upper hand and sometimes even just to be noticed.

To give a concrete illustration of this phenomenon, consider the circumstances surrounding the UK case of *R. v. Stacey* (2012).[26] In March 2012 Liam Stacey, a third-year undergraduate and user of the Twitter internet messaging service, had spent the afternoon watching sports and drinking beer. One of the games he watched was an English Premiership football (soccer) match between Bolton Wanderers and Tottenham Hotspur in which a black player, Fabrice Muamba, collapsed on the pitch with a life-threatening heart attack. Not long after the match Stacey posted this message on Twitter, 'LOL fuck Muamba he's dead.' Several people responded angrily to the message and attempted to censure Stacey. He responded with a string of further hate messages including, 'You are a silly cunt your mother's a wog and your dad is a rapist, bonjour you scruff northern cunt.' These responses elicited a range of more strident attacks against Stacey, such as 'You must be fucking barmy if you think a greasy little welsh sheep shagger could take on a fucking cockney you silly fat wanker.' Stacey replied in kind: 'I ain't your friend you wog cunt.' 'Go and pick some cotton.' This illustrates the problem of relying on ordinary citizens to censure hate speakers. Who is going to successfully restrain individuals who feel the need to resort to hate speech in censuring hate speakers? In the words of Modood, '[i]t is because the absence of a law or some other publicly accountable procedure is inegalitarian and tends toward creating confrontational situations that the issue of group defamation cannot be left entirely to the process of informal pressure and public indignation' (Modood 1993: 151). This, then, is one reason for letting the courts deal with hate speakers appropriately, as they did in *R. v. Stacey*.

## Counterspeech

If the method of censure is flawed insofar as it tends to illicit yet more unhelpful speech, this points in the direction of a different, putatively less inflammatory and more constructive, method commonly known as counterspeech. In the words of US Constitutional scholar Gerald Gunther, '[t]he proper answer to bad speech is usually more and better speech—not new laws, litigation, and repression' (Gunther 1990: 7; see also Craddock 1995: 1058). I shall understand 'counterspeech' to mean speech that states or explains why and how particular instances of hate speech (or even hate speech in general) are factually incorrect, grossly inaccurate, misleading, lacking in judgment, dangerous, inimical to the values of the society, unjustifiable, and so forth, while at the same time falling short of directly attacking or excoriating hate speakers, or lapsing into hate speech. People whose instinct is to believe that counterspeech is a less restrictive but no less effective way of reducing hate speech/the evils of hate speech sometimes cite Holmes' marketplace of ideas dictum (e.g., Browne 1991: 548–550; Majeed 2009: 517). This is evident in Justice McLachlin's dissent in *R. v. Keegstra*.[27] However, one need not think that the spheres of social interaction in which hate speech occurs are like a marketplace to believe that counterspeech could ameliorate hate speech/the evils of hate speech.

One could simply say that counterspeech works by lodging in the minds of hate speakers and potential hate speakers seeds of doubt as to the truth, validity, or desirability of what motivates them to hate speak (e.g., Strossen 1990: 562; Smith 1995: 260). Why cannot university authorities, say, employ campus speech codes regulating hate speech while at the same time permitting counterspeech? Because (so the argument goes) the existence of campus speech codes 'stultifies the candid intergroup dialogue concerning racism and other forms of bias that constitutes an essential precondition for reducing discrimination' (Strossen 1990: 561).

Let us simply assume for the sake of argument that counterspeech is less restrictive; the question is whether it can be as effective or at least sufficiently effective to constitute a reasonable alternative to hate speech law. This question will turn on who is doing the counterspeaking, what form of hate speech/evils of hate speech that counterspeech is supposed to be effective against, and the circumstances in which the counterspeech takes place. One major problem with the idea that counterspeech is a viable alternative to hate speech law is the existence of barriers to speaking back. Azhar Majeed paints a picture of the American university campus as a place in which counterspeech can thrive. 'The efforts of minority students will often be met by a receptive campus audience, one which is curious to hear how they respond to hateful and prejudicial messages, affording these students the opportunity to meaningfully impact the way many individuals on campus think about important issues' (Majeed 2009: 518). However, what about those university campuses in which minorities find a hostile rather than a receptive campus audience? Could it not be the case that campus speech codes have a vital transitional role to play in helping to create the sort of receptive atmosphere in which counterspeech can be effective? Downs declares that '[t]he ideological purpose of [campus speech] codes reinforces a moral, intellectual, and political orthodoxy that casts a pall over the vibrant life of the mind' (Downs 1993: 19). Yet it might be replied that the ideological orthodoxy of campus racism can, if left unchecked by university authorities, cast a pall over the vibrant counterspeech of the minority student (e.g., Delgado and Stefancic 1996: 480–481).

More generally, there is some evidence to suggest that barriers to counterspeech are the greatest for victims of face-to-face hate speech (e.g., the use of racist insults, slurs, or derogatory epithets directed at specific individuals in person). As mentioned in Ch. 3 [3.1], in her study of hate speech Nielsen found that the most common reaction to racist hate speech on the part of those targeted by it is to ignore the remark and simply leave the situation. Only 28% of people of color, for example, reported making verbal responses to racist speech (Nielsen 2002: 277), and even then 'only when they are in situations where they felt relatively safe, such as a crowded public area' (ibid.). This finding undermines the plausibility of the claim that counterspeech by the victims of face-to-face hate speech is a no less effective but less restrictive alternative to hate speech law; at least, that is, when it comes to instantaneous, face-to-face counterspeech. This claim overlooks a powerful psychological mechanism controlling human responses to conflict situations. Nielsen reports that part of the problem is fear that speaking back may provoke yet more hate abuse or even violence (ibid.). This is certainly the reported experience of Matsuda, who in the late 1980s received hate mail as a consequence of speaking in public about her views on freedom of expression and hate speech, and subsequently made a decision not to publish her ideas in the popular press for fear of receiving threats against her person (remarks in Borovoy et al. 1988–1989: 363). Similarly, there is evidence to suggest that this fear has led some complainants in Australia to withdraw complaints about hate speech even under the private processes of dispute resolution established by hate speech legislation (e.g., Gelber 2002: 85). There is also a psychological cost that might be borne by the victims of hate speech if society expects them to take sole responsibility for tackling the problem. If they are made to feel that it is *their* duty or obligation to engage in counterspeech, what happens when they do not? Will this become yet another (illegitimate) source of shame or self-loathing?

Another part of the problem is that dealing with the effects of hate speech can be time consuming, reducing the time that someone might have to actually engage in counterspeech. This is the reported experience of the writer Amanda Hess, who suffered online harassment and intimidation based on her gender. 'I've spent countless hours over the past four years logging the online activity of one particularly committed cyberstalker, just in case' (Hess 2014). At this stage, it might be pointed out that using legal restrictions to combat hate speech also sucks up a lot of time. The victims of hate speech may need to expend a considerable amount of time as complainants, plaintiffs, or even chief witnesses for the prosecution in criminal cases. And then there are the judges and legal scholars who in some cases have spent decades arguing against one another; time that might have been profitably spent doing other things, such as eloquently speaking out against hate speech (cf. Delgado and Stefancic 2009: 360–361). However, it is surely relevant that when victims of hate speech do decide to take a legalistic course of action they can normally expect to receive not inconsiderable support from legal professionals, who share the time burden. Counterspeech undertaken by the victims of hate speech is often without this specialist support.

Of course, the direct targets of hate speech do not exhaust the class of persons entitled to speak back to hate speech. They have other advocates or potential advocates who may speak back on their behalf. Strossen offers the following anecdotal evidence. 'I have seen many situations in which the person who is attacked initially cannot respond [ ... ] but somebody else jumps into the fray and speaks out, and that empowers and encourages the targeted individual victim' (e.g., Strossen 2012: 380). However, Strossen overlooks the fact that similar sorts of problems as those expounded upon above are also likely to confront third parties who are considering speaking back on behalf of the victims of hate speech. For example, it is often assumed that the Internet affords greater opportunities for counterspeech than ever before. It is relatively inexpensive, fast, and open to the whole community. But the fact that the Internet is so public means that it is a place of danger as well as opportunity for potential counterspeakers. Anecdotal evidence suggests that some people, potential "good Samaritans", may be too scared to speak out against hate speakers on Twitter for fear of provoking vitriolic abuse at the hands of these or yet other hate speakers who use this service. It is also worth noting that if internet regulators were granted a legal or even an industry mandate to restrict uses of hate speech over the Internet, this would not deny people the right to speak back to offline hate speech online, and may even empower and encourage more of the very speaking back that Strossen so admires. Intriguingly, Strossen argues that if institutional authorities deny persons the right to engage in hate speech and this successfully deters them from doing so, then the upshot is that people are denied a chance of speaking back against hate speech (Strossen 2012: 386–387). But I think there is perversity in a logic that says we ought to let something harmful happen just to give people the opportunity to speak out against it. Surely the victims of hate speech would say, "Let's just try to stop the hate speech if we can, and not worry so much about the counterspeech if we are successful."

In addition to these observations, Delgado and Stefancic observe that sometimes direct counterspeech is 'simply unfeasible', such as when 'racist remarks are uttered in a cowardly fashion, by means of graffiti scrawled on a campus wall under cover of darkness, or by a flyer placed outside a black student's door' (Delgado and Stefancic 1996: 481). Of course, a person may still have the option of indirect counterspeech, such as scrawling over the graffiti or putting up a different sign with messages proclaiming that hate speech is abhorrent. But, then again, it is also hard to see how any counterspeech could ameliorate some of the psychological harms experienced by the victims of hate speech. As Joshua Cohen puts it, 'it seems especially implausible that the injuries produced by hateful fighting words can be remedied with more speech' (Cohen [Joshua] 1993: 256). This is because '[t]he anger, fear, and suspicion that they produce is not of a kind that is easily addressed by verbal reassurances' (ibid.). Likewise, Stanley Fish maintains that the response that hate speech should be answered not by legalistic constraints but by more speech 'would make sense only if the effects of speech could be cancelled out by additional speech, only if the pain and humiliation caused by racial or religious epithets could be ameliorated by saying something like "So's your old man"' (Fish 1994: 109). This general point seems to hold true of hate speech that rises to the level of a dignitary crime (e.g., *crimen injuria*) or a dignitary tort (e.g., intentional infliction of emotional distress). The point is that if someone is subjected to racist fighting words or demeaning or humiliating verbal abuse on the street or to discriminatory harassment in the workplace, the affront to dignity or the violation of civil rights occasioned by this mistreatment might not be eliminated merely by a bystander or colleague declaring that the hate speaker is in the wrong. Perhaps in some instances counterspeech could cause the hate speaker to retract his or her statements and to apologize for any humiliation or distress or harassment they may have caused. But if such instances turn out to be the exception rather than the rule, counterspeech cannot be relied upon to ameliorate the relevant harms.

Some forms of hate speech pose more technical challenges to speaking back. Langton and colleagues, for example, argue that it can be epistemically difficult to speak back against hate speech that takes the form of negative stereotypes or generics. This is because some statements can be inherently confused or vague as between which kind of generic is being stated. Even under questioning by a competent and confident listener with sufficient communicative standing to ask questions of clarification ("What exactly do you mean by that?"), the meaning of the statement cannot be made precise. This kind of epistemological limit to gaining knowledge of the speaker's meaning can make it difficult to figure out how to speak back, such as by offering relevant counter-examples (Langton et al. 2012). It seems to me that there can be other, non-epistemic barriers to speaking back against generics. For, suppose that a statement is confused or vague as between which kind of generic is being stated but not inherently so in the sense that under questioning by a competent and confident listener with sufficient communicative standing to ask questions of clarification the meaning of the statement could be made precise. However, wherein the listener is subject to hate speech of the relevant sort or similar sorts, this may remove his or her confidence or communicative standing to ask questions of clarification. This kind of barrier to clarification can create a false or unnecessary epistemological limit to gaining knowledge of the speaker's meaning, which can in turn make it difficult to figure out how to speak back, such as by offering counter-examples.

What of incitement to hatred? The idea that counterspeech could be an effective tool to counteract the persuasive and sometimes unduly persuasive influence of words intended to stir up hatred makes certain assumptions that may not hold up to scrutiny. For one thing, the argument assumes that all speakers receive equal time to put their ideas across, but in reality 'some people get a lot more speech than others' (MacKinnon 1993: 72). This is partly a problem of unequal access to public forums among different constituencies of speakers, with minorities who have most need of access to forums in which they can speak back against hate speech having the least access to legislatures and to mainstream TV, radio, or newspapers (e.g., Matsuda 1989b: 2376; Modood 1993: 150–151; Parekh 2005–2006: 219). It is also a function of the way recipients choose to receive ideas. The counterspeech argument assumes a certain model of the way in which persons receive speech to which they are ill-disposed, namely, that they voluntarily and on a regular basis allow themselves to receive such speech. The truth is otherwise. In his *Republic.com 2.0*, for example, Sunstein argues that with the rise of the Internet as a rival to the print media and TV and radio broadcasting the speech market has become increasingly 'fragmented.' This means that many people are choosing to receive the majority of their news, opinions, stories, social commentary, putative facts, and so on from specialist websites rather than from a 'general-interest intermediary' such as a newspaper or news bulletin. Consequently, some members of hate groups are getting most of their information from other members of hate groups (Sunstein 2007: 48–49). According to Sunstein, this puts into doubt 'the idea that "more speech" is necessarily an adequate remedy for bad speech—especially if many people are inclined and increasingly able to wall themselves off from competing views' (78). When there is a 'balkanized speech market' and deliberative enclaves, there is a danger that even counterspeech spread via the Internet 'may work too slowly or not at all, simply because people are not listening to one another' (91).

Partly in response to these various claims about the barriers to speaking back, several thinkers have argued that institutional authorities can, and should, play an active part as counterspeakers against hate speech and hate speakers without becoming censors of hate speech itself (e.g., Wiener 1989: 260–262; Strossen 1990: 562; 2001: 272; 2012: 387–388, 392; Gutmann 1994: 23; Brettschneider 2013: 642). Most comprehensively, Gelber (2002, 2012a, 2012b) advocates a 'speaking back policy' according to which government institutions and officials assume or are charged with a responsibility of speaking back to hate speakers and to hate speech directed at vulnerable groups of citizens by making public declarations about the unwelcome or unacceptable nature of hate speech and hate speech harms. This combines aspects of both the government intervention and counterspeech methods. For example, 'the policy would require an allocation of public funds to the furtherance of specific anti-discrimination messages in a manner which reaches beyond the historical or current commitments of many governments' (Gelber 2012b: 62).

However, it is far from obvious that such proposals are significantly less restrictive but no less effective than banning hate speech. In terms of restrictiveness, there is a question mark about how the policy would be enforced against an elected government that is reluctant to carry it out. If it is a statutory obligation, then this is a form of speech restriction, dictating what governments must say (cf. Strossen 2012: 387). For another thing, it might be asked how restrictive of freedom it is to collect money from taxpayers year after year to spend on anti-hate declarations and associated public information campaigns 'beyond the historical or current commitments of many governments.' *If* this means that government spending will be fenced off from the ordinary democratic cycle by which tax collection and spending plans are outlined in documents and accepted or rejected by the electorate, then the proposal removes *choice* from voters.

Turning to efficacy, Fish is skeptical that university administrators engaging in counterspeech against hate speakers or even for that matter university administrators refusing to engage in any sort of public debate with hate speaker can be effective. Such measures are 'too tame' because they fall 'far short of wounding the enemy at its heart' (Fish 1997: 392). 'A deeper wound will only be inflicted by methods and weapons [...] liberalism disdains: by acts of ungenerosity, intolerance, perhaps even repression, by acts that respond to evil not by tolerating it—in the hope that its energies will simply dissipate in the face of scorn—but by trying to stamp it out' (ibid.). Likewise for state or governmental authorities: it is difficult to believe that speaking in favor of the reasons for people's right not to be subjected to discriminatory intimidation through the burning of crosses, for example, could be as effective in sending out the message that the state disapproves of cross burning as for the state to legislate against cross burning with a bespoke, content-based statute. As Partlett puts it, '[l]egislation is governmental speech of the most potent kind' (Partlett 1989: 468). Why so? Perhaps because it is generally understood that legislative time is in short supply, and because drafting law is fraught with difficulty for legislative authorities, who must contend with objections and challenges throughout the drafting process. These facts may give legislation restricting hate speech all the more symbolic value or meaning. Indeed, the mere fact that the state has opted to refrain from legislating against hate speech may send out the message to citizens that it is not as serious about its anti-hate speech message as it purports to be.

## 9.4 THE AVOIDANCE OF UNINTENDED CONSEQUENCES FOR FREE SPEECH

In this section I wish to examine a general legal doctrine that says laws constraining certain forms of proscribable speech must be drafted so as to minimize adverse unintended consequences for other forms of unproscribable speech and that if those unintended consequences are sufficiently serious, they may override the fact that the constraints serve a pressing social need. This general doctrine supports the Principle of Narrow Tailoring, according to which legalistic constraints on speech or other expressive acts, including constraints on uses of hate speech, are (N-)unwarranted if they are not narrowly framed to meet their own purposes or objectives. In the US, courts have applied a version of the Principle of Narrow Tailoring to First Amendment cases involving time, place, and manner restrictions.[28] They do so under the rubric of the Intermediate Scrutiny Test, which comes into effect when courts review any laws that although do not directly target speech and are ostensibly content neutral may have a substantial impact on certain sorts of ideas or messages. In *Collin v. Smith II*, for example, the Court affirmed as being unconstitutional ordinance No. 77-5-N-994, which required persons seeking to parade or assemble in Skokie village to obtain liability and property damage insurance to cover any injuries to persons or property that might ensue from such parades. The majority ruled that 'the governmental interest [...] could more narrowly be served by criminalizing [...] the conduct (by appellees or others) directly producing any feared injury to persons or property and by marshalling local, county, and state police to prevent violations.'[29] The Court was effectively accusing local authorities of using the ordinance as a pretext by which to ban speech, the content of which they frowned upon. However, it would be wrong to assume that it is impossible for constraints imposed upon uses of hate speech via time, place, and manner restrictions to satisfy the Principle of Narrow Tailoring.[30]

A second principle that falls under the rubric of the general doctrine is the Principle of Overbreadth. It states that legalistic constraints on speech or other expressive acts, including constraints on uses of hate speech, are (N-)unwarranted if they prohibit constitutionally protected forms of speech, even if they also target speech that is constitutionally unprotected. I shall assume for the sake of argument that this principle is, if not fundamentally important, then certainly instrumentally important to the realization of fundamental free speech principles and values, particularly those discussed in Chs. 4 and 7, because it acts as a shield for protected speech. In the US, when a particular hate speech law prohibits a complex, conjunctive expressive act that is itself comprised of subparts that are protected speech as well as subparts that are unprotected speech (i.e., kinds of speech that are categorically excluded from First Amendment protection), the result tends to be that it is deemed overbroad by the courts. Thus, in *Collin v. Smith II* the Court used an overbreadth argument against ordinance No. 77-5-N-995, which prohibited '(t)he dissemination of any materials within the Village of Skokie which promotes and incites hatred against persons by reason of their race, national origin, or religion, and is intended to do so.' Circuit Judge Pell affirmed that even if it were the case (and he expressed serious doubt as to this fact) that the ordinance prohibited constitutionally unprotected speech (e.g., acts of incitement to hatred that have a tendency to induce a breach of the peace), it was also likely to sweep up constitutionally protected speech. For, as well as prohibiting the display of swastikas, uniforms, and placards during a public demonstration it 'could conceivably be applied to criminalize dissemination of *The Merchant of Venice* or a vigorous discussion of the merits of reverse racial discrimination in Skokie.'[31] Of course, in order for ordinance No. 77-5-N-995 to apply to the dissemination of *The Merchant of Venice* it would need to be demonstrated that the disseminator 'intended' to promote and incite hatred against Jews. Yet the mere fact that it could conceivably prohibit the dissemination itself was in the mind of Circuit Judge Pell. Once again, this reasoning was not undisputed.[32]

Along similar lines, in *Virginia v. Black* the Supreme Court held that the *prima facie* evidence provision built into Virginia's cross burning statute rendered it overbroad. Writing for the majority Justice O'Connor reasoned that the statute's provision that any such burning of a cross shall be *prima facie* evidence of an intent to intimidate a person or group of persons has the potential to sweep up constitutionally protected speech, to wit, a person burning a cross as an act of political speech, as well as a person engaging in constitutionally proscribable intimidation.[33] Justice Thomas, however, the only African American Justice on the court, argued in dissent that in fact Virginia's cross burning statute addressed 'only conduct' and therefore 'there is no need to analyze it under any of our First Amendment tests.'[34]

In other cases courts have used the Principle of Overbreadth to strike down laws forbidding hate speech when it amounts to discriminatory harassment because such laws prohibited a complex speech act comprised of subparts that are constitutionally protected (e.g., offensive speech) as well as subparts that although not examples of unprotected speech (e.g., fighting words) are nonetheless sanctionable under federal or state laws. In *Doe v. University of Michigan*, for example, a US District Court ruled that the University of Michigan Policy on Discrimination and Discriminatory Harassment by Students in the University Environment was unconstitutionally overbroad. Judge Cohn justified this finding on the basis of his interpretation of the evidence from the University's discipline files. 'As applied by the University over the past year, the Policy was consistently applied to reach protected speech.'[35] The University did not appeal the decision despite the fact that potentially the evidence from the discipline files could have just as easily supported the opposite finding that the Policy Administrators and the Policy Hearing Panels had actually avoided sweeping up a substantial amount of protected speech.[36]

Of course, US courts are by no means alone here. In *Saskatchewan (Human Rights Commission) v. Whatcott*, for instance, the Canadian Supreme Court concluded that part of s. 14(1)(b) of the Saskatchewan Human Rights Code was *inter alia* 'overbroad' by virtue of the fact that banning a statement or representation that 'ridicules, belittles or otherwise affronts the dignity of' is likely to sweep up protected speech along with any genuine acts of dignitary injury. In *R. v. Zündel* the Canadian Supreme Court made a comparable determination in relation to s. 181 (formerly s. 177) of the Criminal Code, according to which '[e]very one who willfully publishes a statement, tale or news that he knows is false and that causes or is likely to cause injury or mischief to a public interest is guilty of an indictable offence.' The majority of the Court recognized that breach of the peace could be one such public interest threatened by the publication of Holocaust denial literature but held that the term 'a public interest' rendered s. 181 unconstitutionally 'vague and broad' and, therefore, in violation of Section 2(b) of the *Canadian Charter of Rights and Freedoms* (which guarantees 'freedom of thought, belief, opinion and expression, including freedom of the press and other media of communication'). The publication of virtually any controversial or provocative or undesirable opinions could be regarded as capable of injuring some or other public interest by authorities inclined toward censorship.

A third principle that gets to the heart of the aforementioned doctrine is the Principle of Vagueness, that legalistic constraints on speech or other expressive acts, including constraints on uses of hate speech, are (N-)unwarranted if they are so vague that persons who are subject to them cannot reasonably know what they demand of their conduct. A large part of the justification of this principle is the need for predictability, for people to be able to plan their lives based on reasonable predictions about what conduct is and is not likely to attract legal sanction. I take it as read that this is an extremely important legal good, for without predictability it is scarcely likely that law can embody or safeguard the goods of autonomy and self-realization. Of course, in a constitutional democracy concerns about vagueness and predictability begin with the constitution itself, and so First Amendment absolutists and their critics disagree about which version of the First Amendment provides the most predictability.[37] But to focus on statutes, ordinances, and speech codes themselves, what matters is that persons of ordinary intelligence can distinguish between what is permissible speech action and what is proscribed speech action under said law (e.g., Scott 1951: 231). Thus, in *Doe v. University of Michigan* Judge Cohn found the Policy to be vague as well as overbroad. 'Looking at the plain language of the Policy, it was simply impossible to discern any limitation on its scope or any conceptual distinction between protected and unprotected conduct.'[38] Once again, there might have been grounds on which to appeal the Judge's findings. He asserted that '[i]t is not clear what kind of conduct would constitute a "threat" to an individual's academic efforts.'[39] And that '[t]he language of the policy alone gives no inherent guidance' as to 'what conduct will be held to "interfere" with an individual's academic efforts.'[40] But he also recognized as good law[41] the Supreme Court decision in *Meritor Savings Bank v. Vinson* (1986).[42] And in that case very similar language was not deemed unconstitutionally vague.[43]

Both the Principle of Overbreadth and the Principle of Vagueness are concerned with the avoidance of the unintended consequence of censorship. This consequence goes beyond the brute fact of banning the sort of hate speech that ought to be permissible. It also has to do with the putative chilling effect of hate speech law on other categories of speech. Even if a hate speech law is enacted because of a pressing social need, the concern is that in practice any attempt to ban hate speech, no matter how careful or well intentioned, is bound to cause collateral damage in terms of making people overly cautious about what they will say in public. The concern is based on the technical difficulties of framing and wording precise legislation and on the following hypothesis about human psychological and behavior. If law is expressed in a way that is too unclear for a person of average intelligence to reasonably forecast whether or not his or her speech falls under it, then to avoid the risk of adverse legal consequences he or she may refrain from saying anything remotely controversial, critical, or provocative (e.g., Tanenhaus 1952: 218–219; Strossen 1990: 521; McGee 1990: 372, 391; Kors 1991: 25; Laird 1994: 392; Michelman 1995: 274; Baker 2009: 157). This concern was also relied upon by Judge Cohn in his opinion in the US case *Doe v. University of Michigan* Judge,[44] and by Justice McLachlin in her dissent in the Canadian case *R. v. Keegstra*.[45]

When evaluating the chilling effect argument, however, I believe that it is vital to consider the possibility of variations in chilling effect across different clusters of hate speech law. It may be that appeals to a chilling effect may be far more difficult to sustain in the case of law forbidding uses of hate speech when it amounts to discriminatory harassment in the workplace or a university than law disallowing the public expression of hatred or law banning incitement to hatred—by virtue of the narrower frame of reference of the former. At any rate, too often the chilling effect is simply assumed rather than proven. If the chilling effect hypothesis is true, then one would expect to see evidence of a significant diminution in the quantity and quality of political, scientific, artistic, and comedic discourse in institutions (e.g., universities) or even countries that possess and enforce laws/regulations/codes against hate speech as compared to institutions or countries without such legalistic constraints. Yet critics of hate speech law rarely, if ever, present such evidence.

Putting to one side the issue of evidence, a typical argument from the chilling effect proceeds as follows. (1) Hate speech imposes morally significant burdens on those targeted by it. (2) Hate speech law imposes morally significant burdens on the public: namely, the public would be uncertain about the application and enforcement of hate speech law and as a result would be more nervous than they would otherwise be about speaking on subjects of public interest. (3) The harms of chilling outweigh the harms of hate speech. Therefore, (4) hate speech law is N-unwarranted. To illustrate, Kwame Anthony Appiah addresses the particular question of whether it is right to use the law to punish people who make false accusations that all Muslims in a particular area are terrorists or who negatively stereotype followers of Islam as Jihadists or who publish cartoons depicting the prophet Muhammad as a terrorist. His answer is partly that even though hate speech is associated with dignitary and reputational burdens, there is 'already a good deal of suspicion in many quarters that discussion of these issues is conducted without frankness out of a desire to avoid causing offense to the great majority of innocent Muslims' and that this suspicion 'would increase if those who spoke frankly risked not just being thought to be Islamophobic but also fines or imprisonment.' To which he adds this thought. 'If the governments of the world want to do something useful in this area, it is far better to respond to defamatory speech with information and a reminder of the desirability of respectful discussion of these matters' (Appiah 2012: 178).

However, it should be borne in mind that the premises underdetermine this nuanced conclusion in the sense that they also support yet another conclusion. Specifically, they also support the conclusion that hate speech law should be enacted but only on the condition that its enforcement is accompanied by a rigorous public information campaign about the nature and likely application of the law and guidance about what is or is not covered. This would tackle head on the suspicion that merely attempting to speak out about the problem of terrorism within the Muslim community would attract legal sanction. Once again it depends crucially on what category of hate speech law one is talking about. Consider law proscribing group defamation (*sensu stricto*). The information campaign might explain that properly understood group defamation law does not in and of itself prohibit people from contributing to public debate on such issues frankly or even in ways that cause offense or insult. What such law bans is making false statements of fact that are damaging to the reputation or standing of the relevant groups.[46] In other words, what is required is disabusing people of their unfounded fears and misconceptions. This would, if done successfully, lessen the chilling effect but without sacrificing the protection of groups against the dignitary and reputational burdens associated with hate speech. The chances of success for this sort of public information campaign seem no worse than for Appiah's preferred strategy.

At this stage, however, hate speech law detractors might argue that no campaign is up to the task of enabling persons of ordinary intelligence to safely predict when it is likely that comments will land them in trouble with authorities. The history of campus speech codes in the US provides a salutary lesson about law forbidding hate speech when it amounts to discriminatory harassment in the workplace or a university. For example, in *Doe v. University of Michigan* Judge Cohn found that '[t]he language of the policy alone gives no inherent guidance' but that '[t]he one interpretive resource the University provided was withdrawn as "inaccurate," an implicit admission that even the University itself was unsure of the precise scope and meaning of the Policy.'[47] However, it would be wrong to conclude from this one case that no guidance pamphlet is up to the task. Indeed, there is a sense in which Judge Cohn missed the true point about the guidance pamphlet. Speaking in response to the judgment, the University's General Counsel Elsa Kircher Cole made it clear that the Policy and accompanying guidance pamphlet were never intended to be static documents but were to be improved in the light of experience. More generally, the best public information campaigns are iterative and dynamic: they respond and adapt to the response they get from the public.

Of course, the detractor might insist that the prospects of mounting any effective public information campaigns are tied to the kind of law one is attempting to inform people about and that law in the area of hate speech is inherently and irretrievably vague. Yet at present citizens advice organizations and pro bono lawyers give guidance on many areas of tax law, say, that are hard to decipher even for persons of ordinary intelligence, and this apparatus is welcomed and sometimes actively championed by governments. More importantly, the present criticism extrapolates from the fledgling hate speech law of the 1970s, 1980s, and 1990s to a generalization about all subsequent attempts to enact and enforce hate speech law and in doing so ignores the possibility of improvements in response to error. There is evidence to suggest that law in this area has become more acute over time, both through the development of a growing body of case law and in response to comparative studies of hate speech law around the world and the insights that such studies contain as to what sorts of hate speech law works and what does not. In the UK, for example, the first law against the stirring up of racial hatred was presented in the Race Relations Act of 1965 but was substantially refined by subsequent amendments and extensions, which had the effect of widening the scope of protection but at the same time restricting the conditions for prosecution on several counts, including the type of speech, the intent of the speaker, and the sorts of speech protected under the law. Lawmakers responded to the emerging case law in the UK and to the experience of hate speech law elsewhere. Moreover, partly in response to the chilling phenomenon, the Lords insisted on the insertion of protection of freedom of expression clauses into new legislation; for each new piece of law the Crown Prosecution Service has published a guidance document covering the content and meaning of the legislation, the conditions for successful prosecution, and examples of successful and unsuccessful prosecutions.

## 9.5 NEUTRALITY

Finally, according to the Principle of Neutrality, legalistic constraints on speech or other expressive acts, including constraints on uses of hate speech, are (N-)unwarranted if they involve content discrimination, and especially so if they involve viewpoint discrimination. If the intention behind the doctrine of content neutrality is that the state should not use law to suppress public discussion of certain issues or particular subject matter, the intention behind the doctrine of viewpoint neutrality is that it should not use law to suppress only one side of the argument on certain issues, thereby favoring the other side of the debate.[48] The Principle of Neutrality has played and continues to play as significant a role in First Amendment jurisprudence as the Principle of Overbreadth, and perhaps not surprisingly given the obvious connections between the aforementioned intentions and the underlying principles of democracy and legitimacy discussed in Ch. 7. After all, if part of the core purpose of the First Amendment is to provide checks and balances to state power (i.e., to prevent the state from suppressing speech merely in order to cling to power, for example, by silencing critics or by banning certain sorts of speech in an effort to appease a section of society that holds particular electoral influence), then it is not difficult to see how the Principle of Neutrality might serve that purpose, provided that content- and viewpoint-neutral laws are *less likely* to be abused by the state.[49] In addition to this, other academics stress the importance of the Principle of Neutrality for democratic self-governance and the rights of citizens to contribute to public discourse and to participate in the formation of public opinion, upon which a healthy democracy rests (e.g., Weinstein 1999, 2001, 2011b). Yet others emphasize the underlying principle of formal respect for the equal autonomy of citizens (e.g., Baker 2011; Brettschneider 2013).[50] That being said, it is a further question whether what I have called the Principle of Neutrality should be interpreted as a rule (albeit a rule with exceptions) that places precise and absolute requirements on how courts decide free speech cases or instead as a standard or benchmark that is imprecise and not absolute.[51] In keeping with the approach taken throughout this book, and outlined in Ch. 1, I interpret it as a principle.

At any rate, the doctrine of neutrality employed by US courts under the rubric of the First Amendment has normally been understood to preclude the sort of content-based restrictions that characterize a significant amount of hate speech law. Lawrence Tribe makes the point using the example of public discourse. 'If the Constitution forces government to allow people to march, speak, and write in favor of peace, brotherhood, and justice, then it must also require government to allow them to advocate hatred, racism, and even genocide' (Tribe 1988: 838n.17). Similarly, in *R.A.V. v. City of St. Paul*, the US Supreme Court struck down the City of St. Paul Bias-Motivated Crime Ordinance *inter alia* because it involved content discrimination and even viewpoint discrimination. Although the Court, along with the Minnesota Supreme Court, accepted the City of St. Paul's argument that it had intended and interpreted the ordinance as prohibiting fighting words (a category of proscribable speech), the Court extended the requirement of content neutrality even to those laws that seek to draw distinctions between subcategories of proscribable speech. The majority ruled that the ordinance was unconstitutionally underinclusive by virtue of the fact that on its face it proscribed only fighting words with certain sorts of content (i.e., messages relating to race, color, creed, religion, or gender) and as applied it prohibited only particular kinds of viewpoint (i.e., people holding or advocating a certain type of a position on issues of race, color, creed, religion, or gender).[52] That being said, the decision in *R.A.V. v. City of St. Paul* is also notable for its admission of certain 'valid bases' for content discrimination, albeit the majority in this case held that the valid bases did not apply to the St. Paul Bias-Motivated Crime Ordinance. Following on from this, in *Virginia v. Black* the Court also reasoned that there can be valid bases on which a state may ban cross burning carried out with the attempt to intimidate, even if such a ban involved content discrimination. In Ch. 10 I shall argue that the acceptance of these valid bases can be interpreted as a form of principled compromise.

How does American jurisprudence on the Principle of Neutrality compare with the jurisprudence of the ECtHR, say? Arguably something like the Principle of Neutrality has figured in the ECtHR's interpretation of Art. 10 of the ECHR in cases relating to the allocation of access to public spaces or forums[53] and in cases relating to the content of speech. I have in mind this much-quoted dictum from *Handyside v. United Kingdom*.

> [The human right to freedom of expression] is applicable not only to "information" or "ideas" that are favourably received or regarded as inoffensive or as a matter of indifference, but also to those that offend, shock or disturb the State or any sector of the population. Such are the demands of that pluralism, tolerance and broadmindedness without which there is no "democratic society."[54]

Importantly for the present debate, the ECtHR has reiterated this dictum in dealing with hate speech cases, including *Soulas and others v. France*,[55]

*Balsytė-Lideikienė v. Lithuania*,[56] *Féret v. Belgium*,[57] and *Vejdeland and Others v. Sweden*.[58] Despite the demands of pluralism, tolerance, and broadmindedness (which are akin to the demands of content and viewpoint neutrality), the ECtHR permitted content-based restrictions on freedom of expression, and it did so based upon exceptions set out in Art. 10(2) of the ECHR, under its margin of appreciation doctrine. Thus, a comparison between these ECtHR rulings and the US Supreme Court rulings in *R.A.V. v. City of St. Paul* and *Virginia v. Black* suggests the following similarities and dissimilarities. On the one hand, both courts are committed to protecting both favorable and unfavorable speech but at the same time both permit certain valid bases on which to depart from the demands of neutrality, pluralism, tolerance, and broadmindedness. On the other hand, the depth and range of exceptions anticipated by the ECtHR in comparison to those accepted by the US Supreme Court, the fact that the exceptions are written into Art. 10(2) of the ECHR but not the First Amendment, the margin of appreciation doctrine upheld by the ECtHR but not the US Supreme Court, and the difference between the ECtHR and the US Supreme Court in their focus (or lack of) on categories of speech, amount to substantive, doctrinal, and epistemological differences between the jurisprudence of the ECtHR and the US Supreme Court (cf. Feldman 1998: 157).[59]

\* \* \*

In summary, the function of the legal principles discussed in this chapter is to give effect to the conviction that governmental and institutional authorities should be circumspect in using legalistic constraints to tackle the issue of hate speech. Together they provide a formidable barrier to indiscriminate, gratuitous, and irrational restrictions on speech or other expressive conduct. That these barriers do exist, and should exist, in countries and jurisdictions other than the US is clear. Nevertheless, I think it would be an error to assume that they do, or should, constitute an impenetrable barrier to the enactment and effective enforcement of hate speech law. After all, there are numerous clusters of laws/regulations/codes constraining uses of hate speech enacted in many different circumstances and contexts and for a diversity of principled reasons. Recognizing that there is a dilemma between pursuing justifiable objectives in relation to the issue of hate speech and pursuing those objectives employing only justifiable means does not entail that the correct response to that dilemma is to err on the side of striking down all hate speech law.

## NOTES

1. *R. v. Oakes*, at 138–139.
2. See, e.g., the Canadian cases *R. v. Keegstra*, at 745–749; *Canada (Human Rights Commission) v. Taylor*, at 917–919; the ECtHR case *Vejdeland and Others v. Sweden*, Concurring opinion of Judge Yudkivska, at paras. 9–12.

3. See, e.g., the Canadian case *Saskatchewan (Human Rights Commission) v. Whatcott*, at 507.
4. See, e.g., the Canadian cases *R. v. Keegstra*, at 757; *Canada (Human Rights Commission) v. Taylor*, at 919; the ECtHR case *Soulas and others v. France*, at paras. 36–44; the Australian case *Eatock v. Bolt*, at para. 216.
5. See, e.g., the ECtHR case *Féret v. Belgium*, at para. 64.
6. See, e.g., the ECtHR case *Vejdeland and Others v. Sweden*, at paras. 49, 59; the Australian case *Eatock v. Bolt*, at paras. 222–226.
7. *R.A.V. v. City of St. Paul*, at 396.
8. See, e.g., *Rust v. Sullivan* (1991) 500 US 173.
9. 228 F.3d 1003 (9th. Cir.).
10. Art. 47 of the Constitution.
11. Art. 47 of the Constitution.
12. Art. 33(2)(c)(d) of the Constitution.
13. s. 16(2)(c) of the Bill of Rights.
14. Art. 30 of the Constitution.
15. *R. v. Oakes*, at 139.
16. No. 5493/72 (ECtHR, 7 Dec.) (concerning whether or not by confiscating copies of *The Little Red Schoolbook* under the Obscene Publications Act 1959 the UK government had contravened Art. 10 of the ECHR).
17. Separate opinion of Judge Mosler, at para. 2.
18. Of course, Hare might insist that the law does nothing to stop the speech it is designed to stop but at the same time chills speech that it is not designed to stop, but then he would be required to show evidence of these particular effects.
19. *R. v. Keegstra*, at 854.
20. See, e.g., *R. v. Sheppard and Whittle II* [2010] EWCA Crim 65.
21. This type of argument dates back at least as far as Spinoza ([1670] 1958: 227), who defended freedom of thought and speech partly on the grounds that 'it is impossible for thought to be completely subject to another's control'. To which he adds (ibid.): 'This is why a government is regarded as oppressive if it attempts to control men's minds.'
22. See, e.g., *Shelton v. Tucker* (1960) 364 US 479, at 488, 493; *Minneapolis Star and Tribune Co. v. Minnesota Commissioner of Revenue* (1983) 460 US 575, at 586.
23. See, e.g., *R. v. Oakes*, at 139; *Saskatchewan (Human Rights Commission) v. Whatcott*, at 516–518.
24. See, e.g., *Balsytė-Lideikienė v .Lithuania*, at para. 81; *Peta Deutschland v. Germany* (2012) No. 43481/09 (ECtHR, 8 Nov.), at para. 50; *Ricci v. Italy* (2013) No. 30210/06 (ECtHR, 8 Oct.), at para. 55.
25. 'St. Paul has no such authority to license one side of a debate to fight freestyle, while requiring the other to follow Marquis of Queensberry rules.' At 392.
26. No. A20120033 (Swansea Cr. Ct., 30 Mar.) (involving the offence of racially aggravated harassment, alarm or distress of intent to users of the Twitter internet messaging service).
27. *R. v. Keegstra*, at 798.
28. See, e.g., *United States v. O'Brien* (1968) 391 US 367 (involving a prosecution for burning a draft card); *Ward v. Rock Against Racism* (1989) 491 US 781 (involving a city regulation concerning the volume of concerts in New York City's Central Park).
29. *Collin v. Smith II*, at 1209.
30. In his dissent in *Collin v. Smith II*, for example, Circuit Judge Sprecher argued that ordinance No. 77-5-N-994 'seems to impose no greater burden than is necessary to achieve the result desired.' At 1214. In a similar vein, writing

for the majority in *Snyder v. Phelps* Justice Roberts implied that general laws creating buffer zones around funerals could satisfy the Principle of Narrow Tailoring. At _. See also *Phelps-Roper v. Strickland* and *Phelps-Roper v. City of Manchester*.
31. *Collin v. Smith II*, at 1207.
32. When the Supreme Court denied a Writ of Certiorari in relation to this case, Justice Blackmun lodged this dissent (*Smith v. Collin*). 'I also feel that the present case affords the Court an opportunity to consider whether, in the context of the facts that this record appears to present, there is no limit whatsoever to the exercise of free speech. There indeed may be no such limit, but when citizens assert, not casually but with deep conviction, that the proposed demonstration is scheduled at a place and in a manner that is taunting and overwhelmingly offensive to the citizens of that place, that assertion, uncomfortable though it may be for judges, deserves to be examined. It just might fall into the same category as one's "right" to cry "fire" in a crowded theater, for "the character of every act depends upon the circumstances in which it is done."' At 919. He was not alone in anticipating such an analogy. Consider the words of Horowitz and Bramson (1979: 332): 'Without wishing to stretch the analogy, can a strong case be made by the township, that Skokie, with its large Jewish population, is a theatre, in which a small band of self-declared Nazis, in effect, sought to incite a riot rather than hold a peaceful march, and hence to induce the same sort of panic and potential physical harm in the population that would occur if one cried "fire" in a crowded theatre?' In order to buttress this alternative line of reasoning about ordinance No. 77-5-N-995 and overbreadth I would proffer the following remark. The Principle of Overbreadth has to do with law that sweeps up a substantial amount of protected speech. So even if a law against creating unnecessary panic could conceivably be applied to criminalize the enactment of a piece of political performance art consisting of filming oneself standing in a crowded theater and shouting "fire" in order to object to cuts to the public funding of fire services, this sweeping up of potentially protected speech does not suffice to trigger the Principle. Perhaps there is burden on the speaker in terms of lost self-expression or self-realization (i.e., being denied the right to utter these sorts of words), but it seems reasonable to conclude that such burden is not substantial enough. And so it might also be in the case of No. 77-5-N-995.
33. *Virginia v. Black*, at 365.
34. At 394–395. For the argument that Justice Thomas played a special role in framing the terms of the disagreement and final decision in this case, see Charles (2005).
35. *Doe v. University of Michigan*, at 865.
36. I have in mind the fact that the Policy Administrators summarily dismissed a claim of anti-Semitic harassment explicitly on the grounds that the allegation that Jews use the Holocaust to justify Israel's policies toward the Palestinians was protected speech, and the fact that a Policy Hearing Panel unanimously found that the policy was not violated by a student who during a class argued that homosexuality is a curable disease. At the start of his decision in *Doe v. University of Michigan* Judge Cohn quoted a passage from Bollinger's *The Tolerant Society* (1986) in which the author warns of the frailties of the judiciary in matters relating to freedom of expression. '[T]aking stock of the legal system's own limitations, we must realize that judges, being human, will not only make mistakes but will sometimes succumb to the pressures exerted by the government to allow restraints [on speech] that ought not to be allowed. To guard against these possibilities we must give judges as little room to maneuver as possible and, again, extend the boundary of the realm of protected speech into

the hinterlands of speech in order to minimize the potential harm from judicial miscalculation and misdeeds.' At 853. For Cohn, the Principle of Overbreadth constitutes just such a device for ensuring that judges have as little room to maneuver as possible. At 864. However, keeping Bollinger's words at the forefront of our minds it is difficult to avoid the conclusion that even US District Court judges are human and can make miscalculations in divining whether or not as applied a given speech code has swept within its ambit a substantial amount of protected speech. Indeed, it is quite possible that by striking down the University of Michigan Policy on Discriminatory Harassment Judge Cohn succumbed to the pressures exerted by the civil libertarian lobby to not allow any restraints on free speech.

37. First Amendment absolutists believe that the constitutional right to freedom of expression provides maximum predictability when it grants protection to all speech without qualification as to the importance of the public interest served by restricting it or as to the institutions or social practices which form its context and without exception as to the category of speech. It leaves legislators contemplating restrictions on freedom of expression in no uncertain terms as to what the constitution requires of them. With this clarity comes a lack of desirability, however, since few people wish to live in a society in which, say, there are not even time, place, and manner restrictions on speech. As a result, moderate absolutists take the view that the First Amendment ('Congress shall make no law . . . ') stands in need of interpretation like any other part of the constitution but that with the exception of certain kinds of unprotected speech the First Amendment requires that government shall make no law abridging protected speech. This view promises both predictability and desirability.
38. *Doe v. University of Michigan*, at 867.
39. Ibid.
40. Ibid.
41. At 862.
42. 477 US 57 (involving a case of sexual harassment).
43. In *Meritor Savings Bank v. Vinson* the Court recognized certain kinds of sexual harassment as a violation of Title VII of the Civil Rights Act of 1964. Of particular relevance are the guidelines on sexual harassment issued by the EEOC in 1980 as part of its enforcement of Title VII. These guidelines stated that certain conduct constitutes sexual harassment when it 'has the purpose or effect of unreasonably interfering with an individual's work performance or creating an intimidating, hostile, or offensive working environment.' s. 1604.11(a)(3) (Sexual Harassment) of Part 1604.11 (Guidelines on Discrimination Because of Sex), Chapter XIV (Equal Employment Opportunity Commission), Title 29 (Labor), Subtitle B (Regulations Relating to Labor) of the Code of Federal Regulations (CFR).
44. *Doe v. University of Michigan*, at 866–867.
45. *R. v. Keegstra*, at 860.
46. Of course, sometimes frank and insulting expressive acts occur within broader expressive acts that do constitute group defamation, but here the law bans the defamation not the frankness or the insult in isolation.
47. *Doe v. University of Michigan*, at 867.
48. In the words of Justice Souter in *Rosenberger v. Rectors and Visitors of University of Virginia* (1995) 515 US 819: 'It is precisely this element of taking sides in a public debate that identifies viewpoint discrimination and makes it the most pernicious of all distinctions based on content.' At 894–895.
49. For further discussion of, and potential challenges to, this assumption, however, compare Redish (1981) and Stone (1983).

50. Arguably both interpretations can claim a degree of support from the canonical statement of the doctrine of neutrality by Justice Marshall in *Police Department of the City of Chicago v. Mosley* (1972) 408 US 92: 'To permit the continued building of our politics and culture, and to assure self-fulfillment for each individual, our people are guaranteed the right to express any thought, free from government censorship. The essence of this forbidden censorship is content control. Any restriction on expressive activity because of its content would completely undercut the "profound national commitment to the principle that debate on public issues should be uninhibited, robust, and wide-open."' At 95–96.
51. For further analysis of this issue, compare those who regard the doctrine of neutrality as simply one standard or principle that must be considered in the light of others (e.g., Amar 1992; Lawrence 1992; Fiss 1996a) with those who insist that the Supreme Court's approach to neutrality aspires to be more rule-like, and not inappropriately so given the need for precision and predictability and for checks and balances on the tendency of the state to want to suppress problematic viewpoints, such as those which are expressed through racist speech (e.g., Strauss 1988; Kagan 1993). In addition to this, it has been suggested (Kretzmer 1987: 473–474) that there may be a greater need for precise rules in political contexts, such as in the US, where decision-making power, including over the enactment of speech-restricting laws/regulations/codes, is diffuse than where it is concentrated in one main legislative body.
52. *R.A.V. v. City of St. Paul*, at 391–392.
53. See, e.g., *Appleby and Others v. United Kingdom* (2003) No. 44306/98 (ECtHR, 6 May); *Mouvement Raelien Suisse v. Switzerland* (2012) No. 16354/06 (ECtHR, 13 Jul.).
54. *Handyside v. United Kingdom*, at para. 49.
55. *Soulas and others v. France*, at paras. 34–35.
56. *Balsytė-Lideikienė v. Lithuania*, at paras. 20–21.
57. *Féret v. Belgium*, at para. 61.
58. *Vejdeland and Others v. Sweden*, Concurring opinion of Judge Spielmann, at para. 5.
59. Canada is a different context again. Here some laws/regulations/codes that constrain uses of hate speech have been upheld by the Supreme Court and, more importantly, were not criticized by the Court for being, as they are, openly content and viewpoint selective. See, e.g., *R. v. Keegstra*; *Canada (Human Rights Commission) v. Taylor*.

# 10 Toward a Theory of Principled Compromise

Up to this point I have examined whether ten clusters of laws/regulations/codes that constrain uses of hate speech are either warranted or unwarranted based on a collection of key normative principles; each principle has been applied separately. To recap, these principles are the Harm Principle, the Principle of Health, the Principle of Autonomy, the Nuanced Principle of Autonomy, the Principle of Persuasion, the Principle of Security, the Principle of Non-Subordination, the Principle of Non-Oppression, the Principle of Human Dignity (Ch. 3); the Principle of Truth, the Nuanced Principle of Truth, the Principle of Knowledge, the Nuanced Principle of Knowledge, the Principle of Self-Realization, the Nuanced Principle of Self-Realization, the Principle of Human Excellence (Ch. 4); the Principle of Civic Dignity, the Principle of Assurance (Ch. 5); the Principle of Culture, the Nuanced Principle of Culture, the Principle of Recognition, the Principle of Intercultural Dialogue (Ch. 6); the Principle of Democratic Self-Government, the Principle of Democracy, the Nuanced Principle of Democracy, the Principle of Political Legitimacy (Ch. 7); the Principle of Rights-Based Balancing, the Principle of Interests-Based Balancing (Ch. 8); the Principle of Pressing Social Need, the Principle of Efficacy, the Precautionary Principle, the Principle of the Least Restrictive Alternative, the Principle of Narrow Tailoring, the Principle of Overbreadth, the Principle of Vagueness, the Principle of Neutrality (Ch. 9). This is, of course, a very long and diverse list. So it is now time to reflect more closely on those states of affair when a particular hate speech law is N-warranted by one or more principles on the list but at the same time N-unwarranted by one or more (different) principles. I take it as read that such states of affair necessitate judgments of overall warrant. But even if judgments of overall warrant are necessary, and even if making such judgments chimes with our ordinary moral experience of making all things considered judgments, the meaning of overall warrant is not self-evident and can be specified in different ways. The purpose of this chapter is to try to articulate and defend one possible conception: overall warrant as principled compromise. Before introducing that conception, however, I shall begin by discounting an alternative conception of overall warrant that appeals once again to the metaphor of balancing.

## 10.1 WHY OVERALL WARRANT SHOULD BE NEITHER ABOUT LEXICAL PRIORITIES AMONG PRINCIPLES NOR BALANCING BETWEEN PRINCIPLES

One way to think of the idea of overall warrant is in terms of a meta-level principle, the purpose of which is to arrange principles in an order of lexical priority. For example, some theorists believe that freedom to participate in the formation of democratic public opinion is not merely a normatively relevant feature; it is the decisive normatively relevant feature. Therefore, they would argue that the Principle of Democracy trumps other principles. It is not merely a principle of N-warrant; it is a principle of O-warrant. A lexically prior principle is one that must be satisfied before any other principle, such that no amount of satisfaction of other principles can compensate for a failure to satisfy it. It seems to me, however, that resolving dilemmas about hate speech law in fact comes down to numerous principles that together serve a plurality of normatively relevant features, where no one feature has absolute priority over the others. To steal a quote from Shiffrin, 'Isaiah Berlin, with his emphasis on the complexity of social reality and the necessity for tragic choices, explains First Amendment doctrine better than Jurgen Habermas, Professor James Weinstein, or Professor Robert Post' (Shiffrin [S.H.] 2011a: 560).

Of course, Weinstein and Post are not the only free speech scholars to proclaim a single sovereign value. Consider Dworkin's principal contribution to legal and political theory: namely, that whatever our disagreements we can at least be united around our acceptance of the abstract egalitarian principle that each citizen is owed equal concern and respect by his or her government. Taking this hedgehog's creed seriously (some people might argue) challenges Shiffrin's idea of tragic choices. For, the hedgehog's creed seems to suggest that a constructive interpretation of the egalitarian master value can tell us what we need to know about the contents and boundaries of our fundamental rights (i.e., where one right ends and another begins). After all, the abstract egalitarian principle is the foundation stone for Dworkin's own drawing of the boundaries of free speech via the respect owed to people's ethical independence (e.g., 1977: ch. 12; 1985: chs. 18–19; 1996: chs. 7–8; 2012: 342). However, the abstract nature of Dworkin's egalitarian principle means that it is a blank canvas onto which different people can project their own principled concerns. So, for example, in her discussion of campus speech codes Robin M. Hulshizer (1991) begins by quoting this principle but ends up drawing the opposite conclusion to Dworkin about what equal concern and respect mean vis-à-vis such codes. Hulshizer suggests that a campus speech code that forbids discriminatory harassment can be justified because '[b]ias-related verbal assaults undermine human dignity, which all people are entitled to enjoy as free, equal, and autonomous individuals' (Hulshizer 1991: 395). Yet Dworkin insists that the principle undergirds a fundamental right to freedom of expression that is violated by content-based campus speech codes (Dworkin 2009: vi). What this shows, I think, is that appealing to a grand ideal like Dworkin's abstract egalitarian principle is not a panacea for resolving complex disagreements over matters of principled concern (cf. Brown 2007).

Of course, trying to justify why one is more inclined toward value pluralism than value monism in debates over free speech is not easy—no more or less easy than trying to justify the reverse position. But I can at least offer four reasons that strike me as important. First, value pluralism reflects the collective wisdom and experience of a legion of lawmakers, judges, and legal scholars when confronted with dilemmas pertaining to freedom of expression and its limits. This is the experience that there is no decision that rational agents can take about such issues that does not violate or impose a cost to at least one fundamental right, vital interest, basic human good, or value as well as the experience of a residue of regret that attends any such decision. Second, value pluralism avoids a tendency within monist approaches to freedom of expression and its limits to mischaracterize or summarily dismiss other principles or values simply for the sake of ensuring that all relevant considerations can be fitted within the scheme of one lexically prior principle or value. Third, value pluralism provides a check against the possibility that any one principle or value will dominate public discourse and decision-making frameworks surrounding freedom of expression. The risk is that a dominant group in society will also dominate the articulation of the values and principles upon which matters of freedom of expression and its limits are determined. Fourth, value pluralism highlights an important subspecies of speech to which the question of freedom of expression must also be addressed: namely, the freedom to participate in meta-level debate about the principles and values that are important to determining whether or not restrictions on freedom of expression can be warranted. Fully embracing value monism may carry a danger, albeit a dim and distant danger perhaps, of shutting down that vibrant debate.

A slightly different way of thinking about the idea of overall warrant is in terms of a balancing act between principles. If a law can satisfy some principles but not others, if each principle can be met with degrees of success or failure, and if a little more success in satisfying one principle can be traded off against a little less success or failure in satisfying another, the challenge is to judge which outcome strikes a balance. This sort of approach is hinted at by Justice McLachlin of the Canadian Supreme Court, in her account of how the Oakes Test, which is a multipronged test incorporating several of the aforementioned principles, ought to be applied in concrete cases. 'The result in a particular case will depend on weighing the significance of the infringement on freedom of expression represented by the law in question, against the importance of the countervailing objectives, the likelihood the law will achieve those objectives, and the proportionality of the scope of the law to those objectives.'[1]

This approach presupposes the possibility of meaningful judgments to the effect that a particular law/regulation/code is warranted with respect to *all* the principles at stake because it strikes a reasonable balance between those principles. This in turn requires an explanation of how trade-offs can be made between the various principles and the values they safeguard or serve. One potential solution is to appeal to a third value that contains an inbuilt exchange rate mechanism between values. Ruth Chang (1997, 2004a, 2004b) calls this a 'covering', 'comprehensive', or 'nameless' value. According to Change, it may be possible to recast otherwise eclectic values as 'being parts of' or 'contributing constitutively to' a covering value (e.g., Chang 2004a: 119; 2004b: 20n.1). It is part of the essential nature of a covering value that it can 'determine' a 'rational resolution' to questions about appropriate trade-offs between the different values of which it is composed (2004a: 119–120). She cites the example of a keen athlete who is about to win a race when he or she sees a drowning stranger in a pond and nobody else in a position to save the victim. Stopping to save the drowning stranger is accorded high value at the bar of moral value, whereas running on to victory is assigned high value on an index of prudential value. According to Chang, 'it seems clear that the reason to save the stranger is weightier than the reason to carry on in the race' (126). She explains this intuition by positing the existence of a covering value, *prumorality* (125). Now Chang does not address the principles and values discussed in this book, but it is not difficult to extrapolate what her approach might say. If agents share credible intuitions about the right solutions to legal dilemmas in cases involving hate speech, such as when one possible decision is supported by principles and values of autonomy, self-realization, and democratic self-government, for example, and the opposite decision is supported by principles and values of security, non-subordination, and human dignity, then we have ample reason to believe that there is a covering value involved. This may be a value for which we do not yet have a name (hence the term 'nameless value'), but we can always give it a name if needs be, say, *warrantivity*.

However, this approach has two, in my view, fatal flaws. First, the covering value is said to determine the fact that combinations of a little less here and a little more there on one side of the balancing scales outweighs a little more here and a little less there on the other side. Yet how this is done is not fully accounted for. In other words, the covering value explains only the outcomes and not the nuts and bolts of the processes. Chang offers the metaphor of certain types of jigsaw puzzle. 'When values come together in virtue of a "picture" that relates them, they form a more comprehensive value, and it is in virtue of this "picture" that they are normatively related as they are' (Chang 2004b: 17). But to say that basic values are related to one another something like the way pieces of a jigsaw puzzle are put together by a unifying picture raises as many questions as it answers. What is the picture that relates the values implicated in principled dilemmas about freedom of expression and hate speech law? The lack of a clear account of trade-offs may be acceptable in some instances, such as when private individuals are trying to understand their own judgments. However, at the level of public officials it may be disadvantageous if the mechanics of trading off remain mysterious and inexplicable. It bears repeating that we are talking here of supreme court justices, say, deliberating over the potentially divisive and destabilizing issue of how institutional authorities should respond to the issue of hate speech. In a situation where certain groups of people already feel marginalized and alienated in society, how could they have confidence in the fairness of a review court decision to deny them protection against hate speech, and in the legitimacy of the judicial system that produced that decision, if they are informed that the comprehensive value upon which the decision to deny them protection was based is a nameless black box that cannot be opened? And if these groups of people lack confidence in key legal decisions, and in the legal system itself, what adverse implications might this have for the stability of the legal system over time?[2]

Second, the strong intuitions or rational resolutions that are required to posit the existence of nameless values might be obvious in cases of morality and prudence, such as in the case of the runner and the drowning stranger, but things may be different on the terrain of free speech. Perhaps Chang is right to assume that virtually everyone shares the intuition that the runner should sacrifice personal glory in order to save a life. Yet this unanimity is scarcely found when it comes to hate speech law. Few legislatures and supreme courts around the world have tended to reach unanimous decisions about hate speech law. If they did, this book might be redundant. Of course, I do not mean to say that there is never unanimity in hate speech cases. In *Saskatchewan (Human Rights Commission) v. Whatcott*, for example, a unanimous Canadian Supreme Court ruled that the strand of s. 14(1)(b) of the Saskatchewan Human Rights Code that prohibits any representation that 'ridicules, belittles or otherwise affronts the dignity of any person or class of persons on the basis of a prohibited ground' is not rationally connected to a pressing and substantial objective and, even if it were, is not a minimal impairment on people's freedom, in the sense of not being the least restrictive alternative, and is overbroad, in the sense of sweeping up protected as well as unprotected speech. In Ch. 3 [3.6] I tried to cast doubt on the first part of the Court's reasoning, relating to the core objectives of the Code. Notwithstanding this, the point I wish to make here is that the Court did not regard itself as being in the position of having to weigh a prohibition that was N-warranted based on some principles but N-unwarranted based on other principles. On the contrary, it held that the prohibition was N-unwarranted on each of the principles that it considered to be relevant. Therefore, even though the Court's decision was unanimous, and despite the fact that the Court invoked a principle for balancing rights and interests (Is the speech restriction rationally connected to a pressing and substantial objective?), the Court's decision did not actually involve the balancing of *principles*.

Finally, I believe that it is a defining feature of judgments of overall warrant that once the judgment is made there still remains a residue of regret for those principles that had to be forsaken. The tragedy of the situation is that one cannot find any solution to the question of hate speech law that fully satisfies all key normative principles.[3] However, if judgments of overall warrant are boiled down to assessments of the covering value of warrantivity, then it effectively becomes the all-important or supreme value to which all other values must be related and deferred. So provided that given legislative and judicial decisions fully satisfy the value of warrantivity, what could there be to regret? To use Chang's own metaphor, so long as the pieces of the jigsaw puzzle are put in the right places by dint of a picture that relates them together, how could one be regretful if there ends up being more red pieces than blue pieces? So it seems that to embrace the framework of balancing principles could be to lose an important and distinctive feature of judgments of overall warrant.

That overall warrant is not a special case of balancing does not mean, however, that all principles considered judgments are impossible or meaningless. There are other ways to understand the nature of such judgments. Consider the words of Judge Learned Hand.

> Values are incommensurable. You can get a solution also by a compromise, or call it what you will. It must be one that people won't complain of too much; but you cannot expect any more objective measure. (cited in Posner 1990: 129n.10)

Following this suggestion, in the next section I argue that it is more useful to think of overall warrant as an instance of the general practice of compromise.

## 10.2  OVERALL WARRANT AS COMPROMISE OVER PRINCIPLES

Questions of compromise typically come to the fore when no decision can be made that simultaneously honors all of the key normative principles in play. In the case of hate speech, this is summed up in the title of Claudia Haupt's article 'Regulating Hate Speech—Damned if You Do and Damned if You Don't' (2005). The idea of reaching compromises over matters of principled concern has not gone unnoticed by free speech scholars. S. Douglas Murray, for example, proposes 'a compromise solution' to the dilemmas posed by campus speech codes and cross burning statutes: namely, to replace content-restricting hate speech law with penalty-enhancement statutes and regulations covering cases when courts or disciplinary panels have found persons guilty of offenses relating to trespass, damage to property, threats of violence, or harassment, and where the offending was aggravated by bias or a discriminatory motivation (Murray 1997: 279–280). Or consider Shiffrin's vision of the US Supreme Court as nine justices—or 'politicians wearing black robes'—'negotiating to forge compromises' in First Amendment cases (Shiffrin [S.H.] 2011a: 560). Shiffrin is not alone in pointing out the synergies between legal and political compromise. According to Posner, for instance, '[c]ompromise is the essence of democratic politics and hence a sensible approach to dealing with indeterminate legal questions charged with political passion' (Posner 2008: 323). The idea of compromise also crops up in historical accounts of how particular US Supreme Court justices have operated in pursuit of what they regard as just ends. A recent biography of Justice Brennan, for instance, makes much of his readiness to seek, and considerable skill in brokering, compromises among his fellow justices over the scope and application of legal principles in order to hold together majority decisions and opinions (Stern and Wermiel 2010: 409).[4]

However, the particular role that I have in mind for the idea compromise has less to do with accurately *describing* or *explaining* the behavior of supreme court justices and more to do with *theorizing* the concept of overall warrant. I do nevertheless think that the theory of compromise that I will set out can be put to work in *critically reimagining* what it is that supreme court justices could be doing both hypothetically and ideally. My claim is that overall warrant should be theorized as a social practice of compromise over principles and, moreover, that the conduct of compromisers within this social practice is at its best when it is *principled*, which is to say, when it lives up to certain moral ideals or virtues of conduct. I shall say more about these moral ideals or virtues of conduct later [10.6].

Even though my main focus is the concept of overall warrant rather than judicial conduct *per se*, I do take heart from the fact that reaching a compromise over principles is something that judges have on occasion explicitly acknowledged as their guiding light. So, for example, in *Edmonton Journal v. Alberta (Attorney General)* [1989][5] Justice Wilson of the Canadian Supreme Court defended a contextualist approach to the application of the *Canadian Charter of Rights and Freedoms* partly on the grounds that '[i]t seems to be more sensitive to the reality of the dilemma posed by the particular facts and therefore more conducive to finding a fair and just compromise between the two competing values under s. 1.'[6] Plus I reject the distinction that Phillip E. Johnson draws between settling First Amendment disputes 'on the basis of some abstract legal principle' and settling such disputes 'on the give-and-take of legislative compromise' (Johnson 1984: 830). This is a false distinction since it ignores a third possibility: both courts and legislatures settling disputes on the basis of compromises between abstract legal principles and various other sorts of principles, including but not limited to principles of basic morality, civic morality, intercultural morality, and political morality. Johnson's rationale for drawing his distinction is as follows: 'The very act of deciding a dispute on the basis of some abstract legal principle rather than on the give-and-take of legislative compromise tends to identify more clearly one side as the winner and the other side as the loser, with the result of increasing the bitterness of the loser' (ibid.). But, he continues: 'That consideration does not necessarily mean that the Court has acted wrongly because justice, not domestic peace, is the primary aim of constitutional adjudication' (831). However, on the approach that I am advocating, compromise need not be antithetical to justice and may be constitutive of it. My reason for saying this is quite simply that it is a vital ingredient of many legal systems that we may plausibly regard as being just that judges have the prerogative to arrive at compromises over matters of principled concern. Consequently, so long as we continue to think that institutions that embrace this judicial prerogative are more not less just, we have a *prima facie* reason to look upon the results of these compromises as bearing the quality of justice (cf. Jones and O'Flynn 2013: 128).[7]

But what reason is there to think that judicial compromises can be just? Surely without such a reason any endorsement of that practice will be left in a rumpled state. After all, John Rawls famously denounces the practice of 'compromise compelled by circumstances' (Rawls 1996: 169–171), which he equates with mere *modus vivendi* or strategic agreement (147–148). Strategic agreement is the balance of opposing forces (including opposing aims and interests), which holds only so long as it is not within the power of one of the parties to achieve something better for themselves.[8] Nevertheless, compromise compelled by circumstance is by no means the only possible form of compromise. Later in this chapter [10.6] I appeal to a distinction that several philosophers draw between 'pragmatic' or 'tactical compromise' and 'principled compromise.' Principled compromise, as I shall argue, is governed by ideals such as reciprocity, equality, and mutual respect. These will be explained in detail later, but one important aspect is a moral duty on the part of each compromiser to recognize the rights of the other compromisers.

In addition to these preliminary remarks about how the practice of compromise can be just, I also happen to think that it would be churlish to ignore the instrumental value of the practice of judicial compromise, not least in terms of the stability of the entire judicial system over time. In my discussion of the balance conception of overall warrant I hypothesized that the judicial system could be destabilizing if certain groups, who already feel marginalized and alienated by mainstream society, were informed that the value upon which the decision to deny them protection against hate speech was based is a nameless value. Potentially such groups could feel greater confidence in the fairness of judicial decisions, and in legitimacy of the legal system itself, or are less likely to lose that confidence, if they are made aware that the decision was the result of a carefully crafted compromise between two sides, each defending its position as a matter of principle but each prepared to compromise over its principles. It is interesting to note that one of the justified grounds for restricting freedom of expression articulated in Art. 10(2) of the ECHR is 'maintaining the authority and impartiality of the judiciary.' Perhaps something similar can be said for why judicial compromise is necessary in diverse and often fractious societies (cf. Jones and O'Flynn 2013: 129).

Given the fact that many different kinds of compromise are possible, which kinds of compromise are most relevant for dilemmas surrounding hate speech law? In the following pair of sections I discuss two kinds of compromise distinguished by Chiara Lepora (2012).[9] Both kinds seem relevant to forging compromises over matters of principled concern in hate speech cases, but in interestingly different ways.

## 10.3 CONJUNCTION COMPROMISE

The first kind of compromise, *conjunction compromise*, has to do with reaching a compromise by conjoining together a subset of principles taken from two or more sets of either opposing or contrasting principles, where 'opposing' means 'that for every principle in one set there is some principle in the other set such that both principles cannot simultaneously be right' (Lepora 2012: 10n.26), and 'contrasting' means that for every principle in one set there is some principle in the other set such that in a particular context it is not feasible to realize both fully.[10] 'Suppose Agent 5 holds principles {O, P, Q, R}, and Agent 6 holds principles {not-O, not-P, not-Q, not-R}' (10). A conjunction compromise 'may maintain {O, P, not-Q, not-R} as principles for both Agent 5 and Agent 6 to pursue (or anyway allow to be pursued by the other)' (11). This kind of compromise purports to capture a typical ingredient of many forms of compromise: '[Y]ou surrender *one* part of what you want in order to get some *other* part of what you want' (Goodin 2012: 52).

What would conjunction compromise look like for principled arguments about hate speech law? Suppose a group of legislators or a group of supreme court justices are considering a suite of hate speech laws, including a law that bans group defamation (*sensu stricto*) and a law that prohibits the public expression of hatred, such as through the use of insults, slurs, or derogatory epithets or through the dissemination of ideas based on the inferiority of protected groups. Suppose also the legislators or judges are divided evenly down the middle. Some are staunch defenders of free speech and oppose both laws based on a set of four principles that they hold. The remainder support both laws based on a second set of four principles that they hold and that are opposing or contrasting to the first set of principles. A conjunction compromise could emerge that sees the legislators or judges agreeing to a third set of principles that conjoins two principles from the first set and two from the second set. Based on this, they could agree to enact the law banning group defamation (*sensu stricto*) but not the law prohibiting the public expression of hatred. The compromise might be reached because it is attractive and unattractive to each side in equal measure: because each side surrenders two principles in order to retain two principles, and each side would rather have the outcome they favor but at the same time would also rather accept the compromise outcome than be forced to accept the preferred outcome of the other side.

One potential benefit of thinking about hate speech law in terms of compromise is that it provides a response to the following objection that has been leveled at countries that embrace hate speech laws. Hate speech law is often justified by the lights of the Principle of Security, the Principle of Non-Oppression, or the Principle of Non-Subordination. But hate speech is by far from the only category of speech that has the tendency to cause or even enact the evils of insecurity, oppression, or subordination. As Post puts it, '[s]ober, rational communication, communication that conforms to the "decencies of controversy", is extremely unlikely to be suppressed as hate speech, even if it manifestly has the tendency to cause discrimination' (Post 2009: 135). Hate speech laws, therefore, 'are not driven as much by the need to eliminate the objective harms of discrimination as by the more urgent need to suppress speech that violates social norms of respect' (ibid.). But (so the objection runs) this suppression is a threat to free participation in the formation of democratic public opinion (136). As explained in Ch. 2 [2.3], however, some countries possess laws/regulations/codes that disallow the public expression of hatred toward members of groups or classes of persons identified by certain ascriptive characteristics, including publicly disseminating ideas based on the inferiority of such persons. And, pace Post, potentially even sober, rational communication could be suppressed as hate speech in such countries. More importantly, it can be argued that the reason why some societies do not and other societies do enact laws/regulations/codes that disallow the public expression of hatred is because of the different configurations of key normative principles, or conjunction compromises, which they arrive at. It is not necessarily a matter of whether or not societies feel the need to legally enforce social norms of respect or civility.

Notwithstanding all this, I believe that when faced with dilemmas about hate speech law, it is likely that in some instances, perhaps many instances, legislators and judges will be disinclined to conjoin principles from competing sets of principles, leaving the original principles largely intact. Instead, they may be more inclined to create new and more nuanced principles that they substitute for the original principles. This means that compromise is situated around those new principles. It is to this other kind of compromise that I now turn. I wish to make it clear at this stage, however, that I appeal to this other kind of compromise not to show that conjunction compromise is inherently flawed but as a feasible alternative in some cases.

## 10.4 SUBSTITUTION COMPROMISE

A second kind of compromise, *substitution compromise*, involves substituting two or more opposing or contrasting principles with a third principle that speaks to the concerns of the original principles and is influenced by the original principles but which is non-identical with either. Lepora again: '[I] magine that Agent 1 holds principles {A, B, C, D}, Agent 2 holds principles {E, F, G, H}, and those sets of principles are in conflict with (either in opposition to or incompatible with) one another' (Lepora 2012: 8).

'A substitution compromise requires both agents to abandon pursuit of their entire set of initial principles, and to promise to pursue another principle {X} that both Agent 1 and Agent 2 will agree to act upon instead' (ibid.). This kind of compromise captures the thought that in many compromise situations neither side retains the principles that they believe are strictly correct, but both sides nevertheless end up with a principle they can live with.

In Germany, for example, courts have sometimes pursued 'practical concordance' (*Praktische Konkordanz*) in dealing with conflicting constitutional rights or principles. Practical concordance is not about finding a point of balance between conflicting rights or principles, as though they can be traded off against each other. Rather, the method preserves the conflict but seeks to answer it by finding an alternative right or principle upon which parties to the original conflict can agree (e.g., Tulkens 2010: 129–130; cf. Eberle 2002: 106). It has been argued that in *Case of Kruzifix-Urteil* (1987),[11] which was not a hate speech case, the Federal Constitutional Court of Germany reached a practical concordance by substituting opposing or contrasting principles around the displaying of religious symbols in schools with a more nuanced principle: namely, that it is appropriate for schools to display crucifixes and that crucifixes should be removed from classrooms only in the exceptional circumstances that students object to their presence (Kommers and Miller 2012: 68).

Of course, even if substitution compromise is appropriate for disputes over religious symbols in schools, it does not necessarily follow that it is appropriate in free speech cases. After all, the ideal of practical concordance was *not* summoned up by the Federal Constitutional Court of Germany in *Case of National Democratic Party of Germany (or 'Auschwitz Lie')*, a high-profile Holocaust denial case. On the contrary, the Court simply gave lexical priority to the protection of human dignity over the protection of free speech. In essence, it held that statements denying the racially motivated extermination of Jews under the Nazi regime qualify as an attack on the entitlement to human dignity of Jews living today and that the prohibition of such statements is permissible under German constitutional law given the foremost position of the right to human dignity in the German constitution.

Nevertheless, the practices of German courts need not be representative of the approaches that courts could take in dealing with hate speech cases. In the next section, therefore, I want to explore what can be said on behalf of substitution compromise as a way of theorizing judicial judgments of overall warrant in hate speech cases. In order to do this I shall present a detailed illustration that focuses on the Principle of Neutrality. The illustration begins at an abstract level but then looks at two specific cases from the US Supreme Court. At first glance, it might seem that substitution compromise plays little role in the Court's analysis, but I shall try to show that, at least in these two cases, the Court could have engaged in such compromise.

## 10.5 A DETAILED ILLUSTRATION: THE PRINCIPLE OF NEUTRALITY

While the illustration I have in mind does not cover all of the principles discussed so far, and in that sense is not a complete illustration of judgments of overall warrant, it does, I hope, provide a more detailed indication of the role that compromise could play in such judgments by focusing on compromise among particular principles. Overall compromise is likely to depend on iterations of such compromises until all principles have been taken into account.

As explained in Ch. 9 [9.5], the Principle of Neutrality flows from the conviction that the state should not be permitted to restrict speech simply because of its content, including its message, its ideas, its subject matter, its narrative, or, quite simply, what a speaker is saying, and that the state should certainly not be permitted to restrict speech because the state just so happens to favor one particular viewpoint in a debate, or one particular message, idea, narrative, or even one sort of speaker. Nevertheless, I am interested in the fault line that exists between this and other normative principles. On the one hand, the Principle of Neutrality, along with the more fundamental normative principles on which it is grounded—including but not limited to the Principle of Autonomy, the Principle of Truth, the Principle of Knowledge, the Principle of Self-Realization, the Principle of Democracy, and the Principle of Legitimacy—indicates that any hate speech law that involves content or viewpoint discrimination is N-unwarranted. On the other hand, a range of countervailing principles—including but not limited to the Principle of Health, the Nuanced Principle of Autonomy, the Principle of Security, the Principle of Non-Oppression, the Principle of Non-Subordination, the Nuanced Principle of Self-Realization, the Principle of Human Excellence, the Principle of Civic Dignity, the Principle of Recognition, and the Nuanced Principle of Democracy—tend to suggest instead that a hate speech law can be N-warranted even if it does involve content or viewpoint discrimination.

Now it is safe to say that in the context of First Amendment jurisprudence, applying the Principle of Neutrality to hate speech law has tended to be devastating for the latter. US courts have frequently ruled that hate speech law violates the Principle of Neutrality because it differentiates between racist messages and viewpoints, say, and other sorts of messages and viewpoints. However, as I shall try to show in a moment, these decisions have not always been unanimous and in some cases, I believe, could have been the subject of substitution compromises. The particular substitution compromises I have in mind consist in the substitution of the Principle of Neutrality with what I shall call the Nuanced Principle of Neutrality, according to which legalistic constraints on speech or expression are (N-/O-)unwarranted if they involve significant content or viewpoint discrimination, except where the selection of particular content or viewpoints for special constraint is supported by valid bases. I have added both 'N-' and 'O-' to signify the fact that although nuanced principles can involve narrow warrant and, therefore, can be overridden or trumped by yet further principles, in some instances they involve or are the results of judgments of overall warrant.

But before turning to legal cases, I need first to address the place of the Nuanced Principle of Neutrality in the Anglo-American literature on free speech. It is certainly true that several writers in this tradition endorse versions of the Nuanced Principle of Neutrality. It is also the case that some appear to endorse this derivative principle because of their commitment to a single, more fundamental principle—for example, a principle of pluralistic perfectionism (e.g., George 1993: 198–199) or a principle of democratic self-government (e.g., Fiss 1986: 1415–1421; 1996a: 21). However, others look upon the adoption of the Nuanced Principle of Neutrality slightly differently. To take one example, Cohen tentatively endorses a version of this principle because it represents one possible solution to what he calls a 'grim standoff between concerns about expressive liberty and concerns about equality' (Cohen [Joshua] 1993: 263). The motivating thought is that 'some kinds of content regulation seem intuitively less troubling' (214). Thus, according to Cohen, the regulation of 'hateful fighting words' may be a permissible targeting of a subcategory of fighting words because of the 'very great harm' associated with that sort of speech, including 'the role of such words in sustaining racial division and preserving racial inequality' (257). I suggest that Cohen's approach to free speech could be interpreted *as though* he were seeking to reach a compromise between, on the one side, a set of liberty-centered principles that support a blanket embargo on laws involving content and viewpoint discrimination and, on the other side, a set of equality-centered principles that pay little or no head to concerns about content and viewpoint discrimination. The compromise is constituted by a version of the Nuanced Principle of Neutrality. Of course, that is not the end of the story, as even this nuanced principle will need to be considered in the light of other legal principles that have to do with the practicalities of regulating speech, not the least of which are efficacy, minimal impairment, and unforeseen consequences (262). And so the grim standoff has deeper layers.

Moving on from the academic literature, I now want to address a pair of US legal cases, both dealing with cross burning: *R.A.V. v. City of St. Paul* and *Virginia v. Black*. The rationale for exploring these cases is not merely to illustrate what substitutive compromise might look like in practice but also to underscore the fact that such compromise is a dynamic or iterative practice. This means, among other things, that even once a compromise has been reached by substituting one principle with a more nuanced principle, there often remains a need for further substitutions, such as involving the substitution of one reading of the nuanced principle with another reading in order to sustain or carry through the initial compromise in the face of conflicting interpretations. This need arises most clearly when the nuanced principle is implicated in a case before a supreme court and there is disagreement among the justices as to the right way to read the nuanced principle both in light of previous cases and in the context of the case at issue.

## R.A.V. v. City of St. Paul

In his majority opinion in *R.A.V. v. City of St. Paul*, Justice Scalia suggested that the Supreme Court had in its previous decisions replaced an uncompromising approach to content and viewpoint neutrality with a more nuanced approach. Within my proposed conceptual framework this means that the Court had substituted the Principle of Neutrality with the Nuanced Principle of Neutrality. In Justice Scalia's eyes, the Court had made it quite clear that it *is* permissible for the state to draw distinctions between unprotected speech provided that it does so on the strength of certain 'valid bases.' Nevertheless, he opined that none of the valid bases were applicable to the City of St. Paul Bias-Motivated Crime Ordinance, nor to the particular instance of cross burning at issue in the case. In their concurring opinions, however, both Justice White and Justice Stevens rejected that assumption. It is worth running through these disagreements in a little more detail because they shed light on the dynamic nature of substitution compromise.

Writing for the majority Justice Scalia articulated the first valid basis thusly:

> When the basis for the content discrimination consists entirely of the very reason the entire class of speech at issue is proscribable, no significant danger of idea or viewpoint discrimination exists. Such a reason, having been adjudged neutral enough to support exclusion of the entire class of speech from First Amendment protection, is also neutral enough to form the basis of distinction within the class. To illustrate: A State might choose to prohibit only that obscenity which is the most patently offensive in its prurience—i.e., that which involves the most lascivious displays of sexual activity. But it may not prohibit, for example, only that obscenity which includes offensive political messages. [. . .] And the Federal Government can criminalize only those threats of violence that are directed against the President, see 18 US C. §871—since the reasons why threats of violence are outside the First Amendment (protecting individuals from the fear of violence, from the disruption that fear engenders, and from the possibility that the threatened violence will occur) have special force when applied to the person of the President.[12]

He then went on to argue that the content discrimination reflected in the St. Paul ordinance 'assuredly does not fall within' the first exception.[13]

> As explained earlier [. . .] the reason why fighting words are categorically excluded from the protection of the First Amendment is not that their content communicates any particular idea, but that their content embodies a particularly intolerable (and socially unnecessary) *mode* of expressing *whatever* idea the speaker wishes to convey. St. Paul has not singled out an especially offensive mode of expression—it has not, for

example, selected for prohibition only those fighting words that communicate ideas in a threatening (as opposed to a merely obnoxious) manner. Rather, it has proscribed fighting words of whatever manner that communicate messages of racial, gender, or religious intolerance. Selectivity of this sort creates the possibility that the city is seeking to handicap the expression of particular ideas.[14]

In response to this, however, Justice White insisted that 'the majority confuses the issue.'[15] According to White, 'the St. Paul ordinance has not singled out a particularly objectionable mode of communication.'[16] Rather it has singled out a particularly objectionable message. Moreover, this singling out bespeaks the reason why the general class of fighting words is proscribable. 'A prohibition on fighting words,' claims White, 'is a ban on a class of speech that conveys an overriding message of personal injury and imminent violence [. . .], a message that is at its ugliest when directed against groups that have long been the targets of discrimination.'[17] In other words, if the operative reason why fighting words are unprotected speech is because of the message they convey, as in, their *locutionary force*, then in fact 'the ordinance falls within the first exception to the majority's theory.'[18]

I believe that the Nuanced Principle of Neutrality can itself be viewed as the product of a previous substitution compromise involving a conflict between the Principle of Neutrality and other key normative principles that N-warrant the regulation of racist fighting words, such as the Nuanced Principle of Autonomy and the Principle of Security. Furthermore, I believe that the disagreement between Justice Scalia and Justice White can be imaginatively reconstructed as the first stages in the process of forging a secondary substitution compromise over the correct reading of the Nuanced Principle of Neutrality. Under the terms of this reconstruction, we have a conflict between Justice Scalia, who favored what I shall call the Narrow Reading of the Nuanced Principle of Neutrality, and Justice White, who preferred the Broad Reading of the Nuanced Principled of Neutrality. The Narrow Reading focuses on the mode of expression and regards the St. Paul ordinance as falling outside the coverage of the Nuanced Principle of Neutrality, whereas the Broad Reading concentrates on the content of the message and sees the St. Paul ordinance as falling within that Principle. Crucially, however, I believe that they *could have* reached a substitution compromise in which both the Narrow and the Broad Readings are substituted with a third, Middling Reading. The basis for this new reading might have been that neither Justice Scalia nor Justice White quite hit the mark in their understanding of the fighting words doctrine. Another justice could have pointed out that in the canonical statement of the doctrine in *Chaplinsky v. State of New Hampshire*, a key reason that is implied about why fighting words are proscribable is because of what speakers *do* with these words—because of the *illocutionary acts* that speakers perform when they utter fighting words in given contexts. In short, these are words 'which by their very utterance inflict injury or tend to incite an immediate breach of the peace.'[19] The illocutionary acts implied in this definition are *injuring* or *provoking*. Accordingly, a more faithful account of whether or not the St. Paul ordinance falls within the first valid basis for departing from content or viewpoint neutrality must examine more closely the essential features of the relevant illocutionary acts and how instances of racist fighting words relate to those features. According to the Middling Reading of the Nuanced Principle of Neutrality, the operative question is whether or not racist fighting words constitute a particularly extreme mode of *doing* that which the fighting words doctrine is designed to capture, to wit, *injuring* or *provoking*. If the answer to that question is affirmative, then the Court could have had sufficient grounds to believe that the content discrimination reflected in the St. Paul ordinance falls within the relevant exception to neutrality. This is because the reason for banning racist fighting words was a special case of the reason for proscribing fighting words in general.

In my view, the disagreements that emerged with respect to a second valid basis for departing from the Principle of Neutrality were also amenable to substitution compromise. Justice Scalia stated that '[a]nother valid basis for according differential treatment to even a content-defined subclass of proscribable speech is that the subclass happens to be associated with particular "secondary effects" of the speech, so that the regulation is "justified without reference to the content of the . . . speech."'[20] He reasoned that the secondary effects at issue in the St. Paul ordinance, not least of which are the emotional injuries of hate speech, are not qualitatively different from injuries caused by other sorts of fighting words and so the focus on racist fighting words is illegitimate.[21] If two people experience the same degree of emotional distress and the same extent of psychological and physiological damage, why does it matter if some experience these effects as a result of racist fighting words while others from other sorts of fighting words? On the other side, Justice Stevens insisted that the secondary effects doctrine is eminently suitable for racist fighting words. As he put it, 'St. Paul has determined—reasonably in my judgment—that fighting-word injuries "based on race, color, creed, religion or gender" are qualitatively different and more severe than fighting-word injuries based on other characteristics.'[22] In this regard Justice Stevens was expressing a view that had already been articulated by some legal scholars (e.g., Kretzmer 1987: 458; Lawrence 1990: 458–459) and that was subsequently defended by several more (e.g., Amar 1992: 125–126; Cohen [Joshua] 1993: 255–256; Heyman 2002: 690–691, 713–714; 2008: 273n.26). What we have is a disagreement over the correct reading of the relevant valid basis for exception, a disagreement that arguably has its origins in the deeper conflict between the Principle of Neutrality and the Principle of Health. Justice Scalia's Narrow Reading is something like this: racist fighting words *may not* be treated as falling under the secondary effects exception because the injuries that can be caused by racist fighting words are *generic*. Justice Stevens' Broad Reading is this: racist fighting words *may* be treated as falling under the secondary effects exception because the injuries that can be caused by racist fighting words are *sui generis*. I propose a Middling Reading: racist fighting words *may* be treated as falling under the secondary effects exception because even though the injuries that can be caused by racist fighting words are generic, the *risk* of injuries is *far greater* in the case of racist fighting words than in the case of other sorts of fighting words given the background conditions of racist discrimination and oppression in which racist fighting words operate (both historic and current). This is a substitution compromise because it replaces both existing readings with a third reading, which accepts the truth of Justice Scalia's observations about the generic nature of the injuries yet leaves intact the force of Justice Stevens' contextual insights about the particular risk of racist fighting words.

I would suggest that a similar substitution compromise could have been reached in relation to the other sort of secondary effect at issue, breach of the peace. According to the Narrow Reading: racist fighting words do *not* fall under the exception because it is not the case that *only* racist fighting words would cause an immediate breach of the peace. On the Broad Reading: racist fighting words *do* fall under the exception by virtue of the fact that the risk of breach of the peace associated with racist fighting words is greater than that associated with *some* other fighting words. A substitution compromise might be reached on this Middling Reading: racist fighting words *do* fall under the exception by virtue of the fact that the risk of breach of the peace associated with racist fighting words is greater than that associated with *most* other types of fighting words. I do not pretend that this substitution compromise is impeccable, merely that it represents one solution to the impasse.

However, the issue of secondary effects creates yet another possible line of attack against the St. Paul ordinance that cannot be ignored. No compromise worth having is easily won. A staunch defender of the original Principle of Neutrality could choose this moment to protest against the Nuanced Principle of Neutrality itself. He or she might argue that to focus on the secondary effects of hate speech is to emphasize the connection between the ideational content of certain speech and the ensuing effects, and that as a result it is almost inevitable that legislators will be attuned to the ideational content itself. So the threat persists that the state will seek to ban certain content by the back door. Heidi Kitrosser puts the worry in the following terms. 'In the context of unprotected speech, the fact that legislatures might purportedly wish to target secondary effects does not suffice to cure containment-based concerns regarding seemingly superfluous or otherwise suspicious legislation' (Kitrosser 2005: 890). The danger persists that legislatures will use secondary effects as an excuse 'to hone in solely on the most unpopular forms of unprotected speech' (848). 'By so acting, legislatures may skew public discourse, cause intrinsic harms to speakers, and cause intrinsic social harms borne of legislative bad faith' (ibid.). This being the case, it scarcely seems likely that someone who is committed to the Principle of Neutrality will accept a substitution compromise in the form the Nuanced Principle of Neutrality, which so flagrantly violates the spirit of the original principle.

Even so, someone wanting to broker a compromise could delicately insist that the danger of back-door suppression of ideas or ideational content recedes as the true extent of secondary effects is uncovered. The greater the magnitude and severity of the secondary effects associated with particular subcategories of unprotected speech, the harder it becomes to impugn the intentions of the state in seeking to legislate against those effects, and therefore the harder it becomes to cling onto the Principle of Neutrality. This seems especially true given the fact that these are subcategories of unprotected speech (cf. Heyman 2002). In addition to this, advocates of the Nuanced Principle of Neutrality could argue that the valid bases for permitting content discrimination are not exhausted by secondary effects, and that once the full extent of valid bases is recognized, the proposed substitution compromise becomes almost irresistible, even taking into account Kitrosser's fears.

Building on this last insight, another exception to the Principle of Neutrality mooted by Justice Scalia in *R.A.V. v. City of St. Paul* was that 'since words can in some circumstances violate laws directed not against speech but against conduct (a law against treason, for example, is violated by telling the enemy the Nation's defense secrets), a particular content-based subcategory of a proscribable class of speech can be swept up incidentally within the reach of a statute directed at conduct rather than speech.'[23] 'Thus, for example, sexually derogatory "fighting words," among other words, may produce a violation of Title VII's general prohibition against sexual discrimination in employment practices.'[24] Once again Justice Scalia felt compelled to exclude cross burning from the mooted exception, insisting that the St. Paul ordinance *was* directed against speech. In contrast, Justice White opined that it would not be too difficult to bring the St. Paul ordinance under the general class of laws against discrimination or discriminatory harassment.[25] Justice White is not alone in holding this view. According to Guy-Uriel Charles, for example, 'it is not clear why a statute that targets sex-based "hate speech" in the workplace is directed at conduct but not speech, whereas a statute targeting race-based "hate speech" is directed at speech but not conduct' (Charles 2005: 595). Charles has in mind the pertinent fact that the St. Paul ordinance prohibits cross burning, a type of conduct. So whereas other permissible laws incidentally involve content-based restrictions in the course of proscribing discriminatory harassment in the workplace, the St. Paul ordinance could be thought to incidentally involve content-based restrictions in the course of proscribing discriminatory harassment outside of the workplace.

Maybe the list of relevant exceptions need not be limited to illegal acts of discriminatory harassment. In Ch. 3 [3.5] I discussed arguments to the effect that some uses of hate speech constitute illegal acts of pure discrimination. Recall McGowan's example of the elderly white man traveling on a public bus who, through his racist hate speech, putatively enacts a new norm of discrimination, akin to a "Whites Only" sign. It might be argued that cross burning functions in a similar way: it serves to create a new norm of discriminatory conduct according to which "blacks" are not permitted or welcome to live in certain neighborhoods. Once cross burning is uncovered for what it really is, we might think that banning it poses much less of a problem for the First Amendment, even if the relevant laws involve content discrimination (cf. McGowan 2012: 145). Consequently, it seems to me that adding both discriminatory harassment and pure discrimination to the list of valid bases for content-based restrictions captured by the Nuanced Principle of Neutrality would only make the substitution compromise enacted by the adoption of that principle more compelling. Doing so lessens the chance that official suppression of ideas is afoot. I take it that this is not only a point about the *quantity* of valid bases added to the list of exceptions; it is also a point about the *quality* of those valid bases. What is more, it might be argued that adopting this version of the Nuanced Principle of Neutrality represents a substitution compromise in response to a deep conflict between the Principle of Neutrality and the Principle of Non-Oppression.

Having said that, I do not mean to imply that the right compromise is a clear-cut issue. The mere fact that a law is directed not against speech but against conduct may prove insufficient to justify content and viewpoint discrimination in the eyes of those people who fear that *any* valid basis for exception could be used as an excuse by the state, whether that be secondary effects or forms of discrimination. After all, the conduct has the character that it has *partly* due to the *ideas* involved in its enactment. And so for that reason introducing the current valid basis into the discussion could in practice turn out not to be enough to forge a substitution compromise around the Nuanced Principle of Neutrality. Nonetheless, I do think that the inclusion of the aforementioned valid bases would make the substitution of the Principle of Neutrality with the Nuanced Principle of Neutrality more attractive to both sides. At heart, the compromise solution consists of a rejection of the view that *any* risk of official suppression of ideas ought to block laws that involve content or viewpoint discrimination among proscribable speech. Of course, reading the First Amendment in absolute terms (as denying the right of the state to restrict free speech for the sake of certain valid bases) provides greater certainty: so long as the US Supreme Court does not tolerate any risk of official suppression of ideas, we all know where we stand (cf. Partlett 1989: 485–486). But those who are willing to embrace the proposed compromise might do so because they believe that the price of certainty is too high. Certainty is premised upon a jurisprudence of mistrust: it flows from a belief that the state can never be trusted to act in good faith and for sound, principled reasons in the domain of free speech. The relevant compromise is far more optimistic in that sense.

Let us take stock. My overarching aim in running through these arguments has been to show that the act of adopting the Nuanced Principle of Neutrality instead of the Principle of Neutrality as well as the act of adopting some readings of the Nuanced Principle of Neutrality rather than others could be conceived as acts of substitution compromise. The story does not end there, however. I believe that this vision of judicial compromise could cast new light on the Court's reasoning in a subsequent cross burning case in which its reading of the Nuanced Principle of Neutrality continued to evolve.

## Virginia v. Black

In *Virginia v. Black* the Court considered the Virginia Code's cross burning statute. Unlike the ordinance at issue in *R.A.V. v. City of St. Paul*, the Virginia statute treats cross burning as ostensibly a matter of *intimidation* rather than a subcategory of fighting words, and does *not* stipulate 'on the basis of race, color, creed, religion or gender'.[26] The Court ruled that even though the Virginia statute *did* involve content discrimination by virtue of picking out cross burning as a subset of intimidating messages, it was not necessarily unconstitutional on that score (albeit it was unconstitutionally overbroad on account of the statute's *prima facie* evidence provision).[27] Writing for the majority, Justice O'Connor invoked the first valid basis for content discrimination presented by Justice Scalia in *R.A.V. v. City of St. Paul*: that the basis for the discrimination consists entirely of the very reason the entire class of speech at issue is proscribable.

> The First Amendment permits Virginia to outlaw cross burnings done with the intent to intimidate because burning a cross is a particularly virulent form of intimidation. Instead of prohibiting all intimidating messages, Virginia may choose to regulate this subset of intimidating messages in light of cross burning's long and pernicious history as a signal of impending violence. Thus, just as a State may regulate only that obscenity which is the most obscene due to its prurient content, so too may a State choose to prohibit only those forms of intimidation that are most likely to inspire fear of bodily harm. A ban on cross burning carried out with the intent to intimidate is fully consistent with our holding in R.A.V. and is proscribable under the First Amendment.[28]

As Corey Brettschneider puts it, '[Justice] O'Connor's opinion could be interpreted as carving out an exception to the doctrine of viewpoint neutrality when she recognized that threats could be prohibited, even if they were also expressive' (Brettschneider 2013: 609). However, in his concurrence Justice Souter insisted that the Virginia statute did *not* fall within the relevant exception because its grounds for content or viewpoint discrimination did *not* consist *entirely* of the very reason the entire class of speech at issue is proscribable. 'The cross may have been selected because of its special power to threaten, but it may also have been singled out because of disapproval of its message of white supremacy, either because a legislature thought white supremacy was a pernicious doctrine or because it found that dramatic, public espousal of it was a civic embarrassment.'[29] In other words, the Virginia statute picks out cross burning not purely because it is a 'particularly virulent' form of intimidation[30] but also because of its message or viewpoint, and this extra rationale is most certainly not part of the very reason the entire class of speech at issue is proscribable. In fact, Justice Souter argued that the Virginia statute did not merely fail to satisfy the conditions of the first valid basis or exception but also violated a more generalized adequacy test articulated by Justice Scalia in *R.A.V. v. City of St. Paul*: namely, that content discrimination with respect to proscribable speech may be permissible 'so long as the nature of the content discrimination is such that there is no realistic possibility that official suppression of ideas is afoot.'[31] According to Souter, the Virginia statute's inclusion of the *prima facie* evidence provision means that there *is* a realistic possibility that official suppression of ideas is afoot.[32] After all, if cross burning always means intent to intimidate, where does that leave the expressive content of cross burning and the particular viewpoint of cross burners?

I would argue that this underscores yet again why it can be useful to think about these cases through the lenses of substitution compromise. In effect, Justice Souter was attempting to defend a reading of the Nuanced Principle of Neutrality that had the power to cut through relevant cases with the precision of a surgeon's knife, cleaving those cases where the principal rationale for neutrality (i.e., preventing the official suppression of ideas) is in play from those cases where that rationale is not in play. In Souter's mind, for instance, it is one thing to distinguish between obscene publications on the basis of some publications being unusually offensive in their prurience or to pick out for special measures threats against the President because of the special risks and costs associated with threatening the President; it is quite another to reject a general prohibition on intimidation in favor of a distinct prohibition on intimidation by way of cross burning.[33] However, it seems more likely that human affairs do not admit of this level of precision. It may be the case that unusually offensive obscene publications *do* carry a particular message, such as the message that there is no such thing as an inordinate interest in sex and that sexual hedonism is a life well lived. And so there could be a realistic possibility that the state is banning only such material in an effort to repress this pernicious doctrine. Likewise, it is arguable that threatening the President does carry a special message and viewpoint, a particular sort of anti-federalism of which threats of violence against the President are an integral feature. And this means there is always a chance that by meting out special sanctions for threats of violence against the President the state is making a subtle effort to ban a particularly unwelcome message. If these observations are accurate, then perhaps we must accept that there are scarcely any cases in which there is *no realistic possibility* that official suppression of ideas is afoot. As such, Souter's reading of the Nuanced Principle of Neutrality would leave legislators with little real power to pursue compelling state interests, not the least of which would be safeguarding the security (or feeling of security) of potential victims of cross burning practices. I believe, therefore, that it could make sense to think of Justice O'Connor's opinion as attempting to achieve a substitution compromise by replacing one reading of the Nuanced Principle of Neutrality with another. In effect, Justice O'Connor is substituting a Narrow Reading of this principle, which says that *any* risk of official suppression of ideas is enough to invalidate otherwise valid bases for content or viewpoint discrimination, and a Broad Reading of this principle, which says that *not even the highest* risk of official suppression of ideas is enough to invalidate otherwise valid bases for content or viewpoint discrimination, with a Middling Reading, which says that a *sufficiently high* risk of official suppression of ideas is enough to invalidate otherwise valid bases for content or viewpoint discrimination depending on the nature of those valid bases.

Finally, I believe that there is nothing extraordinary about the disputes that characterized *R.A.V. v. City of St. Paul* and *Virginia v. Black*, and nothing unusual about the (hypothetical) substitution compromises that were available to the justices in those cases. In effect, the Court availed itself of a nuanced approach to content and viewpoint neutrality and a substitution compromise between the Principle of Neutrality and the various principles that underpin valid bases for exception, including the Nuanced Principle of Autonomy, the Principle of Security, the Principle of Health, and even the Principle of Non-Oppression. While the influence of the original sets of opposing or contrasting principles upon the ensuing substitution compromises (involving conflicting interpretations of the Nuanced Principle of Neutrality) may not be so explicit, their presence may still be inferred. If I am correct, and these are not freak cases or outlier instances of substitution compromise, then there is no reason to think that this approach would be unsuitable for judicial disagreements about other hate speech law, where substitution compromises of different key normative principles or interpretations of key normative principles are at issue.

## 10.6 THE ETHICS OF COMPROMISE

Thus far I have outlined two kinds of compromise that may be useful for addressing conflicts between opposing or contrasting principles and interpretations of principles: conjunction compromise and substitution compromise. I now want to consider what, if anything, could make such compromises *ethical*.

Now it would be difficult, I take it, to discern the presence of ethical value in the social practice of compromise if compromises were only ever reached simply because one or both sides have an urgent interest in bringing negotiations to an end (e.g., they have run out of resources or can no longer bear the burden of sustaining negotiations) or because the stronger side gains the upper hand over the weaker side (e.g., one side uses its hard or soft power to exert pressure or influence over the other side). Indeed, both the willingness to compromise and the refusal to compromise can sometimes display human vice. Someone who is too ready to reach a compromise is often construed as being spineless. Indeed, the negative picture of someone who capitulates his or her principles at the first sight of opposition is contrasted with the positive image of someone who holds true to his or her principles despite taking flack for doing so. Yet by the same token a refusal to compromise can also be seen as a bad thing. Persons who stick to their original principles come what may and despite hearing sound reasons to set them aside can be viewed as unduly rigid or dogmatic.[34]

One response to this putative ethical deficit in the social practice of compromise is to challenge the core assumption that compromise is something that necessarily occurs between two or more parties: namely, to draw a distinction between *interpersonal compromise*, on the one hand, and *intrapersonal compromise* and *impersonal compromise*, on the other hand (cf. Jones and O'Flynn 2013: 119). If compromise characteristically involves a battle of wills between mutually antagonistic jurors, judges, legislators, policymakers, regulators, prosecutors, police officers, career politicians, pressure groups, and wider political factions, we should not be surprised if the picture that emerges is often unedifying.[35] But compromise may not be exhausted by interpersonal compromise. After all, it is quite normal for the aforementioned agents to experience an inward conflict of principles quite apart from any deliberation with others. Indeed, it may make perfectly good sense to speak of impersonal compromise: to talk meaningfully of compromises over principles in the passive tense, without pinpointing any agents who actually hold the principles or are engaged in the practice of compromising. By removing human beings from the analysis of compromise one removes the stain of human vice. This is not a response that I intend to exploit here, however. For, there remains a disagreement in the literature about the logical priority between interpersonal, intrapersonal, and impersonal compromise that threatens to bog down this response.[36] Besides, many of the examples of compromise outlined in the previous sections of this chapter presupposed at least some degree of interpersonal compromise over principles.

Nevertheless, a second response confronts the problem of ethical deficit head on by drawing a distinction between *pragmatic* or *tactical compromise* and *principled compromise*. The sort of distinction I have in mind rests not in the difference between a compromise over mere interests and a compromise over principles. On the contrary, many pragmatic or tactical compromises are forged in the fire of profound disagreement over matters of principled concern. Rather, the distinction I wish to draw is between different sources of the ethical quality of compromise. Pragmatic or tactical compromises are goal-based and tend to derive whatever moral value they possess from their results. In a pragmatic or tactical compromise the parties may look upon compromise simply as a necessary evil or as a means to morally worthwhile ends, including the realization of principles. It may simply be better, all things considered, if a compromise is reached than if the confrontation is left unresolved (e.g., Jones and O'Flynn 2013: 120–121). In contrast, a principled compromise locates the source of ethical value in an imperative to compromise that does not rest on expected consequences and/or the manner in which compromise is conducted, including perhaps the virtuous dispositions of the agents involved in the practice of compromise. First, principled compromise 'will reflect our acceptance that, in the given circumstances, compromising with others is the intrinsically right thing to do' (120). Second, it may reflect the idea of compromise being conducted in the right way. Accordingly, this second response to the ethical deficit is to say that society should strive to inculcate in people not merely a willingness to compromise over principles but also the ideals or virtuous dispositions that characterize principled compromise.

In what follows, moreover, I shall assume that principled compromise has to do with moderators of compromise and compromisers themselves respecting *procedural ideals* relating to the conduct of compromise rather than as satisfying *end-state standards*, which place demands on what the compromise outcomes should or should not be.[37] What are these ideals? In the remainder of this section I posit three: reciprocity, equality, and mutual respect. In trying to flesh out the nature of these rich ideals I take considerable inspiration from the contemporary literature on virtue jurisprudence and judicial ethics (including work on the norm of *collegiality*) as well as on deliberative democracy, discourse ethics, and communicative virtue.

## Reciprocity

Consider first the ideal of reciprocity. Cast in the terms of this ideal, principled compromise has to do with reaching a compromise 'on the basis of mutually acceptable reasons' (Gutmann and Thompson 1996: 55; see also Bellamy 1999: 105–106, 111; Parekh 2006: 128). That being said, the idea of mutually acceptable reasons could be understood in more or less stringent ways. It could mean simply that the only reasons that may be adduced in favor of reaching a particular compromise solution are reasons that invoke the sort of discourse that all sides can accept as appropriate. So, one side might say that the other sides should support a particular compromise solution because it is "fair" or "reasonable", and this may strike the right tone. This might not be the case if the reasons proffered were framed in terms of the language of "It's in your best interests to accept this compromise" or "You had better agree to this compromise or else." Alternatively, the idea of mutually acceptable reasons could mean something more stringent: namely, that the sorts of reasons that may be adduced in favor of reaching a particular compromise must be reasons whose propositional content is something that all sides can agree upon. So it is not enough that the reason for reaching a given compromise appeals to the right sort of language; it must be the case that the other side can accept the substance of the reason proffered. Suppose the reasons given for a particular compromise outcome are that it is fair because it lets each side retain an equal number of principles (conjunction compromise) or that it is reasonable by virtue of the fact that it is based on a newly created principle the shape and content of which is clearly influenced by the two original sets of principles put forward by each side (substitution compromise). Such reasons satisfy the more stringent constraint of reciprocity only if the other side can accept the content of the propositions from which the reasons are formed.

However, it seems to me that one should not be surprised if, under the less stringent reading, the ideal of reciprocity fails to point judges in the direction of a single, clear-cut compromise solution. For, under the less stringent reading, it is likely that shared discourse will yield multiple compromise solutions. If one side proffers a particular compromise couched in the language of fairness or reasonableness, for example, it is likely that the other side, which favors a different compromise, will also be able to proffer reasons formulated in the language of fairness or reasonableness. So we have two competing compromise solutions both of which use language that the compromisers find acceptable. Furthermore, one should also not be surprised if, under the more stringent reading, compromisers are unable to reach an agreement that satisfies the ideal of reciprocity. One side could proffer as a reason for a particular compromise the fact that it enables each side to retain an equal number of principles, but the other side could reject that reason by insisting that on closer inspection the compromise is unfair because although both sides retain an equal number of principles, only one side had to forego its core, essential, or most valued principle(s).[38] Or, faced with the argument that a particular compromise is reasonable because it is based on a new principle the shape and content of which is clearly influenced by both original sets of principles, the opposing side could maintain that the new principle displays fewer hallmarks or retains less of the spirit of their preferred set of principles than the set of principles favored by the other side.

To come at this issue from a slightly different angle, if the challenge is to find reasons or justifications for compromises that are acceptable to both sides, this creates an injunction not to appeal to controversial reasons or justifications. But even this higher-level injunction might itself prove controversial. In dealing with cases of hate speech members of the judiciary have often been obliged to perform all manner of argumentative contortions just to affirm the Principle of Neutrality. They report both their sincerely held belief that the proliferation of hate speech is repugnant, evil, and born of the worst, animalistic human instincts, and their principled conviction that lawmakers should not lift a finger to stop it if stopping it entails content or viewpoint discrimination.[39] Fish calls this 'the rhetoric of regret' (Fish 2001: 79), which he chides for being 'incoherent' (82). Justice Stevens avoids this rhetoric by grasping the nettle and proclaiming that the secondary effects of hate speech are not trivial or minor and, therefore, should be combated, despite the Principle of Neutrality. But this means that he must also account for why an exception should be made for these secondary effects and not others. With this in mind, Justice Stevens made an appeal to a higher-level norm of justificatory neutrality. He presented the secondary effects of racist fighting words as special kinds of harm and suggested that to appeal to special kinds of harm as a reason for the relevant exception to neutrality is itself to offer a 'neutral' and, therefore, legitimate justification for the exception.[40] Some prominent legal scholars subsequently endorsed this strategy (e.g., Sunstein 1993a: 190–193). The problem is that neither Justice Stevens nor his defenders offered much in the way of analysis of, or argument for, this higher-level norm of justificatory neutrality.[41] Two potential pitfalls merit attention. First, Justice Stevens seems to be saying that the prevention of harm does not presuppose any particular conception of the good or that no matter which conception of the good citizens affirm they can all agree that the threat of severe trauma and riots ought to be prevented. But there is an element of self-delusion in this argument. Supreme Court justices who appeal to the norm of justificatory neutrality in order to justify their preferred reading of the Nuanced Principle of Neutrality are implicitly motivated by a particular set of comprehensive values, such as the virtue of tolerance or the virtue of avoiding appeals to comprehensive conceptions of the good, and this is problematic because the norm of justificatory neutrality explicitly tells them not to appeal to a particular comprehensive conception of the good. Second, it is very far from obvious that Supreme Court justices *should* observe justificatory neutrality and refrain from appealing to comprehensive values in coming to decisions about the requirements of content and viewpoint neutrality in First Amendment cases.[42] The fact that the norm of justificatory neutrality remains controversial for both of these reasons may undermine its usefulness as a tool for brokering a compromise between justices who hold radically different views.

Nevertheless, since actual compromisers may wind up reaching a particular compromise solution even if it transpires that the ideal of reciprocity does not, under the less stringent reading, narrow the field down to one compromise solution, and does not, under the more stringent reading, support any compromise solution, what, in addition to respecting the ideal of reciprocity, can, or should, would-be compromisers do to ensure that any compromise they reach is fully ethical? Happily, reciprocity is not the only ideal that can be used to tell the story of principled compromise.

## Equality

Consider next the ideal of equality. As applied to the practice of compromise, this ideal suggests that, as far as time and other reasonable practicalities permit, there should be equal airing and consideration given to every proposal and alternative proposal that compromisers may wish to put on the table (cf. Cohen [Joshua] 1996: 96; Edwards 2003: 1645; Malik [M.] 2009: 112). In other words, it is important that compromisers proceed with the attitude that 'all have the same chances to initiate speech acts, to question, to interrogate, and to open debate' (Benhabib 1996: 70). Should one side dominate the practice of compromise, this may call into doubt the moral authority of whatever compromise solution is reached.

Interestingly, in his work on the role that collegiality might play in judicial decision-making in appellate courts, the former Chief Judge of the US Court of Appeals for the D.C. Circuit, Harry T. Edwards, differentiates between an 'ordered deliberation in which all views are aired and considered to every judge's satisfaction' (Edwards 2003: 1665)—which he takes to be a constituent feature of the norm of judicial collegiality and a key part of the practice of judges going 'back and forth in their deliberations over disputed and difficult issues until agreement is reached' (1646)—and instances of 'one judge "compromising" his or her views to a prevailing majority' (ibid.). However, I see no reason to regard the ideal of equal airing and consideration of views and the social practice of compromise as mutually exclusive. If there are situations where compromise is fitting, why should we not also expect that compromise to be conducted on the basis of ideals of equality? In other words, assuming that Edwards is correct in thinking that the ideal of equal airing and consideration is an important dimension of what he calls 'principled agreement' (1645), surely it is no less plausible to regard that ideal as an important dimension of principled compromise.

The ideal of equal airing and consideration of views is often formalized in the rules and procedures of legislative assemblies. In my view this ideal should not be thought out of place in the deliberations and negotiations of appellate judges—including justices of the US Supreme Court, for example—even if it is likely to be placed on a more informal footing. The ideal might call for justices to engage in a series of bilateral and multilateral meetings with each justice taking it in turns to open the discussion and to present and defend draft decisions. Dissenting justices who are *not* in support of striking down a particular piece of hate speech legislation, for instance, should be granted as much time to convince the majority to change its opinion as is claimed by justices who *are* in support of striking down the law in the attempt to convince those who initially dissented to join the majority.

## Mutual Respect

Consider finally the ideal of mutual respect. According to one definition, mutual respect 'requires a favorable attitude toward, and constructive interaction with, the persons with whom one disagrees' (Gutmann and Thompson 1996: 79). This ideal goes to the heart of how compromisers, 'who, after deliberation, still fundamentally disagree about an issue should treat one another with regard to that and related issues—even when their deliberations result in legislation that favors one side of the dispute' (80). Mutual respect is a sufficiently abstract ideal to necessitate breaking it down into a series of specific 'communicative virtues' (Rice and Burbules 1993: 35) or 'moral dispositions' (Gutmann and Thompson 1996: 81). Therefore, in what follows I shall posit six virtues of mutual respect that parties to compromises will need to exhibit if their compromises are to truly deserve the adjective 'principled.' Many of these virtues already figure in the account of intercultural dialogue presented by Parekh (2006: 340) (see Ch. 6 [6.4]). But in the present context the virtues will be put to work in understanding the particular phenomenon of interpersonal compromise over principles and are not restricted to instances of intercultural dialogue.

First, there is the virtue of *honesty* or *fairness*, meaning that compromisers will tend to refrain from resorting to underhanded, deceitful, or exploitative tactics (cf. Rice and Burbules 1993: 35). 'We cannot,' as Martin Benjamin puts it, 'acknowledge that an ethical conflict is characterized by the circumstances of compromise and at the same time attempt to secure a competitive edge by exploiting power advantages or employing deception or other forms of manipulation in seeking a solution more satisfactory to ourselves than to opposing parties' (Benjamin 1990: 138).

Second, there is the virtue of *integrity*, which is a matter of parties accepting or rejecting proposed compromises on the basis of principled commitments about what a fair or reasonable compromise would be rather than on the basis of capricious, unprincipled, or purely selfish considerations (cf. Rice and Burbules 1993: 35; Gutmann and Thompson 1996: 81–82). A party to a compromise may be said to lack integrity if he or she dogmatically refuses to countenance a particular compromise solution not because he or she has a principled reason to regard that compromise solution as unfair or unreasonable but simply because it will result in a concrete decision that he or she cannot stomach. This would be evident if he or she offers no objection to a similar form of compromise solution that results in a similar concrete decision in a similar free speech debate. This might happen if, say, someone is more disposed to compromise his or her principled commitment to freedom of expression in the case of anti-pornography law than in the case of hate speech law because he or she just so happens to be someone who is less likely to run afoul of anti-pornography law than hate speech law or because he or she is more ideologically sympathetic to some of the concerns raised by hate speakers than to any expressive content that could be communicated through pornographic material.

Third, there is the virtue of *good faith* or *trust*, which implies that a compromiser is prepared to give others the benefit of the doubt over the status of their reasons (cf. Gutmann and Thompson 1996: 82). Where possible he or she casts the other party in the best light. So, for example, if the other party offers as a reason for accepting a given compromise that it is equitable by virtue of splitting the difference between the two sides, then other things remaining equal he or she ought to assume that the other party is acting sincerely or in good faith and is not merely seeking to shield or obfuscate less worthy motivations with the rhetoric of splitting the difference. By the same token, if the other party presents yet further reasons in support of a given compromise in response to concerns raised about whether in fact it really does split the difference or whether splitting the difference is actually the equitable thing to do, a compromiser who is capable of good faith does not seek to construe the other side as being obstinate, overly demanding, or pleading in a distasteful way. Indeed, the virtue of good faith or trust might extend to how compromisers approach the proposals of people who themselves have been on the receiving end of the sort of hate speech that is ultimately the subject of compromise. For example, it might be an act of good faith to assume that their proposals reflect a kind of personal familiarity with the issues that has special value, rather than, say, dismissing their proposals as intrinsically biased or unreliable (cf. Shiffrin [S.H.] 1999: 85).

Fourth, the virtue of *open-mindedness* is exemplified by a compromiser who is open to listen to what can be said for solutions proposed by other parties and, more importantly, is prepared to be persuaded by sound reasons adduced for those solutions even if those reasons are unfamiliar or require an act of imagination (cf. Rice and Burbules 1993: 35; Gutmann and Thompson 1996: 83–84; Parekh 2006: 128–129). There might be an overlap here with what Delgado and Yun characterize as the need for 'dialogic politics' in the way freedom of expression cases are handled by the courts, especially when they involve hate speech. One of the things they mean, I think, is that supreme court justices who take opposite views or place differential weight on the values at stake or subscribe to competing principles in free speech cases should not merely listen to and consider each other's arguments but should also be ready to be persuaded by good arguments (Delgado and Yun 1995: 1295).

Fifth, the virtue of *reasonableness* is exemplified by the recognition 'by each side of the other's rights, which leads them to make concessions to enable them to meet on a middle ground' (Cohen-Almagor 2006b: 440). This is about compromisers moderating and in part transforming their expectations in the light of the positions taken by persons on the other side of the debate (cf. Bellamy 1999: 111). 'We compromise in a principled way when we act on the belief that we owe it to others to concede something to their position' (Jones and O'Flynn 2013: 120).

Sixth, there is the virtue of *magnanimity*, which I take to mean a preparedness to live with the results of compromise. As Raphael Cohen-Almagor puts it, in principled compromise 'both sides reconcile themselves to the results' (2006b: 440), even results that they otherwise fundamentally disagree with (cf. Parekh 2006: 340). The importance of this virtue rests in the fact that even an otherwise ethical compromise may leave compromisers with unresolved differences. Even when a compromise is reached, in other words, this is a matter of 'agreeing to disagree' (Gutmann and Thompson 1996: 79).

Being prepared to live with compromise solutions matters just as much during the deliberations leading up to the agreement as after the compromise has actually been reached. Parties to a principled compromise should not be held to ransom by the menacing threat that one of the parties will simply refuse to submit to a compromise that he or she finds disdainful—for example, discovering some cunning way to carry on as though the compromise were never reached or as though contrary to fact a different, more favorable compromise were reached. One outward sign of this virtue is a willingness on the part of a supreme court justice, say, to engage in compromise negotiations with other justices and once an agreement has been reached to refrain from writing a bitter dissenting opinion that admonishes and condemns the other justices just because they rejected the proposed compromise solution that he or she put forward and adopted a different solution that garnered greater support.

To recap, I have characterized principled compromise in terms of three ideals—reciprocity, equality, and mutual respect—that are to be understood as moral duties or civic virtues. Before turning to consider two objections, I need first to address the following outstanding question. What makes principled compromise valuable? Or, why should we care whether or not members of the judiciary take the aforementioned ideals to heart? I would argue that principled compromise possesses both endgood value and instrumental value. It is valuable for its own sake or in itself that when parties engage in the practice of compromise, they do so in the spirit of reciprocity, equality, and mutual respect. It may be difficult to justify why this sort of compromise possesses endgood value other than to say that the ideals it enacts or realizes are themselves endgood values. Principled compromise also matters because of the good things that this is likely to bring about. For instance, Edwards claims that a disposition of mutual respect among appellate judges, which he identifies as a core aspect of collegiality, assists with decision-making in cases involving complex matters of principled concern. 'When judges respect one another and are amicable in their dealings, the decision-making process runs smoothly' (Edwards 1991: 858). Indeed, he claims that '[a] deliberative process enhanced by collegiality and a broad range of perspectives *necessarily* results in better and more nuanced opinion' (2002: 329, emphasis added). Perhaps this second claim is exaggerated; perhaps not. But either way, it does not exhaust the possible instrumental value of principled compromise. For, it might also be the case that when members of the public read about judges interacting with each other in the spirit of reciprocity, equality, and mutual respect, they are more likely to hold the court in high esteem or less likely to hold it low esteem, thus potentially aiding the stability of the legal system over time.[43] Then, of course, there is the socially beneficial symbolic value of a racially diverse and mixed-gender supreme court, for example, conducting its own deliberations and negotiations on whether or not to strike down hate speech law in an ethical manner. In this way judicial elites can set a good example for the rest of us to follow.

## 10.7 TWO POSSIBLE OBJECTIONS

The theory of principled compromise that I have advanced in this chapter is characterized by the claim that principled dilemmas surrounding the overall warrant of hate speech law can be usefully theorized in terms of two kinds of compromise, and by the view that such compromises should be principled rather than merely pragmatic or tactical. I shall now consider two possible objections to my theory.

### The Meta-Level Question of How to Respond to Hate Speech

The first possible objection is that by adopting a theory of principled compromise I have merely postponed the question of how we should respond to hate speech and have not, therefore, finally answered it. This is because I have not answered this meta-level question. May or may not parties to principled compromise use hate speech in their deliberations, discussions, and negotiations leading to compromise solutions? Faced with this meta-level question I believe that it is, among other things, fitting to revert back to the ideals of reciprocity, equality, and mutual respect. This echoes an important insight from the literature on deliberative democracy. Here, it is argued that decisions can be valid only if they result from a process of deliberation in which 'all have the right to initiate reflexive arguments about the very rules of the discourse procedure and the way in which they are applied or carried out' (Benhabib 1996: 70). It seems to me that the ideal of reciprocity, for example, may contain enough substance to support meaningful reflexive judgments among compromisers regarding this meta-level question. The ideal of reciprocity calls for parties to proffer mutually acceptable reasons. Thus, within the practice of interpersonal compromise, we might think that reasons adduced for particular compromise solutions must be capable of exerting persuasive force or serving as justifications when uttered by any speaker to any addressee in the compromise situation (cf. Cohen [G.A.] 1992: 280). And it scarcely seems likely that reasons will exert persuasive force invariantly if they are couched in the language of hatred, such as if one party utters a reason that contains hate speech that just so happens to target the addressee.

Nevertheless, I also take the view that the aforementioned ideals of reciprocity, equality, and mutual respect support moral duties or civic virtues, rather than legal duties to be enforced by laws. And so, other things being equal, there is no legal duty to respect ideals of reciprocity, equality, and mutual respect. That being said, judges do not operate in a legal or quasi-legal vacuum and are not above the law. A chief justice might choose to impose codes of conduct relating to proper modes of speech in meetings and might elect to chastise justices under his or her supervision for engaging in what amounts to hate speech. More importantly, some supreme court justices will find themselves operating within legal jurisdictions in which hate speech laws have already been enacted and are applicable as much to *their* modes of expression as to the speech of any citizen. And so, in those circumstances they will be compelled by law as well as by moral rectitude to moderate their use of language accordingly. However, provided that these laws/regulations/codes were themselves the products of prior principled compromises, this state of affairs is not objectionable. Putting the same point another way, if laws/regulations/codes that constrain uses of hate speech are warranted all principles considered, it is only because they are the outputs of principled compromises and not because they represent an enforcement of the normative ideals by virtue of which we can describe compromises as being principled.

## Principled Compromise in Non-Ideal Theory

The theory of overall warrant as principled compromise presented here is not intended as a faithful depiction of what it is that the majority of supreme court justices actually do, for example. Instead, it is presented as an aspirational account of what it is they should be doing or what they would be doing if they were acting in compliance with certain ideals. Now I have not assumed that there is full compliance with the ideals of reciprocity, equality, and mutual respect. Nevertheless, the second possible objection is that I have offered insufficient reason thus far to believe that enough could be done in practice to ensure that my proffered ideals of principled compromise will be complied with to make the theory relevant to, or useful for, the real world.

Before I respond directly to this objection, let me first clarify the sort of theory I am proposing. Since the publication of Rawls' *A Theory of Justice* it has become common practice among political philosophers to specify whether they are offering an ideal theory, in the sense of simply assuming full compliance with the normative ideals advanced in the theory, or a non-ideal theory, in the sense of assuming that there is or can be at least partial compliance with the relevant normative ideals.[44] My theory is intended to be non-ideal in the sense that it assumes that it is probably the case that, other things remaining equal, not every agent will comply with the ideals it sets forth and that the level of non-compliance will be not insignificant unless steps are taken to promote compliance. The task for this non-ideal theory, therefore, is not merely to set out a vision of ethical conduct but also to specify how compliant conduct can be incentivized, non-compliant conduct discouraged, and the ability to discern the difference taught, such that the proportion of agents who are non-compliant and the degree of their non-compliance are minimized. This sort of theorizing is non-ideal but in the moderate sense that it assumes only that full compliance is not probable, as opposed to impossible. It also remains resolutely aspirational in that it articulates standards that ought to be complied with even if they are currently not fully complied with and probably will remain not fully complied with unless steps are taken (cf. Estlund [D.] 2008: 263–270).[45]

Following on from this, do we have any good reason to believe that there is at least partial compliance among supreme court justices, say, to the ideals of principled compromise (reciprocity, equality, and mutual respect)? And, assuming that full compliance is not probable unless practical steps are taken to encourage it, what steps might be taken to promote greater compliance? The correct, if somewhat trite, answer to these questions is that it depends on which supreme courts and in which eras of those courts one is talking about. But sticking with contemporary Anglo-American legal contexts, consider first the norm of equality. In practice, the informal norms of etiquette surrounding time allocated for interpersonal discussion and negotiation among US Supreme Court justices are likely to be the products of a sort of evolving collective bargaining process under the supervision of the Chief Justice. Even so, Jeffrey Toobin's recent history of the Court *does* point to the presence of norms of etiquette concerning the amount of time to which each justice is entitled in trying to persuade other justices to join an opinion, etiquette that is often made visible in the breach (Toobin 2007: 67). He also explains how in the Rehnquist Court, Oral Argument was a particularly important space for justices to set out their competing views. 'Such was the justices' isolation from one another that the best advocacy could be done only in oral argument, when they were a captive audience for one another' (152).

Be that as it may, without the willingness to deliberate and negotiate meaningfully there can be no principled compromise irrespective of how much time justices are forced to spend in each other's company at Oral Argument. Comparing detailed studies of the practices of US Supreme Court justices between the 1970s and the first decade of the twenty-first century (e.g., Woodward and Armstrong 1979; Toobin 2007) gives the impression of not merely a decline in levels of face-to-face and written interaction but also an increase in the tendency to sectarianism and unyieldingness. According to Toobin, many of the justices in the Rehnquist Court were reclusive, and some justices seemed to revel in the unsplendid isolation of separate dissenting opinions (Toobin 2007: 151). Of course, this cuts both ways. A justice cannot remain aloof one day but the next realistically expect his or her peers to compromise their positions in response to his or her valid reasons (cf. 66–67).

Nevertheless, if one way to discern virtues and vices is by looking at the examples set by virtuous and vicious individuals, then no doubt examples of both can be found, even in the Rehnquist Court. One might contrast the dispositions of Justice O'Connor, which were often although certainly not always, studies in magnanimity toward the motives of other justices, open-mindedness in being willing to be persuaded by the best arguments, and reasonableness in being prepared to make concessions in a disagreement (Toobin 2007: 8, 114–115), with the traits of Justice Scalia, which were often disrespectfulness, not least toward Justice O'Connor, dogmatism, close-mindedness, and intransigence (66, 151). There again, Justice Scalia rarely found himself on the side of an opinion that undermined the integrity of his voting record and previous opinions given the clarity and coherence of his originalist approach to the Constitution (65), whereas Justice O'Connor's commitment to a living constitution often meant that she struggled to bring her preferred positions on new cases in line with her voting record and previous written opinions (114–115, 252–253). So it is possible, therefore, to say that each of the ideals and associated collection of virtues that I volunteered as constituent features of principled compromise have been at least partially complied with within the US Supreme Court, provided that one takes a long view and looks at the nine as a whole.

I also believe that at least partial compliance with the ideals of reciprocity, equality, and mutual respect can be seen in the UK Supreme Court. In contrast to the story of declining collegiality told by the studies of the US Supreme Court cited in the previous paragraph, Alan Paterson's recent study of the UK Supreme Court finds that in comparison to the last decade of the venerable institution of the Law Lords—an institution that finally came to an end in 2009—the Court has moved in the direction of more extensive teamwork, interpersonal engagement, and collective decision-making (Paterson 2012: 141–145). Among the evidence that Paterson cites for this generalization are interviews with judges attesting to this new cooperative ethos, the fact that the number of pre-Oral Hearing meetings, Second Conferences, and back and forth exchanges on draft opinions increased during the period, and the raw statistic that in the early 1990s the percentage of single judgments by the Law Lords reached 70%, a number that fell to a low of 15% in the final decade of that institution, but which had increased to 55% by 2013 (ibid.).

But now suppose for the sake of argument that in fact judicial conduct in the US and UK exhibits much less reciprocity, equality, and mutual respect than the foregoing observations indicate. Now the operative question is whether there are any good reasons to doubt that the ideals of reciprocity, equality, and mutual respect could be inculcated. Once again, my instinct is to err on the side of optimism. For, there are at least three things that tell against pessimism. First, there is the integrity and professionalism of the various institutions tasked with the education, training, and oversight of judges. The more integrity and professionalism that exists within these institutions, the more reason we have to be hopeful that they can indeed achieve their primary function, which must surely encompass teaching the ideals and virtues of reciprocity, equality, and mutual respect, along with whatever bureaucratic and technocratic knowledge and skills they must impart. Second, there is a chance that the public will expect, indeed demand, that wherever possible, judicial compromises are forged in an ethical way, and so if the parties to those compromises wish to avoid the censure of citizens, they will need to develop the sorts of traits and dispositions that are viewed as admirable or praiseworthy when it comes to the practice of compromise. Third, it may be possible for selection and confirmation committees to take into consideration whether or not candidate judges or justices possess sufficiently developed moral dispositions of a suitable type (cf. Solum 2003, 2004).

\* \* \*

In this chapter I have attempted to outline a theory of principled compromise for dealing with dilemmas posed by hate speech law. In doing so I have articulated certain ideals, which I conceive as supporting moral duties or civic virtues, as opposed to legal duties to be enforced by laws. In developing this theory I have focused almost exclusively on the example of judicial compromise. I wish to end by asking if the same reasoning can and should be applied to other agents and contexts of compromise besides judges and legal institutions. In short, are ideals of reciprocity, equality, and mutual respect applicable to *any* public officials involved in forging principled compromises over hate speech law, including politicians, legislators, policymakers, media and internet regulators, public prosecutors, and police officers? For that matter, are they applicable to ordinary citizens involved in public discourse around hate speech law? Although I believe that versions of these ideals may be applicable to these other kinds of agents, I do not take it for granted that the content and stringency of the ideals will be invariant. On the contrary, I strongly suspect that a complete theory of principled compromise would need to provide bespoke accounts of its ideals for each of the different sorts of agents involved in forging compromises and for each of the different contexts in which compromises are forged. The high and demanding ideals that might be fitting for supreme court justices in their court rooms and official chambers may not be suitable for politicians in legislatures and still less for ordinary citizens in the public square. One way to proceed is to once again look at work on deliberative democracy, discourse ethics, and communicative virtue in the hope it will shed light on the content and stringency of the moral duties that fall on different compromisers depending on the contexts in which the practice of compromise takes place, including of course the question of whether or not resorting to hate speech is itself compatible with the relevant ideals of principled compromise (cf. Rice 1994; Mann 1995; Flemming 2004; Malik [M.] 2009; Rostbøll 2011).

## NOTES

1. *R. v. Keegstra*, at 845.
2. I pose these rhetorical questions as a *hypothesis* about the likely negative impact on public confidence in the judiciary if nameless values were invoked to justify judicial reasoning to groups of people who find themselves on the

## Toward a Theory of Principled Compromise    311

sharp end of that reasoning. I do not present any evidence here to ground that hypothesis. However, clearly there is evidence of a general problem with confidence in law and legal actors among racial minorities in the US and there is plenty of research on the implications of this lack of confidence for legitimacy, stability, and security. For a survey of this research, see Fagan (2008).

3. In other words, to think that such balancing exercises are possible with regard to the numerous principles discussed in the book may fly in the face of their status as sacred principles. According to Steven Lukes, two principles or values can be said to be 'sacred' when a decision to resolve an issue in favor of one rather than the other is necessarily tragic (e.g., Lukes 1997: 187–188). Part of the evidence for supposing that certain principles or values are sacred is (188–189) 'the attitudes of discomfort, embarrassment, shock, outrage, or horror that we display when such calculation or commensuration is engaged in by others'.

4. Seth Stern and Stephen Wermiel cite the case of *Metro Broadcasting, Inc. v. FCC* (1990) 497 US 547 (involving the constitutionality of affirmative action or minority preference policies adopted by the Federal Communications Commission [FCC] in relation to access to broadcasting). They (Stern and Wermiel 2010: 533–535) claim that Justice Brennan abandoned his own commitment to the Strict Scrutiny Test for affirmative action policies and defended instead the Intermediate Scrutiny Test purely as a means of establishing a 5–4 majority in response to Justice White's inclination toward an even lower standard of review. On this reading, Justice Brennan was willing to forsake his convictions about the correct standard of scrutiny in order to achieve what he believed to be the right decision in the case. He believed that widening access to the broadcasting industry could both serve a legitimate government interest in tackling discrimination within that and other industries (by virtue of the influence that television and radio have on American life) and increase the diversity of views and information on the airwaves and thereby serve important First Amendment values.

5. 2 S.C.R. 1326 (involving publication restrictions on matrimonial proceedings).

6. At 1355–1356.

7. It might be objected that this reason does not extend to the institution of the US Supreme Court, which (so the objection runs) is tasked with interpreting the Constitution as correctly as possible given the historical meanings of the words used in it. On this understanding of constitutional interpretation, "compromise" will turn out to be a dirty word. Consider the views of Justice Scalia on the matter (Toobin 2007: 66): "'Originalists have nothing to trade!" he would say. "We can't do horse trading. Our view is what it is and we write our dissents."' However, this is by no means the only or even the most plausible view of constitutional interpretation. Another is that the Constitution is a living, breathing thing and part of the value of the institution of the Supreme Court lies in its role in continuously reinventing the Constitution for changing times, a role that incorporates the prerogative to cobble together compromises where justices disagree over the best reinvention. Few Supreme Court justices have been at the center of so many compromise deals as Justice O'Connor. This is unsurprising given her view of the nature and value of the Supreme Court (114): "'We're a common law court,' she would say, without a trace of defensiveness.'

8. For the sake of completeness, it should also be noted that not everyone views *modus vivendi* in a dim light. Stuart Hampshire (1998: 163), for example, professes to seeing as much value in a 'smart' political compromise, which involves both sides conceding the most they feasibly can so that they are operating at full stretch or just before their respective breaking points, as in other forms of

9. finely balanced tension between opposing forces, such as the tension that holds together the Heraclitean bow or the performance of a virtuoso singer.
9. Chiara Lepora discusses three kinds of compromise, but I shall concentrate on two.
10. In speaking of either opposing or contrasting principles I have added to Lepora's analysis (which mentions only opposing principles).
11. 1 BvR 1087/91 (involving the issue of displaying of crucifixes in public schools and a principled conflict between Art. 7 of German Basic Law, which legitimizes religious instruction in public schools, and Art. 4, which enshrines freedom from religious indoctrination).
12. *R.A.V. v. City of St. Paul*, at 388.
13. At 393.
14. At 393–394.
15. At 408.
16. At 408.
17. At 408–409.
18. At 409.
19. *Chaplinsky v. State of New Hampshire*, at 572.
20. *R.A.V. v. City of St. Paul*, at 389.
21. At 392–393.
22. At 425.
23. At 389.
24. At 389.
25. At 410.
26. 'It shall be unlawful for any person or persons, with the intent of intimidating any person or group of persons, to burn, or cause to be burned, a cross on the property of another, a highway or other public place. Any person who shall violate any provision of this section shall be guilty of a Class 6 felony. Any such burning of a cross shall be prima facie evidence of an intent to intimidate a person or group of persons.' s. 18.2-423 of the Virginia Code.
27. *Virginia v. Black*, at 361.
28. At 363.
29. At 383.
30. It is worth noting that other writers have questioned the assumption that cross burning is a 'particularly virulent' form of intimidation. Roger Hartley offers this pithy observation (2004: 17): 'What are the principled bases for determining "particularly virulent"? From whose point of view? One is reminded of the Court's observation in *West Virginia Board of Education v. Barnette*, that "a person gets from a symbol the meaning he puts into it, and what is one man's comfort and inspiration is another's jest and scorn." *Black* left all of these questions for another day, that day when government chooses the next symbol for selective regulation.' Hare (2003: 413, 413n.26), a civil liberties barrister based in the UK, also tries to put pressure on what he regards as Justice O'Connor's assumption that cross burning is 'the most' intimidating form of intimidation there is or that the symbol of the burning cross is 'more intimidating than all others.' According to Hare (413), 'it is difficult to see [a raised right arm and clenched fist] as less intimidating than cross burning if used, say, by a group of black youths outside the house of the first white family to move into an all-black neighbourhood.' However, two points need to be made here. First, Justice O'Connor is quite clear, I think, that in her view the first valid basis applies to the Virginia statute because 'burning a cross is a particularly virulent form of intimidation', which is surely not the same as saying that it applies because burning a cross is *the most* virulent form of intimidation.

Second, I disagree that it is difficult to see why a raised right arm and clenched fist might be less intimidating *all things considered*. There is nothing in the history of the Black Power movement in terms of its systematic oppression of, and use of violence against, white Americans that comes even close to the history of the Ku Klux Klan and its direct and indirect association with the systematic oppression of, and use of violence against, black Americans. This means, for instance, that when a raised arm and clenched fist is used, the white family can call on support from other members of the dominant group in American society and can feel reasonably secure in being protected by the police; not so for the black family facing a burning cross, and perhaps not merely historically. Third, when considering whether or not the content discrimination of the Virginia statute is 'neutral enough', to borrow the US Supreme Court's own terminology, it is surely germane that the Virginia statue would no more permit members of the Black Power movement from ironically using a burning cross to intimidate a white family whom it suspected as having ties to the Ku Klux Klan or simply for being white than it would permit members of the Ku Klux Klan from non-ironically using a burning cross to intimidate a black family whom it suspected as having ties to the Black Power movement or simply for being black. With regard to cross burning, then, arguably both sides are required to fight according to the Marquis of Queensbury Rules, and in that limited sense there is no viewpoint discrimination.

31. *R.A.V. v. City of St. Paul*, at 390.
32. *Virginia v. Black*, at 384–385.
33. At 382–384.
34. That being said, blaming someone for being dogmatic in his or her refusal to compromise can belie a deeper judgment on the principles he or she is refusing to compromise. Consider the Ku Klux Klan 'Kreed' (cited in Botham 2009: 107): 'We avow the distinction between the races of mankind as same has been decreed by the Creator, and we shall ever be true in the faithful maintenance of White Supremacy and will strenuously opposed any compromise thereof in any and all things.' If this refusal to compromise is judged harshly by socially progressive sections of society, it may be difficult to disentangle a generalized belief that being dogmatic is a bad thing from a more specific moral disapprobation felt toward theories of white supremacy.
35. That being said, it might still be thought that conflict or confrontation can elicit or even promote the human virtues of endurance, bravery, and strategic acumen.
36. For example, Lepora (2012: 3) argues that a compromise is not a true compromise, as opposed to a bargain, unless it is a compromise over 'fundamental values, moral principles, personal agency, integrity, honour, rights, dignity, and so on.' Moreover, she claims that in order to enter into an interpersonal compromise over matters of principled concern a person must have already established a compromise of his or her own principled concerns. This means that intrapersonal compromise is logically prior to, or forms the basis of, interpersonal compromises; or that intrapersonal compromise is a necessary condition of interpersonal compromise (4, 4n.10). Jones and O'Flynn (2013: 118), in contrast, insist that something is not a true compromise unless it involves two or more parties. On their reading (ibid.), intrapersonal compromises are 'figurative and parasitic upon the standard notion of compromise as an interpersonal or inter-party matter.' Finally, Hampshire draws a parallel between compromise within the hearts of individual men and women and compromise between the members of a society, but says nothing about whether the former is anterior to the latter or *vice versa*. So, for example, Hampshire (1998: 163) writes: 'For the individual also, as for society, compromise, shabby or smart, is both the normal

and the most desirable condition of the soul for a creature whose desires and emotions are often ambivalent and always in conflict with each other.'
37. I do not mean to suggest that end-state standards have no role to play in principled compromise. But I do think that principled compromise ought to be seen first and foremost as a matter of parties living up to procedural ideals, such that if end-state standards have a role to play it is via procedural ideals (cf. Jones and O'Flynn 2013: 122). This might occur if, say, acting in accordance with procedural ideals means that a compromiser should present to his or her opponents a reason for reaching a particular compromise outcome that is based on the fairness of that outcome.
38. In other words, they believe that reaching a fair compromise means that both sides should make concessions or give up part of their demands but at the same time are not asked to cross lines in the sand or to give up certain core demands that are beyond comprise, so to speak.
39. See, e.g., the words of Circuit Judge Pell in *Collin v. Smith II*, esp. at 1200, 1210.
40. *R.A.V. v. City of St. Paul*, at 416, 425.
41. Of course, several liberal political theorists have defended the norm of justificatory neutrality: namely, that in seeking to justify or obtain agreement for its rules the state should not appeal to particular comprehensive conceptions of the good given the fact of reasonable disagreement over such conceptions among the citizens who will be subject to those rules or among whom agreement is being sought (e.g., Dworkin 1978; Ackerman 1980; Larmore 1987; Rawls 1996). Then again, the norm of justificatory neutrality has also been the subject of intense criticism by other notable political theorists (e.g., Barry 1990; 1995; Raz 1986).
42. In Ch. 4 [4.4] I looked at human excellence–centered approaches to evaluating hate speech law. On this approach, *pace* the norm of justificatory neutrality, the promotion of human excellence is a valid basis on which to uphold statutes restricting hate speech, even statutes that constitute content or viewpoint discrimination. Indeed, some pluralist perfectionists insist that it is fitting for the state to justify its rules on the basis of a plurality of human goods. Colin Farrelly (2006: 522), for example, argues that an absolutist approach to free speech that rules out restrictions on the content of speech (e.g., hate speech) 'places too much weight on the moral dimension of toleration, to the detriment of the demands of civility and fairness.' In a similar vein, Brettschneider (2013: 607) defends an exception to the First Amendment doctrine of viewpoint neutrality in the case of laws that target particularly virulent forms of intimidation or true threat that just so happen to be attached to hateful viewpoints—and he does so not by invoking the norm of justificatory neutrality but by 'using a set of substantive, non-neutral values, such as autonomy and equal respect.' Of course, a refusal to rule out an appeal to non-neutral values in the justification of law and legal principles cuts both ways. J.K. Miles (2012), for example, offers a perfectionist justification—grounded in epistemic and intellectual virtues—for courts to be strict in their enforcement of free speech and to embrace wholeheartedly the doctrine of content and viewpoint neutrality.
43. Once again, I offer this purely as a hypothesis and do not providence evidence here to ground that hypothesis. That being said, recent work by Tom Tyler (2001: 234) does suggest that levels of confidence in law and legal actors, not least among racial minorities, is sensitive to the quality of the treatment that persons receive from the courts and the police: 'If they feel that legal authorities are polite and respectful, sincere and benevolent, and do not harass or stigmatize community residents, they are more supportive of law and legal authorities.' See also his (2005).

44. In fact, there are several working distinctions between ideal and non-ideal theory in the literature, but only the issue of compliance need detain us here. For an account of the full terrain, see A. John Simmons (2010) and Laura Valentini (2012).
45. For an opposing view of the ideal/non-ideal theory distinction, according to which questions of socialization, preference formation, and moral education should in instead be viewed as questions of ideal theory, see Alan Hamlin and Zofia Stemplowska (2012: 49–50).

# 11 Conclusion

The first main goal of this book has been to clarify numerous principled arguments for and against hate speech law by articulating a collection of key normative principles. The second main goal has been to disaggregate hate speech law into distinguishable clusters of laws/regulations/codes that constrain uses of hate speech. The importance of being clear about which particular cluster of laws/regulations/codes is the focus of a given principled argument rests in the fact that virtually all of the major principled arguments in the debate are more naturally suited to some clusters than others. The failure to de-homogenize hate speech law into its numerous varieties is like someone trying to decide whether or not a hammer is the right tool for a job without pausing to reflect on the many different kinds of hammer available (ball-peen, cross-peen, claw, dead blow, framing, gavel, rock pick, sledge, stonemason's, tack, and so on).

I shall not attempt to summarize every instance of cluster-sensitivity that has been uncovered in the book. Nor shall I try to draw out a set of definitive conclusions about which clusters of laws/regulations/codes are and which are not warranted all principles considered. This is partly because any such generalizations would inevitably overlook differences between laws within the same clusters as well as subtleties that emerge when laws/regulations/codes are applied to different social practices and institutions. Moreover, it is an important feature of the theory of overall warrant that I defended in Ch. 10 that the principles at stake are compatible with a range of solutions *qua* outputs of principled compromises among citizens, politicians, legislators, regulators, and ultimately legal professionals. Nevertheless, I can offer several points of emphasis that compromisers should bear in mind, which together cover each of the ten clusters of law distinguished in Ch. 2. My first point of emphasis is that laws/regulations/codes that disallow the public expression of hatred and that penalize denying, and so forth, acts of mass cruelty, violence, or genocide are perhaps the most difficult laws to warrant all principles considered. Such laws face a formidable array of principled objections relating to normatively relevant features such as self-realization, the discovery of truth, the acquisition of knowledge, cultural diversity and choice, participation in the formation of public opinion, political legitimacy, and political obligation rooted in respect for formal autonomy, as well as objections relating to more practical considerations such as to do with minimal impairment of liberty and chilling effects. A second point of emphasis is that principled arguments relating to the protection of civic dignity and sensitivity to cultural specificity and intercultural dialogue seem to naturally apply not merely to laws/regulations/codes that proscribe group defamation (*sensu stricto*) but also to laws/regulations/codes that limit negative stereotyping. A third point of emphasis is that principled arguments relating to security are likely to support more than just laws/regulations/codes that prohibit uses of hate speech that threaten public order and laws/regulations/codes that forbid hate speech when it amounts to incitement to discrimination or violence. They might also N-warrant laws/regulations/codes that ban incitement to hatred and laws/regulations/codes that forbid hate speech when it constitutes discriminatory intimidation or provocation. A final point of emphasis is that laws/regulations/codes that forbid discriminatory harassment in the workplace and on university campuses, as well as time, place, and manner restrictions, are likely to draw support from a wide range of different principles and, at the same time, are likely to face a plethora of principled objections. In short, their overall warrant sits on a knife's edge. In the end, what could well make a decisive difference is careful consideration of the point and purpose of the particular social practices or institutions to which these laws/regulations/codes are applied.

All of that being said, I recognize that some people may wish to defend more ambitious generalizations about which clusters of laws/regulations/codes can and cannot be warranted all principles considered. For example, many thinkers draw a distinction between two broad types of hate speech (e.g., Brownstein 1994: 179; Wolfson 1997: 60; Shiffrin [S.H.]1999: 76–77; Peard 2004: 142; Delgado and Stefancic 2009: 362–363; Yong 2011: 394–396; Berger Levinson 2013: 5). The first type is exemplified by immediate, instant, face-to-face, targeted, and individualized hate speech: the type that picks out at close quarters particular subjects for abuse, humiliation, or degradation. The second type is indirect, diffuse, general, and impersonal hate speech: the type that refers to a wide set of targets concerning whom it seeks to express hatred or to create low regard, revilement, or contempt. Following on from this distinction, some people might argue that the first type of hate speech is precisely the sort that should be subject to legal sanctions or remedies, but that the case for laws/regulations/codes is significantly weaker for the second type, so much so that legal constrains are probably unwarranted all principles considered. Along these lines, Kenneth Lasson argues that the first type of hate speech lends itself perfectly to civil actions for the harms of hate speech (harms to health as well as dignitary harms), whereas the second type of hate speech is more suited to criminal prohibitions, and, moreover, that civil actions for hate speech are overall warranted but criminal prohibitions are overall unwarranted (Lasson 1995: 282). However, I believe that such generalizations are hard to sustain, partly because they tend to underestimate the depth and breadth of the principled concerns that apply to legalistic constraints on both the first and second type of hate speech. Perhaps it could be argued that there can be as much harm (broadly construed to include insecurity as well as harm to civic dignity) associated with instances of the second type of hate speech as the first type, and that there can be as much public discourse embedded or enacted in instances of the first type of hate speech as the second type (e.g., Wolfson 1997: 62–63). Consequently, the debate about whether or not to legally constrain hate speech of both types is likely to depend upon complex concatenations of moral, ethical, civic, cultural, political, and legal principles serving or safeguarding a range of different normatively relevant features. This is one of the things that makes talk of compromise so appropriate, I think.

While compromise may be appropriate, not just any compromise can be called "ethical" or "principled", however. And so, the third main goal of this book has been to outline a theory of principled compromise that applies familiar ideals of reciprocity, equality, and mutual respect to the manner in which compromises over matters of principle are conducted. I wish to bring the book to a close by making three things clear about this approach. First, to say that the debate about hate speech law ought to be conducted under ideals of principled compromise is not to say that free speech theory can be reduced to a single principle or value, as some scholars have argued on behalf of self-realization and/or democratic self-government. Rather, it is to say that ideals of principled compromise should be at the pinnacle of how agents go about resolving principled disagreements that reflect a plurality of normatively relevant features. Second, although the aforementioned ideals of principled compromise bear certain similarities with Parekh's vision of intercultural dialogue (discussed in Ch. 6 [6.4]), there are some important differences between the two approaches. My account of principled compromise is primarily focused on interjudicial dialogue rather than intercultural dialogue. My account concentrates on the forging of compromises over matters of principled concern as they relate specifically to debates about hate speech law, whereas Parekh is offering an account of intercultural dialogue across the full spectrum of culturally controversial debates. Finally, Parekh affirms that hate speech law may itself be a precondition for healthy intercultural dialogue,[1] but my account conceives of principled compromise in terms of a collection of moral duties or civic virtues, rather than legal duties to be enforced by laws. In that sense laws/regulations/codes that constrain uses of hate speech are at most only outputs of, and indeed not outputs that are guaranteed by, principled compromise, as opposed to laws that can be foisted upon compromisers *ex ante*. To insist on hate speech law prior to compromise would be to prejudge the outcome of the compromise process and would effectively render that processes redundant. That being said, any process of compromise entered into today must continue to operate within the laws/regulations/codes that were the products of previous principled compromises. And so compromisers who are located in jurisdictions where these sorts of laws/regulations/codes are already in place, via principled compromise, *will* have a legal as well as a moral duty not to engage in hate speech even while attempting to forge new compromises on whether or not hate speech law is overall warranted. Unless and until a new compromise solution is agreed upon, the previous solution stands. However, previous compromise solutions should not be seen as immutable: previous compromises can be subject to review or re-compromise at a later day if parties are in agreement that doing so has become necessary or worthwhile.

Finally, I would like to return to an important dimension of the debate about hate speech law that I briefly touched upon in Ch. 1 but did not fully explore. Which groups or classes of persons warrant protection? I effectively prejudged this question by stipulating that I was interested in laws relating to ascriptive characteristics, which are characteristics ascribed to persons by hate speakers and used to place people into hierarchies of status, merit, morality, humanity, rights, and so on, beyond their control. However, my focus on ascriptive characteristics belies thorny philosophical issues around the distinction between ascriptive and elective characteristics. Some people have argued, for instance, that religious identity ought not to be a protected characteristic as far as hate speech law is concerned because it is voluntarily chosen. I find that argument problematic, but the more important point is that arguments of this nature ought to be aired. Furthermore, in Ch. 1 I provided a semifinite list of 'certain' ascriptive characteristics: namely, race, ethnicity, nationality, citizenship, origin of birth, war record, religion, sexual orientation, gender or transgender identity, disability, age, physical appearance. This list was intended to reflect characteristics that have been specified in hate speech law or that scholars have suggested ought to be specified in hate speech law. Nevertheless, this list raises its own issues. Do all of these characteristics equally warrant protection? Why only these characteristics and not others not on the list? For the most part I have bracketed these issues. One exception was Ch. 5 [5.3] when I argued that Waldron's approach might entail that the characteristics of lacking citizenship or lacking the mental wherewithal to exercise legal rights and powers renders people ineligible for protection through hate speech law, and that he could be criticized on that score. Even so, I believe that the 'Who?' question merits a full and comprehensive research agenda of its own. In Brown (2008) I attempted to make some progress in that direction, looking at possible differences between race and religion vis-à-vis the justification of incitement to hatred legislation in the UK. In their work, other writers have explored arguments for and against extending hate speech law to cover LGBT persons (e.g., Zingo 1998; Cohen [Jonathan] 2000; Goodall 2009), women (e.g., Williams Crenshaw 1993; Lillian 2007), and the disabled (e.g., Cram 2005; Heinze 2009b). These arguments concern the underlying natures of these characteristics as well as more contextually based arguments about extending existing hate speech law under the general principle of treating like cases alike. These are important lines of research that should be strengthened and deepened. Indeed, in my view, it is likely that the 'Who?' question can also be the subject of principled compromise.

**NOTE**

1. For example, springing from his condemnation of the verbal backlash against Muslims in the wake of the Rushdie Affair and more recently the Danish cartoons controversy, Parekh envisages (2006: 317), albeit as a last resort, the use of criminal group defamation law (catchall) in creating a climate of mutual respect in which the vexed issue of restrictions on free speech can be discussed.

# References

Abel, R. (1998) *Speaking Respect, Respecting Speech*. Chicago, IL: University of Chicago Press.
Ackerman, B. (1980) *Social Justice in the Liberal State*. New Haven, CT: Yale University Press.
Adams, W.A. (1958) 'Segregation-Integration: Patterns of Culture and Social Adjustment', *American Journal of Orthopsychiatry* 28: 14–20.
Aleinikoff, T.A. (1987) 'Constitutional Law in the Age of Balancing', *Yale Law Journal* 96: 943–1005.
Alexander, L. (1996) 'Banning Hate: Speech and the Sticks and Stones Defense', *Constitutional Commentary* 13: 71–100.
\_\_\_\_ (2005) *Is There a Right of Freedom of Expression?* Cambridge: Cambridge University Press.
Allport, G. (1954) *The Nature of Prejudice*. Reading, MA: Addison-Wesley.
Altman, A. (1993) 'Liberalism and Campus Hate Speech: A Philosophical Examination', *Ethics* 103: 302–317.
Amar, A. (1992) 'The Case of the Missing Amendments: R.A.V. v. City of St. Paul', *Harvard Law Review* 106: 124–161.
Anand, S. (1997) 'Expressions of Racial Hatred and Criminal Law', *Criminal Law Quarterly* 40: 215–242.
Anderson, E. (1995) 'The Democratic University: The Role of Justice in the Production of Knowledge', *Social Philosophy and Policy* 12: 186–219.
Anti-Defamation League (2006) 'Extremists Declare "Open Season" on Immigrants: Hispanics Target of Incitement and Violence', 23 May. Available at: www.adl.org/main_Extremism/immigration_extremists.htm?Multi_page_sections=sHeading_1 (last accessed 31/07/14).
Appiah, K.A. (1994) 'Identity, Authenticity, and Survival', in A. Gutmann (ed.) *Multiculturalism: Examining the Politics of Recognition*. Princeton, NJ: Princeton University Press.
\_\_\_\_ (2005) *The Ethics of Identity*. Princeton, NJ: Princeton University Press.
\_\_\_\_ (2012) 'What's Wrong with Defamation of Religion?', in M. Herz and P. Molnar (eds.) *The Content and Context of Hate Speech: Rethinking Regulation and Responses*. Cambridge: Cambridge University Press.
Aristotle. [c. 350 BC] (1976) *Ethics*, J. Thompson (trans.). London: Penguin.
\_\_\_\_ [c. 340 BC] (1996) *The Politics*, in *The Politics and the Constitution of Athens*, S. Everson (ed.). Cambridge: Cambridge University Press.
Arkes, H. (1974) 'Civility and the Restriction of Speech: Rediscovering the Defamation of Groups', *Supreme Court Review* 1974: 281–335.
Asquith, N. (2009) 'The Harms of Verbal and Textual Hatred', in B. Perry et al. (eds.) *Hate Crimes, Vol. 2*. Westport, CT: Greenwood.

Assmann, J. (1995) 'Collective Memory and Cultural Identity', *New German Critique* 65: 125–133.
Au, K. (1984) 'Freedom from Fear', *Lincoln Law Review* 15: 45–52.
Audi, R. (2004) *The Good in the Right: A Theory of Intuition and Intrinsic Value*. Princeton, NJ: Princeton University Press.
Austin, J.L. (1962) *How to Do Things with Words*. Oxford: Oxford University Press.
Baker, C.E. (1978) 'Scope of the First Amendment Freedom of Speech', *UCLA Law Review* 25: 964–1040.
_____ (1989) *Human Liberty and Freedom of Speech*. New York, NY: Oxford University Press.
_____ (2009) 'Autonomy and Hate Speech', in I. Hare and J. Weinstein (eds.) *Extreme Speech and Democracy*. Oxford: Oxford University Press.
_____ (2011) 'Autonomy and Free Speech', *Constitutional Commentary* 27: 251–282.
_____ (2012) 'Hate Speech', in M. Herz and P. Molnar (eds.) *The Content and Context of Hate Speech: Rethinking Regulation and Responses*. Cambridge: Cambridge University Press.
Barendt, E. (2005) *Freedom of Speech*, 2nd ed. Oxford: Oxford University Press.
Barry B. (1990) 'How Not to Defend Liberal Institutions', *British Journal of Political Science* 20: 1–14.
_____ (1995) *Justice as Impartiality*. Oxford: Oxford University Press.
BBC News (2005) 'Clarke Unveils Deportation Rules', 24 Aug. Available at: http://news.bbc.co.uk/1/hi/uk_politics/4179044.stm (last accessed 27/11/14).
Bellamy, R. (1999) *Liberalism and Pluralism: Towards a Politics of Compromise*. London: Routledge.
Belton, P.J. (1960) 'Control of Group Defamation: A Comparative Study of Law and Its Limitations', *Tulane Law Review* 34: 299–342.
Benhabib, S. (1996) 'Toward a Deliberative Model of Democratic Legitimacy', in S. Benhabib (ed.) *Democracy and Difference: Contesting the Boundaries of the Political*. Princeton, NJ: Princeton University Press.
Benjamin. M. (1990) *Splitting the Difference: Compromise and Integrity in Ethics and Politics*. Lawrence, KS: University of Kansas Press.
Berger Levinson, R. (2013) 'Targeted Hate Speech and the First Amendment: How the Supreme Court Should Have Decided Snyder', *Suffolk University Law Review* 46: 45–78.
Beschle, D. (2004) 'Kant's Categorical Imperative: An Unspoken Factor in Constitutional Rights Balancing', *Pepperdine Law Review* 31: 949–977.
Bindman, G. (1992) 'Outlawing Hate Speech', *Law Society's Gazette* 89: 17–23.
Blackburn, S. (1996) *The Oxford Dictionary of Philosophy*. Oxford: Oxford University Press.
Blain, M. (1995) 'Group Defamation and the Holocaust', in M. Freedman and E. Freedman (eds.) *Group Defamation and Freedom of Speech: The Relationship between Language and Violence*. Westport, CT: Greenwood Press.
Bleich, E. (2006) 'On Democratic Integration and Free Speech: Response to Tariq Modood and Randall Hansen', *International Migration* 44: 17–22.
_____ (2011) *The Freedom to Be Racist? How the United States and Europe Struggle to Preserve Freedom and Combat Racism*. Oxford: Oxford University Press.
Blim, J. (1995) 'Undoing Our Selves: The Error of Sacrificing Speech in the Quest for Equality', *Ohio State Law Journal* 56: 427–494.
Blum, L. (1998) 'Recognition, Value, and Equality: A Critique of Charles Taylor's and Nancy Fraser's Accounts of Multiculturalism', *Constellations* 5: 51–68.
_____ (2002) *"I'm Not a Racist, But": The Moral Quandary of Race*. Ithaca, NY: Cornell University Press.

Bodney, D. (2009) 'Extreme Speech and American Press Freedoms', in I. Hare and J. Weinstein (eds.) *Extreme Speech and Democracy*. Oxford: Oxford University Press.

Bolotin, L. (2011) 'Disability Hate Speech Has No Place Anywhere – Not Even Online', *The Guardian Online*, 9 Nov. Available at: www.guardian.co.uk/commentisfree/2011/nov/09/disability-hate-speech-online (last accessed 10/09/14).

Bollinger, L.C. (1986) *The Tolerant Society*. New York, NY: Oxford University Press.

Booth, W.J. (2006) *Communities of Memory: On Witness, Identity, and Justice*. Ithaca, NY: Cornell University Press.

Bork, R.H. (1971) 'Neutral Principles and Some First Amendment Problems', *Indiana Law Journal* 47: 1–35.

Borovoy, A.A. (1988) *When Freedoms Collide: The Case for Our Civil Liberties*. Toronto: Lester and Orpen Dennys.

Borovoy, A.A. et al. (1988–1989) 'Language as Violence v. Freedom of Expression: Canadian and American Perspectives on Group Defamation', *Buffalo Law Review* 37: 337–373.

Botham, F. (2009) *Almighty God Created the Races: Christianity, Interracial Marriage, and American Law*. Chapel Hill, NC: University of North Carolina Press.

Boyle, K. (1992) 'Overview of a Dilemma: Censorship versus Racism', in S. Coliver (ed.) *Striking a Balance: Hate Speech, Freedom of Expression, and Non-Discrimination*. London: Article 19 International Centre Against Censorship/Human Rights Centre, University of Essex.

Brahm Levey, G. and Modood, T. (2009) 'Liberal Democracy, Multicultural Citizenship and the Danish Cartoon Affair', in G. Levey and T. Modood (eds.) *Secularism, Religion, and Multicultural Citizenship*. Cambridge: Cambridge University Press.

Braun, S. (2004) *Democracy off Balance: Freedom of Expression and Hate Propaganda Law in Canada*. Toronto: University of Toronto Press.

Brettschneider, C. (2013) 'Value Democracy as the Basis for Viewpoint Neutrality: A Theory of Free Speech and Its Implications for the State Speech and Limited Public Forum Doctrines', *Northwestern University Law Review* 107: 603–645.

Brink, D. (2001) 'Millian Principles, Freedom of Expression, and Hate Speech', *Legal Theory* 7: 119–157.

Brison, (1998a) 'The Autonomy Defense of Free Speech', *Ethics* 108: 312–339.

_____ (1998b) 'Speech, Harm, and the Mind-Body Problem in First Amendment Jurisprudence', *Legal Theory* 4: 39–61.

_____ (2004) 'Speech and Other Acts', *Legal Theory* 10: 261–272.

_____ (2013) 'Hate Speech', in H. LaFollette (ed.) *The International Encyclopedia of Ethics*. Oxford: Wiley-Blackwell.

Brondolo, E. et al. (2011) 'Racism and Hypertension: A Review of the Empirical Evidence and Implications for Clinical Practice', *American Journal of Hypertension* 24: 518–529.

Brown, A. (2007) 'An Egalitarian Plateau? Challenging the Importance of Ronald Dworkin's Abstract Egalitarian Rights', *Res Publica* 13: 255–291.

_____ (2008) 'The Racial and Religious Hatred Act 2006: A Millian Response', *Critical Review of International Social and Political Philosophy* 11: 1–24.

_____ (2010) 'On Behalf of Mill's Assumption of Infallibility Argument', *British Journal for the History of Philosophy* 18: 857–873.

Brown, J.J. and Stern, C.L. (1964) 'Group Defamation in the U.S.A.', *Cleveland State Law Review* 13: 7–32.

Browne, K.R. (1991) 'Title VII as Censorship: Hostile-Environment Harassment and the First Amendment', *Ohio State Law Journal* 52: 481–550.

Brownstein, A.E. (1994) 'Hate Speech and Harassment: The Constitutionality of Campus Codes that Prohibit Racial Insults', *William and Mary Bill of Rights Journal* 3: 179–217.

Brugger, W. (2003) 'The Treatment of Hate Speech in German Constitutional Law (Part I)', *German Law Journal* 4: 1–44.

Buckner Inniss, L. (2007) 'A 'Ho New World: Raced and Gendered Insult as Ersatz Carnival and the Corruption of Freedom of Expression Norms', *NYU Review of Law and Social Change* 33: 43–86.

Burgess, C.R. et al. (2011) 'Playing With Prejudice: The Prevalence and Consequences of Racial Stereotypes in Video Games Media Psychology', *Media Psychology* 14: 289–311.

Butler, J. (1993) *Bodies That Matter: On the Discursive Limits of "Sex"*. London: Routledge.

—— (1997) *Excitable Speech: A Politics of the Performative*. New York, NY: Routledge.

Calvert, C. (1997) 'Hate Speech and Its Harms: A Communication Theory Perspective', *Journal of Communication* 47: 4–19.

Carmi, G. (2007) 'Dignity—The Enemy from Within: A Theoretical and Comparative Analysis of Human Dignity as a Free Speech Justification', *University of Pennsylvania Journal of Constitutional Law* 9: 957–1001.

Caws, P. (1994) 'Identity: Cultural, Transcultural, and Multicultural', in D. Goldberg (ed.) *Multiculturalism: A Critical Reader*. Oxford: Blackwell.

Chafee, Z. (1941) *Free Speech in the United States*. Cambridge, MA: Harvard University Press.

—— (1947) *Government and Mass Communications: A Report from the Commission on Freedom of the Press, Vol. 1*. Chicago, IL: University of Chicago Press.

Chamallas, M. and Wriggins, J.B. (2010) *The Measure of Injury: Race, Gender, and Tort Law*. New York, NY: New York University Press.

Chang, R. (1997) 'Introduction', in R. Chang (ed.) *Incommensurability, Incomparability, and Practical Reason*. Cambridge, MA: Harvard University Press.

—— (2004a) 'Putting Together Morality and Well-Being', in P. Baumann and M. Betzler (eds.) *Practical Conflicts*. Cambridge: Cambridge University Press.

—— (2004b) 'All Things Considered', *Philosophical Perspectives* 18: 1–22.

Charles, G. (2005) 'Colored Speech: Cross Burnings, Epistemics, and the Triumph of the Crits?', *Georgetown Law Review* 93: 575–632.

Chemerinsky, E. (2003) 'Striking a Balance on Hate Speech', *Trial* 39, July: 78–79

—— (2009) 'Unpleasant Speech on Campus, Even Hate Speech, Is a First Amendment Issue', *William and Mary Bill of Rights Journal* 17: 765–772.

Cicero, M. [c. 84 BC] (1949) *De Inventione*, H. Hubbell (trans.). Cambridge, MA: Harvard University Press.

Clark, K. (1995) 'Group Defamation and the Oppression of Black Americans', in M. Freedman and E. Freedman (eds.) *Group Defamation and Freedom of Speech: The Relationship between Language and Violence*. Westport, CT: Greenwood Press.

Code, L. (1987) *Epistemic Responsibility*. Hanover, NH: University Press of New England.

Cohen, G. et al. (2008) 'Identity, Belonging, and Achievement: A Model, Interventions, Implications', *Current Directions in Psychological Science* 17: 365–369.

Cohen, G.A. (1992) 'Incentives, Inequality and Community', in G.B. Peterson (ed.) *The Tanner Lectures on Human Values, Vol. 13*. Salt Lake City, UT: University of Utah Press.

Cohen, J. [Jonathan] (2000) 'More Censorship or Less Discrimination? Sexual Orientation Hate Propaganda in Multiple Perspectives', *McGill Law Journal* 46: 69–104.

Cohen, J. [Joshua] (1993) 'Freedom of Expression', *Philosophy and Public Affairs* 22: 207–263.
_____ (1996) 'Procedure and Substance in Deliberative Democracy', in S. Benhabib (ed.) *Democracy and Difference: Contesting the Boundaries of the Political*. Princeton, NJ: Princeton University Press.
Cohen-Almagor, R. (1993) 'Harm Principle, Offence Principle, and the Skokie Affair', *Political Studies* 41: 453–470.
_____ (2006a) *The Scope of Tolerance: Studies on the Costs of Free Expression and Freedom of the Press*. London: Routledge.
_____ (2006b) 'On Compromise and Coercion', *Ratio Juris* 19: 434–455.
_____ (2008) 'Hate in the Classroom: Free Expression, Holocaust Denial, and Liberal Education', *American Journal of Education* 114: 215–241.
_____ (2009) 'Regulating Hate and Racial Speech in Israel', *Cardozo Journal of International and Comparative Law* 17: 101–110.
_____ (2012) 'Is Law Appropriate to Regulate Hateful and Racist Speech?', *Israel Studies Review* 27: 41–64.
Colby, T.B. (2012) 'In Defense of Judicial Empathy', *Minnesota Law Review* 96: 1944–2015.
Coliver, S. (1992) 'Hate Speech Laws: Do They Work?', in S. Coliver (ed.) *Striking a Balance: Hate Speech, Freedom of Expression and Non-Discrimination*. London: Article 19 International Centre Against Censorship/Human Rights Centre, University of Essex.
Collier, C.W. (2001) 'Hate Speech and the Mind-Body Problem: A Critique of Postmodern Censorship Theory', *Legal Theory* 7: 203–234.
Corlett, J.A. and Francescotti, R. (2002) 'Foundations of a Theory of Hate Speech', *Wayne Law Review* 48: 1071–1100.
Cortese, A. (2006) *Opposing Hate Speech*. Westport, CT: Praeger Publishers.
Council of Europe Ministers of Foreign Affairs (2008) *White Paper on Intercultural Dialogue: "Living Together as Equals."* Strasbourg: Council of Europe.
Cox, P. (1995) 'The Disputation of Hate: Speech Codes, Pluralism, and Academic Freedoms', *Social Theory and Practice* 21: 113–144.
Craddock, J.M. (1995) 'Words That Injure, Laws That Silence: Campus Hate Speech Codes and the Threat to American Education', *Florida State University Law* 22: 1047–1089.
Cram, I. (2005) 'Hate Speech and Disabled People: Some Comparative Constitutional Thoughts', in A. Lawson and C. Gooding (eds.) *Disability Rights in Europe: From Theory to Practice*. Oxford: Hart Publishing.
Crocker, J. and Luhtanen, R. (1990) 'Collective Self-Esteem and Ingroup Bias', *Journal of Personality and Social Psychology* 58: 60–67.
Crossman, G. (2005) 'Religious Hate: A Criminal Offence? Liberty Says No', *Legal Action*, Mar.: 9.
Dahl, R. (1989) *Democracy and Its Critics*. New Haven, CT: Yale University Press.
_____ (2001) *How Democratic Is the Constitution?* New Haven, CT: Yale University Press.
Dan-Cohen, M. (2002) *Harmful Thoughts: Essays on Law, Self and Morality*. Princeton, NJ: Princeton University Press.
Daniels, J. (2008) 'Race, Civil Rights, and Hate Speech in the Digital Era', in A. Everett (ed.) *Learning Race and Ethnicity: Youth and Digital Media*. Cambridge, MA: MIT Press.
Das, E. et al. (2009) 'How Terrorism News Reports Increase Prejudice against Outgroups: A Terror Management Account', *Journal of Experimental Social Psychology* 45: 453–459.

Day, M. (1990) 'The Salman Rushdie Affair: Implications for the CRE and Race Relations', in *Free Speech: Report of a Seminar, Discussion Papers 2*. London: Commission for Racial Equality.

de Villiers, M. (1899) *The Roman and Roman-Dutch Law of Injuries: A Translation of Book 47, Title 10, of Voet's Commentary of the Pandects*. Cape Town: J.C. Juta.

Delgado, R. (1982) 'Words That Wound: A Tort Action for Racial Insults, Epithets, and Name-Calling', *Harvard Civil Rights-Civil Liberties Law Review* 17: 133–181.

———— (1983) 'Professor Delgado Replies', *Harvard Civil Rights-Civil Liberties Law Review* 18: 593–597.

———— (1991) 'Campus Antiracism Rules: Constitutional Narratives in Collision', *Northwestern University Law Review* 85: 343–387.

———— (2013) 'Review of *The Harm in Hate Speech* by Jeremy Waldron', *Law and Society Review* 47: 232–233.

Delgado, R. and Stefancic, J. (1992) 'Images of the Outsider in American Law and Culture: Can Free Expression Remedy Systemic Social Ills', *Cornell Law Review* 77: 1258–1297.

———— (1996) 'Ten Arguments against Hate-Speech Regulation: How Valid?', *Northern Kentucky Law Review* 23: 475–490.

———— (2004) *Understanding Words That Wound*. Boulder, CO: Westview Press.

———— (2009) 'Four Observations about Hate Speech', *Wake Forest Law Review* 44: 353–370.

Delgado, R. and Yun, D.H. (1994) 'The Neoconservative Case against Hate Speech Regulation: Lively, D'Souzu, Gates, Carter, and the Toughlove Crowd', *Vanderbilt Law Review* 47: 1807–1825.

———— (1995) '"The Speech We Hate": First Amendment Totalism, the ACLU, and the Principle of Dialogic Politics', *Arizona State Law Journal* 27: 1281–1300.

Demaske, C. (2004) 'Modern Power and the First Amendment: Reassessing Hate Speech', *Communication Law and Policy* 9: 273–316.

Deutsch, M. et al. (eds.) (1968) *Social Class, Race and Psychological Development*. New York: Holt, Rinehart and Winston.

Deutsch, N. (2006) 'Professor Nimmer Meets Professor Schauer (and Others): An Analysis of "Definitional Balancing" as a Methodology for Determining the "Visible Boundaries of the First Amendment"', *Akron Law Review* 39: 483–539.

Dixon, T. and Maddox, K. (2005) 'Skin Tone, Crime News, and Social Reality Judgments: Priming the Stereotype of the Dark and Dangerous Black Criminal', *Journal of Applied Social Psychology* 35: 1555–1570.

Douglas, L. (1995) 'The Memory of Judgment: The Law, the Holocaust, and Denial', *History and Memory* 7: 100–120.

Dovidio, J.F. et al. (2003) 'Intergroup Contact: The Past, Present, and the Future', *Group Processes and Intergroup Relations* 6: 5–21.

Downs, D.A. (1985) *Nazis in Skokie: Freedom, Community, and the First Amendment*. Notre Dame, IN: University of Notre Dame Press.

———— (1993) 'Codes Say Darnedest Things', *Quill* 81, Oct: 19.

———— (2005) *Restoring Free Speech and Liberty on Campus*. New York, NY: Cambridge University Press.

Dworkin, R. (1977) *Taking Rights Seriously*. London: Duckworth.

———— (1978) 'Liberalism', in S. Hampshire (ed.) *Public and Private Morality*. Cambridge: Cambridge University Press.

———— (1985) *A Matter of Principle*. Cambridge, MA: Harvard University Press.

———— (1996) *Freedom's Law: The Moral Reading of the American Constitution*. Cambridge, MA: Harvard University Press.

———— (2006) *Is Democracy Possible Here?* Princeton, NJ: Princeton University Press.

_____ (2009) 'Foreword', in I. Hare and J. Weinstein (eds.) *Extreme Speech and Democracy*. Oxford: Oxford University Press.

_____ (2011) *Justice for Hedgehogs*. Cambridge, MA: Harvard University Press.

_____ (2012) 'Reply to Jeremy Waldron', in M. Herz and P. Molnar (eds.) *The Content and Context of Hate Speech: Rethinking Regulation and Responses*. Cambridge: Cambridge University Press.

Eberle, E.J. (2002) *Dignity and Liberty: Constitutional Visions in Germany and the United States*. Westport, CT: Praeger Publishers.

Edger, R. (2010) 'Are Hate Speech Provisions Anti-Democratic?: An International Perspective', *American University International Law Review* 26: 119–155.

Edwards, H. (1991) 'The Judicial Function and the Elusive Goal of Principled Decision-Making', *Wisconsin Law Review*: 837–865.

_____ (2002) 'Race and the Judiciary', *Yale Law and Policy Review* 20: 325–330.

_____ (2003) 'The Effects of Collegiality on Judicial Decision Making', *University of Pennsylvania Law Review* 151: 1639–1690.

Ehrlich, H.J. (1973) *The Social Psychology of Prejudice*. New York, NY: Wiley.

Ehrlich, H.J. et al. (1995) 'The Traumatic Impact of Ethnoviolence', in L. Lederer and R. Delgado (eds.) *The Price We Pay: The Case against Racist Speech, Hate Propaganda, and Pornography*. New York, NY: Hill and Wang.

Emerson, T. (1963) 'Toward a General Theory of the First Amendment', *Yale Law Journal* 72: 877–956.

_____ (1970) *The System of Freedom of Expression*. New York, NY: Vintage.

Equality and Human Rights Commission. (2009) *Disabled People's Experiences of Targeted Violence and Hostility*. Manchester: Equality and Human Rights Commission.

Errera, R. (1992) 'In Defence of Civility: Racial and Incitement and Group Libel in French Law', in S. Coliver (ed.) *Striking a Balance: Hate Speech, Freedom of Expression, and Non-Discrimination*. London: Article 19 International Centre Against Censorship/Human Rights Centre, University of Essex.

Estlund, C. (1997) 'Freedom of Expression in the Workplace and the Problem of Discriminatory Harassment', *Texas Law Review* 75: 687–777.

Estlund, D. (2008) *Democratic Authority: A Philosophical Framework*. Princeton, NJ: Princeton University Press.

European Commission Against Racism and Intolerance (2012) *Report on Italy, Fourth Monitoring Cycle*. Strasbourg: Council of Europe.

Fagan, J. (2008) 'Legitimacy and Criminal Justice', *Ohio State Journal of Criminal Law* 6: 123–140.

Farrelly, C. (2006) 'Civic Liberalism and the "Dialogical Model" of Judicial Review', *Law and Philosophy* 25: 489–531.

Feagin, J.R. et al. (2001) 'The Many Costs of Discrimination: The Case of Middle-class African Americans', *Indiana Law Review* 34: 1313–1360.

Feinberg, J. (1984) *The Moral Limits of Criminal Law, Vol. 1: Harm to Others*. Oxford: Oxford University Press.

_____ (1988) *The Moral Limits of Criminal Law, Vol. 2: Offense to Others*. Oxford: Oxford University Press.

_____ (1989) *The Moral Limits of Criminal Law, Vol. 3: Harm to Self*. Oxford: Oxford University Press.

_____ (1990) *The Moral Limits of Criminal Law, Vol. 4: Harmless Wrongdoing*. Oxford: Oxford University Press.

Feldman, D. (1993) *Civil Liberties and Human Rights in England and Wales*. Oxford: Oxford University Press.

_____ (1998) 'Content Neutrality', in I. Loveland (ed.) *Importing the First Amendment: Freedom of Speech and Expression in Britain, Europe and USA*. Oxford: Hart Publishing.

Fish, S. (1994) *There's No Such Thing As Free Speech: And It's a Good Thing, Too*. New York, NY: Oxford University Press.

―― (1997) 'Boutique Multiculturalism, or Why Liberals Are Incapable of Thinking about Hate Speech', *Critical Inquiry* 23: 378–395.

―― (2001) *The Trouble with Principle*. Cambridge, MA: Harvard University Press.

Fishman, E. (2011) 'To Secure These Rights: The Supreme Court and Snyder v. Phelps', *St. Thomas Law Review* 24: 101–115.

Fiss, O. (1986) 'Free Speech and Social Structure', *Iowa Law Review* 71: 1405–1425.

―― (1996a) *The Irony of Free Speech: Liberalism Divided*. Cambridge, MA: Harvard University Press.

―― (1996b) *Liberalism Divided: Freedom of Speech and the Many Uses of State Power*. Boulder, CO: Westview Press.

Flemming, J. (2004) 'Securing Deliberative Democracy', *Fordham Law Review* 72: 1435–1475.

Ford, T.E. (1997) 'Effects of Stereotypical Television Portrayals of African-Americans on Person Perception', *Social Psychology Quarterly* 60: 266–275.

Fraleigh, D.M. and Tuman, J.S. (2011) *Freedom of Expression in the Marketplace of Ideas*. Thousand Oaks, CA: Sage.

Frantz, L.B. (1962) 'The First Amendment in the Balance', *Yale Law Journal* 71: 1424–1450.

Fraser, N. (1995) 'From Redistribution to Recognition? Dilemmas of Justice in a "Post-Socialist" Age', *New Left Review* I/212: 68–93.

―― (2000) 'Rethinking Recognition', *New Left Review* 3: 107–120.

Fried, C. (1963) 'Two Concepts of Interests: Some Reflections on the Supreme Court's Balancing Test', *Harvard Law Review* 76: 755–778.

―― (1992) 'The New First Amendment Jurisprudence: A Threat to Liberty', in G. Stone et al. (eds.) *The Bill of Rights in the Modern State*. Chicago, IL: University of Chicago Press.

Fu, H. (2012) 'China's Hate Speech Conundrum', OHCHR Documents, 14 Dec. Available at: www.ohchr.org/Documents/Issues/Expression/ICCPR/Bangkok/FuHualing.pdf (last accessed 05/09/14).

Gale, M.E. (1991) 'Reimagining the First Amendment: Racist Speech and Equal Liberty', *St. John's Law Review* 65: 119–185.

Galeotti, A.E. (2002). *Toleration as Recognition*. Cambridge: Cambridge University Press.

Ganley, C.M. et al. (2013) 'An Examination of Stereotype Threat Effects on Girls' Mathematics Performance', *Developmental Psychology* 49: 1886–1897.

Gardner, R.C. and Taylor, D.M. (1968) *Ethnic Stereotypes: Their Effects on Person Perception* 22: 267–276.

Gates, H.L., Jr. (1993) 'Let Them Talk', *New Republic* 20 Sept.: 37–49.

Gay, Lesbian and Straight Education Network (2012). *The 2011 National School Climate Survey*. New York, NY: GLSEN.

Gelber, K. (2002) *Speaking Back: The Free Speech Versus Hate Speech Debate*. Amsterdam: John Benjamins Publishing.

―― (2010) 'Freedom of Political Speech, Hate Speech and the Argument from Democracy: The Transformative Contribution of Capabilities Theory', *Contemporary Political Theory* 9: 304–324.

―― (2011) *Speech Matters: Getting Free Speech Right*. Brisbane: University of Queensland Press.

―― (2012a) 'Reconceptualizing Counterspeech in Hate Speech Policy (with a Focus on Australia)', in M. Herz and P. Molnar (eds.) *The Content and Context of Hate Speech: Rethinking Regulation and Responses*. Cambridge: Cambridge University Press.

_____ (2012b) '"Speaking Back": The Likely Fate of Hate Speech Policy in the United States and Australia', in I. Maitra and M. McGowan (eds.) *Speech and Harm: Controversies over Free Speech*. Oxford: Oxford University Press.

Gelber, K. and McNamara, L. (2012) 'The Impact of Hate Speech Laws on Public Discourse in Australia (1989–2009): Preliminary Findings.' Available at: https://lha.uow.edu.au/content/groups/public/@web/@law/documents/doc/uow134359.pdf (last accessed 02/08/14).

_____ (2014) 'Changes in the Expression of Prejudice in Public Discourse in Australia: Assessing the Impact of Hate Speech Laws on Letters to the Editor 1992–2010', *Australian Journal of Human Rights* 20: 99–128.

George, R. (1993) *Making Men Moral: Civil Liberties and Public Morality*. Oxford: Oxford University Press.

Gerber, S.D. (2004) 'Politics of Free Speech', in E. Paul et al. (eds.) *Freedom of Speech*. Cambridge: Cambridge University Press.

Gerstenfeld, P.B. et al. (2003) 'Hate Online: A Content Analysis of Extremist Internet Sites', *Analyses of Social Issues and Public Policy* 3: 29–44.

Gewirth, A. (2009) *Self-Fulfillment*. Princeton, NJ: Princeton University Press.

Gilmore, J. (2011) 'Expression as Realization: Speakers' Interests in Freedom of Speech', *Law and Philosophy* 30: 517–539.

Glasser, I. (1994) 'Introduction', in H.L. Gates Jr. et al. (eds.) *Speaking of Race, Speaking of Sex: Hate Speech, Civil Rights, and Civil Liberties*. New York, NY: New York University Press.

Glensy, R. (2011) 'The Right to Dignity', *Columbia Human Rights Law Review* 43: 65–142.

Goffman, E. (1963) *Stigma: Notes on the Management of Spoiled Identity*. Englewood Cliffs, NJ: Prentice-Hall. Available at: http://en.wikipedia.org/wiki/Special:BookSources/0671622447 (last accessed 11/17/14).

Goodall, K. (2009) 'Challenging Hate Speech: Incitement to Hatred on Grounds of Sexual Orientation in England, Wales and Northern Ireland', *International Journal of Human Rights* 13: 211–232.

Goodin, R. (2012) *On Settling*. Princeton, NJ: Princeton University Press.

Goodpaster, G. (1997) 'Equality and Free Speech: The Case against Substantive Equality', *Iowa Law Review* 82: 645–687.

Gonzales, P.M. et al. (2002) 'The Effects of Stereotype Threat and Double-Minority Status on the Test Performance of Latino Women', *Personality and Social Psychology Bulletin* 28: 659–670.

Gordon, J. (1997) 'John Stuart Mill and the "Marketplace of Ideas"', *Social Theory and Practice* 23: 235–249.

Gunther, G. (1990) 'Should Universities Restrict Expression That Is Racist or Otherwise Denigrating? No', *Stanford Lawyer* 24: 7, 9, 41.

Gray, J. (1983) *Mill On liberty: A Defence*. London: Routledge.

Gross, J.J. and John, O.P. (2003) 'Individual Differences in Two Emotion Regulation Processes: Implications for Affect, Relationships, and Well-Being', *Journal of Personality and Social Psychology* 85: 348–362.

Greenawalt, K. (1987) *Conflicts of Law and Morality*. Oxford: Oxford University Press.

_____ (1989) *Speech, Crime, and the Uses of Language*. Oxford: Oxford University Press.

_____ (1995) *Fighting Words: Individuals, Communities and Liberties of Speech*. Princeton, NJ: Princeton University Press.

Greenberg, J. and Pyszczynski, T. (1985) 'The Effect of an Overheard Ethnic Slur on Evaluations of the Target: How to Spread a Social Disease', *Journal of Experimental Psychology* 21: 61–72

Griffin, J. (1986) *Well-Being*. Oxford: Oxford University Press.

Grimm, D. (2009) 'Freedom of Speech in a Globalized World', in I. Hare and J. Weinstein (eds.) *Extreme Speech and Democracy*. Oxford: Oxford University Press.

Gutmann, A. (1994) 'Introduction', in A. Gutmann (ed.) *Multiculturalism: Examining the Politics of Recognition*. Princeton, NJ: Princeton University Press.

Gutmann, A. and Thompson, D. (1996) *Democracy and Disagreement*. Cambridge, MA: Harvard University Press.

Hafner, H. (1968) 'Psychological Disturbances Following Prolonged Persecution', *Social Psychiatry* 3: 79–88.

Hamlin, A. and Stemplowska, Z. (2012) 'Theory, Ideal Theory and the Theory of Ideals', *Political Studies Review* 10: 48–62.

Hampshire, S. (1998) 'Justice Is Conflict: The Soul and the City', in G. Peterson (ed.) *The Tanner Lectures on Human Values, Vol. 19*. Salt Lake City, UT: University of Utah Press.

Harburg, E. et al. (1973) 'Socio-Ecological Stress, Suppressed Hostility, Skin Color, and Black-White Male Blood Pressure: Detroit', *Psychosomatic Medicine* 35: 276–296.

Hare, I. (2003) 'Inflammatory Speech: Cross Burning and the First Amendment', *Public Law* 2003: 408–414.

_____ (2006) 'Crosses, Crescents and Sacred Cows: Criminalising Incitement to Religious Hatred', *Public Law* 2006: 521–537.

_____ (2009) 'Blasphemy and Incitement to Religious Hatred: Free Speech Dogma and Doctrine', in I. Hare and J. Weinstein (eds.) *Extreme Speech and Democracy*. Oxford: Oxford University Press.

_____ (2012) 'The Harms of Hate Speech Legislation', *freespeechdebate.com*, 23 Mar. Available at: http://freespeechdebate.com/en/discuss/the-harms-of-hate-speech-legislation/ (last accessed 01/08/14).

Harel, A. (2012) 'Hate Speech and Comprehensive Forms of Life', in M. Herz and P. Molnar (eds.) *The Content and Context of Hate Speech: Rethinking Regulation and Remedies*. Cambridge: Cambridge University Press.

Hart, H.L.A. (1973) 'Rawls on Liberty and Its Priority', *University of Chicago Law Review* 40: 534–555.

Hartley, R. (2004) 'Cross Burning—Hate Speech as Free Speech: A Comment on Virginia v. Black', *Catholic University Law Review* 54: 1–52.

Hartman, R.G. (1992) 'Revitalizing Group Defamation as a Remedy for Hate Speech on Campus', *Oregon Law Review* 71: 855–900.

Harvard Law Review (1988) 'Note: A Communitarian Defense of Group Libel Laws', *Harvard Law Review* 101: 682–701.

Haupt, C. (2005) 'Regulating Hate Speech—Damned if You Do and Damned if You Don't: Lessons Learned from Comparing the German and U.S. Approaches', *Boston University International Law Journal* 23: 299–335.

Hauptman, L. (1995) 'Group Defamation and the Genocide of American Indians', in M. Freedman and E. Freedman (eds.) *Group Defamation and Freedom of Speech: The Relationship between Language and Violence*. Westport, CT: Greenwood Press.

Haworth, A. (1998) *Free Speech*. London: Routledge.

Hayakawa, S.I. (1966) *Symbol, Status, and Personality*. New York, NY: Mariner Books.

Heins, M. (1983) 'Banning Words: A Comment on "Words That Wound"', *Harvard Civil Rights-Civil Liberties Law Review* 18: 585–592.

Heinze, E. (2006) 'Viewpoint Absolutism and Hate Speech', *Modern Law Review* 69: 543–582.

_____ (2009a) 'Wild-West Cowboys versus Cheese-Eating Surrender Monkeys: Some Problems in Comparative Approaches to Hate Speech', in I. Hare and

J. Weinstein (eds.) *Extreme Speech and Democracy*. Oxford: Oxford University Press.

―― (2009b) 'Cumulative Jurisprudence and Hate Speech: Sexual Orientation and Analogies to Disability, Age, and Obesity', in I. Hare and J. Weinstein (eds.) *Extreme Speech and Democracy*. Oxford: Oxford University Press.

―― (2013) 'Hate Speech and the Normative Foundations of Regulation', *International Journal of Law in Context* 9: 590–617.

Hemmer, J. (1995) 'Hate Speech: The Egalitarian/Libertarian Dilemma', *Howard Journal of Communications* 5: 307–17.

Henderson, L. (1993) 'Legality and Empathy', in P. Smith (ed.) *Feminist Jurisprudence*. New York, NY: Oxford University Press.

Heyman, S.J. (2002) 'Spheres of Autonomy: Reforming the Content Neutrality Doctrine in First Amendment Jurisprudence', *William and Mary Bill of Rights Journal* 10: 647–717.

―― (2008) *Free Speech and Human Dignity*. New Haven, CT: Yale University Press.

―― (2012) 'To Drink the Cup of Fury: Funeral Picketing, Public Discourse and the First Amendment', *Connecticut Law Review* 45: 101–176.

Heywood, A. (2012) *Political Ideologies: An Introduction*, 5th ed. Basingstoke: Palgrave Macmillan.

Hill, T.E. (1980) 'Humanity as an End in Itself', *Ethics* 91: 84–99.

Holmes, S. (2012) 'Waldron, Machiavelli, and Hate Speech', in M. Herz and P. Molnar (eds.) *The Content and Context of Hate Speech: Rethinking Regulation and Responses*. Cambridge: Cambridge University Press.

Honneth, A. (1992) 'Integrity and Disrespect: Principles of a Conception of Morality Based on the Theory of Recognition', *Political Theory* 20: 187–201.

―― (1995) *The Struggle for Recognition: The Moral Grammar of Social Conflicts*, J. Anderson (trans.). Cambridge, MA: MIT Press.

―― (2003) 'Redistribution as Recognition: A Response to Nancy Fraser', in N. Fraser and A. Honneth (eds.) *Redistribution or Recognition? A Political-Philosophical Exchange*. London: Verso.

Horowitz, L. and Bramson, V. (1979) 'Skokie, The ACLU And The Endurance of Democratic Theory', *Law and Contemporary Problems* 43: 328–349.

Hulshizer, R.M. (1991) 'Securing Freedom from Harassment without Reducing Freedom of Speech: Doe v. University of Michigan', *Iowa Law Review* 76: 383–404.

Hume, D. [1739–1740] (1984) *A Treatise of Human Nature*, E. Mossner (ed.). London: Penguin.

―― [1741–1777] (1994) 'Of the Liberty of the Press', in K. Haakonssen (ed.) *David Hume: Political Essays*. Cambridge: Cambridge Scholars Press.

―― [1751] (2006) *An Enquiry Concerning the Principles of Morals*. New York, NY: Cosimo.

―― [1768] (1932) Letter to Turgot, in J. Greig (ed.) *The Letters of David Hume, Vol. 2*. Oxford: Oxford University Press.

Hursthouse, R. (1999) *On Virtue Ethics*. Oxford: Oxford University Press.

Iganski, P. et al. (2011) *Rehabilitation of Hate Crime Offenders*. Scotland: Equality and Human Rights Commission.

Jacobs, J. and Potter, K. (1998) *Hate Crimes: Criminal Law and Identity Politics*. Oxford: Oxford University Press.

Jacobson, D. (1995) 'Freedom of Speech Acts? A Response to Langton', *Philosophy and Public Affairs* 24: 64–79.

―― (2001) 'Speech and Action: Replies to Hornsby and Langton', *Legal Theory* 7: 179–201.

―― (2007) 'Why Free Speech Includes Hate Speech', in J. Ryberg et al. (eds.) *New Waves in Applied Ethics*. New York: Palgrave Macmillan.

Jacoby, T. (1988) 'Time to Outlaw Racial Slurs?', *Newsweek* 6 June: 48.
Janssen, E. (2009) 'Limits to Expression on Religion in France', *Agama and Religiusitas di Eropa, Journal of European Studies* 5: 22–45.
Jay, T. (2009) 'Do Offensive Words Harm People', *Psychology, Public, Policy, and Law* 15: 81–101.
Johnson, J. et al. (1997) 'Race, Media, and Violence: Differential Racial Effects of Exposure to Violent News Stories', *Basic and Applied Social Psychology* 19: 81–90.
Johnson, P.E. (1984) 'Concepts and Compromise in First Amendment Religious Doctrine', *California Law Review* 72: 817–846.
Jones, P. and O'Flynn, I. (2013) 'Can a Compromise Be Fair?', *Politics, Philosophy and Economics* 12: 115–135.
Jones, T. (1998) *Human Rights: Group Defamation, Freedom of Expression and the Law of Nations*. The Hague: Kluwer Law International.
Kagan, E. (1993) 'Regulation of Hate Speech and Pornography after R.A.V.', *University of Chicago Law Review* 60: 873–902.
Kahn, R.A. (2004) *Holocaust Denial and the Law: A Comparative Study*. New York: Palgrave Macmillan.
Kalven, H. (1965) *The Negro and the First Amendment*. Chicago, IL: University of Chicago Press.
Kant, I. [1785] (1948) *Groundwork of the Metaphysics of Morals*, H. Paton (ed.) *The Moral Law*. London: Routledge.
\_\_\_\_\_ [1793] (2009) *Religion within the Bounds of Bare Reason*, W. Pluhar (trans.). Indianapolis: Hackett.
\_\_\_\_\_ [1797] (1996) *The Metaphysics of Morals*, M. Gregor (ed.). Cambridge: Cambridge University Press.
Karam, N. (2012) *The 9/11 Backlash: A Decade of U.S. Hate Crimes Targeting the Innocent*. Berkeley, CA: Beatitude Press.
Kardiner, A. and Ovesey, L. (1951) *The Mark of Oppression: A Psychosocial Study of the American Negro*. New York, NY: Norton.
Karst, K.L. (1990) 'Boundaries and Reason: Freedom of Expression and the Subordination of Groups', *University of Illinois Law Review*: 95–149.
Kateb, G. (1996) 'The Freedom of Worthless and Harmful Speech', in B. Yack (ed.) *Liberalism without Illusions: Essays on Liberal Theory and the Political Vision of Judith N. Shklar*. Chicago, IL: University of Chicago Press.
Kaufman, G. (1989) 'So-Called Liberals for Whom Some Are More Tolerable Than Others', *Independent*, 1 Mar.
Kawakami, K. et al. (2000) 'Just Say No (to Stereotyping): Effects of Training in Trait Negation on Stereotype Activation', *Journal of Personality and Social Psychology* 78: 871–888.
Kendall, W. (1963) *The Conservative Affirmation*. Chicago, IL: Gateway Editions.
Kennedy, R.L. (1999–2000) 'Who Can Say "Nigger"? And Other Considerations', *The Journal of Blacks in Higher Education* 26: 86–96.
Kernohan, A. (1998) *Liberalism, Equality, and Cultural Oppression*. Cambridge: Cambridge University Press.
Kiev, A. (1973) 'Psychiatric Disorders in Minority Groups', in P. Watson (ed.) *Psychology and Race*. Chicago, IL: Aldine.
Kitano, H.L. (1974) *Race Relations*. Englewood Cliffs, NJ: Prentice-Hall.
Kitrosser, H. (2005) 'Containing Unprotected Speech', *Florida Law Review* 57: 843–905.
Klaff, L. (2010) 'Anti-Zionist Expression on the UK Campus: Free Speech or Hate Speech?', *Jewish Political Studies Review* 22: 3–4.
Klosko, G. (1992) *The Principle of Fairness and Political Obligation*. Lanham, MD: Rowman and Littlefield.

Knechtle, J. (2006) 'When to Regulate Hate Speech', *Penn State Law Review* 110: 539–578.
\_\_\_\_ (2008) 'Holocaust Denial and the Concept of Dignity in the European Union', *Florida State University Law Review* 36: 41–65.
Kommers, D.P. (1997) *The Constitutional Jurisprudence of the Federal Republic of Germany*, 2nd ed. Durham, NC: Duke University Press.
Kommers, D.P. and Miller, R.A. (2012) *The Constitutional Jurisprudence of the Federal Republic of Germany*, 3rd ed. Durham, NC: Duke University Press.
Kors, A.C. (1991) 'Harassment Policies in the University', *Society* 28: 22–30.
Korsgaard, C. (1983) 'Two Distinctions in Goodness', *Philosophical Review* 92: 169–195.
\_\_\_\_ (1996) *Creating the Kingdom of Ends*. Cambridge: Cambridge University Press.
Kretzmer, D. (1987) 'Freedom of Speech and Racism', *Cardozo Law Review* 8: 445–514.
Krotoszynski, R. (2006) *The First Amendment in Cross-Cultural Perspective*. New York, NY: New York University Press.
Kymlicka, W. (1995) *Multicultural Citizenship: Liberal Theory of Minority Rights*. Oxford: Oxford University Press.
Laird, M. (1994) 'Political Correctness Commentary', *Ethics and Behavior* 4: 390–394.
Lakoff, R.T. (2000) *The Language War*. Berkeley, CA: University of California Press.
Lange, E. (1990) 'Racist Speech on Campus: A Title VII Solution to a First Amendment Problem', *Southern California Law Review* 64: 105–134.
Langton, R. (1990a) 'Whose Right? Ronald Dworkin, Women, and Pornographers', *Philosophy and Public Affairs* 19: 311–59.
\_\_\_\_ (1990b) 'Subordination, Silence, and Pornography's Authority', in R. Post (ed.) *Censorship and Silencing: Practices of Cultural Regulation*. Los Angeles, CA: Getty Research Institute for the History of Art and the Humanities.
\_\_\_\_ (1993) 'Speech Acts and Unspeakable Acts', *Philosophy and Public Affairs* 22: 293–330.
\_\_\_\_ (2012) 'Beyond Belief: Pragmatics in Hate Speech and Pornography', in I. Maitra and M. McGowan (eds.) *Speech and Harm: Controversies over Free Speech*. Oxford: Oxford University Press.
Langton, R. et al. (2012) 'Language and Race', in G. Russell and D. Graff Fara (eds.) *Routledge Companion to the Philosophy of Language*. London: Routledge.
Langton, R. and Hornsby, J. (1998) 'Free Speech and Illocution', *Legal Theory* 4: 21–38.
Langton, R. and West, C. (1999) 'Scorekeeping in a Pornographic Language Game', Australasian Journal of Philosophy 77: 303–319.
Larmore, C. (1987) *Patterns of Moral Complexity*. Cambridge: Cambridge University Press.
Lasson, K. (1995) 'To Stimulate, Provoke, or Incite: Hate Speech and the First Amendment', in M. Freedman and E. Freedman (eds.) *Group Defamation and Freedom of Speech: The Relationship between Language and Violence*. Westport, CT: Greenwood Press.
\_\_\_\_ (1997) 'Holocaust Denial and the First Amendment: The Quest for Truth in a Free Society', *George Mason Law Review* 6: 35–86.
Laub, D. (1992) 'Bearing Witness or the Vicissitudes of Listening', in S. Felman and D. Laub (eds.) *Testimony: Crises of Witnessing in Literature, Psychoanalysis, and History*. New York, NY: Routledge.
Lawrence, C. (1987) 'The Id, the Ego, and Equal Protection: Reckoning with Unconscious Racism', *Stanford Law Review* 39: 317–388.
\_\_\_\_ (1990) 'If He Hollers Let Him Go: Regulating Racist Speech on Campus', *Duke Law Journal* 1990: 431–483.

_____ (1992) 'Cross Burning and the Sound of Silence: Anti-Subordination Theory and the First Amendment', *Villanova Law Review* 37: 787–804.
Lawrence, C. et al. (1993) 'Introduction', in M. Matsuda et al. (eds.) *Words That Wound: Critical Race Theory, Assaultive Speech, and the First Amendment*. Boulder, CO: Westview Press.
Lederer, L. and Delgado, R. (1995) 'Introduction', in L. Lederer and R. Delgado (eds.) *The Price We Pay: The Case Against Racist Speech, Hate Propaganda, and Pornography*. New York, NY: Hill and Wang.
Lee, S. (2010) 'Hate Speech in the Marketplace of Ideas', in D. Golash (ed.) *Freedom of Expression in a Diverse World*. Dordrecht: Springer.
Leopold, P.M. (1977) 'Incitement to Hatred: The History of a Controversial Criminal Offence', *Public Law* 1997: 389–405.
Lepora, C. (2012) 'On Compromise and Being Compromised', *Journal of Political Philosophy* 20: 1–22.
Levin, A. (2010) *The Cost of Free Speech: Pornography, Hate Speech, and their Challenge to Liberalism*. Basingstoke: Palgrave Macmillan.
Levy, J. (2000) *Multiculturalism of Fear*. Oxford: Oxford University Press.
Lieberson, S. (1985) 'Stereotypes: Their Consequences for Race and Ethnic Interaction', in C. Marrett and C. Leggon (eds.) *Research in Race and Ethnic Relations: A Research Annual, Vol. 4*. Greenwich, CT: JAI Press.
Lillian, D.L. (2007) 'A Thorn by Any Other Name: Sexist Discourse as Hate Speech', *Discourse Society* 18: 719–740.
Lively, D.E. (1994) 'Racial Myopia in the Age of Digital Compression', in H.L. Gates Jr. et al. (eds.) *Speaking of Race, Speaking of Sex: Hate Speech, Civil Rights, and Civil Liberties*. New York, NY: New York University Press.
Loewenstein, K. (1937a) 'Militant Democracy and Fundamental Rights I', *American Political Science Review* 31: 417–432.
_____ (1937b) 'Militant Democracy and Fundamental Rights II', *American Political Science Review* 31: 638–658.
Love, J.C. (1990) 'Discriminatory Speech and the Tort of Intentional Infliction of Emotional Distress', *Washington and Lee Law Review* 47: 123–159.
Lukes, S. (1997) 'On Comparing the Incomparable: Trade-Offs and Sacrifices', in R. Chang (ed.) *Incommensurability, Incomparability, and Practical Reason*. Cambridge: Harvard University Press.
MacKinnon, C. (1979) *Sexual Harassment of Working Women: A Case of Sex Discrimination*. New Haven, CT: Yale University Press.
_____ (1987) *Feminism Unmodified: Discourses on Life and Law*. Cambridge, MA: Harvard University Press.
_____ (1991) 'Pornography as Defamation and Discrimination', *Boston University Law Review* 71: 793–808.
_____ (1993) *Only Words*. Cambridge, MA: Harvard University Press.
_____ (2012) 'Forward', in I. Maitra and M. McGowan (eds.) *Speech and Harm: Controversies over Free Speech*. Oxford: Oxford University Press.
MacKinnon, C. and Dworkin, A. (1988) *Pornography and Civil Rights: A New Day for Women's Equality*. Minneapolis: Organizing Against Pornography.
MacRae, C.N. et al. (1996) *Stereotypes and Stereotyping*. New York, NY: Guilford Press.
Marshall, G. (1971) *Constitutional Theory*. Oxford: Oxford University Press.
Marshall, W.P. (1995) 'In Defense of the Search for Truth as a First Amendment Justification', *Georgia Law Review* 30: 1–39.
Mahoney, K. (2009) 'Hate Speech, Equality, and the State of Canadian Law', *Wake Forest Law Review* 44: 321–351.
Maitra, I. (2012) 'Subordinating Speech', in I. Maitra and M. McGowan (eds.) *Speech and Harm: Controversies over Free Speech*. Oxford: Oxford University Press.

Maitra, I. and McGowan, M. (2010) 'On Racist Hate Speech and the Scope of a Free Speech Principle', *Canadian Journal of Law and Jurisprudence* 23: 343–372.

Majeed, A. (2009) 'Defying the Constitution: The Rise, Persistence, and Prevalence of Campus Speech Codes', *Georgetown Journal of Law and Public Policy* 7: 481–544.

Major, B. et al. (1998) 'Coping with Negative Stereotypes about Intellectual Performance: The Role of Psychological Disengagement', *Personality and Social Psychology Bulletin* 24: 34–50.

Malik, K. (2005) 'Hate Speech in a Plural Society', talk given as part of an *Index On Censorship* event, 'Incitement, Hate Speech and the Right to Free Expression', Lancaster House, London, 8–9 Dec. Available at: www.kenanmalik.com/debates/freespeech_index.html (last accessed 05/09/14).

Malik, M. (2009) 'Extreme Speech and Liberalism', in I. Hare and J. Weinstein (eds.) *Extreme Speech and Democracy*. Oxford: Oxford University Press.

Mann, P. (1995) 'Hate Speech, Freedom, and Discourse Ethics in the Academy', in D. Caudill and S. Gold (eds.) *Radical Philosophy of Law*. Atlantic Highlands, NJ: Humanities Press.

Marcus, K.L. (2008) 'Higher Education, Harassment, and First Amendment Opportunism', *William and Mary Bill of Rights Journal* 16: 1025–1059.

Massaro, T. (1991) 'Equality and Freedom of Expression: The Hate Speech Dilemma', *William and Mary Law Review* 32: 211–265.

Mastro, D. (2003) 'A Social Identity Approach to Understanding the Impact of Television Messages', *Communication Monographs* 70: 98–113.

Mastro, D. et al. (2007) 'The Cultivation of Social Perceptions of Latinos: A Mental Models Approach', *Media Psychology* 9: 347–365.

Mastro, D., et al. (2009) 'The Influence of Exposure to Depictions of Race and Crime in TV News on Viewer's Social Judgments', *Journal of Broadcasting and Electronic Media* 53: 615–635.

Matsuda, M. (1989a) 'When the First Quail Calls: Multiple Consciousness as Jurisprudential Method', *Women's Rights Law Report* 11: 7–10.

—— (1989b) 'Public Response to Racist Speech: Considering the Victim's Story', *Michigan Law Review* 87: 2320–2381.

Mbongo, P. (2009) 'Hate Speech, Extreme Speech, and Collective Defamation in French Law', in I. Hare and J. Weinstein (eds.) *Extreme Speech and Democracy*. Oxford: Oxford University Press.

McAllister, S. (2010) 'Would Other Countries Protect the Phelpses' Funeral Picketing?', *Cardozo Law Review de novo* 2010: 408–415.

McCrudden, C. (2008) 'Human Dignity and Judicial Interpretation of Human Rights', *European Journal of International Law* 19: 655–724.

McGee, R.W. (1990) 'Hate Speech, Free Speech and the University', *Akron Law Review* 24: 363–392.

McGowan, D.F. and Tangri, R.K. (1991) 'A Libertarian Critique of University Restrictions of Offensive Speech', *California Law Review* 79: 825–918.

McGowan, M. (2009) 'Oppressive Speech', *Australasian Journal of Philosophy* 87: 389–407.

—— (2012) 'On "Whites Only" Signs and Racist Hate Speech: Verbal Acts of Racial Discrimination', in I. Maitra and M. McGowan (eds.) *Speech and Harm: Controversies over Free Speech*. Oxford: Oxford University Press.

McNamara, L. (2007a) 'Salvation and the State: Religious Vilification Laws and Religious Speech', in K. Gelber and A. Stone (eds.) *Hate Speech and Freedom of Speech in Australia*. Annandale, NSW: Federation Press.

—— (2007b) *Human Rights Controversies: The Impact of Legal Form*. Abingdon: Routledge-Cavendish.

Meer, N. and Modood, T. (2012) 'How Does Interculturalism Contrast with Multiculturalism?', *Journal of Intercultural Studies* 33: 175–197.

Meiklejohn, A. (1951) 'The First Amendment and the Evils Congress Has a Right to Prevent', *Indiana Law Journal* 26: 477–493.

_____ (1960) *Political Freedom: The Constitutional Power of the People*. New York, NY: Harper and Brothers.

_____ (1961) 'The First Amendment Is An Absolute', *Supreme Court Review* 1961: 245–266.

Mencap (1999) *Living in Fear: The Need to Combat Bullying of People with a Learning Disability*. London: Mencap.

Meyers, D.T. (1995) 'Rights in Collision: A Non-Punitive, Compensatory Remedy for Abusive Speech', *Law and Philosophy* 14: 203–243.

Michelman, F. (1992) 'Universities, Racist Speech and Democracy in America: An Essay for the ACLU', *Harvard Civil Rights-Civil Liberties Law Review* 27: 339–369.

_____ (1995) 'Civil Liberties, Silencing, and Subordination', in L. Lederer and R. Delgado (eds.) *The Price We Pay: The Case Against Racist Speech, Hate Propaganda, and Pornography*. New York, NY: Hill and Wang.

Miles, J.K. (2012) 'A Perfectionist Defense of Free Speech', *Social Theory and Practice* 38: 213–230.

Mill, J.S. [1825] (1984) 'Law of Libel and Liberty of the Press', in J. Robson (ed.) *Collected works of John Stuart Mill, Vol. 21: Essays on Equality, Law, and Education*. London: Routledge and Kegan Paul.

_____ [1859] (1972) *On Liberty*, in G. Williams (ed.) *Utilitarianism, On Liberty, Considerations on Representative Government*. London: Everyman.

Miller, D. (1999) *Principles of Social Justice*. Cambridge, MA: Harvard University Press.

_____ (2003) *Political Philosophy: A Very Short Introduction*. Oxford: Oxford University Press.

Milmo, P. and Rogers, W.V.H. (eds.) (2008) *Gatley on Libel and Slander*, 11th ed. London: Sweet and Maxwell.

Modood, T. (1990) 'British Asian Muslims and the Rushdie Affair', *Political Quarterly* 61: 143–160.

_____ (1993) 'Muslims, Incitement to Hatred and the Law', in J. Horton (ed.) *Liberalism, Multiculturalism, and Toleration*. Basingstoke: Macmillan.

_____ (2005) *Multicultural Politics: Racism, Ethnicity and Muslims in Britain*. Minneapolis, MN: University of Minnesota Press.

_____ (2006) 'The Liberal Dilemma: Integration or Vilification?', *International Migration* 44: 4–7.

_____ (2007) *Multiculturalism*. Cambridge: Polity Press.

Modood, T. et al. (1998) *Ethnic Minorities in Britain: Diversity and Disadvantage: The Fourth National Survey of Ethnic Minorities*. London: Policy Studies Institute.

Molnar, P. (2010) 'Towards Improved Law and Policy on "Hate Speech": The "Clear and Present Danger" Test in Hungary', in I. Hare and J. Weinstein (eds.) *Extreme Speech and Democracy*. Oxford: Oxford University Press.

_____ (2012) 'Responding to "Hate Speech" with Art, Education, and the Imminent Danger Test', in M. Herz and P. Molnar (eds.) *The Content and Context of Hate Speech: Rethinking Regulation and Responses*. Cambridge: Cambridge University Press.

Mookherjee, M. (2007) 'Permitting Dishonour: Culture, Gender, and Freedom of Expression', in G. Newey (ed.) *Freedom of Expression: Counting the Costs*. Cambridge: Cambridge Scholars Press.

Morgan, G. (2007) 'Mill's Liberalism, Security, and Group Defamation', in G. Newey (ed.) *Freedom of Expression: Counting the Costs*. Cambridge: Cambridge Scholars Press.

Mullender, R. (2007) 'Hate Speech and Pornography in Canada: A Qualified Deontological Response to a Consequentialist Argument', *Canadian Journal of Law and Jurisprudence* 20: 241–255.

Murchison, B. (1998) 'Speech and the Self-Realization Value', *Harvard Civil Rights-Civil Liberties Law Review* 33: 443–503.

Murray, S.D. (1997) 'The Demise of Campus Speech Codes', *Western State University Law Review* 24: 247–281.

Musselman, J. (1995) 'Critical Race Theory on Hate Speech as a Bias Crime', *Contemporary Philosophy* 17: 2–8.

Nagel, T. (1995) 'Personal Rights and Public Space', *Philosophy and Public Affairs* 24: 83–107.

Nash, D. and Bakalis, C. (2007) 'Incitement to Religious Hatred and the "Symbolic": How Will the Racial and Religious Hatred Act 2006 work?', *Liverpool Law Review* 28: 349–375.

Nelson, S.P. (2005) *Beyond the First Amendment: The Politics of Free Speech and Pluralism*. Baltimore, MD: The Johns Hopkins University Press.

Neu, J. (2008) *Sticks and Stones: The Philosophy of Insults*. New York, NY: Oxford University Press.

Neuman, G.L. (1992) 'Rhetorical Slavery, Rhetorical Citizenship', *Michigan Law Review* 90: 1276–1290.

Nielsen, L.B. (2002) 'Subtle, Pervasive, Harmful: Racist and Sexist Remarks in Public as Hate Speech', *Journal of Social Issues* 58: 265–280.

Nimmer, M. (1968) 'The Right to Speak from Times to Time: The First Amendment Theory Applied to Libel and Misapplied to Privacy', *California Law Review* 56: 935–967.

Nockleby, J. (2000) 'Hate Speech', in L. Levy and K. Karst (eds.) *Encyclopedia of the American Constitution, Vol. 3*, 2nd ed. Detroit, MI: Macmillan.

Nussbaum, M. (1988) 'Nature, Functioning and Capability: Aristotle on Political Distribution', *Oxford Studies in Ancient Philosophy 6, Suppl. Vol.*: 145–184.

_____ (1993) 'Non-Relative Virtues: An Aristotelian Approach', in A. Sen and M. Nussbaum (eds.) *The Quality of Life*. Oxford: Oxford University Press.

_____ (2000) *Women and Human Development: The Capabilities Approach*. Cambridge: Cambridge University Press.

_____ (2003) 'Capabilities as Fundamental Entitlements: Sen and Social Justice', *Feminist Economics* 9: 33–59.

_____ (2006) *Frontiers of Justice*. Cambridge, MA: Harvard University Press.

_____ (2011) *Creating Capabilities*. Cambridge, MA: Harvard University Press.

Ogletree, C.J. (1996) 'The Limits of Hate Speech: Does Race Matter?', *Gonzaga Law Review* 32: 491–510.

O'Neil, R.M. (1989) 'Colleges Should Seek Educational Alternatives to Rules That Override the Historic Guarantees of Free Speech', *Chronicle of Higher Education*, 18 Oct.: B1-B3.

Opotow, S. (1990) 'Moral Exclusion and Injustice: An Introduction', *Journal of Social Issues* 46: 1–20.

Ortiz, M. and Harwood, J. (2007) 'A Social Cognitive Theory Approach to the Effects of Mediated Intergroup Contact on Intergroup Attitudes', *Journal of Broadcasting and Electronic Media* 51: 615–631.

Packer, H. (1968) *The Limits of the Criminal Sanction*. Stanford, CA: Stanford University Press.

Parekh, B. (1990a) 'The Rushdie Affair and the British Press: Some Salutary Lessons', in Commission for Racial Equality (ed.) *Free Speech: Report of a Seminar. Discussion Papers 2*. London: Commission for Racial Equality.

_____ (1990b) 'The Rushdie Affair: Research Agenda for Political Philosophy', *Political Studies* 38: 695–709.

_____ (2005–2006) 'Hate Speech: Is There a Case for Banning?', *Public Policy Research* 12: 213–223.

_____ (2006) *Rethinking Multiculturalism: Cultural Diversity and Political Theory*, 2nd ed. Basingstoke: Palgrave.

_____ (2008) *A New Politics of Identity: Political Principles for an Interdependent World*. Basingstoke: Palgrave Macmillan.

_____ (2009) 'Feeling at Home: Some Reflections on Muslims in Europe', *Harvard Middle Eastern and Islamic Review* 8: 51–85.

Partlett, D. (1989) 'From Red Lion Square to Skokie to the Fatal Shore: Racial Defamation and Freedom of Speech', *Vanderbilt Journal of Transnational Law* 22: 431–490.

Paterson, A. (2012) *Final Judgment: The Last Law Lords and the Supreme Court*. Oxford: Hart Publishing.

Peard, T.W. (1999) 'Diana Tietjens Meyers's Remedy for Abusive Speech: Objections', *Law and Philosophy* 18: 1–12.

_____ (2004) 'Regulating Racist Speech on Campus', in C. Sistare (ed.) *Civility and Its Discontents: Civic Virtue, Toleration, and Cultural Fragmentation*. Lawrence, KS: University of Kansas Press.

Peffley, M. et al. (1996) 'The Intersection of Race and Crime in Television News Stories: An Experimental Study', *Political Communication* 13: 309–327.

Peters, J. (2005) *Courting the Abyss: Free Speech and the Liberal Tradition*. Chicago, IL: University of Chicago Press.

Peterson, L.E. et al. (2004) 'The Effects of Intragroup Interaction and Cohesion on Intergroup Bias', *Group Processes and Intergroup Relations* 7: 107–118.

Pettigrew, T. (1997) 'Generalized Intergroup Contact Effects on Prejudice', *Personality and Social Psychology Bulletin* 23: 174–185.

Phillips, A. (2009) *Multiculturalism without Culture*. Princeton, NJ: Princeton University Press.

Plunkett, J. (2006) 'BBC Defends Cartoon Coverage', *The Guardian*, 6 Feb. Available at: www.guardian.co.uk/media/2006/feb/06/broadcasting.pressandpublishing (last accessed 03/08/14).

Pollard Sacks, D. (2010) 'Snyder v. Phelps, the Supreme Court's Speech-Tort Jurisprudence, and Normative Considerations', *Yale Law Journal Online* 120. Available at: http://yalelawjournal.org/2010/12/29/pollard-sacks.html (last accessed 10/09/14).

Posner, R. (1990) *The Problems of Jurisprudence*. Cambridge, MA: Harvard University Press.

_____ (2002) 'The Speech Market and the Legacy of *Schenck*', in L. Bollinger and G. Stone (eds.) *Eternally Vigilant: Free Speech in the Modern Era*. Chicago: University of Chicago Press.

_____ (2006) *Not a Suicide Pact: The Constitution in a Time of National Emergency*. Oxford: Oxford University Press.

_____ (2008) *How Judges Think*. Cambridge, MA: Harvard University Press.

Post, R. (1986) 'The Social Foundations of Defamation Law: Reputation and the Constitution', *California Law Review* 74: 691–742.

_____ (1990) 'The Constitutional Concept of Public Discourse: Outrageous Opinion, Democratic Deliberation, and Hustler Magazine v. Falwell', *Harvard Law Review* 103: 601–686.

_____ (1991) 'Racist Speech, Democracy, and the First Amendment', *William and Mary Law Review* 32: 267–327

_____ (1993a) 'Managing Deliberation: The Quandary of Democratic Dialogue', *Ethics* 103: 654–678.

_____ (1993b) 'Meiklejohn's Mistake: Individual Autonomy and the Reform of Public Discourse', *University of Colorado Law Review* 64: 1109–1137.

_____ (1995) 'Recuperating First Amendment Doctrine', *Stanford Law Review* 47: 1249–1281.
_____ (2002) 'Reconciling Theory and Doctrine in First Amendment Jurisprudence', in L. Bollinger and G. Stone (eds.) *Eternally Vigilant: Free Speech in the Modern Era*. Chicago: University of Chicago Press.
_____ (2005) 'Democracy and Equality', *Law, Culture, and the Humanities* 1: 142–153.
_____ (2009) 'Hate Speech', in I. Hare and J. Weinstein (eds.) *Extreme Speech and Democracy*. Oxford: Oxford University Press.
_____ (2011) 'Participatory Democracy and Free Speech', *Virginia Law Review* 97: 477–489.
_____ (2012) 'Interview', in M. Herz and P. Molnar (eds.) *The Content and Context of Hate Speech: Rethinking Regulation and Responses*. Cambridge: Cambridge University Press.
Potok, M. (2012) 'FBI: Anti-Muslim Hate Crimes Remain Relatively High', *HateWatch*, 10 Dec. Available at: www.splcenter.org/blog/2012/12/10/fbi-anti-muslim-hate-crimes-remain-relatively-high/ (last accessed 02/09/14).
Pound, R. (1915) 'Interests of Personality', *Harvard Law Review*, 28: 343–365.
_____ (1943) 'A Survey of Social Interests', *Harvard Law Review* 57: 1–39.
Powell, J.A. (1996–1997) 'Worlds Apart: Reconciling Freedom of Speech and Equality', *Kentucky Law Journal* 85: 9–95.
Ramasubramanian, S. (2013) 'Intergroup Contact, Media Exposure, and Racial Attitudes', *Journal of Intercultural Communication Research* 42: 54–72.
Rawls, J. (1971) *A Theory of Justice*. Oxford: Oxford University Press.
_____ (1996) *Political Liberalism*, pbk. ed. New York, NY: Columbia University Press.
Raz, J. (1986) *The Morality of Freedom*. Oxford: Oxford University Press.
_____ (1991) 'Free Expression and Personal Identification', *Oxford Journal of Legal Studies* 11: 303–324.
Redish, M. (1981) 'The Content Distinction in First Amendment Analysis', *Stanford Law Review* 34: 113–151.
_____ (1982) 'The Value of Free Speech', *University of Pennsylvania Law Review* 130: 591–645.
Rice, S. (1994) 'Hate Speech and the Need for Moral Standards in Communicative Interaction', in M. Katz (ed.) *Philosophy of Education*. Urbana, IL: Philosophy of Education Society.
Rice, S. and Burbules, N.C. (1993) 'Communicative Virtues and Educational Relations', in H. Alexander (ed.) *Philosophy of Education*. Urbana, IL: Philosophy of Education Society.
Richard, M. (2008) *When Truth Gives Out*. Oxford: Oxford University Press.
Richards, D. (1986) *Toleration and the Constitution*. New York, NY: Oxford University Press.
_____ (1999) *Free Speech and the Politics of Identity*. Oxford: Oxford University Press.
Richardson, D.M. (1982) 'Racism: A Tort of Outrage', *Oregon Law Review* 61: 267–283.
Riesman, D. (1942) 'Democracy and Defamation: Control of Group Libel', *Columbia Law Review* 42: 727–780.
Rosenberg, D. (1991) 'Racist Speech, The First Amendment, and Public Universities: Taking a Stand on Neutrality', *Cornell Law Review* 76: 549–588.
Rostbøll, C.F. (2011) 'Freedom of Expression, Deliberation, Autonomy and Respect', *European Journal of Political Theory* 10: 5–21.
Rowbottom, J. (2009) 'Extreme Speech and the Democratic Functions of the Mass Media', in I. Hare and J. Weinstein (eds.) *Extreme Speech and Democracy*. Oxford: Oxford University Press.

RT News (2014) 'Duma Gives First Nod to Nan on Nazi Rehabilitation', 4 Apr. Available at: http://rt.com/politics/russia-nazi-ban-prison-293/ (last accessed 27/11/14).

Rubenstein, W. (1994) 'Since When Is the Fourteenth Amendment Our Route to Equality? Some Reflections on the Construction of the "Hate-Speech" Debate from a Lesbian/Gay Perspective', in H.L. Gates Jr. et al. (eds.) *Speaking of Race, Speaking of Sex: Hate Speech, Civil Rights, and Civil Liberties*. New York, NY: New York University Press.

Rubin, E.L. (1986) 'Review of Nazis, Skokie, and the First Amendment as Virtue: Nazis in Skokie, by Donald A. Downs', *California Law Review* 74: 233–260.

Sackett, P.R. et al. (2004) 'On Interpreting Stereotype Threat as Accounting for African American-White Differences on Cognitive Tests, *American Psychologist* 59: 7–13.

Sadurski, W. (1999) *Freedom of Speech and Its Limits*. London: Kluwer Academic Publishers.

Sandel, M. (1996) *Democracy's Discontent: America in Search of a Public Philosophy*. Harvard, MA. Harvard University Press.

Sarrazin, T. (2009) Interview, *Lettre International* 86, Fall.

Saunders, K.W. (2011) *Degradation: What the History of Obscenity Tells Us about Hate Speech*. New York, NY: New York University Press.

Saxton, M. (ed.) (2009) *Sticks and Stones: Disabled People's Stories of Abuse, Defiance and Resilience*. Oakland, CA: World Institute on Disability.

Scanlon, T. (1972) 'A Theory of Free Expression', *Philosophy and Public Affairs* 1: 204–226.

―――― (1979) 'Freedom of Expression and Categories of Expression', *University of Pittsburgh Law Review* 40: 519–550.

―――― (1998) *What We Owe to Each Other*. Cambridge, MA: Harvard University Press.

Schachter, O. (1983) 'Human Dignity as a Normative Concept', *American Journal of International Law* 77: 848–854.

Schafer, J.A. (2002) 'Spinning the Web of Hate: Web-Based Hate Propagation by Extremist Organizations', *Journal of Criminal Justice and Popular Culture* 9: 69–88.

Schaff, K. (2002) 'Hate Speech and the Problems of Agency: A Critique of Butler', *Social Philosophy Today* 16: 185–201.

Schauer, F. (1979) 'Speech and "Speech"—Obscenity and "Obscenity": An Exercise in the Interpretation of Constitutional Language', *Georgetown Law Journal* 67: 899–933.

―――― (1982) *Free Speech: A Philosophical Inquiry*. Cambridge: Cambridge University Press.

―――― (1983) 'Must Speech Be Special?' *Northwestern University Law Review* 78: 1284–1306.

―――― (1992a) 'Uncoupling Free Speech', *Columbia Law Review* 92: 1321–1357.

―――― (1992b) 'Speaking of Dignity', in M. Meyer and W. Parent (eds.) *The Constitution of Rights, Human Dignity and American Values*. Ithaca, NY: Cornell University Press.

―――― (1998) 'Principles, Institutions, and the First Amendment', *Harvard Law Review* 112: 84–120.

―――― (2005) 'Towards an Institutional First Amendment', *Minnesota Law Review* 89: 1256–1279.

―――― (2009) 'Is It Better to Be Safe Than Sorry? Free Speech and the Precautionary Principle', *Pepperdine Law Review* 36: 301–315.

―――― (2012) 'Social Epistemology, Holocaust Denial, and the Post-Millian Calculus', in M. Herz and P. Molnar (eds.) *The Content and Context of Hate Speech: Rethinking Regulation and Responses*. Cambridge: Cambridge University Press.

## References

Schneider, D.J. (2004) *The Psychology of Stereotyping*. New York, NY: Guilford Press.
Scott, J.A. (1951) 'Criminal Sanctions for Group Libel: Feasibility and Constitutionality', *Duke Law Journal* 1951: 218–233.
Seglow, J. (2003). 'Theorizing Recognition', in B. Haddock and P. Sutch (eds.) *Multiculturalism, Identity and Rights*. London: Routledge.
Shaman, J.M. (2001) *Constitutional Interpretation: Illusion and Reality*. Westport, CT: Greenwood Press.
Shapiro, J.T. (1990) 'The Call for Campus Conduct Codes: Censorship or Constitutionally Permissible Limitations on Speech', *Minnesota Law Review* 75: 201–238.
Sherry, S. (1991) 'Speaking of Virtue: A Republican Approach to University Regulation of Hate Speech', *Minnesota Law Review* 75: 933–944.
Shiell, T.C. (2009) *Campus Hate Speech on Trial*, 2nd ed. Lawrence, KS: University of Kansas Press.
Shiffrin, S.H. (1983) Liberalism, Radicalism, and Legal Scholarship, *UCLA Law Review* 30: 1103–1217.
_____ (1990) *The First Amendment: Democracy and Romance*. Harvard, MA: Harvard University Press.
_____ (1999) *Dissent, Injustice, and the Meanings of America*. Princeton, NJ: Princeton University Press.
_____ (2011a) 'Dissent, Democratic Participation, and First Amendment Methodology', *Virginia Law Review* 97: 559–565.
_____ (2011b) 'Freedom of Speech and Two Types of Autonomy', *Constitutional Commentary* 27: 337–345.
Shiffrin, S.V. (2011) 'Reply to Critics', *Constitutional Commentary* 27: 417–438.
Shklar, J. (1989) 'The Liberalism of Fear', in N. Rosenbaum (ed.) *Liberalism and the Moral Life*. Cambridge, MA: Harvard University Press.
Simmons, A.J. (1979) *Moral Principles and Political Obligations*. Princeton, NJ: Princeton University Press.
_____ (2001) *Justification and Legitimacy*. Cambridge: Cambridge University Press.
_____ (2010) 'Ideal and Nonideal Theory', *Philosophy and Public Affairs* 38: 5–36.
SimmsParris, M.M. (1998) 'What Does It Mean to See a Black Church Burning? Understanding the Significance of Constitutionalizing Hate Speech', *University of Pennsylvania Journal of Constitutional Law* 1: 127–153.
Simpson, E. (2006) 'Responsibilities for Hateful Speech', *Legal Theory* 12: 157–177.
Simpson, R.M. (2013) 'Dignity, Harm, and Hate Speech', *Law and Philosophy* 32: 701–728.
Solomos, J. and Schuster, L. (2002) 'Hate Speech, Violence and Contemporary Racism', in Evens Foundation (ed.) *Europe's New Racism? Causes, Manifestations and Solutions*. Oxford: Berghahn.
Solum, L. (2003) 'Virtue Jurisprudence: A Virtue-Centered Theory of Judging', *Metaphilosophy* 34: 178–213.
_____ (2004) 'The Aretaic Turn in Constitutional Theory', *Brooklyn Law Review* 70: 475–532.
Smith, A. (1995) 'There's Such a Thing as Free Speech: And That's a Good Thing, Too', in Whillock, K. and Slayden, D. (eds.) (1995) *Hate Speech*. Thousand Oaks, CA: Sage Publications.
Smolla, R. (1990) 'Academic Freedom, Hate Speech, and the Idea of a University', *Law and Contemporary Problems* 53: 195–226.
_____ (1992) *Free Speech in an Open Society*. New York, NY: Vintage Books.
_____ (2011) *The Constitution Goes to College: Five Constitutional Ideas That Have Shaped the American University*. New York, NY: New York University Press.

Special Committee on Hate Propaganda in Canada (1966) *Report to the Minister of Justice*. Ottawa: Queen's Printer.
Spinoza, B. de. [1670] (1958) Theological-Political Treatise, A. Wernham (ed.) *Benedict de Spinoza: The Political Works*. Oxford: Oxford University Press.
Stalnaker, R. (1978) 'Assertion', *Syntax and Semantics* 9: 315–332.
\_\_\_\_ (2002) 'Common Ground', *Linguistics and Philosophy* 25: 701–721.
Steele, C. and Aronson, J. (1995) 'Stereotype Threat and the Intellectual Test Performance of African Americans', *Journal of Personality and Social Psychology* 69: 797–811.
Stefancic, J. and Delgado, R. (1993) 'A Shifting Balance: Freedom of Expression and Hate-Speech Restriction', *Iowa Law Review* 78: 737–750.
Stern, S. and Wermiel, S. (2010) *Justice Brennan: Liberal Champion*. New York, NY: Houghton Mifflin Harcourt.
Stone, G.R. (1983) 'Content Regulation and the First Amendment', *William and Mary Law Review* 25: 189–252.
Stopford, J. (2009) *The Skillful Self: Liberalism, Culture, and the Politics of Skill*. Lanham, MD: Rowman and Littlefield.
Strauss, D.A. (1988) 'The Ubiquity of Prophylactic Rules', *University of Chicago Law Review* 55: 190–209.
\_\_\_\_ (1991). 'Persuasion, Autonomy, and Freedom of Expression', *Columbia Law Review* 91: 334–71.
Strossen, N. (1990) 'Regulating Racist Speech on Campus: A Modest Proposal', *Duke Law Journal* 1990: 484–573.
\_\_\_\_ (2001) 'Incitement to Hatred: Should There Be a Limit?', *Southern Illinois University Law Journal* 25: 243–279.
\_\_\_\_ (2012) 'Interview', in M. Herz and P. Molnar (eds.) *The Content and Context of Hate Speech: Rethinking Regulation and Responses*. Cambridge: Cambridge University Press.
Suk, J. (2012) 'Denying Experience: Holocaust Denial and the Free-Speech Theory of the State', in M. Herz and P. Molnar (eds.) *The Content and Context of Hate Speech: Rethinking Regulation and Responses*. Cambridge: Cambridge University Press.
Sullivan, K. and Gunther, G. (1995) *Constitutional Law*. New York: Foundation Press.
Sumner, L.W. (2003) 'Hate Crimes, Literature and Speech', in R. Frey and C. Heath Wellman (eds.) *A Companion to Applied Ethics*. Oxford: Blackwell.
\_\_\_\_ (2004) *The Hateful and the Obscene: Studies in the Limits of Free Expression*. Toronto: University of Toronto Press.
\_\_\_\_ (2009) 'Incitement and the Regulation of Hate Speech in Canada: A Philosophical Analysis', in I. Hare and J. Weinstein (eds.) *Extreme Speech and Democracy*. Oxford: Oxford University Press.
Sunstein, C.R. (1986) 'Pornography and the First Amendment', *Duke Law Journal* 1986: 589–627.
\_\_\_\_ (1993a) *Democracy and the Problem of Free Speech*. New York, NY: Free Press.
\_\_\_\_ (1993b) 'Words, Conduct, Caste', *University of Chicago Law Review* 60: 795–844.
\_\_\_\_ (2007) *Republic.com 2.0*. Princeton, NJ: Princeton University Press.
Tanenhaus, J. (1950) 'Group Libel', *Cornell Law Quarterly* 35: 261–302.
\_\_\_\_ (1952) 'Group Libel and Free Speech', *Phylon* 13: 215–219.
Taylor, C. (1985) *Human Agency and Language: Philosophical Papers, Vol. 1*. Cambridge: Cambridge University Press.
\_\_\_\_ (1991) *The Ethics of Authenticity*. Cambridge, MA: Harvard University Press.
\_\_\_\_ (1994) 'The Politics of Recognition', in A. Gutmann (ed.) *Multiculturalism: Examining the Politics of Recognition*. Princeton, NJ: Princeton University Press.

Taylor, J. (2006) 'Humean Humanity Versus Hate', in J. Welchman (eds.) *The Practice of Virtue: Classic And Contemporary Readings in Virtue Ethics*. Indianapolis, IN: Hackett.

This Is Derbyshire. (2012) 'Three Jailed for Stirring Up Hatred against Homosexuals in Derby', *Derby Telegraph*, 10 Feb. Available at: www.derbytelegraph.co.uk/jailed-stirring-hatred-homosexuals-Derby/story-15190738-detail/story.html (last accessed 31/07/14).

Thompson, S. (2012) 'Freedom of Expression and Hatred of Religion', *Ethnicities* 12: 215–232.

Timmons, M. (1999) *Morality Without Foundations: A Defense of Ethical Contextualism*. Oxford: Oxford University Press.

Toobin, J. (2007). *The Nine: Inside the Secret World of the Supreme Court*. New York, NY: Doubleday.

Tribe, L. (1988) *American Constitutional Law*, 2nd ed. Mineola, NY: Foundation Press.

Tsesis, A. (2002) *Destructive Messages: How Hate Speech Paves the Way for Harmful Social Movements*. New York, NY: New York University Press.

\_\_\_\_\_ (2009) 'Dignity and Speech: The Regulation of Hate Speech in a Democracy', *Wake Forest Law Review* 42: 497–532.

\_\_\_\_\_ (2010) 'Burning Crosses on Campus: University Hate Speech Codes', *Connecticut Law Review* 43: 617–672.

\_\_\_\_\_ (2013) 'Inflammatory Hate Speech: Offense versus Incitement', *Minnesota Law Review* 97: 101–152.

Tulkens, F. (2010) 'Conflicts between Fundamental Rights: Contrasting Views on Articles 9 and 10 of the European Convention on Human Rights', in Council of Europe (ed.) *Blasphemy, Insult and Hatred: Finding Answers in A Democratic Society*. Strasbourg: Council of Europe.

Tyler, T.R. (2001) 'Public Trust and Confidence in Legal Authorities: What do Majority and Minority Group Members Want from the Law and Legal Institutions?', *Behavioural Sciences and the Law* 19: 215–235.

\_\_\_\_\_ (2005) 'Policing in Black and White: Ethnic Group Differences in Trust and Confidence in the Police', *Police Quarterly* 8: 322–342.

Tynes et al. (2004) 'Adolescence, Race, and Ethnicity on the Internet: A Comparison of Discourse in Monitored vs. Unmonitored Chat Rooms', *Applied Developmental Psychology* 25: 667–684.

Tynes et al. (2008) 'Online Racial Discrimination and Psychological Adjustment among Adolescents', *Journal of Adolescent Health* 43: 565–9.

Underwood, B. and Moore, B. (1982) 'Perspective-Taking and Altruism', *Psychological Bulletin* 91: 143–173.

Unkelbach, C. et al. (2008) 'The Turban Effect: The Influence of Muslim Headgear and Induced Affect on Aggressive Responses in the Shooter Bias Paradigm', *Journal of Experimental Social Psychology* 44: 1409–1413.

Valentini, L. (2012) 'Ideal vs. Non-Ideal Theory: A Conceptual Map', *Philosophy Compass* 7: 654–664.

van Dijk, T. (1987) *Communicating Racism: Ethnic Prejudice in Thought and Talk*. Newbury Park, CA: Sage.

Varden, H. (2010) 'A Kantian Conception of Free Speech', in D. Golash (ed.) *Freedom of Expression in a Diverse World*. Dordrecht: Springer.

Vasquez, M. and de las Fuentes, C. (2000) 'Hate Speech or Freedom of Expression? Balancing Autonomy and Feminist Ethics in a Pluralistic Society', in M. Brabeck (ed.) *Practicing Feminist Ethics in Psychology*. Washington, DC: American Psychological Association.

Viljoen, F. (2005) 'Hate Speech in Rwanda as a Test Case for International Human Rights Law', *The Comparative and International Law Journal of Southern Africa* 38: 1–14.

Volokh, E. (1992) 'Freedom of Speech and Workplace Harassment', *UCLA Law Review* 39: 1791–1872.

\_\_\_\_\_ (2010) 'Freedom of Speech and Intentional Infliction of Emotional Distress Tort', *Cardozo Law Review De Novo* 2010: 300–312.

\_\_\_\_\_ (2011a) 'In Defense of the Marketplace of Ideas/Search for Truth as a Theory of Free Speech Protection', *Virginia Law Review* 97: 595–601.

\_\_\_\_\_ (2011b) 'The Trouble with "Public Discourse" as a Limitation on Free Speech Rights', *Virginia Law Review* 97: 567–594.

Waldron, J. (1999) *Law and Disagreement*. Oxford: Oxford University Press.

\_\_\_\_\_ (2008) 'Free Speech and the Menace of Hysteria', *New York Review of Books* 55, 29 May.

\_\_\_\_\_ (2010) '2009 Oliver Wendell Holmes Lectures: Dignity and Defamation: The Visibility of Hate', *Harvard Law Review* 123: 1596–1657.

\_\_\_\_\_ (2011) 'Dignity, Rank, and Rights', in S. Young (ed.) *The Tanner Lectures on Human Values, Vol. 29*. Salt Lake City, UT: University of Utah Press.

\_\_\_\_\_ (2012) *The Harm in Hate Speech*. Harvard, MA: Harvard University Press.

Walker, S. (1990) *In Defense of American Liberties: A History of the ACLU*. New York, NY: Oxford University Press.

\_\_\_\_\_ (1994) *Hate Speech: The History of an American Controversy*. Lincoln, NE: University of Nebraska Press.

Weatherby, G.A. and Scoggins, B. (2005) 'A Content Analysis of Persuasion Techniques Used on White Supremacist Websites', *Journal of Hate Studies* 4: 9–31.

Weinman, M. (2006) 'State Speech vs. Hate Speech: What to Do about Words That Wound?', *Essays in Philosophy* 7: 1–14. Available at: http://commons.pacificu.edu/eip/vol7/iss1/18/ (last accessed 10/09/14).

Weinrib, J. (2009) 'What Is the Purpose of Freedom of Expression?', *University of Toronto Faculty of Law Review* 67: 165–190.

Weinstein, J. (1992) 'A Constitutional Roadmap to the Regulation of Campus Hate Speech', *Wayne Law Review* 38: 163–247.

\_\_\_\_\_ (1999). *Hate Speech, Pornography and Radical Attacks on Free Speech Doctrine*. Boulder, CO: Westview Press

\_\_\_\_\_ (2001) 'Hate Speech, Viewpoint Neutrality, and the American Concept of Democracy', in T. Hensley (ed.) *The Boundaries of Freedom of Expression and Order in a Democratic Society*. Kent, OH: Kent State University Press.

\_\_\_\_\_ (2009) 'Extreme Speech, Public Order, and Democracy: Lessons from the Masses', in I. Hare and J. Weinstein (eds.) *Extreme Speech and Democracy*. Oxford: Oxford University Press.

\_\_\_\_\_ (2011a) 'Participatory Democracy as the Central Value of American Free Speech Doctrine', *Virginia Law Review* 97: 491–514.

\_\_\_\_\_ (2011b) 'Free Speech and Political Legitimacy: A Response to Ed Baker', *Constitutional Commentary* 27: 361–383.

Weinstein, J. and Hare, I. (2009) 'General Introduction', in I. Hare and J. Weinstein (eds.) *Extreme Speech and Democracy*. Oxford: Oxford University Press.

Weiss, J.C. et al. (1991–1992) 'Ethnoviolence at Work', *Journal of Intergroup Relations* 18: 21–33.

Wells, C.E. (1997) 'Reinvigorating Autonomy: Freedom and Responsibility in the Supreme Court's First Amendment Jurisprudence', *Harvard Civil Rights-Civil Liberties Law Review* 32: 159–196.

Wiener, J. (1989) 'Racial Hatred on Campus', *The Nation*, 27 Feb.: 260–263.

Wiggins, (1997) 'Incommensurability: Four Proposals', in R. Chang (ed.) *Incommensurability, Incomparability, and Practical Reason*. Cambridge: Harvard University Press.

Williams Crenshaw, K. (1993) 'Beyond Racism and Misogyny: Black Feminism and 2 Live Crew', in M. Matsuda et al. (eds.) *Words That Wound: Critical Race Theory, Assaultive Speech, and the First Amendment*. Boulder, CO: Westview Press.

Wolfers, A. (1952) '"National Security" as an Ambiguous Symbol', *Political Science Quarterly* 67: 481–502.
Wolff, J. and de-Shalit, A. (2007) *Disadvantage*. Oxford: Oxford University Press.
Wolfson, N. (1997) *Hate Speech, Sex Speech, Free Speech*. Westport, CT: Praeger Publishers.
Wood, A. (1999) *Kant's Ethical Thought*. Cambridge: Cambridge University Press.
Woodward, B. and Armstrong, S. (1979). *The Brethren: Inside the Supreme Court*. New York, NY: Simon and Schuster.
Wright, R.G. (2006) 'Dignity and Conflicts of Constitutional Values: The Case of Free Speech and Equal Protection', *San Diego Law Review* 43: 527–575.
Yong, C. (2011) 'Does Freedom of Speech Include Hate Speech?' *Res Publica* 17: 385–403.
Young, I. (1990) *Justice and the Politics of Difference*. Princeton, NJ: Princeton University Press.
Zingo, M.T. (1998) *Sex/Gender Outsiders, Hate Speech and Freedom of Expression: Can They Say That About Me?* Westport, CT: Praeger Publishers.
Zipursky, B.C. (2011) 'Snyder v. Phelps, Outrageousness, and the Open Texture of Tort Law', *DePaul Law Review* 60: 473–520.

# Index

ABC (Australian Broadcast Company), 22
Abel, R., 170
absolute weight, 207, 225, 227, 230
academic freedoms, 233
ACLU (American Civil Liberties Union), 59
Adams, W.A., 57
ADL (Anti-Defamation League), 155
adolescents, 58, 246
affirmative action, 311
African Americans, 32, 57, 73, 76, 82–3, 87–8, 95, 99, 102, 104, 122, 145–6, 168, 178, 201, 220, 294, 313
AHRC (Australian Human Rights Commission), 25
Aleinikoff, T.A., 237
Alexander, L., 4, 77, 108, 186, 199, 228
Allport, G., 69, 83, 241
Altman, A., 75–6, 102
Anand, S., 11
Anderson, E., 125
anger, 36, 55, 134, 149, 180, 260
apartheid, 32, 76, 78, 167, 169, 188
Arabs, 43, 78–9, 237
arbitration, 136, 252
aretaic turn, 13, 128, 130
Argentina, 26, 37
Aristotle, 127–8
Arkes, H., 255
Armenia, 26, 242
Arthur, A., 237
artistic speech, 24–5, 30, 82–3, 121, 168, 267
ascriptive characteristics, 4, 7–8, 16, 18, 20–1, 23, 26, 28–31, 33, 35–7, 54, 80, 94, 127, 167–8, 201, 209, 219, 225, 285, 319

ASF (Aryan Strike Force), 71
Asians, 73, 101
Asquith, N., 145
Assmann, J., 171
assurance, 142, 144, 148–52, 154–5, 207, 209, 240, 276; principle of, 148, 276
attitudes, 14, 59, 64, 67, 69–70, 112, 125, 133, 151, 173, 199–200, 204–5, 207, 216, 302, 311
Au, K., 68, 73
Audi, R., 2
Auschwitz, 146, 172, 219, 286
Austin, J.L., 102
Australia, 23–4, 162, 182, 240, 246, 253, 259
Austria, 30, 42
autonomy, 1, 5–6, 8, 11, 17, 21, 24, 49, 58–62, 64, 66, 98, 100, 120, 139, 152, 174, 209–11, 213–14, 217–19, 222, 227, 229, 266, 276, 279, 287, 290, 297, 314; formal, 7, 209–12, 229, 317; nuanced principle of, 60, 64, 276, 287, 290, 297; principle of, 59, 209, 276, 287; substantive, 211
Azerbaijan, 26–7, 242

Baker, C.E., 5, 42, 59, 61–2, 99–100, 139, 210–12, 217, 229, 243, 245, 247, 266, 269
balancing, 11, 17, 28, 104, 108, 198, 207, 218–38, 269, 275–6, 278–81, 283, 286, 311; ad hoc/definitional, 236; principle of interests-based, 223, 225, 276; principle of rights-based, 220–1, 276, 280
balkanization, 224, 234
Bangladesh, 26

Bardot, B., 244
Barendt, E., 11, 52
basic human functionings, 81, 84
basic human goods/values, 6–7, 221, 234
BBC, 22, 29, 254
Belgium, 12, 23, 30, 37, 271–2, 275
Bellamy, R., 299, 304
Belton, P.J., 20
Benhabib, S., 302, 306
Benjamin, M., 303
Berger Levinson, R., 140
Berlin, I., 277
Beschle, D., 91
Bindman, G., 243, 249
Blackburn, S., 117
Blain, M., 245
Blair, T., 108
blasphemy, 16
Bleich, E., 11, 190, 232, 255
Blim, J., 6, 139
Blum, L., 173–4
B'nai Brith, 246
Bodney, D., 16
Bolivia, 23
Bollinger, L., 88, 138, 255, 273–4
Bolotin, L., 196
Booth, W.J., 171
Bork, R.H., 139, 214
Borovoy, A., 244–5, 249, 251–2, 254, 259
Braun, S., 11, 249
Brazil, 31–2
breach of the peace, 20, 24, 28, 115, 159, 197, 214, 264–5, 291–2
Brettschneider, C., 201, 262, 269, 295, 314
Brink, D., 50, 63, 113, 115, 198
Brison, S., 4, 8, 14, 63, 99, 198
broadcasters, 22, 24, 31, 37–8, 48, 70, 107, 120, 244, 254
Brondolo, E., 58
Browne, K.R., 192, 257
Brownstein, A.E., 317
Brugger, W., 159
Brunei, 37
Buckner Inniss, L., 170
bus example, 87–90, 294
Butler, J., 14, 170

Calvert, C., 86
Cambodia, 37
campus speech codes, 34, 75, 85, 102, 114, 116, 129–30, 135–6, 186, 192, 233–4, 238, 252, 268, 277–8, 281
Canada, 11–12, 26–9, 34, 162, 164, 182, 184, 186, 240, 245–6, 249, 271–2, 275; Human Rights Commission, 11–12, 186, 197, 271–2, 275; Supreme Court, 11–12, 17–18, 45, 93, 97, 105, 164, 182, 197, 223, 237, 243, 251, 265, 278, 280, 282
capabilities: central, 81–3, 103; theory, 81–2, 85, 103
captive audiences, 61–2, 131, 308
Carmi, G., 105
Cartesian skepticism, 111
cartoons. *See* hate speech, cartoons
Categorical Imperative, 92, 94–5
Catholics, 15, 41
Caws, P., 173
CCLA (Canadian Civil Liberties Association), 244
censorship, 15, 25, 64, 120, 188, 242, 262, 265–6, 275, 294, 296–7
censure, 253–7, 309
CERD (Committee on the Elimination of Racial Discrimination), 21, 24, 42–3, 245
Chafee, Z., 107, 137, 227
Chang, R., 279–81
Chemerinsky, E., 11, 15
children, 17, 20, 42, 62, 75, 83, 94, 111, 117, 154, 159
Chile, 26
chilling effects, 1, 15, 30, 194, 200, 226, 243, 266–8, 317
China, 26–7, 31, 44
Christians, 20, 42, 62, 101, 117, 138, 176
Cicero, 143
citizens, as legal subjects, 59, 209–10, 213–14
citizenship, 4, 28, 131, 135, 154–7, 174, 319
civic dignity, 1, 6–7, 9, 21, 142, 144–8, 152–5, 157–8, 177, 222, 225–6, 276, 287, 317–18; assurance of, 9, 75, 144, 150, 152, 157, 207–9; principle of, 144, 276, 287; protecting, 236, 240
civility, 54, 77, 158, 179, 181–2, 184, 196, 234, 247, 285, 314
civil or human rights laws/regulations/codes, 8, 17, 29, 33–5, 41, 52, 68, 75, 85, 87, 90, 116, 151,

182, 185, 192–3, 196, 199, 201, 204–5, 214, 241, 249, 265–6, 268, 275, 277, 317
Clarke, C, 29, 101
class, 15
clear and present danger, 68, 98
climate of hatred, 66–70, 75, 93, 101, 108, 119, 224, 240, 252
coercion, 5, 61–2, 255
Cohen, G.A., 306
Cohen, Jonathan, 319
Cohen, Joshua, 260, 288, 291, 302
Cohen-Almagor, R., 4, 11, 15–16, 50, 65, 120, 141, 304
Coliver, S., 4, 249
compromise: compelled by circumstances, 283; conjunction, 13, 284–5, 297, 300; Heraclitean bow, 312; practical concordance, 286; principled, 4, 13, 160, 235, 270, 276–316, 318–19; substitution, 13, 285–97, 300
compromisers, 13, 282–3, 299–304, 306, 310, 314, 316, 318; ethics of, 283, 305–6, 310, 318–19
consequentialism, 223–4, 236
contempt of court, 23, 39
context, 2–3, 13–15, 24, 32–3, 36–7, 72–3, 75–6, 78–9, 84, 87, 99, 102, 115, 130, 138, 143, 153, 159, 161, 166, 168, 174, 177, 182, 191–3, 203, 206, 211, 213–15, 232–3, 248, 252, 271, 273–5, 287–8, 290, 292, 310
Cortese, A., 91, 120
Costa Rica, 31
Council of Europe, 24, 30, 185
counterspeech, 39, 84, 132, 252–3, 257–62; Gelber's speaking back policy, 103, 262
Cox, P., 192, 238
Craddock, J.M., 118, 257
Cram, I., 154, 319
critical race theorists, 8, 51, 53, 58, 75, 80–1, 83–5, 130, 134, 144, 147–8, 169
cross burning, 14, 73–4, 100, 102, 151, 201, 256, 294–5, 297
cross burning statutes, 29, 35–6, 47, 73–4, 85, 101, 134, 165, 183, 201, 214, 220, 263–5, 270, 272, 281, 288–9, 293–6, 312–13

civil libertarians, 5, 10, 15, 35, 39, 92, 184, 192, 198, 205, 251, 274
crowded theater example, 113, 273
cruelty, 9, 94, 130–1, 140, 198
Cuba, 23, 37
cultural: communities, 161, 163–6, 171–7, 179–81, 183–4; diversity, 6, 10, 160–86, 222, 240, 247, 316; hegemony, 166; identity, 1, 6–7, 10, 160, 164, 166–7, 169–74, 222, 229; imperialism, 166; memories, 30, 55, 96–7, 141, 160, 171–2, 184
culture: building, 122–3, 163; nuanced principle of, 164, 166, 276; principle of, 161, 166, 177, 276
cybercascades, 63
cybercrime, 43, 46, 70
Czechoslovakia, 196
Czech Republic, 29–30

Dahl, R., 189, 215
Dan-Cohen, M., 125
Danish cartoons controversy, 121, 178, 249, 254–5, 320
Day, M., 185
Deckert, G., 97, 219
decorum, 32, 196
defamation: civil/criminal, 147. *See also* group defamation
degradation, 16, 30, 80, 169, 178, 317
de las Fuentes, 4, 95, 134
Delgado, R., 4, 8, 17, 49, 51–2, 57, 80–3, 92, 122, 125, 129, 136, 147, 173, 198, 236, 241, 243, 246, 304
Demaske, C., 6, 198
democracy, 1, 14–16, 24, 28, 147, 156, 177, 187–92, 194–202, 204, 215–16, 232, 269, 276–7, 285, 287, 301; collective authorization, 10, 202, 204–5, 207–8; disenfranchisement, 188, 198, 205; militant, 196–7, 201; nuanced principle of, 195–6, 199–201, 276, 287; principle of, 177, 191–2, 215, 276, 287
Democratic Republic of Congo, 26
democratic self-government, 6, 10, 187–90, 192, 214–15, 222, 276, 279, 288, 318; principle of, 188, 276
Denmark, 11, 23, 178–9
deportation, 28, 45, 93, 98

350   *Index*

Descartes, R., 111
destruction of property, 67–8, 70
dialogue, 122, 135–6, 140, 180, 182, 185–6, 192, 318
Dieudonné, 121
dignitary crime or tort laws/regulations/codes, 8–9, 21, 30–1, 52, 82, 93, 129, 221, 260
dignitary rights, 96, 98, 146, 220
dignity: 30–2, 51, 91–6, 105, 108, 117–18, 129, 140, 142–3, 152–3, 155, 157–8, 170, 173–9, 196, 208, 212, 218–22, 234, 260, 265, 267–8, 280, 313; civic, 1, 6–7, 9, 21, 142, 144–8, 152–5, 157–8, 177, 222, 225–6, 276, 287, 317–18; elementary, 144, 207; equal, 240, 256; human, 1, 6, 8–9, 33, 49, 91–8, 104–5, 112, 119, 142–3, 152–3, 157, 175, 177, 184, 217–18, 222, 226–7, 229, 234, 276–7, 279, 286; Kantian conception of, 94, 143; rank, 77–80, 102, 143, 153, 157; social, 104, 176–7
dilemmas, 3, 11, 13, 99, 128, 138, 152, 218, 231, 234–5, 271, 277–9, 281–3, 285, 306, 310
disability, 4, 9, 22, 34, 131, 135, 148, 158, 174, 195, 319
discourtesies, 150
discrimination: acts of, 17, 32, 34–5, 57, 66–8, 73, 86, 93, 108, 112, 134, 146, 204–5, 213, 223, 226, 228, 252, 285, 290, 293–4, 311; content, 64, 92, 269–70, 288–9, 291, 294–6, 313; incitement to acts of, 18, 26, 36–7, 40, 72, 86–7, 221, 317; racial, 21–2, 42–3, 57, 76, 87, 89–90, 245, 264; valid bases for content, 12, 38, 64, 270–1, 287, 289, 291–7, 301, 312, 314; viewpoint, 36, 269–70, 274, 287–9, 294–5, 297, 313–14
discriminatory harassment, 9, 15–16, 33–5, 46–7, 52, 58, 61, 75–6, 85, 114–16, 124, 129–31, 135–6, 192–3, 199, 206, 215, 220, 231, 260, 265–7, 277, 293–4, 317
discriminatory intimidation, 29, 35–6, 40, 58, 85, 103, 165, 173, 199, 201, 214, 221, 247, 263–4, 317

distinctness of persons, 56, 189, 228, 238
Douglas, L., 112, 249
Downs, D.A., 20, 112, 233, 242, 258
Dworkin, R., 2, 5–6, 76, 91, 95, 97, 141, 204–5, 207–29, 217, 277–8, 314

East Timor, 26, 37
Eberle, E.J., 20, 91, 105, 286
ECtHR (European Court of Human Rights), 11–12, 18, 24, 26, 30, 35, 37, 47, 66, 145, 197, 216, 219, 240, 243, 251, 270–2, 275
Ecuador, 23, 37
education, 18, 33, 69, 75, 82–3, 114, 119, 139, 151, 170, 205, 212, 215, 250, 253–4, 309, 312, 315
EEOC (Equal Employment Opportunity Commission), 33–4, 46, 76, 87, 104, 274
efficacy, 3, 11, 103, 242–4, 246–8, 252–3, 262, 276, 288; principle of, 243, 248, 276
eggshell skull rule, 56
Egypt, 28
EHRC (Equality and Human Rights Commission), 154, 185
Ehrlich, H.J., 54, 70, 99
Emerson, T., 14, 120–3, 188
emotional distress, 5, 15, 32, 50–6, 99, 129–31, 147, 206, 220, 223, 235–6, 291
empathy, 9, 131–6
epistemic goods, 99, 116, 118, 225–7, 314
epithets. *See* hate speech, epithets
equality, 4, 6–7, 153–4, 184, 200, 216, 231–2, 234, 244–5, 252, 283, 288, 299, 301–2, 305–10, 318; equal airing and consideration of alternatives, 13, 301–2; formal/substantive, 7, 203; sociolegal status, 145–54, 156, 158, 177
Estlund, C., 192, 308
ethical independence, 95, 141, 208, 217, 277
ethnicity, 4, 9, 32, 35, 37, 114, 131, 135, 142, 148, 154, 158, 173–4, 184, 194, 246, 319
European Commission, 156, 171
European Parliament, 26
European Union, 26, 30, 36

evidence, 6, 9, 17, 21, 28, 33, 42, 49, 54–5, 57–8, 65, 69, 71, 77, 82–3, 97–8, 101, 103, 108, 111–12, 117–20, 138–9, 143–4, 150, 153, 157–8, 171, 185, 196, 198–9, 210, 243–7, 250, 258–60, 265, 267–8, 272, 309, 311, 314
expression of hatred laws/regulations/codes, 7, 23, 31, 33, 36, 41, 54, 80, 123–4, 127–8, 145, 168, 177, 183, 185, 209, 221, 267, 285, 316
expression-oriented hate crime laws/regulations/codes, 8, 16, 18, 35–8, 40, 52, 58, 71–3, 85, 128, 165, 199, 201, 214, 221
expressive conduct, 4–5, 7–8, 14–16, 19, 21, 26–30, 33, 35, 38, 41, 60–1, 73, 85, 90, 107, 113, 117, 119, 121, 127, 139, 151, 161, 171, 188, 191, 202, 209, 219, 239, 251, 263–4, 269, 271, 274
expressive content, 296, 303
extreme and outrageous conduct, 32, 52–3, 130–1, 140, 236. *See also* torts, intentional infliction of emotional distress
extreme speech, 16

Facebook. *See* social networking websites
fairness doctrine, 38, 48, 120, 244
falsehoods, 20, 62, 96–7, 107, 109–11, 114, 117, 119–20, 139, 197, 226
FCC (Federal Communications Commission), 38, 48, 311
fear, 25, 51, 72–5, 84, 100, 103, 115, 134, 137, 159, 165, 172, 184, 194, 198, 208, 220, 240, 243, 250, 255, 259–60, 289, 294–5
Feinberg, J., 2, 222, 230–1
Feldman, D., 249, 271
fighting words, 15, 36, 63, 115, 134, 200, 260, 265, 270, 288–93, 295
Finland, 37
First Amendment, 12, 15, 33, 35, 38–9, 48, 52, 62, 72–3, 76, 83, 99, 116, 131, 133–4, 137, 140–1, 183, 188, 192, 197, 200–1, 203–4, 216, 227–9, 232, 241–2, 251, 266, 269–71, 274, 277, 281, 287, 289, 294–5, 301, 314
Fish, S., 14, 260, 262–3, 300
Fiss, O., 14, 198, 200, 275, 288
football (soccer), 42, 175, 177, 257
Former Yugoslav Republic of Macedonia, 42
France, 12, 20–1, 23, 26, 28–9, 35, 37, 46, 158, 244, 270, 272, 275
Fraser, N., 166, 170, 173
freedom of expression. *See* free speech
free speech, 2–3, 5–7, 10–15, 17, 37–9, 50–1, 58–60, 67–8, 72–3, 77, 82–3, 86, 91, 93, 95, 99–100, 102–7, 112–13, 116–23, 125–6, 128, 133, 135, 137–8, 140, 160–2, 170, 174–5, 177, 180–5, 187–90, 194, 196–7, 200, 202–3, 205–6, 208–10, 213–16, 218–21, 223–4, 227–8, 231–3, 235, 238–40, 242, 247, 249–50, 263–4, 269–71, 273–4, 277–8, 280, 283–4, 286, 288, 294, 303–4, 314, 320; absolutists, 208, 227; values, 20–1, 24, 35, 39, 175, 243
funerals, 26, 38–9, 131, 141, 151, 206, 273

Galeotti, A.E., 163, 240
gangsta rap, 170
Gates, H.L., 129
Gaurady, R., 18
Gelber, K., 4, 84, 103, 198, 203, 247, 253, 259, 262
gender, 4, 9, 16, 22, 24, 36–7, 116, 131, 134–5, 142, 144, 148, 158, 174, 177, 180, 195, 259, 270, 290–1, 295, 319
generics. *See* hate speech, generics
genocide, 8, 29–30, 35–6, 40, 45, 48, 93, 139, 184, 245, 270, 316
Germany, 20–1, 23–4, 26, 28–31, 37, 41, 94, 96–8, 104–5, 110, 141, 146, 156, 158, 171, 196–7, 219, 250, 272, 286
gestures, 5, 35, 220–1
glorification, 16, 30, 94, 128
GLSEN (Gay, Lesbian and Straight Education Network), 246–7
government speech, 242, 263
Greece, 23, 37
Greenawalt, K., 15, 36, 102, 139, 192, 213, 237, 249, 252

352  Index

group defamation laws/regulations/codes, 7, 19–21, 23, 26, 28, 40, 54, 63, 68, 73, 75, 80, 108–9, 117, 127, 143–5, 148–55, 157–8, 177–9, 185, 191, 197, 208, 213–14, 221, 245, 266–7, 270, 290, 317, 320; catchall, 20, 54, 63, 73, 75, 99, 143–5, 148–55, 157–8, 170, 185, 205, 226, 248, 320; civic dignity, 144, 154, 157; false rumors, 62–3, 114, 118; sensu stricto, 20–1, 23, 26, 28, 30, 40, 63, 80, 108–9, 113, 117–18, 127, 145, 178–9, 197, 208, 212–14, 221, 267, 284, 317; truth defense, 21, 23, 27, 40, 107, 178

groups: identifiable, 17, 28, 110–11, 205, 226; ingroups, 63, 70, 131, 133; intergroup contact, 69, 258; intragroup contact, 67, 70; large, 104, 159; minority, 14, 17, 22, 57, 74, 83–5, 122, 134, 149, 151, 154, 156, 158, 170, 179–80, 185, 191, 198–9, 205–6, 208, 215, 223, 228, 248, 255, 258, 261, 311, 314; outgroups, 63, 67, 69–70, 93; powerful, 167, 183, 278, 313; racial or ethnic, 31, 58, 66, 69, 114, 130, 144–6, 179, 202, 226, 234; religious, 40, 124, 152, 170, 173, 176; vulnerable, 9–10, 66, 93, 112, 130–2, 144, 146–8, 150, 152, 159, 207–8, 262

Habermas, J., 277
Hampshire, S., 141, 313
harassment. *See* discriminatory harassment
Hare, I., 15–16, 59, 243, 272, 312
Harel, A., 162, 250–1
harm, 7, 31, 50–4, 59–60, 68–9, 77, 79, 82, 92, 100, 103, 129, 145, 159, 176, 228, 236, 241, 243, 256, 267, 301, 317–18; cumulative, 58; Mill's Harm Principle, 50, 276
hate crimes, 16, 35, 58, 101, 103, 205, 253. *See also* expression-oriented hate crime laws/regulations/codes
hate groups, 67, 70–1, 107, 119, 252, 262

hate mail, 259
hate radio, 243
hate speech: age, 4, 22, 34, 53, 114, 131, 135, 137, 174, 180, 319; anti-Muslim or Islamophobic, 101, 108, 121, 175, 180, 186, 267; anti-Semitic, 57; artistic, asylum seekers, 156; backbiting, 92, 95; banter, 193; breach of the peace, 20, 24, 28, 30, 97–8, 115, 159, 181, 197, 214, 264–5, 291–2; on campus, 15, 17, 34, 47, 62, 65, 75, 85, 99, 102, 111, 113–14, 116, 119, 124, 129–31, 135–6, 186, 192–3, 199, 231–4, 237–8, 247, 252–4, 258, 265, 268, 273, 277, 281, 317; cartoons, 22, 254–5, 267; characterizations of, 4–5, 14, 15, 255; disability, 32, 114–15, 153–4, 319; epithets, 15, 32, 43, 55, 99, 102, 121, 206, 237, 260; ethnophaulisms, 167–8; face-to-face, 31, 33, 147, 219, 308, 317; at football (soccer) matches, 175, 177; at funerals, 38–9, 140–1, 151; generics, 23, 84, 108, 138, 237, 261, 291–2; group defamation, 9, 15, 19, 21, 30, 54–5, 63, 108, 113–14, 118, 144, 156, 170, 177, 212, 221, 225–6, 237, 245, 274; impersonal, 317; individualized, 317; insults, 15–16, 23–5, 27, 40, 53–4, 57, 80, 93, 100, 115, 127, 130, 159, 168, 177–8, 220–1, 236, 267, 274, 284; intimidation, 16, 25, 35, 38, 72–3, 84, 86, 90, 114, 165, 201, 216, 221, 259, 264, 270, 274, 295–6, 312–14; jokes/comedy/satire, 54, 58, 99, 121, 193, 232, 267; journalistic, 25; misogyny, 16, 170, 249; online, 25, 40, 58, 63, 65, 67, 69, 71, 98, 101, 116, 120, 134–7, 151, 156, 160, 170, 189, 248–9, 257, 259–62; propaganda, 94, 101, 184–5; racist, 32, 36, 46, 52–3, 55–8, 61, 64, 75–6, 80–1, 83–9, 91–2, 99, 102, 104, 113, 117, 134, 147, 155–6, 162–3, 184–5, 192, 205, 211, 220–1, 236, 240–1, 245, 258, 260,

Index   353

270, 272, 275, 290–2, 294, 300–1; resident non-citizens, 10, 154–5, 167; scientific, 102, 121; slurs, 15, 23, 32–3, 53–4, 63, 80, 93, 99, 102, 123, 127, 130, 147, 168, 177, 221, 237, 246, 258, 284; symbols, 5, 13, 23, 35–6, 128, 134, 147, 170, 312; undocumented immigrants, 154–6; verbal abuse, 27, 31, 51–3, 55, 64, 129–30, 202, 260, 317; victims, 9, 32–3, 52, 56, 82–3, 92, 103, 111, 113, 124, 129–31, 144, 147, 155, 158, 168–9, 171, 184, 224, 238, 240, 258–9, 279, 297; war record, 4, 114, 131, 135, 159, 174, 319; white supremacy, 196, 296, 313; the word "nigger," 32–4, 46, 85, 87–8, 99, 102, 167–8, 170, 237; in the workplace, 14–15, 32–4, 46, 57–8, 61, 69, 76, 81, 85, 99, 126, 129, 131, 151, 192–3, 199, 214, 220, 260, 267–8, 293, 317

hate speech law: characterization of, 5, 15–16; civil or human rights laws/regulations/codes, 8, 17, 29, 33–5, 41, 52, 68, 75, 85, 87, 90, 116, 151, 182, 185, 192–3, 196, 199, 201, 204–5, 214, 241, 249, 265–6, 268, 275, 277, 317; critics of, 1–2, 15, 25, 27, 35, 49, 72, 77, 112, 114, 151–2, 166, 174, 191, 204, 229, 243–4, 247–9, 267–8; defenders of, 1–2, 60, 77, 129, 174, 183, 207, 214, 218, 228, 246, 249; de-homogenizing, 2, 19, 58, 80, 108, 128, 316; dignitary crime or tort laws/regulations/codes, 8–9, 21, 30–1, 52, 82, 93, 129, 221, 260; expression of hatred laws/regulations/codes, 7, 23, 31, 33, 36, 41, 54, 80, 123–4, 127–8, 145, 168, 177, 183, 185, 209, 221, 267, 285, 316; expression-oriented hate crime laws/regulations/codes, 8, 16, 18, 35–8, 40, 52, 58, 71–3, 85, 128, 165, 199, 201, 214, 221; group defamation laws/regulations/codes, 7, 19–21, 23, 26, 28, 40, 54, 63, 68, 73, 75, 80, 108–9, 117, 127, 143–5,

148–55, 157–8, 177–9, 185, 191, 197, 208, 213–14, 221, 245, 266–7, 270, 290, 317, 320; Holocaust denial laws/regulations/codes, 8, 16, 27, 29–30, 94, 96, 98, 109, 118–19, 137, 146–7, 157–8, 171–2, 197, 316; incitement to hatred laws/regulations/codes, 7, 15–16, 18, 20, 24, 26–30, 37, 40–1, 44, 65–9, 71, 74, 97, 100–2, 110–11, 125–7, 140, 147, 149, 156, 159, 162, 164, 167, 174, 176–9, 181, 191, 197, 203, 208, 210, 212–14, 221, 224, 226, 241, 243, 247–50, 261, 264, 267–8, 317, 319; interpretive nature of, 8, 13; negative stereotyping or stigmatization laws/regulations/codes, 7, 10, 15, 21–2, 35, 80, 83–4, 101, 127, 144–5, 169–70, 173, 178–81, 183, 208–9, 214, 219, 221, 317; sexual orientation, 4, 9, 18, 22, 41, 74, 101–2, 105, 114–15, 131, 133, 135, 140, 142, 144, 148, 158, 164, 174, 176–7, 186, 195, 241, 246–7, 250, 319; ten clusters of, 7–8, 19, 39–40, 276, 316; threat to public order laws/regulations/codes, 8, 28, 30, 97; time, place, and manner restrictions, 8, 12, 38–9, 120, 200, 248, 263–4, 274, 317; warrant of. *See* warrant

HateWatch, 101

hatred: climate of, 66–70, 75, 93, 101, 108, 119, 224, 240, 252; community of, 67; expression of, 7, 15, 23, 33, 36, 40–1, 54, 61, 80, 93, 123, 127–8, 145, 168, 177, 183, 221, 237, 267, 284–5, 316–17; feelings of, 4–5, 15–16, 23–4, 35–6, 42, 66–70, 74–5, 92, 116, 119, 123, 132–4, 147, 152, 156, 193, 224, 250–1; incitement to, 7, 15–16, 18, 20, 24, 26–30, 37, 40–1, 44, 65–69, 71, 74, 97, 100–2, 110–11, 125–7, 140, 147, 149, 156, 159, 162, 164, 167, 174, 176–9, 181, 191, 197, 203, 208, 210, 212–14, 221, 224, 226, 241, 243, 247–50, 261,

264, 267–8, 317, 319; self-, 52, 82, 125, 169, 223
Haworth, A., 111, 138
health, 1, 6, 8, 49–52, 56, 58, 66, 77, 98, 113, 174, 185, 222, 247, 276, 287, 291, 297, 317; bodily, 103; depression, 57–8; emotions, 81–2; headaches, 56–7; high blood pressure, 57, 77; hypertension, 56; principle of, 51–2, 56, 276, 287, 291, 297; psychological symptoms, 54–5, 57
Heinze, E., 246, 249, 319
Heretical Press, 69, 137
Hess, A., 259
Heyman, S., 2–3, 11, 91, 123–4, 140, 201, 217–22, 235–6, 291, 293
Holmes, S., 202
Holocaust denial, 9, 13, 16, 30, 45, 48, 96–8, 110, 119–20, 135, 146, 171–2, 219, 226
Holocaust denial laws/regulations/ codes, 8, 16, 27, 29–30, 94, 96, 98, 109, 118–19, 137, 146–7, 157–8, 171–2, 197, 316
Honneth, A., 126, 166, 169, 173–4, 209–10
honor, 5, 93, 96, 134, 182, 219–21, 281
hostile work environment, 33–4, 46
human dignity, 1, 6, 8–9, 33, 49, 91–8, 104–5, 112, 119, 142–3, 152–3, 157, 175, 177, 184, 217–18, 222, 226–7, 229, 234, 276–7, 279, 286; principle of, 91, 112, 276
human excellence, 6, 9, 106, 127–30, 132, 134, 136, 222, 276, 287, 314; principle of, 128–30, 132, 134, 136, 276, 287
human rights, 11, 33–6, 39, 52, 143, 152, 155–6, 171, 181
human rights law, 23, 26, 31, 34, 36, 72, 160, 239
humans as thinking beings, 117–18
human values, 3, 91, 121, 128, 174, 180
Hume, D., 132–3
humiliation, 16, 25, 30–2, 52, 63, 82, 99, 115, 138, 143, 164, 169, 193, 223, 254, 260–1, 317
Hungary, 23, 26, 29, 135; Supreme Court, 27
Hursthouse, R., 128
hyperbole, 20–1, 72, 138, 178

ideal theory/non-ideal theory, 307, 315
ideational content, 15, 177, 292–3
identity, 30, 35, 82, 84, 90, 124, 126, 140, 162, 164, 166–74, 176, 181; ascribing, 168; cultural, 1, 6–7, 10, 160, 164, 166–7, 169–74, 222, 229; elective, 167; ethnic, 35, 169; group, 173–4; human, 175–6; inferior, 168; LGBT, 4, 131, 135, 174, 176, 319; micro-, 174; narratives, 160, 172–3, 184; politics of, 160, 166–8; racial, 165; religious, 164, 177, 319; social, 169, 173, 176–8
ideologies, 41, 91, 119, 165, 185
imminent lawless action, 68, 98
incitement to crime, 16, 26, 38
incitement to hatred laws/regulations/ codes, 7, 15–16, 18, 20, 24, 26–30, 37, 40–1, 44, 65–9, 71, 74, 97, 100–2, 110–11, 125–7, 140, 147, 149, 156, 159, 162, 164, 167, 174, 176–9, 181, 191, 197, 203, 208, 210, 212–14, 221, 224, 226, 241, 243, 247–50, 261, 264, 267–8, 317, 319
incitement to violence, 15, 18, 29, 41, 220
incommensurability, 229–30, 235, 281
individualism, 129
Indonesia, 23
injuria, 31–2, 46; crimen, 31, 46, 260; racial, 32, 46
injuries: dignitary, 236–7, 265; emotional, 141, 291; personal, 237, 290; psychological, 52, 56, 81; verbal, 220
Instagram. *See* social networking websites
institutional authorities, 3, 129, 133, 235, 240, 248, 253, 260, 262, 271, 280
institutions, 6, 13–14, 87, 135, 167, 175, 181, 192, 196, 204–5, 214, 233, 238, 240, 246, 253, 267, 274, 283, 309, 311, 316–17; cultural, 182; educational, 85; legal, 6, 13, 181, 231, 310; legal-political, 167; non-governmental, 39
insults. *See* hate speech, insults
intentional infliction of emotional distress. *See* tort, intentional infliction of emotional distress

intercultural dialogue, 1, 6, 10, 23, 160, 180–2, 184–5, 222, 276, 303, 317–18; principle of, 182, 276
interculturalism, 160, 182–3
interests, 3, 5–7, 11–12, 17–18, 29, 52, 60, 64, 70, 73, 80, 92, 102, 108, 132, 152, 163, 166, 218, 222–5, 227–36, 238, 241, 256, 278, 280, 283, 297–8; addressee, 223; balancing, 223, 225, 276; commensurable, 230; community, 231; epistemic, 233; general, 29, 231; governmental, 263, 311; speaker, 223–5, 229; third-party, 223–5, 229
intermezzo theory, 81, 92, 95
internet, 39–40, 63, 65, 67, 71, 98, 120, 134–7, 151, 156, 160, 170, 246, 248–9, 254, 257, 260–2, 310
internet messaging services, 40, 248
intimidation. *See* discriminatory intimidation
intolerance, 156, 165, 185, 205, 232, 263, 290
Ireland, 26
Irish people, 22, 73, 193–4
Irving, D., 146
Islam, 27, 37, 48, 101, 176, 180, 184, 197, 267
Israel, 20–1, 29, 273; Knesset, 197; Supreme Court, 197
Italy, 23, 35, 37, 156, 272

Jacobson, D., 85, 200
Japan, 43
Jay, T., 55
Jefferson, T., 137
Jews, 15, 17–18, 20, 30–1, 41–2, 46, 48, 62, 65, 95–7, 100, 109–12, 117, 138–9, 146, 166, 171–3, 176, 178, 201, 220, 244–5, 264, 273, 286
Jihadists, 65, 267
jokes. *See* hate speech, jokes
journalists, 24–5, 27, 43, 48, 86, 165, 196
judges, 11, 23, 25, 51, 68, 74, 95, 128, 130, 133–4, 141, 150, 191, 202–3, 222, 228, 231–2, 252, 259, 273–4, 278, 282–5, 298, 300, 302, 305–6, 309–10; Beaumont, 65; Burgess, 74, 102; Carroll, 31; Cohn, 231–2, 265–6, 268, 273–4; Decker, 203; Dénes, 135; Didcott, 32; Edwards, 302; Grant, 69; Hand, 281; Handler, 53; Meinerzhagen, 98; Mosler, 243–5, 272; Pell, 264, 314; Spielmann, 275; Sprecher, 272; Warren, 230; Yudkivska, 18, 271
judicial decisions, 134, 252, 281, 283, 302, 310
judicial discretion, 23, 32, 234
judicial ethics, 4, 299
justiciability, 3, 100, 174
justification. *See* warrant

Kalven, H., 20
Kant, I., 91–2, 94–6, 104
Karam, N., 101
Karst, K.L., 170
Kateb, G., 50
Kenya, 26, 37, 242, 246
Kitano, H., 57
Kitrosser, H., 292
KKK (Klu Klux Klan), 33, 54, 73, 100, 102, 193, 201, 220, 313
Knechtle, J., 91, 249
knowledge: acquisition of, 1, 6, 9, 13, 17, 71, 106, 109, 111, 116–20, 139, 171, 188, 222, 224–8, 233, 261, 276, 287, 316; nuanced principle of, 119–20, 276; principle of, 117–19, 227, 276, 287
Korsgaard, C., 93, 104, 238
Kretzmer, D., 11, 240, 275, 291
Kymlicka, W., 161
Kyrgyzstan, 26

Lange, E., 125, 192
Langton, R., 4, 76–8, 80, 84, 103, 216, 261
Laramie Project, 141
Latinos, 54, 82, 84, 99, 101
Laub, D., 172
law: civil, 21, 31, 39; domestic, 24, 30, 71, 239; expressive function of, 240–1; good, 128, 266; international, 24, 26, 30, 36, 140; media, 21, 23, 26, 28–9, 37, 179, 181; public gatherings, 26, 39; system of, 143–4, 209
Law Lords, 309; Atkin, 237; Stonham, 100
Lawrence, C., 4, 8, 15, 51, 62, 75, 80–1, 84–5, 114–15, 125, 134, 198, 225, 275, 291

lawsuit, 31, 33–4, 46, 53, 99, 104, 129, 193, 220, 237; class action, 31, 157, 225, 237
lawyers, 46, 99, 131, 143, 168, 252
leaflets, 18, 37, 54, 66, 74, 137, 146, 151, 154, 158, 192, 251
least restrictive alternative, 11–12, 34, 235, 251–2, 276, 280; principle of, 34, 251–2, 276
legalistic constraints, 1, 9, 14, 39, 49, 51, 59–60, 66, 75, 86, 91, 96, 106–8, 113, 117, 119, 121, 128, 144, 148, 157, 160–1, 164, 167, 169, 182–3, 188, 191, 195, 201–2, 209, 218, 220, 223, 231, 239, 251, 260, 263–5, 269, 287, 318
legal principles, 3, 7, 11, 13, 116, 239, 251, 271, 282, 288, 314, 318
legislators, 1, 3, 27, 51, 58, 67, 95, 127–8, 132–3, 149, 189, 196, 202, 222, 228, 230, 232, 244, 252, 261, 278, 280, 284–5, 292, 296–8, 310, 316
Lepora, C., 284–5, 312–13
Levin, A., 77
lexical priority, 4, 277, 286
LGBT, 4, 26, 38–9, 42, 74, 94, 101, 124, 131, 140–1, 146, 151, 162, 174, 176, 205–6, 242, 246–7, 273, 319
liberals, 8, 41, 100, 140, 161, 163, 167, 183, 209, 218, 232, 255, 263, 314
liberty, 1, 6–7, 17, 21, 29, 49–50, 98, 138–9, 143, 168, 174, 185, 200, 216, 221–2, 230–1, 235, 241, 288, 317
Lithuania, 26, 30
Lively, D.E., 129
Locke, J., 153, 219
London bombings, 29
Lukes, S., 311
lynching, 14

Macedonia, 26
MacKinnon, C., 16, 76, 86–7, 104, 189, 206, 261
Madison, J., 137
Maitra, I., 15, 76, 78–9, 86, 102
Majeed, A., 257–8
Malaysia, 26, 28
malice: actual, 185; aggravated, 225
Malik, K., 201, 302, 310
Manning, C., 99

marketplace of ideas, 17, 107, 111, 137, 188, 257, 261
Marshall, G., 107, 117–18, 155
Matsuda, M., 4, 8, 20, 51–2, 57–8, 62, 73, 75–6, 83, 91, 101, 134, 144, 155, 164, 240, 259, 261
McGowan, M.K., 8, 15, 76, 86–90, 104, 145, 253, 294
McNamara, L., 11, 138, 149, 162, 247
media, 22–3, 69–70, 126, 156, 160, 167–8, 170, 184–5, 215, 238, 261, 310; effects, 69, 82. See also law, media; regulators, media
mediation, 34, 136. See also reconciliation
Meiklejohn, A., 187–8, 195–6, 227
menschenwürde, 104
mens rea, 224
Merchant of Venice, 264
Mexico, 23, 26
Michelman, F., 92, 198, 200, 266
Mill, J.S., 50, 107, 109, 116–19, 138–9, 225, 227, 255
Miller, D., 2, 4
misogyny, 16, 249
misrecognition, 10, 160, 166–73, 183–4, 210. See also recognition
Modood, T., 20, 166, 170, 181, 184–5, 254–5, 257, 261
Molnar, P., 253
Mookherjee, M., 20, 173
Morgan, G., 20, 50, 67, 101
Muhammad, 121, 178, 249, 255, 267
multiculturalism, 160, 162, 164–5, 174, 182–5, 244–5
Murchison, B., 139–40
Murray, D., 15, 281
Muslims, 10, 29, 65, 70, 84, 100–1, 108, 123, 138, 159, 162, 164, 176, 178–82, 184–5, 249, 254–6, 267, 320; young disaffected, 180, 184
Musselman, J., 198
mutual respect, 4, 13, 160, 180–2, 283, 299, 302–3, 305–10, 318, 320

Nagy, G., 135–6
Namibia, 27
narrow tailoring, 263–4, 273, 276; principle of, 263–4, 273, 276
nationality, 4, 34–5, 114, 131, 135, 148, 156, 158, 168, 174, 264, 319

necessary in a democratic society, 12, 251
negative stereotypes, 22–3, 69–70, 82–3, 108, 133–6, 138, 156, 167–8, 198, 261; expressed, 18; implicit, 70; threat, 82, 103
negative stereotyping or stigmatization laws/regulations/codes, 7, 10, 15, 21–2, 35, 80, 83–4, 101, 127, 144–5, 169–70, 173, 178–81, 183, 208–9, 214, 219, 221, 317
Nelson, S.P., 17, 121–2, 139–40, 221, 233
neo-Nazis, 97–8, 128, 166
Netherlands, 21, 26, 37, 196
Neu, J., 14, 80
neutrality, 11, 38, 215, 269–71, 274–6, 286–7, 289–97, 300–1; content, 134, 269–70, 288; exceptions to principle of, 12, 38, 64, 270–1, 287, 289, 291–7, 301, 312, 314; norm of justificatory, 301, 314; nuanced principle of, 287–97, 301; principle of, 269–70, 276, 286–7, 289–91, 293–5, 297, 300–1; viewpoint, 12, 39, 242, 269, 289, 291, 295, 297, 314
newspapers, 24–5, 27, 31, 40, 43, 54, 137, 179, 181, 192, 237, 247–9, 254, 256, 261–2
New Zealand, 26, 34
NGOs (non-governmental organizations), 101, 253–4
Nielsen, L.B., 55, 258–9
non-subordination. *See* subordination
normatively relevant features, 1, 3, 5–7, 17, 21, 49, 51, 174, 222, 277, 316, 318
norms, 86, 182–3, 210, 294, 301, 308
Norway, 18, 23
numbskull's veto, 120
Nussbaum, M., 82–3, 103

Oakes Test, 12, 243, 251, 278
obloquy, 21, 144, 158
obscenity, 16, 289, 295
Ofcom, 22, 42
offensive, 22–4, 32, 128, 206–7, 254–5, 273–4, 289, 296
official suppression of ideas, 15, 25, 64, 120, 188, 242, 262, 265–6, 275, 294, 296–7
Ogletree, C.J., 198

O'Neill, R.M., 11, 253
oppression, 1, 6–8, 49, 86–7, 90, 98, 134, 222, 225, 285, 292, 313; principle of non-oppression, 86, 276, 285, 287, 294, 297
ostracism, 93, 256
overbreadth, 30, 34, 36, 105, 215, 264–6, 269, 273–4, 276, 280, 295; principle of, 215, 264–6, 269, 273–4, 276

Pakistan, 26, 246
paradoxes, 110, 112, 255
Parekh, B., 4, 11, 16–17, 20, 67–8, 91, 166, 169, 173–82, 184–5, 198, 204, 221, 248, 261, 299, 303–4, 318, 320
Partlett, D., 60, 225, 240, 250, 254, 263, 294
PCC (Press Complaints Commission), 23, 43
perfectionism, 140, 288
permissibility facts, 87–90, 104
personal development, 9, 106, 116, 118, 123, 127, 137, 215, 235; values of, 106, 139
personality, 94, 126, 220–1, 236
persuasion, 63–4, 114, 120, 276; principle of, 63–4, 276
Phelps family, 33, 38, 131, 140–1, 206, 217, 273
placards, 87–8, 151, 264
police, 18, 28, 32, 57, 65, 149–51, 153, 155, 181, 207, 210, 243, 249, 251, 274, 298, 310, 313–14
policymakers, 128, 134, 155, 298, 310
political legitimacy, 1, 5, 10, 28, 95, 187, 201–4, 206–12, 214, 216, 226, 238, 269, 276, 280, 283, 287, 311, 316; principle of, 202, 226, 276; upstream/downstream laws, 204–8, 226
political obligation, 10–11, 28, 187, 210, 212–14, 317
political speech, 30, 100, 121, 188, 190, 193, 201, 207, 213–14, 220, 224, 264
power, 13, 50, 64, 76–8, 80–6, 103, 128, 130, 132, 149, 153, 158, 167, 170, 179, 181, 183, 189, 202, 209, 242, 252, 256, 269, 275, 283, 296–8, 303
pornography, 15–16, 76, 84, 164, 216, 303

Posner, R., 100, 177, 250, 281–2
Post, R., 4, 10, 14, 19, 54, 84, 121, 154, 182–3, 186, 189–96, 202–3, 215, 233, 237–8, 277, 285
posters, 54, 176
precautionary approaches, 110, 199, 216, 247, 276
precautionary principle, 216, 247, 276
predictability, 174, 265–6, 274–5
prejudices, 22, 37, 57, 65, 69–70, 114, 116, 132–3, 135–6, 180, 198, 205, 207, 234, 241, 244, 253–4
pressing social need, 11–12, 239–40, 263, 266, 276, 280; principle of, 239, 276
principled compromise, 4, 13, 160, 235, 270, 276–316, 318–19. See also equality as equal airing and consideration of alternative, mutual respect, reciprocity
principles: balancing, 4, 104, 218, 281; equal number of, 300; fundamental, 6, 136, 217, 239, 288; general, 117, 319; legal, 3, 7, 11, 13, 116, 239, 251, 271, 282, 288, 314, 318; list of, 276; meta-level, 277; normative, 1–3, 5–7, 30, 41, 81, 239, 276, 281, 285, 287, 290, 297, 313, 316; nuanced, 60, 64, 113, 115, 119–22, 124, 164, 166, 195–6, 199–201, 276, 285–97, 301; pluralism of, 5–6; sacred, 311
prison, 35, 98, 108, 135, 143, 241, 244, 256
probability, 28, 70, 77, 79, 109–12, 226
proscribable speech, 64, 72, 140, 270, 291, 294, 296
protests, 33, 39, 74, 87, 89, 204, 206, 212, 248, 252, 292
provocation, 16, 29, 35–6, 38, 52, 129, 201, 317
public: discourse, 10, 14, 17, 183, 187, 190–5, 199–201, 203, 206, 214–16, 218, 221, 233, 247, 254, 269–70, 278, 292, 310, 318; forums, 185, 261; goods, 9–10, 142, 148, 151, 163, 166, 182–3, 190, 208, 240, 256; interest, 25–6, 97, 131, 185, 188, 217, 219, 265, 267, 274; mischief, 28, 69, 265; officials, 224, 279, 310; opinion formation, 195–6; speech, 7–8, 19, 21, 28–30, 54, 78, 211; sphere, 190–1, 215–16; square, 206, 310

Qur'an, 138

racism, 58, 61, 84, 86–91, 104, 113, 163, 178, 184, 192, 205, 240, 245, 258, 270
radio, 22, 38, 40, 44, 54, 120, 189, 237, 261, 311
rational nature, 92–3, 104
Rawls, J., 283, 307, 314
Raz, J., 139, 161–2, 314
reciprocity, 4, 13, 184, 283, 299–301, 305–10, 318
recognition, 50, 59, 76, 94, 125–6, 136, 140, 160, 164, 166–9, 173, 182–3, 213, 219–20, 229, 234, 236, 276, 287, 304; judicial, 52; legal, 210; principle of, 167, 276, 287
reconciliation, 136, 252
reconstruction era, 169
Redish, M., 5, 11, 139, 274
regulators, 3, 22–3, 26, 39, 120, 128, 133, 179, 200, 202, 260, 298, 310, 316; internet, 39, 71, 120, 134, 260, 310; media, 22–3, 179, 200, 202; press, 181
religion, 4, 9, 16, 18, 22, 27, 32, 34–7, 41, 46, 71, 74, 114–15, 131, 135, 142, 144, 148, 156, 158–9, 162, 173–4, 177–8, 180, 188, 195, 245, 250, 264, 270, 291, 295, 319; religious beliefs, 16, 124, 145, 159, 162, 175, 180
reputation, 96, 146–7, 159, 225; fundamentals of, 142, 144
rhetoric, 231, 243, 300, 304
Rice, S., 150, 253, 303–4, 310
ridiculing, 21, 23–4, 27, 93, 131, 254, 265, 280
Riesman, D., 20, 41–2, 249
rights: balancing, 220–1, 276, 280; civic, 220; equal, 93–4, 254; human: mental tranquility, 220–1; personality, 219–20; reputation, 20–1, 23, 31, 48, 118, 142, 146–7, 157, 169–71, 175–7, 208, 220–1, 225, 236–7, 268
riots, 20, 180, 273, 301. See also breach of the peace
Roma, 18, 22, 42

Romania, 29
Roman Republic, 143
Rushdie Affair, 181, 320
Russia, 26, 35, 48, 148, 177
Rwanda, 23, 28–9, 245

Sadurski, W., 14, 62, 78, 113, 234
Sanctus bells example, 73
Sandel, M., 190
Satanic Verses, 181
Schauer, F., 4, 6–7, 11, 13, 15–17, 105, 108–9, 119, 137, 139, 189, 214, 216, 221, 225–8, 233, 247, 255
schools, 33, 39, 119, 126, 141, 168, 242, 247, 253–4, 286
scientific speech, 25, 102, 121, 267
scrutiny: intermediate, 263, 311; strict, 12, 197–8, 239, 251, 311
security, 6, 8, 29, 49, 66–7, 70–5, 77, 97–8, 100, 103, 108, 149–50, 174, 219–22, 225, 247, 276, 279, 285, 287, 290, 297, 311, 317; educational, 75; national, 65, 100; principle of, 66, 70–1, 75, 276, 285, 287, 290, 297
seditious libel, 42, 62, 159
segregation, 18, 34–6, 93, 192, 234
self-definition, 106, 123–5, 140
self-delusion, 55, 301
self-esteem, 73, 169
self-expression, 14, 223
self-fulfilling prophecies, 83–4
self-fulfillment, 106, 122, 140, 223
self-realization, 1, 5–6, 9, 11, 14, 24, 59, 106, 120–6, 139–40, 177, 222–3, 227, 233, 276, 279, 287, 316, 318; nuanced principle of, 121–2, 124, 276, 287; principle of, 121, 177, 276, 287
self-respect, 17, 81, 106, 125, 210
sexual harassment, 16, 46, 274
sexual orientation, 4, 9, 22, 41, 74, 102, 114–15, 131, 133, 135, 140, 142, 144, 148, 158, 164, 174, 176–7, 195, 241, 246–7, 250, 319
Sherry, S., 4, 136, 141, 186
Shiffrin, S.H., 3, 17, 86, 117, 189, 211, 221, 237, 249, 277, 281, 304, 317
Shiffrin, S.V., 63, 65
Shklar, J., 130, 140
signs, 33–4, 54, 87, 89, 206, 294
Sikhs, 101

silencing, 80, 84–6, 103, 124, 136, 198–200; barriers to speech/counterspeech, 126, 185, 197, 246–7, 258–62, 271
Simpson, E., 50, 55
Simpson, R., 150
Singapore, 26, 28
Skokie Affair, 12, 87–8, 129, 138, 190, 263–4, 273
slogans, 54, 68, 175, 177
Slovakia, 21, 36
Smolla, R., 4, 192, 233–4
soccer. *See* football (soccer)
social exclusion, 29, 145, 195, 223–4
social need. *See* pressing social need
social networking websites, 40, 135, 248
social practices, 2, 13–14, 75, 87, 168, 192, 196, 214, 233, 238, 274, 282, 316
society: members of in good standing, 7, 9, 75, 86, 142, 144, 147–52, 154, 158, 177, 208, 240; multicultural, 164–5, 182
sociolegal status, equal, 145–54, 156, 158, 177
solidarity, 85, 165
South Africa, 26, 31–2, 37, 76, 78, 169, 188, 242
Spain, 21, 29, 37
speaker intention, 37, 104
speech acts, 5, 9, 14–16, 75–8, 102, 116, 131, 139, 183, 191, 214–16, 255, 302; authority problem, 78, 80; cognitive/non-cognitive effects, 5, 15; complex, 265; exercitive force, 104; illocutionary force, 76, 78, 81, 84–5, 102–4, 290–1; legal/illegal conduct, 5, 14–15; locutionary force, 75, 102, 290; perlocutionary force, 75–6, 81, 84–5, 102, 104; pragmatics, 78; pure speech/speech plus, 5, 14
Spinoza, B., 272
stability, 179, 280, 283, 305, 311
statistics, 108, 114, 138–9, 178–9, 246, 309
Stefancic, J., 11, 17, 23, 32, 53, 57, 120, 198, 244, 256, 258–60, 317
stigmatization, 21–2, 52, 74, 80, 82–4, 101, 114–16, 127, 133, 135, 138, 144–5, 169–70, 173, 178–81, 208–9, 214, 221
Stone, G.R., 274

Strauss, D.A., 63–4, 199, 275
stress, 51, 57–8, 232
Strossen, N., 11, 15, 55, 59, 112–13, 150, 205, 243, 249, 252–4, 258–60, 262, 266
students, 116, 125, 215, 234, 258, 260, 286
subhuman, 93, 220
subordination, 6–8, 49, 75–6, 80, 82, 98, 103, 221–2, 276, 279, 285, 287; principle of non-subordination, 75, 80, 82, 103, 276, 285, 287; subordination theory, 8, 75, 77–8, 80–1, 84, 102
Sumner, W., 3–4, 11, 50–1, 67, 223–4, 228, 242–3, 246, 248, 253
Sunstein, C., 5, 14–15, 63, 67, 116, 119, 193, 233–4, 261–2, 301
suppression of speech, 16, 27, 59, 95, 100, 107, 109–10, 112, 117, 125, 137–8, 161, 191, 199, 225, 242, 269, 275, 285, 293
supreme court justices, 13, 128, 203, 280, 282, 284, 304–5, 307–8, 310; Alito, 131, 141; Barak, 197; Blackmun, 273; Brandeis, 139; Bromberg, 25, 165; Cory, 97, 197; Deschamps, 237; Dickson, 110–11; Frankfurter, 170, 202; Holmes, 68, 107, 137, 257; Iacobucci, 97, 197; Jackson, 15, 197, 238; Marshall, 274; McLachlin, 257, 266, 278; O'Connor, 73, 165–6, 201, 264, 295, 297, 308–9, 311–12; Rothstein, 93; Scalia, 64, 134, 231, 241–2, 256, 289–91, 293, 295–6, 308–9, 311; Souter, 296; Stevens, 291–2; Stewart, 142; Stone, 197; Thomas, 264, 273; White, 289–90, 293, 311; Wilson, 282
Swastika, 151
Sweden, 11–12, 23, 43, 66, 100, 145, 158, 271–2, 275; Supreme Court, 145
Switzerland, 26, 29, 31, 275
symbols, 115, 286, 312
sympathy, 9, 111, 132–6, 173

Tanenhaus, J., 20
Taylor, C., 140, 166–7, 169–70, 173
Taylor, J., 132–3

teachers, 17, 65, 110, 119, 141, 193, 242, 253
television, 18, 22, 38, 40, 44, 54, 107, 179, 189, 254, 261, 311
terrorism, 16, 65, 101, 138, 151, 201, 267; attacks on September 11, 2011, 101, 123; attacks on the offices of *Charlie Hebdo* on January 7, 2015, 184
testimony, 112, 171–2, 210
Thompson, S., 53, 101, 125–7, 140, 167, 210, 217
threats, 1, 8, 16, 28–30, 39–40, 50, 53, 65–6, 70, 72–4, 85, 97–8, 100, 103, 144, 146, 178, 181, 197, 220, 247, 259, 266, 292, 295, 301; existential, 171; long-term, 100; true, 72, 314
threat to public order laws/regulations/codes, 8, 28, 30, 97
time, place, and manner restrictions, 8, 12, 38–9, 120, 200, 248, 263–4, 274, 317
tolerance, 62, 141, 163, 165, 180, 234, 252–3, 270–1, 301
torts, 8–9, 21, 30–2, 52–3, 56, 82, 92–3, 129–30, 144, 147, 157, 206, 220–1, 235–6, 241, 250; dignitary, 260; injuria, 31–2, 46; intentional infliction of emotional distress, 32, 52–3, 129–31, 140, 147, 206, 220, 235–6; racial insult, 52, 92, 147, 236, 241
town meeting, 195
traditions, 3, 6, 8, 27, 86, 129, 161, 176, 181, 219, 246, 288
treason, 62, 293
Tribe, L., 270
trust, 15, 60, 64–5, 215, 303–4
truth, 20, 25, 27, 86, 97, 106–15, 117, 119–20, 137–9, 157, 217, 226–7, 229, 258, 261, 276, 287, 292; discovery of, 1, 6, 9, 13, 96, 106–8, 110, 112–16, 118, 137, 222, 225–6, 228–9, 233–4, 316; exchanging error for, 107–10, 112–14, 137–8; falsification, 21, 77, 119; livelier impression of, 109, 116–17; nuanced principle of, 113, 115, 276; principle of, 107–13, 115–7, 138, 276, 287; theories of, 137–8; true beliefs, 109, 116–19, 226

Tsesis, A., 11, 67, 73, 75, 198
Tunisia, 26
Turkey, 11, 18, 23, 28, 35, 47, 197, 219, 235
Twitter, 249, 257, 260, 272. *See also* internet messaging services

UK (United Kingdom), 20, 22–3, 26–7, 29, 34–6, 41, 65, 69, 74, 100–1, 126, 140–1, 149, 156, 159, 176–7, 181, 184, 232, 241, 243–4, 248, 254, 257, 268–9, 272, 309, 312, 319; Supreme Court, 309. *See also* Law Lords
Umati Project, 246
UN (United Nations), 21, 24, 72
unintended consequences, 11–12, 51, 263
university campuses, 15, 17, 34, 47, 62, 65, 75, 85, 99, 102, 111, 113–14, 116, 119, 124, 129–31, 135–6, 186, 192–3, 199, 231–4, 237–8, 247, 252–4, 258, 265, 268, 273, 277, 281, 317
Uruguay, 26
US (United States of America), 15, 18, 20, 23, 32–5, 38, 43, 46–8, 52–3, 55, 67–8, 87, 100–1, 113, 120, 133, 137, 139, 151, 157–9, 164, 167, 169, 184, 188–9, 199, 203, 215–16, 220, 233, 235, 238–9, 242–3, 246, 251, 263–6, 268, 271–2, 274–5, 288–9, 309, 311; First Amendment, 12, 15, 33, 35, 38–9, 48, 52, 62, 72–3, 76, 83, 99, 116, 131, 133–4, 137, 140–1, 183, 188, 192, 197, 200–1, 203–4, 216, 227–9, 232, 241–2, 251, 266, 269–71, 274, 277, 281, 287, 289, 294–5, 301, 314; Supreme Court, 12, 33, 36, 38, 48, 72, 151, 165, 182, 188, 201, 206, 216, 224, 227, 231, 239, 270–1, 281–2, 286, 302, 308–9, 311, 313
Uzbekistan, 26

vagueness, 116, 265–6, 276; principle of, 265–6, 276
value monism, 278
value pluralism, 5, 51, 278; problem of incommensurability. *See* incommensurability

values: basic, 60, 256, 279; communicative, 255; comparative, 229, 232–3; competing, 231, 282; comprehensive, 279–80, 301; endgood, 305; ethical, 208, 297, 299; extrinsic, 238; fundamental, 139, 241, 313; independent, 124; liberal, 301; moral, 94, 279, 298; nameless, 279–81, 283, 310; non-neutral, 314; political, 99; secular, 16; symbolic, 263, 305
Varden, H., 96
Vasquez, M., 4, 95, 134
Venezuela, 28
verbal abuse. *See* hate speech, verbal abuse
video games, 69
Vietnam, 26
violence, 8, 15, 18, 28–30, 35–7, 40–1, 57–8, 66–8, 70, 72–3, 93–4, 108, 112–13, 140, 159, 186, 220–1, 223, 228, 240, 252, 259, 281, 289–90, 295–6, 313, 316–17; incitement to. *See* incitement to violence; threats of, 281, 289, 296
virtue ethics, 128, 140
virtue jurisprudence, 4, 9, 128–9, 135, 299
Volokh, E., 10, 15, 137, 140, 192–4, 217

Waldron, J., 4, 9–10, 41, 75, 92, 143–59, 177, 190, 204, 207–9, 226–7, 236, 238, 240, 319
warrant, 1–4, 9–11, 13, 19, 25, 51, 60–1, 66, 73, 75, 86, 91, 99, 107–9, 112–19, 121, 124, 128, 136, 138, 144, 148, 162–4, 166–7, 179, 182, 187–8, 191–2, 195, 200–2, 209, 211, 218–20, 223, 235, 238–9, 241, 251, 263–5, 267, 269, 276–83, 286–7, 307, 316–17, 319; narrow, 3, 9–11, 41, 49–50, 58, 61, 73, 75, 82, 103, 108–9, 112, 114–15, 117–18, 124, 132, 136, 138, 163–4, 182, 187, 191–2, 199–200, 202, 218, 223, 235, 238, 276, 280, 287; overall, 3–4, 9, 13, 51, 99, 116, 179, 235, 276–8, 280–3, 286–7, 306–7, 316–17, 319

Weinstein, J., 10, 16, 20, 190–2, 194, 198–9, 206, 215, 241, 269, 277
Wermiel, S., 282, 311
Westboro Baptist Church, 26, 33, 38–9, 131, 206
Westergaard, K., 121
white Americans, 76, 78, 85, 88, 102, 129, 162, 166, 312–13
"whites only" signs, 34, 76. *See also* signs
white supremacists, 124, 166

Wilders, G. 121
Williams Crenshaw, K., 170, 319
Wolfson, N., 15, 317–18
women, 16, 32, 76, 79, 84, 138, 172, 176, 185, 216, 313, 319
Wright, R.G., 91, 94

Yong, C., 4, 317
Young, I.M., 149, 166–7

Zündel, E., 97–8, 216, 219, 249, 265